WORK
RELIEF
to
REHABILITATION

WITHDRAWN

HAROLD E. SIMMONS
M.S.W., A.C.S.W.
Deputy Director
Employment and Rehabilitation Branch
California State Department of Social Welfare

Edited by THERESA W. EMLEY

Cover Design by RALPH HANAMAN

SBN 87312-002-7

TABLE OF CONTENTS

PREFACE

THIS BOOK is concerned with man's need for dignity, worth, and self-realization through meaningful work, and with the role of society in rehabilitating those who cannot meet this need without assistance.

Since human relations have been breached by enmity between the haves and the have-nots throughout recorded history, research for this book has covered material as venerable as the ancient philosophies and as contemporary as yesterday's public welfare hearing. The most significant findings from the source materials, as well as from the most recent hearing attended by the author prior to publication of this book, are that continuous impoverishment and humiliation of one segment of the population eventually degrade an entire society.

Today's affluent society appears to accept with composure the marked contrast between rich and poor and to accept the breach between their life styles as irrevocable and even necessary, perhaps, to protect the status quo of those in power. Any transition from this archaic attitude will require comprehension of the nature of poverty and dependency. It is the author's conviction that poverty must be recognized, not as a condition willfully produced by those who suffer from it, but as a disease endemic to and perpetuated by the present power structure of our society which will not risk legislating and programming beyond the most ignorant of its constituency.

The crippling effects of poverty cannot be mitigated by applying the quack therapy of work relief or subsistence handouts or by instructing its victims in techniques of adjusting to their handicaps.

The middle class, burdened in conscience and pocketbook by the existence of the unemployed, the disabled, and the dependent, negotiates endlessly to render them "invisible" and to avoid any direct confrontation. The persistent detail of this book is therefore partially designed to reveal the intractable nature of traditional approaches to welfare.

When traditional approaches are currently measured against those of the 1930's, the totality of the strands brings forth the startling realization that the major problem today is not generational poverty, as believed, but generational middle-class provincialism. The ignorance of educated, middle-class citizens in the United States is unbelievable when tested in respect to the nature and significance of human behavior. Scientists, engineers, physicians, lawyers, businessmen, and farmers cast off any scientific approach, logic, or good judgment when assessing human problems, and put on the cloak of mythology and folklore. While these good citizens

5

also have the power to insure that their ignorance prevails in law and administrative regulation, they fail to realize that the fruit of their beliefs and labor is the historical persistence of poverty, dependency, and crime throughout the generations.

This book exposes the universal expression of this middle-class phenomenon in welfare directors' and county supervisors' associations, in farmer's organizations, in legislatures, and in bureaucracy. In observing the pattern of their practices and attitudes, we become pessimistic for the future, because it reveals the repetitive nature of the middle class syndrome through the ages. We marvel at the power of this group which never yielded in the past to such authors as Bellamy, who advocated relief for the oppressed, and we recognize the present-day politics which insure the generational aspects of poverty and dependence.

To understand the grinding poverty of the poor, the intractable generational qualities of the power structure, and the ineptness and clumsiness of legislative and administrative organisms, the reader must walk slowly and thoughtfully through descriptive and analytical, individual, administrative, and legislative case material.

The importance of the power structure must not be minimized. Many approaches are sought by experts to influence the power structure—by organizing it, expanding it, confronting it, and assisting it. While this book may carry a bit of all these approaches, the author particularly sought to *reveal* the nature of the power structure, because unless we understand its nature, its methods, its insidiousness and callousness, its generational qualities, and its conspiracy of forces, the society will never mobilize to modify it. This book seeks to clarify the impotence of poor people against such powerful forces.

While middle-class provincialism seems hopeless, we see hope in the spirit of poor people. The fundamental need of men and women to become engaged in meaningful activity is reassuring. The author therefore focuses on methods of overcoming obstacles to the achievement of a meaningful life, and in the chapter on women at work, stresses that women receiving AFDC feel like social outcasts, as do their children, and that they seek help to emerge from their trapped environment.

Men want work, not relief, and government must intervene when necessary to insure every man and woman the right to work. Yet national government under conservative administrations mimics the impotent attitudes and approaches of the Hoover regime. In fact, the Nixon administration has added a new dimension by admittedly developing an economic strategy in early 1969 to permit a substantial rise in unemployment by as many as 750,000 workers to reduce inflation. The author takes strong exception to the strategy of a labor secretary, an economist, who makes economic pawns of poor people. Social and behavioral scientists should be commissioned to develop policies to insure that human need and dignity are considered first.

Throughout our history the world of things has taken precedence over human values. Today, it would be well to remember John Dewey's statement of 50 years ago: "Our disagreements with one another as to conclusions are trivial in comparison with our disagreements as to problems; to see the problem as another sees, in the same perspective and at the same angle—that amounts to something. Agreement as to conclusions is in comparison perfunctory." Implicit in this profound statement is the understanding that unless problems are understood, no real commitment can be made to overcome them. Both President Kennedy and President Johnson brought hope to the 1960's by beginning a spiritual as well as a practical war on poverty. President Nixon started his tenure as Commander-in-Chief by ordering a retreat. It does not augur well for the 1970's that the administration favors deliberate increases in unemployment as an antidote to inflation. Expansion of the forces of unemployment in this manner is a form of collaboration with the enemy—poverty. The unemployed become prisoners of war, wasting away in the concentration camps of our ghettos while the diplomats of our economy negotiate an ineffective truce.

The reactionary forces in our society which remain unresponsive to human need are, because of that unresponsiveness, promoting a revolution in this critical period of protest because there is no other alternative open to achieve needed social reform. The critical nature of the issue was revealed by a report carried in the news media on March 19, 1969: "I'm not against people who need help," a California County Supervisor said, "it's the influx of agitators I object to." If there were no agitators, he was asked, would he favor letting his county join the nationwide food stamp program? "If there were no agitators," he replied, "they wouldn't be asking for food stamps." At a given point in time, at the state level, the administration may see the big welfare problem as a fraud issue with implications of traditional "crackdown" approaches; at the county level, it may be the agitators who disturb the complacency of the Establishment; and at the federal level the administration may seek solutions to inflation by further punishing the poor through increased unemployment.

Despite the swing of the pendulum away from constructive confrontations between the affluent and the impoverished, solutions to these problems of our society are clearly within the realm of possibility because the seeds of changed value systems are known and ready for sowing. It is possible to have a world with meaningful life style for every person, with poverty and bigotry abolished, if it can be recognized that whenever the seeds of change start to germinate, some reactionary force stifles their emergence through misguided approaches. Since poverty and crime are a sickness, the Establishment must learn to stop its barbaric practice of punishing or further depriving the afflicted when a helping hand is needed instead. Those who retain the power to thwart change defeat the higher impulse of man to overcome his baser, synthetic value judgments, but they cannot be allowed, interminably, to set these degrading judgments as the goals for an entire society. To the end that this issue may be understood, this book seeks to clarify the intractable nature of unenlightened middle-class provincialism, the exploitation of the impotent poor, and the latent surge of poor people to escape their entrapment through use of instruments which provide opportunity, and on balance, this book presents some signs of hope for fundamental change in attitudes and methods of intervention for poor people.

CHAPTER 1

MEANINGFUL WORK

THE UNIVERSAL NEED FOR PRODUCTIVE ACTIVITY

MAN'S CAPACITY FOR WORK AND LIFE-FULFILLMENT appears to have always been submerged in his social relationships. From primitive to modern times, his need to maintain status through productive activity has been based upon his own and his community's point of view of the usefulness and desirability of such activity. Although there has been a growing awareness of the fact that all men must be engaged in meaningful work, the need has never been fully understood or met in terms of the social and cultural factors involved, and has been confused with purely economic values.

Historical perspective now makes it possible for men of good will to recognize the direct moral consequences of disturbing the motivational bases for socially meaningful work in a specific culture without providing appropriate substitutes for the lost values. It can now be demonstrated that when a man loses the dignity and self-respect essential to his own work traditions and social standing, not only does he deteriorate as an individual, but the culture of which he is a part also tends to become a downgraded subculture. Both the individual within his own cultural group, and the subculture within society as a whole are reduced to outcast status.

SOCIAL AND CULTURAL BASES FOR WORK NEEDS

Man's absolute need to work within the specific context of his own social values can be better understood in the light of many research studies and analyses made within the past 40 years. New concepts for understanding this universal need are required if society is to bridge the gaps, not only between the affluent and the poor, but also between constructive and destructive approaches to daily living.

Work in the modern culture of Western man may be likened to the stone ax of the Yir Yoront tribe on the North Coast of Australia. This tribe was stable and well integrated, although living with a stone age culture as late as 1900. The most important tool that a man could own was his ax, its handle fashioned with care and fitted with bark and gum to a stone which came from a quarry 400 miles away. The ax was used to build huts, cut firewood, and make hunting and fishing tools. It was a status symbol reflecting the owner's masculinity, and as a cherished possession was handed down to his male heirs. As civilization infiltrated, more efficient steel axes were brought in and distributed by missionaries as gifts and rewards. By 1915, not only a man, but also his wife and son might have a steel ax. Since man was no longer the controlling factor in his own work nor the sole owner of the means of production, he felt that his masculinity and self-worth were destroyed. His wife and children, with their own power symbols, became independent and disrespectful, and the culture deteriorated, as no appropriate belief system was substituted for the original one.

Work is modern man's stone ax, without which his individual culture system is drastically disturbed in terms of loss of feelings of self-worth and the respect of the family and community.

Studies of the aged offer clues to the effect upon man of changing occupational roles. Primitive cultures varied in their treatment of the aged, some providing valued roles for the aged, others leaving them to die in walled-up igloos or in the jungle. In many tribes in North Australia, old men received great respect and obedience, were provided special goods, and had the power of command in peace or war. Among the Dieri, the sole qualification for eminence was being the oldest member of the tribe. Councils of old men maintained power and commanded the respect of their tribes, and this tradition gave all old men status and value. Reverence was given to the aged for their knowledge of tribal lore, food resources, and survival through difficult life events, and for their contributions to the psychic life of the tribe through the retention of tribal secrets, rites, and ceremonies.

Samoan women who gained increasing skill in the manufacture of baskets and fine mats could become teachers of these skills or they might become midwives or physicians. Therefore, old women had great influence in Samoan households. Likewise, the oldest women in Dahomey, Africa, carried great prestige but for a different reason—their intimate relationship with the dead.

In modern society, women weather the aging process better than men because there is less discontinuity between women's earlier life patterns and their lives as aged persons. The common life element for women is continuity of household duties which provide meaningful activity, familiar routines, and the sustained sense of feeling needed. Man, on the other hand, experiences a sudden change when, upon retirement between the ages of 60 and 70, he is cut off from familiar work activity, routine functioning, group associations and meaningful actions. Modern society makes no place for the aged as some primitive societies did. Theoretically, retirement from the modern world of work is symbolized as a desirable goal, yet the shame of the reality is soon revealed to the retired man as little more than a shelving of himself as a useless commodity—one easily replaced. The continuity of familiar life patterns is disturbed, and most aged persons are incapable of restoring life patterns which are satisfying and meaningful. The consequence of this failure is inevitable deterioration and death.

Aristotle deduced that "virtue" (excellence) is "activity," by which he meant the exercise of the functions and capacities peculiar to man. Happiness, which is man's aim, results from meaningful activity, and the use of his powers. It is not a quiescent possession or state of mind. Explaining his concept of activity, Aristotle said: "And, as in the Olympic Games, it is not the most beautiful and the strongest that are crowned, but those who compete (for it is some of these that are victorious), so those who act, win, and rightly win, the noble and good things of life. The free, rational and active man is the happy person. The way to increase human tranquility is through meaningful activity, not activity as an end in itself, but as an accommodation to a feeling of purposeful life."

It is the author's concept that productiveness is an intrinsic human faculty and that this concept contradicts the popular idea that man is lazy by nature and has to be forced to be active. For centuries man has been obsessed by the idea of work, by the need for constant meaningful activity. He is almost incapable of being lazy for any length of time. There is a difference between symptoms of laziness and compulsive activity. Although we often find the inability to work as the main symptom of the neurotic, and the ability to enjoy ease and repose characteristic of the "well-adjusted," compulsive activity is not the opposite of laziness. The opposite of both is productiveness.

The disturbance of productive activity can result in passive dependency or overactivity. Hunger and force cannot motivate productive activity. On the contrary, a meaningful life derives from freedom, economic security, and the provision of work to enable the expression of man's tendency to make productive use of his powers. Productive activity is characterized by the life rhythms of activity and repose. Freud, in fact, defined maturity as the ability to love and to work.

Erick Fromm[1] evaluated man's capacity for adaptation to adversity by suggesting that man can adapt himself to slavery, but he reacts to it by lowering his intellectual and moral qualities; that he can adapt himself to a culture permeated by mutual distrust and hostility, but he reacts to this adaptation by becoming weak and sterile. Man can adapt himself to cultural conditions which demand the repression of sexual strivings, but in achieving this adaptation he develops neurotic symptoms, as Freud has shown. He can adapt himself to almost any culture patterns, but insofar as these are contradictory to his nature, he develops mental and emotional disturbances which force him eventually to change his nature. Fromm suggests that many life examples show the person who lives productively before he is old by no means deteriorates; on the contrary, the mental and emotional qualities he developed in the process of productive living continue to grow, although physical vigor wanes. The unproductive person, however, deteriorates in his whole personality when his physical vigor dries up. The decay of the personality in old age is a symptom—it is proof of the failure of having lived productively. The fear of getting old is an expression of the feeling, often unconscious, of living unproductively; it is a reaction of our conscience to the mutilation of ourselves.

In public welfare, AFDC-U means Aid to Families with Dependent Children—Unemployed. An AFDC-U family's central problem is lack of employment. It is important to see clearly why the unemployment and attendant financial dependency of able-bodied men is a moral issue. The moral debate over public assistance payments to the unemployed husband with a wife and children centers on the issue of dependency versus self-reliance. To the public, receipt of income without work is unacceptable. Public morality is offended, and a particular concept of the welfare family develops: If self-reliance is stressed as the key virtue, then the welfare client is a lazy and inadequate person. These traits are believed to be the cause of unemployment and welfare status. Therefore, partly as a punitive measure, the public attitude is that the recipient should receive only the minimum subsistence from welfare agencies. If the public could think of the welfare client as a person ready for and capable of work, but without the opportunity for adequate employment, then welfare payments sufficient to maintain a minimum standard of health and decency would be made available to him. To gain acceptance of a less punitive and more dignified concept of welfare, the public must be educated in a fuller understanding of man's need to work.

It is important to understand that the relationship between the lower-class worker and the world of work is different from that of the middle-class worker. Herbert Gans[2] states that with the middle-class worker, the character of the work is intertwined with his self-definition. Achievement, status, contribution, and service are the symbols that have most significance for him. Work and income, in and of themselves, are taken for granted. The investment of self in work tends to be maximized and his work is seen as an extension of himself. When extended to its maximum degree, this orientation produces a pathological type that has been labeled the "work addict" by Nelson Bradley.[3] Such cases represent supremacy of the protestant ethic over all other considerations or values.

For lower-class workers, as Friedman and Havighurst[4] have indicated, the character of the work appears secondary to the fact of working. Work and income are most important and are goals to be achieved, in contrast with the middle-class assumption of taking these elements for granted. For the lower-class worker, work and income arise from the same source. Hence income, and particularly the prospect of steady income, is foremost as the goal to be achieved. His first identification is with the working process that produces income.

The second factor involved in achieving fuller understanding of man's need to work is that of the microculture or subculture of the informal social system associated with the work setting. Characteristic of this system are the horseplay, jokes, resentment against bosses and authority, and the sharing of gripes and complaints that come into play in the social relations that focus around the work setting. The microculture involved in work is also related to the use of tools, machinery, materials being worked on, and work rhythms and routines. The cultural elements and informal social relations emerging from work settings constitute a system of male sociability. Studies by Burleigh Gardner[5] of human relations in industry have documented the character of such relationships in work settings, and have demonstrated the importance of such relationships to lower-class male workers during the time they are at work.

It can be seen that working, income, and male sociability are interconnected aspects of a particular work setting. The worker can shift from one job to another, and one job can be more taxing or more pleasant than another, but the three elements of work, income, and sociability are relatively constant, all-continuing aspects of the work setting itself and are tied up in the worker's concept of himself as a breadwinner. His self-definition as a breadwinner, in turn, is tied up with his self-definition as a man. Thus, his male ego—his concept of himself as a man—is expressed and reinforced by working, by income, and by participation in the microculture of informal social relationships on the job. Given the fact of such linkages between the lower-class worker and the work world, the strength of these linkages is difficult to assess unless more is known about the other aspects of the worker's life that may have to do with his self-definition. Robert Dubin[6] stated that if the worker's basic life interests are focused on areas other than work, then these linkages to the work world may be offset by other more powerful motives or social forces. The concept emerging from studies on the lives of lower-class workers is that the local social world of kin, friends, acquaintances, and neighbors is a dominant interest. This world of buddies, chums, kinsmen, and pals is a major source for the expression and reinforcement of the male ego. Family and church may also be focal points of identification but are usually thought to be less significant than the informal peer groups.

William Dyer[7] states that if the local social world is a dominant focus for male identification, the crucial question to be answered is whether or not this world interfaces at any point with the world of work. For the lower-class worker are these two spheres of life totally separate, closely connected, or somewhat connected? The interconnection between his work and nonwork worlds is primarily through friendships and informal social relationships. Some of the friends met at work are subsequently involved at various points in his local social world. The sources of friendship are a sensitive index to the relative psychological importance of various sectors in a man's life. Furthermore, the interconnections between circles of friendship are one clue at the social level to the social-psychological process of identification. In the case of the lower-class male worker, the first source of friends is from the neighborhood, the second source from work, and the third source from family and kin. There are linkages between his work and nonwork worlds even though the nonwork world may be his dominant life interest. Consequently, his concept of himself as breadwinner is not separate from his participation in his local social world. We would conclude that work is very important to the male worker in maintaining his self-image.

Morse and Weiss state that[8] the psychological and social interconnection between the work and nonwork worlds is most apparent when work is absent and long-time unemployment takes place. If these two worlds were quite separate for the lower-class worker, and he had no identification with work, but only with money, then the unemployed, long-time welfare recipient should show the same pattern of social relationships as is shown by the working person. The only disturbance manifested would result from the lowering of income level, and there would be little or no disturbance if the continuity of the welfare checks was superior to the continuity of income created by intermittent employment. The fact of the matter is that studies of unemployment[9] point to significant changes in the worker's self-definition and to developmental patterns of social withdrawal which accompany his long-time unemployment.

While we are considering in this discussion the unemployed and poor as a special class it must be recognized that man's need for work is universal even though the expression of this need varies in reference to the subculture. Kimball Young[10] observed that the importance of work to the individual can be tested by viewing man without work. Unemployment often is anticipated and thereby preceded by anxiety which is greatly accentuated when work loss occurs. Such emotional reaction varies by individual, depending upon his personality, the extent of previous unemployment, reactions within his family, and the like. Following the first shock, he actively seeks work, and unable to obtain work to his liking, he will ultimately settle for lesser jobs. If work is not found, then apathy, depression, and a sense of hopelessness ensue. The loss of job routine plus family complications contribute to feelings of inferiority in relation to his wife and children.

In an analysis which deals more broadly with the subject, but is applicable also in that it evaluates the motives of man in groups, Karl Polanyi[11] states: "The outstanding discovery of recent historical and anthropological research is that man's economy, as a rule, is submerged in his social relationships. He does not act so as to safeguard his individual interest in the possession of material goods; he acts so as to safeguard his social standing, his social claims, his social assets. He values material goods only in so far as they serve his end. Neither the process of production nor that of distribution is linked to specific economic interests attached to the possession of goods; but every single step in that process is geared to a number of social interests which eventually insure that the required step be taken. These interests will be very different in a small hunting or fishing community from those in a vast despotic society, but in either case the economic system will be run on noneconomic motives . . . With the Trobriand Islanders of Western Melanesia the sustenance of the family—the female and the children—is the obligation of their matrilineal relatives. The male who provides for his sister and her family will mainly earn credit due to this good behavior, but will reap little immediate benefit in exchange; if he is slack it is first and foremost his reputation that will suffer. It is for the benefit of his wife and her children that the principle of reciprocity will work, and thus compensate him economically for his acts of civic virtue. Reciprocity helps to safeguard both production and family sustenance." Polanyi builds a case for noneconomic values as related to man's motivations and describes the devastation that follows disruption of these values: "Not economic exploitation, as is often assumed, but the disintegration of the cultural environment of the victim is then the cause of the degradation. The economic process may, naturally, supply the vehicle of the destruction, and almost invariably economic inferiority will make the weaker yield, but the immediate cause for that reason is not economic; it lies in the lethal injury to the institutions in which his social existence is embodied. The result is loss of self-respect and standards, whether the unit is a people or a class, whether the process springs from so-called cultural conflict or from a change in the position of a class within the confines of a society . . . The condition of some native tribes in Africa today carries an unmistakable resemblance to that of the English laboring classes during the early years of the nineteenth century. The Kaffir of South Africa, a noble savage, than whom none felt socially more secure in his native Kraal, has been transformed into a human variety of half-domesticated animal dressed in the unrelated, the filthy, the unsightly rags that not the most degenerated white man would wear, a nondescript being, without self-respect or standards, veritable human refuse . . . Their crafts have decayed, the political and social conditions of their existence have been destroyed, they are dying from boredom . . . While their own culture offers them no longer any objectives worthy of effort or sacrifice, racial snobbishness and prejudice bar the way to their adequate participation in the culture of the white intruders."

The social withdrawal that follows unemployment includes both kinship and nonkinship relations. As unemployment lengthens and welfare dependency increases, the local social world of the unemployed man includes loss of the friends first met at work. Concomitant with social withdrawal is an increase in feelings of dependency. These feelings of dependency are interconnected with welfare dependency because of the interaction of psychological and social processes. Long-time unemployment, social withdrawal, and changes in self-definition which contribute to increased feelings of dependency are all interconnected.

UNEMPLOYMENT AND WELFARE DEPENDENCY

It is important to recognize that unemployment is the initial condition that weakens the linkage between workers, their local social world, and the world of work. Paralleling the economic factors of unemployment, factors of social withdrawal and subsequent alterations in personality result, in turn, in increased feelings of psychological dependency and defeat. Financial dependency, as indexed by public assistance, is not necessarily related to psychological dependency. Therefore, the meaning of psychological dependency has to be assessed in terms of the economic and cultural framework of the individual.

Psychological dependency arises and has significance only in the context of changes in the economic and social circumstances of a particular worker's relationship to a specific labor market. Thus, a long-time aid case shows strong feelings of psychological dependency caused by a cycle of economic, social, and psychological changes that destroy the relationship between himself, his local social world, and the world of work.

Many researchers of the subject agree that for most men a job serves more functions than just earning a living, and that even with sufficient money they would still want to be employed, because work gives them a feeling of being tied into the larger society, of having something to do, of having a purpose in life, functions evidently not available in nonwork activities. The finding that work has essential meanings other than earning money is consistent with observations on the effects of unemployment. If men work only for money, there is no way of explaining the degree of dislocation and deprivation which retirement, even on an adequate salary, appears to bring. The results of the Morse and Weiss[8] national sample study on the meaning of work show that: (1) Work is more than a means to an end for the vast majority of employed men; (2) a man does not have to be at the age of retirement or be immediately threatened by unemployment to be able to imagine what not working would mean to him; and (3) work serves other than monetary functions for men both in middle-class and working-class occupations, but that the nonmonetary functions are somewhat different in these two broad occupational classifications.

It is mostly through productive activity that the majority of men tie into society, and for this reason and others, most men find the producing role important for maintaining their sense of well-being. Freud stated that work has a greater effect than any other technique of living in the direction of binding the individual more closely to "reality;" in his work at least, he is securely attached to a part of reality, the human community. To the typical man in a middle-class occupation, work means having a purpose, gaining a sense of accomplishment, expressing himself—a meaningful "reality." He feels that not working would leave him aimless and without opportunities to contribute to his world. To the typical man in a working-class or farming occupation, work means having something to do; not working would leave him no outlet for physical activity; he would just be sitting around. But work has even more pervasive importance for the farmer than for men in other occupations, since the boundaries between work and home life are not as sharp for him, and life without work is apt to be difficult to consider. The development of means by which individuals can gain, through substitute activities, the same satisfactions which they obtain from work is one possible long-range solution to nonwork. Morse and Weiss[8] suggest another solution— the development of methods by which individuals might remain productive in their later years. In either case, it would seem necessary that the occupation give the individual an opportunity for activity which is meaningful and socially integrating in his own terms.

The demoralization of the wage earner as a result of unemployment will also profoundly affect his family. Children suffer loss of prestige with their peers and through disturbed parental relationships which often lessen the warmth and affection of parental care. Continued presence of a man in the home during working hours leads to marital friction. One of the values of work relief during the depression was noted by a number of observers as being the restoration of normal family life rhythm. The wage earner regained respect for himself and from his family and peers even though the work had lesser status because of its association with relief. If a father experiences chronic unemployment, and the mother works, this disturbs the son's identification with the father. Several generations of dependency, to the extent that it exists, may be ascribed partially, at least, to chronic unemployment which has established parental dependency as a model for the children.

Wight Bakke's[9] two-volume opus on the unemployed was based on studies conducted by the Institute of Human Relations, Yale University, between 1932 and 1939. During the course of these studies, the researchers used a wide variety of methods designed to analyze adjustments and reactions of the unemployed. These methods included participation by the researchers in the life practices of the unemployed for several periods, as well as intensive case studies, budget investigations, interviews with the members of many unemployed families, interviews with social workers, public officials, and employers, and other appropriate research devices. Bakke's summary of both volumes is a source of insights into the thinking, behavior, and motivation of working-class people.

In the Yale study, researchers emphasized how close to the possibility of realization people tailor their hopes, stressing the point that results must not fall too far short of hope, or the hopes will be adjusted downward to be consistent with the anticipated results. In this connection, the author poses the following question: If objectives are lowered in anticipation of decreased economic resources, may they not also be raised to conform to increased economic resources?

Bakke emphasizes the basic importance to the individual of having a socially respected role as well as having control over his own affairs, and concomitant with these two ideas, finds that the doing of work for wages is an essential component of the practices and relationships which lead to social status, independence, and control. His belief that life on relief contains few possibilities of renewing progress toward individual goals leads him to the conclusion that this fact can be counted on to stimulate development of alternative practices which carry greater promise of success. He also concludes that when no alternative is available, this fact can also be counted on to lower the unemployed worker's objectives to the level of possible dependency on relief, and can cause him to reorganize his structure of living on this foundation. Since retention of the material symbols of former success is a necessary condition for postponing such modification, it follows that their loss is the signal for it, so that results may not fall too far short of the unemployed worker's hopes. The author concurs in this, deplores the welfare laws and regulations which tend to pauperize the individual, and agrees regarding the advantages of work relief over direct relief in enabling the worker to maintain a socially respected role.

Certain studies in depth of family life, unemployment, and welfare dependency, which were carried out separately during the depression era by Ruth Cavan and Katherine Ranck,[9] and by Mirra Komarovsky,[12] remain classic sources for analyzing dependency in terms of the relationships between the pre-unemployment and the unemployment family patterns of living. Bakke's reports on some of these studies and on his own case studies of 24 families over an eight-year period during the depression era led to his formulating a theory of stages in family adjustment to unemployment and welfare dependency. These stages involved concepts of stable and unstable equilibrium, disorganization, and readjustment. He pointed out that the first internal changes in family life and response to loss of work were associated with external changes and that "The journey of the families through these several stages is relevant. The economic changes are accompanied by social changes in family and community relationships. The two are closely related and react upon each other." He added that as a family moves through this set of stages, few changes occur in the division of labor, but shifts take place in the relative power and authority of husband and wife. Psychological practices of rationalization are used by both husband and wife in coping with these changes with the wife assuming more control over managing, planning, and money. Family ritual declines and there may be increasing health problems. Readjustment does not take place unless the family head is able to obtain work relief. Family breakup follows the stage of disorganization unless the husband's role in the family can be stabilized by work relief, since the job of the head of the family provides not only an income but a social role for which there is no adequate substitute in a working-class culture.

Cavan and Ranck's[9] earlier study of 100 families resulted in much the same general conclusions as Bakke's. They stated that a family's reaction to the crisis of unemployment and relief status rested on family organization in the past, susceptibility to disturbance, type of economic impact experienced, necessity of requesting relief, and family modes of coping with crises in the past. Adjustments were found to include denial that a crisis existed, acceptance by the husband of dependency status, change in husband-wife roles, and various attempts at escape. The mechanisms of escape include daydreaming, contemplation of suicide, living in the past, absorption in religion, ill health, and actual suicide. They made the observation that: "It is characteristic of the families that were well organized before the depression that other crises do not complicate the situation, and of the families that were disorganized before the depression, that crises either supersede the depression or complicate it some way (many of these crises involve illness or death and suggest that ill health may have been an unrecognized factor in the disorganization that characterized the family before the depression)."

Mirra Komarovsky's[12] study of 59 unemployed relief families during the depression focused on the impact of unemployment on the husband's authority within the family. Her findings indicate that one-fifth of the men experienced loss of such authority. The variables involved in the adjustment of these families included prior patterns of relationships between husband and wife, their personalities, and social relations outside the family. Three changes in the husband's status resulting from unemployment and welfare dependency were noted as loss of the provider role, the stigma of economic failure, and loss of daily work routine. Komarovsky stated that: "The general impression that the interviews make is that in addition to sheer economic anxiety the man suffers from deep humiliation. He experiences a sense of deep frustration because in his own estimation he fails to fulfill what is the central duty of his life, the very touchstone of his manhood—the role of family provider."

It may be concluded from these studies that (1) unemployment and welfare dependency interact with a family's previous equilibrium and methods of coping with crisis in determining the family's pattern of response; (2) unemployment and welfare dependency erode the authority of the husband within the family; (3) shifts in husband-wife relationships usually do not involve shifts in the division of labor, but in terms of respect, authority, and power; and finally, (4) shifts within the family system are interrelated to changes in their social life outside the family.

It seems clear that long-term unemployment and welfare dependency produce a variety of orientations on the part of the husband, all of which weaken his potential response to opportunities for employment. If his self-definition as a male breadwinner can be maintained by participation in a local social world that is linked with the male sociability arising from work situations, his role as father and parent operates to maintain a satisfactory self-image. But changes in interpersonal relations within the family, which are the result of unemployment and welfare dependency, will operate to weaken his self-definition as the head of his own household.

The final report on *Family Life Styles Below the Poverty Line*,[13] a Federal welfare administration supported research program, is one of the most comprehensive single pieces of survey research produced by public welfare agencies in California. This research came about as a result of the need of numerous groups, including the California State Senate, to obtain information about how welfare families and comparable low-income families meet their conditions of deprivation.

Extensive interviews with a sample of 1,200 low-income, intact families with children, one-half of whom were currently receiving public assistance AFDC-U, affords a detailed picture of the life conditions of families living at or close to the welfare standard. Major findings showed the following:

1. Their employment and income records reveal a fixed position at the bottom of the social and economic ladder. This is equally true of aided and nonaided families. Few differences were found between the two groups in the father's age, education, and skill level or in family size. Indeed, they all suffer from chronic underemployment and consequently earn too little to maintain their families, which average four or five children.

2. Many factors indicate that the families have little ability to cope with the crises associated with combinations of health, psychological, cultural, and familial relations factors, no one of which is dominant.

3. Families receiving public assistance differed from other low-income families in a combination of handicapping factors: More illnesses which caused time-on-job losses, less stability in employment, slightly lower occupational skill levels, more social alienation, and more psychological dependency.

4. Families receiving long-term aid showed a combination of handicapping factors in their life histories and present circumstances, including a pattern of social withdrawal; a lower level of living, occupational status, income, and economic security; poor health; and attitudes of hopelessness, defeat, and despair. The fathers' previously limited and irregular relationships with the world of work and their consequent failure to develop work concepts of generally accepted value led to their toleration of public assistance as a way of life.

Further research is needed to validate the conclusion drawn in this report that dependency status is the most powerful factor patterning the life style of families receiving long-term aid. It will be argued by many who read the report and consider its supporting evidence, that dependency is not the cause, but the effect of the variables studied, despite certain indications that continued conditions of poverty render some families more vulnerable than others to surrender and acceptance of dependency.

DEPENDENCY AS A FORM OF ALIENATION

The alienated worker, whether public welfare recipient or not, has been described as one who lacks attachment to the labor force, suffers from family instability, low continuity of productive activity, high rate of unemployment, chronic illness, malnutrition, sleeplessness, and a very low level of living. He may also manifest high psychological dependency and anomie, though there is no direct evidence from research studies to substantiate such a hypothesis. In the system of adaptation that emerges from these characteristics, widespread mutual aid and sharing are used as mechanisms to cope with fluctuating levels and sources of income.

The typical alienation pattern constitutes a subculture of mutual expectations in which the breadwinner role is negated and the role of nonworker becomes acceptable or even desirable. Fulfillment of the nonworker role is built around almost total insecurity, and undoubtedly involves a strong emphasis on the con-man connotations. Since participation in the labor force is intermittent and only for brief periods, considerable effort and energy may be directed toward obtaining money, but the definition of such activity makes it qualitatively different from legitimate work. The participants in such subcultural patterns may constitute a changing population, and at the periphery may include families in various stages of disintegration. The tragicomic aspects of such behavior can be found in the case of the man who requested and received a living allowance of $175 per month as a work experience project trainee, and then disappeared. When he returned, unabashed, several months later, he had a new Cadillac and a complete wardrobe bought from the winnings of crap games financed by the project funds.

The routes which lead to alienation of the low-status worker vary, depending upon whether he is a young adult without much work experience or family of his own or is an individual who has had stable work periods, but has been finally subjected to all the forces that result in family breakup and loss of his capacity to fulfill the breadwinner role.

In contrast, the very low-status worker whose work provides a modicum of job stability, successfully fulfills the breadwinnner role and retains an intact family. His linkage with kin and his participation in a local social world are extensive. Judged in terms of the statistical characteristics of lower-class persons, he tends to be healthy, shows relatively low psychological dependency, and does not have strong feelings of hopelessness and despair. His orientation to life and his family relations may be as strongly patterned by his ethnic background as by his low socio-economic status, but this does not affect his participation in the labor force. While his family suffers from a high degree of economic insecurity, he engages in such limited foresight practices as his meager income level will allow. His frustration due to lack of status achievement may be high, but the other elements in his life offset the debilitating effects of such frustration insofar as his work orientation is concerned. Stuart Rice,[14] as early as 1925, viewed these sociological aspects, asserting that it was the job around which the life of the workingman pivoted, providing the worker a large number of his social norms, with codes of usage and social responsibility. He believed that the sharing of the common life of the group through a job became the workingman's coat of respectability, and that when this central element of the mores and folkways of the society disappeared from the workingman's life, the accustomed understandings and status within the group were destroyed.

While unemployment which leads to dependency on public aid becomes a serious form of alienation, the provision of work relief tends, at least partially, to modify the degree of alienation. Contemporary approaches which provide more sophisticated educational and vocational rehabilitation and on-the-job experience will modify the alienation more extensively.

Bakke[9] stated that the contribution work relief made to the desire of workers to play a socially respected role depended partly upon whether the relief job was being compared with former maintenance by direct relief or with a "regular" job. He acknowledged the difficulties involved in maintaining any desirable social status while labeled a "reliefer." There was little question that for many of the unemployed, work relief, coming after a contrasting experience with direct relief, meant an opportunity for a "comeback," particularly for the unskilled worker. In cases where the men have done similar work all their lives, work relief is a renewing of their "regular" occupation. Moreover, the ordinary project type of work, if purposeful, socially useful, and efficiently managed, could provide a basis for social adjustment and status similar to and in some cases superior to former jobs for a private employer, and the worker himself knew, whatever the general public might think, that he was participating in a valuable and effectively managed job, and the status he derived from such work would be proportionately high. If, on the other hand, the worker felt that the work was a mere gesture or excuse for giving his money for the support of his family, or if he was allowed to loaf on the job under poor supervision, or the quality of the service he rendered was poor, these conditions provided little self-respect.

In raising questions about the values of work relief in retention of skills, Bakke considered that the preponderant type of job required manual labor, road building, sewer digging, or other types of construction jobs. Obviously, if unskilled workers were employed there was little question about the possibility of retention of skill, for it was the retention of a general fitness for work which was sought. There was ample evidence in the testimony of the unemployed that the daily work routine, the necessity for using one's muscles, and the outdoor life were beneficial in maintaining the worker's general health and physique. It is questionable, however, whether those who were formerly engaged in more skilled occupations were equally benefited by such a course of training. Many men complained that their ability to perform highly skilled jobs was impaired by the necessity of doing manual labor. Particularly was this true of men whose former jobs

required the performance of very delicate operations. Far from retaining their skills they felt they were losing them. Bakke found that
in work relief, the retention of work habits was theoretically possible
and frequently realized, but that to the extent relief-work projects
permit slipshod and careless work habits, they might actually be
ingraining in the workers habits which would have to be undone.
That the work habits required by private enterprise were not too
seriously damaged by an experience with relief-work conditions,
however, was indicated by the fact that among the 50 employers interviewed in a hiring-policy survey, those who had knowingly hired
WPA or CCC workers during 1938-39, found no difficulty in working them into the production schedule required by their enterprise.
Bakke concluded that work relief was valued because it avoided the
stigma of charity characterized by relief. Part of the social status
involved in work relief came from the reality of an employer behind
the phrase used by those who were working on projects: "I am
working for the city," or "I am working for Uncle Sam," a status
superior to: "I am on relief;" although this value existed only when
the job being done was an obviously useful and desirable one from
the point of view of the community.

In addition to the social status of the worker as a "producer,"
work was also the foundation of social status in other community
relationships, as within the family, giving the head of the family an
opportunity to approximate his normal schedule as chief breadwinner, going out each day to work as when in private industry. So far
as the family was concerned, his routine was the same, and the fact
that he brought home wages at the end of the week was a duplication
of an event with which all of them were familiar. Such an approxi-
mation of normal conditions ought not to be underestimated, according to Bakke. The constant reminder when the family was on direct relief that the function of the chief breadwinner had changed from
that of worker and provider to that of a messenger boy to and from
the relief office was as demoralizing to the family relationship as any
other single accompaniment of unemployment. The primary source
of family discord under the strain of unemployment was that the
father was not performing his normal function as required by the
division of labor laid down in the folkways. This discord was partially alleviated if money came as the result of work performed,
whereas the securing of money by application for relief did not reinstate the husband and father to his functional place.

In rehabilitation processes it was important to maintain the highest
possible morale of the individual, yet the conditions under which
public aid and services were rendered seriously undermined morale
and thereby rendered rehabilitation even more difficult. Being on
relief was an obstacle for any worker who had previously been suc-

cessful in finding a self-supporting place in society, and the anxiety, despair, and desperation attendant upon his first application for relief was evidence of that fact.

At the onset of the depression in 1929, the attitude of the community toward the unemployed on relief was that any willing worker could find a job, and that any who did not were inferior individuals. Only the "ill, the lame and the lazy" found their way to charitable societies or public relief. Attacks were made through the press and on campaign platforms during 1936, on the efficiency and soundness of WPA. Stories were afloat that WPA workers soldiered on the job, preferred to stay where they were rather than accept jobs in industry, and that WPA was a political racket, and men working on the projects saw some evidence that political influence counted in securing the "gravy" jobs.

While Bakke decried the degradation of public aid by society in its constant barrage of "public opinion" against the unemployed and relief clients, Eli Ginsberg[15] noted the personal indignities attached to public aid. He observed the unemployed were able to adjust to the loss of their jobs, the exhaustion of their savings accounts, even to the cashing in of their insurance policies, but that they broke down on the day they asked for relief even though many families were better off after being accepted on relief than they had been during the preceding weeks when they could not be sure of a roof over their heads and something to eat. Ginsberg believed people struggled so hard to stay off relief because they knew from the experience of relatives and friends that relief was not solely a matter of asking, but that once a person applied, his past, present, and even his future were subject to the scrutiny and control of officials in the Department of Welfare. Such control was not easy to contemplate and things were not made any easier during the filling out of detailed forms, trips for lengthy office interviews, and investigations in the home. After all, most had always been self-supporting and though their incomes had never been large, they had been masters of their own fate in deciding where to live, what to eat, and what clothes to buy. They became still more uneasy when, on making application, they were forced to answer many intimate questions which they had never discussed with relatives and certainly not with strangers.

The fear of "relief" held by the society which extends it has been a constant attribute through the ages. That fear has been expressed through development of punitive and restrictive measures, can be excused because of man's lack of understanding of the causes of dependency. However, the fact that improper remedies were chosen to alleviate man's problems, in no way lessens the validity of man's intuitive concern for the problem. These concerns can be capsulized by the statement of Josephine Lowell more than 70 years ago: ". . . relief is an evil—always. Even when it is necessary, I believe it is still an evil. One reason that it is an evil is because energy, independence, industry, and self-reliance are undermined by it, and since these are the qualities which make self-support and self-respect possible, to weaken or undermine them is a serious injury to inflict on man."[16]

The meaning of welfare dependency arises from the position of indigent persons in general society. Welfare status has a unique quality in that the state accepts obligations for an individual only because of his inability to hold any other status from which he can claim rights. Each welfare family shares a common condition, which results from lack of any other organic position that gives the family a claim to recognition within society. Hence, the obligation that the state incurs for the welfare of indigent families creates a common status that is unconnected to any other status position within society. The quality of this welfare status emerges from lack of reciprocity between the rights of welfare clients and the obligation of the state to care for them.

In his article on poverty, George Simmel[17] summarizes this unique condition of the welfare client as follows: "To deprive those who receive alms of their political rights, adequately expresses the fact that they are nothing but poor. As a result of this lack of positive qualification, as has already been noted, the stratum of the poor, notwithstanding their common situation, does not give rise to sociologically unifying forces." There is nothing that the welfare person does, by virtue of his status, that matches the responsibility assumed by the state. This lack of reciprocity, along with his indigent condition, creates a status that carries no social respect, and there is nothing that the welfare client can do within the context of his dependent condition that merits respect. If it is not possible for him to remove himself from this condition, then some form of adaptation must take place, leading either to self-redefinition and adoption of alternative values, or some form of escape, or acceptance of defeat.

In order to see the importance of this underlying quality of welfare status, we can contrast it with the status of persons who accept vows of poverty. Historically, such vows have been taken by members of a group claiming status on grounds other than poverty, usually religious, and their claim to public charity is a voluntary choice and an avowal of intense attachment to another status that carries rights and duties. The recipients of public welfare are in exactly the opposite position because their lack of attachment to any group that epitomizes their status designates them as public welfare cases. Religious vows of poverty give rise to social respect, whereas poverty that designates only the individual's inability for self-maintenance evokes disrespect.

The social outcast element in the life of the welfare client is counterbalanced by a second force in his life—the utilitarian need for money to maintain a livelihood, and the social and psychological needs to preserve his sense of self-worth. The operation of these contradictory forces—the outcast status and the need to adapt—can be seen in the attitudes of welfare clients to acceptance of public welfare as an income source and in their attempts to maintain self-respect. The need to adapt forces the welfare family to de-emphasize the outcast quality of welfare income and to treat it as simply another source of money in making ends meet. In his study of AFDC mothers in Boston, Sidney Bernard[18] found that acceptance of public assistance as an income source varied with the individual's welfare experience. Bernard summarized his respondents' attitudes as follows: "The distribution of these views of AFDC function among the user-types was clearly as expected: the more the use, the more favorable the view." He also pointed out that kinsmen and friends of welfare users did not disapprove of the respondents' resort to public assistance, and concluded that the use of AFDC is a recognized and accepted aspect of lower-class life. However, there was a difference in attitudes of welfare recipients to the use of welfare as an income source by others and such use by themselves. The further removed they were from direct public assistance experience, the less likely they were to look upon this income source as acceptable for their own use. The respectability of one's income source is a value shared by those in the lower class and the middle class, but the practical exigencies of lower-class life result in a generalized tolerance and acceptance of public assistance, despite its nonrespectable qualities. While these qualities of welfare income represent only one force differentiating the status of the public assistance recipient from that of the breadwinner, another general quality of welfare status—loss of self-reliance—widens the gap between welfare and nonwelfare recipients. Bakke's description of the impact of welfare status on the self-reliance of the client follows: "It is one of the tragic consequences of the lack of jobs in which the worker can prove he is capable of self-support that many must learn new ways of proving that they cannot support themselves. When a man's chief problem, which must be solved if he and his family are to survive, is to prove that he has no resources and has been unable to find ways of renewing them, the stimulus to self-reliance is severely curtailed. The basic cause of this curtailment, however, lies in the nature of the task he must perform and the factors that he must manipulate in the performance. Men become what they practice. What they practice must be adapted to the nature of the problems they face."[18]

Since welfare status unconnected to any form of work relief interferes with the self-reliance central to a breadwinner role, and extended exposure to welfare status weakens a man's capacity to fulfill this role, it is important to initiate early, goal-oriented education and training programs for welfare recipients. At the very first point of an individual's application for public assistance, discussions should begin around planning for rehabilitation toward independent living, thereby restoring hope of improved functioning. The life of workers at the bottom of the American lower-class is a product of contradictory forces which create a life style centering on family stability and continuity of work. Since the breadwinner role is at the very center of this life style, participation in this role is vital in maintaining the self-respect of the very low-status worker and in attaching him to the values of the larger society. Identification with the values of occupational achievement and rising standards of living are manifested mainly in their aspirations for their children while welfare dependency functions as a temporary refuge. There are no adequate statistics to document the number of low-status workers who have had welfare experience during their working lives, the number of such experiences per worker, or their aggregate length, but it seems plausible that welfare experience is much more common for these workers than is popularly supposed. The refuge of welfare dependency, while necessary for survival, threatens the worker's self-respect and tends to produce social isolation, weakening his linkage to the very mode of life that he is struggling to maintain.

ALIENATION AS A CAUSE OF STRESS

Since unemployment is a serious stress condition for most men, it is important for those in the field of welfare administration to understand man's emotional response to stress in order to assist rehabilitating the unemployed. Scientific research on the subject is limited, but connections with other related circumstances and studies can be established. Alexander Leighton's[19] study of Japanese-Americans in evacuation camps in the United States during World War II is one such study. The principles which Leighton developed regarding human response to displacement can be applied to the unemployed, because both experiences represent severe stress, and require new environmental adaptations and modification of belief systems. He stated that the concentration camp situation was not simple, neither was it so complicated or chaotic as to be incomprehensible. The causes and the consequences of the human acts and attitudes within these camps were encompassed in many well known functions of biology, individual psychology, and society.

The hardships of evacuation produced extensive mental and emotional stress, greatly affecting the ways in which the evacuees reacted to the camps' administrative policies and practices. They became unstable and inefficient, and strong differences of opinion amounting to considerable antagonism divided them into various groups, thereby affecting their adjustment to the relocation program. As a reaction to feelings of insecurity, the evacuees struggled hard to achieve self-confidence, and there was a continuous striving for recognition on the part of individuals. On the other hand, a tendency on the part of the administrators to think of the evacuees in terms of emotionally colored stereotypes and sweeping generalizations was an obstacle to cooperation between them. Leighton observed that as administrative efforts to rehabilitate the evacuees and protect their interests became recognized, many of the adverse influences of evacuation were counteracted.

Similarly, the stresses of unemployment are not simple, nor are they so complicated as to be incomprehensible. The feeling of inadequacy of the unemployed may be compared with that of the evacuees. The struggle of both groups to regain security, and their search for recognition, dignity and status—not easily found under the circumstances—is similar. The tendency of society as a whole to view the unemployed as lazy, work-shy malingerers with families who prefer living in their degraded circumstances, and the middle-class stereotype of the poor disturbs communication between groups with differing belief systems.

Better understanding of the problems of communication with the poor and unemployed must emerge before progress can be made. The middle-class helping agent often has little association with the belief systems of the poor and therefore tends to adopt antagonistic rather than rehabilitative approaches toward helping them. Conversely, to the extent that indigenous staff and enlightened professionals establish helping methods which are recognized, their assistance tends to relieve individual and group tensions, and is appreciated.

In noting basic characteristics inherent to human nature among the different people of the world, as well as profound differences in belief, sentiment, habit, and custom among various communities, tribes, and nations, Leighton observed common types of stress disturbing to the emotions and thoughts of individuals. Those equally pertinent to unemployment include loss of means of subsistence, whether in the form of money, jobs, business or property; enforced idleness; rejection, dislike, and ridicule from other people; and capricious and unpredictable behavior from those in authority and upon whom one's welfare depends. It is apparent that enforced idleness and loss of job and social status produce extreme stress, and that there is a universal need of human beings for life purpose, whether they live in Japanese relocation camps, mental institutions, prisons, or general society. There have been many instances of the unreliability, unpredictable behavior, and even capriciousness of the helping professions to the poor and unemployed. As a result, education, employment, and welfare agencies are attempting gradually to re-examine inappropriate and ineffective practices.

Cooperation, withdrawal, and aggressiveness are three universal kinds of behavior with which individuals react to authority when subject to forces of stress that are disturbing to the emotions. When cooperation and compliance operate to free the individual from the forces causing disturbed emotions, they may also lead him to extremes of blind submission which rob him of the ability to take care of himself. Withdrawal, apathy, and indifference arising from disturbed emotions may protect the individual from the forces causing the disturbed emotions, and may enable him to survive until conditions improve, but may also lead to extremes of selfishness, isolation, personal deterioration, and unreliability. Aggression arising from disturbed emotions may stimulate the individual to take decisive actions that will free him from the forces causing the disturbed emotions and may also lead to confused and violent action. As Leighton found, in his study, when aggression is combined with fear, causing the spread of and belief in "pathological" rumors such as atrocity stories, betrayal stories, and suspicions of plots, it may lead to attacks on persons who have little or nothing to do with the cause of stress. Following such an outburst of aggressive action, there is usually a period in which the individual has a sense of relief and well-being. We recognize such violence and its causes and effects in urban rioting today. The welfare recipient who is already emotionally disturbed by chronic stress situations may be further alienated from rationality by tragic world events or may be triggered to violence by real or imagined rebuffs from a helping agency. A case in point is that of the AFDC mother who faced eviction shortly after the assassination of Dr. Martin Luther King in 1968. She threatened to "burn to the ground" the house of her Caucasian landlord, demanded that the welfare consultant call the county supervisor, the county welfare director, and the Governor, and was heard telling her children after the interview that she "got absolutely nothing," and that "we are going to have a riot this summer, and we're going to riot hard and long."

Leighton noted that in the control of human behavior, whether cooperative, apathetic or aggressive, punishment and reward were equally important. He suggested that people respond to stress according to their systems of belief, that they become intolerant of belief systems other than their own, and portray those in systems alien to them as stereotypes, with unaccountable, inferior, or repugnant traits. The belief systems of a community undergoing such stress become more emotional and less rational, increase in number, variety, and tendency to conflict, and are subject to instability and change. The longer and more intense the stress, the more extensive the changes, and the community becomes less able to deal with its stresses until some new equilibrium is established. Out of the confusion, there is likely to arise a single radical system of belief which may or may not bring a new stability but will bring at least a sense of temporary relief from stress.

Leighton acknowledged that the members of administrative staffs, like other human beings, also have their systems of belief, and these may or may not facilitate carrying out the administration's aims. To be effective, all measures aimed at correcting stresses must be applied in accordance with the belief systems of both the administration and the people administered. In summary, he stated that people perceive stress and react to it through their systems of belief, and that an administrator must be aware of these systems, both among the people administered and among the members of his administration if he is to understand, communicate with, and direct both groups.

In his evaluation of the effects of governing men in a war-based situation, Leighton pointed out that forcible alienation and its concomitant extreme emotional stress could be counteracted by the use of rehabilitative techniques. During the quarter century since then, the poor and the unemployed in our cities have shown by protest and by acts of violence that our welfare programs have been administered counter to the socially meaningful work needs and belief systems of welfare recipients. In this regard, one may reflect on the Watts area riots in 1965 and other protest areas. With or without leadership, the frustrated, angry, impatient, negroes and other members of minority groups will revolt in the streets of many American cities to defend and vindicate their humanity.

Warren Haggstrom[20] succinctly identified the social dilemma of the poor in our society as contrasted with opportunities in the middle class structure. He proposed that "motivation, hope, confidence, and skills are provided through childhood socialization and continue as relatively permanent personality components." Since such childhood socialization and subsequent opportunities are available to the middle class, not the poor, Haggstrom assumed that "dependency is not a neurotic need to be dependent, but rather results from lack of social resources during important periods in the lives of the poor." The conditions of the poor are hardened by the repetitive nature of their failures and further established by the rejection, segregation, and censure of the middle class.

Haggstrom's assumption, as well as parallel concepts of adult socialization in anthropological and psychological studies, provide a basis for applying the theory of socialization to rehabilitative techniques for the poor and unemployed. Originally used to conceptualize the processes through which children learn to function within their own social groups, it has more recently been used in studies of adults, especially those in the process of becoming members of professions, and those who are institutionalized as deviate.

Social work interventions that would result in socialization of public assistance clients seem to offer possibilities for testing and comparison with similar interventions derived from psychoanalytic techniques. Adult socialization interventions would include instruction on the social role of the client and the values of the society in which he is expected to become a full-fledged member. Activity would be the key concept, in contrast to the passivity and permissiveness of techniques derived from psychoanalysis, since the goal of socialization is to learn how to function within a specific group. Variables essential to socialization include the agent, aim, timing, and transition rituals. McBroom[21] has emphasized that in the public assistance agency, the worker is the agent of socialization. His aim is to socialize the adult client to his role as a worker, a parent, and independent person, and to help him acquire a repertoire of behaviors adequate to the complex demands of these roles. Major techniques of socialization are teaching, providing a model, inviting participation, offering gratifications and deprivations, inducing cooperation, and preventing back-sliding.

To summarize the psychoanalytical and socialization points of view as alternative models for social work interventions, it may be said that within the psychoanalytic model, the client is perceived as an individual who suffers from psychological maladaptations traceable to remote causes, and within the socialization model, he is seen as a person unprepared for the performance of an adequate repertoire of adult roles, and especially in the case of an AFDC client, for the worker and parental role. The social worker who applies psychoanalytical techniques, attempts to effect improvement in the client's ability to adapt by interviewing him, and through handling of transference phenomena, by correcting his distortions of present reality. The social worker as socializing agent provides alternative opportunities, gives explicit explanations, rewards and punishes, and offers himself freely and consciously as a model for identification, one whom the client can imitate and whose values can be acquired.

In approaches to understanding the alienation of the unemployed as a cause of emotional stress, and in our attempts to restore them to meaningful roles in society, it is important to return to and emphasize the social outcast status of public assistance recipients when dealing with questions of rehabilitation and motivation. In our work-oriented culture, able-bodied men or women feel the stigma of non-work. These feelings are of two kinds—those of personal inadequacy, and the humiliation imposed by society in general. The social outcast phenomenon is pervasive throughout the family structure. Public assistance to the aged, disabled, or blind can often be rationalized as having been earned through payment of taxes if the recipient is aged, or acceptable for other reasons, if he is disabled. But for the able-bodied man no such rationale exists, and the able-bodied AFDC mother can no longer rationalize child care as justification for receiving public aid when a third of the labor force today consists of working women, many with children.

The social outcast phenomenon becomes extremely important to understand as a debilitating feature in one sense and as a motivating feature in another. Recent studies have shown that, contrary to general public opinion, AFDC mothers are extremely motivated to work, but that the initial incentives to obtain work become destroyed by loss of hope, fear of capacity to engage in a working situation, and myriad obstacles such as poor education, lack of work skills and inadequate resources for child care and work-connected expenses. Such frustrated hopes and feelings of being rejected by society often lead to imbalance in the individual's emotional and physical health, and the resultant lack of stability may further weaken any original motivation toward active responsibility or work.

PSYCHOLOGICAL AND PHYSICAL BASES FOR WORK NEEDS

When unemployment requires an individual to rely on public assistance for his livelihood, it may reactivate old psychic conflicts which were resolved when he was gainfully employed. He is viewed in a different manner by his family, because he is no longer the wage earner and head of the household, and by the community which may consider him unwilling to work. This combination of internal and external pressures can create conditions of stress and considerable imbalance between the individual and his community. If he cannot adapt by securing employment, other kinds of adaptation may occur, and the intensity of his emotional responses will depend upon his basic stability.

In medical terminology, "homeostasis" refers to the tendency of the human body to maintain internal and external stability, as when it retains even temperature despite exposure to extremes of heat or cold. The term can also be applied to the relatively stable state of equilibrium that must be kept between man's social and cultural relationships if he is to stay physically and mentally healthy. The maintenance of homeostasis requires that the individual adapt to the society in which he lives in a manner which is acceptable to the group and without detriment to himself.

Although it is well known that when the self-regulating power of the body fails in its capacity to regulate body temperature, disease and death may follow, it is not as well known that when man fails to establish appropriate and satisfying adjustments to his group, disease and death may also follow. It is much easier to comprehend cause and effect in the former example than in the latter, because understanding the reaction of the human organism to disturbance of the condition of homeostasis requires some knowledge of the several processes related to this phenomenon. Consider unemployment, for example, as a circumstance which would establish a stress situation. Aside from the necessity for working in order to provide money for the essentials of life, other basic cultural characteristics associated with employment establish it as a basic requirement for men in our culture. In most instances, the return of homeostasis would occur when the unemployed individual obtains employment, because he would regain balance with the society in which he lives. Prolonged unemployment, however, with the attendant imbalance between man and society, creates problems of several kinds. Since it has been recognized that sustained emotional response to stress situations creates mental and/ or physical ailments, the question arises as to how unemployment can cause physiological changes within the body of an unemployed man.

We must first look to the means that the body has of communicating stress. We know that the two coordinating systems which connect all parts of the body are the nervous system and the blood system. Therefore, messages concerning the stress of unemployment would be carried to the brain through the nervous system, and in the brain these messages are transmitted from the nervous system to the blood vessels. The pituitary gland, which is the intermediary between the nervous system and the blood vessels, picks up the message from the nervous system and transmits it through other endocrine glands within the body. These glands produce hormones which activate appropriate portions of the body to meet the stress situation. This system, however, is designed to cope only with temporary periods of emergency. In accordance with the Psychogenic Theory[22] of the author, chronic stress due to persistent anxiety about prolonged unemployment creates abnormalities in the hormonal system, which in turn, may tend to break down body tissues, and as a result, mental or physical disease can occur.

From the considerable body of knowledge in the field of psychosomatic medicine, it is well known that unemployment, bankruptcy, loss of a loved one, marital discord, and many other tragic life events can cause disease. It becomes apparent that one of the objectives of modern society should be to assist individuals in adapting to serious life events when it is not possible for them to make these adaptations alone. Since so much of life's stress arises out of environmental problems, it is appropriate for those in the field of social work to become engaged in alleviating such problems and thus assist in restoring people to a condition of homeostasis.

Public welfare agencies receive a majority of those who encounter environmental stresses of varying kinds without being able to make adaptations satisfying to themselves. It is important that public welfare agencies establish services, facilities, programs and assistance, all directed toward the restoration of a homeostatic condition for such people. There must be a healthy adaptation on the part of the individual, not adaptation to the ailment. This means that he should not be asked to adapt to life in a nursing home so as to live a bit more comfortably with his illness. Rather, he should be assisted in relieving his environmental stress so as to return to some kind of useful activity in the community.

Charlotte Towle[23] stated that the adult lives by his work in more ways than one, and that the unemployed man's countless pleas for work, complaints of boredom, and intense dissatisfaction, expressed in terms of not having anything to do, as often as in terms of not having enough money to spend, made it clear that work has more than mere survival value. This conviction is supported by modern insights into human personality which have been gained through scientific study. Students of human behavior are convinced that the adult normally wants to work, has an imperative need to work, and is deeply frustrated in his growth impulses when denied work opportunity. It is not idleness itself, but the frustration produced by the idleness which sets in operation the regressive processes through which men break down.

Towle also recognized the adverse influence of unemployment on the family. Out of affectional and economic deprivation in earlier years, a woman may bring to marriage a childlike and excessive need to be loved and cared for. Her husband may be able to meet this need as long as he is feeling adequate through satisfactory work, with status as head of the family and in the community. Some of the gaps in the relationship may have been filled and the marriage sustained through his ability to provide for her, but loss of satisfying work and status may create feelings of inadequacy in the husband which make him temporarily dependent on her. Unable to meet his affectional need, she may be irritated, particularly when he is showing less affection and providing so little, and she becomes even less able than usual to meet his need. Mutual frustration may lead to a breakdown in a relationship which might have continued had not unemployment brought a shift in the balance of needs. In its varying consequences, unemployment can create crises in family life which must be relieved before normal family functioning can be restored.

Public assistance caseloads include a relatively large proportion of persons who are physically, mentally, and emotionally disabled and hence unemployable. Among these we may encounter some legendary instances of generational dependency. A study of the background of these people may give us a better understanding of this condition.

Employability from the standpoint of physical fitness is sometimes carefully determined by medical examination. When physical unfitness has been ruled out, an individual's disinclination for work, continued complaints of physical symptoms, and ineffectual attempts to get or to hold jobs, are commonly designated by lay staff under terms such as "work-shy," "lazy," or "malingering." Until it is understood that man wants to work, and that disinclination for work may be a symptom of emotional or physical illness, appropriate services will not be employed for study and treatment. Meanwhile, we fail to be helpful to persons who might be helped, and we treat unjustly those who are incurably ill. Use of social casework and other resources might throw valuable light on the problem of the work-shy individual. In addition, many public welfare social workers have long understood that adequate assistance grants would aid greatly in the rehabilitative process.

Several investigators have pointed to the difficulties encountered by the adolescent in contemporary society in choosing a satisfactory job from the myriad available vocations. They have also recognized the difficulties which are associated with the marginal status, social and economic, of adolescents. It has been suggested that restrictions on the freedom of vocational choice in adolescence may be associated with increased mental health problems and anxiety over the ambiguity of the future job situation. The marginal status afforded the adolescent is also detrimental to his self-esteem and may have serious consequences relating to his mental health. Studies in other cultures have suggested that such responses are a peculiarly complex and western phenomenon associated with the lack of predetermined work-role-definition for the adolescent. From these studies it appears that the mental health of adolescents is related not only to work opportunities but also to the range of opportunities present, to the social status accorded the adolescent, both before and after the employment is secured, and to the stability of role expectations which impinge upon him. In view of this, it is reasonable to assume that the work and mental health relationships of adolescents vary with personality, family cohesiveness, socio-economic class, and demographic factors. A fuller understanding of the psychological aspects of childhood and adolescence in reference to job choice and life-plan patterns will clarify the generational aspects of dependency on public aid.

It is important to observe that physical and psychological factors are associated with work and the lack of it. Inactivity torments a healthy human being. Every fibre is alive with the impulse toward activity. The usual forms of activity in our culture are play, for children; work and intermittently, play, for adults. Activity for the adult finds expression in work and in games and sports and illustrates the impulse to bodily activity as important in its own right. The instinct for activity is, however, more than an urge to expend bodily energy; it is generally directed toward creation of something which has been imaginatively conceived, a constructive impulse. Interference with the free expression of this human instinct to activity is sufficient to induce grave disturbances in physical and emotional health. This is illustrated in prison life, with the system of confinement in separate cells an additional torture. In prison, the most trifling occupation is welcomed with relief. Man has been able to equate mental activity with physical activity, but still requires a rhythm of physical activity interspersed even if in the form of play or hobby.

Unemployment is intolerable to the average manual worker as soon as the normal craving for rest and leisure has been satisfied, because his life rhythm has become conditioned to physical action. Dixon Wexter[24] observed psychological and physical deterioration in the unemployed as follows: "Bewilderment, hesitation, apathy, loss of self-confidence were the commonest marks of protracted unemployment. A man no longer cared how he looked. Unkempt hair and swarthy stubble, shoulders a-droop, a slow dragging walk, were external signs of inner defeat, often aggravated by malnutrition. Joblessness proved a wasting disease. What social workers called 'unemployment shock' affected some men as if they were in the grip of panic, driving them to frenzied search for work by day, sleepless worry at night . . . a mood of lost self-esteem, perplexity, or bitterness toward old employers and life in general. The sum of these effects upon the former breadwinner added up to weaker morale, by a vicious cycle making him still more unemployable." Wexter's report on a survey of idle engineers conducted in 1933 revealed that three out of every four showed morale inferior to that of the average job holder. The physical expression of job losses was revealed in flabby muscles, faulty coordination and lack of stamina when work was resumed. Similarly, when a group of 40 unemployed stenographers were set to work in a New York office, all quickly showed signs of nervous fatigue under the old routine and several grew hysterical. More than two-thirds needed from two to three week's readjustment before they could take dictation without breaking down.

James Williams[25] described the physiological need of the human organism to function, and suggested that unemployment and inactivity contributed to changes in human values as from "right to work" to "right to relief." In lamenting the fact that our social order does not meet the need for character building work and recreation in periods of unemployment, he stated: "Essential in morale is the attitude to work. It is the nature of the organism to function, to be active in the satisfaction of its needs. The whole animal creation is active in getting subsistence. The human organism is not different from any other in this respect. The glands pour their hormones into the blood stream, the cortical and other nerve reserves are in unstable equilibrium. There is, then, an organic desire for action, just as there is an organic desire for food. The desire for action cannot be denied satisfaction any more than can the desire for food without weakening the organism. During unemployment men have not the proper nourishment, they are forced to be inactive, they lose muscular tonicity, vitality runs low. They become submissive, apathetic, incapable of exertion on their own behalf."

In acknowledging that men want to work because they acquired the cultural attitude from our rural heritage, and that the worker is socially approved as contrasted with disapproval for the one who will not work, Williams maintained that men's sense of a right to relief was much weaker than their feeling of a right to work, and that some even attempted suicide rather than ask for relief. He identified our social heritage as well as the physiological drive toward action as motivating man's desire to work and identified this desire as essential to morale. He stressed the conditioning of man through habits and attitudes built up by the environment of the independent farmer and the artisan who always had gainful work to do, and stated that these ideas were then handed down from father to son and preached from the pulpit. Williams recognized that if a man is inactive long enough, he loses the habit of action and is conditioned to inactivity, loses the pride of the worker, and no longer condemns lazy people or feels that he has a right to work. Being no longer averse to asking for charity, he feels most keenly the right to relief, although this change in the morality of a person comes slowly. In noting that social workers in 1933 could see men's bodies becoming soft, their minds losing objectivity, and their emotions becoming unstable, he concluded that without the initiative which they once had as workers, men showed an aversion to making any effort at all. His insight predicted our present concern for generational poverty and dependency.

Eisenberg and Lazarsfeld[26], in a study of the psychological effects of unemployment, agreed with other authorities that unemployment tends to make people more emotionally unstable than they were previously. They examined reports of clinicians which identified the effects of unemployment as a personal threat to an individual's economic security with fear playing a large role. They found that the individual's sense of proportion was shattered, he lost his common sense of values, his prestige was lost in his own eyes and in the eyes of his fellow men, he developed feelings of inferiority, and lost self-confidence and morale. It was found through questionnaires and numerous tests analyzed in this study that three groups of unemployed office workers tended to be slightly more neurotic than the general population, that poorer general adjustment, in terms of attitude to-

ward the future, the home, and the social environment characterized
the unemployed; and that the unemployed as compared with employed groups were more negative and more depressed in the sense
that they expected greater failure in various situations in the future.
They tended to resemble mental patients suffering from anxiety neurosis in this respect. It was noted that when the unemployed regained
jobs the effects were almost immediate. The individual bright-
ened up, regained his status in society and his emotional stability. If
the unemployment was too long-lasting it was noted that the individual may have suffered to such an extent that it was very difficult
for him to regain his stability.

It is generally agreed that lowering of morale, discouragement, a
sense of hopelessness, particularly with reference to finding a job,
general depression, and distrust of one's fellow man are characteristic
of the unemployed. It is important to note, however, that a job must
provide, plus other satisfactions, a feeling of economic security. Those
who are economically insecure, employed or unemployed, will have
lower morale. The length of time that an individual is unemployed seems
to play an important part in determining the change in his attitudes. In
an analysis of life histories of 25 unemployed English workers, Beales
and Lambert[27] described the progression from optimism through
pessimism to fatalism, the increase of inferiority feeling, the destruction of family relationships, and the weakening of interest in politics
and organization with an increasing length of unemployment. Gatti[28]
described very much the same course of moods of the unemployed,
stating that first, there was surprise, particularly if the individual had
never before been unemployed; then fear, with renewed hope while
the worker was actively looking for a job, and then anxiety. But
when hope failed, the unemployed had the feeling that "life had forgotten them" and became apathetic. Gatti felt that unemployment
had its most marked effects at this stage, and that it was the point of
greatest crisis, with long duration of unemployment making the individual even more apathetic.

Robert Frumkin's[29] study of occupational and mental disorders
concluded that "there is an inverse relationship between rates of first
admissions to a mental hospital and income and prestige as manifested
in occupation, but there are definite sex differences in this relationship which indicate that occupation is generally more important to
the mental health of men than of women; occupational prestige is
more significant to mental health than is occupational income; occupational income is more significant to the mental health of men than
of women, probably because occupation is not the only source of
income for women; because occupational income and prestige are
considered as valid indices of socio-economic status, it can be stated
that rates of admission, in general, are inversely related to socio-

economic status." He believed it important to the sex role of the adult age level that the normal man have a job related to social status in general, and that only in very exceptional cases could an adult man be genuinely self-respecting and enjoy status in the eyes of others if he did not earn a living in an approved occupational role. Not only was it a matter of his own economic support, but, also the primary source of income and class status of his wife and children. In relating work with the satisfaction of basic needs, Frumkin stated that all men must have . . . "an opportunity to provide for himself and his family which means more than an ability to take care of the financial needs of the persons for whom he is responsible. The individual must prove that he is providing for his family. Many patients returning to mental hospitals after periods of unsuccessful adjustment away from the hospital, report they were unable to tolerate a situation where their wives or children had to work to provide an income for the family. A man needs work that will be related to his basic vocational interests. He wants work that is meaningful, and job activities to which he can constructively apply his energies. Man wants a job which will give him a feeling of accomplishment. He must feel that he is making a contribution to his community and society. The satisfied worker is one who gains from his job, among other satisfactions, a sense of achievement through his own efforts. He wants a job with which he can identify. This is difficult to attain in some vocational areas today because of the breakdown of jobs, however, satisfactions are gained as a member of a work group."

J. P. Kahn's[30] analysis of reactions to dependency suggested that a certain amount of independence is essential for the mature individual whose self-directed functioning rests on the maintenance of his sense of personal capacity, because adult status in our culture implies relative independence and earning one's own living. Therefore, when an adult is in need of financial help from public sources, a reversal in the relationship between the individual and reality takes place. He is thrust back into a state of helplessness and passivity. The loss or absence of money to live on has the effect of weakening techniques of mastery, and the disappearance of ordinary resources inhibit usual modes of action. Established standards and patterns of living break down and the person finds himself blocked in discharging simple responsibilities with less security in carrying familiar relationships. The ego loses part of its functioning capacity; change in the outer world is accompanied by inner confusion and shrinkage in ability to operate. The construction of the ego span is similar to the reaction that takes place when the organism is physically damaged and the individual becomes oblivious to all but his physical hurt. The problem of having no money impinges on every part of the individual's life and relationships. Kahn stated that since dependence on

others for assistance is for most people an undesirable, severely restricted way of life, respect for the client in need entails an ability
and willingness on the part of the caseworker to recognize the client's
real and justified dislike and fear of public assistance. The client
should be helped to regain and strengthen his own self-direction and
self-responsibility.

The psychological problem with which public welfare agencies
must deal is to provide clients with an economic base for repairing
and strengthening the damaged structure of their living in a way that
enables them to assert again their own capabilities for self-respon-
sible decision and action. The agency can restore the minimum essential elements of the economic reality that the individual has lost, and it
should present these elements to him in a manner that engages him
as a functioning adult with the capacity to carry adult responsibilities
and the right to exercise adult prerogatives. An understanding of the
social, cultural, psychological and physical aspects of human behavior
in reference to unemployment and public aid gives direction to establishment of appropriate services and facilities. The importance of the
attitudes and practices of the social worker in rehabilitation of the
unemployed cannot be overstressed.

In her studies of motivation, capacity, and opportunity, Lillian
Ripple[31] examined the forces at work in human behavior which combine to provide success for the individual in the casework treatment
process. She found that the most important variable was the provision
of services, rather than environmental conditions, and that skill in
specific service activities was not as important as the amount of encouragement given the client during and immediately after the first
interview. Of 178 clients who were discouraged by caseworkers in
the first interview, only eight continued to a fifth interview. Discouragement could result from negative attitudes or actions on the
part of the caseworker, as first, from an uninvolved, neutral or bland
appraisal of the client's problem, leaving little hope that the condition
could be relieved; and second from a positive response followed by
placing the client on a waiting list with the next appointment three or
four weeks later. The positive aspects which encouraged continuance
with the casework service were characterized by warm, specific
efforts to relieve discomfort, assurance of improvement, and development of a plan for work on the problem in the next interview. Restrictive or unmodifiable environmental influences resulted in client
discontinuance or other unfavorable outcome. Similar conditions
which were modifiable resulted in favorable outcome. It was also
found that if change had occurred by the fourth interview, 9 out of 11
cases had favorable outcome. If the client had complicating psychological problems, the attitude and behavior of other persons became
determining, as when another person opposed the client's efforts, he

was likely to discontinue. High motivation and capacity resulted in favorable outcome. Ripple concluded that the client must have discomfort about his condition and hope that something can be done about it before casework can begin, and the case services must positively identify with the client's hope.

Motivation was clarified by Thomas French[32] as composed of two parts, first, a negative process involving the need to get away from something such as pain, fear, unrest, or tension; and second, hope stimulated by opportunity for satisfaction along with desire to realize anticipated goals. The possibility of movement by an individual toward an identified goal depends, according to French, upon his "integrative capacity." The hope, capacity and opportunity must be synchronous for success. Ripple expanded French's theory and agreed with his general premise. Both authors agreed that deficiencies in motivation and/or capacity in reference to the goal (opportunity) would tend toward failure. When the goal sought exceeds the integrative capacity, disintegration of the goal-directed behavior occurs. French believed that confidence of success was the most important factor in maintaining the integrative capacity, and Ripple found that when the casework helping process was supporting and highly encouraging, the prospects of success increased markedly over passive helping methods and other discouraging casework practices. French found that the most important ingredients for success in maintaining integrative capacity for goal-striving were confidence of success, opportunities for satisfaction of needs or memories of previous satisfaction, and aid in the establishment of hope and confidence of success.

An essential message emerging from French and Ripple's independent studies is that there is a need to evaluate capacity and motivation, to tailor opportunity to the individual, and to offer supportive casework or other services as needed to remove obstacles which interfere with rehabilitative processes. Since mutual engagement between caseworker and client is vital to the rehabilitative approach, the caseworker should go out of his way to also provide a protected vocational environment for selected disadvantaged unemployed. It is only when the client's hopes have been revived that he may be newly directed toward work motivation and sometimes casework alone is insufficient to restore hope.

TRADITIONAL METHODS OF INTERVENTION AS ADDITIONAL CAUSES OF STRESS

The evidence is sufficient today to develop conceptualizations on the dynamics of human behavior in respect to man's need for work and his defensive adaptations to nonwork in the form of physical and emotional illness, dependency, and social disorganization. Knowledge is being gained as to appropriate methods of intervention as well as to understanding conditions which exacerbate rather than relieve work disability. Historical evidence will clarify for the objective scholar the fact that traditional methods of intervention to a large extent have tended to worsen the condition of the unemployed person. When public aid was given to relieve the distress, its conditions of meagerness, humiliation, shame, and degrading work relief all tended to add stressful conditions to an already over-stressed family. The consequences of increasing psychological and social problems and generational dependency could be expected and predicted. The studies of French and of Ripple offer new intervention clues and the myriad studies and reports either of scientific or less structured nature also support alternate systems of services and public aid. The conditions sought will contain elements of supportive help, adequate financial aid, and provision of upgrading opportunity in the form of education, vocational training and protective work experience; and most important, work must be available to all adults to prevent the debilitating consequences of nonwork.

During the height of the great depression, President Roosevelt said in his message to Congress on January 4, 1935: "The Federal Government must and shall quit this business of relief." In this instance, the fervor of the sentiment against direct relief, the dole, was traceable to abhorrence of its waste and destruction of morale when given to men and women able and willing to work. When productive activity has been recognized as of tremendous consequence to the individual, how do we go about and how can we promote marshaling the forces of public and private competency to achieve the desired objective? Achievement of objectives requires more than intellectual realization of the validity of newer concepts on the part of a few. General change in practice will require a complete cultural reorientation to new concepts. The belief that some men are, by nature, lazy, shiftless and no-good is so firmly ingrained in our culture that modification of this belief will require herculean efforts, including research, experimentation, demonstration, dissemination of knowledge, and the full attention of cooperative public and private activity. Since societal attitudes and beliefs will require more than conceptualization, the ensuing discussion will consider attitudes and beliefs of man in our society.

REFERENCES

1. Fromm, Eric: Man for Himself. New York, Rinehart & Co., Inc., 1947.
2. Gans, Herbert J.: The Urban Villagers. New York, Free Press, 1962.
3. Bradley, Nelson: The work addict. Sales Management, July 7, 1961.
4. Friedmann, E. A., and Havighurst, R. J.: Work and retirement, Man,

Work, and Society, edited by S. Nosow and W. Form. New York, Basic Books, Inc., 1962.

5. Gardner, Burleigh: Human Relations in Industry. Chicago, Richard D. Irwin, Inc., 1945.

6. Dubin, Robert: Industrial Workers' Worlds: A study of the central life interests of industrial workers' worlds. Social Problems, Vol. 3, No. 3, January, 1956.

7. Dyer, William G.: Work and the family, Man, Work, and Society, edited by S. Nosow and W. Form. New York, Basic Books, Inc., 1962.

8. Morse, Nancy C., and Weiss, R. S.: The function and meaning of work and the job, Man, Work, and Society, edited by S. Nosow and W. Form. New York, Basic Books, Inc., 1962.

9. Baake, E. Wight: The Unemployed Worker. New Haven, Yale University Press, 1940.

Baake, E. Wight: Citizens Without Work. New Haven, Yale University Press, 1940.

Cavan, Ruth S., and Ranck, Katherine H.: The Family and the Depression. Chicago, University of Chicago Press, 1938.

Angel, Robert C.: The Family Encounters the Depression. New York, Charles Scribner's Sons, 1936.

10. Young, Kimball: Personality and Problems of Adjustment. New York, Appleton Century, 1940.

11. Polanyi, Karl: The Great Transformation. New York, Rinehart & Co., Inc., 1944.

12. Komarovsky, Mirra: The Unemployed Man and His Family. New York, Dryden Press, 1940.

13. Stone, Robert C., and Schlamp, Frederic T.: Family Life Styles Below the Poverty Line. Sacramento, Report of the California State Social Welfare Board, 1966.

14. Rice, Stuart A.: Psychological effect of unemployment on the jobless man. American labor legislation review, 15:46, 1925.

15. Ginsburg, Eli and others: The Unemployed. New York, Harper Bros., 1943.

16. Lowell, Josephine Shaw: The Evils of Investigation and Relief, National Conference of Charities and Corrections. Boston, George H. Ellis Press, 1898.

17. Simmel, George: The poor, translated by Clair Jacobson. Social Problems, Vol. 13, No. 2, Fall, 1965.

18. Bernard, Sydney E.: The Economic and Social Adjustment of Low-Income Female-Headed Families, A report of a research project supported by the Federal Welfare Administration and Social Security Administration Cooperative Research and Demonstration Grants Program. Florence Heller Graduate School for Advanced Studies in Social Welfare. Waltham, Mass., Brandeis University, 1964.

19. Leighton, Alexander: The Governing of Men. Princeton, N.J., Princeton University Press, 1945.

20. Haggstrom, Warren C.: The power of the poor, Mental Health of the Poor, edited by Frank Riessman, Jerome Cohen, and Arthur Pearl. New York, Free Press, 1964.

21. McBroom, Elizabeth: Helping AFDC families—A comparative study. Social Service Review, Vol. 39, 1965.

22. Simmons, Harold E.: The Psychogenic Theory of Disease—A new Approach to Cancer Research. Sacramento: General Welfare Publications, 1966.

23. Towle, Charlotte: Common Human Needs, Public Assistance Report No. 8, Bureau of Public Assistance, Social Security Board, Federal Security Agency. Washington, D.C., U.S. Government Printing Office, 1945.

24. Wexter, Dixon: Age of the Great Depression, 1929-1941. New York, MacMillan Co., 1948.

25. Williams, James M.: Human Aspects of Unemployment and Relief. Chapel Hill, University of North Carolina Press, 1933.

26. Eisenberg, Philip, and Lazarsfeld, Paul F.: The psychological effects of unemployment. Psychology Bulletin, Vol. 35, 1938.

27. Beales, A. L., and Lambert, R. S.: Memoirs of the Unemployed. London, Victor Gollancz, Ltd., 1934.

28. Gatti, A.: La Dis occupazione come crisi psicologica. Archives Italia di Psicolog, Vol. 15, 1937.

29. Frumkin, Robert M.: Occupation and major mental disorders, Mental Health and Mental Disorders, edited by M. Rose. New York, W. W. Norton Co., 1955.

30. Kahn, J. P.: Attitude toward recipients of public assistance. Social Casework, Vol. 36, 1955.

31. Ripple, Lillian: Motivation, Capacity, and Opportunity—Studies in casework theory and practice. Chicago, University of Chicago Press, 1964.

32. French, Thomas M.: The Integration of Behavior. Chicago, University of Chicago Press, 1952.

CHAPTER 2

ATTITUDES OF SOCIETY TOWARD WORK

PHILOSOPHICAL AND ETHICAL DETERMINANTS

THERE IS HISTORICAL EVIDENCE that man has viewed work as abject drudgery, a curse on mankind. In his poetry, Homer alleged that the Greek gods hated mortals, and out of spite condemned them to toil. Xenophon, the historian, called work the painful price the gods charged for the goods of life. The Talmud stated in ancient Hebrew that "If man does not find his food like animals and birds but must earn it, that is due to sin." Although hard work was expiation for sin and a drudgery to some Jews, it was not the same fateful necessity that was the basis of many of the Greek tragedies. In some respects, work took on a spiritual quality in Hebrew literature, yet in Ecclesiastes, the question is asked: "What gain has the worker from his toil?" "The labor of man does not satisfy the soul." An alternate viewpoint in later rabbinical literature predicted that the kingdom of God would emerge slowly from earthly reality in terms of the good will and work of man in brotherly relations with his fellow man. In this context work acquired dignity and value. The Pharisees, the reactionary Jewish sect of the century before the birth of Christ, exalted manual labor: "Blessed the man who bows himself like an ox under the yoke, and like an ass to the burden." The Hebrew heritage which places spiritual value on work has in the twentieth century found expression in the modern *kibbutz* (communal farm) of Israel.

The New Testament indicates that Jesus coupled labor with material gain: "Behold the fowl of the air; for they sow not, neither do they reap nor gather into barns; yet your Heavenly Father feedeth them. Are ye not much better than they?" . . . "And why take ye thought for raiment? Consider the lilies of the field, how they grow: they toil not, neither do they spin: And yet I say unto you, that even Solomon in all his glory was not arrayed like one of these." . . . "Take therefore no thought of the morrow; for the morrow shall take thought of the things of itself. Sufficient unto the day is the evil thereof." Jesus saw no value in accumulating material goods and viewed efforts to gather such goods as barriers in the road to God.

St. Augustine attempted to equate religious doctrine with earthly needs by declaring that work for monks was obligatory only in supplying the needs of the monastery, fostering brotherly love, and purging body and soul of evil pleasures. His Rule XLVIII stated:

47

"Idleness is the enemy of the soul and therefore at fixed times the brothers ought to be occupied in manual labor, and again at fixed times, in sacred reading." This early Catholicism gave work a spiritual dignity, supporting the earlier Hebrew concepts.

It was protestantism which historically became the moving force in a spiritual development of the concept that work was the key to life. Luther became the founder of the protestant ethic which declared both the penal and the educational virtues of work. To Luther work became a form of service to God, its benefits falling equally amongst all professions, and an ingredient necessary to a good life. The religious dignity bestowed upon work by Luther was further exalted by the subsequent declarations of Calvin who believed that all men, rich and poor alike, must work to fulfill God's will. As the followers of Calvin became strong-willed and hardworking from religious conviction, his antithesis was seen as an idle, lazy, soft-souled person. While work pleased God, Calvin believed that the fruits of labor should not be hoarded, but used to finance new ventures, thus developing religious approval for the beginnings of modern capitalism. The hard, disciplined, rational, and uniform nature of Calvin's concept of work, as opposed to the easygoing ways of the independent artisan, formed one of the bases for the rigorous discipline of modern factory life. Calvin, unlike Luther, favored an upward movement from class to class in work and the professions, setting aside the caste system, and imploring men to strive for improved occupational status.

It is difficult and perhaps of relative unimportance for historians to judge whether Calvin's precepts were used to dignify a change which was inevitable in any event, since religion in any era has reflected and supported man's culture as it evolved. While work values emerged initially from a religious heritage and then gradually lost their pious flavor, they have become firmly entrenched in the modern world culture. Profit has finally become the end product, the rationale for all endeavor. Today, in industrialized society, profit represents the basis for measurement of success or failure, motivating man to develop cost cutting methods, research new systems and products, install machines, and sell.

Throughout history, philosophers, writers, and artists have theorized about men and work. In the fifteenth century Leonardo da Vinci adopted the Greek concept that the gods sell man the goods of life and exact the price of labor and travail. While less bitter than the Greeks, Leonardo rejoiced in the thought that although a man's life work was a search which would fail in goal achievement, it would never be given up in his search for perfection. In the sixteenth century in Italy, Giordano Bruno glorified work as a tool of human conquest and as an arm against adverse fortune. He described the past golden age as an age when men lived in idleness and as stupid brutes, while the new society with its blessing of work saved man from life's deadly monotony. Tommaso Campanella, a generation later, idealized workers who became joyful because each had work suited to his character. England's Sir Thomas More sought to develop a utopian society without social classes but even more significantly, a utopia where all men are at work. In France, Rabelais promoted the study of the arts and liberal sciences, the practice of gymnastics and military exercises, and admonished Gargantua's tutor not to forget to train his pupil in skills in the humblest, most common manual work.

In the seventeenth century, the English philosopher, Locke, idealized labor as the source of all economic values; and Adam Smith, the Scotch economist, applied Locke's principle in the eighteenth century in greater depth through development of the theory that any act is truly productive which helps make over raw material into something useful to man; that labor, in effect, creates the mass of goods which man consumes. Smith's views became the root of the emerging science of political economics of modern times.

Because of the wide range of philosophers' intellects some more than others inevitably became caught up in the provincialism of their time. In the eighteenth century, France's Rousseau believed the small artisan in his frugal village environment was ideal and the happiest of men, while Voltaire, the satirist, threw his logic on the side of work which produced cities with their wealth, luxury, commerce, industry, the arts. Voltaire's *Candide*, reflects the basic value of work. In the conversations of the three characters who agree that work, not optimism, is the best possible solution to life's problems: "Man was not born for repose," says Pangloss; Martin agrees: "Work without arguing about it is the only way to make life endurable;" and the book closes with Candide's: "Let us cultivate our garden." At this time, Hume, the Scot, glorified luxury, wealth, and work in his philosophy, suggesting that man differs from animals because of the work and struggle through which he secures the goods of nature after having been thrown poor and naked into the world. He believed that necessity was the mother of activity as well as invention.

The nineteenth century became the principal era for full development of new concepts of work. European philosophers exercised great influence as they promoted work to a position it had never previously held in religion or ethics—the cause of all human progress—material, intellectual, and spiritual. This movement was begun toward the end of the eighteenth century with the theories of Kant, who stated that work is a productive activity of the spirit operating out of a law inherent in itself, and that it forms a cosmos which is the ordered world of nature from the chaos of data given by the senses. The spirit is activity which, from within, generates order and harmony. To know is to do, to act, to produce order and harmony. Kant's *Critique of Pure Reason* gave depth to the concept of the spirit as productive activity, semi-divine creativeness. Fichte also made a connection between the spirit of man and activity, stating that in activity alone can man find happiness. The source of vice is sloth, similar to the inertia found in most forms of matter. Man, born from matter, is naturally slothful, but because of complex needs can satisfy them only by conquering his natural laziness and by battling forces of nature. Work therefore becomes its own reward, bringing to man the joys of strength and activity.

During the latter part of the nineteenth century and the early part of the twentieth century, Bergson critically pursued the connection between intelligence, human labor, and technology. Man's intelligence meant he could invent, make tools, become an artisan; and his artisan and mechanical intelligence, turning its back on life to work with inert matter, in effect allowed man to cast off the bonds of instinct and enabled him to act as he pleased, continually surpassing earlier efforts. Bergson, more than any other philosopher, celebrated the productive labor of man and, in fact, believed that as a productive worker, man achieves divinity. Freud considered work the chief means of binding an individual to reality. Carlyle stated: "All work, even cotton spinning, is noble; work alone is noble . . . A life of ease is not for any man, nor for any God . . . Even in the meanest sorts of labor, the whole soul of man is composed into a kind of real harmony the instant he sets himself to work . . . Blessed is he who has found his work; let him ask no other blessedness."

In their theories on work, Ruskin, the English critic and reformer, and Tolstoi, the Russian philosopher and mystic, brought forth views which tended to differ from traditional thought in the 1890's. Ruskin believed that profit as an end in itself tends to cut men off from their brothers, withering the soul; that earned money should be spent; that the only appropriate sources of wealth should be work and personal savings; and that profit taken on capital alone was highway robbery. He went so far as to suggest that all work be done by hand with no aid from machinery except devices set in motion by wind and water.

Although Tolstoi believed it was the duty of each man to earn his living by the sweat of his brow and that "calloused hands make independent and virtuous men," he was not persuaded work was essentially merit or virtue, but rather a necessity like food. He was convinced that his view of work would eliminate the possibility of any injustice or exploitation arising from the idea that work was a burden. Although Ruskin's ideal was of free artisans paying their way with work which they loved as an art, frequently pausing for rest and play, and all resulting in peace and contentment, and Tolstoi preferred a homogeneous anarchical society of peasants and artisans paying each other with their work to fulfill a humble existence, both believed work an absolute necessity for man just as eating and breathing—a tranquil activity without any element of the hectic rush toward ever-receding goals.

Ruskin's considerable understanding of the nature of working conditions included the suggestion that the greatest material results could be obtained between employer and worker, not through antagonism, but through affection for each other. If the employer, instead of endeavoring to get as much work as possible from the worker, would seek rather to have the work performed in a manner beneficial to the worker, in the final analysis such unselfish treatment would produce the most effective return. He likened the employer-worker relationship to a father-son affinity, and drew the analogy of a youth entering a commercial establishment, having left home, and viewing his employer as a father. Ruskin noted that the employer's authority, together with the general atmosphere of his business and character of his associates on the job, would have more pressing weight than the home influence. In other words, he noted in the 1890's what is more readily apparent today, namely, that the father-son relationship model is reenacted throughout life in differing situations.

Ruskin's reflections on the value of work caused him to propose methods of ensuring that work would be available to all. He suggested that men or women out of employment be placed at once in a government school and allowed to work at tasks appropriate to their training and at a reasonable wage, but if found incapable of work because of lack of education, they should be taught new skills in this setting. If the individual could not work because of illness, he should be treated. Ruskin believed that if the individual was unwilling to work, he should be compelled to work, with wages, in a painful and degrading form of toil. While we would consider Ruskin's belief regarding compulsive work distasteful today, it is interesting to note that his concept of man's need to be at work, and the nature of governmental responsibility to ensure the right to work can be likened to the movement toward education, training, work experience, and provision of work for man in present society.

Ruskin disapproved of the accumulation of wealth, considered the desire for riches essentially a desire for power, and suggested that the art of making oneself rich also involved keeping one's neighbor poor. He added, however, that if the use of riches was such that it was to the advantage of the nation, it might be justifiable. In other words, it would be appropriate to grow rich justly. It appears that Ruskin was concerned that the power which wealth provided should not be used for exploitation of man, and to the extent that it was not,

it might be appropriate for individuals to obtain wealth. Later discussion in this book of the use of power by agri-business interests in
California to exploit men gives credence to Ruskin's concern. He
apparently also foresaw the possibility of automation, complicated
by modern man's incapacity to understand the value of work. His
prophetic concept therefore included such ideas as guaranteed income, which, as he predicted, may be perverted to support men in
idleness. Ruskin conceived that man should not work for profit but
rather as a social service, and that work should be guaranteed to all.

Many social, political, and economic practices of the past were
based upon psychological, religious and philosophical assumptions
about the nature of man which have relevance to his motivation to
work, or lack of it. Thomas Hobbes, the seventeenth century contemporary of John Locke, developed the "egoistic" concept of ethi-
cal hedonism, justifying conduct motivated by desire for that which
aids the "vital motion" of the individual, a selfish system. Hobbes believed that man was by nature self-seeking, that he might employ
elaborate subterfuges to conceal this self-interest by pretense at
obeying the King, conforming to law, organizing into groups; but
that, basically, these activities were only expressions of self-interest.
Locke suggested that the good or evil in man were nothing but expressions of pleasure or pain, a concept which was widely held at
that time and influenced such thinkers a century later, as Adam
Smith, who also took the selfish system for granted. By 1800, Jeremy
Bentham developed the philosophy of psychological hedonism, partly
based on the writings of Locke, but differing from the concept of
Hobbes in theorizing that human conduct was motivated by the desire for pleasure, seeking that pleasure which was most certain, most
intense, and of longest duration.

Ancient Greek concepts of individualistic hedonism gave way
to more social and philanthropic concepts. It was suggested that
human action must be induced, that in the absence of enticement
provided by pleasure or advantage the organism would remain
quiet and inert. Thus developed in mid-seventeenth century philosophy the concept of "quietism," a system of mysticism which
suggested that man would avoid the pain of effort, work, or labor,
unless compensated by the enticement of a correspondingly greater
amount of pleasure. On the basis of this concept, Malthus, toward
the beginning of the nineteenth century, believed that even the
desire for the means of subsistence did not suffice to overcome
the indolence of man. Others theorized that there was real need
for pestilence, floods, famine, and other disasters to shatter the
complacency of man, render him very uncomfortable, and thus
thrust him into greater activity for self-preservation. It was suggested that the lower classes would need to be kept poor, otherwise

they would never be industrious, a concept that rationalized a ready source of cheap labor. Thus man, particularly the lower class of man, was construed by some to be a rather low form of animal life, poorly motivated, with the need to be prodded into productivity by high adversity and/or high pleasure potential.

The all-pervasive nature of philosophical generalizations belittling the nature of man has been found in the literature of politics, economics, labor movements, reform movements, and administration. Systems of social classes, slavery, and other forms of human bondage all attest clearly to man's lack of concern and respect for his fellow man. The history of the labor movement shows clearly the way early English landowner-legislators established dominance over laboring classes after shortages of labor resulted from the Black Death in the year 1350, by enacting strict residence and vagrancy laws. Remnants of these early laws and attitudes still strongly persist.

ATTITUDES OF SOCIETY—APPLICATION TO FIELD OF ADMINISTRATION

Later historical records cite judicial action against protective labor unions in rulings against the rights of men to band together to enforce better working conditions. Such representations of some men's concepts of other men is found in all aspects of social life. To further illustrate these concepts the field of administration has been chosen as a specific representation.

The field of administration has been strongly influenced by early traditional theory and philosophy as to the nature of man. This can be noted in writings in the Conference of Charities and Corrections Proceedings.[1] Consider the argument in 1891 about the disadvantages of outdoor relief. Levi Barbour of Detroit presented his argument at this meeting as follows: "No man or woman, or family, ordinarily sound in body and mind need starve or lack the comforts of life, if industrious and frugal, or in general lack if forethoughtful, a sufficient surplus in the treasury to provide for old age, sickness and disaster . . . It is the weak, the lazy and the imposter who demand outdoor relief, and for them we have provided the workhouse, the hospital and the prison . . . It has been found unwise, unsafe and wasteful to trust any of these classes with money to expend in their own behalf, unless doled out to them as their daily or hourly needs may require . . . A careful examination of the list will show that very few who get on the list, willingly resign . . . Indeed, the inference of outdoor relief furnished to families but prepares them and reconciles them to poorhouse life . . . It is universally recognized by all who have watched its effects that it demoralized the neighborhood, tempting everyone to apply for it who knows that his neighbor is thus assisted . . . It demoralizes the officers who distribute it. They come to own the cattle they feed, and keep themselves in place by the votes of such dependents . . ." Mrs. James Codman, a conferee from Massachusetts, related that her community had discontinued outdoor relief in favor of the almshouse and stated that as a result: "The moral effect of the change has been very great . . . And that to come upon the town, at one time looked upon as a natural and proper thing to do, is now looked upon as a disgrace . . ." Such attitudes and beliefs directly influenced principles of welfare management.

Let us look at the writings of an administrative theorist, one of the first in this country, who wrote in 1911: "A long series of experiments coupled with close observation had demonstrated the fact that when workmen of this calibre (ore handlers) are given a carefully measured task, which calls for a big day's work on their part, and that when in return for this extra effort they are paid wages up to sixty percent beyond the wages usually paid, that this increase in wages tends to make them not only more thrifty but better men in every way; that they live rather better, begin to save money, become more sober, and work more steadily. When, on the other hand, they receive more than a sixty percent increase in wages, many of them will work irregularly and tend to become more or less shiftless, extravagant, and dissipated . . . Now one of the first requirements for a man who is fit to handle pig iron as a regular occupation is that he shall be so stupid and so phlegmatic that he more nearly resembles in his mental make-up the ox than any other type. The man who is mentally alert and intelligent is for this very reason entirely unsuited to what would be for him grinding monotony of work of this character. Therefore, the workman who is best suited to handling pig iron is unable to understand the real science of doing this class of work. He is so stupid that the word percentage has no meaning to him . . . These two elements, the task and the bonus constitute two of the most important elements of the mechanism of scientific management.[2]" Thus we see clearly in administrative policy-making the expression of psychological assumptions about man. Furthermore, we recognize that the values placed on man as a result of these assumptions are low, as in the foregoing evaluations, where man is referred to as "cattle" and "ox."

While many such historical concepts about the nature of man still persist in current administrative practice, they are gradually becoming modified or replaced with more enlightened ones. One of the most significant developments in the evolution of modern administrative theory has been disposal of the assumption that man is motivated largely by financial gain, and by struggles with his fellow man for the means of survival. Elton Mayo and his group of Harvard associates have done much to offset this assumption through experimentation. Mayo states: "Economic theory in its human aspect is woefully insufficient, indeed it is absurd. Humanity is not adequately described as a horde of individuals, each activated by self interest, each fighting his neighbor for the scarce material of survival . . . Realization that such theories completely falsify the normal human scene drives us back to study of particular human situations. Knowledge and acquaintance of the actual event, intimate understanding of human relationships, must precede the formulation of alternatives to current economic abstractions. This is the clinical method, the necessary preliminary to laboratory investigation."[3]

The first inquiry of this Harvard group which Mayo represents and which he describes more fully in another publication[4], relates to the large percentage of turnover in the mule spinning department in a textile mill near Philadelphia, whereas other departments of the mill had only a 5 or 6 percent turnover. When the Harvard group found that all the mule spinner workers had histories of minor illnesses and and general pessimism, it instituted the plan of four rest periods in the 10-hour day. Production went up and was further implemented when workers were allowed to decide for themselves how to plan the rest periods. Turnover went down to 5 or 6 percent. These workers had been transformed from a horde of solitaries into a social group. Prior to the Harvard group's entry into the problem, four efficiency experts had worked on it, offering incentives of various kinds, and had failed. Mayo states that "The efficiency experts had not consulted the workers; they regarded workers' statements as exaggerated or due to misconception of the facts and therefore to be ignored . . . The experts' assumptions of rabble hypothesis and individual self-interest as a basis of diagnosis led nowhere." He concludes that "First, in industry and in other human situations, the administrator is dealing with well-knit human groups and not with a horde of individuals. Man's desire to be continuously associated in work with his fellows is a strong if not the strongest human characteristic. Second, the belief that the behavior of an individual within the factory can be predicted before employment upon the basis of a laborious and minute examination by tests of his technical and other capacities is mainly if not wholly mistaken. Examination of his developed social skills and his general adaptability might give better results. Third, directly one in an administrative position discards the absurdities of the rabble hypothesis and endeavors to deal directly with the situation that reveals itself on careful study, the results accomplished are astonishing."

The movement from the complex, many-faceted components of the artisan's creation to the over-specialized work of the watch factory worker responsible for punching holes in watch plates every ten seconds, reflects a full range of the swinging pendulum. Mass production emerged from "scientific" methods of dividing up the work into minute fragments. Peter Drucker[5] explained this in terms

of three basic principles: the breakdown of a complex, skilled operation into its component elementary and unskilled motions; the syn-
chronization of the flow of raw or semi-finished materials with the
operator's movements; and the interchangeability of parts. Drucker
was highly critical of the assembly line because it atomizes labor,
reducing it to a single movement, thereby increasing fatigue and
producing such psychogenic results as nervous tics, headaches, deaf-
ness or neuritis; the worker is chained to the slowest pace of other
workers on the line, disallowing work at personal rhythm; and
finally, never completing a whole job which can be identified as his
own personal product, the worker suffers from lack of interest and
sense of justification.

Complaints of workers against the assembly line led to a series of
experiments designed to cope with the problem and improve conditions. Some of these efforts attempted to improve conditions such as
lighting, space, rest periods, and social relationships of the work
groups. More substantive experiments dealt with a reexamination of
the system. The pendulum was swung back a bit toward the artisan
by providing more than a single function for the worker to perform.
A management expert at Sears, Roebuck & Co., stated in 1951 that
Frederick Taylor's theory of scientific management and the disciples
of this theory were all engineers dealing with human problems in
industry as they were taught to deal with machines. The expert was
also critical of Taylor's methods in their failure to secure the participation of workers in the life and progress of the firm. Work lost
meaning for the specialized employee, who felt little responsibility
for his job. Attempts by management to overcome worker apathy
often resulted in tension, or active or passive resistance. Sears, Roebuck & Co. established management practices which recognized the
advantages of the flexible, versatile, general practitioner in contrast to
the narrow specialist. In addition, the company established a profit-
sharing arrangement for its employees, which improved employee
morale.

According to Drucker, when World War II forced industry to
new production methods, Taylor's "scientific" management methods
were further dislodged. A Detroit auto plant, for example, employed
inexperienced women to finish an entire component of aircraft
engines, and it took no longer to train these women for the job than
for normal assembly-line work. The advantages of the change were
found in avoidance of repetitive activity, allowing various work
rhythms and offering the satisfaction of completing something.

To further illustrate his theory, Drucker in 1943 studied two tank
manufacturing plants in different cities but under administrative
control of the same company. Plant A was housed in old buildings,
while Plant B was in a brand new building especially adapted to tank

production. Plant A had low labor turnover, low absenteeism and accident rates, and good labor relations. Plant B had high turnover and accident rates with work relations strained. Production rates were 16 percent higher in Plant A than in Plant B. Drucker's analysis of these two plants disclosed that the new plant was organized according to scientific methods with workers following carefully detailed instruction charts, routinely, and repetitively, and working silently lest they fall behind schedule. Plant A, the ramshackle, improvised factory without the careful Plant B preparation, had done overall planning and engineering but left the execution of plans to foremen and their teams. No attempt was made by management to interfere with work distribution. The work crews intuitively introduced work rotation and job enlargement, about which the engineers were worried, and apologized for such lack of neatness to visitors. Drucker observed that a year later both plants adopted Plan A methods with success.

Elliott[6] described experiments at Detroit Edison in 1953 related to job enlargement. The customer billing department originally maintained three groups of tabulating-card, key-punch, and calculating-machine operators. Work was highly subdivided, organization rigid, and morale poor. Complete reorganization enabled each employee to operate all three kinds of machines, and rotation of tasks was arranged. Other segments of Detroit Edison were similarly reorganized. General conclusions reached from this experiment indicated that enlargement of workers' jobs tended to simplify and unify operations which formerly were dispersed among a crowd of specialized employees. This reorganization resulted in a decrease in absentee rate and a rise in productivity. Job enlargement does not completely capture the essence of job satisfactions found by the artisan, yet it captures some of its essence.

Frederick Taylor, an engineer, and the "father of scientific management," developed through the use of time and motion studies and the stop watch in 1893 a synthetic, mechanistic system which inevitably would be displaced with methods which took into account human needs, yet a system which was to be a forerunner for scientific methods of dividing up the work. Evidence is overwhelming that unskilled workers engaged in repetitive, monotonous, overspecialized work cannot find interest, meaning or even dignity in such occupation. This observation does not preclude some values gained from the work in terms of work group association, respect of family, and a form of economic security. Taylor was despised by the workmen, as evidenced by his later writings: "I was a young man in years but I give you my word, I was a great deal older than I am now, what with the worry, meanness and contemptibleness of the whole damn thing. It's a horrid life for any man to live not being able to look any work-

man in the face without seeing hostility there and feeling every man
around you is your virtual enemy."

The mechanistic approaches, pecuniary values, and inhumane
atmosphere of the intensely competitive business community have
received substantial treatment by American novelists. *The Man in the
Gray Flannel Suit*, by Sloan Wilson, *Babbit*, by Sinclair Lewis, and
The Hucksters, by Frederic Wakeman are typical examples. In their
works, these and many other novelists have sought to indict American
business as inhumane, materialistic, overly bureaucratic, depersonal-
ized in outlook, and generally alienated from more substantive cultural values, and have pointed out that the business value system takes
precedence over loyalty to religion, common humanity, and social
institutions. The psychological point of view is beginning to replace
mechanistic business management devices, and there is recognition of
the reality that in the long run, efficiency in industry cannot be
achieved by sacrifice of human for economic values. Industrial psychology has conceded that those scientific methods which improved
efficiency in industry were most appropriate when adapted to the
maximum well being of the worker. Thus, the view of society of
work and poverty has been modified in recent years through studies
of human behavior in reference to the work setting. However, many
organizations are still administered by authoritative, unfeeling ex-
ecutives, without reference to a humane, scientific approach to
management.

ATTITUDES OF SOCIETY—APPLICATION TO FIELD OF PUBLIC WELFARE

Negative approaches to human distress are exemplified in many
ways in public welfare law, regulations and practices. To illustrate
with the following example, the effects of repressive residence laws
are chosen, since they have relevance to restricting mobility, thereby
limiting man's opportunity to freely seek work throughout the
nation.

It is not possible to consider man's right to work without a review
of man's right to freedom of movement in this nation to seek work.
Residence laws in public welfare which preclude the opportunity
of free movement must be examined, understood, and modified. To
understand this issue we must first review the general welfare clause
in the Constitution of the United States. Section 8 of Article 1 states:
"The Congress shall have power to lay and collect taxes, duties,
imposts and excises, to pay the debts and provide for the common
defense and general welfare of the United States; . . ." The meaning
of the term "general welfare" has been a subject of debate since the
original writing. A true laissez-faire interpretation might suggest
that the general welfare considered solely our relations with other

nations and the policing of our own nation against the aberrations of criminals. Does the preservation of general welfare suggest responsibility for prevention of malnutrition and exposure to the elements because of lack of individual resources for the necessities of life?

Court decisions related to the interpretation of the general welfare clause of the Constitution favor such an interpretation. An advisory opinion of the Supreme Court of New Hampshire, rendered in 1931, states in part: "The validity of pauper acts has never been assailed . . . The support of paupers has long been accepted exercise of valid authority under the police power in promotion of the general welfare . . . In the avoidance and relief of pauperism the state acts for its own benefit and welfare.[7]" Two decisions of the Supreme Court of Pennsylvania are also of great significance. In the first of these[8] the court declared: "The care and maintenance of indigent, infirm and mentally defective persons, without ability or means to sustain themselves, and other charges of a like nature . . . became direct charges on the body politic for its own preservation and protection. As such, in the light of an expense, they stand exactly in the same position as the preservation of law and order . . ." Several years later, when the same court was again called upon to pass upon the constitutionality of a relief measure[9], it reiterated the opinion that . . . the obligation of the government to care for poor persons was not a charitable undertaking any more than the performance of any other public function is a charity. . . . the support of the poor, meaning such persons as have been understood as coming within that class ever since the organization of the government, persons who are without means of support . . . is and has always been a direct charge on the body politic for its own preservation and protection. . ."

While state and local responsibility for providing relief has been long recognized and approved by the courts, assumption of such responsibility by the Federal Government has only recently been accorded formal recognition and approval. The legal basis for recognition of the validity of federal efforts in this field was laid down in a decision on the federal Agricultural Adjustment Act, announced by the United States Supreme Court in 1936[10]. Speaking therein of the power conferred upon Congress by the constitutional provision to "provide for the common defense and general welfare of the United States," the court stated: "The view that the clause grants power to provide for the general welfare, independently of the taxing power, has never been authoritatively accepted . . . The true construction undoubtedly is that the only thing granted is the power to tax for the purpose of providing funds for payment of the nation's debts and making provision for the general welfare . . . the power of Congress to authorize expenditure of public moneys for public purposes is not limited by the direct grants of legislative power found in the Constitution. Funds in the Treasury as a result of taxation may be expended only through appropriation . . . They can never accomplish the object for which they were collected unless the power to appropriate is as broad as the power to tax. The necessary implication from the terms of the grant is that the public funds may be appropriated 'to provide for the general welfare of the United States.' These words cannot be meaningless, else they would not have been used. The conclusion must be that they were intended to limit and define the granted power to raise and to expend money." Building upon this interpretation of the welfare clause, the Supreme Court, in a decision upholding the constitutionality of Title IX of the Social Security Act[11] declared in 1937: "During the years 1929 to 1936 when the country was passing through a cyclical depression, the number of unemployed mounted to unprecedented heights . . . Disaster to the bread-winner meant disaster to dependents . . . It is too late today for the arguments to be heard with tolerance that in a crisis the use of moneys of the nation to relieve the unemployed and their dependents is a use for any purpose narrower than the promotion of the general welfare." In another case decided the same day, involving Titles II and VIII of the Social Security Act, the Supreme Court declared: "Spreading from state to state, unemployment is an ill not particular but general which may be checked, if Congress so determines, by the resources of the nation . . . The ill is all one, or at least not greatly different, whether men are thrown out of work because there is no longer work to do or because the disabilities of age make them incapable of doing it. Rescue becomes necessary irrespective of the cause." This appears to concede the power of the federal government to come to the aid of needy people regardless of whether their want results from unemployment, old age, or any other cause that might deprive them of work or render them incapable of working.

How, then, do we reconcile residence laws in counties and states which influence in some cases the right to free movement within the nation? The practice of transferring dependent persons from one locality to another in order to avoid supporting the nonresident has been carried on in this country and abroad for centuries. It came to this country from the old parish system in England and continues even today. There have been certain advances in the techniques with which persons are transported from one locality to another, yet the essential regressive characteristics are retained. Edith Abbott cited the following typical case history of a family victimized by such policies in the 1930's: "Mr. X, with wife and six children, left Yonkers, New York, in 1930 to seek work in California. He found it and for two years supported himself and family. But in May 1932 he had to ask for relief in Oakland, California. Relief was denied because he had no 'settlement.' That is, he had not lived in California for three years. At the same time, however, Mr. X had lost his 'settlement' in New York because of his absence from there for more than one year. Nevertheless, the Oakland authorities shipped the X family back to Yonkers. When they arrived there the Yonkers authorities deported them back to Oakland.[12]"

If a person does not have residence and becomes dependent upon public welfare for aid, communication is established with his former state of residence to determine whether or not he still retains residence in that state. If the assumed state of residence reports that he is such a resident, then arrangements for his transfer back to this state are made, regardless of whether or not the individual wishes to return. In fact, if he should decide not to return, financial assistance is withheld. If the individual has lost residence in his former state, the new state of residence might assume responsibility for him as a "stateless" person. It should be noted in this regard that residence is far easier lost than attained. In many states, residence is lost after an absence of one year, while it may take from one to five years to become a resident. The policy of "derivative residence" where the members of the family take residence of the husband or father creates other complications. A person may have resided in a state all his life yet not have residence.

More recent case histories illustrate that society has not changed these practices over a period of more than 30 years. "Negro mother, father and two pre-school children, in California two months, came for work. When the family requested aid they were returned by the county to Alabama even though there was no assurance of aid there." "Man, wife and four children—home Virginia, lived in Santa Clara County about six months and became dependent and were returned by the California county to Virginia in 1955. They liked California, and in 1956 left Virginia to return. They stopped in Alabama and Arkansas, arrived in Santa Clara County in early 1957, then later moved to San Mateo County. Because of lapse of time, they lost residence in Virginia and had not gained it elsewhere. San Mateo County carried them on G.A. as stateless."

The harshness of residence laws as an influence on policy change favoring the enactment of an AFDC Unemployed Parent program is further illustrated by the following: "The father of this family was aged 52, the mother, 42, and the three children, 6, 7, and 8. The father an unemployed carpet and linoleum layer applied for assistance at a time when the family had only 21 months' residence in the State of California out of the required 36. He at first was unwilling to return to his state of origin, but later signified willingness to return because he had been unable to find employment of any kind. The agency cleared with the state of origin, which refused to authorize return on the basis that the family had left with the intent of establishing permanent residence in California. In spite of this refusal on the part of the original state, the county welfare department informed the family that they must return, that they were not eligible for assistance, and that the county would pay for the family's return. The father had tools of his trade but was informed that the cost of shipping them back to the midwest was too great and that they could not be returned with him. He was advised to use them as a resource and he objected because he could realize such a small proportion of the replacement cost by selling them. Arrangements were made for the family's return, but the father then obtained a promise of employment. The agency checked with the employer, who stated that two jobs were available but that he could not guarantee the man a job until he started work and proved his competence. On this basis, the agency again decided that the family must go back to their former state. The family subsequently decided not to return. Some months later, the family again applied for assistance, which was denied on the basis of their unwillingness to return to the state in which they no longer had legal residence. This became a permanent reason for denial of assistance, with the result that the family sought assistance from the Salvation Army."

The California "County Aid and Relief to Indigents" law provides that "whenever the respective boards of supervisors deem it best for the welfare of a family or in the pubic interest that an indigent remain in a county not responsible for his support, the county responsible for the support of the indigent may agree to support him in the county not so responsible; but no indigent supported in this manner shall be deemed to have acquired a residence in the non-responsible county." While this provision makes it possible to work out intercounty agreements, procedures are often extremely complex and time consuming. The following is an illustration of many such cases: "Family of parents, grandmother, and eight children had resided in County A since 1950, receiving occasional General Relief when the father was out of work. In 1959 they moved to County B, where they applied for General Relief after several months. An 'informal bicounty agreement' was made whereby County A agreed to reimburse County B for assistance payments to the family in County B. Assistance was paid for only two months, until the man again found work. Several months later the father had a heart attack, and reapplied for assistance and medical care. County B contended that the family was not its responsibility, even though they by now had lived there for 19 months, because of the two months aid given under the bicounty agreement. The issue now resolves about payment for medical care. The county physician in County A declares that he is not bound by the welfare department's 'bicounty agreement' and that the family has lost residence for purposes of medical care. Besides adding to the insecurity experienced by this family, the procedures for establishing county responsibility take valuable administrative and casework time."

Various methods of determining residence creates administrative problems. The requirement of physical presence on a continuous basis is common. In many jurisdictions a person would be excluded from residence during those periods of time he was in receipt of public assistance or in a mental or penal institution. The Public Assistance Handbook of the Federal Social Security Administration, Department of Health, Education and Welfare, states: "We recommend that states eliminate all eligibility requirements that relate to length of residence in the state." Residence requirements are not mandatory under the social security laws. However, the Social Security Act has maximum standards for residence which, to a large extent, have tended to become the standards adopted by the states. In the Old Age Assistance, Aid to the Blind, and Aid to the Permanently and Totally Disabled programs, the Social Security Act requires that the state cannot have standards requiring more than five years of the last nine years residence, with one year of the five immediately preceding the application. For the Aid to Dependent Children, the Federal Social Security Act prohibits a residence requirement of more than one year preceding application.

There is considerable debate about the legal implications of population mobility. The question revolves around the constitutional right of free movement, the right to leave one's place of residence, and to go to any other place one might choose. The evacuation of Japanese-Americans from the West Coast during World War II, though an apparent denial of this right, resulted in a reaffirmation of it. The Federal Government conducted this movement and the Supreme Court gave constitutional sanction to it. The court did not state the rights of the individual did not exist, but rather that the circumstances were special and that the war conditions were of such pressing necessity that they justified a movement which would not otherwise be allowed constitutionally. This interference with the rights of thousands of loyal citizens will be debated for many years to come. The same sort of evacuation, without any justification of war, takes place frequently, though on a smaller scale.

One such incident with a promising outcome is the case of *Fred Edwards* v. *the People of the State of California*. Fred Edwards went to Texas from California in 1939 and met his wife's brother-in-law, Frank Duncan. Arrangements had been made for Edwards to bring Duncan to California, with the hope that he might find gainful employment there. Duncan had been employed by the Works Project Administration for some time before he left Texas. Thus he was an employable person, although at the time he left Texas he was not actually employed. Edwards knew that Duncan was not employed and that he had only twenty dollars when they left Texas January 1, 1940, for Marysville, California. Since this money was exhausted before Duncan arrived in California, he remained at the Edwards home for a period of about ten days after which he was granted assistance by the Farm Security Administration. He later obtained remunerative employment and became a self-supporting person. On February 7, 1940, Fred Edwards was convicted by a court in Marysville of a violation of a statute known as Section 2615 of the Welfare and Institutions Code of the State of California. This 1860 statute states that: "Every person, firm, or corporation, or officer or agent thereof, that brings or assists in bringing into the state any indigent person who is not a resident of the state, knowing him to be an indigent person, is guilty of a misdemeanor." Edwards was found guilty under this section for bringing his wife's brother-in-law, Frank Duncan, from Spur, Texas, to Marysville, California. Edwards appealed his case to the Superior Court of California on June 26, 1940. The Superior Court upheld the decision of the Justice Court. Edwards then appealed his case to the Supreme Court of the United States. The American Civil Liberties Union and the Committee on Defense Migration, a Conpressional Committee headed by Representative Tolan, each made representations before the Supreme Court. The American Civil Liberties Union, citing the Fourteenth Amendment to the Constitution, testified that: "The dispossessed and economically disinherited must have a legally guaranteed minimal right of freedom of movement. The right to seek the improvement of their fortunes, to seek help, to change their social environment as those more fortunately situated. No democracy can afford to permit the legal status of the individual's liberty to fluctuate with his economic condition . . . California is obviously seeking to prevent indirectly what it cannot prevent directly. It is attempting to prevent indigent persons from taking up residence in California by intimidating those who would assist them. A state may not bar one whom it may consider a potential relief recipient from entrance and, similarly, it may not make one who makes his entrance possible a criminal." Justice Byrnes of the Supreme Court stated that the concept underlying Section 2615 of the Welfare and Institutions Code of California is based on the philosophy that each community must care for its own indigents, but that recent times have proved that the theory of the Elizabethan Poor Laws no longer fits the facts. He said: ". . . We are of the opinion that Section 2615 is not a valid exercise of the police powers of California; that it imposes an unconstitutional burden upon interstate commerce and that the conviction under it cannot be sustained." Justice Cardozo added that: "The Constitution was framed under the dominion of a political philosophy less parochial in range. It was framed upon the theory that the people of the several states must sink or swim together and that in the long run prosperity and salvation are in union and not in division." Thus, the Supreme Court invalidated the California statute as an unconstitutional invasion of the national power over interstate commerce. It is hoped that ultimately some provision of the Constitution will be found which will treat the problems of people in a way different from that suggested by the term "interstate commerce." In this regard, in the Edwards case, Justice Jackson said: ". . . that he possesses nothing that can be sold and no wherewithal to buy do not fit easily into my notions as to what is commerce. To hold that the measures of his rights is the commerce clause is likely to result eventually either in distorting commercial law or in denaturing human rights."

The 1960 Advisory Council to the Federal Welfare Administration report on public assistance recommended the following residence requirements:

"The great majority of states have residence requirements that, with much resultant hardship, exclude many financially needy persons from public assistance. Federal grants-in-aid should be available only for those public assistance programs imposing no residence requirement that debars any needy person in the state from help to which he would otherwise be entitled.

"When the Social Security Act was enacted in 1935, the States were permitted the option of having residence requirements. If they chose to have them, the law prohibited requiring longer residence than set maximums. Today, in the three adult categories, the states may not require residence for more than five years of the nine preceding application for public assistance. In the aid to dependent children program, they may not require more than one year's residence of the parent or other relative who is the child's caretaker and receives money on his behalf.

"For some years there was a trend toward the liberalization of residence requirements in the states. Since 1950, however, very little has been done to relax them. Today only a few states provide that assistance be given without regard to residence. The remainder have varying requirements up to the maximums permitted by the Social Security Act. Many states take no responsibility for the nonresident group.

"Free movement of people is encouraged by our economic system, which enables the individual to improve his own situation. Many persons move to seek employment. Others, especially older men and women, move to be near relatives or for reasons of health. The head of a dependent family, or a feeble old person, may find himself stranded far away from home, destitute and resourceless, when something happens that through no fault of his own dashes his hope of employment or changes his living plans.

"Most of us regard residence requirements as an anachronism, and see no reason why a needy person should be precluded from getting essential aid solely because he is caught in the technicalities of residence laws. We find no evidence that people move solely to qualify for public assistance. Athough in general we firmly uphold the states' rights to have wide latitude in determining the nature and scope of their public assistance programs, we think that state residence requirements are inconsistent with the high degree of national interest reflected by the extent of Federal participation in the public assistance program."

William MacDougall, General Counsel and Manager, California County Supervisors Association, disagreed with the Advisory Council recommendation on residence and made the following minority statement:

"The proposal to deprive states completely of their historic right to impose residence requirements on those who seek financial support from the states' taxpayers is the most drastic recommendation of the Council.

"Since the earliest days of any record anywhere of public relief being granted to the needy, there is record of some type of residence requirement. While approximately one-half of the costs of public assistance continues to be provided by the states and the localities, it seems undesirable and impractical to deny them the right to ask that assistance be granted by the state government of the applicant's legal residence. This is particularly true for the 'permanent types of public assistance' as exemplified by the aged, blind and disabled aid program, and by some long-term cases of aid to dependent children.

"It may be that the present lengths of time permitted to the states to be used as residence requirements need some shortening. It is possible that a '2 years out of the last 3' or that even a single year's residence requirement may be practical for future years, but objection must be registered to the proposal to wipe out completely all permission to the states to impose residence requirements in their welfare laws."

The plight of the poor, the unemployed, is invisible to the average middle-class person. A number of recent publications refer to the invisible poor, to the "trap ghetto," and to generational poverty and dependency. These concepts reflect economic, social and cultural entrapment of the poor which the adult poor cannot escape and the children inherit. Moreover, to the middle-class masses, these poor are off the freeways, largely invisible. Yet these conditions and concepts are not new; they reflect conditions of the ages, inherited from our forefathers. As the poor are generational, so too is the cultural inheritance of the middle class with its traditions of meaningless and useless solutions, compendiums of folklore and magic which wish the problem of the poor away but settle for its invisibility. In reference to man's right to move freely in this nation for purposes of seeking work or for any other purpose, the following principle should be established: The right to freedom of movement between local and state jurisdictions within the nation for all the peoples of the nation is inherent in law, tradition, and practice. The inherent right to settle in any state or locality is similarly available to all persons. These basic freedoms cannot be withheld from some people because they have different characteristics than other citizens. Economic dependency of people shall not abridge or modify these fundamental rights to free movement and settlement. Fiscal problems encountered by the several jurisdictions of government related to financial dependency of people shall be managed between these units of government through fiscal agreements in such a manner as not to interfere with the basic rights of people to freedom of movement and settlement.

We know that today settlement laws satisfy no reasonable purpose and, in fact, only increase the stress on already overstressed persons, another example of man's inhumanity to man. Some communities feel they save money by transporting nonresidents back to their state of residence. However, most of the public assistance load today is carried by the federal and state government. If it is determined that monetary loss by some states occurs, this should be treated as a fiscal problem to be managed by the federal, state, and local governments in a way that will assure freedom of movement to the individual.

With the development of the Office of Economic Opportunity, legal services to the poor became available, and in 1964, a program was initiated for the purpose of testing various aspects of current welfare laws. The durational residence requirements immediately came in for a major share of the interest. By 1967, there were formal legal actions pending in at least four states, all challenging the constitutionality of durational residence requirements in federally supported aid programs. The states were California, Pennsylvania, Connecticut, and Washington. Most of the cases were filed in federal courts and were based on provisions in the federal law which allow "class" or representative actions to be brought in instances where the constitutionality of a law is attacked. These cases were required to be heard by a trial court consisting of three judges. The main arguments against constitutionality of durational residence requirements were as follows:

1. Such laws represent unconstitutional interference with the right of a citizen to move freely from state to state.

2. Congressional power to regulate the interstate movement of people prohibits the states from setting up residence barriers.

3. These laws are at odds with the purpose of the Public Assistance Titles of the Social Security Act, which is to feed hungry people regardless of where they happen to be at the time they become hungry.

Arguments in favor of residence laws were as follows:

1. Congress authorized these laws by express language in the Social Security Act.

2. Public Assistance is not a full-blown right and therefore not completely protected by the Due Process and Equal Protection clauses of the Constitution.

3. State remedies should be exhausted before relief is sought in the Federal courts.

In May, 1968, a San Francisco three-judge federal court enjoined the State of California from enforcing its residence laws. While the State prepared an appeal to the U.S. Supreme Court against this great historical decision, on fiscal grounds, the social work profession, at least, applauded the long-awaited event. Other state cases had also been appealed to the Supreme Court and the expectation was that a decision favoring the abandonment of the residence laws was imminent.

Over the centuries our society has believed that dependency can be treated by methods designed to deter people from becoming dependent. This belief rests on the concept that all men have control over their actions and can will themselves out of such actions. The logical conclusion from this set of beliefs is that if a man persists in abnormal behavior it is simply because of the perversity of his nature; this is, he is lazy, hostile, or stubborn, and does not choose to change. In order to treat this perverse nature of man, society logically assumed that if he were humiliated, harassed, deprived and otherwise punished—the uncomfortable nature of these conditions would motivate the person to change. This, in essence, is our cultural heritage.

Current scientific knowledge about the dynamics of human behavior largely refutes such folklore. Public welfare officials, social workers, and psychologists have been trying for decades to correct general community attitudes in this regard. Beliefs are so basic and firmly established, however, that correction is difficult. Community leadership generally reflects the outmoded concepts and federal, state and local law and policy continue prescribing long outmoded "remedies." During the past quarter of a century the leaders in public welfare have achieved—through persistent action—some legislative and procedural modification of practice.

Many states still retain humiliating, harassing, and depriving provisions in public welfare law and policy, as follows:

HUMILIATION

1. Publications of lists of public assistance recipients.
2. Payment of aid-in-kind.
3. Non-useful, demeaning work-for-relief.
4. Requiring the applicant to solicit support from relatives (other than from parents of minor children).

HARASSMENT

1. Requiring the public assistance mother to file legal action against her absent spouse as a condition of eligibility.
2. Requiring the maintenance of a "suitable home" as a condition of eligibility.
3. Requiring the unmarried mother to file filiation action against the child's father or, as in a few states, denying aid to certain unmarried mothers, thus requiring chastity as a condition of eligibility.

DEPRIVATION

1. Requiring residence as a condition of eligibility, thus depriving applicants of their rights to free choice of settlement.
2. Establishing maximum grants, or applying ratable reductions to grants, thus depriving applicants and recipients of adequate allowances for the necessities of life.
3. Establishing citizenship as a condition of aid, thus denying assistance to certain classes of persons.
4. Requiring applicants and recipients to "lien" or "assign" their property to the government as a condition of eligibility.

Public welfare in its modern form has attempted, during the past quarter century, with concerted effort to dignify public assistance as a social instrument which is available to people as a matter of right. Against great odds, small gains have been made, yet our briefly described law and policy suggests that the programs are still restrictive in nature.

Our society holds many paradoxes directly resulting from this lag between knowledge and practice. Not the least of these is the fact that we organize public welfare agencies to help those who need help, and then run them so that they offer as little help as possible, instead of as much as is needed. Old-fashioned laws and administrative regulations force us into practice of harassment, deprivation, embarrassment, and punishment that we know to be not only useless but injurious. Social engineering covering broad fields of human problems designed to correct faulty cultural patterns or other social conditions basic to cause of individual problems, is needed.

While the United States has strangely disregarded the poverty stricken who comprise one-third of the nation, it has sought to influence the world of nations with its beneficence in a nouveau riche manner. Economists and sociologists have commented on the more than $30 billion in aid given to nations of Western Europe since World War II as unnecessary and unwise policy, since these gifts have not created gratitude or a basis for friendship. In fact, those nations have helped to create a gold shortage. A policy of making loans rather than gifts to war depleted nations would have been wiser policy. In regard to aid to underdeveloped countries our share has been similarly disproportionate. The United States grants billions of dollars in aid to the people of other nations, yet allows federally subvented welfare programs to exclude aid to our own needy people if they do not meet residence requirements in the state and locality in which they presently reside.

ATTITUDES OF SOCIETY—MIDDLE-CLASS APATHY AND INDIFFERENCE

It has literally taken centuries to achieve justice for poor men in respect to their freedom to travel as they choose. And poor men everywhere are treated with casual disdain. The plight of distressed, unemployed men evokes differing responses from fellow man, dependent on what is seen, and on the cultural attitudes of the viewer. In 1934, after a professor of economics accepted the invitation of a friend to go and see one of the emergency shelters serving thousand's of Chicago's unemployed single men, he remarked that "if this were a fair sample of the group served in all the shelters, the world would be better off if eighty-five percent were loaded onto a raft, towed out into Lake Michigan, and scuttled."[13] A commissioner of Cook County in Chicago, delegated by that body to investigate and report on relief services to single men prefaced his report with the following: "During my visit, I was astonished that I was not able to pick out of the line, men who gave any indication that they were the self-respecting type of good citizen; men who would some day again be leading the life of good citizens. Most of the men were the dregs of humanity. No one can tell me that in four years time they . . . have sunk to the depths of degradation that inspection of these men showed. Most of them were dirty and shabby—the regular railroad-yard type of bum. Many had liquor on their breath. My impression was that they were just plain bums and hoboes living off the taxpayers."[13] A similar comment was made by a private family relief agency executive who spent 20 minutes observing the shelter and the men receiving care. He noticed the beaten look on the faces of the men, their extremely shabby appearance, and the impersonal routine. He concluded that most of the men were casuals who were accustomed normally to a living standard about on the level as that on which they were then existing; that they composed the well-sifted end-product of human beings who long ago ceased to desire independence; and probably they would not live differently if offered the opportunity.

In 1965, a member of a California County Board of Supervisors, speaking to a small group of welfare officials, likened welfare recipients to his cattle. In the spring he gradually lessened the amount of winter feeding to stimulate foraging for their own food, and so with welfare recipients, reduced grants to force them to work. "Practical" men do not understand the dynamics of human behavior, the impact of loss of hope for improved functioning; and seemingly, have little compassion. The overriding concern in American society has been the economics of the issue as opposed to the human values. In spite of the reduction of feed to cattle in the spring, as described, cattle still do better than some people. The U.S. Department of Agriculture issued a report in May, 1968 showing that California cattle are better fed than the people in one-half of the households in the United States. The report stated that 50 percent of all the households have diets falling below established nutritional standards for a good diet, and 20 percent have poor diets. In contrast, Walter Rodman of the California Beef Council stated that cattle from California's feedlots had been fed scientifically compounded rations measured and evaluated through use of computers.

The American Institute of Public Opinion reported in 1964 on attitudes of conservatives and liberals in respect to poverty. Typically, the conservatives blamed lack of individual effort as a major cause of poverty, and the liberals more often ascribed poverty to circumstances beyond the individual's control. This opinion poll further studied attitudes toward the cause of poverty without reference to political views, and found that 30 percent attributed it to lack of effort; 34 percent to circumstances; and 34 percent to both of these. Thus 64 percent believed wholly or partly that lack of individual effort causes poverty in spite of overwhelming scientific evidence which reveals complex, multi-causal associations with poverty status.

The simplistic stance of middle-class American society toward poverty and work is found also in relation to crime. Arthur Goldberg stated that "Practical distinctions between the rich man and the poor man are found throughout the area of criminal law. The rich man may be summoned to the police station; the poor man is more often arrested. The rich inebriant may be escorted home by the police; the poor drunk is almost always tossed in jail. The rich accused is released on bail; the poor defendant cannot raise bail and remains in prison. The rich defendant can afford the best legal advice . . . ; the poor defendant . . . is denied many other important tools of advocacy. After conviction when a fine is imposed the rich man pays it and goes free, but the poor man who cannot afford to pay a fine goes to jail. The rich man who can be guaranteed a job may qualify for probation or parole; the poor man lacking a job more often goes to or remains in prison."[14] Moving from work to crime to welfare, we observe a continuum of simplistic approaches and beliefs.

The 1965 Report by the Governor's Commission on the Los Angeles Riots[15] reviewed public welfare in Los Angeles and its relationship to the Watts riot. While noting that 70 percent of the AFDC families were from the South or Southwest (by implication, Negro or Mexican-American), that seven out of ten of these families included illegitimate children, and that AFDC expenditures have been "increasing dramatically," the report applied traditional attitudes regarding these facts. Commission members were "profoundly concerned" by the accelerated trend of expenditure; by the migration of Negroes and Mexican-Americans due to the "generosity of the California program compared with southern and southwestern states;" by uncertainty whether recipients wished work rather than welfare; by payments of $177-$238 per month per family, therefore reducing incentive to find work; by the example of an 18-year-old girl excluded from the grant by age, who "may have considerable incentive to become a mother herself so as to be eligible again as the head of a new family group;" and by insufficient cooperation between welfare and the employment agencies. Thus, traditional attitudes reflecting the folklore and myth of sixteenth century practice were expressed by the Commission.

The plight of the poor is little understood, and enlightenment on the subject has not been sought traditionally by the public. The recent surge of books on the subject of the poor stress the invisibility of these people in the sense that the poor are in pockets off the main thoroughfares of American life. This invisibility may be intentional public dismissal of the problems of the poor, rather than actual physical obscurity. Moreover, the phenomenon may reflect fear of the potential power of the poor as a vital force seeking political and social justice. The characteristics of "invisibility" have been noted before: Carey McWilliams wrote in 1942: "Not only is the agricultural migrant almost invisible, but he is voiceless as well. One can read the debates in Congress on agricultural legislation and never find a reference to agricultural workers. So far as social legislation is concerned, it would seem that agricultural workers do not exist. Since they are politically impotent, no one is concerned with their welfare."[16] Elsewhere he referred to the farm laborer as "a voiceless fellow who looks for a job somewhere else if he cannot find it on the farm and not much is heard from him." The essence of "invisibility" is, then, the disregard of a disdainful public and a reflection of the political impotence of the poor. The segregated ghetto off the freeways of middle-class life is the symbolism of the voicelessness and despair of the poor, and the apathy of American middle-class society.

Yet it is more than the apathy of society—it is a way of life. The synthetic value system of a materialistic American society prizes rugged individualism as a cultural objective for all, camouflages exploitative, acquisitive tendencies, and provides indignities and humiliation for the "improvident" poor. It is not so much the taking of public money to relieve the distress of the poor that is offensive, since businessmen and farmers receive huge amounts of public subsidy, with dignity—it is also the protocol of "Madison Avenue" dress and aplomb missing with the poor, which offends middle-class sensibilities. Historians may look back on the 1960's in the United States as representative of a latter-day primitive society with many paradoxes. Public welfare systems will be viewed as an archaic fulfillment of all that was expected by England of their 1601 "poor law," with perhaps some more modern embellishments, to heap indignity on the poor. The paradox will be noted—as the social and behavioral sciences stagnated, the physical sciences launched men in space.

REFERENCES

1. Barbour, Levi: Arguments Against Public Outdoor Relief, National Conference of Charities and Corrections Proceedings. Boston, George H. Ellis Press, 1891.

2. Taylor, Frederick: The Principles of Scientific Management. New York, Harper & Bros., 1911.

3. Mayo, Elton: Social Problems of an Industrial Civilization. Boston, Harvard Business School, 1945.

4. Mayo, Elton: Industrial Fatigue. Personnel Journal, December, 1924.

5. Drucker, P. F.: The Way to Industrial Peace. Harpers, November, 1946.

6. Elliott, J. D.: Increasing Office Productivity Through Job Enlargement, Office Management Series No. 134. New York, Ames Management Association, December, 1953.

7. In re Opinion of the Justices: 85 N. H. 562, 564; 154 Atl. 217, 221.

8. Busser et al. v. Snyder et al., 282 Pa. 440, 453; 128 Atl. 80, 84; 37 A.L.R. 1515.

9. Commonwealth ex. rel. Schnader, Attorney General v. Liveright, Secretary of Welfare of Pa. et al., 308 Pa. 35, 76-77; 161 Atl. 697, 709-710.

10. U.S. v. Butler et al., U.S. 1, 64-66; 102 A.L.R. 914.

11. Steward Machine Co. v. Davis, 301 U.S. 548, 586-587; 109 A.L.R. 1293.

12. Abbott, Edith: Public Assistance: American Principles and Policies. Chicago, University of Chicago Press, 1940.

13. Notes and Comments. Social Service Review, 8:137, 1934.

14. Moynihan, Daniel, Defenses of Freedom—Public Papers of Arthur J. Goldberg. New York, Harper & Bros., 1965.

15. Governor's Commission on the Los Angeles Riots: A report on violence in the city—an end or a beginning? Sacramento, The Commission, 1965.

16. McWilliams, Carey: Ill Fares the Land. Boston, Little, Brown & Co., 1942.

CHAPTER 3

THE DEPRESSIONS

As EARLY AS 1857, New York City witnessed the spectacle for the first time in America of American skilled laborers roaming the streets, and existing on the free soup of charity. The problem, however, had not reached national proportions. Watson[1] observed that in 1873 there occurred one of the worst panics and one of the most protracted periods of industrial depression in American history, creating a problem of unemployment and suffering unprecedented in extent and degree. Multitudes were thrown out of work. Their ranks were augmented by soldiers of the Civil War, who had not yet found a place in the industrial life of the nation. There was an increase of tramps. For the first time, unemployment as a national problem faced the country. The period proved in many cities the heyday of soup kitchens and bread lines.

The extraordinary drafts on the charity of individuals and communities ultimately led to an examination of the prevailing methods of relief. This disclosed the fact that the methods of charity were incredibly wasteful and inefficient, and led finally to the launching in the seventies of a number of charity organization societies.

The unemployed able-bodied man, often without family, presented to these early societies a problem which seemed to require special machinery. The societies often provided some systematic form of relief by offering employment in stonebreaking, streetwork, or woodyards, usually the last. These were regarded as "work tests." Such men were often in need of temporary sleeping quarters. It was customary in many places for them to find lodging at police stations or in free shelters having no "work tests." Society recognized the evils of such a solution and opened several wayfarers' lodges and secured legislation which recognized them as desirable substitutes for police lodgings. The law empowered the city authorities to close the station houses as sleeping places, and gave the lodge superintendents the right to arrest any men who refused to do woodyard work in exchange for the care given. The city authorities took advantage of this plan to reduce vagrancy and closed the station houses to lodgers until they were again thrown open during the depression of 1893-94. Since municipal lodging houses were largely unknown, similar wayfarers' lodges were opened, often under the direct control of the local charity organization society, in a number of cities.

Woodyards and temporary shelters were also frequently used to curb the evils of street begging and vagrancy. Some of the most constant work in this direction was undertaken by the New York

Society, which as early as 1883, appointed special officers to cooperate with the New York Police Department in solving the problem. This service was continued until 1897, when the city established a police detail of 12 men to form a "vagrancy squad."

Watson also observed that the conditions prevailing during the depression of 1907-08 brought about industrial paralysis of the country, and charity organization societies on all sides reported an increase in distress. The number of applicants for relief during the three winter months was in many places double that of the winter before, while the number during the spring had more than quadrupled the corresponding figure of the previous year. There was a phenomenal increase in the numbers of unemployed single men.

As soon as it became evident that another industrial depression had gripped the country, a number of societies prepared for the aftermath of distress. There was a disposition not to repeat the mistakes made during the depression of 1893-94, and to profit by the lessons then learned. The judgment of the societies was to avoid treating the problem en masse, and as far as possible to so decentralize its handling that it would not get beyond control and stampede them into lowering their standards. In many cities, the societies for organizing charity were able not only to discourage centralized general schemes for dealing with distress, but also to differentiate between plans for the homeless and those for family distress. Frequently, they urged the expansion of existing agencies to meet the situation and sought a logical division of work among them.

An effort was made in many places to secure work for able-bodied men with families rather than to grant relief direct. In some places this took the form of cooperation with the city and other social agencies in the work of street cleaning in less privileged neighborhoods, the men so employed being from families which the local society would in any event have to help. Such also served as a work test. In other places it took the form of cooperation with manufacturers who increased their forces in the production of staple articles, and in rotation of employees so as to give some work to the largest possible number of men.

One of the results of the 1907-08 depression was a large increase in the number of charity organization societies launched immediately after the worst of the storm had passed. Many unemployed who could weather one year of hard times could not weather two, and so went over the poverty line the second year. Societies were launched in reply to citizen appeals that something be done to meet these conditions, for not until 1910 had the industrial storm completely spent its force. Watson noted that the causal relation between unemployment and poverty had frequently been driven home. Previous attempts had, however, been limited in the main either to emergency measures at times of industrial crisis or to work for the handicapped. However, it should be added that from no quarter was there any persistent agitation for a nationwide system of labor exchanges that would function in seasons of prosperity and depression. Approximately half the states of the Union had established free employment offices, following Ohio's lead in 1891.

An industrial depression during 1914-15 once again brought us face to face with a winter of distress surpassing even that of 1907-08. New York City, like Chicago, Kansas City and Seattle, is a reserve city where the unemployed congregate during the winter awaiting distribution to new kinds of employment, however, the fact that 400,000 to 440,000 were simultaneously unemployed in New York City in the early months of 1915 indicated conditions of nationwide unemployment of great seriousness. An estimate of two million jobless in the United States during the winter of 1914-15 is conservative.

The relief task proved so impossible that certain societies were led to take the initiative in creating opportunities for work. Outstanding among these was the New York Association for Improving the Condition of the Poor. Finding so many of the problems resolved themselves largely into a question of relief, giving groceries and rent, where the one thing needed and wanted was work, the association arranged with the city to clear lands of the Bronx Botanical Gardens and the Zoological Park, and to do the incidental trenching, grading and roadmaking. This was work which was needed to be done but for which the city itself had no funds. The money which the association had been paying out as relief was converted into wages for the men. The work kept the men in physical trim to swing back into their own occupations when the wheels of trade and industry should quicken, at the same time affording a work test that separated the shirkers, loafers, the inefficient, and the physically incapacitated from those willing and able to work.[2] Every precaution was taken to keep the plan from savoring in any way of relief, in recognition of the fact that "doles of work" for "doles of pay" do not deceive men, and that a work test falls short of its purpose except as the jobs offered are for a fair wage and under conditions which do not tend to destroy a man's self-respect. Accordingly, arrangements were made whereby the men reported to the park superintendent for the jobs. Supervision and discipline were left to the regular park foreman, the understanding being that a good day's work would be required of every man sent, and failure to comply with such requirement would mean dismissal. Wages were paid weekly by the park paymaster, who was reimbursed by the association. The wage rate was $2 a day. Thus a man was assured $6 a week for three days' work, and on the alternate days he could do other part-time work or search for an opening at his regular occupation. Although urgent at the time, the whole plan was launched on the assumption that the need for it would be transient.

The secretary of the New York Associated Charities reported that the men employed took pride in working for the betterment of their sections of the city, and the men in charge of the work became personally acquainted with men needing employment, and so were able to help them in other ways.

At a meeting held in New York City under the auspices of the Society for Sanitary and Moral Prophylaxis, October 16, 1913, Dr. Richard C. Cabot of the Massachusetts General Hospital declared that judging from his field of observation, if any comparison could be made in regard to the morality of the rich and poor, the comparison would be favorable to the poor.

If one man with reasonable intelligence and a social conscience could have experienced the 1873 national depression and all subsequent ones to the great depression of 1929, he would surely have utilized the learnings of that half century to develop a sophisticated system of social insurance, public works and assistance. The repetitive nature of economic depression and its consequences should somehow have enabled man to scientifically examine cause and effect and provide appropriate social and economic remedies. Yet even today a large segment of our population carry beliefs and attitudes and propose solutions to unemployment and dependency which clearly characterize attitudes, beliefs and solutions of 1873 and earlier. Fortunately, progress has been made, though limited, and out of the depression of 1929 emerged social and economic changes with profound significance.

The mass unemployment that came with the major depression of 1929 required the provision of public aid at first to thousands, and later to millions of persons who had formerly lived self-sufficient lives. The existing provisions for aid to dependent persons in 1929 were totally inadequate to cope with the problem. Local, state and federal governments were required to improvise ways of meeting mass problems that were so urgent that they could not await thoughtful development of sound theory, principles and administrative structure. The local and state governments were not equipped financially, because of inadequate tax systems to meet the needs of the unemployed. It became necessary for the Federal Government to act. Thus began a long series of innovations during the next decade designed both to relieve the current emergency and to provide a framework of social legislation which would avoid future depressions. The earliest action by the Federal Government occurred during the Hoover administration when, on July 21, 1932, the Emergency Relief and Construction Act authorized the Reconstruction Finance Corporation, under Title I of the Act, to loan a maximum of 300 million dollars to the states. These loans were "to be used in furnishing relief and work relief to needy and distressed people and in relieving the hardship resulting from unemployment." Requirements for repayment from the states were subsequently repealed. Title II of the Act authorized loans of certain kinds of projects, and Title III of the Act appropriated about 322 million dollars for the construction of federal public works and for emergency construction on the federal-aid highway system. This Act came many months after the depression began and had little time for operation prior to the beginning of the Roosevelt administration in 1933.

The Roosevelt administration quickly passed new legislation relating both to financial assistance and public works. The Federal Emergency Relief Act, approved May 1933, authorized "grants to the several states to aid in meeting the costs of furnishing relief and work relief and in relieving the hardship and suffering caused by unemployment in the form of money, service, materials, and/or commodities to provide the necessities of life to persons in need as a result of the present emergency, and/or to their dependents, whether resident, transient or homeless.[3]" This Act provided for a Federal Relief Administrator. This administration later became the Works Progress Administration (WPA). In its initial form, the Federal Emergency Relief Administrator (FERA) made grants of federal funds to the states and left the administration of the funds with the states. While the Act made money available to the states for work relief, it did not provide for any federal projects to furnish employment. Harry Hopkins was appointed Administrator of the Federal Emergency Relief Administration. Provision was made for such federal work relief in Title II of the National Industrial Recovery Act (NIRA) approved June 16, 1933. This Act provided for loans and grants to non-federal public bodies for eligible work projects approved by the Federal Government, and grants could not exceed 30 percent of the total cost of the project. Eligible public works were highways, parkways, public buildings, development of natural resources, low cost housing and slum clearance. Administrative authority was vested in a newly created agency, the Federal Emergency Administration of Public Works (PWA). President Roosevelt appointed Secretary of Interior, Harold L. Ickes, to the position of Federal Administrator of Public Works, and during the life of PWA, Ickes held both offices. PWA was very slow in beginning operation. Laws had to be passed in state, and local governments; project plans had to be drawn, contracts let and material secured. The projects were relatively large and Ickes maintained high standards. Thus long periods of time elapsed between the inception of a project and the employment of men.

Since PWA was not relieving unemployment as anticipated, the

President, in November 1933 under authority given him by Title II of the NIRA, established by executive order the Federal Civil Works Administration. The objective of this program was provision of immediate employment to four million unemployed workers about one-half of whom were on relief at the time. Within a month of inception of the CWA, one and one-half million were at work, and by January of 1934, a full four million persons were receiving CWA checks. The CWA program was short-lived. Its cost was high and many nonrelief persons were dissatisfied because of their inability to receive CWA jobs. Moreover, many of the projects elicited criticism and even ridicule because of their improvised nature. In April of 1934, after about five months of operation, CWA was discontinued. The program had cost 931 million dollars, of which the federal government had contributed 90 percent.

The CWA offered valuable aid in understanding how a work program should be developed. Moreover, it represented the Federal Government's attitude that distress of able-bodied unemployed persons should be relieved by provision of work rather than relief. The conviction of the federal government that work rather than relief should be provided to help the unemployed resulted in the approval by the Federal Government of the Emergency Relief Appropriation Act on April 8, 1935. This Act was designed "to provide relief, work relief and to increase employment by providing for useful projects."[5] Over four and a half billion federal dollars were made available to carry out the objectives of this act. The WPA received full-blown administrative authorization by the President under the powers he received from this act. Harry Hopkins directed both the FERA and the WPA. The President's Executive Order 7034 stated of the WPA that it "shall be responsible to the President for the honest, efficient, speedy and coordinated execution of the work relief program as a whole, and for the execution of that program in such manner as to move from the relief rolls to work on such projects or in private employment the maximum number of persons in the shortest time possible." Thus in 1935, we observe two agencies concerned with provision of work to the unemployed.

The PWA under Harold Ickes had developed into essentially a financing agency and was not in itself a construction agency. The projects financed through PWA used largely private contractors who, in turn, hired the bulk of the employees. The WPA, on the other hand, created jobs of the type which could be filled by persons on relief. WPA officials learned that the program could achieve its objectives more effectively by designing projects which gave such employment and by operating these projects with its own directors, supervisors, and foremen. In one sense, the programs of PWA and WPA were complementary in nature. Yet out of the sameness of their general objectives evolved highly significant competition. While much of the competition related to the nature of the programs, it is interesting to note that this implicit rivalry was personalized in the interactions between Harry Hopkins and Harold Ickes. Gradually, however, as the work programs developed they tended in the main toward the type of projects especially designed to take people off relief and give them work. Thus emerged the growing concept of *governmentally operated projects.*

Even during the heavy unemployment of the depression years, it was observed that unemployment was a selective economic disease often related to the efficiency, productivity, and skill of the individuals. It was found that the skilled, efficient employee was the last to become unemployed and the first to be reemployed. Accordingly, the unemployed during the depression years, just as today, did not represent a true cross-secton of the labor force. As a result of this phenomenon WPA had to select projects which would employ large numbers of unskilled and semi-skilled workers. Moreover, for those persons who had less efficiency, the projects needed to offer some shelter and concomitantly offer opportunity for improvement of efficiency. Generally, selection of projects for WPA was dominated by highway, road and street work. Erection and rehabilitation of public buildings, development of recreational facilities, and building and improvement of sewer systems constituted a large percentage of the projects. Airports and airways were built and improved. Conservation and sanitation projects and certain kinds of professional services completed the bulk of the kinds of projects developed by WPA. By June 30, 1940, WPA had spent a total of just over nine and a half billion dollars. The dominant WPA projects constituted fields in which state and local governments and private contractors functioned prior to the depression. The issue raised was whether WPA's work in these fields tended to retard the improvement of the equivalent section of the economy. Such questions remain essentially academic when consideration of the emergency needs of the moment for food, clothing, and shelter for millions of unemployed are reviewed.

Selection of Workers. The ill-fated experience of CWA proved that to try to provide work for all who would work, whether need existed or not, was a stupendous undertaking. Accordingly, WPA required that the unemployed applicant had to be in need. Such need determination was made by the relief agencies. In addition, the unemployed person needed to be considered employable in order to be certified to a work program. It was found that often the needs of a particular project and the resources of personnel available through this certifying process were incompatible.

Wages and Hours. Earning one's relief represents a concept that has maintained favor for centuries. WPA, after accepting this philosophy

82   WORK RELIEF TO REHABILITATION

for its purposes, was confronted with the problem of relating in some
manner the work done with the wage given. The administration developed the concept of a security wage. Project workers were not paid
by the hour or day but by the month. The monthly wage was theoretically designed to give the worker a security wage. Payment of wages
was related to prevailing rates of pay. Accordingly, an old principle
in relief administration was violated—belatedly, we might add—that
life on public aid should be less desirable than independent self-support. The monthly wage on WPA did not take into consideration
the need of the family. One worker might live well, while his associate with a larger family would be unable to manage on the wage.
Wage concepts and relief concepts accordingly were often found to
be in conflict. While this was true, it must be recognized that one of
the chief assets of the WPA was its social point of view. Personnel in
key administrative positions were either social workers or others with
social work orientation. This undoubtedly resulted in expediting
early projects. Had trained construction personnel and engineers
been in charge, as with PWA, they would undoubtedly have been
hampered by their professional standards in establishing projects
expeditiously. This factor may acccount for later criticism of WPA
projects. Yet we must measure WPA effectiveness, not solely in its
material accomplishments, but in its conservation of human values.

     Did WPA fulfill its social obligation to provide gainful employ-
ment to all in need? It has been estimated that from the beginning of
WPA in the summer of 1935, through June 1940, the WPA employed
about 7,800,000 different persons. The size of the program ranged
from 1,454,000 in September 1937, to about 3,330,000 workers in
November 1938. Yet, in spite of this tremendous demonstration of
the potentialities of a work program, it must be acknowledged that
the nation did not succeed in providing jobs for all the unemployed
and particularly did not cover all persons in need. For example, in
January 1936, there were 9,434,000 unemployed and 2,880,000 on
WPA, or 30.5 percent of the unemployed on WPA. In January 1940,
there were 9,163,000 unemployed, 2,203,000 on WPA, or 24 percent.
At no time during this five-year period did the percentage of unemployed on WPA exceed 40 percent of the total unemployed.
Major defects of WPA are listed as follows:

     1. WPA at no time during its existence provided jobs for all un-
employed, employable persons in need. Such employment was contingent upon closed-end appropriations from Congress which were
usually deficient to meet the need.

     2. Some persons in need received more than their budget deficit
while others received less. An efficient assistance program would have
met budgetary needs first.

     3. WPA was not closely integrated with other assistance pro-

grams at the state and local levels. This created problems in local planning for needs of people, since the exact amount of WPA funds available was never known at the local level.

These are serious criticisms of the WPA. The values of such a program, however, with its national standards of social philosophy which were vastly superior to local work relief philosophy, cannot be underestimated. It has been suggested that aside from giving aid to persons in need, the WPA made these additional contributions as follows:

1. WPA preserved the morale of the unemployed.
2. It preserved the skills of workers.
3. The public received a return in construction of public works and in services.

At the beginning of the great depression many persons feared loss of local control more than the consequences of the depression itself. The leaders of the federal administration and the leaders of business alike feared that the populace would demand federal appropriations which would eventually lead to federal taxation to meet those needed appropriations.

When Walter S. Gifford took the chairmanship of the President's Organization on Unemployment Relief in August, 1931, Silas H. Strawn, President of the Chamber of Commerce of the United States, made strenuous efforts to get important business men to act in their own states on the advisory committee. On December 16, 1931, the Committee on Public Works of the President's Organization on Unemployment Relief sent a long report to Mr. Gifford. Five major suggestions had been presented to this committee of the Gifford organization, which was headed by James R. Garfield. The suggestions called for acceleration of federal projects already authorized by Congress under the federal ten year program of public works; congressional appropriations for projects already authorized but for which funds had not yet been made available, and appropriations for new projects recommended by departments of the government but not yet acted upon by Congress; appropriations by Congress of large sums to be given or loaned to the states and municipalities for public works to be constructed by the states and the municipalities; additional federal road appropriations; and the floating of federal bond issues to raise five billion dollars for public works.

The committee of the Gifford organization evinced negative reactions to all of these suggestions. In its opinion, the federal ten-year program of normal public building had been expedited as much as possible. The committee was also of the opinion that large appropriations by Congress to be loaned or given to the states and municipalities "are unsound in principle." First of all, the committee maintained, it had never been done before. Secondly, it would lead to ever increasing demands, and "would necessarily weaken the sense of responsibility of the municipalities and states to provide for their local needs and welfare, and would postpone, if not prevent, the adoption by the localities of wise, local, long-time construction plans." The committee also doubted whether sufficient numbers of unemployed workers could be found in some parts of the country to carry on a large public works program. It reported that "the advocates of vast appropriations for public works as a means of relieving unemployment during the present winter seem to assume that labor can be shifted readily from its normal work to emergency construction, or moved from home surroundings to new localities." This should not be done, the committee felt. It insisted that "unemployment should be met by private resources marshalled locally to grapple with a problem predominantly local in character. In the long run the real problem of unemployment must be met by private business initiative if it is to be permanent." In the meantime, the committee had no recommendations concerning what was to be done with the millions of unemployed except that it indicated it was the duty of their local communities to take care of them out of hopelessly depleted tax resources, and that "the problem of unemployment can not be solved by any magic of appropriations from the public treasury." President Hoover had told Congress the same thing in December, 1930. The committee's report continued: "Under our political system, government is not nor should it be the general employer of labor. There are times when private enterprise fails; in such periods society must assume the care of those who are unable to help themselves and their children: the primary obligation is upon the local political division where such conditions exist. The response of our great and small cities to meet such conditions shows that our citizens will not shirk their obligations."

Opposed to federal relief and a federal public works program, the Gifford organization confined its activities to propaganda to induce the states and the local communities in the states to care for their unemployed. Mr. Gifford himself testified concerning the work of his organization before the committee holding hearings on the La Follette-Costigan Bill, which called for large appropriations for public works and direct federal aid to the states. He stated to the committee: "I think what we need is that everybody go back to work and have full pay for all jobs." When Senator La Follette asked, "Do you feel that the problem of unemployment relief is now being adequately met?" Mr. Gifford read a short statement: "It so happens I just made a check within two or three days of the situation by telephone, with each state representative in order to be up to date as possible. A check of the unemployment-relief situation by states which I have just made emphasizes again the existence in some parts of the country of great hardships resulting from unemployment. At the same time it indicates that, subject to action by legislatures in possibly some four or five instances, each State will care for its own who must have help this winter. These private and public funds, however, do not include what is called 'invisible' relief. I refer to the cash aid and the board and lodging extended to relatives, friends, and neighbors; to the aid, voluntary or involuntary remission of debts by merchants, landlords, and others; and to the aid—quite real in this depression—extended by business concerns to former employees. These are only a few of the items, but it seems clear that if the total of this invisible relief, which is obviously incalculable, were known it would be found that the private contributions very greatly exceed the public."

The testimony of representatives of social work organizations before the same committee revealed that each state was not able to take care of its own adequately, and had not done so during the winter of 1931 to which Mr. Gifford referred. Other witnesses, including social workers and municipal officials, testified that the landlords, the victims of "invisible" relief methods, were at the end of their own resources and were going on relief themselves, that relatives and friends granting "invisible" relief were cracking under the strain, that families were being broken up, and that the condition of the unemployed was the worst it had ever been and was rapidly growing even more desperate.

Gifford told the La Follette-Costigan committee: "In brief, the principle underlying the relief activities throughout the country has been that first, if possible, the individual community would look after its own. Next, if necessary, the county would help, and then, if the county were unable to meet the needs the state would help. It would seem that the combined efforts of communities, counties, and states can take care of the situation this winter." Other witnesses maintained that, first it was impossible for the individual community to look after its own, to say nothing of the hundreds of thousands of transients wandering into individual communities throughout the country. It was necessary for the county to help, but with taxes delinquent, the counties did not have the resources to aid effectively. In many of the states there were constitutional barriers to raising relief, loans, and levying state income taxes, and while the constitutions could be amended, the process was slow and the unemployed suffered in the meantime. But even where there were no constitutional limitations on their ability to raise money by loans and taxes, in some states resources were insufficient to care for the unemployed. The result was that during the winter of 1931 the unemployed were not adequately cared for according to the unanimous testimony of those actively engaged in relief work.

Mr. Gifford was afraid of what would happen if "local responsibility were lessened by federal aid." He told the La Follette-Costigan committee: "Should such community and state responsibility be lessened by federal aid, the sincere and whole-hearted efforts of the hundreds of thousands of volunteers engaged both in raising and administering relief funds would doubtless be materially lessened. Individuals would tend to withdraw much of the invisible aid they are now giving; private funds raised by popular subscription would become less; efforts to spread work and provide work that would not be done except for the emergency would be lessened; business organizations would tend to do less for former employees. Communities, counties, and states undoubtedly would appropriate less public moneys. The net result might well be that the unemployed who are in need would be worse instead of better off. Also, the effect of federal aid on federal government credit should be considered. If this were adversely affected, the real cure for unemployment, which is obviously the restoration of normal business, would be retarded."

When Senator Costigan asked Mr. Gifford: "What evidence of human need in America would be required to satisfy you that the federal government should make an appropriation?" Mr. Gifford answered: "I think if a state government were absolutely broke and could not raise any more money by taxes or otherwise, that would be pretty satisfactory, assuming now that the local communities and counties could not do the thing directly and state aid was asked and the state legislature met and they could not sell any bonds and the tax limits had been reached and they could not tax anybody. I think that would be pretty good evidence."

President Hoover told Congress on December 9, 1931: "The evidence of the Public Health Service shows an actual decrease of sickness and infant and general mortality below normal years. No greater proof could be adduced that our people have been protected from hunger and cold and that the sense of social responsibility in the Nation has responded to the need of the unfortunate." This statement caused protest from social workers and from hospital officials who were in direct touch with conditions. Jacob Billikopf, executive director of the Federation of Jewish Charities, quoted the President's statement at a hearing on the La Follette-Costigan Bill, and added evidence from the speech of Mr. Appel, Secretary of Public Health of Pennsylvania, before a joint session of the Legislature of Pennsylvania, in which he claimed that malnutrition was prevalent among children in the rural sections of that state, that the number of new patients in tuberculosis clinics had nearly doubled since 1929, and that waiting lists at sanatoria were two and a third times their average.

The Committee on Economic Security in 1935 stated that the need of the people of this country for "some safeguard against misfortunes which cannot be wholly eliminated in this man-made world of ours is tragically apparent when 18,000,000 people including children and aged were dependent upon emergency relief for their subsistence and approximately 10,000,000 workers had no employment other than relief work. Many millions more had lost their entire savings, and there had occurred a very great decrease in earnings. The ravages of the worst depression of all time have been accentuated by greater urbanization, with the consequent total dependence of a majority of our people on their earnings in industry.[6]" While progress would be made toward recovery, the committee noted that even in the "normal times" of the prosperous twenties a large part of the population had little security. From the best estimates which were obtainable, it appeared that in the years 1922 to 1929 there was an average unemployment of 8 percent among industrial workers. In the best year of the period, the number of the unemployed averaged somewhat less than 1,500,000.

The Committee stated that "since most people must live by work, the first objective in a program of economic security must be maximum employment. As the major contribution of the federal government in providing a safeguard against unemployment it suggested employment assurance—the stimulation of private employment and the provision of public employment for those able-bodied workers whom industry cannot employ at a given time. Public works programs are most necessary in periods of severe depression but may be needed in normal times as well, to meet the problems of stranded communities and overmanned or declining industries. To avoid the evils of hastily planned emergency work, public employment should be planned in advance and coordinated with the construction and developmental policies of the government and with the state and local public works projects."

The Committee noted that "a program of economic security for the nation that does not include those now unemployed cannot possibly be complete. They, above all, are in need of security. Their tragic situation calls attention not only to their own desperate insecurity but to the lack of security of all those who are dependent upon their own earnings for a livelihood. Therefore, any program for economic security that is devised must be more comprehensive than unemployment compensation, which of necessity can be given only for a limited period. In proposing unemployment compensation, we recognize that it is but a complementary part of an adequate program for protection against the hazards of unemployment, in which stimulation of private employment and provision of public employment on a security payment basis are other major elements."

The Committee agreed that in our economic system the great majority of the workers must find work in private industry, if they are to have permanent work. The stimulation and maintenance of a high level of private employment should be a major objective of the government. All measures designed to relieve unemployment should be calculated to promote private employment and also to get the unemployed back into the main channel of production. The Committee believed that provision of public employment in combination with unemployment compensation would most effectively serve these purposes. Both would operate to maintain purchasing power, and public employment would indirectly give work to many more persons in private industry who otherwise would have none. At the same time, it would stimulate workers to accept and seek private employment when available.

What the federal, local and state governments would be called upon to do in providing work depends upon many complicated factors: Financial resources, advance planning, the general industrial trend and methods; but it is a sound principle that public employment should be expanded when private employment slackens, and it is likewise sound that work in preference to relief in cash or in kind should be provided for those of the unemployed who are willing and able to work.

The experience of 1934-1935 demonstrated that making useful work available is a most effective means of meeting the needs of the unemployed. Further, it has been demonstrated that it is possible to put large numbers of persons to work quickly at useful tasks under conditions acceptable to them. The social and economic values of completed projects represent a considerable offset to the losses occasioned by millions of unemployed workers. The required expenditures have an important stabilizing effect on private industry by increasing purchasing power and employment and the completed works frequently produce self-liquidating income. Work maintains occupational skill.

Lewis Meriam presented statistics to refute the suggestion that work relief preserved skills, pointing out that "unskilled workers constituted the largest single group with which WPA had to deal. The second largest group was the service skilled . . ." About skilled workers, Meriam stated: "WPA could not supply them with jobs to maintain their skills unless it competed directly with private enterprise . . . these statistics strongly suggest that the argument regarding the preservation of skills was more a talking point than an actuality. The unskilled had relatively little in the way of skills to preserve: What they needed to preserve was more good work habits than skills, and it is questionable how far WPA promoted good work habits."" With regard to the public receiving a return in construction of public works and in services, Meriam says: "The people got some useful and valuable public works and services from WPA. That is unquestionably true, but it is not the real issue. The real issue is, which would have given the people the most for their money: (1) WPA as it was actually conducted, or (2) payments of direct relief to persons in need to the extent of their budget deficiencies, and use of the balance of the money and credit in ways that would stimulate private enterprise and normally conducted public enterprise." Meriam admits that data is not available to answer the question fully but he suggests that better selection of projects and more efficient operation could have resulted in greater public value from the expenditure. Judgments of this kind, however, fail to consider the human equation.

WPA project work was classified by reference to 250 standard job classifications. Each worker was given his project assignment on the basis of a work history and although it was the intent of WPA to make assignments paralleling previous work experience, it was not possible to do this because the type of work available precluded such assignments. At the end of June 1940, about 3 of every 4 project workers employed by WPA were working on construction projects. In this regard, the National Resources Planning Board stated: "By and large, only some of those workers usually employed in the building trades and other construction work and a relatively small number of professional, technical, and white collar workers could continue their usual type of work while on WPA.[8]"

Apart from the difficulties of initiating so vast a project as WPA, the lack of experience derived from any previous program on the same scale, the shortage of trained administrative personnel, and the legislative and financial restrictions upon matching jobs with men prevented WPA from competing directly with private industry. Moreover, it was required by statute that projects should not be of a character to benefit private interests. These limitations seriously restricted the variety and representative character of the projects that could be developed. Finally, the use of the work program for relief purposes during a period in which the funds had been inadequate for provision of work to all needy unemployed, created the need to develop projects which would spread the available funds by giving as large an amount of direct employment as possible from a given appropriation. The development of projects requiring considerable machinery or expensive materials was not to be expected.

The National Resource Planning Board, in a research study[9] on maintenance of work habits in WPA, illustrated the quality of performance of over 1,400 skilled workers, and evaluated the quantity of output of over 1,200 such workers. More than 75 percent of the group were classified as passable or better on the basis of both quality and quantity of the work completed. About 40 percent were rated excellent on quality, 30 percent excellent as to quantity. Only 9 and 8 percent, respectively, were rated inferior. Actually, it could be expected that efficiency would be less from employees on a work relief project. They were required to pass a means test which most often meant they had undergone long demoralizing months of unemployment and deprivation. Employers tended to employ the most efficient and younger workers. Outdoor projects often needed to continue during periods of adverse weather because of the relief objectives of the work. These objectives also tended to inhibit the prosecution of a vigorous policy related to high standards of performance. Thus, attempting to relate maintenance of work habits to efficiency on the job was a complex and inconclusive task.

The difficulties of developing work projects adapted to the previous occupation and skills of the unemployed led to the tendency to emphasize the maintenance of work habits as a major objective of any work program. The Yale Institute of Human Relations conducted a study of the reactions of a sample group of WPA workers in New Haven in 1938, and concluded that "there was ample evidence in the testimony of the unemployed that the daily work routine, the necessity for using one's muscles, and the outdoor life were beneficial in maintaining the workers' general health and physique except during the most severe weather.[10]" There is essentially little evidence in available literature based upon the testimony of workers themselves to support the theory that work relief aids in the maintenance of work habits.

In periods of depression, public employment should be regarded as a principal line of defense. Even in prosperous times, it is necessary, on a smaller scale, when "pockets" develop in which there is much unemployment. Public employment is not the final answer to the problem of stranded communities, declining industries, and impoverished farm families, but is a necessary supplement to more fundamental measures for the solution of such problems. And it must be remembered that since a part of the population has not been covered by unemployment compensation projects to give employment assurance, it should be recognized as a permanent policy of the government and not merely as an emergency measure.

In 1939, Paul Kellogg[11] stated that until state and local governments can measure up to the basic responsibility for relief, we should be chary of turning over to them our second line of countrywide defense—the WPA. By middepression, with private industry stalled, private charity overwhelmed, and public works requiring much material and machinery, the heavy end of the load of finding substitutes for regular jobs was taken over by the WPA. Its scheme of work projects had been the one outstanding American contribution to ways for combating enforced idleness. Kellogg believed that to throw out the WPA would be the scuttling of the first promising demonstration that the American people had the good sense to make use of idle workers and idle time in such a way as to produce needed services and enduring utilities for the benefit of our common life.

Speaking in 1939, William Hobson[12] agreed that every relief administrator was anxious to return a maximum number of the needy unemployed persons on his rolls to self-support as quickly as possible; and that we need and must have a vigorous and aggressive public employment service which will not only concern itself with securing employment for those receiving unemployment insurance benefits, but will also provide adequate and efficient service for the general population, including persons on relief. The employment services ought to make available to those on relief the largest possible number of job opportunities, not primarily because these workers are on relief, but because they are in need of work. Public welfare departments should not be expected to set up competing employment services when such services already exist. To do this would be a wasteful duplication of facilities, Hobson declared. He added that the WPA had been an absolute necessity, without which it would have been impossible for the local community to carry their relief rolls and without which there would have been tremendous loss of morale by reason of the inability of workers to use the skills which they have or can acquire. Hobson believed thoroughly in the fundamental idea behind the WPA program and wished it were possible for America to provide a job for every man willing to work, either in private industry or through the public works or through the WPA.

The author agrees with this view and strongly emphasizes in our contemporary society that the basic needs of man for meaningful work remain the same.

DEPRESSION UNEMPLOYMENT—ITS EFFECT ON MAN

The plight of an unemployed man in 1933 was described at a social work conference by Helen White, District Secretary of the Charity Organization Society in New York, in a manner which transcends all conceptualizations of the impact of lack of work on contemporary man:

"Recently a man sat in the office of a family agency. In silence he looked down at his hands—hands knotted, their muscles strengthened by hard toil of the past through which a livelihood had been earned. Fear in his eyes, fear in his voice, he whispered: 'They are growing soft and white.' The words of this man may symbolize a fear which is everywhere—a fear with which caseworkers come daily into contact. It is, I think, in a role of activity which senses the nature of the individual's fear, psychological and practical; shares his experiences with him to the extent of enabling him to carry on—an activity which resorts neither to argument nor to persuasion, but stimulates the client to self-expression and to the facing of his difficulties—that casework for the present can fulfill its greatest usefulness to a people who are frightened and confused.[13]"

At this same conference another agency executive, Frederick H. Allen, M.D., Director of the Child Guidance Clinic, Philadelphia, stated that the first reaction to loss of work is severe and a personal affront, a feeling of personal failure. Later, perspective is gained and the second reaction is less personal, a recognition of the universality of the problem with resulting restoration of values. The third group of reactions are those characterized by apathy, indifference, and feeling of "What's the use?" Dr. Allen reported that in the summer of 1932, Philadelphia went for three months without any relief funds. Thousands of families were left without any means of support. Several workers, interested in knowing how people were meeting this situation, visited many of the families and were impressed with the amount of apathy they observed. Many seemed like lost children who had passed through a period of anxiety and were now dulled into a state of little feeling. A man, previously energetic, dulled into a state of helplessness by continued efforts to find work, stayed in bed a good share of the day until prodded by an irritable wife to get out, and then he wandered around the neighborhood. The fourth group of reactions is quite different and is characterized by action and aggression. In the milder forms there is irritability and quarreling, particularly in the family groups. In the more exaggerated expressions there is rebellion, bitterness, and hatred not unlike that noted today in high unemployment tension areas like Watts in Los Angeles. Physical conditions around the home favor the development of these reactions, Allen observed. Everyone is on edge. Husbands out of work are around the house during the day, and to preserve their feelings of self-respect many become autocratic with wife and children. Wives in turn, worried about the situation, taunt the man because he is not working and urge him to get out. Children, sensitive to tension, become fretful and quarrelsome and frequently become the target for adult irritability.

Paul H. Douglas of the University of Chicago noted[14] that during the early part of this depression, many thought it wicked to feed the unemployed from state funds because it was believed that this would undermine the concept of rugged individualism which was to be held sacred, at all costs. As a consequence, localities were compelled to stagger under this burden and to give grossly inadequate relief because it was believed that federal grants would violate the principle of local responsibility, which was held most dear. Throughout the whole gloomy period of the four and a half years of the depression, there had been large sections of the more comfortable classes who agreed to relief only because by reducing the pangs of hunger could the fear of revolution with its threat to their property be lessened or removed. Professor Douglas also disclosed the opposition of real estate interests to slum clearance and housing projects because of their fear of an increase in the total number of apartments and subsequent decrease in their rents. These groups kept the people penned up in slums and living in shanties in order that all existing properties, however inadequate, might continue to draw as large an income as possible.

Rexford G. Tugwell, Undersecretary of Agriculture in 1934, expressed grave concern for people undergoing severe privation during the depression.[15] He acknowledged that Americans want no pity, no one crying for them, that they wanted opportunities to use their energies and their talents. He was concerned that there seemed scant recognition of the human deterioration which had been going on with increasing speed among the unemployed, and to the proverb men live by more than bread alone, he added, "they demand jobs, not only reasonable security in receiving their bread, but the sense of being useful to, and of being used by, society." He also believed that we must get rid of the oversimplified notion that face-to-face relationships with those who are insultingly described as the "deserving poor" are sufficient without any sense of the general situation which produces poverty, whether deserved or undeserved; and that we must modify the old idea of personal salvation and casework, wherein it is said to be sufficient to adjust the individual to a society which itself needs to be changed and is changing. The task is not only to help the individual but also to assist in attacking the causes of his distress. Tugwell claimed that it was arrogant to assume that we have any right or power to change people, that people are pretty much the same with respect to their basic wants, urges, and passions as they were five thousand years ago. Men establish ways and means by which they satisfy these wants, needs, urges, and passions. What changes is our institutions. These institutions take many shapes and forms and constitute the organized milieu of society. When we talk of social changes, we talk of changing these institutions, not the men who use them. When we speak of the need for social change, we mean that these institutions are failing, that they do not provide effective instrumentalities by which people's urges, wants and desires are satisfied.

William Hobson, Commissioner of the New York City Department of Public Welfare in 1934 stated[16] that society learned from experience with the FERA that no system of relief, however soundly conceived or ably administered, can be successful in coping with the by-products of unemployment, and that no system of relief can take the place of work opportunities. During the depression, the morale of workers had been shattered, their health undermined, and their homes disrupted. They had changed from self-respecting, independent citizens into self-confessed unemployables, dependent upon relief for their continued existence. Hobson believed that the depression, with its relief methods, had done this to the American workingman, and he stated that no society can long exist that does not furnish to men and women an opportunity to make their own way in life. He emphasized that technological advancement, instead of being accompanied by the tragic human waste of unemployment, should be matched by new social machinery for the retraining and replacement in other jobs of the men thrown out of their former lines of employment. Harry Hopkins, Federal Emergency Relief Administrator, echoing Mr. Hobson's concerns, insisted that unemployment should not be handled on a relief basis but rather through the provision of dignified work opportunity.

Aubrey Williams, Deputy Administrator of the WPA in 1936 stated that he believed no one questioned the desirability of a job for the unemployed able-bodied man or woman. He said: "There is work that needs to be done and there are people who are competent to do it. What more logical responsibility has the government than to bring the two together! Public work for the unemployed is socially desirable in that it uses for the public benefit the talents and capacities of those people whom industry has rejected . . . There is something deep-rooted in a democracy like ours that demands that each person shall pull his own weight, that despises the parasite.[17]" He did not believe that any direct relief program for the able-bodied can fail to humiliate and degrade the individual who receives it, and he could think of nothing more unfair to the unemployed person than to add to the misery of insecurity and want the humiliation of idle uselessness and the sense of being despised by his neighbors for that uselessness. He added that WPA had increased the average benefit paid to the unemployed from $25 under our federal relief program to $50 under a federal work program; that to the American people a laborer is worthy of his hire, but the able-bodied man who depends on charity for his livelihood is thrown a pittance in contempt; and that this is a trait in our American character which we should not despise, but must accept along with its inevitable corollary —a public responsibility to see that every able-bodied worker has the opportunity to take his rightful place in our democratic society not only through the exercise of political rights, but through a job.

Fiorello La Guardia, Mayor of New York City during the depression years, presented an evaluation of the contributions of both WPA and PWA in New York City. In reviewing these years of relief work, Mayor La Guardia found that: (1) A very high percentage of skilled workers, as compared with laborers, were employed on many of the projects and there was in consequence a shortage of skilled workers very soon after the work program had been launched, while the construction work undertaken by WPA did not take care of the great mass of unskilled workers; (2) that the work provided by the Division of Women's and Professional Projects was generally adapted to the experience and skills of those employed; and (3) as to the white collar workers, a sufficient number of acceptable projects had not been available, and in his opinion it was almost impossible to devise worthwhile white collar jobs which would not displace regular employees. Of special interest was his following opinion of the efficiency of the WPA workers: "As to the quality of the workmanship, there is little question. PWA work was executed under contract. The quality of PWA work has been uniformly as high as that done under contract. On the other hand the efficiency of the work, measured in units of time, is considerably below the maximum that should be attained. This is due in large part to the small sums available for materials and equipment, and in part to the constant shifting of forces made necessary by the fact that mechanics work only part time. It cannot be denied, either, that some of the inefficiency is the result of the haste in which the work was organized, the class of supervision available, and some is due to the workers themselves. Many of them are beyond the age when full activity may be expected of them.[18]"

CHICAGO STUDY

The depression period produced a few studies designed to evaluate specifically the dynamics of human response to lack of work. Throughout the United States in 1934 there was an increasing emphasis on work relief as part of the program of public assistance to unemployed wage earners. The School of Social Service Administration at the University of Chicago took advantage of the opportunity that was offered in the winter of 1934 to study the system as it was working in Chicago. The study was undertaken at the request of the Illinois Relief Commission and was carried on as an educational research project under the FERA.[19] It was concerned primarily with seeking answers to the question: What are the values to the client given work assignments of receiving his relief in this form?

Case records which were studied contained reports of statements made by some member of the family, for example: "He or she gets on my nerves" or "I am not used to having him home all day, I never can get any work done." A careful survey of 407 case records showed that 222, or 54 percent of the cases, gave evidence of definite psychological and emotional problems which appeared to be associated with the need for employment or at least a need for some type of constructive activity. It appeared from the evidence at hand that 188 of the 222 had problems of the type for which treatment by work relief might be appropriate. Of these, 93 were grouped together as suffering from general despondency—men who had been diagnosed as being psychopathic, or who had attempted suicide apparently because of unemployment, or whose cases of restlessness were associated with despondency. An example was the case of Mr. Lane, who had been laid off from his last job as an insurance salesman because he lacked ability and was "not suited to the job." Both he and his wife were upset over the difficulty. The caseworker thought that Lane needed work relief because of his mental attitudes toward himself and his feeling of inferiority toward his own ability. For 51, the problem was one of domestic friction. This group included men who had previously deserted their families where the desertion appeared to be caused by unemployment, men whose wives were constantly "nagging" at them, men who didn't get on with relatives, or men in whose families general discord had come into evidence only after unemployment had become a problem. Mr. Harrison, for example, had been deserted by his wife because he had no work. The mother-in-law with whom Mr. Harrison lived was very ill, and both she and he were very much worried. It was thought that if he had work his wife might return home. Another example was Mr. Adams, who felt that he could not sit around at home all day long. Mrs. Adams was constantly complaining of her illness; and when Mr. Adams was at home, he seemed to be annoyed at her constant repetition of her complaints. Finally, there were 44 whose personal pride demanded some opportunity to work for their relief. Some had been dependent upon their wives' relatives and needed the chance to be self-supporting; some were young men who felt the responsibility for their mothers and younger brothers and sisters because of the death or incapacity of the father; and one was a man over 60 years of age who had been living with his married son but felt that the son was unable to care for him and therefore he wanted to be self-supporting. Also included in this group were seven men on probation, parole, or just recently discharged from institutions. In all 44 of these cases, the men had asked for work relief in order to demonstrate their intentions to make good and to show their families that they could furnish the necessary support if given a chance. The following examples are typical of the cases in this group:

The Harris family, a very proud family, was humiliated to have to apply for relief. They were facing eviction but would not accept rent from the agency since the landlord did not know that they were receiving relief. Mr. Harris, a tailor by trade, thought that the laboring job was very degrading, but his attitude seemed to improve after he started to work.

Mr. Barbes, 46 years old and suffering from peptic ulcers, wanted work relief so that his 19-year-old son would not have to carry the complete responsibility of the family. At first he was not referred for work relief because of his health, but since he wanted it, an assignment was made. No medical report was received as to the effects of the work.

Roy S., 24 years old, had just returned from serving a jail sentence and was almost "pathetic" when he begged to have work given to him so that he could support his younger brothers as he had done previously when he was working. Both of his parents were dead.

Bristol and Wright, the authors of this Chicago case study article, concluded that the value of work assignments in lessening emotional tension and despair and in maintaining self-respect stood in clear relief. In spite of the irregularity of the work, in spite of difficulties caused by inadequate clothing and carfare, and in spite of objections to work that they considered beneath them, an overwhelming majority of the men interviewed liked the work assignments and wanted more. The evidence on this point, however, came largely, almost' exclusively, from men who had been generally supposed to be most suitable for work relief, able-bodied workers with good work records.

A later Chicago study[20] compared that city's work relief program with the Civil Works Administration (CWA), and found similar morale problems. Some of the limitations in the city work relief program, especially the uncertainty and irregularity of the work, were not found in the Civil Works Administration program; and it was believed, therefore, that a better idea of the possibilities of work relief in this direction could be obtained by studying a group with CWA assignments. This study was made by a caseworker in the Unemployment Relief Service and included 61 families whose members were given such assignments. She worked with all the families after their return to the relief rolls, and with all but a few before their assignments as well. Thus the descriptions of the families and the reports on their reactions to the work assignments are based on a more intimate knowledge than could be gained by an outside investigator. The following are typical examples.

The G family came to the attention of the Unemployment Relief Service in February, 1933. Mr. G lost his job after ten years of service for one firm in October, 1932. He was extremely irritated by unemployment and requested work at each visit of the caseworker. He was restless and irritable, and Mrs. G. stated that she had to be extremely careful with him. A 16-year-old daughter of Mrs. G's by a former marriage was also complicating the family situation. She had dropped out of high school shortly after the family applied for relief because of their inability to give her the necessary clothes or the other small things her friends in school had. At home she was restless and unhappy and seemed to feel no responsibility for the family. Her relations with her mother were not good, as her mother clearly identified her with her father, with whom Mrs. G had been very unhappy. In this situation, the assignment to work under CWA helped appreciably. Mr. G found great satisfaction in his work; he enjoyed being busy and was no longer moody and irritable at home. The daughter was immediately returned to school and she too seemed happier. The improvement in her case, however, was very temporary. A few months after the family returned to relief she was expelled from school and was again at home, as unhappy and disturbing as before.

The W family, consisting of Mr. W, 48 years old, and his wife, 52 years old, had been known to the Unemployment Relief Service since August 1932. Mr. W. had a good history of employment as a maintenance man. The family was ashamed of being dependent on their friends for rent and worried constantly about making payment to them. Mrs. W was ill with an advanced case of diabetes. She was receiving medical care at a clinic and the budget had been adjusted with a special diet allowance. The family, however, still found it difficult to buy the necessary food for her. Mr. W keenly felt his inability to provide for his wife. He finally doubted his ability of ever finding employment and ever being independent. He attempted to face the situation calmly, but occasionally he would break into tears before the caseworker. He was again able to take care of his wife when he was employed with CWA. He was easily able to buy the food required, and rent was paid to the friends who had sheltered them during his unemployment. His confidence in himself returned. He again felt that he could sell himself to an employer. His moodiness disappeared. "I was working," he proudly told the caseworker, "and I could again hold my head up when I met people."

These families were typical of the group where unemployment was followed by a loss of self-respect, loss of self-confidence, and irritation. CWA, by providing employment, helped to restore their self-confidence and relieve the tension. The number of families studied was obviously too small to allow general conclusions about the effects of the CWA program on those who shared it. However, the study noted that with negligible exceptions, the 61 families benefited by the work assignments and received help in the maintenance of general morale. The intimate accounts of some of the families made clear the value of the work assignment with its accompaniment of cash and independence, and made clear, too, the increased hardship for many of the families when the CWA program came to an end and they were forced once more to reapply for nonwork relief funds.

Comments in a 1939 edition of the *Social Service Review*[21] gives some information on the hardships of the depression in Chicago, as revealed by a special study commission. When the next to the last

Illinois relief crisis was impending in the early winter of 1937-38, Governor Horner appointed a special Council on Public Assistance and Employment, composed of well-known businessmen in the community. Later, in January 1938, the Council issued a preliminary report on the administration of relief in Chicago, with a report on a survey of the Chicago relief rolls, made not by social workers but by persons loaned from the various business offices. The Council reported that 15 percent of the relief families were living under "utterly poverty-stricken conditions," that many of them were living in condemned buildings, and that they were living in buildings where the electricity had been shut off, the water had been turned off, and there was no heat. The report also showed that a large number of children had been unable to attend school because of lack of proper shoes and clothing.

The Council presented an example of a family on WPA consisting of father, mother, and five children—seven people to be fed and clothed and rent to be paid out of $65 a month. This was originally a Chicago Relief Administration supplementation case prior to the 35 percent reduction in the budget. The total minimum budget for this family of seven, and this is only a minimum health and decency budget and nothing more, was $97.72 a month. They were reduced to only the $65 WPA wage and with the 35 percent relief reduction, any hope of supplementation came to an end. They had a stove-heated flat. This WPA mother went to the Chicago Relief Administration and asked for medical care and clothing for her five children. The results of the examination in a good clinic to which they were sent showed malnutrition and early rheumatic heart disease for two children, malnutrition and upper respiratory infection for the third child, malnutrition and secondary anemia for the fourth child, and malnutrition, eight pounds under average weight, for the fifth child. Special diets were recommended by the clinic for each of these five children. Can the WPA $65 a month provide for the needs of this family, was the question raised by the Council.

NEW YORK STUDY

New York Governor Herbert H. Lehman appointed a commission to study unemployment relief, and this commission reported its findings to the Governor on August 10, 1936.[22] The commission found that work relief in New York State embraced the following principles: (1) The recipients were, in the main, selected from persons eligible for public relief by reason of destitution; (2) the weekly wage was, with few exceptions, limited to the recipient's budget deficit as determined by the relief needs of the individual family, minus any other income which the family may have had; and (3) continued employment under work relief was contingent upon demonstrable continued eligibility for public relief, with persons placed on work relief jobs retaining their status as relief cases.

The commission agreed that the major factor which caused the continuance and expansion of work relief was the assumption that it offered definite benefits to the workers when contrasted with home relief. Principle among these benefits were: (1) The preservation of morale, skills, work habits, employability, normal family relationships, self-respect, self-reliance, initiative, and independence; (2) a somewhat more liberal relief grant per family per week as compared with home relief; (3) the provision of a solution to the problem occasioned by thoroughly needy people who refuse to accept home relief but will accept work relief; and (4) the superior effect of a cash wage as compared with a home relief order.

Retention of Skills—The commission observed that protracted subsistence upon home relief tends to render a person unfit for the resumption of a state of self-support. This condition arises partly out of the gradual loss of skills and work habits; it hinges more definitely upon a decline in confidence and initiative. That the problem is a real one is shown by the inclination of employers to hire persons on relief only after exhaustng other resources. Work relief clearly had some value in point of preservation of both skills and work habits; but it appeared to the commission that its merits in this respect had been exaggerated by some people, particularly as to the skills of the workers. This is evident when it is observed that the majority of the workers were unskilled manual laborers. Some workers in the skilled and white collar groups, on the other hand, risked losing the capacities peculiar to their respective callings. For example, stenographers decline in performance through the lack of practice consequent upon unemployment. Nevertheless, it appears that too much emphasis may have been attached to this condition in respect to skilled persons in general, both because it is doubtful whether the loss of skills is as great as is frequently assumed and because a return to activity is often productive of a very rapid return of the skill formerly possessed.

Work Habits—It appeared to the commission that employable persons commonly lose their work habits in part as the result of the inactivity consequent upon unemployment. The longer the period of inactivity the more pronounced this phenomenon tended to be. Work relief employment operates to preserve work habits to the extent that the discipline and efficiency are of good caliber. Obviously, the performance of slip-shod work with inefficient and unsatisfactory supervisors does not maintain work habits satisfactorily. It may be even more injurious to the retention of work habits than complete unemployment in the sense that the development of unsatisfactory working methods may be carried over to a subsequent period of normal employment.

Normal Family Relationships—The commission found the most important value of work relief is that it affords the family head an opportunity to approximate the conditions of usual family life which he would obtain if he were regularly employed. Any normal family is accustomed to seeing the head of the family engaged in a certain routine in connection with having a job. There is a regularity in the household governed by his going to and coming from work, and the weekly pay envelope creates prestige for him as the head of the household. The commission added that no single factor contributes so greatly to family disharmony as the continued presence of the family head in the home during a period of unemployment. When the man is working, his daily absence helps in avoiding the strain on family relationships that come from enforced idleness and close proximity. Family harmony is frequently and seriously disrupted in consequence of the presence of the head of the household who has no place to go and nothing to do.

The New York Governor's Commission on Unemployment Relief took particular note of the effect of unemployment upon morale, and attached the greatest importance to work relief in its effect in preserving and maintaining the morale of the individual workers. The belief was that work relief fostered the retention of a favorable emotional state and of a normal and well-balanced psychological attitude on the part of the worker toward himself, his responsibilities, and his environment. This involved, among other things, the prevention of injury to his normal outlook, self-respect, self-reliance, initiative, and independence, insofar as these attributes are the result of employment. It appeared that the tone of the recipients of this form of aid was superior to that of home relief cases; not that the morale of persons on work relief had not suffered nor that it had remained at the same level as in predepression days. Much damage was done to many individuals before they were reduced to the point where their personal resources were exhausted and they found themselves forced to apply for relief of any kind. Moreover, work relief had not been of equal value to all workers with regard to morale preservation, and some recipients had apparently not benefited from the employment.

It was clear to the Commission that the idleness and unemployment which necessarily accompanied a period of subsistence upon home relief constituted serious impediments to the preservation of normal attitudes and healthy relationships. Relief recipients were likely to brood, lose faith in themselves, their families and their country, and their whole confidence was seriously impaired.

The Commission found that before the beneficial effects of work relief could be fully realized, the project must be worthwhile and the detailed operations performed must be useful and purposeful; if the workers conclude that the work is a mere gesture or a means of keeping them busy, they do not receive much benefit; and the supervision of the workers must be adequate and the management of the work efficient. If the worker is regarded as a ward of society whose rewards are the same whether he be a model worker or an unreliable loafer, or if the community attitude toward the work relief enterprise is unsympathetic or derisive, then the value of work relief, in point of morale preservation, is very largely lost. Low efficiency and lax discipline have a peculiar bearing, since morale hinges very substantially upon the worker's feeling that he is earning the funds which he receives through work relief. Moreover, it was noted that advantages to the worker were inevitably limited because of the relief character of the undertaking. Obviously, the morale preservation values of any form of work relief are in no respect equal to those of normal employment. The necessity of undergoing a period of idleness and dwindling resources before acquiring eligibility for relief, plus the recognition of the fact that work relief is, after all, relief, and is secured and retained only because of a state of destitution, detract from the value of the employment. The extent, therefore, to which work relief is dissociated from relief has a bearing upon its morale value.

The Commission also found that while work relief possesses the morale values previously stated, there are strong reasons for suspecting that its advantage in this respect will wear off; that its values are of maximum importance in a situation which is in fact temporary and emergency, and that in a longer period, when the concept of lasting employment begins to infiltrate and when awareness of the shortcomings of the enterprise grows cumulatively to sizeable proportions, the morale value diminishes. Work relief on a more lasting basis, as in a permanent institution, does not have the same effect as such an enterprise on a temporary basis. This would suggest that work experience programs in welfare departments may have temporary value for the individual but should not be prolonged or they lose their benefits.

The Commission's conclusions on the principal advantages of work relief are as follows:

1. It avoids the particular stigma of charity which is commonly attached to home relief.

2. It tends to maintain the morale, self-respect, self-reliance, security and social stability of the participants.

3. It produces a valuable return to the communities of the state for the relief outlays.

4. It preserves, in part, the skills and work habits of the persons who participate; and, in some cases, cultivates new skills.

5. It directs available public employment to persons who are destitute.

6. The benefit of the work opportunity afforded by the expenditure of a given sum of money reaches more people than it would under other methods of employment, since it is spread thinner than it otherwise would probably be.

The Commission's conclusions on the disadvantages of work relief are as follows:

1. It costs more than home relief.

2. It is less efficient as a means of doing work than the usual processes.

3. If conducted on a scale sufficiently large to accommodate a relatively large proportion of the present needy population, and if centered upon projects of such character as to be beneficial to the morale of the workers and of economic value, it is inevitably competitive with public enterprise and, in a few of its activities, with private enterprise.

4. It fails to provide adequate incentives for the workers to put forth effort as diligently as they would normally be expected to, since most of the elements of competition are lacking. There are fewer dismissals for inefficiency than in normal enterprise and fewer opportunities for advancement. Generally, work relief is subject to the effects of employment upon the basis of need.

5. It causes the workers, in some measure, to become accustomed to work relief and to fail to seek private employment because it offers too much security. Some tendency has developed to regard work relief employment both as a matter of right and as a continuing job.

6. It has affected adversely the contrasting organizations which engage in public works construction.

7. It has attempted to combine the giving of relief with the doing of governmental work and has thus had dual objectives which give rise to some confusion and conflict.

8. It has tended to be cumulative and self-perpetuating because it provides a distinct economic advantage to local communities to do their necessary work through work relief.

In considering the problem of work relief for the future, the Commission proceeded on the theory that a large number of persons would probably require public relief for some years to come and that if the size of the relief burden should ever decrease to the predepression level, work relief should no longer be continued as a form of relief. The advantages of work were so obvious when compared to the unplanned idleness of home relief as to admit of no question.

Finally, the Commission expressed the belief that insofar as government is to provide work for those able-bodied persons who are not absorbed in private industry, such work should be placed upon an open competitive basis, and the conditions of work should be those of normal employment. Therefore, individuals should be chosen on the basis of their fitness and ability to fill the specific demands of the job without regard to their economic needs, and they should be retained only so long as they demonstrate satisfactory efficiency in their work. The Commission recognized that the use of normal work methods in preference to the methods of the work relief system reduces the number of persons to be employed, unless greater sums of money are made available. It believes, however, that the greater values of normal competitive employment for the workers and the greater efficiency which will be achieved in the doing of governmental work justify the policy.

CONCLUSIONS

The National Resources Planning Board stated . . . "there appears to be almost unanimous agreement that work relief as it has operated under Federal leadership is less demoralizing than direct relief . . . The fact that the payment received is a return for work performed has not merely removed the sense of dependence upon public or private charity, so repugnant to the vast majority of people, but has also given the unemployed worker a renewed sense of independence, for he has been answerable to no one for the way in which he spends the income he has thus earned. Finally, in giving the worker an opportunity to participate in normal productive activity and to conform to the mores of the society in which he lives, work relief has helped sustain the worker's sense of self-respect as a worker and as a citizen. But while federal work relief has thus undoubtedly proved superior to direct relief payments which offer the worker no opportunity to perform useful work, the extent to which morale has thereby been enhanced must not be overestimated. For while work relief enhances the unemployed worker's sense of self-respect as a citizen, certain aspects of the work program, as it has operated in the past, have limited the measures of achievement.[23]"

The National Resources Planning Board along with other authorities believed that a major problem related to morale was that the average project worker must have experienced a period of demoralization before securing project work. Bakke's conclusions, in concurrence with those of the Board were that: "Work relief as at present administered . . . gives him an opportunity for a 'comeback' rather than an opportunity to maintain unbroken his position as a worker in the community . . . If the work relief project is worthwhile, if the supervision of the workers is adequate, and if management of the work is efficient so that the worker himself knows, whatever the general public may think, that he is participating in a valuable and efficiently managed job, the status that he derives from said work will be proportionately high.[24"]

In regard to morale building aspects of WPA employment, it was considered that some of the attributes of WPA projects were: (1) The right to organize in unions; (2) the right of project workers to have grievances adjusted through committees of their own choice; (3) the right to appeal grievances to Washington, if necessary; (4) coverage by Workmen's Compensation; and (5) the standing of project employment in the eyes of the community.

Those characteristics of WPA employment which might operate against morale were: (1) Lack of job security on project work: (2) placement of some workers on jobs at a lower level of skill than that to which they are accustomed; (3) lowering of the degree of pride in work when standards of performance on projects are lower than those in private industry; and (4) the security wage paid on WPA projects, although higher than general relief, was for many workers insufficient to meet elementary needs, and in practically all instances was below wages in private industry.

The experience with WPA indicates that for a job to be morale-producing to its fullest extent, it must approximate standards of working conditions, income, and general usefulness to the community similar to those found in private employment. However, when such similarity exists, it becomes more difficult to make private jobs attractive enough to attract the men from work projects, particularly private jobs of a marginal nature. It is generally conceded that while the benefits of WPA were immeasurable, they did not nearly approximate the optimal conditions for producing morale. Consider the wage structure, for example. No allowance was made for size of family. A single person or small family was able to live marginally on the wage, while a large family could not manage on it. There is much factual data available to support this generalization.

The grinding poverty of large families during the depression, and the tragic effects of loss of self-respect upon the individual members of such families was expressed in the literature. Social workers of the 1930's could easily recognize and identify many a client like Willie Pond, "hero" of a novel of the times, who lived with his family on a starvation diet in a dirty, damp, verminous apartment. In recognition of his own degradation, Willie observed that: "A man like me, with a wife and seven children, gets twelve or fifteen dollars a week, if he don't get cut . . . He looks down on me," he thought, speaking of his son, "a man that can't give a boy like George five dollars ought to get looked down on" . . . and his wife, recalling her husband's application for work relief, sobbed: "It just broke him all up, . . . none of his people, or mine either, ever asked for charity . . . they wouldn't give him work only if we was fit for relief.[25]"

Authorities on the subject are in general agreement that in order for work to be morale-building it needs to be a useful project of benefit to the public. In this regard, MacMahon, Millett and Ogden stated: "Usefulness, it was assumed, was essential, not only to avoid waste of public funds, but also with at least equal force, in order to realize a fundamental objective of the program: the preservation of the morale of the workers. But the criteria of usefulness presented several difficulties. It had already been decided to avoid extension of the principle of self-help in ways and on a scale that might create an economy within the national economy. The program must not be competitive with private enterprise, but it must produce useful things. Useful to whom? In collaborating with public bodies the program must not take over their normal functions. What was normal? A fundamental tenet of the works program was that sponsorship might only be public bodies, including autonomous units. This restriction was agreed upon early, seemingly without hesitation and for obvious reasons. It was admitted that refusal to recognize semi-public entities as sponsors might reduce the flexibility and even the scope of the program, but the rule seemed a necessary safeguard. Certainly scrupulous care must be taken that the benefit rendered by the expenditure of public moneys, especially national funds spent far from their source, was public, not private. There could be no objection to this principle, but its application was inherently difficult . . .[26]"

Not all authors believed that work relief was morale-building. Lewis Meriam[7] concluded that preservation of morale was largely a talking point not supported by fact. "It seems reasonable to assume that by the time it became necessary to apply for a certification of need and a WPA job, the applicant's morale had been seriously impaired . . . If WPA had been able to supply a worker with a job where he could exercise such skill as he possessed and make him feel that he were an efficient member of an efficient working organization, morale might have been improved, but in many instances that could not be done . . . morale depends on the prestige of the organization . . . what do the neighbors, associates, former or prospective employers think of the place the worker is employed? Although WPA may not have deserved the bad reputation it gained in many localities, and many of the stories were funny rather than truthful, yet such things prevented the agency from being a real morale restorer. What a worker needs to retain or restore his morale under our existing system is a real job in a private enterprise or in a normally conducted public enterprise. Employment on a sheltered project especially conducted by the national government for the needy unemployed employable that segregates the worker from the more fortunate and possibly the more effective did not improve his standing in the community, with his family, or possibly himself.'"

Edith Abbott's address[27] to the National Conference of Social Work in 1937 is applicable to national developments 30 years later. She stated that as dark as the picture was, she did not want merely new relief funds, but a continued development of new methods of abolishing relief by making other kinds of provision for those in despair, namely, an emphasis on the problem of prevention and a refusal to accept relief as a proper way of life for people. She sought a way to do something better for the group mislabeled "unemployables," a large proportion of whom were really employable or near-employable and believed some way should be found to lead these men and women back into the labor market. In spite of the good intentions of the administrators, and the vast sums of money spent on the program, it is only too true that the present system of work relief does not do this.

The depression experience with work relief revealed that: (1) Man must be occupied in meaningful work to remain at peace with himself and his surroundings; (2) idleness and dependency upon public aid tend to stigmatize, demoralize and seriously disrupt individual and family life; (3) normal channels of private industry and government offer the most desirable type of meaningful activity; (4) work relief can be an acceptable substitute if work placements are made in terms of the worker's aptitudes and interests, and work conditions are dignified, productive and properly managed; and (5) problems arising from notable increases in unemployment can best be prevented or overcome, not through work relief, but by augmenting job placement opportunities, and by promoting rehabilitative educational and training programs for the unemployed.

REFERENCES

1. Watson, Frank Dekker: Charity Organization Movement in the United States. New York, The Macmillan Co., 1922.

2. Edwards, Grace O.: Clean-up by Unemployed. Survey, 34:96, 1915.

3. 48 Stat. 55, Title II.

4. 48 Stat. 200, Title II.

5. 49 Stat. 115, Title III.

6. Economic Security Act—Hearings before the Committee on Ways and Means, House of Representatives, Seventy-fourth Congress, First Session on H.R. 4120. A Bill to Alleviate the Hazards of Old Age, Unemployment, Illness, and Dependency, to Establish a Social Insurance Board in the Department of Labor, to Raise Revenue, and for other Purposes. Washington, D.C., U.S. Govt. Printing Office, 1935.

7. Meriam Lewis: Relief and Social Security. Washington, D.C., The Brookings Institute, 1946.

8. Security, Work and Relief Policies. Washington, D.C.: National Resources Planning Board, 1942.

9. Curtis, Wm. R.; Klein, Walter A.; and Berman, Edward: The Skill of Brick and Stone Masons, Carpenters and Painters Employed on WPA Projects in Seven Cities in January 1937. Washington, D.C., WPA Division of Research, Statistics, and Records, 1937.

10. Bakke, E. Wright: The Unemployed Worker: A Study of the Task of Making a Living Without a Job. New Haven, Yale University Press, 1940.

11. Kellogg, Paul: Buffalo and Points West—National Conference of Social Work Proceedings. New York, Columbia University Press, 1939.

12. Hobson, William: Integration of Unemployment Compensation, Unemployment Relief and Works Programs—National Conference of Social Work Proceedings. New York, Columbia University Press, 1939.

13. White, Helen C.: Activity in the Casework Relationship—National Conference of Social Work Proceedings. Chicago, University of Chicago Press, 1933.

14. Douglas, Paul H.: The Concept of Social Justice in the Light of Today—National Conference of Social Work Proceedings. Chicago, University of Chicago Press, 1934.

15. Tugwell, Rexford G.: Relief and Reconstruction—National Conference of Social Work Proceedings. Chicago, University of Chicago Press, 1934.

16. Hobson, William: The Social Worker in the New Deal—Presidential Address, National Conference of Social Work Proceedings. Chicago, University of Chicago Press, 1934.

17. Williams, Aubrey: The Progress and Policy of WPA Administration—National Conference of Social Work Proceedings. Chicago, University of Chicago Press, 1936.

18. This was published in mimeographed form by the WPA's headquarters in New York City.

19. Bristol, Margaret Cochran, and Wright, Helen R.: Some Aspects of Work Relief in Chicago. Social Service Review, 8:628-652, 1934.

20. Mack, Dorothy: Psychological and Emotional Values in CWA Assignments: A Study of 61 Families on Relief Before and After CWA. Social Service Review, 9:236-268, 1935.

21. Notes and Comments. Social Service Review, 13:691, 1939.

22. Work Relief in the State of New York. New York Governor's Commission on Unemployment Relief, 1936.

23. Security, Work and Relief Policies. Washington, D.C.: National Resources Planning Board, 1942.

24. Bakke, E. Wright: The Unemployed Worker: A Study of the Task of Making a Living Without a Job. New Haven, Yale University Press, 1940.

25. Slade, Caroline: The Triumph of Willie Pond. New York, Vanguard Press, 1940.

26. MacMahon, Arthur Whittier; Millett, John David; and Ogden, Gladys: The Administration of Federal Work Relief. Chicago, Public Administration Service, 1941.

27. Abbott, Edith: Public Assistance—Whither Bound? National Conference of Social Work Proceedings. Chicago, University of Chicago Press, 1937.

CHAPTER 4

WORK RELIEF TO REHABILITATION

—An Innovative Approach
San Mateo County

A CHRONOLOGY of the author's experience as a public welfare director will serve as a framework for analysis of the policies and principles associated with providing educational and vocational training for public welfare recipients. As Superintendent of Social Services in California's San Mateo County from 1954 to 1960, and since 1960 as Deputy Director of the California State Department of Social Welfare, the author has had the privilege of developing substantive new vocational service programs for Californians; and as federal vocational programs have emerged, he has been closely associated with the process of adapting state programs to the new federal provisions.

The 1950's and 1960's have been characterized by growing concern on the part of welfare personnel and the public for deficiencies in traditional public welfare programs. Yet, new approaches to providing greater opportunities for welfare recipients have been received, more often than not, with suspicion both by the community and by welfare staffs. One of these innovative approaches, which set a precedent in establishing new rehabilitative objectives in public assistance programs for welfare recipients, was first conceived in San Mateo County in 1954, offered as a county welfare vocational services program in 1955, and is still functioning today as a comprehensive program with one unique feature, the sheltered workshop, remaining the only one of its kind in the State of California. The development of this program, its inception in project form, and the findings and reports on its effectiveness within the community are documented in the following account.

During July of 1954, the author became the new Superintendent of Social Services in San Mateo County at a time when a deficit in the General Assistance fund had occurred and the agency had just asked the county board of supervisors for $90,000 to supplement the budget because of increasing costs in general assistance caseloads. Within six weeks of his arrival, the Superintendent suggested to the administrative staff in the Social Service Division that a survey be conducted to determine the causes of these increases. Although the supervisors of the business section and the adult section, which included the general assistance program for both family and adults in 1954, were opposed to making such a comprehensive study, the Superintendent developed a survey which was concluded and reported on in November 1954. The report showed that the basic reasons for increases in public assistance expenditures in general assistance caseloads were related to such factors as population increases, cost of living index, incidence of unemployment, size of family, mental or physical disability on the part of the recipients, and lack of education and vocational training. These findings were then used to develop a rationale for attacking the causes of dependency. Although the report showed that the factors related to increased costs of the General Assistance Program were beyond the control of the Agency, since there were broad social and economic conditions existing in the community, the new Superintendent observed that there was still opportunity for decreasing caseloads through utilization of improved services. In stressing the need for the agency to focus on rehabilitation, recommendations for organizational changes, and suggestions for improving service resources were made, and the report became a focal point for many things which were to occur later in relation to development of improved service and rehabilitative objectives.

Favorable public relations aspects of such a program were recognized as necessary to the achievement of objectives, and in this connection, an interesting development occurred. In October 1954, a reporter for the *Redwood City Tribune*, telephoned the Superintendent. The reporter's publisher had requested that she write a story on welfare chiselers, because he had related the need for increased general assistance funds to an increase in such chiselers. The Superintendent, recognizing this as typical of community thinking about the nature and cause of dependency, replied that it would be possible to find examples of chiseling, but that there was always some of this in welfare cases, just as in income tax return and unemployment benefit falsifications. He pointed out, however, that the small amount of chiseling had little relationship to the increased costs of public assistance, suggested that if the publisher would be willing to wait another 30 days, the agency would give the newspaper a full description of the nature of causes of increased costs, and described the general assistance survey that was being conducted at the time. The reporter stated that she would review this with her publisher, and on the following day, advised that the publisher had agreed to await the results of the survey. When the survey was completed, November 29, 1954, the newspaper reporter was so informed, but when she asked the Superintendent to tell her about it by telephone, he requested a personal interview, indicating that the material was rather comprehensive in nature. Since the reporter could not come to the agency, the Superintendent went to the newspaper office and spent a couple of hours reviewing the survey. He then left a copy of the survey with her.

About a week later, the news story was published with the heading: "Most Relief Recipients Can't Work." It presented a very positive picture as related to the welfare situation in general, and described in detail the recommendations made by the Superintendent. The story was then picked up by the San Francisco newspapers. The end result of this cooperation on both sides was that although the newspapers had initially planned a completely negative story about the general welfare program, they came forth finally with highly positive statements about the program, noting that the majority of General Assistance recipients were ill, disabled, and unable to support themselves, and establishing a community introduction to the need for new services.

In September of 1955, the Superintendent of Social Services, in conjunction with the Director of the Health and Welfare Department and other staff, established a vocational rehabilitation project designed to offer rehabilitative services and if possible, measure the results. A formalized rehabilitation team was established and the Supervisor of the Special Services Section was set up as the coordinator of this team. The findings of the project, which was concluded July 1956, nine months after its beginning, fully substantiated the view that given proper personnel and administrative structure, rehabilitative services for public assistance recipients could achieve important results.

After 200 copies of a report on this project survey were multilithed and distributed to newspapers and interested persons in San Mateo County and to state organizations such as the Tax Payers Association, the Chamber of Commerce, the Supervisors Association, newspaper accounts on the survey were carried by most local newspapers and by some of the San Francisco newspapers. The San Francisco Chronicle, for example, published its account of the program on Sunday, August 11, 1957, with the headline: "New Welfare Policy of Self-Help," and stated that "Social workers are excited about the early result of a new policy that places the emphasis of public welfare aid on problem solving rather than financial help."

The substance of the report on the 9-month survey was contained in the following cover memo, dated September 6, 1956, from the Superintendent of the Social Service Division to the Director of the Health and Welfare Department.

On November 29, 1954, the Social Service Division transmitted to you the report of a General Welfare Survey. This survey was designed to evaluate the characteristics of general assistance recipients and the causative factors related to fluctuation in caseloads and expenditures. It was observed in that study that cause is multiple in nature. Increases or decreases in assistance expenditures were related to such factors as: (1) Population increases; (2) Cost of living index; (3) Incidence of unemployment; (4) Size of family.

In addition to these items, which have no possibility of control by the agency, it was suggested that there were circumstances within the caseload over which the agency had some control. It was observed in the study that approximately 58 percent of our General Assistance recipients were in poor health. It was known at that time also that many others were handicapped because of emotional problems. In order to provide services which would get at the problems which could be alleviated by the agency, it was recommended in November of 1954 that the agency: (1) Realign administratively their medical and psychiatric facilities; (2) Develop and utilize vocational counseling services; (3) Improve the agency's resources for training and employment of able-bodied and medically rehabilitated persons.

You will see in the pages following that many of the agency's objectives as proposed in the 1954 survey have been achieved. You will note also that certain refinements in procedures and the extension of some facilities and services will be required. It is encouraging to realize that the agency has taken note of its problems; has suggested some remedies, and has then been able to implement the improvement of its services.

One of the most significant findings from our experience with assistance recipients relates to the residual hard-core nature of the cases served. In the study itself it will be observed that many of the cases had characteristics which appear generally to relate to chronic dependency. Outstanding in this regard were these characteristics: (1) The wage earning client was over forty years of age; (2) He or she was unskilled and not in the labor force; (3) He or she had less than high school education.

These three factors would obviously handicap any individual with respect to his being able to obtain satisfactory employment and support himself and dependents. When we add to these characteristics the physical and emotional problems characteristic of many of our recipients, we begin to realize the difficult nature of the problem of rehabilitation.

Our study, and studies of similar nature, clearly indicate that problems of economic dependency are often associated with problems in the other two areas of social maladjustment and health. It is recognized that economic dependency with its demoralizing influence upon individuals can become causative of physical disability and emotional maladjustment. Inversely, it is also recognized that emotional and physical handicaps create economic dependency. It is fully understood that the combination of these factors, if not corrected, tends to create in time a more chronic kind of disability and dependency.

The importance in our culture of adequacy in the economic area is of such a nature that it is almost impossible to achieve adequacy in other respects while failing to function adequately in the economic area. When the normal wage earner is unable to meet the economic needs of himself and his dependents through his own efforts, his loss of self esteem and social status becomes so great that it creates other problems.

Historically, these problems have been served by a general assistance program, particularly, and other programs in general, which have tended to focus their emphasis on ineligibility of such persons for aid; on disposing of cases, rather than trying to correct the problem which brought about financial need. Restrictive policies have been established for the purposes of reducing expenditures and keeping cases off the county rolls. Devices have been employed, such as the giving of aid in kind, and the provision of inadequate assistance, to achieve the objective of discouraging dependency. We are coming to realize that such inadequacy and tenuous nature of assistance may of itself so undermine the individual client's feelings of adequacy that in a sense these restrictive measures actually contribute to the development of chronic assistance cases. Thus, rather than relieve the agency of its assistance burden, such practices tend to increase the burdens of the agency. These practices derive from our cultural belief that causes of dependency arise from "wilful laziness" and other over-simplified generalizations. Fortunately, in this agency, our objectives are related more to the determination of actual cause of dependency and the alleviation of those factors which bring about the dependency.

Our recognition that cause of disability and dependency is complex in nature suggests that correction of these problems becomes necessarily a complex process. Simplified single remedies will not suffice. More often correction requires the application of a variety of services and facilities well integrated into a therapeutic whole. The Social Service Division is in the process of achieving such an integrated program in the following ways:

Aid

It is important that adequate assistance be given individuals so that they will be relieved of financial stress and thus be able to concentrate on other important factors related to their achievement of self-sufficiency. Payment to recipients of aid is given in cash and without restrictions as to the method of expenditure of the grant. These payments are made with recognition of the fact that a recipient of public assistance, because of financial dependency, does not lose his capacity to determine how, when, and whether he shall make expenditure for each of his budgetary requirements. The agency eligibility conditions are administered in such a way as to respect the dignity and worth of the individual and are applied by the social worker with an impartial, non-judgmental attitude. Aid is not withheld to force a change in the standards of behavior of individual clients, nor are recipients forced to work out aid given. The assistance budgets are generally adequate and the calibre of the casework staff issuing assistance is of very high quality. As a result, out of the enlightened issuance of aid has come considerable impetus to the agency's focus on rehabilitation of clients.

Services—Casework

Casework services are an essential requirement in the rehabilitation process. The caseworker in the public assistance agency must assume responsibility for coordinating all other services and facilities which are made available to the client. In addition to this coordinating function, the caseworker must assume the ongoing responsibility of casework services to the individual client.

There has been considerable strengthening of casework services in the Social Service Division in the past two years. While we had seven classified positions calling for trained social workers approximately two years ago, today we have 30 casework positions requiring graduate training. This has been achieved largely through the reclassification of positions. An intensive recruitment program has virtually filled all of these positions. Administrative reorganization which combined the Family and Childrens Services has given further emphasis to the achievement of the most highly skilled casework services possible. This, in conjunction with the casework services already existing in the agency, has stimulated the achievement of rehabilitative objectives for our clients.

Medical Services

The Social Service Division is a part of a combined Health and Welfare Department. As such it has always enjoyed excellent coordination of the services of the division with those of the Health Division, the Out-patient Clinic, Community Hospital, and the T.B. Sanatorium. It was believed that the coordination of these services could be improved through the establishment of one medical doctor who would be responsible for welfare recipients. Such a medical position was established in February 1955. A doctor was employed on a part-time basis to assume this responsibility. His offices were located in the Health Department. The study will indicate the value of such a medical arrangement. It is believed from the experience that we have had in this regard that it will be profitable to continue the use of one physician. It is suggested, however, that this physician would be more appropriately located in the Out-patient Clinic where he will be closer to the other medical specialists and facilities. The medical person will be responsible for a medical evaluation of all clients referred to him. The physical examination will be done by the physician, and his work will be coordinated with other clinic physicians. He will also participate in the Social Service Division's staffing of cases and be available for medical consultation as needed.

Vocational Counseling and Work Placement Services

During the past nine months we have employed on a part-time basis a vocational counselor. He has interviewed clients referred to him and given them appropriate tests. We have found this service of real value and one which we believe must be continued. While he has assumed a small amount of responsibility for coordination of our services with the employment services existing in the community, his time has been most limited in this respect. We are recommending that his functions be strengthened to include responsibility for employment placement as well as counseling. It is anticipated that we will utilize to the fullest extent existing services in the community prior to utilization of our own vocational and placement services.

Psychiatric Services

During the past nine months the agency has attempted to utilize existing psychiatric services available through other departments. Out of this experience we have come to realize that, as with medical services, the psychiatric service must be more closely related to the Division. This person will need to be available for consultation and for staffing of cases when it is appropriate. Obviously, it will not be necessary for the psychiatrist to participate in the evaluation of all clients.

Facilities—Crystal Springs Home

Crystal Springs Home, an administrative part of the Social Service Division, is the primary rehabilitation facility in the Division. This facility just two and one-half years ago was considered an institution for custodial care of persons. It offered very little in the way of treatment and as a result persons residing there tended to stay. In February of 1954, the function of the institution took different form. It has gradually become a rehabilitation center for the chronically ill. The institution now has the services, either full or part-time, of a consulting psychiatrist, a vocational counselor, a physiatrist, an occupational therapist, a physiotherapist and a dietician. These services are in addition to the regular medical and nursing services. In addition, there are improved facilities for rehabilitation in the institution. The occupational therapy room has looms for weaving. Instruction in weaving, art and crafts, ceramics, woodworking, textile painting and stenciling are available. There is physical therapy apparatus such as bars and exercise mats. There is a fully equipped carpenter shop, which is used for occupational therapy, and a beauty shop. Gardening, maintenance and clerical activities are available for work experience for patients interested and able to participate. Crystal Springs Home has become an integral part of our rehabilitation program. Those patients who cannot be served through the resources available on an out-patient basis may be referred to the institution for in-patient care. The facility is being used primarily for those individuals who have some rehabilitation potential.

In October 1955 we established in the Community Hospital a diagnostic team composed of one physician and a medical social worker. This team assumes full responsibility for all referrals of patients to Crystal Springs Home and to the private nursing homes. Eligibility for rehabilitation services at Crystal Springs Home is based on capacity of the individual for improvement. This does not mean that the person must have potentiality for employment, although an employment objective is one of the considerations. We are just as interested, however, in seeing the individual regain self-sufficiency. For example, we recently referred an 82-year old woman to Crystal Springs Home because of certain kinds of rehabilitative potential. The facility is available to all ages and to highly varying kinds of disabilities. While we have not done a recent study on the successes of Crystal Springs Home, we know from personal observation of cases and from the statistics on rate of turnover that this facility is rendering an important service to the community. Its achievements have resulted in decreasing population in the institutions to the point where we have recently begun reviewing patients in nursing homes to determine whether or not there are persons who might benefit from the services at the Home.

Work and Training

Out of the experience that the Social Service Division has had in the vocational rehabilitation project we have come to realize that the application of an increased number of services and the intensification of these services is not entirely sufficient in some cases to fulfill our rehabilitative objectives. Some of the persons served by the agency have had such tragic experiences and have endured these experiences for such prolonged periods of time that they have come to passively accept their dependency and disability role. Accordingly, it is recognized that the satisfactions coming from productive activity will be required to complement the other services. Inasmuch as there was no available community resource to meet this need, it became necessary for the Division to construct its own program, and a work experience project was established in the county departments. This project differed from the usual ones. Historically, we think of the county work projects as being established to provide mass employment for assistance recipients, with relatively little regard for the individual's capacity and interest. Thus one might find a potential office worker raking leaves in the Park Department, or vice versa. It is recognized that such inappropriate work placements create new problems for the individual, thus retarding rather than accelerating his movement toward self-sufficiency.

The Division obtained the cooperation of other county departments in the establishment of this work program. Clients were evaluated by the rehabilitation team and if they were unavailable for private employment because of their handicaps or low motivation, such persons might be considered and referred to a work placement. The staff in conjunction with the client would determine the kind of placement he preferred and then an attempt would be made to find a placement that would fit the needs of the individual, both from the standpoint of his interest and ability. This work program has developed very slowly, as you will see from the report. There are some individuals who can accept and utilize effectively this kind of placement and there are others who are unable to use it. Accordingly, it must be placed on a selective basis. It is hoped that private industry and business can be utilized in some way in a similar kind of work experience program.

Our experience has shown that existing employment agencies are unable to place in private employment welfare clients requiring such placement. The employment services are able to place some persons, but for the many who remain it is considered desirable to develop such services within the Social Service Division. It is recommended that we extend the services of our vocational counselor to that of work placement officer as well. It will be expected that he will make employer contacts, will coordinate Social Service Division activities with those of employment services and rehabilitation agencies. It is recommended that in conjunction with this work the vocational counselor will develop a small Citizens Advisory Committee composed of representatives from business and labor and other appropriate individuals. This committee will assist in evaluation of the training and placement problems which arise.

The Division considers the need to offer vocational counseling and placement services to the young people served as well as to older clients. The children in foster homes and in Aid to Needy Children (ANC, currently AFDC) and in General Assistance (GA) families should have such services available to them when, in the opinion of the caseworker, these facilities are necessary.

You will observe that this study is not conclusive in its findings. There is evidence of productive use by clients of the services and the facilities of the agency in their search for self-sufficiency and independent living. It will be seen that some savings in money have occurred as a result of the application of these services. We have particularly observed that the problem of rehabilitation of individuals coming to our agency is a most difficult process because of the serious nature of the social, physical and emotional problems of individual clients. The complexity of their problems, while difficult to manage, does not deter us in our conviction that for significant numbers of individuals it is possible to achieve rehabilitation. This complexity suggests rather that we exercise more ingenuity in the development of our services and facilities in their application to these difficult problems. We did not have sufficient time in nine short months to fully demonstrate the adequacy of the vocational rehabilitation plan. The study, however, gives us considerable encouragement. We believe that rehabilitative services and facilities should be extended and improved.

Summary

In summary, the following recommendations are made:

1. Extend the function of the vocational counselor to include responsibility for liaison with employment agencies and for actual work placements.

2. Develop training programs where indicated for those clients not eligible for training in other agencies. Evaluate both public departments and private industry for resources in this regard.

3. Improve and extend the county work experience program. Evaluate possibilities of achieving a similar program in private industry.

4. Develop a Citizens' Advisory Committee to offer consultation on the work and training programs.

5. Continue the medical internist, but place him in the Outpatient Clinic rather than in the Health Division.

6. Improve casework orientation to the rehabilitation process as follows: (a) Give caseworkers greater responsibility in the rehabilitation process; (b) Improve the agency's diagnostic methods at the point of intake and develop improved methods for evaluation of continuing cases.

7. Provide funds for the employment of a part-time consulting psychiatrist.

Finally, we must continue to examine those forces which tend to liberate incentive and motivation of people. We must alleviate anxieties and fears of insecure people which tend to decrease their motivation, and for this substitute a sense of security and a feeling of hope. While we should make adequate services and facilities available, we will avoid becoming unduly preoccupied with diagnostic processes. We cannot shunt the client from specialist to specialist, unless there are impelling reasons to do so. The risk of overspecialization may result in loss of the values people receive from friendly relationship with others. We hope to avoid this potential "laboratory objectivity" through utilization of the caseworkers as the person who maintains a sustaining relationship to the client. The caseworker will assume responsibility with the client for determination as to which specialists and facilities will be needed to aid the client to self-sufficiency, thus avoiding routinized systems of referrals from one specialist to another.

The worker will utilize all other existing agency services, such as the State Bureau of Vocational Rehabilitation and the U.S. Employment Service before considering our own agency specialists. Through this kind of selective referral it is anticipated that the part-time services of a psychiatrist, a combined vocational counselor and placement worker, and a physician will be sufficient to meet the current needs of the Division. Thus the cost of this integrated program will be kept at a minimum.

The following study is a progress report. It describes where the agency has been in the field of rehabilitation. It suggests some new directions for the future. Recommendations for improvement are modest and of little cost. Our experience suggests that we have much to learn as to how to most effectively use existing serivces and facilities.

Rating Factors

Approximately 50 percent of the group included in the 9-month survey were men, and these tended to be older than the women, although there were some women between the ages of fifty and sixty included in the project. In general, the men's employment in the past had been more substantial than that of the women and a proportionately larger number of men were married and living with their spouses. The men tended to fall in such chronic illness groups as alcoholism, pulmonary disease, hypertensive vascular disease, and neurological, or orthopedic disease whereas the majority of the women either had no pathology, or diagnosis indicated they suffered from emotional problems. It was noted both among the men and the women that many problems existed along with organic disease or physical disability, indicating a need for psychiatric evaluation. In general, the group had less than a high school education and at least one-third had never attended high school. There was a distribution of 25 percent with IQ's of 95 or more; 50 percent with IQ's between 80 and 95; and 25 percent with an IQ of 80 or less. Although 50 percent of the group had been receiving assistance for less than a year, the majority had experienced months of inactivity during which time they had not been gainfully employed. These factors, on a case-by-case basis, determined the ratings which were given at the evaluation conference and the recommendations that were made regarding clients. A principle that was used throughout the conference was that the client's potentialities and assets would be assessed and recommendations made at the level where he would be able to function with some interest and satisfaction to himself. Assisting clients to gain some self-confidence was considered particularly important.

The following ratings were used by the team at the time of the conference:

1. High motivation: fair or good physical condition; some skills and abilities; and favorable psychological and social factors.

2. Fair motivation: fair physical condition, but with some limitations, either due to age or physical handicap; some skills and abilities; and favorable emotional and social conditions.

3. Fair motivation: some physical limitations; skills and capacities limited because of physical condition; emotional and social problems of a mild nature.

4. Fair or low motivation: moderately impaired physical condition which would severely restrict mobility; skills and abilities minimal or lacking; and serious social and/or emotional problems.

5. Poor motivation: severely impaired physical condition; skills and abilities minimal or lacking; and serious social and/or emotional problems.

The ratings were used by the vocational rehabilitation team consisting of a social worker, vocational counselor, physician, and others as needed in the individual case situation. While the rating scale was useful in reference to the survey, it is not recommended for normal case evaluation purposes. We must avoid categorizing people, because this tends to establish impediments to rehabilitation. For example, a social worker or rehabilitation counselor may believe that a person with an IQ of 75 is incapable of rehabilitation and employment when, in fact, the individual may have real potential.

The findings of the survey were useful. Men and women were rehabilitated, and the survey revealed human values and monetary savings accruing from the approach. Case illustrations were used in the report as follows: Mr. Johnson, a 50-year-old married man without children, has been receiving General Assistance since July, 1955. His wife became a patient at the tuberculosis sanitarium a few months before he came on aid. Mr. Johnson had been extremely dependent upon his wife. The loss of her companionship, the development of physical ailments, and his inability to obtain employment culminated in his application for General Assistance. When the agency first observed Mr. Johnson, he was very poorly clothed and his entire appearance represented utter dejection and demoralization.

Mr. Johnson was referred to the vocational rehabilitation project and on December 2, 1955, he was recommended for placement on a trial basis with a County department to assist in automobile maintenance. One could observe Mr. Johnson's progress merely by looking at him from time to time. His dress gradually became neater, his carriage erect, and attitude pleasant. The first tangible evidence of improved motivation toward independence occurred a couple of months after the work placement in the County Department. Mr. Johnson began passing out cards inscribed as follows: "M. Johnson, proprietor, I do light gardening, odd jobs, light hauling," revealing that hope for improved functioning had been restored.

The County department expressed its confidence in Mr. Johnson by taking him on the regular department payroll on two different occasions a few weeks at a time to fill in during vacations of regular staff. Finally, in June 1956 Mr. Johnson received full paid employment at one of the County institutions as a permanent employee on the maintenance staff.

Through the cooperative efforts of the several specialists in our vocational rehabilitation project, Mr. Johnson was enabled to become completely self-supporting and a much happier and better adjusted individual. It is speculated that without these combined services and facilities Mr. Johnson would still be dependent upon the agency for General Assistance. His success was shared by his wife who was released from the T.B. Sanitarium within weeks of his employment.

Mary O'Brien is a 26-year-old woman who married at an early age and had three children: ages 8, 6 and 5. Her husband had deserted her, and she had since obtained a divorce. She had been receiving an Aid to Needy Children grant for six years. Mrs. O'Brien had no work experience, although she had completed all of her high school work with the exception of four credits.

She took good care of the children and provided well for them within the limits of the Aid to Needy Children budget. In her contacts with the social worker, Mrs. O'Brien indicated that she would like to have some type of training so that she could work in an office situation and have more stimulation than she had from housework. Since her children all would be in school in another year and would not need so much of her attention at home, it was considered a realistic plan. She was in good health although slightly obese. She had poor vision which had been corrected. In the vocational testing she rated high in intelligence. Her interests were in the business field and the test results showed she had clerical aptitude.

It was agreed that Mrs. O'Brien should be given further vocational counseling and information about the possibilities of training in private and public schools which offered secretarial, clerical, and accounting work. Her vocational rehabilitation rating was "A."

The social worker assisted Mrs. O'Brien in working out plans to enter a secretarial school. She did excellent work in her training and made arrangements to proceed at an accelerated rate through outside practice which ordinarily students are not expected to do. In the course of training, however, she decided to remarry.

It was the social worker's impression that the encouragement that Mrs. O'Brien had in the vocational rehabilitation process had given her self-confidence which was an asset not only in her ability to work but also to consider a suitable marriage plan. Although her training was not completed, she was no longer in need of public assistance. She has knowledge that at a later date, should she wish to pursue vocational training, she has aptitude which could be developed.

The value of the vocational rehabilitation project was of many kinds: Value to the community, of people served, and as a model for administrative practice.

The values were as follows:

1. Planning—The findings established a framework of knowledge which enriched program planning for services.

2. Coordination—Promotion of team concept among workers, multidisciplinary approach accomplished; ability to be flexible and shift goals as indicated by change in clients' situations and motivations; established mechanisms of coordination such as case review committee and special interdepartmental arrangements.

3. Policy Development—Procedure was tested for expediting case handling; embraced a more liberal interpretation of policy; case actions flowed from evaluation team decisions; agency movement toward development of self-sufficiency services.

The project findings particularly emphasized the importance of the caseworker remaining fully involved in the rehabilitation process, because the introduction of other specialists and the case review committee often caused the social worker to feel that somehow her responsibility had been transferred to others. Agency practice was altered to refocus the social worker to the important role social work must maintain in the vocational rehabilitation process.

The vocational services reports from San Mateo County caused interest in rehabilitation programs to spread to other counties. After the Superintendent of the Social Service Division was asked by the County Welfare Directors Association to organize and chair a rehabilitation committee for the Association, he organized such a committee, and in 1956, with the committee, developed a program for rehabilitation of public assistance recipients at the annual meeting of the County Welfare Directors Association. The proceedings from this particular panel discussion on rehabilitation were later published by the American Public Welfare Association in a pamphlet, "Teamwork in Services for Rehabilitation in Public Assistance."

By early 1967, the San Mateo Social Service Division vocational services program included vocational training, work experience placements in county governmental agencies, and employment placement to supplement other community services. Oriented to rehabilitative objectives, the program included medical, psychiatric, vocational testing and counseling and social casework services.

Sheltered Workshop—An Innovative Approach

The Superintendent of the Social Service Division decided in 1957 to augment the work experience and training program by developing a sheltered workshop. The objective was to develop a production workshop which would contract for production jobs from the community. The workshop would be a protected resource to which public assistance recipients could be referred for opportunity to test vocational skills which some recipients had long believed lost without possibility of restoration. The workshop could also provide the function of evaluating an individual's work capacity and training needs, particularly for those persons who needed help in working to overcome fear of failure in employment and training, the sheltered workshop offered an opportunity for the individual to develop work skills and improve readiness for work in a less competitive and less threatening situation.

In effect, the sheltered workshop was viewed as an extension of the training and work experience programs, enabling the agency to be more selective about placements of individuals who required a more sheltered type of initial placement, and increase the variety of work experiences available to individuals. Since it had not been possible to make arrangements, as hoped, for work placements in private industry, it was necessary to attempt to establish training and experience programs in the workshop which would have some relevance to the private industry field.

The first contract was negotiated with a wine company to manufacture fiber jackets for wine bottles. The wine company had been contracting with a firm in Czechoslovakia but was planning to bring the operation back to the United States. Agreements were reached to manufacture between 8,000 and 10,000 wine bottle jackets per month with the wine company providing all of the materials. The Superintendent proceeded to make arrangements for space and staff for this operation. Space was finally obtained in the new hospital building in a location that was originally designed for a laundry. The space was very rough and it was necessary to improvise at the outset. The occupational therapist who was employed by the Superintendent to manage the workshop and train the public assistance recipients had no previous experience in the needle trades industry, so arrangements were made for her to obtain training. The Superintendent then rented three power sewing machines, obtained the materials from the wine company, and the workshop started operation. The workshop gradually increased its functions to the point where it had contracts of a wide variety, including electronics assembly, floral decorations and the servicing of in-flight motion picture headset kits for airlines, as well as manufacturing the straw jackets for wine bottles. In 1968, the workshop handled approximately $100,000 worth of contract materials.

Problems of the workshop at the outset were manifold. In October 1957, when the District Attorney of San Mateo County was asked whether or not the welfare department had authority to establish a revolving fund to handle the income to the workshop, he went far beyond this question and ruled that the buying and selling of goods could not be handled by the County. After raising substantive questions about the propriety of the County entering into private business through this contract plan, he declared the operation illegal. The letter to the Board of Supervisors from the District Attorney, dated November 1, 1957 follows:

"Your office has referred to this office for study and report, the letter requesting authorization for the establishment of a revolving fund for control of receipts and expenses in connection with work experience projects for welfare recipients. The Social Service Division desires to establish a program whereby welfare recipients as a part of a retraining plan, will perform certain work under the direction of an occupational therapist. Some of this work will consist of the manufacture and sale to a wine company of straw jackets for wine bottles. The material for this work will be furnished by the wine company. Other work will consist of the repairing of bottle crates for compensation.

"We have carefully reviewed the law on this matter and have concluded that it is extremely doubtful that the County has the legal authority to embark upon such a program. Therefore, on this ground alone, the establishment of a revolving fund for this activity would appear to be improper.

"The reason for our conclusions are as follows: The functions of counties are exclusively governmental and are only such as have been imparted to them by the state. Also the powers of a County are only those expressly granted by law and such other powers as may be necessarily implied from those expressed. (See 13 Cal. Jur. 2nd, page 349.) There appears to be no question that the activity proposed is engaging in business. It has been held that, in the absence of express legislative sanction, municipalities have no authority to engage in any independent business enterprise or occupation such as is usually pursued by private individuals. (See *Ravettino* v. *San Diego*, 20 C.A. 2nd 37, Vol. 12, *McQuillin-Municipal Corporations*, page 702.) The same principle is applicable to counties. It would be immaterial whether the proposed business is one which will compete with private industry. The question is whether there is authority to engage in business at the outset. Section 2505 of the Welfare and Institutions Code provides that counties may require work of welfare recipients who are not incapacitated by reason of age, disease, or accident, as a condition of relief. Such work shall be created for the purpose of keeping the indigent from idleness and assisting in his rehabilitation and preservation of self-respect. Section 2508 provides that work relief projects conducted pursuant to section 2505 which consist of work of repairing or maintaining any shipping facility or public building shall not be subject to the competitive bidding statutes. These two sections clearly authorize the County to establish work projects for welfare recipients. However, such work would be limited to projects which the County would be authorized to undertake in its ordinary conduct of governmental affairs. Thus welfare recipients could do such work as maintenance of county buildings, perform labor on public projects, make furniture and other equipment for county use, and work of a similar nature. However, the manufacture or repair of goods for use in private industry would not come within the purview of the above section of the Welfare and Institutions Code. However laudable the plan, it seems not to be authorized under the present statutes."

The Superintendent was determined to maintain somehow the operation of the sheltered workshop. He arranged a meeting with the local Society for Crippled Children and Adults to determine whether or not the board of directors of that agency would agree to the operation of the workshop for the county welfare department. After considerable discussion and negotiation, the private agency decided, because it was embarked on new building plans of its own, that it would not take on the program. The Superintendent deferred closure of the workshop pending evaluation of other alternatives, and on Febraury 4, 1958, called a meeting of interested community persons to discuss the problems related to the workshop. Represented at this meeting was the National Association of Manufacturers, labor, a newspaper, and others. The Superintendent pointed out that the District Attorney's recent opinion precluded the continuation of the workshop under county auspices.

The committee strongly supported continuation of the workshop, and the representatives from both labor and industry indicated their whole-hearted approval of the workshop objectives. They did not believe that the training objectives of this program would inter-fere in any way with management or labor concepts.

Seeking county governmental examples of contract work, the Superintendent telephoned Rancho Los Amigos, which was func-tionally a part of the Department of Charities in Los Angeles and was contracting with private industry. As an example, they received the sweepings from a local automobile factory, sorted the nuts and bolts from these sweepings, and returned them to the automobile factory and received payment. They also made small souvenirs which found their way into the retail market, although the organiza-tion did not retail these articles themselves. The Superintendent re-ceived copies of the Los Angeles Ordinance related to the Rancho Los Amigos project and a letter from the director of that organiza-tion describing the projects. These materials established an excellent precedent for the workshop program in San Mateo County.

The Superintendent described the nature of the project to the District Attorney, who commented that it appeared to establish a precedent but he later decided, in spite of the Los Angeles model, that the San Mateo Workshop was illegal and should be abandoned. At this point, the Superintendent of the Social Service Division decided to appeal the District Attorney's opinion to the Attorney General, and requested the District Attorney himself to prepare such an appeal. While the District Attorney believed this was a strange request, in which he would be required to appeal to the Attorney General to overturn his own decision, he agreed to do so. The Superintendent continued to operate the workshop pending the appeal. Later the Attorney General overruled the District Attorney, thereby clearing the workshop for continuing operation. The At-torney General's opinion, dated October 28, 1959 read as follows:

"The District Attorney of San Mateo County has requested the opinion of this office on the following question: May a county contract to sell goods to private firms or render services to such firms, the goods to be made by and the services performed by welfare recipients who are required to work pursuant to Welfare and Institutions Code section 2505?

"The conclusions may be summarized as follows: A county may establish a work program for recipients of indigent aid pur-suant to division 4, chapter 2 of the Welfare and Institutions Code the primary purposes of which are to keep the indigents from idleness, and to assist in their rehabilitation and the preservation of their self-respect. As part of the program the county may con-tract with private firms for the sale of goods made by or the rendi-tion of services performed by welfare recipients.

"ANALYSIS—Counties must by law relieve and support all incom-petent, poor or indigent persons and those incapacitated by age, disease or accident, who are lawfully residents within the county when such persons are not supported or relieved by their relatives or friends, by their own means, or by state hospitals or other state or private institutions (Welf. & Inst. Code, section 2500; all section references hereinafter are to the Welfare and Institutions Code unless otherwise stated).

"We are advised by the district attorney that the County Welfare Department, as part of its rehabilitation program for the recipients of aid under section 2500, desires to embark on a program whereby recipients who desire such work will manufacture straw jackets for wine bottles for the 'X WINE CO.' The company will supply all the materials and the work of the recipients will consist of making the straw jackets, putting them on the bottles and returning the bottles to the company. The X Company will pay compensation for this service. As part of the rehabilitation program it is also contemplated that the recipients will repair bottle crates for a soft drink company at a fixed rate per crate. We assume that the rates to be paid by the company in each case will be commensurate with the value of the work to be performed.

"The stated purpose of the program is to retrain the recipients and to aid in their rehabilitation. At the same time the plan will provide some revenue for the rehabilitation program. All the work performed will be under the direction of an occupational therapist.

"The question is whether this program may be carried out pursuant to the provisions of the Welfare and Institutions Code. Section 2505 of that code provides as follows: 'Work may be required of an indigent, who is not incapacitated by reason of age, disease, or accident, as a condition of relief. Such work shall be created for the purpose of keeping the indigent from idleness and assisting in his rehabilitation and the preservation of his self-respect.'

"Section 2506 provides, in part: 'The board of supervisors of every county as a board, or by committee or by such person or society as it may authorize, shall . . . devise ways and means for bringing persons unable to maintain themselves to self-support . . .'

"Section 2508 provides as follows: 'Work relief projects conducted pursuant to section 2505 which consist of the work of repairing or maintaining any shipping facility or public building shall not be subject to the competitive bidding statute expressed in sections 25450 and following of the Government Code where the work is to be done entirely by indigents, except that those providing supervision need not be indigents. In counties employing a purchasing agent, the materials and supplies used in such a project may be purchased by the purchasing agent without limit and without the formality of obtaining bids, letting contracts, preparing specifications, and the other formalities otherwise required by law.'

"There can be no question but that under the above mentioned code sections the county may require welfare recipients to perform work of the general nature outlined in the information supplied by the district attorney if such work were for public use or upon public property. It has been suggested, however, that the activity will amount to the county's engaging in a business enterprise beyond any power granted to the county by law.

"Although a county is not authorized to engage in a project solely for the purpose of conducting it as a business enterprise, a county may engage in activities similar to those of a private business as an incident to conducting the county's public functions. Thus, in *City of Los Angeles* v. *Lewis*, 175 Cal. 777, it was held that a county could not be authorized to engage in the manufacture and sale of Portland cement merely for commercial purposes and without limitation to manufacture and use for public needs. On the other hand it has been held that where a county adopts measures primarily designed to carry out a legitimate function of the county, such as protecting the public health and welfare, a county may, for the purpose of eradicating pests, manufacture and sell pesticides in the county (*Farley* v. *Stirling*, 70 Cal. App. 526).

"The court in the Farley case reasoned that the gain to the county was not the object or the result intended by the project but rather the preservation of the health and welfare of the people of the county by the eradication of pests.

"On various occasions this office has held that certain quasi-commercial transactions of a county may be valid where the transactions implement one of the express powers of the county. For example, in 15 Ops. Cal. Atty. Gen. 141 this office held that in the course of carrying out a reasonable personnel policy a board of supervisors may operate a lunch room in a county courthouse. In 27 Ops. Cal. Atty. Gen. 30 this office held that a county registrar of voters may make available a set of punch cards showing the information contained on the affidavits of registration of voters provided that all costs of the preparation are borne by the person requesting the duplicates. In passing, it was stated at page 32: 'Under our analysis it is not necessary to now decide whether the county can bring property into existence merely for the purpose of sale. Certainly, the county can do so where the sale happens to be a proper method of implementing one of its express powers (*Farley* v. *Stirling* [1925], 70 Cal. App. 526), and we have no intention of writing an opinion which impinges on this implied power.'

"The general theory upon which *Farley* v. *Stirling* and the two cited opinions of this office proceeded is that a county has all implied powers necessary to execute the powers expressly granted to it. (See Gov. Code section 25207.)

"It has been suggested that section 2508 modifies section 2505 so that any project conducted pursuant to the latter section must relate to work on public property or consist of other public works. However, it is the view of this office that section 2508 does not require that relief projects be confined to work of that nature, but rather the section merely exempts the work relief projects mentioned in it from the competitive bidding statute and other formalities required by law.

"The essence of the plan is to relieve idleness and to assist in the rehabilitation and preservation of the self-respect of the recipient of indigent aid. In this respect the plan is merely one means of carrying out the duties of the county and is in no way to be deemed merely a commercial enterprise (See 16 Ops. Cal. Atty. Gen. 198; Ops. Cal. Atty. Gen. No. N.S. 10272, dated October 15, 1935). The fact that the supplies are to be furnished by the companies rather than by the county has also been considered. The Legislature has expressly permitted such arrangements with regard to work performed at institutions for the blind under the jurisdiction of the State Department of Education (Welf. & Inst. Code, section 3341). There appears to be no reason why a similar plan cannot be adopted by the county under the indigent aid program. This would seem clear from the grant of power to the county to create work and from the imposition of the duty upon the board of supervisors to 'devise ways and means for bringing persons unable to maintain themselves to self-support.' (Sections 2505, 2506.) Since the power given to the county is unqualified, the county has the power to devise other means reasonably related to the purpose expressed in sections 2505 and 2506 (*Lewis* v. *Colgan*, 115 Cal. 529).

"The only restriction imposed upon the county with regard to work relief projects is that the indigent persons who may be required to work upon them must not be incapacitated by reasons of age, disease or accident (Welf. & Inst. Code, section 2505). Aside from this restriction, the county is left free to prescribe reasonable conditions of work and hours, to adopt reasonable standards relating to which recipients of aid should be admitted to the work program, and to determine what credits, if any, should be given for work on the projects (*Patton* v. *County of San Diego*, 106 Cal. App. 2d 467, 470).

"Another objection to the program has been suggested, based on the belief that requiring indigents to work in this fashion is an interference with the free competitive labor market. This objection has been advanced with regard to the working of convicts, but is not expressed in the law with regard to indigents (cf. Calif. Const., Art. X, section 6). What little California law there is seems to recognize the right of the county to the indigent's services and earnings (*McBurney* v. *Industrial Accident Commission*, 220 Cal. 124). At this time it is not necessary to determine or inquire into the limits of these rehabilitation programs. Whatever impact this particular project has on the free competitive labor market, it is merely incidental to the welfare program, and by the same token, whatever business aspects there may be, they are also incidental to the welfare program. Consequently, this office concludes that the project under examination is within the statutory powers granted to the county." The San Mateo Workshop continues today as the only public welfare workshop of its kind in the State of California.

The San Mateo experience was an exciting revelation of the capacity for change of so-called hard-core public welfare recipients. The responsiveness of such people to the provision of opportunity was clearly illustrated. The human values of the vocational rehabilitation program was shown, case by case. Although social workers were slow at first to accommodate vocational objectives because the administrative arrangements fragmented case responsibility, and the vocational training of women was accepted with hesitation, the social work input, in time, was strongly supportive of rehabilitative objectives.

Social welfare in San Mateo County had added a significant new dimension to the services program—the vocational training, adult education, on-the-job work experience, and motivational and conditioning experiences in the sheltered workshop. When the hundredth mother who had been receiving Aid to Families with Dependent Children (AFDC) was graduated from the nurses aid training program it was noted that 99 had been placed in employment. When a class of six AFDC mother graduates of the welfare department's electronics assembly training program was rejected by the Employment Department because of failure to pass their tests, the Social Service Division took pride in placing the mothers with private employment.

During the 1950's the educational, employment and rehabilitation agencies were largely unresponsive to the needs of poor people. Most adult education programs served educated people. The Employment Department selected well-qualified persons for very discriminating employers and the Vocational Rehabilitation Service served very few welfare cases because they were viewed as poor risks and termed "economically nonfeasible." The welfare system had required routine referral of able-bodied welfare recipients to employment departments since the inception of the Social Security Act in 1935—an empty gesture. Such referral was a gesture since most welfare recipients were not acceptable to discriminating employers and the employment department did not offer rehabilitation services. There was no community resource able to provide opportunity to welfare recipients, so they remained on welfare and were maligned by society for doing so. The innovative approach in San Mateo County led to responsiveness to the needs of the clientele served.

By establishing a full and sophisticated range of vocational services, beginning in 1955, employment and rehabilitation agencies viewed these developments with some alarm, and as similar programs developed in other counties and states, took a variety of counteractions to offset welfare programming which they considered inappropriate to welfare functions.

As public relations aspects of welfare in San Mateo County improved, the community became supportive. Labor and industry, after understanding the rehabilitative objectives of the program, gave it strong support. When on one occasion the San Mateo Grand Jury became very critical of the Social Service Division as having social workers who were too "client oriented," the local newspaper called the Superintendent for his version before printing the story. The front page of the newspaper displayed the Grand Judy indictment and then noted, in contrast to the Grand Jury opinion, that the Superintendent cited rehabilitation successes resulting from concentrated client orientation of social workers. Consequently the Grand Jury report received no further attention in the community. The community had become strongly responsive to constructive methods of social welfare rehabilitation.

CHAPTER 5

REHABILITATIVE APPROACH
—A State Program Emerges

WHILE SAN MATEO COUNTY in California and a handful of communities in other parts of the nation experimented with sophisticated vocational programs for the rehabilitation of the unemployed, welfare departments in most American counties still struggled with work relief or had no programs at all associated with work or vocational training programs, or dealt with the problem only in terms of traditional pauperism.

Work relief was initiated under England's sixteenth century "poor laws" authorizing the setting to work of able-bodied paupers in work-houses, labor yards, public roads, streets, and other projects as a test of willingness to work. The operation of poor laws did not notably change during the ensuing centuries. In the United States prior to 1930, emergency work relief was resorted to in some communities under private or state and local governmental auspices during periods of acute unemployment. The work-test for able-bodied needy persons was not uncommon.

Work programs received their first federal financial support in 1932 under the Emergency Relief and Reconstruction Act in a period when more than 12 million persons (24 percent of the civilian labor force) were unemployed. In successive measures during the thirties, as decribed in earlier chapters, federal funds were used in work programs under the Federal Emergency Relief Administration (FERA), the Civil Works Administration (CWA), the Works Projects Administration (WPA), the Public Works Administration (PWA), the Civilian Conservation Corps (CCC), and the National Youth Administration (NYA).

The WPA was the most significant of these various programs in both the scope and variety of the work accomplished. By June 1940, it had provided more than 13 million man-months of employment to about 7.8 million different individuals. However, even this program was rationed on the basis of urgency of need in order to keep its costs to a minimum, covering only half the estimated number of the able-bodied needy unemployed. On the premise that employable people should work for their subsistence when they could, state and local work relief programs continued to grow. In May 1940, even with improved economic conditions, it was estimated that such work relief projects in 25 states employed up to 180,000 workers.

When the WPA program was discontinued in 1943, the Federal Government assumed no further financial responsibility for meeting need due to unemployment through public assistance programs. States and localities tried to meet such need under state and/or locally financed General Assistance programs, many of which operated work relief projects.

Little attention was given on a nationwide basis to the question of work relief during World War II when there were heavy demands for labor (only 670,000 persons or 1.2 percent of the civilian labor force were unemployed in 1944) and during most of the postwar period when employment levels were generally high. But unemployment increased in 1949, 1953-54, 1957-58, and 1960-61. During the recovery period following each economic recession, the rate of unemployment tended to be higher than its pre-recession level. As of September 1961 there were 71.1 million persons in the civilian labor force, and 67.0 million of these were employed. The other 4.1 million, or 6.8 percent (seasonally adjusted) of the labor force were unemployed. This rate was below the postwar peak unemployment rate (seasonally adjusted) of 7.6 percent in August 1958, when 4.7 million persons were out of work. The seasonally adjusted unemployment rate fell steadily from September 1961 to 5.5 percent in March 1962 and remained at about that level through November 1962. The Vietnam war tended to influence reductions of unemployment since 1962 to just under 4.0 percent by 1968.

A relatively small number of unemployed persons were engaged in work relief projects in September 1961, according to a nationwide inquiry made by the Bureau of Family Services. Work relief projects then employed some 30,400 persons in 348 local jurisdictions in 27 states. Of those assigned to work relief projects, 86 percent were concentrated in seven states, primarily in the northern industrial area bordering the Great Lakes (Michigan, Illinois, Ohio, Wisconsin, and Pennsylvania) together with West Virginia and California. Work relief recipients represented only a small proportion of the General Assistance caseload in these states. Projects ranged from brush cutting along remote country roads to training oriented projects in big city hospitals. Most projects, in the order named, consisted in maintenance of streets and roads, custodial work in public buildings, care of park and recreation facilities, and distribution of surplus food commodities. Urban areas offered a greater variety of work than rural areas. A majority of the projects served a useful purpose for the community, such as training work relief recipients for jobs as nursing home attendants and kitchen helpers. In other instances, however, inadequately financed counties used work relief recipients to perform essential custodial services, a type of work usually performed by regular employees.

Most of those assigned to work relief projects were unemployed family men. Women were employed to a limited extent in about a fifth of the communities. The determination as to whether a recipient was able to work was usually made by the welfare worker at the time the recipient applied for assistance. A recipient claiming disability was usually referred to a physician for examination; in only a few instances were all recipients required to have a physical examination. Most agencies assigned workers to projects; a few delegated work assignments to the sponsor of the project; and some assignments were made by elected officials.

Rising unemployment remained a threat. Unemployment insurance benefits were insufficient in scope and coverage to overcome economic hardship of unemployed families, and the public assistance programs subvented by the Federal Government did not cover unemployed parent families. Under the provisions for Aid to Dependent Children (ADC), federal grants-in-aid were available to the states only for the assistance of children deprived of support or care because of the absence, death or incapacity of one parent. The result, ironically, was that in many states, destitute children living with two able-bodied parents were actually penalized. On the premise that a hungry, ill-clothed child was as hungry and ill-clothed if he lived in an unbroken home as if he were orphaned or illegitimate, the ADC program required expansion to include any financially needy children living with any relative. One argument for change was that the ADC program encouraged desertion, that fathers who were unemployed would desert because they could see no other way to get their hungry children fed.

The recurring recessions with accumulating hardship for unemployed families in the 1950's stimulated strong national pressures to provide federal aid to the unemployed. In 1960, the National Advisory Council on Public Assistance recommended amendments to the Social Security Act to include the unemployed family in the ADC program. A study of public welfare by the New York School of Social Work of Columbia University was organized November 1960, and financed by the Marshal Field Foundation. The report on the study[1] discussed questions of employability and assistance, and strongly recommended aid to the family of an unemployed or underemployed father. The impact of this study cannot be underestimated in the final development and passage of the amendment to the Social Security Act. Public Law 87-31, which amended Title IV of the Social Security Act to authorize federal participation in aid to dependent children of unemployed persons was passed May 8, 1961, by the Federal Government.

Public Law 87-31 included provisions for cooperative arrangements with public employment agencies and vocational education offices in the states to provide maximum services. These provisions support, by statement, the encouragement of retraining and reemployment, and assure that aid will not be granted those who refuse without good cause to accept employment or retraining for reemployment. The optimism and outlook of the Kennedy administration, the sense of conquering old problems with new vigor and vitality, in part made the passage of the amendment possible. The strategy was such that the new change in assistance focus created little criticism or furor in legislative debate or in news media. The recession in the economy, caused in part by loss of the consumer market through reduced purchasing power, was also a force in the passage of the amendment, since financial circles discussed the need for pump priming through the use of federal funds to the consumer as well as other methods of financial manipulation.

For the first time, those families in need because of unemployment whose only earlier resources was help under whatever General Relief program was available, could now qualify, if a state so determined, for help under a federally aided category. When a state's ADC plan was extended to children in need because of the unemployment of a parent, any amounts paid by a state or local government to unemployed parents of needy children as wages or compensation for work done or services rendered were not subject to federal financial participation, because such amounts were not assistance. There was no federal law or departmental policy prohibiting any work relief project that a state or locality wished to operate. The determination that wage payments on such projects could not be included for federal participation under the assistance titles of the Social Security Act was made by the Social Security Board in 1936. This limitation had been included, with others, in letters to states when each state plan was approved. It had been carefully reviewed several times since that date but each time had resulted in a decision that the language of the law does not provide authority for matching such payments as assistance. Thus the federal law and its interpretation restricted states from establishing a Work Experience and Training program in association with the Unemployed Parent program, a deficiency that was later remedied. In May 1961 for the first time in Social Security history, needy families received ADC payments because of a parent's unemployment. The legislation was to be effective through June 1962, and Public Law 87-543, enacted in 1962, extended the program to 1967.

Payments to eligible families began immediately with nearly $1.5 million going to families in Illinois, New York, Pennsylvania, and Rhode Island. Nine out of ten persons added to the expanded federal assistance program had been receiving General Assistance. By 1962, the following 14 states were participating in the ADC-U program: Connecticut, Delaware, Hawaii, Illinois, Maryland, Massachusetts,

New York, North Carolina, Oklahoma, Oregon, Pennsylvania, Rhode Island, Utah and West Virginia. Washington started, but later withdrew from the program.

NEW PERSPECTIVES

In October 1960, the author resigned as welfare director in San Mateo County, California, to accept an appointment as Deputy Director, California State Department of Social Welfare, responsible for policy development in all programs. This new position offered a unique opportunity for engagement in development of ADC-U program and Work Experience and Training programs in all of the counties. A new director had been appointed to the California State Department of Social Welfare by Governor Edmund Brown in 1959. The Director of Social Welfare and the author agreed that every possible method and instrumentality should be used to influence legislative and administrative change toward establishment of an assistance program along with sophisticated programs of education and vocational training for the unemployed in California.

It was sad that Congress did not mandate the unemployed parent program in 1961, but left it permissive and therefore open to the vagaries of local financing and power politics. It would take a battle in California to gain the Unemployed Parent program. The initial instrument to be used toward this end soon emerged in the form of the Welfare Study Commission, appointed by the Governor of California in 1961. In preparation for the Commission's work, Governor Brown asked the State Department of Social Welfare to conduct a study of of unemployment. A report on the impact of the recession in 13 California counties was delivered to the Governor on February 17, 1961. The report was based on first-hand confidential interviews and investigations made by State Department of Social Welfare and county welfare department social workers during the week of February 5, 1961, in 13 representative counties: Los Angeles, San Diego, Alameda, Santa Clara, Contra Costa, Riverside, Kern, Stanislaus, Fresno, Marin, Humboldt, Mendocino, and Shasta. State welfare representatives talked to county welfare officials, businessmen, bankers, union leaders, educators, nurses, auto dealers, private charity agency officials, finance company officials and others.

The report indicated that in all counties checked unemployment was substantial and increasing; not only greater than a year ago, but in some instances, the worst since the depression of the 1930's. Union groups reported as many as 50 percent of their membership unemployed or working on a part-time basis, and in one small lumbering community, unemployment was as high as 90 percent. Unemployment affected a wide variety of occupational groups, but was particularly prevalent in the construction, aircraft, steel, and lumber industries. Although persons laid off were frequently the unskilled and semiskilled, counties reported that for the first time in years skilled laborers were also applying for assistance. Much of the unemployment was among young people with families, particularly among those below the age of 25. Many reports stressed the substantial numbers from the minority groups, Negroes and Mexican-Americans. All reports indicated the increasing exhaustion of unemployment benefits, and many stressed the fear of the workers and community leaders that further depletion of these benefits in the next two or three months would bring about substantially worse conditions than now existed.

County welfare departments met the needs caused by this unemployment only on an emergency basis and in inadequate amounts. With some exceptions, the needs of shelter and utilities were met only when there was danger of eviction. Additional hardship was created by contingent provisions such as liens on property, which caused families to deprive themselves rather than apply for assistance under these circumstances. Aid was not usually given by the public agencies to single employable men or to nonresidents. The use of surplus commodities varied greatly. Some counties issued them as supplemental to cash aid and granted them only when there was eligibility to General Assistance, others supplied them to other needy families in the community, and still others made no use of this resource.

Voluntary agencies in all communities tried to assist in a variety of ways but were unable to meet the demands made upon them. Private agencies stated that there was considerable distress on the part of families moving together and living in overcrowded conditions, and reported there would be increased family disorganization, particularly among young married persons, because of lack of adequate income. There were a number of incidental occurrences such as increased army enlistments in one area, illegal cattle rustling and shooting of deer in another, a substantial movement away from a few communities, and evidence of increased tension of children in school.

The study of 13 California counties was used as a backdrop for the beginning of actions by the Welfare Study Commission. Following a news release on the 1961 recession, the Commission began its deliberations, and preparation for that portion of the study which would consider an ADC-Unemployed Parent program, the staff of the State Department of Social Welfare began an analysis of the subject. In August 1962, representatives from the Department visited Oregon, Illinois, New York, Pennsylvania, and Maryland for the purpose of getting first-hand information for program planning and for estimates with respect to the extension of the ADC program to cover children of unemployed parents. The eastern states were unequivocally in favor of the program. Oregon staff were more mixed in their reaction, in part because of considerable local opposition to it, in part because General Relief seemed to offer greater control of those aspects of the program which worried them most. There was general agreement among the states that the two most persistent problems which this program brought in its wake were large grants to some families and grants in excess of what a family had ever been able to make before on their own and in an amount which they were not likely to receive in the future from their own employment. Oregon, and to a lesser extent Illinois, were looking for ways out of the dilemma which this posed for them, whereas New York, Pennsylvania, and Maryland had such firm philosophical convictions about the importance of meeting need at a minimum adequate standard that the issue resolved itself in terms of a clear-cut enunciation of the appropriateness of the payments made.

Each of the five states had come into the program with a minimum of preplanning, and all except Maryland aimed to obtain federal funds for families already eligible for and receiving assistance under the General Relief program operated under statewide standards, with state participation in the grants. Generally speaking, the states had accepted minimum federal requirements for eligibility and attempted to treat these families as they did all other ADC families. Since they were already aiding families with employable adults, they were in all instances already working closely with their state employment offices, and in most states all that was required was either the formalizing of their procedures or restating them in written form in order to meet federal requirements. Although state assistance standards varied in terms of items of coverage and allowances, all states except Maryland, which had a maximum payment, attempted to meet total need within these standards. Most gave the impression that they were chary about providing "special circumstances" allowances, especially for families who appeared likely short-termers. In one respect, all differed diametrically from California in that they permitted no cash reserves. Some states exempted certain property resources, such as automobiles and insurance with a low cash surrender value, especially during the first few months of aid. All states (Oregon somewhat uncertainly) emphasized the short-term nature of the program in relation to the "regular" ADC program and saw it as having considerable seasonal variation.

Not only was there minimum preplanning for this program, but it had received little attention in most of these states except in terms of the problems common to ADC generally high grants, adequacy of grant management, and the like. What attention had been given the program was in terms of employability and employment. Procedures were carefully worked out for referral for registration and for possible benefits, and some limited work had been done with Departments of Education around vocational education training courses. No state had much success with referrals of cases to its Vocational Rehabilitation Agency, mainly attributing this to lack of funds on that agency's part and on lack of candidates who could meet their requirements. All states had some experience with work relief, and reactions to it varied from complete and uncritical acceptance (Oregon, Illinois), to cautious acceptance with a critical reaction to some of its aspects (Pennsylvania, New York), to outright opposition (Maryland).

To summarize in capsule form, each state described the ADC-U families as large in size, composed of adults either beyond their prime working years (late forties) or just entering the labor market after school dropout, with less than average education, few job skills and those mainly at a menial level, heavy concentration among the ethnic minorities groups, and living at a minimum subsistence level prior to application. The general description which fits this group was "not likely to be full-time, self-sustaining families except in periods of fullest prosperity." Despite this, most states expressed optimism, pointing out that many of these families worked part of the year and that they were the public assistance agency's best candidates for training and employment. Both New York and Pennsylvania described this segment of their ADC load as the "preferred" group for whom there was less public criticism than for the regular load; whereas to some Oregon staff these were the disreputable unemployed who, given public assistance, become long-term dependents on aid.

Following this review of programs in selected states, the author and his policy development staff prepared a proposed Unemployed Parent and Work Experience and Training regulation as a model to be considered by the California Welfare Study Commission and by the Legislature. While it was unprecedented action to write regulations before the enactment of a law, it turned out to be a useful one since it formed a base for deliberation and, interestingly, emerged in legislation with relatively little modification.

The Unemployed Parent and Work Experience and Training legislation could not be sold on its merits alone. The County Supervisors Association had reservations about the program, including increased county costs, fear of increasing dependency of able-bodied people, and fear of loss of unemployed labor pool, particularly in the agricultural districts. The Welfare Study Commission accommodated the county cost argument by developing a legislative proposal to relieve county costs of county hospitals by transfer of such costs to the California State Medical Care program for public assistance recipients. It was finally agreed after numerous meetings of the Commission that the law containing the Unemployed Parent program would contain a variety of benefits, including the medical care provision, and under no circumstance could the various elements be dealt with separately. Since the County Supervisors Association and the Legislature were represented on the Commission, this agreement prevailed in later legislative actions. The original model of the Unemployed Parent regulation, as drafted by the Department staff before statutory enactment, emerged with essential features intact. The draft proposed that all county welfare departments would establish a Work Experience and Training program for all able-bodied ADC recipients which emphasized education, vocational training, and work experience in contrast to traditional work relief approaches.

The Welfare Study Commission report to the Governor and Legislature in January 1963, reviewed the rationale for enactment of an ADC-Unemployed Parent program by considering, first, its general relief aspects.

GENERAL RELIEF—THE "RESIDUAL" PUBLIC ASSISTANCE PROGRAM

The Commission observed that the function of General Relief (GR) sometimes referred to as General Assistance, (GA), since the enactment of the Federal Social Security Act in 1935 had been to provide for needy families and individuals who were not eligible for the special types of assistance for which states receive federal grants-in-aid. In California, this "residual" program was expected to take care of a potentially larger group of needy persons than in some other states because California, for a variety of reasons, had not taken advantage of the Unemployed Parent provisions of the Social Security Act. Specifically, the full burden of aiding needy children whose parents were unemployed was to be borne and could be provided for only by General Relief. In a 1961 winter month, when unemployment was relatively high, approximately 22,000 families consisting of nearly 110,000 persons received General Relief to help meet basic living expenses. In the summer months, the numbers decreased to about half. Financed entirely by local funds, General Relief in all counties was provided on a lower standard of adequacy than the assistance programs that were federally reimbursed. Thus, "County Aid and Relief to Indigents," as it is designated by law, approaches in concept and administration the early poor laws from which it was derived.

The families who received General Relief in California averaged between four and five persons, compared with slightly over three in ADC. The level on which their needs were met was far below that for ADC, which itself is the least adequate of the federally reimbursed programs. In March 1962, for example, the average General Relief payment for family cases was $58.33, compared with the ADC monthly average of $156.72 per family for the quarter ending March 31, 1962. In the winter months, the average General Relief payment for family cases was only slightly above the average payment for one-person cases, and in the Central Valley section, was less than the average per one-person case. The findings of this study substantiated those of a study of General Relief made in July 1960 by the State Department of Social Welfare, which showed that recipients of General Relief were paid about half the amount of assistance paid to recipients of other types of assistance who were living in similar circumstances.

County policies regarding assistance to families with unemployed members varied widely. In answers to questionnaires from the Welfare Study Commission, four of the 58 counties in California reported that they made no provision for unemployed families other than through the federal surplus food program; 12 gave aid to such families only occasionally, in circumstances described variously as "extreme hardship," "dire emergency," "in periods of general unemployment," "extreme destitution," and the like; and 22 provided aid only during periods of seasonal unemployment, ususally between the months of November or December and April or May; and only 20 counties granted General Relief because of unemployment without regard to the season of the year. The majority of the 22 counties that gave assistance on a seasonal basis had predominantly agricultural economies. However, three large counties, in which a considerable part of the economy was urban and industrial, also continued to place seasonal limitations on the granting of General Relief. Together with seasonal limitations, many of this group of counties limited the period during which assistance would be granted to an individual family. Several would not provide assistance beyond 30 days, others, for 90 days, one limited assistance to a period of two weeks in any given 30-day period, and another limited the amount to seven days' emergency assistance.

During periods of prolonged unemployment, families were in serious straits because of these arbitrary limits which were unrelated to their needs.

CASE 1. A family consisting of parents and eight children received temporary General Assistance in April 1962 because of unemployment of the father. He had been a clerical worker at a military base but had been laid off nearly one year previously and in the interim period had received unemployment benefits, and later supported his family by odd jobs and a janitorial night job. He had left this job because his family was alone at night and feared prowlers. The length of time during which a family may receive General Relief was determined in this county by the rate of unemployment. When the rate fell below 5.5 percent, General Relief was paid to an individual family for only 15 days. The period increased up to a total of 60 days when the unemployment rate rose to or over 7.5 percent. This family had received 15 days' assistance and was denied further help because the rate of unemployment was below 5.5 percent. Since the father had not been able to find employment, the family was in serious trouble, as they were eligible for nothing additional from the county except federal surplus commodities.

Personal interviews were conducted by Welfare Study Commission staff with 38 families who received only short-time assistance in the winter and spring of 1961-62 or were denied such assistance. Of those who received aid, the plight of those who were given only federal surplus commodities warrants the most attention. Two examples follow:

CASE 2. The father in this family was aged 39, a farm laborer, who had a third-grade education. The mother, aged 28, had completed the ninth grade. Four children ranged in age from 1½ to 8 years, and a fifth child was expected early in September. The family's estimated annual income from farm work was $2,700. The mother customarily worked in the fields in the summer, but because of her pregnancy had not done so this year, and was greatly concerned about meeting expenses in the coming winter. The family was purchasing their small, two-room house for $1,600, balance due, $277. The meager furniture consisted of a table, chairs, refrigerator, and gas stove in the kitchen; television set, two double beds, and one chest of drawers in the bedroom. Housekeeping standards were good. The mother spoke hopelessly about the decrease in farm work in this section of the state. The most pressing problem was clothing for the children. The oldest boy started school in 1961, and the second child would start in the fall. Athough the children wore old, patched clothing, the mother noted with pride that her boy had never been sent home from school with a note about being dirty. In 1961, the mother was in a hospital for tuberculosis for nine months, and the children lived with relatives, who received Aid to Needy Children for them. The mother remarked that then the oldest boy had "good clothes." Besides the clothing problem, the sleeping arrangements—two double beds for a father, post-tuberculous mother, and four growing children—must be considered grossly inadequate. Further, a surplus commodity order in the winter of 1962 provided only the following items of food for two weeks, for a child who at that time was ten months old, a toddler, two school-aged children, and the parents: flour, cornmeal, rice, dried beans, dried milk, cheese, lard, chopped meat, canned tomatoes, butter, oats or wheat, and peanut butter. This family received three such orders for a total of six weeks. They received no whole milk, no eggs, no fresh vegetables, no fresh meat, and less than one pound of canned chopped meat per day for a family of six. The county in its promotional material describes itself as "one of the richest agricultural areas in the world."

CASE 3. This family consisted of father, aged 58, mother, 44, and four children, aged 7 to 15. An older son, his wife, and three pre-school children shared the four-room house that the family owned, making a total of 11 people in four small rooms. The father had been a railroad worker for many years but suffered a back injury several years ago and since then had been able to do only farm work. Because of difficulty in bending, he was limited in work he could get. The family went to "the welfare" for the first time two years earlier and again during the winter of 1961 which was more difficult because of the long rains. They had no money for transportation to the commodity warehouse, 20 miles distant, and the county made no provision for delivery of commodities except for disabled persons. The mother commented that, "We were hungry," but that the children fared somewhat better than the adults because of school lunches. The older son finally managed to earn a dollar for gasoline from odd jobs and was able to get to the warehouse to pick up surplus foods for the "emergency."

These cases are cited as typical of the situations in 23 home visits made in this county. It is possible that these families fared better than many others, from the mere fact that they were available for interviews, which reflected their more stable living situations. Attempt was made to interview a total of 87 families, but nearly half of them had moved, their whereabouts unknown to their neighbors. Another 20 percent were reported by relatives or neighbors to be working elsewhere but with the intention of returning to their homes in this county when the various harvests ended. Several families declined to be interviewed, some of them openly suspicious of the interviewer's intentions. In the counties that did not place seasonal limitations on General Relief, the assistance standards were well below those for the federally-aided public assistance programs, including ADC. In the majority of the counties, General Relief to unemployed families was regarded as a short-term or emergency type of assistance. The usual items provided were food, shelter, and utilities, but a substantial number of counties gave only food. Other counties paid rent and utilities only when the family was in danger of being evicted or had received shutoff notices from the utility company. In most counties, clothing was rarely provided unless, again, the family was in dire straits.

Of the eight counties included in the field study, those with the most adequate standards used the ADC cost schedules as a base, but generally with some scaling downward. Food standards for unemployed families in one county, for example, were 10 percent lower than for ADC; in another, food costs were based on the 1956 ADC cost schedule rather than the 1962 revised standard. These were the counties with the most generous policies.

The effect of the differences in standards between ADC and GR can be illustrated by the cases of two families receiving General Relief because the fathers were unemployed:

CASE 1: Family consisted of father, mother, and eight children whose ages ranged from 3 to 17 years. GR payment was $325.30. Need according to ADC standards was $488, and ADC payment would have been $360, the maximum ADC allowance regardless of budgeted need.

CASE 2: Both parents in this family were 25 years old. The oldest child was seven, and the youngest under one year. The two oldest children had been treated for tuberculosis, which was inactive at the time that the father, a laborer, applied for aid because of unemployment. They were granted $242 General Relief. In addition, this county was able to provide a layette for the baby, shoes and clothing for the other children, and a refrigerator. According to ADC standards, this family's basic need would have been $356. The payment, because of the legal maximum, would have been $343, which, though less than minimum need, was $100 more per month than the General Relief payment.

A substantial proportion of General Relief was paid in kind, either by voucher or through county commissaries, again in contrast to the federally-aided programs which require the more dignified method of cash payments. Of the 58 counties, 13 had local commissaries through which food, and in some instances, clothing, were issued to needy families. Los Angeles had a clothing commissary but by policy provided for other items of need in cash unless it was found that the family had a money management problem. Less than one-third of General Relief was given in cash by 16 counties, and approximately 14 gave no cash whatsoever. An additional four counties paid an inconsequential proportion or less than 5 percent of General Relief in cash. Statewide, 42 percent of General Relief was provided either through commissary assistance or voucher payments to vendors.

Besides the limited provision of consumption items for these families, any income received, whether casual, intermittent, or inconsequential, was taken into account to the last penny. The following case, by no means an unusual occurrence, is an example:

CASE X: This family consisted of the father, aged 39, a mother aged 36, and 11 children, who ranged in age from 2 to 18 years. The father was a laborer and was assigned to the county work project when he applied for assistance because of unemployment. He reported regularly to work and, though an unskilled worker, apparently did a satisfactory job and had a good attendance record on the project. The mother had worked occasionally as a domestic servant but gave this up when she found she was not able to make satisfactory arrangements for the care of the children and the school complained because of irregular attendance of some of the older children, who stayed home to take care of the younger children. In February 1962 the caseworker learned that the mother had earned $15 in domestic work the previous Christmas. As a consequence, $15 was deducted from the March assistance payment. The family was told by the agency that, "all income regardless of how small must be reported," and the father was cautioned that if any other unreported income were discovered, his case would be closed.

Answers to the question on supplementation of full-time earnings indicated that 22 counties supplemented under certain circumstances and that supplementation was generally given in great emergency for a short period of time when "other community resources" could not be found. In the field study, it was learned that "other community resources" were usually the Salvation Army or another voluntary agency that might give aid on a short-term basis. Also, it was found that some emergency supplementation was given to very large families for short periods to tide them over an emergency. No county, however, supplemented full-time earnings regularly as a means of meeting families' ongoing needs.

In contrast, a majority of the counties by policy would provide supplementation of unemployment insurance benefits. More than three-fourths of the counties responded that they supplemented such benefits. Similarly, disability insurance benefits were supplemented with General Relief by a large majority of counties. In the cases reviewed, however, it was observed that families tended to exhaust unemployment or disability benefits before applying for General Relief even though the benefits did not cover total living expenses. The differences between standards of assistance for General Relief and ADC were so great that they could have a built-in deterrent to reuniting a broken family. For example:

CASE Y: The family of a mother and three children received $215 ADC during a period when the father was in jail. After he returned home, he had trouble finding work and when ADC eligibility ended, the family, now five persons instead of four, received $177 General Relief. The agency's efforts to help this family work constructively on problems of relationships between the parents and on the father's employment and retraining plans were seriously handicapped by an assistance standard that seemed to the family to be a penalty for the father's return.

Personal interviews conducted by the Welfare Study Commission as part of the follow-up study in two counties threw further light on the problems of unemployed parents. A substantial proportion of these families were stable, cohesive family groups who were struggling against great odds to provide a satisfactory living for their children and to make it possible for them to attend school. In the agricultural county, several of the families had sought assistance for the first time in the unusually severe winter of 1961-62. A substantial number were attempting to purchase homes, little more than shacks. Not all of these families were migrant workers, and several worked steadily for the same employer. In one case, the employer was a small farmer who tried very hard to keep a stable labor force. Another family worked regularly for a large farm-labor contractor. Still others were men with skills in running and repairing farm machinery and able to work in this line when it was available. The families, generally speaking, had many children, and this, coupled with the fact that full employment was available during only nine or ten months of the year, meant that in spite of careful planning most of them had little reserve with which to meet prolonged periods of bad weather or unexpected illness. These were mostly young families, with fathers in their twenties and thirties. Many had grade-school education, some not more than the third or fourth grade, and several had completed the tenth or eleventh grade in school. Many of the families spoke of the decline in agricultural work available in the communities. Every family interviewed spontaneously mentioned the serious problem of obtaining clothing for their children who were attending school. The children's feelings of difference from their classmates was a factor, but more important was the lack of warm clothing in the winter.

The Welfare Study Commission recommended to the Governor that California enact legislation making ADC available for all children who were in financial need because of unemployment of their parents. The Commission commented that simple justice demanded that a great and prosperous state like California guarantee that no child shall be hungry or wear ragged clothing because he happens to live in a section of the state that cannot provide food, clothing, shelter, and other minimum needs on a standard giving children a chance for wholesome growth and full development of their abilities. The inequities between General Relief and ADC were so glaring that assistance to needy unemployed families should not be left to the 58 counties with their individual and widely differing standards.

The California State Legislature passed Assembly Bill 59 containing the unemployed parent provisions, and the Governor signed it May 21, 1963. The unemployed parent and work experience and training provisions contained in this bill were so controversial it probably would not have been successful had it not been contained in the "package" bill. The conservative county representatives on the Welfare Study Commission and in the Legislature would surely have defeated it. Masterful Welfare Study Commission actions and reports and liberal legislative strategy prevailed. The Unemployed Parent law was combined with a medical care section of law which allegedly rewarded the conservative counties in such a manner that the county could enjoy a substantial net gain. To illustrate the importance to the County Supervisors Association of California of the medical care bonanza, a letter from the Association to all county supervisors and welfare and county hospital administrators, dated May 21, 1963, is quoted as follows:

"Urgent special briefing to discuss mechanics of realizing the greatest possible immediate gain to counties from the new federal funds provided for the first 30 days of hospitalization in county hospitals under the Medical Aid to the Aged Program.

"Assembly Bill 59 (omnibus welfare legislation) cleared the Legislature yesterday and was sent to the Governor for his signature. Effective on the Governor's signature, AB 59 will permit the granting of Medical Aid to the Aged for patients in county hospitals during the first 30 days of their confinement on the basis of 50 percent federal — 50 percent county and zero state participation. In addition, there will be some retroactive claim possible for county hospital care during February, March, and April.

"The MAA extension feature of AB 59 will provide substantial cash savings to counties this year. It is imperative, therefore, that every county act now to gain the maximum return under the new law."

Many counties later expressed regret at the passage of AB 59 because they had not realized the alleged medical care savings. To illustrate the protest of some counties against the Unemployed Parent Program the following resolution of the Solano County Board of Supervisors is of note:

"WHEREAS, there is now under consideration by the California State Department of Social Welfare, a proposed regulation pertaining to unemployment of a parent (C-161.40) in the following language:

Either parent is unemployed if:

1. He is not working or is working less than the number of hours per week considered full time by the industry for the job, AND he is available for and seeking employment and/or is receiving training essential to his future self-support. The cause of unemployment is immaterial to this determination, or

2. He is working full time but is incapacitated to the degree that he is able to accomplish less on a job than a normal person and is paid on this basis; and

"WHEREAS, interpretation by local welfare agencies of such regulation, if adopted, would be subject to many and varied interpretations leading to inevitable excesses in many instances due to the broad coverage and general wording of the regulation; and

"WHEREAS, it is believed that further consideration and examination of the proposed regulation by the State Department of Social Welfare would reveal the uncertainty and possible undesirable consequences that are inherent in the present wording; it is therefore

"*Resolved* that in its present form, the proposed State Social Welfare Regulation C-161.40, is not considered desirable or feasible since it tends to design a program to meet a need created by unemployment by establishing a regulation which could result in a total family income higher than that which is available to the family when in its normal employed status, or higher than the income of a similar neighboring family which has not suffered the misfortune of unemployment; and be it further

"*Resolved* that such regulation can have serious consequences for the relative value which the recipient family may place on employment as compared with the receipt of aid. It can have serious consequences for the effectiveness of the local welfare department in maintaining its integrity and usefulness in the eyes of the community it serves. It can have serious consequences ultimately for the general acceptance of the fundamentally important aims of the state in its concern for the best interests of all of its people; and it is further

"*Resolved* that it is unacceptable that eligibility should not be conditioned by the cause of unemployment. It does not appear possible that local government could defend such a ruling against the charges which will undoubtedly be leveled by employers, employer groups, and others. When considered with the subject of the previous paragraph this ruling would appear to make it reasonable and desirable for certain families to become voluntarily unemployed; and it is further

"*Resolved* that the State Department of Social Welfare give further serious consideration to all adverse implications involved should proposed regulation C-161.40 be adopted."

AID TO FAMILIES WITH DEPENDENT CHILDREN

Excerpts from the (AFDC) Unemployed Parent (formerly ADC) section of Assembly Bill 59 read as follows:

"1500. Aid, services, or both, shall be granted under the provisions of this chapter, and subject to the regulations of the state department, to families with related children under the age of 18 years, in need thereof because they have been deprived of parental support or care due to:

*   *   *

(c) The unemployment of his parent or parents.

*   *   *

"1500.4. For the purposes of this chapter, unemployed parent means a natural parent, adoptive parent, or stepparent with whom the child is living, and who:

(a) Is not working but is available for and seeking employment or, as a result of unemployment, has been accepted for or is participating in a training project essential to future self-support, or

(b) Is employed only part time as determined in accordance with such standards as may be developed by the State Department of Social Welfare in its rules and regulations . . .

"It is the intent of the Legislature that the employment and self-maintenance of parents of needy children be encouraged to the maximum extent and that this chapter shall be administered in such a way that needy children and their parents will be encouraged and inspired to assist in their own maintenance. The State Department of Social Welfare shall take all steps necessary to implement this section. . .

*   *   *

"1503.1. The provision of useful work experience and constructive vocational training for unemployed recipients is a matter of statewide concern.

"Insofar as practical each county department shall establish a community work experience and vocational training program for unemployed persons and others for whom such experience and training is deemed desirable as part of a plan to help them become self-supporting.

"Such programs shall be conducted in accordance with standards and regulations established by the Department of Social Welfare as desirable and necessary to qualify for such federal funds as are available.

"The cost of materials, equipment, and supervision provided by agencies cooperating with the county department in community work experience and training programs shall not be charged as an administrative expense under this chapter or with respect to other public assistance programs.

"Work projects developed under this section shall be confined to projects which serve a useful public purpose, do not result either in displacement of regular workers or in the performance of work that would otherwise be performed by employees of public or private agencies, institutions, or organizations, and (except in cases of projects which involve emergencies or which are generally of a nonrecurring nature) are of a type which has not normally been undertaken in the past by the state or community, as the case may be.

"All public entities, including state agencies, are authorized to cooperate and participate with the county department in the establishment of community work experience and training projects.

* * *

"1523.7. Aid shall be denied to an unemployed parent and his family if it is determined by the county welfare department, in accordance with regulations of the State Department of Social Welfare, that:

(a) He fails to seek and to keep himself currently available for employment as required by standards set by the department, or

(b) He refuses without good cause to accept part-time, full-time, temporary or permanent employment without reference to his customary occupation or skill. Good cause for refusal of employment shall be deemed to exist, when:

(1) The offer of employment is not for a specific job at a stated wage comparable to the prevailing wage for that type of employment in the community, or

(2) The job is available because of a bona fide labor dispute, the existence of which has been established by the State Department of Employment, or

(3) The job is not within the physical or mental capacity of the person, as established, when necessary, by competent professional authority, or

(4) Acceptance would be an unreasonable act because of hardships imposed upon the person or his family due to illness or remoteness; interruption of a program in process for permanent rehabilitation or self-support; or conflicting with an imminent likelihood of reemployment at his regular work.

"1523.8. The State Department of Employment shall report immediately to the county welfare department whenever an unemployed parent willfully fails or refuses to comply with the provisions of Section 1523.7.

"1523.9. An unemployed parent shall be denied aid for himself and his family if without good cause:

(a) He refuses to accept assignment to a community work or training project, or

(b) He willfully fails to report to an assigned community work or training project.

* * *

"1550.2. When aid is granted under this chapter to an unemployed parent and his family, whenever practical or feasible such parent or

other employable family member shall be assigned to a community
work or training project established and conducted under the provisions of Section 1503.1 of this code.

*   *   *

"1552.4. Payments made under this chapter shall be issued at
periods most nearly consistent with prevailing patterns for wages in
local industry."

Based upon the preceding law, regulations were presented to the
Director of the State Department of Social Welfare at a public hearing by the author, in his capacity as Deputy Director of the department. The presentation, accompanied by an evaluation, is summarized as follows:

The proposed regulatory material deals with implementation of
the unemployed parent and the community work and training law.
As a beginning I will describe some of the history of this program
development. It goes back to the past work that has been done by
the State Department of Social Welfare and serves the need in cities
and counties for unemployed people. It incorporates the work of the
Welfare Study Commission which was appointed by the Governor
and finally, of course, the action of the Legislature itself. The particular phase that we are discussing here is part of the package of legislative action contained in AB 59. I would like to first identify a few
principles which we feel emerge from the law and which certainly
reflect the objectives of the State Department of Social Welfare. The
first principle is that we believe that most people want to work, and it
is out of that basic principle and belief that these programs have been
developed. Men do not wish to settle for public assistance alone, if
work were available they would choose to work, and to the extent
that it is not available they would seek every other way possible to
survive, viewing public welfare only as a stop-gap. Second, that men
without work must not be forced to desert their families to qualify
their children for public assistance. To some extent this eventuality
will be overcome by the legislation and new program. Third, if as a
last resort, men must seek public aid they must not remain idle on aid
but must be provided with the opportunity for education, vocational
training, and work experience. In this manner their education and
vocational skill will be upgraded, their work skills and work habits
maintained, and their morale, their feeling of self-worth, their respect
from family and community retained. All of these elements work for
the return of the individual to self-dependence. Fourth, that public
welfare is not a vocational service and educational or employment
agency, and that other educational and vocational services will be
fully utilized to the extent that they exist in state and local agencies.
Public welfare, however, has for a quarter of a century avoided its
service responsibilities by development of a so-called referral prin-

ciple. Assistance recipients were referred to employment offices who could not place them; to vocational rehabilitation agencies who could train only a few of those referred, and most recipients weren't qualified for referral at all, because they weren't disabled or economically feasible. Our department had no alternative except that of provision of the rehabilitative services from the public welfare agency itself. With these principles as a backdrop, we may view AB 59 as one of the most significant pieces of social welfare legislation in the history of public welfare in this state.

The policy material before you today fulfills the intent of this progressive legislation. The community work and training regulatory material specifically establishes (a) A community work and training program in each county and sets standards and conditions for this program; (b) requires that every unemployed adult recipient become engaged in educational, vocational training, or a work experience placement; (c) requires the State Department of Social Welfare to enter into agreements with state agencies of education, vocational rehabilitation, and employment; (d) requires the development of county advisory committees to initially evaluate and periodically review the community work and training program; (e) finally, the material identifies the responsibility of the county welfare departments to insure adequate child care during the absence of the caretakers.

The policy material emphasizes:

(1) Diagnosis of the individual to insure work, training or educational assignments appropriate to the individual's interest and aptitude

(2) Protection of the person's safety and health

(3) Provision of wage credit for community work performance

(4) Protection of business and labor interests through avoidance of displacement of regular employees or competition with private industry

(5) Provision of money and service to sustain and protect the family during the temporary emergency

In summary, I believe this is a realistic program with exacting expectations of education, work or training, yet a program with a scientific approach in its expectation of diagnostic evaluation, selective work or training assignments, plus other forms of work conditioning and work retention elements. I use the term "scientific" to describe this program because it is built upon current knowledge regarding the dynamics of human behavior which substantiate that conditions set forth in this program are rehabilitative and carry hope of future independence for those individuals served. The program also illustrates the concern of the State of California for disadvantaged people who are experiencing the impact of fundamental economic change in this era of mechanization and automation which outdates work skills almost before they are attained and provides practically no work opportunity for the underprivileged, uneducated, and unskilled.

Based upon AB 59, the State Department of Social Welfare promulgated Unemployed Parent and Community Work and Training regulations effective February 1, 1964.

These regulations plus a September 3, 1964 departmental bulletin clarified the responsibility of counties for implementing the work experience and training program as follows:

"The public welfare amendments of 1962 (PL 87-543) included provision for federal participation in aid expenditures in the AFDC program which are made in the form of payments for work performed under community work and training programs by one or more of the relatives with whom a child is living. The purpose of this provision is to encourage the conservation of work skills and the development of new skills through work and training programs of a constructive nature under conditions which are designed to assure the protection of the health and welfare of the families and children involved.

"Taken together with the SERVICES provisions of the Social Security Act already implemented by Bulletin 629, the Community Work and Training provisions which are the subject of this Bulletin provide a sound basis for establishing and carrying out plans to prevent or reduce dependency and helping individuals attain or retain capability for employment and self-support. It is anticipated that these plans will be achieved through coordinated maximum use of education, constructive work experience, training, counseling and guidance, and special job placement services. . . .

"Assembly Bill 59 enacted during the 1963 sessions of the California Legislature provided for the establishment of a 'community work experience and vocational training program for unemployed persons and others for whom such experience and training is deemed desirable as part of a plan to help them become self-supporting'.

"These provisions are applicable to the entire AFDC caseload regardless of reason for deprivation.

Program Goal

"The goal of the Community Work and Training program is to aid the recipient to compete more effectively in the labor market and increase his chance for self-support. Assignment to work-training projects which serve a useful public purpose is one way in which recipients are aided in gaining or retaining necessary work skills and habits.

"This goal can be accomplished by finding gainful employment through effective job hunting; by acquiring needed education and improved skills; and by maintaining and developing good work habits, attitudes, morale and skills through constructive work experience. Work-training assignments are not goals in and of themselves but steps in an individual plan toward employment, self-support, and independence.

Establishment of Community Work and Training Program— Requirement to Establish Program

"Each county shall establish a community work and training program commensurate with the volume of cases receiving assistance and the requirement to improve the employability of employable or potentially employable recipients by conserving and developing their work habits and skills. This program may be designed to serve one person or many. The program may be developed and extended on a progressive basis over a two-year period. It is not planned to replace existing programs, but rather should build on those which already exist in a supplementary and complementary manner. If community work training plans are not feasible in a particular county, consideration may be given to securing the training from an adjacent county, if distances are not too great for the trainees to travel (travel costs in such instances would be a legitimate part of the training plan). . . .

"If no community work training is considered feasible by a county, the county welfare director shall submit a statement of justification to the area office of the SDSW stating the facts and reasons, and the steps taken in arriving at the decision. In this instance, the SDSW makes the final decision on the appropriateness of the decision not to undertake a community work and training program.

County Plan of Operations

"Each county welfare department shall develop a plan for implementation of the community work training program. This plan, together with descriptions of each project undertaken shall be filed with the area office of the SDSW.

"Exception will be taken by the SDSW to any plan or project found upon subsequent review to be in conflict with any requirements of this Bulletin. . . .

"The following general standards are established for the planning, development and administration of community work and training programs by county welfare departments. In addition to these general standards, county welfare departments will adhere to the specific standards set forth under the succeeding sections of this Bulletin.

A. The program in all of its aspects must be designed to contribute to the maximum development of the recipients' potentials for self-support through developing good work habits, attitudes and morale; overcoming the effects of educational deprivation; conserving or improving existing skills; and developing new skills.

B. The program must be so administered as to give consideration to individual needs, capacities, abilities and aptitudes.

C. The program must provide for the coordinated and appropriate use of two major elements:

1. WORK-TRAINING PROJECTS: These are projects in which one or more recipients are assigned to a sponsoring agency (another public agency or the county welfare department) for the dual purpose of performing work of benefit to the public, and of gaining useful work experience and on-the-job training.

2. ORGANIZED GROUP INSTRUCTION: This is the means through which remedial and/or vocational education is provided to enable recipients to overcome educational deficiencies blocking their chances for employment or vocational training and to upgrade their work skills and increase their earning capacity.

Interagency Relationships

"Agreements between the State Department of Social Welfare and State Departments of Employment, Vocational Rehabilitation Service, Industrial Relations, and Education are designed to further the SERVICE aspects of the public assistance programs and to encourage the maximum cooperation with community work training programs.

"The training available in some communities under the Manpower Development and Training Act shall be coordinated with the community work experience training program; the community work and training program complements and supplements the federal and state manpower, training, employment and rehabilitation programs.

Advisory Committee

"The county welfare director shall appoint an advisory committee to assist in formulating and evaluating the county's Community Work and Training Program. An already-existing committee may be designated to assume this function. The services such a committee can provide include:

1. Interpretation of the program to the community.

2. Advising the welfare director on program planning and development, including review of the county's plan of operation for the program prior to its being filed with the SDSW.

3. Bringing labor and management together in the development

of an acceptable program and working out problems related to work-training projects.

4. Reviewing periodically the county's plan of operation for the program and advising the welfare director as to the effectiveness of particular projects and the progam as a whole.

"Membership of the committee must include representation from labor, management, employment, education and apprenticeship training, as well as representation of significant ethnic groups in the county. Staff services to the committee should be provided by the county welfare department.

Work-Training Projects

"Work-training projects are designed to provide constructive work experience and training for participants and to serve useful public purposes. Development of projects should be geared to the needs of recipients rather than being exclusively concerned with the needs of potential sponsors. The work performed must not displace nor adversely affect regularly employed workers, nor provide a service normally and continually met by a federal, state, county, municipal, or other public agency.

Types of Projects

"All work-training projects must have an emphasis on training. The degree of this emphasis will depend upon the background, skills, and training needs of the workers. Suggested work-training projects may be classified under the following three broad types:

1. Projects designed to develop new or improved skills through the planned coordination of work experience, training and related instruction. Participants will need to be carefully selected on the basis of their ability to absorb the training and instruction. These kinds of projects would be closely geared to the purpose of producing well-trained workers for a competitive labor market.

2. Projects designed to improve, or conserve existing skills. Workers will be given an opportunity to use their acquired skills and through useful job experience and related vocational instruction or adult education to increase their employment opportunities.

3. Projects designed to precondition persons who do not have a recent employment history, who have been unable to adjust in private employment, or who lack motivation for work or to maintain work skills and habits. Such projects are to be designed to develop work habits, attitudes and morale under close supervision on the project, coupled with casework services and counseling. Participants in such projects shall be encouraged to improve their basic education through adult education courses. Reassignment to more advanced work and training shall be made as soon as indicated.

Physical Examinations

"A preassignment physical examination when (a) the caseworker has any reason to suspect that a health problem exists or that there is a health problem, or (b) whenever a participant requests such an examination.

"Each potential assignee must be advised of his right to request, without prejudice, a physical examination.

Safety Standards

"Project workers must be provided with the same safety features as are provided regular employees of the sponsoring agency.

Work Standards

"Work-training projects must be operated in accordance with the following commonly accepted work standards:

1. Credits for work must be at the prevailing rates for similar work in the community, or at the minimum rate established by California Labor Code for such work, whichever is higher. The rate credited applies to the work performed not to the worker.

2. Workers will be assigned to projects commensurate with their vocational potential and physical and mental capacities in order to develop skills and improve employability.

3. Work assignments may not exceed the number of hours necessary to meet the family assistance payment at the credited hourly rate, nor may they exceed 36 hours in any one week or eight hours in any one day . The assigned hours do not have to match the amount of assistance payment exactly but may not exceed it. Exception to the eight-hour day and 36-hour week may be made in a bona fide emergency.

4. Necessary provision must be made for allowing appropriate time off for job hunting during normal business hours. When organized group instruction is an integral part of the training plan for an individual, his work hours must be adjusted to class hours.

5. Work assignments which are punitive, degrading, abusive, or which would tend to cause public ridicule of the worker are prohibited.

Workmen's Compensation Protection

"All persons assigned to work-training projects must be covered by Workmen's Compensation Insurance or comparable protection.

Project Review

"All projects should be visited by the county welfare department at least monthly to see that project standards are complied with and to maintain a close working relationship with the project supervisor. There will be periodic review of projects by SDSW.

A. Organized Group Instruction

Relationship to Total Community Work and Training Program: As indicated in Section 111, Program Standards, *organized group* instruction, together with *work-training projects* constitute the two major elements of a community work training program. The goal of the program to help people conserve work skills and develop new skills requires the coordinated use on planned basis of remedial education, work experience, vocational education, and job training. The remedial and vocational education required to supplement and complement the work experience and job training afforded by assignment to work-training projects is provided through the medium of organized group instruction.

B. Types of Instruction

1. *Remedial Education*—So far as the Community Work and Training program is concerned, remedial education is in effect prevocational in that it involves instruction designed to remedy educational deficiencies which preclude the successful pursuit of vocational education, job training or employment. This includes:

a. A course or series of courses of instruction in basic elementary subjects designed to overcome illiteracy.

b. A course or series of courses of instruction in secondary subjects when these are required as prerequisites for successful pursuit of vocational education, job training or job placement.

2. *Vocational Education*—This is a course or series of courses of instruction that deal specifically with the acquisition of skills, understandings, attitudes, and abilities that are necessary for entry into and successful progress within a particular occupation.

C. Sources of Instruction

Adult educational services of the public school system of the state are the primary resource for the provision of organized group instruction. State colleges and University of California Extension are additional resources.

As established by the policy in Department Bulletin 629, Section 216.40, county welfare departments may organize and establish educational programs only after determination that the local school district or districts involved are unable or unwilling to provide needed service even if reimbursed. Adult education programs are currently offered by many regular high schools, by adult schools, which include evening high schools, and evening junior colleges, and by junior colleges. Any secondary or unified school district is authorized by law to set up and offer classes for adult and out-of-school youths as a part of their regular high school program.

Program Operations

"The Community Work and Training program in effect represents an extension and elaboration of the SERVICES program described in Department Bulletin 629.

The clients involved in the Community Work and Training program will all have priority needs in the area of self-support. In the operation of the Community Work and Training program, county welfare departments will be guided by all of the relevant policies set forth in the SERVICES bulletin.

A. Determination of Potentials for Work Training Assignments

This determination will be made as a consequence of the social study process.

In this connection, the services provided by the State Employment Service, school districts, and Vocational Rehabilitation Service may be helpful. These services include testing and vocational counseling. If these services are not available from public sources, the county department shall provide them.

B. Social Services in Connection with Work Training Assignments

With respect to all clients involved in the Community Work and Training programs, county welfare departments will provide the following SERVICES related to the priority need for self-support, in addition to the minimum SERVICE activity of counseling: Health care; family counseling; employment counseling.

All assignments made to activities in connection with the Community Work and Training program shall be consistent with the diagnostic results of the social study and with the case plan developed as a consequence of that study. Assignments should be time-limited, based upon the individual's particular needs, abilities and capacity. Periodic reviews should be made for each individual to determine his progress with particular attention to his readiness for regular employment.

"In making assignments the following additional factors shall be taken into account:

1. *Criteria for Assignment to Projects to Develop New or Improved Skills.*

Participants in these projects will need to be carefully selected on the basis of their ability to absorb training and instruction. In addition, the decision to assign a client to such a project shall be based on the following criteria:

a. The individual's present occupation and skills in relation to the market demand for that occupation is such that his earning capacity is insufficient to prevent periodic or continuous dependency on aid.

b. The occupation for which he would be trained would so increase his potential earning capacity that the likelihood of the family's dependency on aid would be substantially reduced.

2. *Effective Market Demand for Particular Occupation*

When through the combination of assignment to a work-training project for job training, and vocational education, we would be helping a person develop *new* skills and train for a *new* occupation, such assignments will be made only on occupations for which there is an effective market demand as determined by the State Employment Service. Where a work-training assignment would be designed to conserve *existing* skills, such assignment will not be made in occupations known to be of declining importance, or where there is a particularly heavy surplus of labor as determined by the State Employment Service.

3. *Priority of Employment*

Referral to and acceptance of employment will always have top priority over any assignment on work training projects under the Community Work and Training program.

4. *Priority of Manpower Training Programs*

When an individual appears to meet the requirements for any of the manpower training programs, he will always be referred to the State Employment Service for possible selection. Assignment to such programs will always have top priority of any assignment under the Community Work and Training program.

5. *Priority of Vocational Rehabilitation Services*

When a physical examination indicates that a potential trainee has a handicap which may bring him within the scope of vocational rehabilitation services, referral to VRS will be made. Acceptance of the client by VRS will always have top priority over any assignment under the Community Work and Training program.

6. *Child Care*

The county welfare department shall assist in providing for the care and protection of children during the absence of the caretaker assigned to a work or training activity."

It will be noted that the preceding clarification of policy made no mention of work-connected expenses to recipients. The omission of specific legislative provision for this item became a major impediment to full implementation of the program. The SDSW through regulation prescribed a standard for work-connected expenses— a flat $25 allowance plus actual cost of transportation. While this amount was appropriate for inclusion in the recipient's grant, most persons were at the legal maximum which they could receive, so if they were to gain work-connected expenses it could only be provided at county expense. Hard-pressed counties could not obtain sufficient budget allocations for this purpose. SDSW regulation provided that recipients could not be expected to participate in work training or education programs if work-connected expenses were not provided. The result was that some recipients volunteered to participate and used money from an already inadequate grant, and many remained idle at home. Legislation subsequently initiated in 1967 to remedy this problem, passed both the California Assembly and Senate, but was vetoed by Governor Reagan for fiscal reasons.

What, then, was the effect of the deficiency in work-connected expenses? There was considerable unevenness in meeting the work-connected expense requirement. State policy provided that the costs of additional expenses attributable to engagement in a Community Work and Training Program be allowed in the grant in addition to basic needs. Allowances were to be included for transportation, child care, paper, supplies, books, and the like; and for those involved in community work and training for 30 hours per week or more, $25 would be allowed to meet the cost of additional food, clothing, and personal incidentals.

There is a fact of budget life in California social welfare known as the "State maximum." This is a ceiling on the base for State financial participation which was as follows:

Number of eligible children in the same home with one parent	Maximum participation base per month	Number of eligible children in the same home with one parent	Maximum participation base per month
1	$148	6	330
2	172	7	355
3	221	8	373
4	263	9	386
5	300		

Plus $6.00 per child for each additional child

The ceiling on State financial participation resulted in a ceiling on grants, or a grant maximum. Counties were authorized (but not required) to supplement the statutory participation maximum to meet total need through the use of county funds. Some counties did, most did not. There was an abortive attempt to make it mandatory for counties to provide work expenses from local funds but the state withdrew the proposal. State policy later provided that if the expenses of community work and training were not included, this was a good cause for refusal by a welfare recipient to participate in the program. On the other hand, a county could authorize the amount of training expense, in which case the recipient would be expected to participate. Some counties attempted to supplement the expenses relating to community work and training through provisions of goods and services to meet these needs, but such arrangements resulted in uneven treatment.

Counties which could supplement the grant did so in a creative, constructive fashion, and clients tended to be well-motivated, with much enthusiasm and self-involvement. Selected interviews of welfare recipients by State and Federal representatives found that conditions varied in counties which could not supplement grants because of local fund restrictions. In the largest county, several of the clients who were interviewed seemed unaware of the goals, purpose, and extent of work training assignments, were uninformed as to whether additional items were allowed, or of their right to refuse to participate. As one participant put it, "I don't know anything. I was just told to report—or else." This same recipient indicated that he had not been informed of any changes, actual or projected, in his grant, nor had the matter of community work and training expenses been discussed. Although this was not true of all project participants in that locality, it was true of some.

Clients interviewed in both supplementing and nonsupplementing counties were involved in constructive programs which included basic literacy, education, and training needs, along with work training experience. At times, because of the county's inability to provide cash supplementation, voluntary participation was at considerable sacrifice and hardship to recipients and families. In other instances, participation had to be delayed or ruled out. In spite of these difficulties, most recipients remained highly motivated and enthusiastic about the opportunities made available to them. One outstanding instance was that of several clients who were required to travel over 20 miles to attend night classes in basic language skills for Spanish-speaking illiterates. In spite of the fact that transportation allowances were not available, classes were well attended and students seemed most sincere and interested in their class work. Even so, the problem of a maximum grant was serious and long standing, one which hampered state and county efforts to serve AFDC families.

Child Care

The provision of opportunity to AFDC mothers in the form of education and vocational training was contingent upon availability of adequate child care. Funding for child care services was seriously deficient. As with work-connected expenses the cost of child care was not generally available within the maximum grant. If the recipient received some income from an absent parent or from employment, the income was deducted from the grant, thereby lowering it and allowing use of the grant structure for child care costs. The assistance grant, therefore, became a child care resource for a few welfare recipients. Another resource was Federal funds entitled Child Welfare Services (CWS) from the Children's Bureau. The annual allocation to the State of California of CWS money in 1968 was approximately $3,000,000, whereas California spent about $40,000,000 for a wide range of Child Welfare Services. Thus, federal matching of Child Welfare Services amounted to about 7 percent of the amount spent by the state. On the other hand, the federal government provided 75 percent of the cost of certain administrative services in the AFDC program.

The State Department of Social Welfare in California sought 75 percent federal subvention for day care of AFDC children to enable mothers to engage in community work and training programs. The author discussed this with representatives of the welfare administration in Washington, D.C., in October 1964, and was advised that day care services were the responsibility of the Children's Bureau and therefore could not be funded with AFDC administrative funds. When the author pointed out that California had only $300,000 from a meagre CWS allocation to use for day care services, while the need would amount to several millions of dollars, he was asked to submit a request in writing to the federal agency.

The Director of the California State Department of Social Welfare, in December 1965 and again in August 1966, wrote the federal agency seeking clarification of the issue, emphasizing that the federal decision was an artificial interpretation, since work training programs in Aid to Families with Dependent Children required full day care services for children. To designate such services as inappropriate for this group, but appropriate to Child Welfare was inconsistent, since day care is definitely an essential service to families as a public social service. SDSW recommended that the Department of Health, Education and Welfare policy be reinterpreted so that day care could be considered appropriate to both Child Welfare and to Aid to Families with Dependent Children.

Despite the apparent legal and regulatory obstacles to funding Day Care Services through public assistance administrative funds, these same federal regulations provided a strong base for arguing that this should be made possible. Under the AFDC provisions, all states were required to "assist in assuring appropriate child care and in relieving multiburdens resulting from employment" when mothers are "working full or part-time with problems in arranging satisfactory care for children or with multiple burdens from employment and homemaking." According to the Federal Handbook Section, the full range of these and all other prescribed services must be available in fact to all families in need of them by July 1, 1967. The SDSW emphasized that were it not for the specific exclusion, the provision of day care could very well be considered as one of the "Complementary Services," more specifically, Special Service for Self-Care and Self-Support, as described in Federal regulations. The provision of day care meets the overall criteria for complementary service in that "it is of unique value in meeting certain needs, usually requires staff in addition to the casework staff for planning, directing, or for providing direct services that are complementary to the services of the case-work staff." Further, it is clearly apparent that Day Care Services are, in fact, often needed to "help the person develop, improve and/or restore capacities for self-care and self-support."

The SDSW letter further noted that the state would be required, by July 1, 1967, to assist in assuring appropriate Day Care Services for all Aid to Families with Dependent Children mothers who would need them in connection with their efforts to become self-supporting, and at the same time, these clients were denied access to what, in many instances, would prove to be only adequate source of funds to carry out the Federal mandate. The letter closed by suggesting that the SDSW could see its proposal as the only solution to providing needed, adequate Day Care Services for families eligible for public social services.

Late in 1966, the Federal Welfare Administration advised the California SDSW that AFDC administrative funds could not be used for purchase of Day Care Service, and strangely, while this negotiation proceeded, California received approval from the federal agency to provide compensatory education to AFDC children. The State Legislature appropriated $4,000,000 for compensatory education for preschool children, thereby gaining 75 percent federal matching funds of $12,000,000 making a total of $16,000,000 for compensatory education for preschool AFDC children. The result of the strange federal fiscal deteminations for California was that mothers were unable to engage in education or training programs because of lack of day care for their children while these same mothers might place their children for part of a day in a compensatory education program which was amply funded through AFDC administistative funds. The compensatory education proved to be a valuable program with relevance to reduction of dependency through preparation of children in poverty for their school experience. The example is not designed to negate the values of an excellent compensatory education program, but rather to illustrate the vagaries and clumsiness of entrenched bureauocracy. The issue of fiscal inadequancy for day care and work-connected expenses was strongly relevant to slowness of growth of the Community Work and Training program in California during the early developmental years.

COMMUNITY WORK AND TRAINING

A California report dated September 1964, on the distribution of recipients in Community Work and Training Programs showed that 3,836 adult recipients were assigned to work training projects; 2,027 in organized group instruction; 248 in Manpower Development Training Act (MDTA) training; 792 in vocational rehabilitation training, and six in apprenticeship programs. In addition, 88 young adults between the ages of 16 and 20 were involved in these activities, 63 in organized group instruction. A subsequent report on community work and training activities for the month of February 1965, showed that the number of cases involved in projects had more than doubled since September 1964. From inventories prepared in January 1965, it was revealed that the number of active work and training projects exceeded 500. By early 1968 the number of projects exceeded 1,000.

Work experience and training projects were located in county, city, and state agencies in the communities and covered a wide variety of occupational assignments. In some counties, projects were initially developed on a "recruitment" basis, i.e., public agencies and organizations were invited and encouraged to establish projects, and clients were assigned as available. At times the response was greater than the supply of recipients, and welfare departments were occasionally seduced into trying to fill these requests regardless of recipient needs. Some counties proceeded differently, developing projects as the need for them arose, and assuring that assignments were sound and specifically related to recipient needs. The use of Federal agencies as work project sponsors was uncertain. Counties knew of facilities which had great potential for use as training and work experience settings, but were unsure of the ground rules in this area, and apparently the Federal agencies which had been tentatively approached were noncommittal or generally uninformed about the Community Work and Training Program and its goals.

Responsibility for assignment and placement of recipients on projects was usually handled by special community work and training staff who also maintained liaison and supervisory relationships with sponsors. Periodic site visits, written reports, and client contacts were utilized as the main supervisorial tools. Each project sponsor utilized its staff resources of supervisors or experienced employees to supervise participant performance. Sometimes trainees were given "lead man" or foreman responsibilities if they demonstrated supervisory capabilities. Foremen and supervisors displayed great interest in the successful performance of participants, and in many instances were serving as "caretakers" by assisting trainees in preparation for examinations to qualify for regular jobs, providing employment leads, and generally lending other supportive help. Supervisors usually had responsibility for timekeeping and progress reports on work performance, and were in close contact with community work and training staff or case-workers to work through problems.

Equipment, work materials, tools, and safety gear were supplied for participants in the same fashion as for regular employees. Some projects did not permit assignees to use power equipment or automotive equipment. Others imposed no such restrictions, in recognition of the fact that knowledge of safety procedures and of responsible handling of expensive equipment was an important aspect of the training process. There was liberal use of badges and other devices to play down the identification of assignees as welfare recipients. This kind of practice apparently had a morale-boosting effect on recipients, particularly those in institutional settings where badges, uniforms, and other paraphernalia somehow imparted status. Training needs such as books, tuition, and watches required by the training facility, as well as special work clothing, uniforms, and the like, were provided by the welfare departments.

All counties had some leaf raking and other types of menial labor. The recipient was assigned to "work out his public assistance grant." In these projects, little effort was made to train, upgrade, or generally improve the skills and morale of the client. The author personally observed large scale work relief practices in the hospitals of Los Angeles County.

Some projects which had been established as work experience and preconditioning assignments had actually developed into work training assignments, and recipients were either hired by the sponsor or referred by them to other employers known to have jobs available in the same or similar line of work.

Physical examinations were not generally routinely given, unless the sponsoring agency had such a requirement, and in such instances, these were usually furnished by the sponsor as for regular employees. A recipient who either appeared or claimed to be ill or disabled was provided with a physical examination.

In some projects, day rooms, lunch rooms, and coffee breaks were available as for regular employees, and if time cards were required of regular employees, they were required of assignees also. In other words, participants were generally treated the same as employees with no special treatment or disadvantages accorded them. In fact, during visits to some projects it was often impossible to distinguish trainees from regular employees unless they were pointed out.

Cooperative Agreements and Working Relationships with Other Agencies

At the state level, formal agreements established working relationships with the State Departments of Education, Employment, and

Vocational Rehabilitation. The agreement with the State Department of Education provided for the purchase of adult educational services for welfare recipients by county welfare departments from local school districts when such services were not otherwise available. Classes were to meet recipient needs for vocational, remedial, and other kinds of education necessary to further preparation for self-support. A joint policy statement by the departments and guide materials developed by the State Department of Social Welfare were made available to facilitate use of these educational resources, including secondary, unified, and junior college districts. Local development of such arrangements proceeded slowly on a state-wide basis. In localities visited, three counties had not been required to pay for classroom instruction established for welfare recipients, but rather the regular average daily attendance formula had been utilized to an almost unlimited extent. One county had to supply classroom facilities but this was the only limitation on the availability of educational resources. In two of the counties where purchase of services was required, development of classes had not progressed as much as hoped for. This was most often due to lack of budgeted funds for this purpose. Two other counties purchased educational services successfully.

The State Department of Employment also entered into an agreement with the State Department of Social Welfare aimed at assuring maximum use of employment services on behalf of welfare recipients at the local level. All counties indicated that relationships with local departments of employment were excellent, and some had become sponsors of projects for recipients. The views concerning the extent and availability of useful services varied, however. Since welfare departments felt that their recipients generally needed a different kind of focus and handling than employment service agencies were geared or able to give, some set up employment referral and development services within the agency as more adequate for their needs. For 30 years, welfare agencies required referral of able-bodied recipients to the Department of Employment for placement, and the department generally could not place the referred recipients because they were not job ready. Some critics believed the department was too employer-oriented. The dilemma was not appropriate employer orientation, but rather that the department was not equipped to serve the welfare recipients who needed education and vocational training before they could become acceptable to any employer. It is sad that the welfare and employment systems engaged in a useless referral process for 30 years before they came to realize they were harming instead of helping discouraged welfare recipients.

The State Department of Social Welfare and local welfare agencies also had long term agreements with the State Department of

Vocational Rehabilitation. Traditionally, relatively few recipients were rehabilitated because they were not "economically feasible." Both the State Department of Employment and the State Department of Rehabilitation served broad population groups. There was a natural tendency to screen out the best candidates for the scarce services available, so hard-core welfare recipients rarely qualified.

The author, as a representative of the California State Department of Social Welfare, requested a meeting with staff from the State Department of Vocational Rehabilitation to discuss the issue, in early 1964. The topic chosen was rehabilitation of Aid to Blind (AB) welfare recipients who were automatically qualified for vocational rehabilitation services because of blindness. The author requested a survey of the blind caseload in the State of California. It was found that 1,500 persons between the ages of 18 and 65 were potentially feasible for training. Vocational rehabilitation was asked to accept these persons for training. The referrals could not be accepted because of limited resources and priority allocations of the resources. The vocational rehabilitation representative explained that there were approximately 100,000 persons in California at that time needing services, and the department could serve 10,000 annually, or only 10 percent of those in need; and was serving 300 blind welfare recipients, 20 percent of those needing services. The representative emphasized that welfare was receiving twice as much service for the blind as the remainder of the general population group received. The author indicated welfare could not settle for anything short of training the entire eligible blind recipient group because of the untenable alternative for the recipients themselves of remaining on welfare in idleness. This impasse was resolved by agreement that a joint project would be established in Alameda County to test employment feasibility of blind recipients and to provide a model for the entire state.

The project served long-term recipients and was designed to determine whether an intensive effort could result in helping an appreciable number of AB recipients to be placed in employment. A coordinated approach was used (not only as between interested agencies, but through a team approach consisting of a rehabilitation counselor, a placement counselor, and the client's social worker). The three-year project terminated March 1968. It was concluded that many blind persons can be helped by low visual acuity aids; that there were virtually no clients who were trained and ready for immediate or direct placement, but rather intensive counseling and training were first required; that a competent placement man can find job openings for blind persons in competitive industry (some 59 such openings were found in the first nine months of the project, but trained clients were not available); and with adequate training and motivation, even hard-core cases could be placed in employment. Of the 244 cases accepted by the project, 46 percent were not found feasible for employment, due chiefly to multihandicaps, even though they were between the ages of 20 and 49. Of the 112 found feasible, 38 percent were placed in employment. It was anticipated that additional numbers of feasible persons would achieve the employment objective. The project experience affirmed the severe nature of the handicaps of blind persons on welfare, yet reinforced the author's conviction that with patience and skilled help many blind persons could find renewed hope of independent living and a more satisfying, meaningful life.

The following examples of the Community Work and Training Program in a few counties will illustrate the nature of local programs in late 1964, about 8 months after the inception of the Community Work and Training Program.

LOS ANGELES COUNTY

In Los Angeles County the county relief work project program developed in 1948 expanded into Community Work and Training on February 1, 1964. From 1948 through 1963, county aid recipients worked over 12 million hours in public agencies for the assistance they received, and most of these hours provided services which taxpayers could not otherwise afford. Prior to February 1, 1964, the Bureau of Public Assistance had 1,833 county welfare recipients assigned to 68 work projects. Since that date, the Community Work and Training Program under federal and state legislation enabled the county to expand its program to approximately 100 projects. In August of 1964, approximately 3,500 welfare recipients were assigned to the Community Work and Training Program. Of this number, 2,600 were recipients under the Aid to Families with Dependent Children Program, while the remaining 900, recipients of County General Relief, were mostly single men and women in the upper age bracket who did not qualify for aid under one of the state programs.

Under the old county relief work project program, the number of those rehabilitated and actually placed in private industry or elsewhere was not large, although the program did experience some success. Although this was attributed by the county to the fact that more than 60 percent of the recipients on projects were over 40 years of age, and many had various illnesses or handicaps, the quality of the program was also relevant.

Some projects which were redesigned to suit the needs of recipients and to meet the requirements of the Los Angeles County Community Work and Training Program are listed as follows:

(a) Los Angeles County Parks and Recreation Department—This project was designed to provide experience for parks and recreation helpers and to provide landscaping experience.

(b) Los Angeles County Road Department—Construction and road repair experience was provided. Also, fork lift operators and light equipment operators were trained.

(c) Los Angeles County Hospital—Project offered a variety of experiences in hospital jobs, including attendants, custodians, laboratory helpers, and animal caretakers.

(d) Los Angeles County Mechanical Department—Garage and service station attendants were trained to help keep the county's fleet of automobiles in shape.

(e) Los Angeles County Probation Department—Recipients were engaged in the repair of damaged toys for use by needy children.

Some new projects included the following:

(a) Los Angeles County Flood Control District—Junior engineering aids and draftsmen were trained by this department to help highly qualified recipients return to well-paid permanent jobs.

(b) Los Angeles County Bureau of Resources and Collections—Typist clerks were trained.

(c) Los Angeles County Bureau of Public Assistance—Initiated its own project to help train typist clerks and key punch operators in its accounting and processing functions.

(d) Maclaren Hall (Los Angeles County Probation Department)—Work training in PBX operation, power machine operation, and food service.

New approaches were attempted in training clients to perform work for public agencies, but these were not client-oriented or innovative. In one instance, a new structure was built entirely by work project recipients to increase the facilities at one of the county hospitals. In another instance, a crash program was developed to clean county hospitals, which resulted in better looking, more sanitary facilities for hospital patients throughout the county, although training benefits for welfare recipients were questionable. The Community Work and Training Program inspired some new approaches in Los Angeles County during the first year of operation, but the pervasiveness of old work relief concepts persisted in most of the projects serving the bulk of the assignees.

Client Characteristics—In Los Angeles County, 60 percent of the AFDC-U applicants were unemployed for three months or longer; 40 percent unemployed six months or more. It was a relatively young group of persons with two-thirds of the applicants between the ages of 21 and 39, and more than one-half of these in the 30-39 age group had physical ailments which are important in employment consideration, but not severe enough to block consideration for aid under the AFDC employable provision of the law.

CITY AND COUNTY OF SAN FRANCISCO

Unlike many counties in California, the city and county of San Francisco did not operate work-relief projects following the termination of those operated by the WPA (Works Progress Administration) during the depression years of the 1930's. With the rapid expansion of shipyards and other war industries in San Francisco immediately prior to and during World War II, the number of employable persons receiving public assistance was virtually reduced to zero. (There were 6,025 families or individuals receiving General Relief in San Francisco in July, 1941, of whom 4,000 were determined by medical examination to be unemployable. By July, 1946, the number of cases had been reduced to 970 because of war-time employment.) After the end of the Korean War, however, employment again became more difficult to obtain and the Public Welfare Department in 1952 established an Employment Division, which was later called a Vocational Services Division. This division started with 2 or 3 social workers working as vocational counselors under part-time supervision. As of July, 1963, full time supervision was provided for the division with a staff of four vocational counselors, and by late spring of 1964 the staff was increased to six.

The work of the division consisted of vocational counseling and guidance, referral of employable recipients to educational and vocational training courses, stimulating and co-sponsoring such courses, obtaining aptitude and achievement tests from San Francisco schools and the State Department of Employment, and referring well-qualified recipients to the Department of Employment for special interviews and assistance in job recruitment and job referral. In recent years, approximately 700 employable persons were registered with the San Francisco Employment Division at any one time—mostly employable mothers in AFDC families. An average of about 10 percent of these secured employment each month.

Anticipating the extension February 1, 1964, of the AFDC program to children of unemployed fathers in the home, the Public Welfare Commission applied in 1963 to the State Department of Social Welfare for County Demonstratiton Project funds to purchase consultative services in planning and developing a full-scale and broadly based vocational services program in San Francisco. The state approved this grant of funds late in January, 1964. In March and April, 1964, the San Francisco Public Welfare Commission adopted a Community Work and Training Plan for San Francisco and appointed a Community Work and Training Program Advisory Committee to the Public Welfare Commission. A clerical work-training project was started in the Public Welfare Department in August, 1964, one in the San Francisco office of the State

Department of Social Welfare in September, and two in the San Francisco Office of the State Department of Mental Hygiene and the Social Security Administration of the Federal Department of Health, Education, and Welfare. In September, a training course for orderlies was started at Laguna Honda Hospital by the Adult and Vocational Education Division of the San Francisco Unified School District, and similar training courses began in October for hotel, motel and hospital maids. Six work-training projects at the San Francisco Library were also established to provide work training for 48 to 50 persons.

During the fiscal year 1963-64, a total of 901 employable recipients of public assistance secured employment with help from the Vocational Services Division. Of these, 522 were for full-time work and 379 for part-time work, with 180 placed through the California Department of Employment, 379 by the Welfare Department's Vocational Services Division, 284 finding their own jobs, and the balance placed through special training courses.

During the 1963-64 fiscal year, 174 persons participated in vocational and educational courses. This included a total of 34 separate courses with 125 persons receiving vocational training under MDTA, 39 persons enrolled in remedial or regular educational or vocational training courses under the Adult and Vocational Education Division of the San Francisco School Department, and 10 persons attending other schools or agencies for instruction. Physically and mentally handicapped individuals needing specialized guidance and training were referred to the Division of Vocational Rehabilitation of the State Department of Rehabilitation. A total of 236 recipients of public assistance received the services of this division during the year. Of these, 121 were AFDC recipients, 68 received Aid to Totally Disabled, 46 received Aid to the Blind, and 1 received Old Age Security.

With the start of the AFDC-U program in February 1964, the number of employable recipients of assistance registered with the San Francisco Vocational Services Division increased to 1,269. In the spring of 1964, special County Demonstration Project funds were requested by the San Francisco Public Welfare Commission from the State Department of Social Welfare for expansion of operations of the Vocational Services Division for the next three years by doubling the number of vocational counselors and allowing for a vocational psychologist and additional clerical and supervisory personnel. The state approved this expanded project as of October 1, 1964.

While San Francisco did not have the handicap of Los Angeles in overcoming out-moded work relief concepts it had problems of another kind. San Francisco, strangely, was not motivated to develop in its own right a viable community work and training program. It required an initial and supplemental 100 percent money grant from SDSW to initiate its program. The early growth and development of the community work and training program in San Francisco was less than inspiring.

SANTA CLARA COUNTY

The Santa Clara County Welfare Department, through its Reemployment Bureau, had operated a progressive program of self-support planning with assistance recipients since 1956. Legislation requiring Community Work and Training programs on February 1, 1964, posed no problem because of the long experience in operating an almost identical program. The department emphasized rehabilitation in administering public assistance, and its Reemployment Bureau provided specialized help to recipients to become self-supporting. The Bureau had developed methods of identifying people's vocational needs, as well as services to meet these needs, so that recipients became employable through vocational counseling, testing, on-the-job training, work assignment, vocational training, and job placement. Social workers focused on employment possibilities in working with applicants and recipients, many of whom were enabled to obtain jobs through counseling and other social services and to resolve problems that prevented self-support. Reemployment Bureau staff regularly advised applicants and recipients, consulted with social workers, and placed recipients in training programs and in jobs.

During the fiscal year 1963-64 the Reemployment Bureau conducted 3,915 interviews with applicants and recipients. In 3,883 cases, it was consulted about the development of training or employment opportunities for applicants or recipients. It assigned 1,587 people to job-focused activities. Of these, 327 persons went into on-the-job training; 419 undertook work assignments to maintain or increase their skills and as credit against their aid payments; and 841 were engaged in learning skills necessary for employment through formal group training. During this time, the department discontinued 1,201 public assistance payments because recipients or members of their families obtained employment. In a large number of other cases, the amount of the monthly aid payments was reduced because of part-time work. The Reemployment Bureau influenced these results directly through its placement of recipients in specific job openings and indirectly, to a significant degree, through its employment referrals, its vocational counseling and guidance, and the opportunities it created for recipients to learn or to maintain employment skills. The Bureau referred 1,698 people for possible employment and placed 833 of them directly in job openings.

The Santa Clara experience showed that people who received aid responded to the encouragement and support of the reemployment interviewer-social worker team. Most accepted early the opportunity to equip themselves for self-support and some mobilized themselves with amazing speed to overcome their handicaps and difficulties and take their places in the labor market. In 1964, Santa Clara County examined a sample of parent recipients of Aid to Families with Dependent Children, who were referred to the services of the Remployment Bureau. In one-parent families, nearly 66 percent of the mothers were younger than 30, and almost 80 percent had not completed high school. Almost 33 percent had no work experience at all; less than 10 percent had commercial or industrial experience; and others had some experience in farm labor, canneries, in-service industry, or as domestics. The number of children in these families ranged from one to eight—an average per one-parent family of two and one-half. In two-parent families, almost 60 percent of the fathers were younger than 40, and 75 percent had not completed high school. Almost 50 percent had some experience in industry, construction work, or as truck drivers; slightly more than 25 percent had been employed in service, clerical, or semi-professional jobs; 18 percent had worked as farm laborers; and 6 percent had experience in part-time work. The number of children in these families ranged from one to ten—an average per two-parent family of four.

The program of Santa Clara County and the earlier described program of San Mateo County were the most extensive and sophisticated welfare vocational service programs in California, and probably in the nation as a whole. These programs had started in the mid-1950's and had provided leadership for later development of state and national programs.

SAN BERNARDINO COUNTY

Upon enactment of the 1962 Social Security amendments, and implementation by the State Department of Social Welfare, the San Bernardino County Welfare Department established a Community Work Training Program, February 1, 1964. Conferences were held with the County Administrative Officer and the heads of several departments, such as the County Forestry Department, County Highway Department, Department of Public Works, Aviation Department, and County Hospital, for the purpose of establishing work training projects throughout the county. This group served as a committee to advise the welfare director on the development of programs that would help promote good work habits, attitudes, and general rehabilitation of welfare applicants and recipients. Work projects were designed to accomplish one or more of the following:

(1) Develop new or improved skills through the planned coordination of work experience, training, and instructions.

(2) Improve, or conserve existing skills, and/or

(3) Pre-condition persons who did not have a recent employment history, had been unable to adjust to private employment, or lacked

motivation for work or the maintenance of good work skills and habits.

As a result of these conferences, 12 work projects were established in various state, county and city agencies. A separate unit of 7 social workers was set up within the welfare department and trained to carry out the specialized job of working very closely with the recipient group. Caseloads were reduced to allow for at least bimonthly contacts with the unemployed fathers, and recipients were assigned to work a maximum of 32 hours per week to give them sufficient time for job hunting. The work project sponsoring agencies expressed uniform satisfaction with the program and felt, in general, that the recipients were doing a good job, although absenteeism, especially on the less challenging work projects (more menial routine) proved to be a serious problem.

The county placed emphasis on organized group instruction as a means through which remedial and/or vocational education was provided, enabling selected recipients to overcome educational deficiencies. In order to accomplish this, immediate contacts were made with adult education, Valley College Extension, California State Employment Office, Manpower Development, vocational rehabilitation services, and other related community services. By October, 1964, the county had expanded the Community Work Training Program to a total of 85 work training projects, representing 18 sponsoring agencies. The referral and placement procedure was set up in such a way that the social worker acquainted with the overall family circumstances retained the key role of responsibility. Trainees who were not performing satisfactorily were removed from the program for reassignment, further counseling, employment placement, or discontinuance.

The San Bernardino county program was generally reflective of slow development of modest, relatively unsophisticated vocational services characterizing programs in a large number of California counties. Whatever the agricultural valley counties like San Bernardino accomplished, it was always within the framework of historic practices respecting agricultural needs for farm labor. The community work and training programs were inevitably developed in such a manner that they did not interfere with recruitment of welfare recipients for farm labor.

FRESNO COUNTY

Fresno County comprises a large and wealthy agricultural area where the farm products and its climatic conditions require a peak labor force during certain periods of the year and a minimum need for such labor at other periods. Farm workers comprise the largest single labor force and the bulk of this labor force is unemployed approximately six months in a calendar year. Unemployed families who are recipients of AFDC-U in Fresno County are the largest in the State of California, with an average of seven children per family. In 1960, the United States Census report indicated that Fresno County residents were comparatively low in educational achievement, with only 40 percent of all of the residents 25 years of age and older high school graduates, and adult welfare recipients with much lower levels of education than among the general county population.

In November 1961, the Fresno County Board of Supervisors authorized the welfare department to conduct a retraining and re-employment project for mothers of dependent children. As a part of the project the Board authorized the employment of a research specialist from Fresno State College to evaluate results. The project was initiated in April 1962 with 400 mothers as participants, and the random selection of 200 assigned to a project group, the other 200 to a control group. The project group was placed in relatively small caseloads, 45 per social worker, and the control group was scattered through a number of larger caseloads. The identities of the project group were known to the workers and other staff members. The names of the control group were known only to the project evaluator and the selection screening committee.

The project continued from April 1962 to June 1964. The evaluation pointed to several interesting conclusions. Fifty of the participants obtained gainful employment and became fully or partially self-supporting. Workers assigned to small caseloads were able to work more effectively with recipients in the areas of training and employment than those who were assigned to larger caseloads and whose workers did not know the identity of the control cases in their caseloads. Mothers with young children were less successful in training and employment than were mothers of older children. Mature women were more successful than young women and young mothers of illegitimate children were least successful of all. Some social workers, even where caseloads were small and equal in number, achieved considerably better results than others. The most meaningful and important conclusion, however, was that the biggest single bar to the employment of mothers of dependent children in Fresno County was lack of formal education. Although this was a select group from a caseload of approximately 5,000 cases, the average educational level of the 400 women was completion of tenth grade.

The findings from the evaluation of the project formed the basis for development of an intensive educational and training program. Shortly after the results of the project were apparent, the department surveyed the total adult welfare recipient population in Fresno County as to educational achievement. This survey revealed that 23 percent of the adult recipients had not completed the fourth grade, 48 percent had not completed the eighth grade, 68 percent had not completed the tenth grade; and only 5.4 percent had completed high school. The characteristic most common to all welfare recipients in Fresno County was lack of formal education. At that time, a number of recipients attended night school, and although results were generally satisfactory, completion of high school by night school attendance was a slow process.

At a joint meeting of the administrative staffs of the welfare department and the Fresno City Schools it was agreed that a day school for adult welfare recipients would be established, the Adult Education Department of the Fresno City Schools would employ the teachers and be responsible for administration of the school, and the Welfare Department would provide the physical facilities. An abandoned hospital building on welfare department grounds was cleaned and repaired by unemployed welfare recipients. The Adult School obtained discarded furniture and books and opened on January 6, 1964, with three teachers and 60 students. In March 1968, there were 12 teachers and 560 students. Most of the classes prepare recipients for graduation from high school, and some upper level elementary classes are conducted in preparation for high school entrance. Since June 1964, 102 mothers of dependent children have been awarded high school diplomas, and 55 have completed high school entrance requirements. Of the 102 graduates, 60 are employed and self-supporting, 10 are engaged in on-the-job training, 12 are enrolled in college and business schools, 8 have married, and 12 have moved from Fresno County. The Fresno City Schools organized a preschool nursery staffed with two full-time employees aided by mothers on a voluntary rotating basis for 60 children whose mothers were attending the Adult School. Teachers were paid from State Education funds based on average daily attendance of students. Nursery staff salaries were paid from State education funds for preschool education. The financing of the Adult School and the nursery which featured the use of existing facilities and resources, involved relatively small sums of welfare money.

The following is an example of a former recipient of aid who graduated from the Fresno school and is now employed:

Sally was the sixth child in a large farm labor family. At age 16 she left school and married. Two children were born to this union and shortly thereafter her husband deserted. She came to the Welfare Department in February 1961 to apply for aid. Her teeth were badly decayed and she had a back ailment. She tried to obtain employment but her lack of education and experience were insurmountable barriers. She attempted to attend night school but was unable to arrange child care during the evening hours. Sally's social worker encouraged her to enroll in the Adult School for welfare recipients from which she was graduated in June 1964. After graduation she was placed in on-the-job training and was assigned to the Welfare Department. In the beginning, her attendance was irregular and she failed to notify the department when she was going to be absent, but after several months of training and counseling by a clerical supervisor, her attendance improved and her work became neat and accurate. Her teeth were repaired with welfare medical care funds and her general health and appearance improved. In February 1965 she passed a civil service test for junior typist clerk and was employed by Fresno County, beginning at a salary of $365 per month.

It is obvious that not all of those enrolled in this school will complete their high school education and become self-supporting. But there are other discernible and important by-products of their adult school attendance, such as better individual grooming, standards of housekeeping, and child care; and more participation in community and governmental activities such as registering and voting for the first time. The most important by-product was the effect upon the children of mothers attending the school. Some of these children re-entered school after dropping out and made marked improvement in scholastic achievement. A sixth grade teacher in a local public school told of a boy in her class who was above average in intelligence but at the bottom of the class in achievement. The teacher had utilized all her resources and skills but the boy had failed to respond. At a given point the boy began a marked improvement which continued until he assumed his proper position among the best achievers in the class. The teacher was puzzled and approached the boy and said, "I am the same teacher, you are the same boy, this is the same classroom. You were failing and now you are among the leaders in the class, what happened?" The boy replied, "That's easy to explain. My Mom is going to the Welfare School and I'm helping her with her homework."

Enrollment of an adult in literacy classes does not come easily or on a strictly voluntary basis. There is a great deal of self-consciousness and a feeling of shame attached to the inability of a 50-year old man to sign his name except with an X. Enrollment and attendance at literacy classes for those unable to read or write was a condition of aid in Fresno County. Some resistance to the initial attendance was experienced, but once this barrier had been hurdled there was enthusiastic participation by the overwhelming majority. A more constructive approach to resistance to attendance in adult classes would have included individual group and individual counselling.

Experience with attempts to place in employment recipients who have completed formalized education has demonstrated the need for on-the-job training. As a part of the overall education and training program, the welfare department placed recipients in its own offices and in other public offices in Fresno County. The department successfully trained and placed in employment all classes of clerical personnel, key punch operators, mechanics, school custodians, golf course groundsmen, switchboard operators, and nurses aides. On-the-job training included instruction in proper grooming and demeanor on the job and counseling and instruction by supervisory personnel. From 40 to 70 recipient trainees were engaged in on-the-job training at any given time. Work projects involving unskilled activities of the brush-cutting type were participated in by temporarily unemployed agricultural workers, who returned to full-time work on farms and ranches in the Spring. Some 400 to 500 men were engaged during winter months in work relief jobs on public parks and highways. Some unemployed men were assigned to literacy classes, which softened somewhat the work relief aspects of this portion of the Fresno program, although does not camouflage the intent of the work relief system to reserve a labor supply for farmers.

In March 1967, at the request of the Welfare Director, the Fresno County Board of Supervisors authorized the establishment of a scholarship fund for welfare recipients who were enrolled in college. In the first year of its operation, more than $1,900 had been contributed and pledged by welfare department employees, clubs, organizations, and individuals. Six graduates of the Adult Day School were awarded scholarships and enrolled in Fresno State College and Fresno City College. Scholarship funds included, books, fees, and tuition, with the welfare grant providing maintenance. Additional scholarships will be awarded each year.

The adult education program in Fresno County became the most extensive and sophisticated program of its kind in California in spite of some of its objectionable features. This was an unusual accomplishment for a county which otherwise maintained the most archaic, conservative, and punitive approaches to welfare administration.

BUTTE COUNTY

The Butte County Counsel took issue with the SDSW rule on work connected expenses. He wrote in May 1967 to the California Supervisors Association asking their help on the matter. He stated that: "The part that has caused concern is under Section C-204.70 B 1, subsection b, entitled 'Persons engaged in education or rehabilitation.' The explanation of the heading is that the cost of items of service which cannot be arranged for through the county welfare department or other agency in the community is to be allowed in the budget as follows. B under this section reads: 'The cost of food, clothing and personal incidentals. For persons working on a work training project or engaged in a full time course of organized instruction, the $25.00 standard allowance for employed persons shall be allowed for these costs.' It is the position of the county, pursuant to Sections 11301 and 11305, that if the parent does not respond to a notice to work on a county project, there will be no welfare check forthcoming. The particular circumstances with which we are concerned is the interpretation of the above quoted section as to the payment of the $25.00 allowance. The interpretation this office has placed on it is that after investigation by the welfare director or welfare worker assigned to the case, they find there is a *need* for additional food, or clothing, or additional personal incidentals to enable the person to work, then he will be allowed additional funds up to a maximum of a $25.00 allowance."

The SDSW emphasized in discussions with Butte County that code sections and regulations all spell out that a Community Work and Training Program should be basically a training program aimed at developing skills which help recipients better compete in the labor market. The emphasis throughout is on training, not work for the sake of work. Plans for Community Work and Training are to be made on an individual basis to fit the needs of a particular recipient and all decisions regarding assignments must be based on a total study of the individual and family. A recipient cannot be placed on a work experience or training program unless work connected expenses are provided. SDSW advised the county that against these standards and criteria Butte County's Work and Training Program was far short of meeting standards and needs of people:

1. The lack of a working relationship and coordination between the Community Work Training Coordinator and the social workers. Social workers were referring clients directly to work experience projects which had been set up by the coordinator but without any relationship to the cordinator's efforts and without even providing him with information as to their activities.

2. Case records did not indicate what was happening to the client with whom the worker discussed work or training. In some instances recipients who were able bodied men received assistance for over a year without any apparent attempts to develop a plan for participation in a Work Training Project or to interest the recipient in upgrading his skills.

3. In many situations there was no way of telling from the records whether or not a client was assigned or participating in a Community Work and Training project.

4. There was no indication of the number of hours a recipient was expected to work or the rate of credit which he would receive against his grant.

5. Work connected expenses in connection with Community Work and Training Projects were not fully met. In one particular

case where a young woman was in training and received a contribution from her former husband, not all of her needs were met even though they could have been met in the AFDC grant at minimal county cost.

6. The Community Work and Training Program in Butte County did not encourage recipients to participate and recipients had been allowed to drift with respect to work and training, then suddenly in January, 1967, all AFDC-U recipients were required without preparation to report to public works projects which appeared to have had little or no training components but were purely work for the sake of work with the overtone of punishment. This sudden reversal appeared to have had a very poor effect on morale of recipients. In general, the Community Work and Training Program in Butte County needed to be set up on a coordinated, consistent basis. The emphasis should have been on training and upgrading levels of marketable skills of recipients and not to be used for punishment or for providing the community with free labor. Case records in Butte County, indicated clearly that the county did not meet the extra expenses of the Community Work and Training assignments except when they were made under the maximum participating base at little county cost. Since Butte County did not meet the regulations in regard to covering extra work connected costs in Community Work and Training assignments, the refusal of an assignment by a recipient should not have affected his eligibility for AFDC. The refusal could not be considered a basis for discontinuance of aid unless the extra costs were met. However, the Butte County Counsel, through delaying actions, avoided compliance with SDSW rules to September 1, 1968, the time when the new Work Incentive (WIN) program became effective.

The extent to which a county would go to maintain its regressive practices and the power used by the Board of Supervisors and the County Counsel in Butte County to offset progressive program development is surprising. While the County Counsel's action is surprising, it is well known that the legal profession through County Counsels and District Attorneys[2] support regressive practices against poor people. Since the legal profession has a strange way of rationalizing such practice and staying within legal bounds, questions of social justice and equity remain unresolved; but hope lies in counter forces such as later described defense of the poor by CRLA.

SUTTER COUNTY

Sutter County, a small, rural county located in the middle of the Sacramento Valley, contains some of the most fertile and productive land in the state. The political attitudes of the peope are basically conservative. Sutter County was one of the few counties that favored Barry Goldwater in the 1964 Presidential election and Ronald Reagan swept the county in the 1966 gubernatorial election.

The population of the county is small, estimated in 1965 at 39,000 people. The people have less formal education than those in the rest of the state, with 11.2 the median number of school years completed as compared to 12.1 statewide.

Sutter County ranks high in the area of poverty and deprivation compared to the rest of the state. Approximately 30 percent of the families residing in Sutter County have incomes falling below the $4,000 or "poverty" level. The statewide average is 21.4 percent. Another 24 percent have incomes at the deprivation level of $4,000 to $6,000 per year. Ethnic minority group families are relatively more poverty stricken, with 78.2 percent falling below the deprivation level and 58.4 percent below the poverty level. Unemployment is high, in the Yuba City-Marysville labor market area ranging from 5.1 percent to 13.8 percent for a 10.4 percent average, while the state average is 5.9 percent.

On June 1, 1965, the Sutter County Economic Opportunity Act Advisory Committee submitted its report on the need of federal assistance under the Economic Activity Act of 1964 to the Board of Supervisors. The Committee reported that federal assistance was unnecessary, that there was no poverty in Sutter County, or at least, not serious enough to warrant correction—shades of the Hoover Administration!

Sutter County Supervisors responded to SDSW regulations on Community Work and Training by appointing an Advisory Committee on Welfare. The Committee recommended the appointment of a staff person to establish a Community Work and Training Program in Sutter County. A program was developed consisting of employment development for trainees through formal education and vocational training plus work projects. Out of 84 work projects developed by the county, only 18 could fit any category of skilled training. Classifications included clerk typist (6 positions), librarian (2), data processing (1), stenographer (1), orderly (1), cook (1), fireman (3), county printer (1), and janitor (3). The landscaping, maintenance, and other specialized training assignments did not offer any skilled training. The men training at Richland Housing Center were assigned to projects labeled as painting (hand and machine), electrical, plumbing, woodworking, tree surgery, and the like. The director of the government housing center stated that the men do general tasks, accompany the regular maintenance men around and assist them in changing screens, installing new wall plugs, raking leaves, pruning trees, and filling lawn mower gas tanks. There was no skilled training involved in these menial tasks. Fairground projects were the same, with the "trainees" raking leaves, helping mow lawns, sweeping, and changing sprinkler pipes.

Yuba College is a resource to the welfare department in Sutter County. Some men take welding and other vocational courses there, but this training is limited to a few recipients because they must compete with the regular students who have an educational advantage. Yuba College also provides a licensed vocational nursing program which is used to train AFDC mothers.

Generally, the Sutter County program did not meet the requirements of the SDSW, and this was typical of a number of California counties. The failure to provide meaningful work experience and the failure, in general, to promote an effective program resulted in several hearings with the SDSW. In one such hearing, the county was reprimanded for misplacing a recipient on a project. In this case, a woman was denied AFDC and her husband was referred to an inappropriate work training project, a menial assignment to the Live Oak, Public Works Project. The hearing comments included the following:

"It cannot be said that the training project to which the claimant's husband was referred met the requirements of the Bulletin (636) that such projects provide training for the participants. Nor can it be said that the project to which he was assigned . . . provided related vocational instruction or adult education to increase his employment opportunities. The project to which the claimant's husband was referred did keep him busy while he was out of work. The duties thereunder were of a menial type which did not teach him anything new . . . In short then, the project to which the claimant was referred was inappropriate to his circumstances because it contained no training or educational component. The county, therefore, failed to meet its administrative responsibilities to the claimant and his rights were thereby abridged." In another hearing an AFDC-U recipient was assigned to a project for four days in April and eight days in May 1967. The county contended that even though there may not have been a training component, the assignment was legitimate because it served a useful public purpose. The Hearing Officer declared that, "Such interpretaion is in conflict with the express provisions of Department Bulletin 636. In view of these requirements, it is found that, since the projects to which the claimant was referred did not contain a training component, the referral was inappropriate and not in accord with the provisions of Department Bulletin 636."

There was evidence that recipients sometimes worked in projects which displaced regular employees. The fairground project had more training openings in the summer, especially in the months immediately preceding and after the fair when more training opportunities existed because more needed to be accomplished. Whether this could be considered displacement of regular employees is questionable. More substantial evidence of displacement of regular employees occurred in Live Oak, California, where the Director of Public Works testified that the work training was successful and beneficial to both the trainee and the city because otherwise, "the city would have to hire men to do some of the work in the busy season if it wasn't for the trainees." If this view is correct, this project was in conflict with the law, as stated in the Welfare and Institutions Code: "work projects . . . shall . . . not result either in displacement of regular workers or in the performance of work that would otherwise be performed by employees."

Sutter County has gained the reputation of being the most regressive, most restrictive county, the one with the least human compassion of all the counties in California. This is a record difficult to achieve in a state with many backward counties operating programs based on the attittudes and principles inherent in the 1601 English Poor Law. In such counties, Community Work and Training Program envisioned by the author would fall far short of expectations for years to come, given the continuation of a county administered, state supervised welfare program. In spite of this discouraging prediction, the SDSW continually sought methods of upgrading service in such counties, and the author had the privilege of administering a project program in the SDSW which sought improvement in county services.

THE PROJECT METHOD—A MEANS OF PROGRAM IMPROVEMENT

In California, projects have become an important method of developing vocational services. The Project Program of the State Department of Social Welfare was an outgrowth of legislation enacted by the 1961 Legislature in accordance with recommendation of interim committees of each house. Two separate project statutes were passed, one providing for the promotion of local community activities in behalf of older persons, and the other directed toward improvement in the local administration of public welfare. Prior to these two important enactments of California law, the State Department of Social Welfare had engaged in a limited way in special demonstration projects in the child welfare field.

The enactment of Public Law 87-534, known as the 1962 Public Welfare Amendments to the Social Security Act, added an important means of testing and developing public welfare methods to the project program. Through project funds, local public welfare departments were encouraged to try new and novel methods and procedures designed to improve their capability to meet the problems presented by families and individuals coming to them for help. A group of projects were developed which enabled 16 county welfare departments to provide specialized services for applicants and recipients of public assistance with some potential for employment. Three of these projects provided specialized services to assist unemployed youth and mentally impaired adolescents and adults in securing training or employment. In 13 additional projects, a variety of methods were used to assist recipients to develop vocational goals, determine auxiliary services necessary to implement vocational plans, and provide for each person vocational evaluation, counseling, training, supervised work experience, or job placement.

The project program became an important method of introducing vocational services in Welfare departments. The process was not without difficulty, however. Some counties developed their mandated Community Work and Training Program only within the limits of the project as described earlier in reference to San Francisco. In Sacramento County, the Community Work and Training Program was initiated through use of the State 100 percent funded project program. Later, when Federal Title V, Economic Opportunity Act project money became available, it was with great difficulty that the SDSW was able to persuade the County to assume local responsibility for the SDSW project in order to qualify for a Title V funded greatly expanded vocational services program.

The Community Work and Training Program in California cannot be fully comprehended without some awareness of the "farm labor problems." Newspapers and other mass communication media have given exceptional coverage to the problems and issues related to the labor force needs of the agricultural industry in California since the termination of the bracero program under which Mexican labor was imported to perform farm labor.

At least two points of view have directly or indirectly affected the unemployed welfare recipient. The first of these, the view most often expressed by domestic farm worker organizations and organized labor, is that the domestic labor force would be adequate in supply and skill to meet farm labor needs providing the agricultural industry came up to standard in terms of working conditions, salaries, and protections. The second, or industry point of view is that the recurring need for farm labor far exceeds domestic resources, and therefore importation of foreign labor is essential; that domestic labor is either generally unskilled or disinterested in farm labor; and that any who has the grit and determination can make an adequate living at farm labor employment. There are other points which come into play in these opposing views, so that it is difficult to unravel all the threads. One important result, however, has been that the Community Work and Training Program and, accordingly, some recipients, became entangled in the problem.

Many counties in California have some proportion of agriculture in their geographic area, and in some of these counties, "agri-business" is the main force in the economy. Welfare departments, caught between opposing points of view, were involved in recruitment of farm labor by referral of potential employees from the unemployed on welfare rolls. If large numbers were not immediately forthcoming, the accusation was made that welfare departments were withholding employable persons from bona fide employment offers. This occurred despite the fact revealed in unofficial studies that many unemployed AFDC recipients were not fully employable. At the same time, if recipients were referred, often they were not hired or were dismissed after less than a week of work, and some counties developed the practice of discontinuing aid as soon as an individual was referred, on the basis that jobs were available.

Several instances were reported where large numbers of farm laborers were requested, recipients were pulled off work-training or work-experience assignments to meet the demand, and the farmers who had requested perhaps as many as 500 employees would show up with one truck which might hold 50, and select 10 or less of the several hundred who had reported for hiring. This showed that there had been no intention of hiring the numbers requested, and it was both frustrating and demoralizing to recipients. Staff, too, were unhappy over these incidents, but felt in no position to take a stand or refuse to continue in this fashion. Sacramento County had a body of citizens, prominent in business and agriculture, who serve without pay as an Advisory Commission on welfare to the Board of Supervisors. In the month of April 1964, the Advisory Commission, recognizing that farm labor was open between April and October, questioned the fact that there were farm jobs available while able-bodied men were being placed on work projects. The Commission recommended forcing able-bodied men into farm labor by deducting their anticipated income in advance, and the welfare director adopted this policy. This action was later ruled illegal by the State Department of Social Welfare.

The preceding summary of a sampling of implementation of the Community Work and Training Program in California reveals modest progress. The county heritage of work relief practices impeded sophisticated movement in many counties, while a few others made significant advances. The scientific approaches envisioned by the author at the advent of the program did not characterize early county developments, yet incipient elements of program development offered real hope in some counties. In other counties, the possibility of overcoming traditional oppressive practices seemed hopeless. Some of the backward counties were urban, more were agricultural, and some which had become urban had never overcome their earlier rural attitudes and practices. In preparation for a substantive discussion of the farm labor-welfare issue Chapter 7 is designed to provide perspective on the exploitation of the California farm worker and attempts to forestall such exploitation.

REFERENCES

1. Wickenden, Elizabeth and Bell, Winifred: Time for a Change. Public Welfare, New York, University Publications, 1961.
2. Simmons, Harold E.: Protective Services for Children: A Public Social Welfare Responsibility. Sacramento, General Welfare Publications, 1968.

CHAPTER 6

WORK FOR AFDC MOTHERS

THE NUMBER OF PERSONS receiving public assistance in the United States in January 1968 totaled more than 9 million. AFDC accounted for 60 percent or 5,401,000 of these persons on aid, including 1,326,000 families and 4,075,000 children. Almost 30 percent of the AFDC recipients were in California or New York, 790,000 and 813,-000 respectively. Through its official sanctioning of aid payments which are indaquate to the stated objectives of the program, AFDC has perpetuated abject poverty and deprivation more than any other element in American life. In Mississippi, a child receives an average of $8.40 per month while an aged person receives $38.45, more than 4 times as much. In fact, the aged person in Mississippi receives an average of $3.55 more per month than the entire AFDC family consisting of over 4 persons. In the affluent state of California, where 14.5 percent of all the AFDC recipients live, the child receives an average of $45.70 as compared to a $104.95 monthly average for the aged person. The subpoverty level of grants to the aged further accentuates the starvation grants provided children. In spite of the incredibly meagre grants to mothers and children, middle-class criticism of the AFDC program is based on misguided notions of its generosity and on the belief that mothers have more children solely to qualify for additional aid! The following table shows these average grants in relation to the type of aid.

AVERAGE MONTHLY AID PAYMENT TO RECIPIENTS BY CATEGORY OF AID IN SELECTED STATES

State	AFDC Recipients Family	AFDC Recipients Individual	Aged	Disabled
Mississippi	$ 34.90	$ 8.40	$ 38.45	$ 45.70
California	180.90	45.70	104.95	119.40
New York	242.50	60.75	92.15	101.55
Alabama	64.35	15.50	63.05	49.90

The federal-state-county fiscal alliance, in funding the public assistance program, has developed methods for making a major contribution to poverty in the United States. AFDC mothers have been seeking a way out of this entrapment. The abject poverty to which AFDC families are subjected is accompanied by an even lower social outcast status than in any other public assistance category. A federally supported research project revealed, March 1968, that 70 percent of all the mothers on AFDC in New York preferred work instead of receiving AFDC payments. The typical public welfare worker disagrees with the survey, persisting in the belief that mothers prefer to remain home with their children.

The employment of women was a major public issue during the decades prior to and following the turn of the century. Strong public aversion toward employment of women outside the home was based on a variety of reasons. The feminine role was viewed in traditional terms as that of mother and guardian of the home. The female qualities peculiarly adapted to homemaking and child care were believed to be inadequate for the work requirements involving energy, daring, intelligence, and other rugged attributes reserved for men. Not only were traditional concepts of the feminine role incompatible with the idea of women at work, women were also considered downright inferior in intelligence, endurance, and aggressiveness in comparison to men. Since women were solely the caretakers of children, the myth prevailed that the working woman's children were bound to be neglected and delinquent. This myth persists today in spite of research evidence to the contrary. In addition, women at work were a threat to men. Each depression brought complaints that women were taking jobs that belonged to men, that the employment of women tended to lower wages for men, and that single women who lived at home worked only for pin money.

Great concern was expressed by many Americans in 1890 because 4 million women were in the labor force. Today women comprise one-third of our entire labor force. In relation to the total labor force in other countries, the proportion of workingwomen varies widely from 6 percent in Pakistan to 45 percent in Russia to almost 50 percent in Thailand. Low participation rates in Brazil, Egypt, Mexico, and Pakistan reflect cultural patterns which tend to discourage women from engaging in economic activity. Although patterns become modified as countries move from agricultural to industrial economies, as in the United States, such change alone cannot account for increased numbers of women at work. A variety of influences—labor saving devices in the home, emancipation of women as independent persons, and educational opportunities, among others—affect the situation.

Over a decade ago, in a report on the employment of women and its impact upon children, Katherine Oettinger[1] acknowledged the irreversibility of trends in the womanpower revolution, and in view of the increased number of workingwomen, emphasized the importance of evaluating the impact of the industrial revolution on the welfare of their children. Although stating that working mothers with children under six and particularly those with children under three were less able to fulfill their children's needs during these first six crucial years, she agreed that it was possible but very difficult to provide adequate substitute care for them. She emphasized the importance of allowing the mother to make a choice in the matter, rather than forcing her, by public welfare rules, to work if she preferred to remain at home with her children. She believed such rules were shortsighted because long-range economic gain might accrue from the psychological advantages to children with mothers in the home. While the author agrees with this concept of free choice, he thinks that it must be weighed against the average AFDC mother's feelings of shame on the one side, and strong motivation on the other to lead a more meaningful life, one which loss of hope often obscures. The mother's choice of life style must be made in the context of her understanding that there is a possibility of breaking out of AFDC through opportunity provided by the welfare agency. Although Oettinger acknowledged that some are better mothers if they are working, her conflict on this point was demonstrated by her approval of halting the trend toward employment of mothers by improving their status as homemakers.

We must conclude, 34 years after the AFDC program emerged in 1935 to secure homes for children from disruption by economic adversity, that it has partially failed, because it has fed and clothed children insufficiently, maligned them for receiving the pittance, and has made the mothers feel as social outcasts, incapable of providing the envisioned security for their children. Yet the 1935 illusion that AFDC was the best of all possible alternatives persists in spite of the evidence of failure. In 1960, the author discussed problems of AFDC working mothers with members of his SDSW staff in the Family and Children Division. The author proposed that all such mothers should be considered potential candidates for education and vocational training leading to employment since the issue was not whether the mother should work, but rather how they could be prepared for work. The staff literally gasped in amazement at such an unusual proposal and argued that mothers should remain at home with their children. This attitude which permeated federal, state, and county welfare staffs has retarded the movement toward upgrading the education and the vocational skills of AFDC mothers.

With the advent of social legislation supporting Community Work and Training programs in the early 1960's, the issue of mothers working came into sharper focus. The Federal Welfare Administration set staff to work on clarification of federal policy on the subject. On May 20, 1966, Ellen Winston, U.S. Commissioner of Welfare, sent a communication to the states in which she stated that the issues concerning mothers working were of primary concern to the Administration and its Bureaus which were charged with specific responsibilities for strengthening family life, protecting children, and reducing economic dependency to the fullest extent possible. She specified that in the administration of programs designed to fulfill these social and economic purposes—Aid to Families with Dependent Children, Child Welfare Services, and Title V of the Economic Opportunity Act—the Federal Welfare Administration and the State welfare departments had the obligation as well as the opportunity to assure that these objectives would be appropriately achieved in respect to the situation of each family served. Emphasis was placed on viewing the question of economic independence for AFDC mothers and other mothers similarly entrapped socially and economically in the light of an even more important value to society—the opportunity for home life and maternal care for healthy growth and development of children.

In 1962, Congress confirmed this priority value in setting forth the purpose of the AFDC program: ". . . to help maintain and strengthen family life and to help such parents or relatives to attain or retain capability for the maximum self-support and personal independence consistent with the maintenance of continuing parental care and protection." Similarly, Title V, Part 3, Public Welfare Amendments of 1962, defined requirements with respect to child welfare services to include ". . . such safeguards as may be necessary to assure provision of day care under the plan only in cases in which it is in the best interest of the child and the mother and only in cases in which it is determined, under criteria established by the State, that a need for such care exists . . ." Commissioner Winston attached a statement to her communication which set forth the position of the Welfare Administration and which would govern all staff of the Welfare Administration in activities related to mothers working or preparing for employment. State welfare departments were urged to incorporate the principles and guides in the position statement in the administration of their own programs for mothers and their children. In addition, a joint statement of the Bureau of Family Services and the Children's Bureau, providing further guides for assessing the appropriateness of mothers working and the quality of plans for substitute child care, was issued as follows:

Premise

"Two values of society relate directly to the employment of mothers. One is the high value placed on the economic independence of families. The other, and deeper, value is that children have the maternal nurture and care essential to their healthy physical, mental, and social development.

"Many families, particularly poor families, can achieve economic independence only through the employment of the mother. For such mothers, these two values often create tension and conflict between the expectations of society and their own desires regarding the fulfillment of their maternal responsibilities and achievement of economic independence.

"Generalizations that all needy mothers should work or that no mother should work are equally untenable. Where adequate substitute care for children is available and other family and personal circumstances permit, employment of the mother can provide personal and family satisfactions and values in addition to income. For many other families, however, employment of the mother would be deterimental to the welfare of the children and to the stability of the family. For them, society has established institutions, such as public welfare and social insurance, to permit and assist the mothers to fulfill their maternal roles.

"Adequate income maintenance resources, day care facilities, adult education and vocational training programs, and social and health services are necessary to guarantee to each mother the opportunity to choose the course which best fulfills the needs and responsibilities of her particular situation.

Basic Principles

"Decisions that affect the discharge of maternal responsibilities and the well-being of children should be made by the mother within the context of her family situation. The needs of the child must take precedence over all other considerations.

"The function of public welfare and other social agencies is to assist mothers to arrive at sound family decisions in respect to employment or training for employment and care of children and to make appropriate plans to carry out those decisions.

"The goal of economic independence is best served when it is carried out within the broad context of strengthening individual and family functioning; is directed to the achievement of stable employability status and employment that is rewarding to the mother and her family and is advanced by helping mothers who are currently needed in the home to plan for future employment, including training plans to improve their general educational level and employment skills.

"Adequate substitute care for children requires planning that is differentiated in accordance with the ages of the children and their special needs or problems, e.g., children under school age, older children who are free from school in the afternoons, and individual children with health or behavior problems.

Implementation of the Principles—Guides for Assessing Availabilty of Mothers for Work or Training for Employment

"The following guides are intended to assist public welfare agencies in carrying out their responsibility for helping mothers to decide on the feasibility of entering into training or employment activities. The guides relate to factors that are essential in assessing the appropriateness of current work and the immediate and longer range employment potentials of mothers and in helping them to make sound decisions as to immediate and future plans:

"What are the interests, concerns and motivations of the mother in respect to immediate or future preparation for employment or to current employment, and in respect to the needs of her children for her care and guidance? Is the mother's assessment of her employment interests and capacities sound? Are the needs of her children viewed realistically?

"Do the ages, health or other special needs of the children require the mother to be at home all or part of the time? What are the attitudes of the children toward their mother working? Can the older children be involved with the mother in making a family plan?

"Are the health conditions and physical stamina of the mother adequate for the multiple burdens of employment, home management and child care? Are there older children or relatives in the home who can assume some of the home management responsibilities?

"Are there responsibilities for other family members that require the mother's care, e.g., incapacitated husband, ill mother or father?

"What are the educational attainment and capacities of the mother? Previous work experiences, interest in and capacities for preparation for employment? Does she have employment skills that are currently marketable? If not, what education, training or other services are necessary to achieve an appropriate employment goal?

"Is her current or prospective employment suitable as to the nature and hours of work; travel time; fair remuneration and meaningful net return for the family after work expenses; and personal satisfactions or changes for improvement or advance? Does or would the prospective employment permit the mother to have adequate time to maintain home life and emotional ties with her children?

"Are there plans for substitute care of all of the children that are adequate for their physical care and safety and their social protection? Are these plans dependable? Are costs of care to be paid by the mother from her salary? Is this a reasonable expectation in terms of her total net income and the needs of the family?

Summary

"On the basis of the above considerations, mothers can be helped to make sound decisions for themselves and their children about the appropriateness of immediate employment or training or plans for training and/or employment at a later and more appropriate time."

The foregoing statement lacked a definite position on the working of AFDC mothers. It offered no real leadership to states. Implicit in the statement is the belief that ADFC families are more secure and stable when the mother is not at work, a conclusion which has no basis in fact, whereas research has shown that the meagre grants, social outcast status, and feelings of less worth, all work against a stable family life. The Welfare Administration obviously favored traditional approaches to the question of AFDC mothers at work. Let us consider the issues in greater depth.

Women at Work

The long-range trend in America toward increasing numbers of women at work has been inevitable due to a variety of forces. Wars have accelerated the trend. The United States was in World War I less than 20 months. Although this had a temporary effect in increasing the numbers of women in the labor force, cultural and economic factors of the times did not promote such status, and World War I had no significant impact upon women in the labor market. Before the end of World War II, however, the numbers of women in work increased substantially. By April 1945, there were 19.5 million women in the labor force as compared to 13 million in 1940. The startling change is illustrated by the following statistics from a California aircraft assembly plant:

Date	Total Employees	Women
November 1940	14,000	0
November 1941	20,600	300
December 1941	24,600	900
April 1942	24,700	3,600
November 1942	24,000	13,000

In 1965, when 26 million women were employed, they represented 35 percent of the total labor force and 37 percent of all women of working age. Of these women workers, 38 percent (9.5 million) had children under 18 years of age; 3.5 million had children under 6 years of age; and 2 million had children under 3. About 6 million mothers had children from 6 to 17 years of age. In 1964, about 7.9 million working mothers were from homes where the husband was present. The other 1.6 million were widowed, divorced, or separated from their husbands for other reasons (a total of 44 percent of all mothers in these categories).

In 1965, the 3.4 million women from ethnic minorities who were working, represented 13 percent of the workingwomen and 41 percent of the ethnic labor force, and about 90 percent of the minority group women workers were Negro. The most striking change was the decline in the traditional type of work for Negro women—household labor. In 1940, domestic workers comprised 60 percent of all employed Negro women; in 1950, only 42 percent. Sharp gains were noted in the employment of Negro women as operatives and service workers; and these employed in professional, managerial, and white collar occupations rose from 6 to 12 percent of the total. This upgrading of work was actually less dramatic than it appears to be, since many domestics merely shifted to work as cooks, waitresses, or practical nurses.

We have witnessed a marked social change since the turn of the century, when less than 50 percent of the women had ever worked outside their own homes, while today, 90 percent will work at some time in their lives. Currently, of the 26 million or one-third of all the women in the United States who work outside the home, 50 percent are over 40 years of age, and 60 percent are married. Of all the married women, 30 percent are working; and of all the mothers with children of school age, 40 percent are working, including about 2.5 million whose children are under six years of age.

The revolution which has occurred in women's employment and in the lives of working wives and mothers in this century is fully documented. The social, psychological, and cultural implications of that revolution are less well-known and documented. Why do married women work? Does a mother's absence jeopardize the healthy development of her children? Does working contribute to juvenile delinquency? Where does responsibility lie for providing adequate child care facilities?

Why do women work? Since labor-saving devices in the home may make the housewife role less demanding and challenging, boredom or the distastefulness of housework may be involved. Moreover, work in the home is lonelier now than it was a few generations ago considering the change from extended kinship to more centralized family patterns. Motivation toward work may be based on the desire to use new leisure in a more meaningful way. Some may work to escape problems at home. The personality of the woman may be such that she cannot tolerate sustained relationships with her children, husband, in-laws, or parents. A life rhythm pattern which varies work and home life often is more satisfying for such women, thereby making it possible for them to be better wives and mothers than they would be without the diversion of work.

A primary cause for the decision of women to work is economic necessity. Wives and mothers wish extra income to purchase more goods or services, or to relieve an impossible debt load. Advertising strongly influences new tastes and desires, often transforming former luxuries into present necessities. It has been alleged that advertising not only creates new standards of material satisfaction, but also tends to create extravagant temptation and anxious restiveness. General use of new products by relatives and friends also tempts their purchase. Material goods reflect status even though the value judgments are largely synthetic. In addition, the natural inclination of a parent to provide a good standard of living for the family is an overriding consideration. A wife may consider work to enable the family to engage in some extra-ordinary experience such as a trip abroad, further education of the husband, or lessons of varying kinds for especially talented children, or emergency expenditures for medical or dental care, funerals, or support of aged parents may force the wife to work. For some, money has other meanings, as when it symbolizes independence, power, or freedom from the tyranny of a controlling husband.

In our society, orientation toward meaningful work is a strong cultural trait for both men and women. Since other facets of the American way of life have changed toward apparently less meaningful and supportive views, the tendency is to seek a more meaningful life in work and work group associations. The completion of education at higher levels has also led women into a search for life values which go beyond homemaking. The fulfillment derived from the development of talent through work, group status, and recognition provides women with a sense of achievement often not found in homemaking. That they can encompass work outside the home and homemaking itself is presently demonstrated by millions of married workingwomen. Society may be moving toward the condition where women may eventually feel the need to justify staying at home rather than the need to justify working, a complete reversal of earlier attitudes. Since 26 million married women are actually at work it is useless to regret the fact, as many still do. Rather, this irreversible trend should be accepted, and methods of enhancing the experience should be sought. Particular attention must be given to the development of enriching children's experiences under substitute parental care during the mother's working hours.

The Feminine Mystique

The public welfare concept of 1935, that women should remain in their homes to care for their children, bake their own bread, and perform other homemaking duties, may have been reinforced by the "motherhood mania" of the 1940-1957 era. This period was characterized by an enormous upsurge in the fertility rate in the United States that demographers could not explain in traditional terms of postdepression or postwar babies. Jessie Bernard[2] offered an explanation of this strange interlude in terms of a psychoanalytically-spawned and widely accepted doctrine, the "feminine mystique," wherein women who seek self-fulfillment in work and activity outside the home are categorized as a "lost sex." Consequently, some women turned to extravagant motherhood, weaving, baking, and food preservation to reinforce their concept of femininity. One might speculate that this was one of the last reactionary protests against the inevitable movement of women toward their emerging role in the world of work; and since all progress is marked by occasional regression, Margaret Mead's[3] explanation of the phenomenon becomes strikingly applicable. She suggested that some women, through maternity, regressed "to the Stone Age arrangement in which women's main ambition is to acquire and hold a mate, to produce or adopt children who are to be the exclusive delight and concern of a single married pair, and in which work outside the home . . . holds no attraction by itself, unless it is subservient to the demands of an individual household . . . Woman has returned, each to her separate cave."

The era of the feminine mystique did not keep millions of mothers from jobs, although it did help maintain a rationale for those who thought that mothers on welfare should be supported at home. The "femininity" of the 1950's became even more ludicrous when, in the 1960's, many young people displayed a unisex stance in their dress and coiffure, thereby minimizing the traditional outer symbols of sex differences.

Mothers at Work: Influence Upon Children

The working of a mother is only one of many factors relating to a child's growth and development. Others include the child's inherited physical and intellectual capacity, the parents emotional stability, the number and kinds of other children in the family, the nature of the community in which the child lives, the influence of his peer group, whether his family has an extended kinship or nuclear pattern, plus many other contributing factors.

The general public tends to hold the concept that children of working mothers are delinquency prone. Some studies are available which refute this concept. In the 1940's, Sheldon and Eleanor Glueck studied a group of 500 delinquent boys in comparison with a control group consisting of nondelinquents who were similar in intelligence, ethnic background, age, and residence in underprivileged areas.[4] While there was no difference between these two groups in relation to mothers who worked *regularly* outside the home, the delinquency group did contain a larger proportion of boys (11.9 percent) whose mothers worked *intermittently*. It is apparent that the sporadic employment may have reflected personality traits which caused the delinquency, rather than the irregular work itself. The Gluecks' study, in fact, revealed that these irregularly employed mothers tended to have histories of delinquency themselves, and married husbands who were emotionally disturbed and had poor work habits, factors more likely to have relevance to the delinquency of children rather than the sporadic working of the mother. The Gluecks' findings did reveal the importance of insuring good substitute care for children while the mother worked, showing that if a mother arranged adequate care for her child while she worked, he was no more likely to become delinquent than the well-supervised child of the nonworking mother. The Gluecks' study did show, however, that in the late 1940's a majority of the mothers did not make appropriate arrangements for their children during their absence.

The *kibbutz* or communal farm settlement of Israel has often been referred to as a model of substitute care for children while their mothers work. Shmael Golan[5] discusses the unique system of education which has been developed in the *kibbutz*. Children live in children's homes from birth, while making strong emotional daily contacts with their parents, and are raised in groups: infants, toddlers, kindergarten, grade school, and high school. However, there are no set designations for these stages. Through endless devotion and dedication of the *metaplot* (caretaker of children), health standards have been raised so high that infant mortality in the *kibbutz*, as of today, is lower than in any other place in the world. Of late years, much has been and is being done toward turning the children's house into a home which is warm and open both for the child and his parents.

As regards the emotional life of the child, during the first year of life, the infant is mainly in charge of its mother, and a strong emotional bond is developed between mother and child. At this stage, the *metaplot* is of secondary importance. Aside from seeing to the cleanliness of the house and taking care of equipment, she carries out observations on each child and gives guidance to mothers who need it because of lack of experience or for other reasons. From his second year, the child is mainly cared for by the *metaplot* and is with his parents in their room for about two hours daily. Each *metaplot* assumes responsibility for 4-6 children, sees to the satisfaction of their physical and emotional needs, serves as an additional mother figure, an object of love and identification, and the training of instinctual drives and habit formation is in her hands. She is the one who makes demands on the child; the parents hardly participate in the process. Such simultaneous relations of the child to his family members, on the one hand, and to his *metaplot*, on the other, are bound to bring about changes in the formation of or avoidance of the Oedipus complex, freeing him from its characteristic burden of conflicts. The concept of "separation from the mother" is inapplicable to conditions in the *kibbutz*, because the life of its young children cannot be compared to life in a foster home or in an institution away from the parents. By and large, there is a great deal of opportunity for intimate relationships between parents and child in the *kibbutz*.

Doubts have been expressed as to the advisability of such multiple emotional bonds and their effect on the integrity of the child's personality, possible impoverishment of his emotional life, or the development of a "flat" personality, incapable of forming deep emotional attachments. Also discussed is the question as to whether the contant shifting from one emotional and mental climate to the other —an intimate, permissive atmosphere in the parents' room and a matter-of-fact, demanding atmosphere within the children's home —might not result in the formation of conflicting areas and contradictions within the child's personality. Experience seems to have answered these doubts. Over 2,000 youngsters who have graduated from *kibbutz* high schools and grown into maturity exhibit wholesome personalities with excellent adaptive capacity, and their personalities vary over a wide range of intellectual, artistic, and emotional types. The *kibbutz* youth appears to be stable and well balanced, cooperative, courageous, and devoid of envy and aggression. There are, of course, disturbed and neurotic children within the *kibbutz*. A study carried out on a population of 1,800 children between the ages of 7 and 12 revealed 5-6 percent of these children to be disturbed to the extent that they could not adjust to the regular framework of educational requirements. In a survey of children within this age framework, it was found that, for the most part, the causative factor in the neurotic syndrome was the relationship with the parents, and only a small minority of these disturbances could be traced to the system of collective education.

George Mohr[6] suggests that the infant in the *kibbutz* is much more on his own and for longer periods of time than the child in the conventional family setting, and he points out that the *kibbutz* nurseries make much more of an institutional impression than do the houses for toddlers and older children. The *metaplot* is generally a warm and interested person who offers much to the child, but must be shared perhaps too much and too soon. The child reared as an active participant in family life, where parents and siblings are active in relating themselves to him, is subjected to many stimuli to which he can respond positively although a child is not exposed to these stimuli in the *kibbutz* nursery setting, it cannot be compared to that of the large institution in which children receive minimal attention, are deprived of mothering care, do not experience the normal mother-child symbiotic relationship, and develop the capacity for self-differentiation and object relationship. The *kibbutz* child does not experience this order of deprivation; he is always a cherished object. It must be remembered that the mother plays an important role during the first year of the child's life, and at no time is the child deprived of daily contact with the parents. Since more than one mothering-person is involved, there may be an initial developmental lag, but by and large, the child's developmental potential is not damaged and he is able to recoup his developmental loss later. Since children normally begin to relate themselves to group situations around the third year of life, the group situation becomes more effective as a growth stimulating environment than during the earlier years.

Dr. Rabin[7] points out that the attitudes of society toward various practices within its institutions are subject to change, and that this is especially true of one particular aspect of intrafamily relationships— the rearing of children. He notes that the current trend is in the direction of "continuous mothering" or close mother-child relationships, especially during the first few years of life, and that an impressive amount of data, clinical and scientific, has been amassed in support of this kind of early maternal care for later favorable personality development and mental health. Also, a number of child psychologists state that for proper mental health, it is essential for the infant and young child to experience a warm, intimate, and continuous relationship with his mother (or permanent mother-substitute) in which both find satisfaction and enjoyment. Dr. Rabin discusses behavior research on a group of 24 infants between nine and seventeen months old who lived in five different *kibbutzim*. Tests and comparisons were made between these infants and a control group from families from ordinary Israeli villages in which nuclear structure of the family had been preserved, and another group of 40 children ranging in age from nine to eleven years were similarly compared. Results indicated that the control group of infants was superior to the *kibbutz* group in tests involving social and interpersonal responsiveness, but that by and large, the *kibbutz* ten-year-olds seemed to excel in ego and intellective factors. Rabin poses the question: "What are the experiences which turn retardation to normalcy or advanced status?"

Although the considerable amount of research on *kibbutz* children is still not definitive, it offers some reassurance to mothers with children who prefer to work, since it tends to verify that when proper substitute parental care is provided, hordes of delinquents will not result from mothers working. The subtleties of personality development of such children needs further research.

The conclusions of a conference on womanpower[8] coincide with the author's belief that quality of the relationship between mother and child is most important during the time they spend together. If the mother provides poor care and rejects the child, this will result in serious personality disorder for the child, whether the rejection is part-time or full-time. The author would emphasize the importance of a consistent mothering relationship with one person during the first three to five years of life of the child. While some research has suggested that children may develop well during the first three years of life with intermittent care by the same mother figure, a much safer approach favors the child receiving full-time mothering from his own mother during these crucial years. If the mother prefers to work when her child is under three, child care arrangements should be made, since a mother frustrated from work choice may be a poorer mother, but the child should receive substitute care in a foster home caring for no more than two children under three years of age.

Public welfare has accepted and applied in the program prevailing attitudes of society regarding child care. Bowlby[9] synthesizes these beliefs in the following statement: ". . . It is sufficient to say that what is believed essential for mental health is that the infant and young child should experience a warm, intimate, and continuous relationship with his mother (or permanent mother substitute) in which both find satisfaction and enjoyment." Bowlby further cites the necessity of close association with the mother figure without separation for the first three years of life, and considers that "inconstancy, or changes from one mother figure to another during the first three years of life" is deleterious to mental health and personality development.

The effect of separation of the child from his mother may take a variety of forms, a question which has been considered by many experts. Heinicke[10] in England conducted a study which compared two groups of two-year-old children, one group in a residential nursery and another group in a day care nursery, and he observed the two groups during a three-week study period. The day care group were children of working mothers. This study sought to clarify differences between the effects of day care separations and longer-range separations. Heinicke found that on the first day, both groups of children cried for their parents, and as the three-week period progressed, the crying almost disappeared with the day nursery children, but the residential nursery group continued to cry for their parents frequently and throughout the three weeks. The day nursery children sought substitute attention with staff, but the residential group sought attention more intensely and cried more. While hostility expressed by the day nursery children was normal, that expressed by the residential children was often severe. The day care children showed continuing eagerness to see their parents at the end of each day, whereas the residential group cried when their parents visited and occasionally failed to recognize them. The Heinicke study suggests that the child of the working mother is initially upset when placed in a day nursery, but quickly adjusts and then maintains a close affectionate relationship with the mother when they are together; and that long separations for the child who does not go home are initially more disturbing; and the disturbance persists, lasting beyond the time when the child returns to his own home.

The mother's relationship to the child will be influenced by the marital relationship. If the mother has a work schedule compatible to that of her husband so that the couple can spend time together alone and with their children, this will reflect in a more satisfying parent-child relationship. The marital relationship, of course, must be marked by love and acceptance, if the mother is to become a loving and accepting parent for her child. The influence of the father upon the children is an important factor, although the mother is most important for young children. The father figure is particularly important in the life of the Negro male child who, living in a matriarchal culture, frequently carries the consequences of the burden of a weak father image.

The issue for AFDC mothers, working or not, cannot be considered by others—solely with reference to the effects of out-of-home care on the child. An equally important question for society is: "What are the effects of the care of an AFDC mother on her child?" The author would postulate an assumption that because of the social outcast status, economic adversity, and probably underprivileged conditions of childhood of AFDC mothers themselves, the environment that they can provide for their children would be hazardous. Surprisingly little research has been conducted on the subject.

Alice McCabe studied one aspect of the subject in regard to children in deprived urban areas who seemed doomed to repeat all the problems of poverty inherited from their AFDC mothers. Forty families were studied[11] by a jointly financed project (Welfare Administration, U.S. Department of Health, Education, and Welfare; and the Community Service Society of New York) with the hope of developing programs to meet their needs. They were selected at random according to four criteria—there was no father in the home; the mother was under 40 years of age and head of the household; two or more children were in the home, the oldest being a school-age child under ten; and acting-out behavior, considered prognostic of antisocial tendencies, was shown by the oldest child.

Of the 40 mothers studied, 21 were Negro and 19 Puerto Rican. Most had dropped out of school before graduating because of work, marriage, or pregnancy, had grown up in broken homes, overwhelmed by loneliness and poverty, and without developing the inner strengths necessary to create family solidarity for their own children. Though these mothers hoped for a permanent relationship with a man, they revealed enormous economic and emotional deprivations which caused them to make poor judgments and brought, instead, a series of unsatisfactory relationships. They tended to be overprotective, underprotective, or competitive with their children. Most realized clearly that they were responsible for physical care, but were rated poor or very poor in the emotional nurturing of the children. The energy level for most mothers was judged to be very low.

Though appealing and expressive, the children showed a wide range of acting-out behavior caused by the deprivation and disorganization to which they were exposed. This resulted most seriously in a diminished capacity for learning. Ego functioning was impaired and resulted in a loss of identity. The children coped with their environment in ways necessary for survival and were devoted to the family as a defense against a hostile world. The survey concluded with the "impression that these children were not even doing as well in school as their mothers did."

DAY CARE AS A LEARNING PROCESS

Persons doing research in child development have, for a long time, given attention to problems of the young child, his behavior, his learning, and his emotional development and have established several hypotheses. Two of the most important of these are as follows:

1. Children under five years of age, even as early as infancy, are innately ready to absorb basic skills which are prerequisites in learning to read, write, and understand mathematics. The utilization of educational practices appropriate to the learning potential of infants and young children can promote later learning, and increase motivation to attend school and to achieve academic success.

2. Children who are deprived of adequate emotional and intellectual stimulation during their first five years of life are likely to develop severe learning problems later on when they attend school, making them prone to become truants, to drop out of school entirely, and to become delinquents.

Let us examine some of the research proving the validity of the first hypothesis, namely, that children under five years of age are ready to learn basic skills which are prerequisites in learning to read, write, and understand mathematics. Research in the field of cognitive studies has followed the pioneering work of the Swiss biologist-psychologist Piaget,[12] whose theories of how children learn developed from his detailed day-by-day observations of his own three children in Geneva. He described stages of intellectual development beginning in the first five months of life and carried forward into adolescence.

Piaget reasoned that there were certain critical periods in the life of each infant and child. In the beginning, the child's brain and nervous system in general were capable only of receiving a variety of sensory stimulations—through the eyes, ears, and skin particularly—through which the infant's nervous system was able to automatically coordinate his neurological reflexes. But repeated experiences at looking for things *heard*, of reaching for and grasping things *seen*, of sucking things *grasped*, not only helped his brain to develop but brought him pleasure which, in turn, motivated him to seek further stimulation. Starting with a signal from outside, like a noise, a cycle was set up which prompted the baby to become alerted, to turn his eyes and his head, and as he was able to see the source of the noise, he found pleasure. Such pleasure prompted him not only to be alert for more pleasure, but even to try to initiate it himself by using his hands or his voice.

In the second six months of life, the baby is able to experience a greater variety of situations which he increasingly recognizes, in which he develops an interest, and on which he can act in a manner that either prolongs or reproduces that which interests him. This is the period when babies recognize their parents, smile, and begin to establish emotional attachments. If such an attachment is to one person alone, the baby shows anxiety at separation. From this standpoint, mothering by more than one person, such as day care provides, may have the advantages of inoculating the child against separation anxiety, building into him a more finely differentiated set of perceptual ability, thereby widening his range of curious interest in human behavior.

The third stage in Piaget's scheme is that from ten months to one and one-half years of age, the child begins to explore and to try out his new found muscle development, and to learn the effects of his efforts. For example, as he has opportunity to throw things and watch their trajectory, as he has an opportunity to climb and walk freely, to manipulate objects, he begins to develop conceptions of space, time, and causality. As parents are able to mesh into the child's natural proclivities to use his body in exploration, by talking to him, playing with him, and giving him the opportunities to experiment with various objects, they enhance his performance as well as his development. In this period, when the child's play is very often imitative and not yet the result of his own conceptualizing or preplanning, it is found that given a greater variety of models to imitate, his skills increase, not only for the play at hand but in intellectual performance later on. As J. McVicker Hunt of the University of Illinois states, "Evidence independent of Piaget's observations for this point are hard to come by," but experiences in several schools lend some degree of confirmation. For example, the headmistress of a small private coeducational school in Rhode Island believed that the basis for arithmetic can be taught in the nursery school and kindergarten. She considered it unfortunate that children are often introduced to addition, subtraction, multiplication, and division before they have had sufficient opportunity to discover, at the concrete level, what these operations mean. In consequence of her opinion, teachers of children between the ages of three and five encouraged their young pupils to play games containing concrete number experience. Thus, playing games in which blocks were arranged in rows and columns to form rectangles or three-dimensional buildings gave the teachers opportunity to talk about areas, count the number of stories in buildings, or blocks, and the like.

Such talk was aimed not only at communicating enthusiasm, but also at helping the children to make useful discriminations. Time was regularly given for such games every day, and the teachers would ask questions about the number of rows and the number of columns in a way which would reinforce the children's interest and knowledge about figures. By kindergarten age, children could define what was meant by area and volume, not as physicists might, but nevertheless in definitions which had pertinence and meaning to the teacher and the children. In the first grade, these children were also given repeated opportunity to learn to use figures when they played store, using play money in addition and subtraction.

The pay off from such teaching became evident not immediately, but when the children reached higher stages of learning in the fifth grade. The testing of the children and comparison with past results of children from the same background and environment who had not had this experience showed no special benefits to them by the time they reached third grade. However, by the time they had reached fifth grade, they tested higher on the achievement tests. Obviously, it was impossible to separate the effects of the nursery school experience from the techniques of teaching used in the grades, but the fact that those children who had not had the nursery school experience did less well than those who had matriculated through the nursery school indicates that the early experience was probably a factor.

An article in the British publication, *The Lancet*, in April 1965, calls attention to the revolution in the "2 Rs" via the infant schools, termed "the most boldly experimental sector of British education." Here the new math concepts are used where children play with rods of differing lengths representing units one to ten, through which they are gradually introduced to activities that help them grasp how smaller numbers can be combined to make larger numbers, and how larger numbers can be decomposed into smaller ones. In the new initial teaching alphabet of 24 traditional letters and 30 new symbols (I.T.A.) introduced by Sir James Pitman in 1959, young children have secured a dependable base to master the relation between symbol and sound. *The Lancet* article concludes "that infant logic may not be adult logic, but it is valid within its range. . . . It is beginning to look as if our infants can understand a good deal more than we supposed. They are not ready for formal instruction: they *are* ready for mastering the fundamentals of number and language in a climate of informality, play, and discovery."

Other researchers also have found that children have the ability to profit from experience which is appropriate to and meshes with their innate scheme of biological development, as exemplified in studies by Baldwin, Kalhorn, and Breese[13]. Studying children between the ages of 4 and 7 years, or what Piaget calls the intuitive phase of learning, when a child is continually bringing his intuitions in correspondence with reality, these researchers found that children who are reared in families where the parents take pains to understand the child's questions, explain the reasons for actions, and discuss the nature of things, show a more rapid rate of intellectual development than children whose parents ask for unquestionable obedience and require that children be only seen and not heard.

In addition to the laboratory research reported, there is much clinical evidence stemming from the work of teachers in good nursery schools, especially in various universities where they serve as laboratory schools in departments of child development. Such educators, for many years, have been impressed with the preschool child's native curiosity, his motivation to learn, his ability to ask basic questions, and his freedom to experiment. When these traits have been assisted and promoted by providing learning experiences in the use of objects to give these children understanding of the physical properties of objects—such as flatness and roundness, bigness and smallness—and when they were permitted to use their muscles spontaneously in games and in other group activities, their total learning seemed stimulated. In other words, it has been shown that children who are stimulated through their sense organs—the eyes, the ears, the skin—begin to learn not only about the things in the world which surround them and with which they have daily contact, but they begin to learn about symbols and the interpretation of symbols in reading and writing.

Although all this looks like child's play, not education, physiologists agree with Piaget that the development of the central nervous system of the brain and of the mind proceeds in a healthy fashion only when there is adequate and appropriate stimulation in the sensory organs. Cognition, reasoning, and ability to read and write follow the development of language, and this comes only through contact with people who talk and in other ways communicate well. It follows then that the kind of experience received by a preschool child in a day care center or nursery school is far removed from the custodial service of other times, but is now an indispensable support for his future individual growth and success. Thus, for public assistance recipients, day care of children is not only a holding operation while the mother is becoming educated and trained, but could be a desirable learning experience for the children as well.

Several important studies of school failure in the first five grades have shown that the basic difficulty is an inability to communicate because these children had problems in speaking and in understanding words spoken to them. They had no anatomical defects of the nervous system, of hearing or vision, or of the vocal apparatus, but they did suffer from a deficiency in function which resulted from a lack of stimulation, especially the experience of being spoken to and responding with language.

In studying such children, a style of family life is observed in which the relationships of parents to the children is so nonverbal that use of language is not developed or encouraged. For example, instead of giving a child an explanation to his questions, he is given a reply of yes or no, maybe just a nod of the head, or even worse, a harsh injunction against "talk." No models of speech and no clues are given to the child as to how to use words in response or ways of articulating ideas by the use of appropriate words, phrases, and sentences. Although mealtimes in most families are occasions for conversation, in many of the families studied this is not so. Either there is no family gathering for mealtime or when parents and children come together they do not talk. While this is more true of the more disadvantaged and lower social classes, such cultural deprivation is also found in some middle-class families where, for some reason or another, conversation is kept to a minimum.

In some of the studies, children from fatherless homes showed significantly lower IQ scores by the time they got to the fifth grade than did children who came from intact families. The researchers ascribed this deficiency not so much to the absence of the father as to a diminution of organized family activity. Children who started out with this inability to communicate with their parents accumulated their deficiencies as time went on, so that by the time they were in the fifth grade they had severe learning problems and communication was almost impossible between them and their teachers. They were frequently passed on from one grade to another, as unfinished articles on an assembly line, and in time, got into trouble, attended school irregularly, became truant, got into difficulties with the law and finally, left school. Most children who come to the juvenile courts are found to have learning problems, many of them not being able to learn to read though well along in age. This is not because they are mentally retarded, but because they have not received the proper stimulation and other advantages of learning to speak and to use their minds and bodies appropriately from infancy onward.

Beginning with the studies of Piaget and going through the great numbers of American psychological studies, particularly of scientists interested in the development of cognition, the conclusion has been reached that for academic learning to be successful it must be viewed as developing in a continuum, beginning with infancy and early childhood. All the early learning experiences, those intellectually stimulating as well as those emotionally satisfying, tend to foster good learning later on. Each child learns by phases or stages, and if any one of these is unfinished, there is a block in his intellectual functioning, in his progress of learning. These interruptions may be due to physical illness, economic and social deprivation, lack of stimulation, or emotional illness in a child or in his parents.

Longitudinal studies of child development carried on by a number of research centers have shown that the major development of personality takes place in the earliest years. By the age of two, certain trends are already evident, at least in such matters as intellectual interest, dependency, and aggressiveness. Just as there is a spurt in the development of a child's height in his first five years of life, there is also a spurt in his intellectual development when conditions are optimally right. This is not to say that all learning potential is tapped or cultivated to its utmost by the age of five, since considerable change takes place later on, again depending upon the opportunities provided each individual, but it is very likely that the greatest receptivity for one's innate potential exists in the first few years of life, a time which is uncluttered with nonessentials. Like seeds already sprouted and needing cultivation, with some growth assured but with the greatest growth guaranteed through appropriate and designed techniques, the growing child requires intellectual nourishment given by persons who are affectionate, kindly, and sympathetic to his needs.

The day care center can supplement those elements which are lacking in the home. Even where the home is more or less ideal, a good day care center can still complement its efforts. The further dimensions which research has contributed to the fostering of child growth and development can be incorporated into existing day care centers and nursery schools as their significance and value become apparent. Just as levels of high and low quality exist in other educational systems, the same variance can be found in day care centers and nursery schools. It is imperative that day care centers which cannot provide optimum benefits do nothing which is detrimental to a child physically, intellectually, socially, or emotionally. It is not inconceivable that certain unfortunate day care or nursery school experiences may be seriously disturbing to children, according to evidence from the clinical field of child psychiatry. This is obviously not the model we seek, but it gives us due warning of pitfalls and dangers. If we follow the standards set by the Children's Bureau and others, we may be assured that children in AFDC families will gain from day care or nursery school experience.

CHILD CARE

The Federal Interagency Requirements for Day Care approved May 25, 1968, by the Department of Health, Education and Welfare, the Office of Economic Opportunity, and the Secretary of Labor, describes day care as "a service for the child, the family, and the community and is based on the demonstrated needs of children and their families. It depends for its efficiency on the commitment, the skill and the spirit with which it is provided." Day care should be a community sponsored service under public and/or voluntary agency auspices for children of preschool and school age, designed to promote and maintain stable family evironments and relationships for children. These services must be based on the best possible plan for the child and his family and coordinated so that a wide range of services are available to the family.

A variety of organized services are essential today in every community if family life is to be sustained and strengthened, and if children are to receive the care they need to develop into healthy adults. Day care is one of these services, which include foster family care, homemaker services, group care and institutional care.

TYPES OF CARE AND SERVICES

A day care facility is any place where day care is provided, including family day care homes, day nurseries, group day care homes, and day care centers. If the day care facility does not provide a full range of services, then the administrative agency must directly or indirectly provide those services which are essential. These include but are not limited to educational, social, health and nutritional services. Community programs for day care require different types of facilities so that the particular needs of the individual child and his family can be taken into consideration in planning for the utilization of services.

Family Day Care Home: The family day care home serves only as many children as it can integrate into its own physical setting, and pattern of living, and is especially suitable for infants, toddlers and sibling groups. This type of care should, in accordance with federal regulations, include no more than six children, including the family day care mother's own children. The number of children in special homes may be extended to ten only with the permission of the licensing agency.

Group Day Care Home: The group day care home offers family-like care to school age children in an extended or modified family residence. It utilizes one or several employees, provides care for 12 or less children, is suitable for those who need before and after school care, do not require a great deal of mothering or individual care, and can profit from association with their peers.

Day Care Center: The day care center serves groups of ten or more children. It utilizes subgroupings on the basis of age and special need, and provides opportunity for learning appropriate to a mixing of age groups. Day care centers should not accept children under three years of age unless the care available approximates the mothering of the family home. Centers may be established in private dwellings, neighborhood houses, schools, churches, social centers, public housing units, and other facilities especially constructed for this kind of care.

Cooperative Day Care Center: The cooperative day care center is one in which the children are usually given care for a limited number of hours a day and in which parents participate along with the staff in the program. This care is usually not suitable for children of working parents, since it requires the active participation of the parent and is of limited duration.

Neighborhood Family Day Care Services: These services are provided in low income neighborhoods by parents who are recipients or potential recipients of public assistance, are employed by the public welfare department, and are trained and supervised to provide care for the children of other public assistance recipients. This is an important development in day care services, since children remain within easy walking distance of their own homes and the care which they receive is similar to that in their own home environment.

In-Home Care: In-home care is provided in the child's own home when it is the best plan for the child and family, and is desirable for infants and young children who have had no experiences outside their own homes and is also appropriate for siblings. This type of care can be effective if the mother, caseworker, and in-home mother work together in providing the care needed in each home. The caseworker draws upon other professional disciplines and resources as they become necessary. In-home care may be used as a substitute for out-of-home care for a child when an emergency arises which necessitates his remaining in his own home.

Federal and State Requirements: The Federal Interagency Requirements for Day Care approved by the U.S. Department of Health, Education and Welfare, the Office of Economic Opportunity, and the Department of Labor on May 25, 1968, set forth the conditions which day care programs must meet if they receive funds under any of the following programs:

Title IV of the Social Security Act; Part A—Aid to Families with Dependent Children; Part B—Child Welfare Services.

Title I of the Economic Opportunity Act (Manpower Program).

Title II of the Economic Opportunity Act; Head Start and Versatile Community Action Programs.

Title III of the Economic Opportunity Act; Program of Migrants (except that these standards will not apply in full to migrant programs until July 1, 1969).

Title V of the Economic Opportunity Act! Part A—Work Experience Program; Part B—Day Care.

Manpower Development and Training Act.

Title I of the Elementary and Secondary Education Act; Programs funded under this Title must be subject to these requirements at the discretion of the state and local school education agencies administering these funds.

The requirements are supplemented by a series of recommendations, and the requirements and the recommendations, taken together, constitute the *Federal Interagency Day Care Standards*. Agencies administering day care programs, as a condition of federal funding, must assure that requirements are met in all facilities which the agencies establish, operate, or utilize with federal support. Requirements apply to all day care programs initially funded and to those refunded after May 25, 1968, and administering agencies are expected to initiate planning and action to achieve full compliance within a reasonable time. If a facility does not provide all required services, the administering agency must assure that those that are lacking are otherwise provided. Administering agencies must also develop specific provisions and procedures within the framework of the federal requirements and recommendations in order to maintain, extend, and improve day care services. Additional standards which are developed locally may be higher than federal requirements, but must be at least equal to those required for licensure or approval.

Enforcement of Requirements: The basic responsibility for enforcement of the requirements lies with the administering agency. Acceptance of federal funds is an agreement to abide by the requirements. State agencies are expected to review programs and facilities at the local level for which they have responsibility and make sure that the requirements are met. Noncompliance may be grounds for a suspension or termination of federal funds.

Program Standards for California Day Care Services for Children: The State Department of Social Welfare Program Standards for Social Services, Day Care of Children, include the requirements for day care services in California, are based on the Federal Interagency requirements, and became effective July 1, 1968. The objectives of day care services are to provide protection, care, and developmental experiences through use of group facilities or family day care homes for children of preschool and school age who have special needs or whose parents or caretakers are at work, engaged in training or education, or are away from home for other reasons. These services are a comprehensive and coordinated set of activities providing direct care and protection for infants, preschool and school age children outside of their own homes during a part of the day.

Day care as a public service had not been funded by the Federal Government prior to the 1962 Amendments to the Social Security Act. These amendments recognized day care as one of the components of child welfare services, and made it possible for public welfare agencies to establish and strengthen day care services in the communities, whereas prior to this legislation, communities provided such care only through private or voluntary funds on an extremely limited basis and served, for the most part, children of parents who could afford to pay for their care. The "war on poverty" has led to renewed interest in day care programs for children of all ages, and major emphasis has been placed on providing services so that mothers, through employment, can become self-supporting.

During the 1966-67 fiscal year, $407,893 of federal child welfare services funds were allocated to the county welfare departments in California for day care services. The 1967-68 department budget included $401,000 for county welfare department day care programs. The counties requested additional funds, totaling approximately $650,000, but these funds were not available. This caused dire need for day care in some areas, since local government did not provide funds for such care.

Day Care Advisory Committee: A county welfare department administering day care services on behalf of 40 or more children must have an advisory committee with not less than one-third parent representation selected by parents or their agents.

Administration of Day Care Services Programs: County welfare department must provide for the development, publication, and dissemination of policies and procedures governing:

Required program services—health, education, constructive development experiences, social services, nutrition, parent involvement and education.

Intake and eligibility for care and services; Financing, expenditures, budgeting; Relationships with community; Continuous evaluation, improvement and development of the program in quality and expansion as needed; Records and reports as required; Coordination with other agency and community facilities; Training for all staff involved in day care services which include professional, nonprofessional and volunteer staff.

Families Eligible for Day Care Services: Day care services are required for children in all of the following groups:

AFDC families with parents in training for employment or receiving educational or rehabilitation services; Children of Aid to

Totally Disabled (ATD) parents in training for employment or receiving vocational or rehabilitation services; Employed AFDC mothers requiring day care; Any assistance family or potential or former recipient family where day care is appropiate as a part of the provision of social services by the county welfare department.

Day care is *recommended* for low income, non-AFDC families who are potential or former recipients receiving training for employment, educational or vocational rehabilitation services, or are residents of a target area of special needs such as migrants.

Purposes for Which Day Care Funds May Be Expended: Day care funds may be expended for purchase of care for individual children or by contract for families eligible for these services; for direct operation of day care centers; for additional staff in county welfare department; and for operation of neighborhood day care facilities.

Services Required: Social services, health and nutritional services, and educational services are required for day care.

Social Services—Each family shall receive help in determining the appropriateness of day care, the best facility for a particular child, the care of siblings, and referral to additional resources as needed. Continuing assessment must be made with the parents and the facility when the child is in placement. Service aides must be used in a meaningful role in the provision of social services.

Health and Nutritional Services—The county welfare department shall assure that the health of children is supervised adequately. Arrangements must be made for medical and dental care and treatment for each child. In the absence of financial resources for health care, county welfare departments must assume responsibility to assure that no child is denied health services because his parents are unable to carry out an adequate health plan.

Educational Services—Educational opportunities appropriate to every child's age, regardless of the type of facility in which he is enrolled, shall be provided each child.

Location and Use of Day Care Facilities: Members of low income or other groups in the population and geographic areas which have the greatest relative need shall be given priority in the extension of day care facilities.

PRESENT AND FUTURE NEEDS

Immeasurable benefits would result if day care services were available to all families and children, regardless of financial need for these services. Day care services would free taxpayers from the support of many families who could be self-sustaining if this kind of care were available for their children, and the children could grow up to become self-sustaining adults. This would be a major factor in breaking the cycle of dependency.

The rate at which employment of women increases is more rapid than the rate at which day care programs expand to meet the needs of their children. Until July 1, 1968, California's day care program did not include employed parents' children, providing day care only for public assistance families with parents preparing for employment.

Since group day care facilities cannot always be located within neighborhoods in which the children live, a development of additional family day care homes will be necessary. Urban areas have, in many instances, established group and family day care programs, but these will need extending to meet the increasing needs of families and children. There is substantial need for additional day care services in rural areas.

It is not possible without an assessment to pinpoint all areas of need for day care services. However, county welfare departments have, since 1964, requested funds in addition to those available to provide for day care for children in families needing this kind of service. Each county welfare department and community must survey the need for day care and must, at the same time, ascertain the resources available to provide these services. Many county welfare departments, stimulated by federal funding, are currently planning for the development of day care services, and as an early part of this development, are assessing the need for additional resources in all areas of their counties.

RELATIONSHIP BETWEEN DAY CARE AND HOMEMAKER SERVICES

Every community should have available a variety of child welfare services, including care for children in their own homes. Homemaker services and day care services are closely related in the public welfare program. A casework evaluation should determine which service is most appropriate for each child and family. The homemaker cares for the child in his own home, rather than in the home of a caretaker, and is also directed toward working with parents in order to supplement parental care and strengthen family life. It is one of the most practical services and should be available to families and children in need of care in their own homes. This care is especially important when an emergency arises, if there are very young infants, sibling groups, and in special situations in which a child should remain in his own home environment. Homemaker services can be used in conjunction with out-of-home day care for children for part of the 24-hour day.

The homemaker is trained to work with families and is supervised by the child welfare services worker, who has determined that homemaker services are the best possible plan for the family. Home-makers are trained to work under difficult situations and to consider the strength as well as the weaknesses in each home. Homemaker training may well be coordinated with day care training. Development of standards for in-home care should be considered in relationship to homemaker services, as they share many common elements, and training and other program requirements can be coordinated. Since homemaker services as well as day care services are now required in all county welfare departments, concurrent development of these services can have far reaching effects in all areas of the state, and can do much toward the attainment of child welfare services in every community where such care is necessary.

CHARACTERISTICS OF GOOD DAY CARE PROGRAMS

Day care programs should meet the emotional, physical, social, and educational needs of children; provide for parent participation, including effective communication between parents and nursery school personnel; and insure that the children and their families receive such medical care or social services as they may need apart from the day care program.

While the child is in day care, he needs sympathetic help in the growing process, and protection from hazards he is too young to handle alone. Therefore, the good day care program must offer opportunities for vigorous play, quiet, creative activities, acceptance and establishment of relationships with children of all types, races, religions, and economic levels. The children need assurance that they are loved and valued as individuals, and that they have the support, understanding, and protective care of the adults with whom they have these early close contacts away from their own families.

The day care experience can and should form the basis for the child's belief in himself as a worthwhile person and for his ability to trust others. While parents remain the primary source of a child's "inner sturdiness," the adults who spend a great deal of time with him, as in the day care program, play a vital part in his wholesome development. Each child must have an opportunity to realize his own growth potential and capacities for a good life in a democratic world. These are the years in which the foundation of the child's character and personality is being laid, and the strength or weakness of this foundation is greatly influenced by the actions and feelings of the people who surround him. A young child sees himself as others see him. If they approve of him, he feels worthwhile. If they disapprove of him, he suffers self-disapproval, and his capacity for wholesome development may be damaged.

In order to establish and maintain an emotional tone in the day care setting which will give children a feeling of comfort and security, the supervising adults must accept and like children for what they are, must understand how children grow, and how they may behave at different stages of development. Although this means that adults need to be able to accept anger, jealousy, disobedience, and other disturbing behavior as natural and to be expected, it does not mean that they allow children to behave in uncontrolled or destructive ways. Children need and want limitations. Complete freedom is frightening, because it demands self-limitation beyond the child's ability. It is the responsibility of the adults in the nursery to help each child learn what is expected of him as an individual and in relation to the group and understand that his own desires and rights are limited by considerations of his own safety and the rights of others.

The methods and techniques used by adults in teaching control are of great importance, but the feelings and attitudes of the adults about children and their behavior are of even greater significance. The adults must act in a calm, relaxed, and gentle manner. This means that they must feel calm, relaxed, and gentle about the children, and must have confidence in the methods they choose for controlling children's behavior.

General Atmosphere. A good day care program provides a stabilizing atmosphere which includes the following minimum requirements: Security which makes it possible for the child to have a safe, wholesome, happy time; Protection from hazards to health and safety; Protection from disease, and promotion of good emotional and physical health; Nutritionally balanced diet; Exercise; Rest; Love and self-confidence; Companions and friends; Development of acceptable behavior patterns; Development of appropriate degree of independence; Intellectual stimulation; Development of skills appropriate to age level; Opportunities for creative experiences.

Physical Setting. The physical setting must be safe, not crowded, conducive to easy supervision of the children, and must provide the essential components of day care, including rest, toileting, cleanliness. The environment must be adjustable to a child's individual moods and needs, such as chances to be alone, have additional rest, or times of "not sharing." Studies have demonstrated that crowding creates increased aggression and hostility in children, and that attractiveness and convenience of surroundings make a major contribution to the development of the sense of well-being and self-worth in the child as well as to his ability to play, grow, and learn appropriately at his age level. Buildings must be free from fire as well as health hazards. (Fire drills in day care centers for preschool children have demonstrated that during naptime children cannot be waked up quickly, that staff must carry them outside.)

Emotional Hazards. Some of the emotional hazards of day care from which the child must be protected are as follows:

He may feel deserted by his parents.

He may feel the adults do not approve of him and that he is unloved and unwanted.

He may need to relate to several adults during the day with inconsistent handling.

He may be disciplined in ways which reenforce rather than correct his undesirable behavior.

He may feel the other children do not like him.

He may feel that he does not have a place where he belongs or that there are none with whom he comes first.

Extended Day Care. An extended day care program for children should provide opportunities to develop friendship groups; freedom from scheduling and regimentation; opportunities to be alone; interesting, fun, and creative activities; vigorous outdoor play and quiet indoor play. It should also provide for appropriate nutrition, sufficient rest to avoid fatigue and overstimulation, and temporary care when a child becomes ill during his time at the center. The child also needs chances to form friendship groups outside the center during play hours after school, and opportunity to exercise some of the independence in his goings and comings that he might have in a well-ordered home.

Parent Participation. The importance of parent and Family Day Care mother or Group Day Care staff working closely together cannot be overestimated. The child in Family Day Care must adjust to a dual living environment in which there are many similarities. He needs to be able to differentiate between the Day Care mother and his own mother, and must not become a victim of rivalry between the "parents." In the Group Day Care setting the child may be less likely to develop confusion between the two ways of living because of the greater dissimilarity between home and group care, but there still are problems of adjustment to separation, differences in methods of child rearing, and the need to relate to a variety of adults, to many children of nearly the same age, and to keep pace with group living. One of the skills of the providers of the day care service must be to help parents increase their feeling of adequacy as parents and gain self-confidence and self-esteem in this role.

Licensing Program. California law, as in most states, requires that persons who receive care for children outside of their own homes in the absence of their parents be licensed. This includes such persons in family day care homes and all private group day care facilities. Federal regulations require that federally-funded day care must meet the new Federal Interagency Day Care Requirements and the licensing laws of the individual states.

One of the major issues in the current developments in day care is adequate standards and their relationship to need for care. There are pressures on this issue from community groups who are fighting for high standards; from those who seek to exploit care of children for personal gains; and from grass-root movements in poor areas where community strength is mobilized to provide care which may be of grossly inadequate quality. The licensing program, which is charged with assuring reasonable standards in family day care homes, private day nurseries, and centers under county welfare department administration, is frequently caught between conflicting pressures, especially in relationship to need for adequate standards and support of grass-roots community "ground swells" to provide services.

Individual staff members of the licensing program must have direction, courage, social work, and supervisory and administrative skills. The SDSW administration provides overall direction in terms of achieving balance and sometimes becomes involved in individual decisions because of their complexity and far-reaching implications. Licensing in itself is not a panacea, and there are weaknesses as well as strengths in the program, but if it is to continue to be a vital force in raising the level of care for young children as one method for accomplishing our goals, these decisions must be made in the direction of strengthening the quality of care within reasonable boundaries of feasibility.

An example of the way in which the day nursery licensing program has sought to accommodate to some of these problems, is the regulation known as "Special Circumstances," which was passed in California in 1965 for a three-year period and readopbted in 1968 for another two-year period. This regulation provides for waiver of licensing requirements under circumstances of unusual need when the emotional health and physical safety of the children will not be in jeopardy. The "special circumstance" clause was developed to accommodate special needs in deprived urban and rural areas where child care could not be provided within the context of full application of all licensing standards.

CALIFORNIA COUNTY DAY CARE AND RELATED PROJECTS

The day care allotment to California made by the Children's Bureau of the Department of Health, Education and Welfare have funded a variety of services and projects in many of California's 58 county welfare departments, which have utilized these funds to strengthen and extend day care services in areas where such services were particularly needed. All of these counties purchased day care for children in AFDC and low income families (less than $4,000 a year annual income) from existing day care facilities. Some county welfare departments also purchased services for mentally retarded children and children in families of migrant seasonal agricultural workers. The facilities included licensed day nurseries, licensed family day care homes, and child care centers operated by the local school districts and supervised by the California State Department of Education. Several counties, in addition to purchasing day care for children, used day care funds to make available professionally trained caseworkers as consultants, coordinators, and counselors to assist in providing adequate services.

Projects set up to demonstrate a need for day care services, and to offer day care in areas where none was available, were administered by county welfare departments in cooperation with other public or private agencies, and with the State Department of Education. These projects were set up in accordance with a state agreement to establish additional child care centers in areas with a high percentage of public assistance and low income families.

Madera County

The Madera County Welfare Department established and is operating the only county operated day care center in California. This center, which provides services for 30 children of AFDC parents engaged in work training projects or employed in seasonal agricultural work, was established because no group facility was available in Madera County to care for children needing this kind of care. A 1964 report from the Madera County Welfare Department in relation to this day care center contained the following statement: "The Madera County Department of Public Welfare established a day care center under the supervision of the Child Welfare Services, September 27, 1964. The day care center is financed by federal funds for the purpose of establishing day care services for families receiving rehabilitation and other types of educational training and also for migrant workers' children where the family income is less than $4,000 a year. A child Welfare Services Worker II assists the family with problems relating to adjustments to employment and areas involving emotional problems and problems that occur in the families of children attending this center. The Child Welfare Services Worker also evaluates children in Family Day Care. . . . Observation of children in the day care center has established a different approach in casework services to families. Other than emotional situations observed in a day care center, extensive medical examinations, and clinical tests, including dental examinations and pediatric examinations, focus on extensive dental and medical care needed for culturally deprived children. . . . Private organizations and citizens have contributed to the Madera County Welfare Day Care Center. The Lions Club donated funds for Christmas toys for every child in the center. The Camp Fire Girls assisted in the Christmas program. Citizens also made contributions to the float which was entered under the name of the Day Care Center in the Christmas parade. . . . A Catholic Youth Organization consisting of sophomores, juniors and seniors in high school are currently planning volunteer services to give each child in the day care center individual attention by assisting in reading, mathematics, play, singing and art classes. . . ."

The judgment of the SDSW, upon reviewing this program, was that it has produced some of the most visible, interesting, and convincing results. The day care center operated by the Madera County Welfare Department in a building constructed under the WPA program, and at one time used as a detention home by the probation department, has provided a rallying point around which the board of supervisors, civil service commission, county administrator, community leaders, and the county welfare staff have all lent their support. Similar results have been achieved by the practical work and training projects promoted by the welfare director which led into job placements for welfare recipients. Fresno State College secured a grant from HEW to enable the school to provide a field work supervisor and place six second-year students at the Madera Day Care Center.

Los Angeles County

Los Angeles County utilized day care funds principally to provide specialized staff to assist AFDC workers in making sound day care plans for children in families engaged in work and training projects. This specialized staff also engaged in developing new and badly needed resources in many areas of Los Angeles County. Some of the funds were also used to provide day care services for retarded children in connection with an employment training program. The county indicated that this spade work was done by the specialized staff to plan proper day care services which will be the most beneficial kind of day care service to Los Angeles County's day care program under the Economic Opportunity Act. Los Angeles County was granted over $400,000 to contract for day care centers under Title V of the Economic Opportunity Act.

Ventura County

Ventura County was involved directly in one of the earliest programs funded under Title V Economic Opportunity Act. On February 19, 1965, the county received formal written approval of its application to establish combination training and day care centers with a grant of $94,100 for the one-year period beginning February 1, 1965. Plans called for the establishment of two combined day care and training centers, where children of AFDC recipients could be cared for during the day while their mothers were in training at the centers or elsewhere in other training facilities. Part of the training of some of the mothers at the center would be geared to child care, whereby they would be assisting staff in caring for the children.

Some difficulty was experienced in locating suitable facilities. Since the project provided funds for leasing only, not for capital investment, the solution was a cooperative plan between the Welfare Department and the Cities of Oxnard and Ventura, whereby the county located suitable buildings, which the cities then proceeded to obtain, move onto city property, and refurbish for leasing. In Oxnard, the administration building of the Dale Park Oxnard Housing Authority was obtained and moved by the City to Colonia Park, opening its doors on June 21, 1965. In Ventura, it was necessary to lease an old house in the downtown area, where operations began on July 19, 1965. Later, the City arranged to move onto City property in West Park. Each center was licensed to care for up to 40 children and was equipped to train up to 25 adults at one time. Training was provided in the following areas: Food services, clerical, teacher aid, maintenance, and high school equivalency training. Over 55 welfare recipients, as a result of training at the centers, passed their General Educational Development test, giving them the equivalent of a high school diploma and opening many doors for further training and employment. A report covering the period from September 1966 to September 1967 showed a total of 25 men and 123 women received training at the two centers, while a total of 247 children received care. The care for the children was not just simple day care, but day care designed to assist and prepare the children in coping with the cultural deficiencies in their lives. During the preceding year 21 adults went directly from training into employment, while others went on to further training elsewhere.

CONCLUSIONS

Emerging evidence tends to affirm that day care, instead of being the harmful experience that the mythology would have us believe it is, can become an enriching educational and socialization experience for children. The importance of good standards for day care facilities is emphasized to insure that the experience is a constructive one for children. Thus a major impediment to the education and vocational training of AFDC mothers is being lifted as we provide appropriate child care programs. The enrichment of family life accrues from a multiplicity of values: To the mother whose life values and strengths are enhanced; to the children whose life experience is enriched; and to the family structure which becomes ennobled and unified.

In the United States Federal funds were made available for day care for the first time under the Lanham Act during World War II, when there was a critical need for women in the labor force. The

160,000 children were receiving care in nurseries under this act as of June 30, 1945. At the end of the war, Federal funds were terminated, and despite the fact that women continued to work in increasing numbers there was no Federal provision for day care until the 1962 Amendments to the Social Security Act. At that time, out of the $25 million Child Welfare Services allotment, part was earmarked solely for day care "to assist the States to provide adequately for the care and protection of children whose parents are working, or otherwise absent from the home or unable for other reasons to provide parental supervision." The amounts earmarked were $4 million in 1964 and 1965 and $7 million in 1966. These funds were used to stimulate licensing laws and to develop programs that would offer protection as well as to pay for day care. Under the leadership of Senator Ribicoff (former Secretary of the Department of HEW) the specific earmarking of funds for day care was deleted in the 1965 Amendments to the Social Security Act and instead the total Child Welfare Service authorization was increased to $45 million.

The Economic Opportunity Act was passed in 1964, and in 1965 the Head Start program was launched. Head Start demonstrated that imaginative and creative compensatory programs can be devised for 4- and 5-year olds from socially disadvantaged backgrounds which will improve both the child's opportunities and achievements. On a cost benefit basis alone, aside from social considerations, this program has shown that investment in pre-school educational and child development experiences for the very young will in the long run effect a monetary savings. Reductions occur both in the present cost of remedial instruction and the long range impact of costs of juvenile delinquency, unemployment and other social and economic problems.

The next major legislation at the Federal level pertaining to day care was passed in 1967. An amendment to the Economic Opportunity Act directed the Secretary of the DHEW and the Director of the Office of Economic Opportunity to coordinate their child care programs to attain common standards and regulations and to develop mechanisms for State and local coordination. In accordance with this legislative mandate, interagency requirements for day care were adopted. Day care is defined as, comprehensive and coordinated sets of activities providing direct care and protection of infants, pre-school, and school-age children outside of their own homes during a portion of 24-hour day. Comprehensive services include, but are not limited to, educational, social, health, and nutritional service and parent participation. Such services require provision of supporting activities including administration, coordination, admissions, training and evaluation.

The Federal interagency requirements must be met by day care programs receiving funds under the Social Security Act, the Economic Opportunity Act, the Manpower Development and Training Act or the Elementary and Secondary Education Act. Waivers may be given when necessary to advance innovation, experimentation and to extend services. The requirements apply whether the day care program is operated directly by the administering agency which receives Federal funds or indirectly by contract for purchase of day care from a facility operated by a public voluntary or proprietary organization. The standards require that there be provision for: (1) full-range of services—social, educational and health; (2) parent participation, and (3) opportunities for employment of low-income persons. Specific requirements are spelled out re size of groups and child to adult ratios. These ratios must be met by new facilities prior to Federal funding and existing programs may be granted up to 3 years, provided there is evidence of progress and good intent, to comply.

Major amendments to the Social Security Act also were passed in 1967 which will have far-reaching implications for the day-care field. As a result of its concern over rising caseloads under the AFDC program, Congress enacted a "package" of provisions designed to assist welfare families to become self-supporting. Part of this "package" declares that all appropriate AFDC recipients over 16 years of age are to be referred to the Department of Labor for employment, training or special work projects. Adequate child care must be provided for any person so referred. The costs of child care and other supportive services are reimbursable from Federal funds at the rate of 85% prior to July 1, 1969 and 75% thereafter.

The magnitude of this program will be seen when it is realized that of the persons receiving public assistance, there are over 1 million mothers with 4 million children in the country as a whole. In California alone there are 172,500 AFDC families headed by mothers. The 194,900 children in these families are under 6 years of age and 298,700 are between 6 and 17 years of age. Contrast these figures with the total capacity of licensed facilities in this country, namely 500,000 children.

Day care facilities must be expanded if the objective of reducing dependency on public assistance is met. Not only is day care needed for persons now receiving AFDC, but it is essential that other low-income families have such services to prevent their becoming recipients. In a recent Department of Labor study of unemployment and underemployment in ten areas of high poverty concentration, it was found that one out of five slum residents who were not in the labor force but who wanted a regular job gave their inability to arrange for day care as the principal reason for not looking for work. In this regard, under the AFDC program Federal matching for day care services is available for potential and former recipients which includes practically all such low-income families. In California, by purchase from the Department of Education, the California State Department of Social Welfare is providing compensatory pre-school education to potential recipients of AFDC as well as current recipients. The 13,000 children were receiving pre-school compensatory educational services under this arrangement as of June 30, 1967. The California State plan also includes the potential recipient group for day care services.

In recognition of the need to improve and expand day care programs as well as to coordinate presently diverse and fragmented programs, the President in 1968 requested the Secretary of HEW to establish the Federal Panel on Early Childhood Development, an interagency group on which are represented all of the Federal agencies having a direct or indirect part in the planning, funding, operation or support of programs for children. The panel includes membership from agencies having a primary concern for services to family and children, e.g., Department of Labor, Agriculture, Housing and Urban Development, Office of Economic Opportunity, Bureau of the Budget and Department of Health, Education and Welfare, including Public Health Service, National Institute of Mental Health, Office of Education and Social and Rehabilitation Service. The associate Chief of the Childrens Bureau, Department of Health, Education and Welfare is Chairman.

As one of its first actions the Federal Panel initiated a proposal for coordination of child care called the 4 C's, or Community Coordinated Child Care Program. The basic concept of the "4 C's" program is that those agencies responsible for services required for a comprehensive child care program coordinate their resources for a more efficient and economical operation. Social, health and educational agencies must be included from both the public and voluntary fields. Among the ways such coordination may be achieved in the local community are:

1. Chartering a central planning organization to oversee the needs of all children and setting priorities for types of care to be set up or expanded.

2. Through agreements covering the kinds of families and geographic areas to be served by each agency.

3. Subcontracting by one agency with another to provide a total program of child care.

4. Arranging for one agency to supply a specific service to other agencies, e.g., Head Start providing educational activities for pre-school children in family day homes.

5. Establishing central training programs and depositories for lending equipment, books, etc.

Such methods require a willingness on the part of the individual agencies to give up some of their autonomy. Also needed is similar coordination at the State and Federal levels from which public funds flow and where overall standards are established. Governors hopefully will establish coordinating procedures for State agencies in which State-wide voluntary organizations also will be asked to cooperate. The Panel on Early Childhood Development is the major mechanism for coordination at the Federal level. However, before the "4 C's" plan can be fully implemented there are several crucial issues to be resolved by the Federal government. They are:

1. Approval of the joint funding regulation;

2. Agreement among the agencies to establish a system of priority and to earmark specific funds;

3. Development of a single funding application.

While the "4 C's" program offers promise, other problems remain: (1) In order to stimulate initial expansion there is critical need for demonstration funds. Financing is particularly needed for costs during the planning stage of a coordinated program with respect to development of eligibility criteria, joint staff training, comprehensive personnel policies, evaluation system of service programs, uniform reporting systems, and financial integration. Authorization was given for grants to pay up to 90% of the cost of special day care projects serving low income families under amendments to the Economic Opportunity Act in 1967, but no money was appropriated. Even with Federal funding available under the 1967 amendments to the Social Security Act, States are hard pressed to come up with their proportionate share. (2) While better utilization of existing resources will help to some extent, there is still a critical need for trained teachers and other staff. (3) Licensing laws vary drastically between States and sometimes even between localities within the same State. (4) Complex zoning regulations often hinder development of family day care homes as well as centers. (5) Lack of adequate physical facilities indicate the need for Federal funds to finance construction similar to that provided under the Hill-Burton Act for medical facilities. (6) Finally, the potential impact of Federal financing for day care programs on existing services should be recognized. Concern has been expressed that if the comprehensive quality care required under the Interagency standards is provided it may inflate costs beyond the reach of middle income families. This may force our society to face up to the need for adequate public financial underpinning for basic services needed to fully develop our most important human resource—children.

REFERENCES

1. Oettinger, Katherine: Maternal Employment and Children; Work in the Lives of Children—Proceedings of a Conference on Womanpower. New York: Columbia University Press, 1958.

2. Bernard, Jessie: The status of women in modern patterns of culture; The Annals, 37:519, 1968, and Friedan, Betty: The Feminine Mystique; New York: W. W. Norton, 1963.

3. Mead, Margaret: Introduction to American Women: The Changing Image, Edited by Beverly B. Cassara. Boston: Beacon Press, 1962.

4. Glueck, Sheldon and Eleanor: Unraveling Juvenile Delinquency. New York: Commonwealth Fund, 1950.

5. Golan, Shmael: *Collective Education in the Kibbutz*, American Journal of Orthopsychiatry, 28:549-56, 1958.

6. Mohr, George J.: A Discussion on Behavior Research in Collectives in Israel, American Journal of Orthopsychiatry 28:584-86, 1958.

7. Rabin, A. I., *Infants and Children Under Conditions of "Intermittent Mothering" in the Kibbutz*, American Journal of Orthopsychiatry, 28:577-84, July 1958.

8. National Manpower Conference—Proceedings of a Conference on Womanpower—Work in the Lives of Married Women. New York: Columbia University Press, 1958.

9. Bowlby, J.: Maternal Care and Mutual Health. Geneva: World Health Org., 1951.

10. Heinicke, Christoph M.: Some effects of separating two-year-old children from their parents—a comparative study. Human Relations: Vol. IX, 1956.

11. McCabe, Alice R.: *Forty forgotten families*. Public Welfare: Vol. 24, No. 2, April 1966.

12. Piaget, Jean: The Psychology of Intelligence. New York: Harcourt, Brace and Co., 1950.

13. Baldwin, Alfred L., Kalhorn, Joan, and Breese, Fay Huffman: Patterns of parent behavior, Psychological Monographs, Vol. 58, 1945.

CHAPTER 7

THE EXPLOITED
CALIFORNIA FARM WORKER

FARM WORKERS IN CALIFORNIA are so deeply locked in abject poverty that they are set off from all other categories of the "poor." At least 150,000 farm laborers and their families, and at peak employment, over 300,000 domestic farm workers are available. Seasonal employment is one cause of their marginal existence. Only 36 percent of all those for whom farm labor was the principal occupation worked between 50 and 52 weeks in 1960 as compared with about 68 percent of all workers. Low wages were standard for California farm laborers at an average of $1.35 per hour. Very few other occupational groups had such a low percentage of full-time employees and in all these groups, with the one exception classified as "private household workers," the median income was two or three times that of the farm laborer, whose median income was $1,940 and whose average annual income was $1,378. Only 30 percent of sailors and deckhands worked for 50 to 52 weeks, but their median income was $4,875; and 36 percent of plasterers and cement finishers worked 50 to 52 weeks, but their median income was over $6,000. Only the private household workers earned less than farm laborers.

The majority of farm labor families are economically marginal even with multiple family employment and some shelter provided. The median income of the farm labor family is about $3,800 as compared with about $7,300 for all families and $5,600 for rural families, statewide. About 54 percent of farm labor families had an income of less than $4,000 as compared with 14 percent for all families and 31 percent for rural families. These disparities are heightened by the fact that the income of farm labor families typically includes the work of more family members than is the case in any other category. The economic deprivation of these families is further intensified by the fact that they have been virtually uncovered by any form of social insurance. In the United States as a whole, the Labor Department reported that during 1965, farm workers averaged only 104 days of work at an average yearly income of $805.

Stanislaus County in California's rich, agricultural San Joaquin Valley had unemployment varying from 4.8 percent in October to 16.3 percent in the winter of 1967, and 25 percent of the county population was either on public welfare or receiving unemployment insurance during these winter months. It is ironic that in this, the richest agricultural valley in the world, the county sought a $75,000 poverty grant to provide food for the poor people there. This wealthy farm area is a 200-mile belt which stretches from Sacramento to Bakersfield and has a 9-month growing season. The eight counties in the valley include 8,500 farms, each with an annual average gross income of $50,000 and more foodstuff is produced here than in 47 of our 50 states.

A Yugoslavian agricultural official on a recent visit to Stanislaus County stated in astonishment, "This is the top, this is the best in the entire world." As an agricultural expert he saw only the richness of the land. Had he been a humanitarian, he would have been more impressed with the abject poverty, the deplorable working conditions, and the hunger of a third of Stanislaus County's population who live below the poverty level. The contrasts of wealth and poverty on the farms of California reflect the impotence of the poor and the exploitative power of agri-business.

When measuring the farm worker's impotence, it should be noted that he is excluded from the protections of the National Labor Relations Act, which guarantees other workers the right to bargain collectively; the Federal Fair Labor Standards Act, which sets the basic minimum wage and maximum hours for industries engaged in interstate commerce; and the Federal Unemployment Tax Act, which subsidizes 60 percent of the State's unemployment insurance programs. At the state level, the farm worker is not covered by unemployment insurance or by maximum hours provision. His wife and children may receive a minimum hourly wage of $1.65, effective February 1968, if they undertake farm work, but this rate does not apply to employers hiring less than five women and children, does not extend to 20 percent of the piece work which is performed for any employer, and is not accompanied by maximum hour or overtime provisions. Moreover, growers were alleged, by the California Attorney General in July 1968, to be flagrantly violating the payment of the minimum wage to women and minors. The growers sought court help to restrain enforcement of the new minimum wage!

As far as the rural poor are concerned, the familiar saying that "we are a society of laws and not of men" is, at best, a half-truth. It is true that laws are passed, interpreted, and enforced by men, but legal rights depend upon political, economic and legal representation, and this is what the rural poor, particularly the farm workers, have consistently lacked. Those who migrate from job to job are unable to comply with the residence requirements which must be satisfied to qualify for voting and for receiving welfare assistance, so that by and large, they are unrepresented by the politician and unaided by the welfare worker. Excluded from the provisions of the National

Labor Relations Act, agricultural workers are not afforded the protection of the National Labor Relations Board. Largely non-unionized, they have had no organization which can bargain collectively on their behalf, nor can they expect much assistance from their employers, for as the President's Commission on Migratory Labor has observed: "What the employer of migratory farm-labor hires is usually not a man to fill a job, but rather labor service. . . . The employment relationship is highly impersonal. Often the employer maintains no payroll and he does not know the names of his employees nor how many on any given day are working for him. When the work is ready, such matters as experience, prior employment, or residence in the area count for little or nothing. Hiring is on a day-by-day basis. Labor turnover in a harvest crew may be 100 percent within a week or less. . . .The insecurity and obscurity of the employment relationship are aggravated when labor contractors are used. Workers testifying in California told us that it was difficult and often impossible to obtain a job directly from the farmer; instead, they were referred to labor contractors. Parallel with the obscure relationship of the individual worker to the farmer when a labor contractor stands between them is that introduced in some but not all instances when growers' or processors' associations undertake many of the functions performed by the labor contractor."[1]

Legal assistance for farm workers and other rural poor persons has not been available to any appreciable degree. The poor man can neither afford to pay a lawyer, nor can he expect free legal services from the rural practitioner who appears loath to give him legal assistance relating to wages, working conditions, and labor relations, for fear that such legal advice will strengthen his economic bargaining position in his dealings with the local farmer and grower. Private organizations such as the American Civil Liberties Union operate bare-bones programs in rural areas. Recent law school graduates who have been found most likely to provide free legal services on indigent defense panels and other legal aid programs do not, on the whole, settle in rural areas. In California, 34 rural counties have no legal aid or lawyer reference services whatsoever, and in counties which have such services, the programs are likely to be understaffed and the staffs overworked and underpaid.

In view of the lack of legal representation, it is not surprising that the laws which are intended to protect the rural poor frequently go unenforced. Section 923 of the California Labor Code guarantees to the individual worker full freedom of association and the right to organize and engage in concerted activities; but in practice, organizational picketing by farm workers, which is essential to any successful organizational campaign, is often enjoined. Under present California case law, trial courts possess broad discretionary powers to enjoin picketing, even where the acts enjoined are nonviolent, so long as the court determines as a matter of fact "that future picketing, even though conducted peaceably, would probably, if not necessarily be regarded as sinister in purpose."

The State of California has extensive housing codes governing the operation and upkeep of labor camp housing, but the President's Committee on Migratory Labor estimated that only 25 to 33 percent of the labor camps comply with these laws. Working conditions in the field are also regulated. Employers are required to provide their workers with drinking water, toilets, hand-washing facilities, and periodic rest periods; yet it has been observed that less than 20 percent of the employers in the State comply with these requirements.

The California Labor Code and the Education Code contain extensive regulations governing the employment, working conditions, and hours of minors, but inspectors from the Department of Labor find children working illegally on 60 percent of the farms they inspect. Criminal prosecutions are permitted under the Labor Code, but they are rare. In 1957, for example, only one California farm employer was prosecuted for violating the Labor Laws. Many violations of the law go unreported because farm workers are fearful of retaliation or because they are unaware of their rights.

Employers are required to furnish their workers an itemized written statement showing income earned and deductions made, but the nebulous, constantly changing work relationships between farm workers and employers, and the common practice of paying workers on a piece-rate basis mean that accurate records are rarely kept or made available to employees. As a result, the benefits of the Social Security Act and the Old Age Survivors and Disability Insurance Program are frequently not received by workers, even though they are legally entitled to such benefits.

EXPLOITATION—A GENERATIONAL PROBLEM

The number of farm workers in the labor force is gradually diminishing as a result of agricultural mechanization. The workers are thus transferred from one category of displacement to another—from seasonal unemployment to technological unemployment. Characterized by low educational levels, and composed of a high proportion of Mexican-Americans and other ethnically disadvantaged groups, these workers are not equipped to move into California's modern economy.

In 1939, the plight of the migrant farm worker, made uncomfortably visible by John Steinbeck's *Grapes of Wrath*, inspired the Congressional La Follette Committee to convene in California, where it discovered the industrialized farm and the processes that were rapidly transforming American agriculture. The investigation was followed by the creation of the Congressional Tolan Committee in 1940. The trail of inquiry spread from California across the country. Soon people in Florida, Michigan, Texas, Ohio, and Colorado were reminded of the fact that they too had a migratory labor problem; that something was happening to agriculture in their farming sections. Before the Tolan Committee had concluded its inquiry, it had established that in the heart of such agricultural empires as Iowa and Illinois, the industrial revolution was working much the same havoc that had set thousands of farm families adrift in Texas and turned many on their way to California.

On December 6, 1939, the La Follette Committee hearings opened in San Francisco in an atmosphere of tension and defiance. One of the leaders of the Associated Farmers demanded that the Senator cease "giving aid and comfort to the Communists" and that he return to Wisconsin and mind his own business.

The tensions occasioned by the impact of the dust-bowl migration upon the agricultural economy of California were outlined in an opening statement to the La Follette Committee prepared by Henry H. Fowler, its counsel. Between January 1, 1933, and June 1, 1939, the years of greatest migration to California, approximately 180 agricultural strikes had occurred in 34 of the 58 counties of California, which included every important agricultural community and every major crop. Vigilantism characterized the general picture of conditions in California. The Committee's investigation of the 1937 apricot strike at Winters in 1937 revealed a typical pattern of vigilante activity: evictions, the use of special deputies, the formation of an "Apricot Patrol," and the usual "rough stuff." In this strike, some 3,500 or 4,000 migrants were involved. In investigating the strong-arm methods used by the Associated Farmers in Contra Costa County (where no one worked in the fields without first having been registered and interviewed by the sheriff), the same pattern was indicated. Documentation in the transcript of the La Follette Committee revealed the systematic and thorough going vigilantism practiced by the Associated Farmers of California: strike breaking and resisting the right of self-organization; black listing, the use of thugs, the technique of whipping a local community into a frenzy against strikes, and the subservience of law enforcement officials to private interests.

One observer of events in California from 1938-1942 was Carey McWilliams, Commissioner at that time of the California Housing and Immigration Division, Department of Industrial Relations. McWilliams, currently editor of a periodical, *The Nation,* was an astute observer of conditions on the farms of California and reported them well.

In a book, McWilliams[2] noted that a political upset had touched off the revolt against the impoverished migrants who, like the Joads in the *Grapes of Wrath* had become displaced persons in California. From 1896 to 1938 there had been only Republican governors in California, and with the exception of Hiram Johnson's administration, reactionary interests had long kept a close grip on the apparatus of state government. The new Olson administration in 1938 had an important program for farm labor in California. It proposed to give liberal administration of relief; eliminate "work or starve" edicts; set up a system of agricultural labor wage-rate boards; safeguard the right of collective bargaining in agriculture; and consolidate the sounder parts of the production-for-use plan into a cooperative program for the unemployed. But the Old Guard, having anticipated such a situation, retained a strong grip upon the State Senate. Los Angeles County, with half of the population of the state, had but one Senator. As a result, virtually every item on Governor Olson's legislative program was defeated, and the people were robbed of the victory which they had won at the polls in 1938. The Associated Farmers denounced the *Grapes of Wrath* as obscene, vulgar, and immoral, and were successful in having its circulation banned in the public libraries of Kern County.

A campaign was launched to slash relief appropriations and increase eligibility requirements in California. Relief appropriations were cut to the bone, the 1 to 3 year residence requirement was raised to 3 to 5 years, and finally, the State Relief Administration was abolished altogether. McWilliams reported that, under these circumstances, the migrants in rural areas in California did not have any alternative but to go to work in the fields at whatever rates were offered. Twice during 1939, at the request of Governor Olson, McWilliams in his role as a state official held wage-rate hearings in the San Joaquin Valley in an effort to bolster up the declining wage structure and in each instance, the hearings were denounced from one end of the valley to the other. In 1940, a local county health officer had placards printed and distributed throughout the county which read: "MADERA COUNTY HEALTH UNIT BOASTS OF 2,600 CABINS IN GROWER LABOR CAMPS; TO HELL WITH THE GRAPES OF WRATH AND FACTORIES IN THE FIELD." Even prior to the time when this interesting placard was distributed, McWilliams had rated the camps in Madera County among the worst in California. He described the migrant worker as invisible and voiceless, noting that in 1942, there were 5,474 private labor camps in agriculture, yet one could drive the main state highways from one end to the other and never see a labor camp. Since the owners who built these camps did not want them located near highways, motorists scarcely got a passing impression of the fact, even during the peak of the season, that 150,000 migrants were at work in the San Joaquin Valley alone. According to McWilliams, one could read the debates in Congress on agricultural legislation and never find a reference to agricultural workers; so far as social legislation was concerned, it seemed that agricultural workers did not exist; and since they were politically impotent, no one was concerned with their welfare.

McWilliams had observed[3] that for the first few months after Federal relief had been inaugurated in 1933, the relief agencies managed to remain fairly neutral, but by the spring of 1935, reports appeared in the press throughout California that relief clients were being forced off the relief rolls and given orders to report for work in the fields. In the period from 1933 to 1935 the growers had endeavored to accomplish the same end by demanding that the relief allowance be cut to such a low point that its recipients would quit in desperation. Failing in this effort, they began to demand that the relief agencies deliver workers to them and, by and large, the relief agencies succumbed to this pressure. On April 23, 1935, the State Emergency Relief Administrator entered into a written agreement with the head of the National Re-employment Service in California, and with a representative of the State Employment Coordinators "to supply whatever labor might be needed in the fields," and in May, 2,396 persons were "turned over" by the relief agencies to the growers in the San Joaquin Valley. The growers were elated and various chambers of commerce throughout the state passed resolutions in praise of the new cheap labor mechanism.

In June, seeking to ward off the growers' demands, relief administrators in Los Angeles County appointed a citizens' committee to hold hearings and to fix an hourly scale to guide the various relief agencies in determining whether, in a given case, workers should be forced to accept employment. It was revealed at these hearings that in the citrus industry, second richest industry in the state, the average period of yearly employment was only 150 days and the annual average wage $300. Although finding that agricultural wage conditions in California were "deplorable," the committee fixed the prevailing wage at 30 cents an hour for field workers in the citrus and avocado industries, 25 cents an hour in other types of orchard work, and 22 ½ cents an hour in all types of agricultural employment except orchard labor. Relief administrators instructed their clients to accept these wages or to get off the relief rolls.

Throughout the state in the spring and summer of 1935, thousands were struck from the relief rolls and ordered into the fields, and in most cases no attempt was made, as in Los Angeles, to fix a prevailing wage. About 4,000 men were taken off the relief rolls in Northern California and ordered to work in the Sonoma orchards and vineyards. In Solano County, workers were ordered into the fields and in cases where they refused to work for the wages offered, they were automatically and permanently removed from the relief rolls. This procedure was highly praised by the growers. "It enables us," they said, "to get our share of available unemployed labor without having to impossibly compete with union wages." They continued to demand that the relief agencies "jar labor loose" and protested that relief administrators were "unwilling to send out a Mexican worker if he has a sore thumb or an ingrowing nail." In the face of these relief policies, the few unions left in the state were powerless to maintain the gains achieved in 1933 by strike action.

After 1,000 workers had been dropped from the relief rolls in Los Angeles County and told to report for work in the San Fernando Valley, the Los Angeles County Relief Administration was deluged with protests and complaints. Some of these complaints indicated that one man worked 29 hours picking tomatoes and earned $1.60; a married couple worked in the fields 10 days for only $9.00; the head of a family of five, who had been getting the lucrative sum of $15.57 on relief, was only able to earn $7.50 in five days in the fields; and hundreds of workers who had reported in the fields at their own expense had been unable to secure any employment whatever.

When the cotton harvest started in the fall of 1935, the growers demanded that 4,000 workers be cut off the relief rolls in Los Angeles and ordered to report for work in the cotton fields of the San Joaquin Valley, some 200 miles away, at their own expense. After the County Relief Administrator stated: "we have to solve the farmers' problem, even if it does work hardships," relief workers were sent to work in orchards in Northern California 500 miles removed from their homes. Reports of similar conditions continued to appear in the press throughout 1935. Wherever relief clients failed to accept work orders in the fields, they were permanently dropped from the rolls. The net result of this system was lessening of the tax burden for the grower and the lowering of wages for the farm worker.

Despite this evidence of the subserviency of relief officials and a prosperous year for the growers, McWilliams reported that they continued to criticize the relief situation, and in conferences later in the year at Santa Cruz, became more insistent in their demands, informing relief administrators, in no uncertain language, that they were to conform. In fact, the growers began to lobby for merging relief agency and unemployment services so as to bring the whole situation more firmly under their own control. That they were already entrenched in the relief agencies was shown when the head of the State Emergency Relief Administration sent out confidential instructions to his staff in various parts of the state that, henceforth, they were to "cooperate in labor matters with the Associated Farmers." The relief administrators were excessively conciliatory. "We realize we cannot dictate wages to farmers," was the theme of their remarks. When asked what would happen if a relief client who took a field job were to be discharged, one relief administrator replied: "We will not take them back. We shall be vigilant to make certain that they do not get back on relief. We are just as anxious to get them off relief as the farmers are to take them."

Growers persuaded relief officials and WPA officials to avoid establishing work projects in rural areas in order to keep workers on direct relief during off seasons and force them into the fields during the harvest. Relief administrators and unemployment service officials worked out a plan for short-term projects involving some 60,000 workers, the completion of the projects being timed to coincide with the commencement of the harvest season. In March 1936, the head of the Federal Emergency Relief Administration in California stated that, "We will close down our projects whenever there is a shortage of labor in the farming sections." This can readily be interpreted as meaning "whenever the farmers want a superabundance of workers to force wages lower." Every effort was made in 1936 to facilitate the transfer of relief workers to the farms, and the whole relief administration was tightened up. The State Relief Administration announced that it would no longer give assistance to strikers in agricultural areas; and in Los Angeles County, workers were told that unless they employed their children to assist them in the walnut harvest, relief woud not be granted.

The Chamber of Commerce in the City of Fresno, September 4, 1937, passed resolutions endorsing the relief program as administered. On the same date, in response to growers urgings, Governor Frank Merriam issued an ultimatum that all able-bodied workers receiving relief "must help the State's harvest or get off the dole." This order was headlined in the press as a "Work or Starve Order." Officials of the unemployment service went through the relief rolls, selected the names of those whose work had proven satisfactory the previous year, and ordered these people into the fields. The entire quota of hop pickers was recruited in this manner.

McWilliams stated that in a number of instances, relief workers attempted to rebel. When they refused to chop cotton for 20 cents an hour in the San Joaquin Valley in April and May of 1936, their action was denounced by the growers as a "Communist conspiracy." When 30 clergymen (Protestant, Catholic, and Jewish) remonstrated on behalf of the workers after investigating conditions, they in turn were roundly denounced for having "stepped out of their pulpits" and for "lining up on the side of professional agitators." In May 1937, several hundred men who had been ordered to pick peas in Sacramento County returned to relief headquarters and protested against "intolerable conditions in the pea fields under which no white man, Mexican, or Oriental, or any other human being should work." In this instance, the WPA director upheld their action, stating: "We do not intend to force these workers to become peons or slaves to the pea-picking contractors."

Men ordered into the cotton fields from Los Angeles in the fall of 1937 rioted at local relief offices. In the summer of 1937, ranchers in Sonoma County flooded Los Angeles County officials with telegrams demanding that 20,000 workers be detached from the relief rolls and sent north to work in the orchards. At this juncture, the *Los Angeles Evening News* sent Tom O'Connor to Sonoma to investigate conditions. He reported that, originally, there had been no labor shortage; growers could get all the labor they wanted if they would pay a decent wage; hundreds of migratory families were destitute; state unemployment services was openly cooperating with the large growers in jailing union officials and in terrorizing the workers; and when the Resettlement Administration had attempted to build a migratory labor camp in Sonoma, the growers had protested, fearing that a semipermanent labor supply might be easily organized. The failure of the relief officials to cooperate, in this instance, provoked a storm of protests from the growers, who demanded that all relief be shut down.

Since the 1940's the condition of the migratory worker has changed relatively little. Wages continue low, housing and sanitary conditions poor. The Mexican braceros have come and gone. In 1941, Kelley's Army of the Unemployed marched on Sacramento. In 1965, Cesar Chavez led his Delano grape strikers on a walk to Sacramento and subsequently captured a labor contract with a major grower.

Although the attitudes of those opposing any progress for the farm worker have undergone very little change, the cause of this oppressed minority has begun to receive more responsive assistance than in the past from some governmental agencies, private organizations, and foundations. There appears to be a development of more than well-intentioned good will among men of conscience about the oppressive conditions under which their fellow men live, and in some instances, this has taken the form of active participation in improving living and working conditions for the farm laborer and his family. The agonies of poverty and humiliation to which several generations of these people had been subjected can truly be likened to the sowing of a crop which, in the end, could only be harvested as "grapes of wrath." When the Delano grape strikers went into action in 1965, they were motivated not only by a sense of outrage at their situation, but also by an awareness of their rights and the hope that others stood ready to assist them in asserting these rights.

The San Francisco Rosenberg Foundation funded a project in

1964 which provided funds to the California Migrant Ministry, affil-iated with the National Council of the Churches of Christ in the United States. The Ministry has worked for years with farm laborers in the California central agricultural valley. The goal of the project, as described in the Rosenberg Foundation 1965 Annual Report, was to develop a self-supporting organization of Mexican-American farm workers who would make decisions for themselves as to how to meet their problems. Two young Protestant ministers and a Mexican-American subprofessional were provided to help the group help itself. By early 1965, approximately 100 farm families had devel-oped a self-help group, the Farm Workers Organization of Tulare County (FWO). Within a few months, the FWO voted to join the National Farm Workers Association (NFWA), at that time a little-known organization in Delano, California. A major incentive to affiliation was the availability in the NFWA of a credit union, a co-operative from which much-needed gasoline and tires could be purchased, and an insurance plan. FWO and the Migrant Ministry inevitably became involved in the successful grape workers' strike for improved working conditions and wages.

A real challenge was given the Migrant Ministry and, in effect, the Rosenberg Foundation, when FWO requested help in July of 1965, in staging a rent strike against the Tulare County Housing Authority, which had substantially raised rents on the small metal shelters housing FWO members. Remembering the project pledge that the FWO could determine their own objectives, the Ministry assigned a staff member to work on the rent strike and provide case counseling to the workers. Later in the fall of 1965 the NFWA, in-cluding then the FWO, embarked on their famous grape picker strike by picketing a number of vineyards in Tulare and Kern counties. The Migrant Ministry staff joined in the strike with the approval of the National Council of Churches. In addition, the Migrant Ministry project provided help to Mexican-Americans who had difficulty with welfare departments, health agencies, and immigration authorities.

The work of the Migrant Ministry, supported by the Rosenberg Foundation, influenced powerful events during the 1965 project year—events which struck heavy blows against a wide variety of entrenched power structures. It is remarkable that the Rosenberg Foundation, the Migrant Ministry and the National Council of Churches sustained their strong support of FWO during the course of these events. The Rosenberg Foundation renewed its grant for 1966 to the Migrant Ministry for established purposes, and added the proviso that funds would also be available to keep clergy and others on "the other side of the tracks" informed of its work.

The last day of 1964 marked the end of the importation of thou-sands of Mexican workers under Public Law 78. Thus deprived of a cheap and abundant foreign labor supply, some growers turned to section 214 of the Immigration and Nationality Act (Public Law 414), which provides for importing temporary foreign labor if a domestic labor shortage exists. In order to determine such need, the Labor Department established base wages, which varied from state to state ($1.40 in California), and with which a grower would first have to comply in his recruitment of domestic workers before he could request foreign workers.

Many American workers reasoned that they must be worth the same $1.40 hourly minimum, whether or not the grower wanted to qualify for a foreign labor force. During the May 1965 grape harvest in the Coachella Valley, southeast of Los Angeles, no braceros were used. The going wage was a minimum of about $1.20 an hour, plus a piece rate of 15 cents a box. Members of the Agricultural Workers Organizing Committee (an affiliate of the AFL-CIO) working in the area then struck for $1.40 an hour minimum, the Labor Secretary's criteria wage for the state, plus a 25-cents-a-box incentive piece rate. Within a week, the growers agreed to the higher wage. Said one grower: "This strike re-enforced our earlier decision to pay the rate." The men went back to work.

By late summer, some of these grape workers had moved into Delano for the second grape harvest. Their resolve to demand the Labor Secretary's recommended wage was accompanied by the growing conviction that the only way to secure certain reforms was to organize. This message had reached tenants in two public housing projects consisting of one-room metal shacks with no windows or running water, located just outside the Delano grape area. These huts, ovens in the summer and iceboxes in the winter, were built as temporary housing in 1937. In May 1965, the local housing authority decided to raise the rents from the usual $18 a month to a new high of $25 a month and $10 was charged for each additional shack used by one family, instead of the previous fee of $5. Under the leadership of the National Farm Workers Association, an independent farm union, the tenants organized and picketed. When the housing authority compromised at $22 and $8, a rent strike was called and many tenants, all of whom were farm workers, began paying rent into a trust fund at the old rate. The Farm Workers Association organized a 7-mile march from one of the projects into the housing authority offices. Many civil rights and welfare workers from all over the state showed up to march in the 105-degree heat. The authority commissioners canceled their regular meeting, and at a later conference, decided to sue the tenants for back rent. The tenants won the suit in a November ruling. These limited victories in the May grape harvest and the midsummer rent strike set the stage for the Delano struggle.

When the Delano harvesting began in August 1965, the pay rate was about 10 cents a box plus an hourly minimum of $1.20. The workers demanded a piece rate of 25 cents a box plus a $1.40 hourly minimum. When there was no response from the growers to this demand, several union meetings were held, and on September 8, 1965, the men decided to stage a sitdown in their camps. Of some 1,500 men in the camps, 1,300 struck. Ten days later, National Farm Workers Association members joined the strike, initially pulling out about 1,500 workers. With virtually no resources, the two unions were challenging the powerful Delano grape industry.

The National Farm Workers Association had been founded four years earlier by former members of the Community Service Organization, a Mexican-American civic and political group. Cesar Chavez, formerly the National Director of the Community Service Organization, and in 1965, the Director of the National Farm Workers Association, decided that a strictly political approach would not result in the overall reforms necessary for improvement of farm labor conditions. The National Farm Workers Association, an independent organization attempting to develop some countervailing power in the farm communities of Central Valley, managed a credit union, a buying cooperative, and a biweekly newspaper, *El Malcriado*. The Delano grape strike was the Association's first broad effort to win union recognition from growers.

The initial approach of the Agricultural Workers Organizing Committee was a sit-in with no picketing. This held for a few days, but when the growers began to move strikebreakers into the grape fields, AWOC organized crews of pickets who roamed the countryside trying to talk those working into joining the strike effort. They used logic, ridicule, and loud voices and were remarkably effective. The Committee also put picket lines at packing houses and cold storage plants. Truck drivers and railroad workers honored the lines to the extent that their contracts would permit. When the National Farm Workers Association joined the strike, field picketing expanded. Both unions were now in full accord on the dispute, and adopted additional tactics, such as picketing the homes of "scab herders," people who recruited workers to pick grapes behind the lines.

On October 7, 1965, the California State Department of Employment formally certified (Trade Dispute 65-3289a) that the Schenley workers had a legitimate dispute with the Schenley ranch, second largest in the area, and the Department thereafter refused to refer workers to the Schenley vineyards. While similar action had been taken against additional ranches, a lack of substantial evidence in certain other cases made it necessary for the Department of Employment simply to inform potential workers of the dispute situation if they decided to work at these ranches. On December 16, 1965,

Walter Reuther, president of the United Auto Workers and head of the Industrial Union Department of the AFL-CIO, pledged a Christmas contribution of $5,000 with an additional $5,000 a month for "as long as it takes to win this strike, and we are going to stay with you until you do."

During the uneventful sit-ins of the first few days, the growers considered the strike a minor irritation, even a harmless community joke, but as soon as the Agricultural Workers Organizing Committee began to organize roving pickets, the atmosphere quickly altered. Electricity, gas, and water were turned off in some of the camps in order to force the strikers back to the fields. When this failed, the growers began to evict the workers, some of whom had lived in the barracks for 30 years. In a few places, workers' belongings were thrown on the ground and the buildings were nailed and padlocked. Other strikers were ordered to leave by growers accompanied by sheriff's deputies. At the end of two weeks, all strikers had been evicted.

Some growers tried to provoke incidents by shooting at picket signs, by displaying shotguns in a menacing manner, and by playing off one group of workers against another. At one field the rancher urged Mexican-American strikebreakers to ignore Filipino pickets, "because I'm just beginning to trust you Mexicans." Another grower gave guns to two Negro strikebreakers and encouraged them to attack Mexican-American pickets. They gave the guns back to him. Armed guards were hired to patrol the fields where the strikebreakers were working. When the National Farm Workers Association entered the strike, Kern and Tulare County Sheriffs' patrols were doubled and redoubled. All deputies carried Instamatic cameras; some had movie cameras and tape recorders. They took repeated photographs of all pickets, particularly close-up shots. The deputies began conducting what they told reporters were confidential investigations. These probes took two forms: First, several carloads of police would stop a car full of strikers, spend a half hour taking down names and addresses, while a pro-grower newsman pointedly made mug shots of each striker, and no tickets were issued, nor complaints filed. Second, deputies would stop cars with out-of-town strike supporters, particularly ministers, for identification purposes and discussions of the dispute.

A member of the California Migrant Ministry who was a Farm Workers Association organizer was arrested for disturbing the peace when he read Jack London's definition of a scab to strikebreakers in the field, a description which reads in part: ". . . a two-legged animal with a corkscrew soul, a water-logged brain, a combination backbone of jelly and glue . . . a traitor to his God, his country, his wife, his family . . ."

While the growers claimed it was a local issue, national church organizations have found in the Delano story a valid example of the need for increased church involvement in secular affairs. The Rev. Wayne C. Hartmire, Director of the California Migrant Ministry, affiliated with the National Council of Churches, commented on this shift in a recent article in *Christianity and Crisis*: "The present situation poses a difficult dilemma for the churches. Charitable services, long the mainstay of Protestant penetration into poverty areas, now are problematic. The expectations of low-income people are revolutionary and not evolutionary. . . . Farm workers want to be organized so they can have enough power to change their situation. They will not for long tolerate programs that either evade the issue of power or get in the way of organizing. . . . Churchmen could lead the way in approaching the underlying social, economic and political issues. A good beginning point is to understand and give support to basic attempts at organizing workers."

While the Delano strike resulted in agreement with some grape growers, others were unwilling to agree to a labor contract. The labor union shifted its tactics from full reliance on local picketing to a national boycott of the grape growers corporate products. Some parts of the United States were responsive to the boycott, so the growers sought relief from traditional sources such as the California State Legislature, the U.S. Congress, and the California Governor's Office. But the growers found that times were changing. One federal legislative committee requested three large growers to testify and they initially refused, because, according to two of the growers, there was a 3 to 4 margin of the congressional committee favoring the boycott. The arrogance of the growers was revealed when they publicly telegraphed the congressional committee that, "this so-called hearing is a propaganda sideshow to promote an illegal boy-cott . . . it is a political fakery." The wrathful congressional committee then issued a subpoena for the growers to appear.

Senator Harrison A. Williams, Jr., New Jersey, made a statement to the Senate on October 11, 1968 supporting the farm workers as follows:

"Mr. President, in September the United Farm Workers Organizing Committee, AFL-CIO—UFWOC—began the third year of their strike and boycott against California growers of fresh table grapes. They are solemnly dedicated to nonviolent, direct action as a tactic to obtain human dignity, and to guarantee by contract improved living and working conditions through collective bargaining with their employers.

"The recent impact of the boycott is indicative not of worker desperation, but of increasing worker commitment to their cause, which heretofore has been frustrated by grower intransigence. Employer importation and use of strikebreakers, presence of Mexican alien greencarders, and court injunctions severely limiting the union's right to picket, left no recourse for the workers but to seek public support through a consumer boycott of grapes. . . .

"The reports from the Department of Agriculture indicate a slowdown in the transporting, wholesaling, and distribution of grapes; the prices are lower than in previous years; and, the number of sales on consignment have increased. The response from the industry to the boycott, rather than an expression of purpose to mediate with the union, has been a resort to an extensive newspaper, radio, and television campaign allegedly to inform the public of the industry's position.

"The zeal of the growers in resisting progress has been accompanied by the raising of the strawmen as issues; reliance on misleading and untruthful statements; and, the imposition of unacceptable conclusions on the public. . . .

"*The growers say that 90 percent of their workers are local people; not migrants, and that they have year-round work in table grapes.*

"The figures of the Farm Labor Service say something else. There are three major work periods in table grapes; in Kern County, California, in 1967-68, for example:

"Pruning and tieing peak: December 18-January 27, 6 weeks, 3,200 workers needed at peak.

"Thinning and girdling peak: May 13-June 1, 3 weeks, 3,500 workers needed at peak.

"Harvest peak: August 7-September 2, 4 weeks, 6,000 workers needed at peak.

"There are migrants at work in each of these seasons. At the peak of the harvest approximately 50 percent of the fieldworkers are migrants. At other times of the year there is less work; for example, October 28, 1967: 3,000 workers; December 2, 1967: 200 workers; February 24, 1968: 200 workers; March 30, 1968: 0 workers; July 13, 1968: 800 workers. In the United States, there are well over 1 million migratory seasonal workers. In California, there are over 200,000—about one-third migrants and two-thirds local seasonals.

"*Recent full-page advertisements have asserted that farmworkers have said publicly that the real workers do not want a union.*

"This is not true and there is no evidence to substantiate it. The only public evidence that we have—elections and card checks—proves the opposite: that fieldworkers want the protections of a contract negotiated by UFWOC. From the beginning of the strike the growers have supported and made use of labor contractors, local business people, and a small number of farmworkers in their efforts to oppose unionization. The first group was the Kern-Tulare Independent Farm Workers, exposed by the late Senator Robert Kennedy in hearings of my subcommittee as a 'company union' with no actual farmworker leadership.

"Subsequently there has been the Facts from Delano group, Mothers Against Chavez, Men Against Chavez and now the Agricultural Workers Freedom to Work Association—AWFWA. The AWFWA has been sued by UFWOC as an employee organization financed and controlled by employers in violation of the California code. This case is pending. It calls UFWOC a Communist conspiracy, and is alined with the National Right to Work Committee and other antiunion forces of the State and Nation. This organization appears to be only another pitiful example of man's willingness to sell out the rightful aspirations of his brothers for the sake of personal gain.

"*Opponents of the union say that California grape workers make $2.50 per hour and more.*

"It is true that some workers earn more than $2 per hour during certain parts of the harvest season. Of course, the work is backbreaking. But the harvest season is short and families should live in decency year-around. Through the whole year, day in and day out, hourly wages in California agriculture average $1.62. Even this low wage level has been reached as a result of union pressure for higher wages, and the recent termination of the bracero importation program. Add to these low wages the seasonal nature of farm labor and it is then easy to understand why annual income for male farmworkers in California is just under $2,000 and family income is between $2,500 and $3,000 per year.

"Average hourly wage for all farmworkers—including year-around hired hands—in 1967 was $1.33 for the entire Nation, and $1.62 for California.

"In 1965, average hourly earnings of farmworkers in the United States and California was one-half that of factory workers.

"Average annual earnings for migrant workers in the Nation in 1967 was $1,307.

"The average migrant only finds 82 days of farmwork a year and supplements his meager income with other low-paid work. Very few workers get any free food, transportation, or housing. Even for those who do, the value does not come close to the paid insurance, vacations, and other fringe benefits common in America. . . .

"*The growers say they favor unionization, but that UFWOC and Cesar Chavez are untrustworthy.*

"Some agricultural organizations have consistently opposed the extension of the NLRA to agriculture. The Council of California

Growers, the California Farm Bureau Federation and the American Farm Bureau Federation are among the major opponents of present efforts to extend the NLRA. The big business segments of the agricultural industry have given lip service to the rights of their workers to organize but in every specific instance they have bitterly opposed unionization. . . .

"*What are some of the provisions of the existing UFWOC contracts?*

"There are now nine contracts negotiated between organized workers and their employers. These contracts provide for better wages, establish grievance and arbitration procedures, and make provision for job security, overtime pay, rest periods, a jointly administered health benefit plan, certain holidays and vacations with pay, health and safety protections on the job, and other benefits. The contracts include 'no-strike' clauses for the life of the contract with stringent immediate binding mediation and court action in the event of a violation of this clause. . . .

"*Growers say that the migrant is surviving and working.*

"Death rates of migrant farmworkers as a percent of the national rates in 1967 are shocking:

"Infant mortality: 125 percent higher than the national rate.

"Maternal mortality: 125 percent higher than the national rate.

"Influenza and pneumonia: 200 percent higher than the national rate.

"Tuberculosis and other infectious diseases: 260 percent higher than the national rate.

"Accidents: 300 percent higher than the national rate.

"Life expectancy for migrants is 49 years, as opposed to 70 for all others. . . .

"Farmworkers are specifically excluded from unemployment insurance and collective bargaining laws. They are discriminated against in minimum wage coverage—$1.15 for farmworkers, $1.60 for others—and social security laws. Children working in agriculture are excluded from child labor and school attendance laws. Without contracts, farmworkers do not have protections that other workers take for granted; for example, job security, overtime pay, holidays and vacations with pay, sanitary toilets and drinking water, health insurance, grievance procedure, rest periods, and so forth. . . .

"*What do the farmworkers intend to accomplish by their boycott of grapes?*

"The primary goal is to obtain union recognition and assurance of good faith collective bargaining from their grower and farmer employers.

"The best way to achieve this goal would be to include the agricultural industry under the protective provisions of the National Labor Relations Act.

"With the elementary rights of union recognition and collective bargaining, in addition to all the other protections of the NLRA, the farmworkers and farmers and growers would have access to the same legal protections and forum that has been so very successful in the past 30 years for all other industry, so that they can work together with their employers toward:

"A living wage, so that their children do not have to quit grammar school to help earn food;

"Sanitary facilities placed in the field to protect themselves and the consumer, from disease;

"The right to work and live with dignity;

"Recognition of the workers basic humanity and dignity as a free moral agent who may exercise his right to help form his own destiny and to responsibly better his own conditions;

"Securing collective bargaining agreements, similar to the nine already signed, that provide for higher wages, grievance procedures, overtime pay, job security, rest periods, health insurance, holidays and vacations with pay, and other benefits;

"Strong and strict enforcement of laws already on the books that are intended to regulate farm labor contractors and crewleaders, transportation, sanitation, child labor and school attendance, discrimination in employment, workmen's compensation insurance, minimum wage, wage payment and collection, State labor relations acts, unemployment insurance, temporary disability insurance, health and welfare benefits, and social security laws.

"The grape strikers do not ask for pity or charity, only their rights. They are not rejoicing in the boycott. It is tragic that the grape industry will not talk with representatives of their employees."

These unusual events favoring the exploited California farm worker signalled the gradual shift of sentiment and power from its concentration with agribusiness. Yet the battle was only beginning and other political forces emerged.

On August 15, 1968, the Governor of the State of California became responsive to the plight of the growers by denouncing the boycott of California grapes. He sent telegrams to the Vice-President of the United States and to selected governors and mayors. The Governor stated in his wire that "The boycott, along with the misinformation, is causing serious and unwarranted damage to California grape growers, is affecting employment opportunities for farm workers and is depriving consumers of needed fresh fruits . . . The boycott is an attempt to compel employers to force farm workers to join the United Farm Workers against their wishes. It has nothing to do with working or living conditions." The Governor asserted that federal statistics place California farm worker earnings as the highest in the nation, well above those of agricultural workers in either New York or Michigan where grape boycott efforts were concentrated. He said working conditions for California farm workers also rank high and added: "California grape workers are not strike breakers but are legal residents of the United States and are bona fide employees, many of whom have long standing work records and who have refused to join the farm workers union out of their own choice, although the union has had ample opportunity to solicit their membership. Concerned growers are preparing legislation to be presented at the next session of the legislature to establish procedures for handling agricultural labor problems that will protect both workers and growers. I have been advised that charges have been filed with the NLRB claiming that this boycott is illegal and not in the best interest of the public. I trust you will consider all the facts before giving any support to this boycott."

By late 1968 the process of strikes and boycotts had continued for over three years. The prospects of farm workers gaining bargaining rights long held by industrial workers appeared hopeful. The hope was not found in California where state and local politicians tended to follow traditional approaches favoring agribusiness. The hope was found, rather, in national support in the office of the Vice-President, parts of Congress, some governors and mayors offices, and in national unions. These powerful forces became the hope for a lessening of the exploitation of farm workers.

LEGAL SERVICES—AN ANTIDOTE TO EXPLOITATION

While the historical and contemporary uncivilized oppression of poor farm workers persists in spite of sporadic attempts to overcome the deplorable working and living conditions, other forces also are at work offering hope that improvement may occur. The Rosenberg Foundation, Migrant Ministry, Council of Churches, National Farm Worker's Association, and more recently, the California Rural Legal Assistance (CRLA), all have achieved some success and support for their cause in the 1960's as never before in the history of agriculture in California.

CRLA was funded by the federal Office of Economic Opportunity (OEO) in May of 1966 as a statewide organization of 30 lawyers to insure justice for the rural poor, and their impact upon individual and class justice has been phenomenal. CRLA lawyers brought actions on behalf of their clients to enjoin the Madera County Board of Education from closing the schools so that the students could help in the fields, the Governor of California from eliminating some services offered by the state's Medi-Cal program, and the United States Secretary of Labor from issuing a certification for the importing of braceros. CRLA has been denounced by the Governor, several California congressmen, the Kern County Association of Cities, the Republican Central Committee of Kern County, the *Los Angeles Times*, the Stanislaus County Bar Association, the McFarland City Council, the Council of California Growers, and the California Raisin Advisory Board.

A California congressman was so angered when CRLA and the Department of Labor settled the bracero case out of court that he called the agreement "a new low in groveling submission to blackmail." The California Governor was very angry when an injunction was granted against his Medi-Cal cuts, when CRLA began "harrassing" the Sutter County Welfare Department by appealing a number of its decisions to the California State Department of Social Welfare, and when James Lorenz, Jr., the young Los Angeles attorney who founded CRLA, informed him by letter that "Of the 13 decisions which have thus far been rendered by the California State Department of Social Welfare 12 have been in favor of our clients." California's Senator Murphy called the financing of both sides of a lawsuit by the taxpayers "a ludicrous and ridiculous situation," and introduced an amendment to the poverty program bill that would have prevented lawyers who receive OEO funds from suing any government agency. The amendment was defeated. The OEO, backed by a legal services advisory board which includes the President of the American Bar Association, contended that a lawyer is entitled to bring any suit that may be in his client's interest.

When Guimarra Vineyards Corporation attempted to evict some striking workers who had continued to live in its labor camp and CRLA won two injunctions against the eviction, the Corporation lawyer's astonished reaction was: "CRLA advised those people that they could stay on the property, even though they no longer worked there. That's not right."

CRLA, following priorities agreed upon with a group of poor people who serve as a local advisory board, gives preference to cases that could be of benefit to more than one poor person. These cases often come about through what California's Governor in 1968 thinks of as "actively and unethically promoting litigation," and what CRLA thinks of as interpreting and attempting to solve, in legal terms, the problems of uneducated poor people.

In rural areas where lawyers are rare and often limited in experience, sophisticated legal skill is a powerful weapon. When a street department worker in Delano was fired in 1968, the city found itself holding a personnel board hearing and facing a battery of CRLA lawyers. The mayor of Delano felt that CRLA used its power "wrongly, immorally, and frighteningly," whereas CRLA hopes that legal power can eventually be used to make groups of poor people, as well as those who deal with them, aware of the fact that the poor have rights and the means to protect them.

For several years, two tracts in the poorer section of Wasco, a small town in Kern County, were served water by a private company that, according to the residents, charged much higher rates than those of the public water company that served the rest of the town. The neighborhood organized the Wasco Water Committee to protest these rates, and CRLA took the case. After complaints had been filed with the proper state boards, and suits had been threatened in the courts, a settlement was reached that included a rebate for past over-charges.

CRLA has been testing, through these and other cases, how far publicly paid lawyers can go in representing the poor. After extensive evaluations by OEO, it has been judged to be "one of the best legal services programs in the United States." Although it functions with 30 or less lawyers, it is the largest rural legal services program in the country, and the first to provide legal aid to farm workers. It represents a bold new venture in law because it seeks to provide the same high quality of service which a wealthy client could expect of his lawyer, even though this may mean a decrease in the total number of cases that are handled; represents groups of poor people, as well as individual indigents, recognizing that poverty is a social as well as an individual problem, and recognizes the importance of long-term research into the underlying causes of the farm worker's economic deprivation and political powerlessness.

During the first six months of 1967, CRLA attorneys handled over 4,000 civil cases. These were some of the results:

1. The water company which supplied contaminated water to the low-income area of a town has purified the water, and refunded more than $4,500 on water bills.

2. A grower conceded that wage bonuses, payment of which he made contingent upon staying until the end of the season, were actually sums immediately earned and therefore payable to the employee at the employee's option.

3. Several finance companies reduced their interest charges by 50 percent after they were found to be charging exhorbitant interest rates; and over 50 contracts were nullified on grounds that the sellers were guilty of exerting undue influence on the buyers.

4. The U.S. Public Health Service agreed to construct immediately a water system for an Indian Reservation after having originally told the Indians that they would have to wait 3 years to remedy their contaminated water supply.

5. A farm laborer who was fired as a result of successfully pursuing a complaint to the Labor Commission was awarded $1,500 in damages.

6. A Rural Development Corporation has been established to assist farm workers in the planning, financing and management of at least six low-income housing projects which will provide new housing for more than 3,000 people.

7. In three rural counties, actions have been taken to protect the rights of Mexican-Americans who wish to qualify and serve as deputy voting registrars.

A typical test case not yet settled is that of a private company which owns cattle feed lots located adjacent to the Mexican-American section of town. The residents have complained to the county because swarms of flies have gathered near the cattle and have infested their neighborhood and their homes. Neither the cattle company nor the city have taken any steps to abate the nuisance. CRLA is preparing to file suit against the county and possibly the County Health Department. They may also sue the company to stop them from continuing to house beef cattle on the lots without taking measures to abate the nuisance caused by the flies. One of the cases which did reach settlement after CRLA's intervention was when the U.S. Public Health Service agreed to construct a water system immediately for the Kashia Indian Reservation, although it had originally told the Indians that they would have to wait 3 years to remedy their contaminated and often nonexistent water supply.

More recently, CRLA was instrumental in getting a school district, which has been discriminating against Indians with regard to school bus service for some years, to provide the same service for Indian children it was providing for non-Indians. In another instance, following CRLA investigations which disclosed that in the memory of dozens of Indians living in the area no Indian had been requested to serve on the County Grand Jury, four Indians immediately received requests to serve. A high priority is given to cases concerning the preservation of Indian lands because they are a unique asset, available to no other poor ethnic group, and once lost they are forever gone. A second high priority is the improvement of tribal charters, organization and operation. A third is the reinstatement, expansion, or obtaining of special governmental programs available to Indians in other states but presently unavailable or insufficient in California. For example, Johnson-O'Malley funds for Indian education were withdrawn from California many years ago and never substantially replaced, although Indian students in other states continue to obtain hundreds of thousands of dollars in Johnson-O'Malley benefits.

During 1968 the CRLA budgeted its time between cases defending individual rights and law which could influence an entire class of cases. Selection was made of cases which could set precedents in striking at abuse and exploitation of large numbers of people such as defending the right to join unions. A typical case was that of two negroes and seven Mexican-Americans who worked many years for a Salinas carrot grower. They enjoyed their employment and were considered good workers, but were fired because of their union membership in the NFWA. The National Labor Relations Act prohibits employers in interstate commerce from firing workers because of union membership, but agricultural firms, regardless of their size, are exempt from this law. A CRLA attorney represented the nine men and gained an unusual settlement: reinstatement in their jobs, and a job guarantee for the rest of their lives at a minimum wage of $4,500 a year. If any of the workers are subsequently discharged, an impartial arbitrator selected by the American Arbitration Association will be chosen to resolve the dispute.

The bracero issue also illustrated the selection of cases dealing with class justice. In September 1967, CRLA attorneys brought suit against and then entered into an historic agreement with the U.S. Department of Labor, forcing it to abide by its own regulations, which prescribe the basis for declaring when a shortage of labor exists before certifying Mexican braceros for use in California farm work.

Another most significant CRLA achievement was realized in respect to the Public Welfare Medical Care Program. Governor Reagan had ordered a multi-million-dollar cutback in medical benefits to poor people, discontinuing dental care, eye care and glasses, and the provision of most drugs except the minimal lifesaving types. CRLA obtained a court injunction against the cutback, and much to the surprise of state officials, both the Superior Court and the California State Supreme Court ordered restoration of the medical benefits. Later events proved that the alleged fiscal bankruptcy of the Medical Care program was an illusion since the program ended the fiscal year in the black. Without the attempted curtailment of medical benefits, 1,200,000 public assistance recipients in the State of California benefited in a highly significant manner from the class justice medical issue. These examples strongly support the original CRLA decision to divide their time between class and individual case activity.

The author has observed and in a later chapter will discuss specifically another important feature of CRLA activity, their participation in hearings on governmental policy-making at state and national levels. CRLA attorneys argued at great length for revision of SDSW regulations which the author, as Deputy Director of the Department, presented to the Director for action. CRLA's representation of public assistance recipients at these hearings was welcomed by the author as an inestimable contribution. It is rare, indeed, to find such knowledgeable and effective representation of clients' rights. CRLA had made similar written and oral representations to the Federal Welfare Administration on cases such as the Sutter County's irregularities in welfare administration.

Could CRLA approaches and successes have evolved if the Office of Economic Opportunity had funded traditional organizations in California providing legal services to the poor? It is unlikely, since legal aid societies were long known by welfare agencies to offer very little relevant legal service and to rarely initiate cases for purposes of class justice. In 1966, nationwide, legal aid offices served 426,000 poor people on civil matters, while 200 public defenders defended the poor in criminal cases. The average caseload of a legal aid attorney ranged from an average of 541 (in 22 offices) to 1,792 (in 27 offices). In New York City the average caseload of a private attorney is 50 per year with the top 2 percent handling 500 or more cases. It has been generally agreed, as stated in the 1964 Annual Report of the President of the National Legal Aid and Defender Association, that Legal Aid Societies provide but an illusion of a service—an attractive facade.

On a national basis, OEO delegated to local Comunity Action Agencies the responsibility for choice of whether an existing legal aid society would run the OEO funded legal service for the poor, and of 250 OEO funded legal services, in the nation, 40 percent were administered by existing legal aid societies. OEO established local standards involving decentralization of services, expansion of scope of services and, most important, development of law reform as a major goal. While the American Bar Association endorsed the OEO standards for legal service to the poor in February 1965, Levitan and Burt concluded "that some of the pre-OEO legal aid societies accepted legal services program funds without changing their scope of activities."[4]

Many lawyers favor provision of legal services to the poor through an English-type plan termed "Judicare," which would channel business to local attorneys, ensure bar association control, minimize federal interference, and eliminate neighborhood legal offices. Such a proposal would insure that legal services to the poor would be provided, but disdainfully, as in medicare. The OEO Legal Aid Services experimented with Judicare in Wisconsin, Montana, California, and Connecticut, and concluded that: (1) Judicare negates the concept of a "coordinated attack on the legal problems facing the poor . . . Full term lawyers can provide the necessary concerted and thoughtful analysis to challenge the basic legal problems of the poor on a consistent basis; (2) Costs of Judicare are nearly three times higher than under the neighborhood law office approach —$139 per case compared with $48; (3) Judicare involves governmental investigation of fees charged and services rendered, a control which the Legal Services Program does not involve."[5]

In terms of reform, and class justice, the author questions that Judicare could, in 50 years, have equaled the few months achievements of CRLA in California. In addition to legal reform and class justice, the Legal Services Program has provided the urgently needed divorce service to the poor, a service consistently refused by traditional legal aid societies.

The author is particularly grateful that the Legal Services Program has successfully attacked barbaric injustice against poor people involving residence laws, responsible relative laws, man-in-the-house rules, and maximum grants, which devise establishes an equitable amount of need and then pays less than needed. Social workers had been absolutely impotent for decades in respect to achieving reform of the kind that the Legal Services Program is achieving in a few short years. The author's bitterness at failure of social work inspired reform does not obscure the hard facts of failure, but knowledge of such injustice and social work failure tends to make the Legal Services Program successes awesome. The author, as Deputy Director, California State Department of Social Welfare, was responsible for writing and defending welfare regulation, yet gained great personal satisfaction as CRLA attacked and destroyed great impediments to justice for the poor in welfare law—a feat the author was incapable of achieving in an unresponsive entanglement of law and regulation strongly supported by the county and state entrenched establishment.

The output of California's land is immense and diverse, including over 200 farm crop and livestock commodities. Always at the top of the ten leading farm producing states, California's 4 billion dollar crop tops second place Iowa by 470 million. The three leading agricultural counties in California, as well as the nation, are all located in the San Joaquin Valley. These three counties—Fresno, Tulare and Kern, with their abundant crops, are the most regressive, restrictive, reactionary, and exploitive in their actions toward farm labor. It was in such counties that birth was given to reform authors' books, such as Steinbeck's *Grapes of Wrath* and McWilliam's two books, *Ill Fares the Land* and *Factories in the Field*. Such California counties treat their livestock with more care and consideration than farm labor families, and approaches to the problem in other states do not differ.

Agribusiness must be considered as a powerful force in the economy of the state. The farmers and their associations have dominated the State Legislature, County Boards of Supervisors, and sheriffs, city police, and other officials to influence the necessary protective measures favoring the industry. The effect of this dominance has been to hold wages and working conditions at deplorable levels, and has degraded the welfare system whereby through force, welfare recipients have been used as pawns to hold down wages. The following chapter further describes contemporary problems related to welfare and the farm labor issue.

REFERENCES

1. Report of the President's Commission on Migratory Labor: Migratory Labor and American Agriculture, Washington, D.C., 1951.

2. McWilliams, Carey: Ill Fares the Land. Boston, Little, Brown & Co., 1942.

3. McWilliams, Carey: Factories in the Field. Boston, Little, Brown & Co., 1939.

4. Levitan, Sar A., and Burt, Jeffrey: The Poor and the Law, OEO's Legal Service Program. Poverty and Human Resources Abstracts, Vol. 3, No. 3, 1968.

5. Young, Patrick: Legal Help for the Poor. National Observer, August 21, 1967.

CHAPTER 8

PUBLIC WELFARE AND
SEASONAL FARM LABOR
—An Administrative Case Study

THE NEW LAW AND REGULATIONS extending the AFDC program to include unemployed parents injected a new element in traditional county welfare and employment department practices, particularly in regard to farm labor. The usual local community practices were not in conformance with the new law and regulations. While this situation was widespread throughout California, Alameda County has been selected to illustrate the general problems by means of the following series of events, practices and case examples.

The Farm Labor Office of the Employment Department notified the Welfare Department in Alameda County, that the manager of the Oakland Farm Labor Office and the manager of the Union City Farm Labor Office held a meeting with the Sunol strawberry growers on April 30, 1964, for the purpose of finalizing the plans for a day haul. The various terms and conditions of day haul requirements were re-emphasized to the growers, and after considerable discussion, were accepted.

It was agreed that the haul would start on Tuesday, May 5, 1964, with the bus departing from the Oakland or the Union City Farm Labor Office at 5:30 a.m. and returning at 6:00 p.m. The jobs, described as stoop labor, at $1.05 an hour, were open to both men and women who had normal use of both hands and were not colorblind. Payday was every Wednesday, but the pay period ended the preceding Saturday. Workers were to be reminded to take their own lunch and water canteens; wear hats, long-sleeved shirts and sturdy shoes; and women were to wear jeans or slacks. Employers were solicited individually, and orders for 40 workers were received. A bus with a carrying capacity of 40 was to transport them to and from the job. Registering, interviewing, screening, and referral of applicants was the responsibility of the Oakland Farm Labor Office, and employers were urged to feel free to direct any questions they had regarding applicant qualifications, etc., to this office. It was understood that the total number of workers requested by the employers might fluctuate from day to day depending on crop conditions.

On April 29, 1964, the Alameda County Welfare Department (ACWD) Employment Unit advised its staff that the strawberry harvest was expected to start rolling the following Tuesday, May 5, 1964, although there would be some work before then. The work was expected to continue into the Fall, offering a fairly steady work opportunity for men, women, and teenagers. Women were considered well-suited to the job. The Farm Labor Office of the Alameda County Department of Employment had asked the County Welfare Department to set up crews of recipients who would continue with the harvest through the summer months, and stated that if welfare could not furnish an adequate and regular number of workers, Mexican nationals would be called in to do the work. Each welfare worker was instructed to advise recipients about the specifics, and then submit lists of individuals who have been referred (giving name, address, case number, and worker number). Then, by letter, the Welfare Department advised 300 recipients of AFDC-U that it had been assured by the Farm Labor Bureau in both Oakland and Union City that farm labor was plentiful in these communities. In addition to the strawberry harvest, work was also available for men in both lettuce and corn, with transportation for a fee leaving from the Oakland Farm Labor Office at 5:00 a.m.

The Welfare Department asked recipients to contact the Farm Labor Offices as soon as possible, as this was considered acceptable employment under the Aid to Families with Dependent Children program, and failure to make such contact might jeopardize their eligibility. Any recipient who believed that his health did not permit participating in this type of work was to contact the welfare worker for arrangements for a medical examination.

On May 19, 1964, the following directive was issued to welfare department staff on the farm labor subject:

1. Recipient to report at office at 810 - 14th Street in the early A.M. (from 3:30 to 6:00) the hour varying with the crop and the season. Note AC transportation available all night from various parts of city. He is to present a green I.D. card Form No. 2650 at the counter. If there is a welfare representative present, Farm Labor representative will, when finished with recipient, send him to report to the welfare representative. The Farm Labor representative will stamp date on card and initial and return to recipient. If this is the first time reporting, the recipient will also present Form No. 17-29 (orange). The Farm Labor representative will date 17-29 and sign the back of one copy and show disposition and return it via mail to the County Welfare Department Employment Unit which will in turn forward to welfare caseworker. If the 17-29 is already on file at the Farm Labor Office and the recipient has not reported for a length of time, the Farm Labor representative will send a 17-33 "no show" back to caseworker. If there is a change in the status at ACWD, the case worker should forward Form No. 17-30 by mail to the Farm

Labor Office. (Discontinuance, physical disability, etc.) See procedure 20-7 for details.

2. If there is no ACWD representative at the counter and there is a welfare bus, the recipient is assigned to go on a bus. If there is no welfare representative or welfare bus, the Farm Labor representative at the counter will maintain a list of those reporting to the Farm Labor Office, and those referred to various buses, and those who were referred via their own transportation.

If there is not sufficient or applicable Farm Labor, recipients are to sign up for casual labor—especially for the current and/or next handbill passing crews. Recipients are to report daily unless otherwise excused.

On May 25, 1964, the welfare department notified its staff that large families as well as small families would be discontinued from AFDC-U because of the availability of farm labor. The possibility of men deserting their families because of the farm labor program was discussed. It was decided that if a man deserted his family the woman was to be referred to the Family Support Division to sign a complaint, and the case would be carried as an AFDC-U for 3 months before it was changed to a regular AFDC case. If the man returned to the home and was eligible to participate in farm labor, he would be referred to the farm labor program.

People were to be referred to farm work for the hourly rate of pay programs rather than piece work. If some preferred to do piece work rather than work at $1.05 an hour minimum wage, they could do so, but if they could not earn more by piece work they were to be referred to the strawberry crop at the hourly wage. A staff member was to check out the $1.05 per hour for the strawberry crop and obtain from the California State Employment Service (CSES) the amount the average worker could make at piece work in the various crops.

In June 1964, the SDSW conducted a review of Alameda County Welfare Department practice of referral of AFDC-U parents to farm labor. This review showed the following deviations from requirements as specified in the AFDC Manual, Department Bulletin 636 (Community Work-Training) and Department Bulletin 629 (Services):

1. Persons requesting AFDC are discouraged from signing applications by warning the parent the request for aid will be denied, since full-time farm labor is readily available.

2. Active AFDC cases are being referred to farm labor routinely without reference to required department procedures or use of proper referral forms.

3. Verification of a specific full-time job is not secured.

To bring your practice into conformity with existing regulations the following steps will need to be taken:

1. An application must be accepted when a person requests aid (AFDC Manual Sections C-011.20, C-011.30). This requirement relates to persons applying on any basis of deprivation (death, absence, incapacity, unemployment).

2. An applicant or recipient must be screened to determine his physical and mental ability to work (AFDC Manual Section C-171.1). When there is question regarding his ability he must be referred for a medical examination. After an applicant or recipient has been determined physically and mentally able to perform work, referral procedures outlined in Department Bulletin 629, Supplement 318 must be followed.

3. Applicants or recipients must be referred individually to a specific job at a specific wage. Since mass referrals to "available work" are not permissible, no individual shall have aid denied or discontinued on the basis that "farm labor is available." (AFDC Manual Section C-172).

4. In considering eligibility for assistance of a person who has accepted farm labor, the following practices must be observed:

a. Anyone who works 40 hours or more shall be considered fully employed. In such an instance, the warrant may be withheld until the outcome of the job placement is verified. Assistance may be discontinued if employment continues at the level of 40 hours or more per week.

b. If an individual works less than 40 hours in a week, he shall not be considered fully employed. In such a situation his net earnings shall be deducted from the total budget of the family.

c. There can be no arbitrary deductions from the grant on the assumption that future earnings will be a certain amount.

d. If a person fails to report to a job or fails to stay on a job, the grant may be discontinued only if the provisions of AFDC Manual, Section C-174 indicate that discontinuance is the proper course of action.

On July 3, 1964 to facilitate accommodation of Alameda County welfare staff to the SDSW regulations, procedures were clarified as follows:

If it appears that the family meet the regular eligibility requirements, a CA 200 is to be signed. After the signature has been taken, a very careful explanation of farm labor should be given. Be sure that the applicant has the opportunity to tell his full story. Explain to the applicant that under the AFDC-U Law, effective February 1964, a recipient (to be eligible) must be willing to accept employment without reference to his customary occupation or skill if he is physically and mentally able to do so. It should be explained to him that full-time employment in farm labor is now available through referral to CSES, and that a person employed in full-time work or refusing full-time employment is not eligible for aid under this program. It should be explained that it is recognized that the work is not easy, but that it is honest work which is a means of providing support for the family. If the person is unable to earn enough to cover the needs of the family, he should be told that his earnings may be supplemented. He must know that such supplementation will be made only if he has worked regularly and has put in full effort on the job. The system of clearing daily with the Farm Labor Office regarding average earnings and names of those persons going to farm labor should be described.

The regular referral system should be followed: Form 17-29 as well as the green Farm Labor card are given with the explanation of the use of the green card. Applicants should then be advised that as long as there is full employment available their applications will be denied. Applicants should also be told that the law indicates that an employer must give a complete statement of wages at the time of payment and that they should always request such a statement.

If an applicant has skills which might be in demand, a clearance should be made with the Employment Unit to see if there is any work available for him through that source, and he should be referred to CSES on the regular referral form, as well as to Farm Labor. Any situation in which it appears that regular employment might be lost by referral to the Farm Labor Office should be brought to the attention of the section head for a decision.

APPLICATION: On July 24, 1964, a sample case was submitted to welfare staff as a model: On July 6, 1964, William Jones was in office to sign an AFDC-U application for himself, wife, and minor child, Billy Joe. (Wife should also be recognized as having signed the application in the dictation if she was in the office.)

PROBLEM: Mr. Jones reports that he has been unemployed for six weeks. He last worked as a car washer but was laid off due to the lack of business, and he doesn't know when he will be recalled. This has been his only skilled employment. (State whatever skilled work the man has, if so indicated.) Mr. Jones reports he has no unemployment benefits due him. He states he reports regularly to CSDE; and he showed his notice indicating "exhausted," as verified through the California State Employment Service. He advised the worker that he was physically and mentally able to do any type of work. He reports no health complaints. (If he has any health condition which does not interfere with his employability, so indicate.)

Mr. Jones was informed that clearance with the California State Employment Service Farm Labor Office each day has verified the need for both skilled and unskilled farm workers. These jobs are available from the office at 810 - 14th Street and the Union City Office at 300 E Street, Union City. They are full-time jobs, eight hours or more per day, seven days a week if desired, and will last continuously through the summer and into the fall. The daily reports indicate that unskilled farm laborers are now averaging $8 per day or $173.33 per month for 5 days a week work. The family's welfare budget was explained to Mr. Jones. (If the budget exceeds the income, use the following wording: Mr. Jones was informed that if he went regularly and was unable to earn sufficiently to cover his welfare department budget, the welfare department would assist him in meeting the deficit.) It was explained that farm labor earnings are usually paid daily or at least once a week. If the family could not manage for a week, Mrs. Jones could contact the welfare department concerning her needs, and assistance could be considered upon confirmation with the Farm Labor office of his employment status. The method of referral to the employment was explained, including Form No. 1729 and the green Farm Labor Card.

Mr. Jones accepted the referral to employment and stated he would be able to manage until the first payday (or, Mr. Jones stated he was not a farm laborer and could earn more at other types of employment, and that he did not want to accept the farm labor referral.) He was advised of the regulations which do not permit payment under the AFDC-U program if full-time employment is available, (or, he was advised of the regulations which do not permit payment under the AFDC-U program if full-time employment is refused). Mr. Jones stated he would make his own plan. August 7, 1964, a review of the daily reports from the Farm Labor Office indicates that Mr. Jones failed to report for farm work, nor has he returned to the welfare department to report any change in his physical or mental health or any reason for failing to accept full-time farm employment.

APPLICATION DENIED

REASON: Code B-1, applicant refused full-time employment through Department of Employment.

The real need for such elementary training case examples eloquently speaks to the desperate nature of county practice. A review of some cases of families on AFDC-U follows:

FAMILY A: The father of this family is 58 years of age. He has had "two ulcer operations and one bowel operation." He needs to eat small amounts through the day. The case was reported as discontinued June 1, 1964, because of availability of farm labor. The record indicated the father missed reporting for farm labor only three days from May 12 to the 31st. On two occasions he was fired. Mr. A was attempting to comply with department demands but he was finding it physically more difficult each day. The client was seen by a private doctor on June 11, 1964; and on June 27, 1964, the June check was granted. The doctor told the department that this client was only eligible for light labor and then only if he ate eight small meals a day. A medical exam finally resulted in the family receiving AFDC on the basis of the father's incapacity.

FAMILY B: On May 2, 1964, the county notified the family that the June check had been suspended due to availability of farm labor. Mr. B, the father, was not fast enough working in strawberries and therefore switched to peas, where he was only able to earn an average of $2 per day. He paid $1.25 per day for transportation. The man was 53 and was willing to work but was incapacitated due to high blood pressure. This was verified when a medical exam was completed on him. Checks were released to the AFDC family on June 16, 1964, as the case was transferred to basis of deprivation—incapacity. This man had been a bicycle mechanic and it appeared that farm labor was not a satisfactory referral. Considerable time was lost in social service and vocational planning because of the determination that this man should take farm labor. There was no evidence in the record that he had ever had experience as a farm laborer. There were six children in the home ranging from 6 months to 6 years of age.

FAMILY C: Mr. C has not been able to earn enough at farm labor to feed his family. He claims that he has worked faithfully at farm labor for the past 12 summers but this summer the pressure is too great. Even though he goes out every day, he cannot earn enough. He stated that he cannot get on any of the buses because the crews are already selected. He shows up regularly at the farm labor office but is thrown off the buses when he gets on. There is a question as to whether farm labor is actually available to this individual. The record showed that between June 22 and June 30 he reported each day for farm labor between 4 and 5 a.m. but was not hired. Aid was not restored. There is a suggestion that the man's physical and/or mental incapacity prevented him from accomplishing much on a job and for this reason he was thrown off the buses and was not able to work full time at farm labor. Several of the children in the home had medical problems; home conditions were not satisfactory; and there was a report that two of the children passed away just after birth. One of these died from pneumonia and the cause of the death of the other child was not recorded.

FAMILY D: The mother was notified that AFDC was to be discontinued as of June 1, 1964, due to availability of full-time farm labor. The husband left home to seek other types of work since he knew from previous experience that he could not make a living at farm work. The mother signed nonsupport papers against the father. The father was jailed for four days for nonsupport. The mother was about to deliver (overdue) and no child care plan had been made for the period of confinement. When the father refused farm labor, aid was discontinued for the father and his children but continued for the stepchildren. The 16-year-old son who acts as interpreter and helps out around the home, could have been included in the budget under Section C-201.1 if he had been placed on a work-training activity. The county had not implemented this section of the policy. The father had employment in previous years both in farm labor and cannery work. It was his pattern to leave home periodically in order to take this work during the summer, and at times in the winter months. From the time he was requested to take farm labor there had been so many changes in the family's health status and jail sentences of the father that it appeared aid could have been continued for the total family in this case without interruption. The father claims to have completed the sixth grade and the mother the second grade, therefore some effort should be made to determine both parents' potential. Some vocational or employment planning should be initiated for the older children in the home, particularly the son.

FAMILY E: As farm labor was available, the family's aid was discontinued May 15, 1964. Although the father went to the fields he was fired because he was too slow. He is a member of a laborers union and was concerned that if he did not report every day to the hiring hall, his plug may come up for work and he would not be available to take it. On June 29, 1964, his plug dropped because he was absent. State policy does not allow for an individual to be exempt from taking any form of employment because it is necessary for him to plug in at the union office. The record has shown that this 26-year-old father had unskilled work experience in lumber and casual labor which generally made it unnecessary for the family to receive assistance from the welfare office. At the time the family applied for aid the father was drawing Unemployment Insurance Benefits (UIB) in the amount of $39 weekly. There are five children in the home, from 5 years of age to 2 months. The social service plan developed for the father at the time the family began receiving aid in April 1964 showed that employment counseling should have been directed toward the father's return to construction work or as an automobile mechanic. Although he had training in the army as a mechanic nothing in the record suggested he had been evaluated for future vocational training in this field, and there had been no plan in the record except to send the individual to farm labor. The stability of the father's prior work experience and family life suggests that he had vocational potential greater than farm labor and this should have been explored.

FAMILY F: This family "was broken up by the Farm Labor Program." The mother reported that they separated because they argued over money matters. Mr. F, 20 years of age, refused to go to farm labor because he and his wife felt they could not survive on what he could earn. Mrs. F is now receiving aid for herself and one child and her unborn child. The father had attempted to pick strawberries but was fired. He then tried beans at 65 cents a basket but was not fast enough. He had to hitchhike 20 miles back from the strawberry field, having earned just $1. He was fired because he had stepped on the strawberry plants. It appeared probable that Mr. F had worked on farms previously but his usual work was with a cement contractor as a laborer. He was a school dropout in the eleventh grade. He had done a good job of filling out the preemployment interview questionnaire. The services plan showed he needed vocational counseling and testing but received none before the Farm Labor issue arose.

FAMILY G: Prior to the farm labor referral, the county had done an outstanding job in respect to a vocational evaluation for Mr. G. He was very cooperative, was attending job preparation classes, and was enthused about it. He had worked at the post office, as a truck driver, and as a nurse's aide; however, there was no recording of farm labor experience. His wife's earnings as a domestic amounted to a net of $81 per month. Under the present policy it would have been possible to continue the father on AFDC until a tooth extraction problem had been settled. This man was a musician in the Navy from 1948 to 1954, and training in relationship to his music background should have been explored. He has had trouble obtaining employment since his arrest for possession of marijuana in 1963. Since the Probation Department, Department of Corrections, was involved in working with the father, closer coordination with probation services on planning would have been of value.

On September 15, 1964, the Alameda County procedure regarding AFDC-U applications was described by the welfare department at the request of the State Department of Social Welfare. When an applicant comes to the waiting room, he briefly indicates to the clerk the reason for his visit to the office. If it appears that an application for assistance is being requested or is needed, the clerk asks for identifying information and then tells the person that he will be interviewed by a social worker. The case is cleared with Index, and if there has been a former case record, it is obtained. If the applicant has not been known to the office previously, a case number is assigned and the clearance returned to the waiting room.

A Social Worker III then interviews the applicant. Information is obtained on the applicant's work history for the past 3 years, as well as information regarding union affiliations. The basic eligibility requirements are discussed—residence, real and personal property, etc. If these requirements appear to be met, an application is signed by both the man and wife, or by whichever one is present. Information is secured about the applicant's plan for seeking employment. Status of his UIB is also explored. His physical and mental ability to work is discussed.

An applicant who has any skills which might be in demand is referred immediately to the ACWD Employment Unit. Either an Employment Counselor will interview him or the job file is made available to the social worker who will clear to see if there is a potential referral which can be made. Where a job is available, the applicant is given a referral card to the employer and is then asked to notify the worker of the results of the interview. In some instances, although a definite job is not available through the Employment Unit, the Employment Counselor will make a file on the applicant and will inform him that he will be contacted if any job opportunities become available. The applicant with skills is also referred to CSES on Form 17-29.

If it appears that a farm labor referral is indicated, careful explanation of the farm labor situation is given to the applicant. He is told that clearance each day with the California State Department of Employment, Farm Labor Office has verified an ongoing need for both skilled and unskilled farm workers. He is given the addresses of the Farm Labor Offices where the work is available and is told that the jobs are full time (8 hours per day or more), 7 days a week if desired, and that they will continuously last through the summer and into the fall. He is also given information regarding the average earnings of the unskilled worker as verified regularly by the Farm Labor Office. The family's budget is then explained to the applicant, and he is told that if he is unable to earn enough to cover the family's needs, his income may be supplemented by the county, providing he works regularly and puts in full effort on the job. He is told that a daily report is received from the Farm Labor Office regarding the availability of jobs and the rate of pay, and that farm labor is usually paid daily but in some instances pay may be made weekly. If he is unable to support the family until payday, he is told that his wife may contact the office and that assistance could be considered until payday upon confirmation of his employment status with the Farm Labor Office. If the applicant indicates he is not willing to accept the referral, he is given the opportunity to explain his decision in the matter. If it appears that the applicant might lose regular employment by referral to the Farm Labor Office, the social worker has been instructed to bring the situation to the attention of the Section Head who will make the determination as to whether the farm labor referral is in order in such a case. In those cases on which the farm labor referral appears in order, the regular referral system is followed. A referral card is presented daily at the Farm Labor Office, it is stamped, and the applicant's name is phoned to the welfare department with information regarding the job to which he was referred.

The applicant is advised that during the period full-time employment is available, there is no eligibility for AFDC-U, and that unless circumstances change, his application will be denied. The applicant is also told that according to law, an employer must give a complete statement of wages at the time of payment, and that the employee should always request such a statement. He is advised that if he does not accept the referral to the full-time work which is available, he is not eligible for assistance. He is told that if for any reason he does not secure employment, and if there is any other change which he feels would affect the situation as discussed with him, he is to contact the office. He is told that his case will be kept open for about two weeks to make sure that he has secured full-time work. He is also told that at any time there is a change in the farm labor situation, he may contact our office.

Situations in Which Farm Labor Referral Is Not Made: If the social worker learns from the applicant that he does not feel that he is physically or mentally able to do farm work, verification of incapacity for this type of work is discussed with the applicant. He is told that he may secure a doctor's statement or if he has no doctor or does not wish to secure the statement himself, an appointment may be made with the county physician who will make the determination as to his ability to do this type of work. If upon completion of the medical examination it is found that the applicant is able to do farm work and there are no other extenuating circumstances, the farm labor referral is completed. If the medical report indicates that the applicant is employable but is unable to do farm work, the application for AFDC-U is processed in the usual manner and a referral to the Employment Unit is made.

The foregoing Alameda County Welfare Department practices on AFDC-U clearly emphasize farm labor placement, although they allow for referral to other types of labor and training. An evaluation of these practices, however, indicates that local welfare and employment agencies cooperated with the growers in mass employment of welfare recipients. Following complaints from welfare rights organizations and case appeals, the State Department of Social Welfare conducted a survey to determine whether Alameda County administrative direction and practices in referral of AFDC-U applicants and recipients to farm labor were consistent with SDSW policy; and to determine whether the relations with the Department of Employment present problems in carrying out policies on referral of AFDC-U parents to farm labor. The findings were drawn from:

Interviews with the Chairman of the Board of Supervisors; administrative staff, supervisors, and caseworkers of the county welfare department; staff of the Department of Employment, San Francisco SDSW Area Office; and Farm Labor Offices in Alameda County.

Review of directives and instructions of the Alameda County Welfare Department concerning AFDC-U and farm labor.

Examination of 97 AFDC-U case records of (1964) May and June denials and April, May, June discontinuances: a detailed review of 49 case records involving implementation of the farm labor policy; and interviews with 19 of the 49 recipients who were discontinued or denied as a result of the farm labor policy.

Application Process of AFCD-U re Farm Labor: In May, when full-time labor was available, it became Alameda County Welfare Department policy that there be no eligibility under AFDC-U except in cases of verified physical disability. A 15-minute screening interview was conducted to determine whether or not farm labor referral was appropriate. Denial of aid was inevitable either on the basis of refusal to report for full-time work or on the basis of full-time farm work. This practice continued in effect with the July 3 modification asking the applicant to sign the CA-200 as a beginning of the application process although this did not move beyond the screening interview unless physical disability was proven, or verified union plug-in found essential to imminent employment. Case findings revealed no determination of readiness or lack of readiness for the labor market or for a program of self-support planning, nor was consideration given to the problems of transportation or undue hardship which farm labor might cause. Of the reviewed cases which were discontinued or denied because of the availability of full-time employment in farm labor, some were automatically discontinued without specific referral to farm labor, others were discontinued without evaluation of the effect on the employment which had been held immediately prior to denial. There were few who were known to have had previous farm labor experience. In none of the discontinuances was there any actual verification of wages.

Referral of Active AFDC-U Cases to Farm Labor: Contrary to the intent of Supplement 318 of Bulletin 629 (Release 5), arrangements for farm labor referral were made directly between staffs of the Farm Labor Office and the Alameda County Welfare Department. The welfare department made a commitment to the Farm Labor Office in April to meet the anticipated need for an agricultural labor force of 300 men by means of the referral of men and women on the AFDC-U and General Assistance rolls. This commitment was made without proper consideration and protection of the needs and rights of the welfare recipient or applicant and without careful review and evaluation for job referral in light of the emphasis on rehabilitation and family planning.

A form letter No. 3-24 (5/64) was sent the first week in May to approximately 300 recipients of AFDC-U and G.A. Staff interviews and records indicate that the mass mailing of the letter was not preceded by adequate screening and evaluation for referral. The appropriate farm labor referrals were overshadowed by those which were inappropriate and detrimental.

The case findings of 49 records of April, May, June discontinuances and June, July denials authenticate the lack of appropriate screening for physical, mental, or emotional ability to do farm work. Where some evaluative statement was made, it was meager, uninformative, and not in conformity with Regulations 171.1 and 172.1.

Physical examinations for the determination of ability to do farm work were the only clear-cut effort at screening; and during the undifferentiated referral to farm labor, these were hastily and superficially performed. The doctor states that under the present administration, the medical statement re a recipient's ability to work carries almost the complete weight in the case worker's decision re farm labor or any employment.

On September 24, 1963, the Board of Supervisors passed a resolution establishing the required caseload standard and supervisor-supervisee ratio in order for the welfare department to qualify for the 75 percent federal reimbursement on service. The department is not properly evaluating and assessing personal, family, social, or economic functioning on AFDC-U cases for farm referral as defined in the criteria for social study. The review of 49 cases revealed a high percentage of incorrect actions because of lack of appropriate screening; verification of specific job secured, and/or wages; and consideration of other compelling reasons for refusal to accept farm labor. Administrative directives corroborate the fact that recipients on AFDC-U were, in the first instance, considered eligible for farm labor referral. By resolution, at its meeting on September 8, 1964, the Board of Supervisors approved the welfare work policy. In conference, the Chairman of the Board did express regret that the county had not developed a greater number of work training projects and speculated about the value of farm labor training.

Staff Orientation re AFDC-U and Farm Labor: It is significant that the Alameda County Welfare Department was one of the few county departments which did not participate in the state program of staff training on AFDC-U in January, 1964. Although the Director and Assistant Director state that staff meetings on this policy and farm labor in particular were held, there was little evidence of its substance and effectiveness.

The directives concerning practice in the implementation of policy are restrictive and prohibitive. There was little or no evidence of staff or administrative understanding of the basic intent of the

AFDC-U program nor acceptance of the principle that parental unemployment is a basis for deprivation.

In implementing the unemployed parent addition to the AFDC program, the intake responsibility was assigned to the program section with responsibility for General Assistance intake. Concurrently, the ongoing General Assistance caseload was screened for transfer to AFDC-U. Such organization of functions is indicative of the county department's view that AFDC-U was actually an extension of the General Assistance program with a more liberal budget and with state and federal participation.

Observation of Practices in Hiring, Transportation, and Payment of Farm Laborers: The early morning trip by SDSW representatives to the fields was informative and significant. The physical facilities of the Farm Labor Office, as well as the trucks, were adequate. A Farm Labor Office representative believed that the farm contractors exploit the workers and the farmers. It is known that one contractor in particular over-charges the farmers and charges workers for transportation, even though he is paid for it by the farmer as well. Although he claimed he gave wage vouchers, he could not produce a sample.

The staff in both the Oakland and Union City offices has an accepting and understanding attitude toward recipients and others in farm labor. They support and are active in a rehabilitative approach through MDTA projects and regret the lack of referrals from the county welfare department.

The Farm Labor Office has detailed comments on individual recipients who reported for employment. It could not be determined that this information (reported to the welfare department) was evaluated and used in continuing rehabilitative planning with the family. All interviewed members of the Department of Employment staff in farm labor and area office felt that in light of recipients referred, there had been no attempt to screen or evaluate cases individually, and that in many instances the recipient indicated that the social worker had reflected her attitude that they needed only to check in, not to work. Farm labor records indicate that of the recipients or applicants who got to the fields, some quit in the middle of the day; some were met by friends and driven back to town as soon as they got off the bus; some created scenes; a few did a good job, but didn't work more than a day or two; and a very few became consistent farm workers.

Relations Between Department of Employment and County Welfare Department: The Department of Employment did appear to have expected the county welfare department, through pressure placed upon the welfare office directly and through the Chairman of the Board of Supervisors, to meet the farm labor need. The welfare department, in turn, committed itself to supply 300 strawberry pickers without consideration of the AFDC-U program requirements. Both departments failed to operate under the interdepartmental agreement established between the State Departments of Social Welfare and Employment.

SUMMARY

Many factors influenced the attitudes and actions of persons involved. The phasing out of the bracero program meant that the Department of Employment would have to meet farm labor needs with an increasing number of domestic workers. This had been foreseen, as evidenced in the department's 1963 Annual Farm Labor Report, which describes, in part, its reorganization to strengthen local management of farm labor functions and programs.

The AFDC-U addition to the welfare program on February 1, 1964, resulted in the transfer of a group of "socially unemployable" General Relief cases to AFDC-U without careful screening and case planning. In April, the Department of Employment, as in previous years, let the welfare department know the beginning farm labor need for workers. The Director of the Alameda County Welfare Department was motivated by strong convictions that a man should choose to work rather than receive aid; that the intent of AB 59 could better be met by the Department of Employment as an employment problem; and furthermore, that AB 59 sustains a built-in group who would try to avoid work in order to continue on aid. He believed that the increase in grant under AFDC-U made it more attractive than General Assistance was, thus lowering a man's incentive to work. He stated that, as an individual, he was concerned about the low wage for stoop labor, the hardship placed on the farm laborer, and other work conditions which made the job untenable, but as director, he could not take cognizance of these factors. The Welfare Rights Organization seized upon these issues and the civil rights unrest, thus bringing the matter to the attention of a larger group which insisted upon action. It is possible, as the Welfare Director claims, that the activity of the Welfare Rights Organization interfered with the recipient's normal access to his social worker. All of these factors contributed to the problem and resulted in a smoke screen which made it difficult to examine the directives and practices of the welfare department in line with the survey intent.

The Welfare Rights Organization (WRO) in Alameda County took strong exception to welfare department practices in regard to farm labor referrals of AFDC-U applicants and recipients and organized picket lines and sit-ins. The farmers newspaper, *California Farmer*, on June 6, 1964, tooks strong issue on the subject, editorializing as follows:

"Things have come to a pretty pass. The Welfare Director of the Alameda County Welfare Department, has the gall to suggest that people work for a living. With this sort of crazy thinking on the loose, who knows what to expect next? But never fear, he is not getting away with it easily. He's being picketed by the World Owes Us a Living Committee, or as they prefer to be called officially, the Welfare Rights Committee. The Director has taken the position that so long as there are jobs, agricultural or otherwise, open within the county, no welfare checks will be sent to those physically able to fill these positions. The Welfare Rights Committee maintains it is the right of those unemployed to sit around home and expect the working people to support them.

"Alameda County has a total population of just under one million people, and 26,780 cases on welfare involving 49,272 people. Of these, 13,289 are on Old Age Security; 792 are blind, and 2,045 are totally disabled. This leaves 613 cases as of March 1, on the new AFDC-U program (Aid to Families with Dependent Children with Unemployed Parent). These cases involve 613 men, 2,306 children and a total of 3,441 individuals. Of these 613 cases, 80 have claimed a disability which requires that they have a physical examination. After the examination by a doctor, 50 of these were said to be fit for work and 30 were certified disabled.

"This welfare load amounts to $50 million per year in Alameda County, of which 18 percent is collected in the county. The remainder is split about 50-50 by the state and federal governments. It doesn't require an advanced math degree to figure a $50 million welfare tab divided among just under 1 million people comes out $50 for every man, woman and child.

"What started all this, anyway? We're told by State Department of Employment officials that it really began to get out of hand April 20. On this date, a discussion was held between the employment and welfare department officials in an effort to figure how to get welfare receivers who did not have transportation into strawberry fields. After some discussion and after checking with the strawberry growers in the Sunol area, it was decided the growers would provide a bus at their expense to haul welfare people from Oakland to the fields.

"This was not as easy as it sounds, either. It was necessary to go to Sacramento for an official State Department of Employment ruling on what constitutes a reasonable haul. It is now official, 50 miles or one hour travel time one way is considered reasonable. In other words, no one can refuse work because it is too far from home if it is within 50 miles or requires not more than one hour to get there.

"Growers arranged for a 42-capacity bus at a cost of $40 per day and the welfare department agreed to have a crew of strawberry pickers ready on May 5. The bus showed up at the Farm Placement Office in Oakland and one worker showed up. Startled welfare office people couldn't believe it and said things would be better from there on in. The second day, things improved 100 percent—two women showed up. One was the same lady who came the first day. By now, the welfare department was getting fed up and told one and all they were going to hold up checks if those on the welfare rolls did not accept jobs. This scared the hell out of ambitious folks on the public dole and on the third day, six showed up for the bus. At this point the Department officials figured it would be cheaper for the growers to provide a taxi. But the Assistant Welfare Director was determined, so he arranged to have a bus from the sheriff's office and for a few days as many as 30-35 welfare recipients showed for the ride to the fields as the word got out that checks were being held up.

"Then growers began to complain about the work being done by these so-called workers. The Assistant was told many showed up at the field, then walked off. He found this hard to believe and told the Department of Employment folks that these were good people. To settle this hash once and for all, the Assistant Chief of farm placement, picked up the Assistant Welfare Director on May 13 and drove to the field. They drove up unannounced and found eight people lying or sitting down on the side of the road outside of the field at 11:00.

"When asked why, the welfare people said the work was too hard, they were fired for being too slow, or they didn't want to pick strawberries. The Assistant Welfare Director told them if they did not work they would have their checks cut off. In checking with the growers, it was discovered this was about par for the work they were getting from the welfare office referrals. They were taking 1 hour and 45 minutes to pick a crate of berries. Growers informed the Assistant Welfare Director they couldn't afford to pay $1.05 per hour when it was taking almost two hours for these people to pick a crate. The berries picked hardly covered the wages paid. The situation got no better. On May 14, 29 workers went to the field in the morning but only nine were on hand for the bus ride home in the evening. With this situation, the Department of Employment finally certified braceros to do the strawberry picking in Alameda County, thus providing another victory for the loafing class. The first day the braceros arrived there was one fellow who didn't know if he was to pick the leaf or the berry. He filled his first crate in 30 minutes, after about five minutes' instruction.

"At this point, the tremendous job turned in by one and all to recruit workers should be pointed out. Growers spent $300 for advertising in Oakland, Berkeley and Hayward newspapers. Spot announcements were aired on five Bay Area radio stations. A call for strawberry workers went out statewide through the state farm labor placement offices. And last, but by no means least the welfare office tried, and still the bracero had to be brought in. We are only talking about 162 acres of strawberries requiring a maximum of 300 workers. An all-out effort has failed to provide these workers in a county with a million population. If it can't be done this year what happens next year when the bracero is no longer available?

"Fifty people have actually lost checks in the county because they have refused to accept available work, and 200 checks have been held up pending investigation to determine why they did not accept positions offered. The average check lost amounted to $162, which is maximum for a man and wife and one child. Small family cases are generally referred to agricultural jobs, because they can make more in agricultural jobs than they can make on welfare. Large families on welfare in California can't afford to work. They make more money letting you and me support them with our tax contributions. As you might expect, the loafing class is not about to take this sort of thing lying down. This is the one thing that will get them up and moving— in a picket line. About half a hundred objectors showed up at the county welfare department headquarters in Oakland and expended as much energy marching up and down the sidewalk as they would have doing a day's work.

"The picketing was sponsored by a newly formed Welfare Rights Committee, which claims that a man performing forced labor, such as picking strawberries at $1.05 an hour, actually loses money. This happens because his earnings are deducted from his aid to families with dependent children payments.

"A Berkeley attorney is legal advisor to the rights committee. (You didn't know the unemployed had lawyers?) They also have support from the International Longshoremen's and Warehousemen's Union, according to business agent Bill Burke of Warehouse Local 6.

"The welfare committee is headed by a Berkeley hospital speech and hearing specialist. Committee members maintain that 'children are the real victims, should a father be unwilling to work'. The committee chairman said families are being broken up because fathers are being forced to work long hours in the field. The Welfare Director says, 'I don't see how a father working eight hours a day breaks up a family'."

The *Oakland Tribune*, on September 17, 1964, supported the Alameda County official job policy position on the welfare issue in the following statement:

"The County Welfare Director declared today there will be no change in Alameda County's policy of referring welfare recipients to farm employment. He made the statement following a telephone conversation with State Social Welfare Director. Earlier this week the State Director met with 17 members of the Alameda County Welfare Rights Organization, which conducted a five-day demonstration at the county welfare building two weeks ago to protest the policy. The Director of the State Department of Social Welfare staved off the threat of a similar demonstration at the State Capitol by promising to discuss the policy. He also pointed out that some changes are being made in the regulations governing farm labor for welfare recipients, including *one which provides that they be directed to specific farm jobs rather than employment placement bureaus.* 'Based on my telephone conversation with the State Welfare Director,' the local Director told members of the County Welfare Commission yesterday, 'I can say there will be no change in the basic county policy. The state is studying the farm labor question, and we would, of course, obey any new policy directives.'

"Benny Parrish, former social worker who was fired in Alameda County and who resigned in San Francisco to take part in the demonstrations, has claimed that 300 families had been illegally cut off Alameda County relief rolls because the family heads had refused to take farm jobs.

"The County Welfare Director said the WRO was told by state welfare officials that the county's farm referral program does not violate the intention of the Legislature and that it conforms with state law. He explained the practice is followed to varying degrees, by several other counties, including Contra Costa. One of the primary weaknesses of the system, he continued, stems from the difficulty in obtaining complete records of what recipients earn in the fields. The Director explained that since some labor contractors refuse to give their workers statements of earnings, the county has to accept average farm pay figures as the basis for determining the amount of additional aid payments. He told the commissioners that sit-in demonstrators were allowed to stay in the welfare building over the Labor Day weekend because the county had no policy against citizens remaining on public property after closing hours. However, he added, an emergency ordinance adopted by the Board of Supervisors last week gives department heads power to have buildings cleared. From now on, he said, any demonstrators will be removed from the welfare building by sheriff's deputies at 5 p.m.

"The commission unanimously adopted a resolution supporting the County Welfare Director and commending him for his handling of the crisis. They also cited the Oakland police and fire departments and the sheriff's office for their cooperation in controlling the pickets."

Thus the biased reporting in newspapers combined with Board of Supervisor's support, as usual, downgraded the exploited farm workers position in favor of the growers.

The State Department of Social Welfare reviewed the Welfare Rights Organization activities. It was observed that the Welfare Rights Committee and its group "sat-in" at the Alameda County Welfare Department's premises Friday evening, from 5 o'clock through the Labor Day weekend, and until approximately 5:30 p.m., September 8, 1964. On Saturday afternoon everything was quiet. There were three people in front of the building talking, and one person sleeping on a cot in front of the entrance doors. Other members inside were seated and quiet, and the Sheriff's Deputy on duty said there had been no difficulty. However, the Sheriff's Office was not allowing food to be brought in and, if people left the building, they were not allowed to return.

On September 8, the County Welfare Director and three members of his staff met with Welfare Rights Committee representatives and SDSW representatives without resolving the problem. The Alameda County Board of Supervisors passed a resolution on September 8 against sit-ins in any county buildings or premises. As a result of this resolution, the Welfare Director and the Sheriff's Department of Alameda County, at the conclusion of the conference, ejected all of the Welfare Rights Committee and their sit-in demonstrators.

The WRO maintained that they had demonstrated by picketing and sitting-in only when all other means failed. They claimed that on many occasions they had gone back with applicants and recipients, insisting that Alameda Welfare Department employees accept applications, and that on many other occasions they had review conferences with the supervisors without success. They did admit that in some cases they were able to convince the supervisors that the applicants were entitled to assistance and the applications were processed. On other occasions they went further and had the cases reviewed by Division Chiefs and by the Assistant Welfare Director. They indicated that on at least four different occasions they had attempted to contact the Director, only once had he ever made an appointment with them, and on that occasion he had broken his appointment. They felt strongly that he was not available to them as a final resource in adjusting complaints of applicants and recipients. Their second demand was that the SDSW review all 300 plus cases that had been discontinued at the beginning of Alameda County's mass referrals to farm labor. They insisted that SDSW review all denied applications during this same period and that the results of this review also be made public. The final demand of this group was that the State Social Welfare Director meet with them on Monday, September 14, in San Francisco. In addition to meeting with them, they demanded that the SDSW revise its policies:

1. So that union men who have "plug-board" responsibilities not be referred to farm labor;

2. So that men in training status, either on welfare department projects or in training classes, not be required to go to farm labor;

3. So that it redefine and make clear the "reasonable" provisions in the sections whereby travel time and travel distance are stated specifically, and 4 to 6 hours a day will not have to be spent by farm laborers in travel to and from the field.

One of the areas of conflict became apparent. The Welfare Rights group and clients, in general are apparently blocked from getting to top administration in the Alameda County Welfare Department. Regularly available to them are the social worker, and Grade I and Grade II Supervisors; however, less regularly, they are able to see the Division Chief; on a number of occasions, they have seen the Assistant Director; but never the Director. Finally, on September 8, 1964, the Alameda County Welfare Director, and representatives of the SDSW, met with representatives of WRO, as members of the "sit-in" demonstrators in the Alameda CWD building, and six cases were discussed. Running throughout most of these cases was the Welfare Rights Committee's insistence that farm labor was unreasonable, the travel distance and time unreasonable, and the wages atrociously low.

The first case was that of Mr. and Mrs. T. There was considerable discussion of the fact that the welfare department has insisted that Mr. T accept Farm Labor employment. He was a member of the laborer's union, was required to plug-in at least once a week, and if he was at the union hall and someone else whose name came up on the list did not accept the job, he could accept it. He had gone to Farm Labor Employment on several occasions and as a result had missed his name being at the top of the list at least twice. However, he finally managed to be there when his name came to the top of the list, and he is presently employed at construction labor. Mrs. T indicated that the family had no money, in fact they had not even had money for carfare for Mr. T to get to the Farm Labor Office to accept farm labor employment. The Welfare Director authorized granting of General Assistance to the T's until Mr. T's first paycheck came through.

The second case was that of Mr. P, whose record showed that he had been released from Alameda County's prison farm on April 1, 1964. He had received a physical examination and had been found able to do farm work. Although Mr. P had given his consent to have the record read to the group there was an increasing awareness on the part of several members of the group, during the reading, that the man was seriously emotionally disturbed. This particular case was on appeal, and after the Director had a chance to review the county's record that was there, he indicated that the man should be granted assistance, probably ATD, on the basis of presumptive eligibility.

The third case was that of Mr. M. There was a long discussion about the discrepancy between the amount workers report they receive from farm labor and the amount reported by the CSES Farm Labor Office. It was at this point that the Welfare Rights Committee mentioned the Catholic organization that is now called the West Oakland Farm Workers' Association. This organization, according to the Committee, had proof that farm labor wages were nowhere near the amounts reported by the farm labor office of CSES. There was a very long discussion that involved such things as working conditions in the fields, and the payment of money for the use of toilet facilities and for water to drink. It also involved the fact that the labor contractors who picked up the men at the CSES Farm Labor Office refused to give the workers a statement as to how much they could earn. It was indicated that Alameda County Welfare Department was using an average for what workers were supposed to be making in the field; that there was as much discrepancy as $8 and $9 between what the workers report they earned and what CSES reported earnings were in the field. One worker stated that he had been working in the fields and that he made from $3.50 to $4.50 a day, whereas the Farm Labor Office reported that in the work he was doing the average worker made $10 to $13 a day. There was increasing suspicion that the farm labor contractors were not paying the farm laborers the total of what they earned. It appeared that farm laborers honestly reported their earnings and that growers or farmers honestly reported what they paid for the produce picked or harvested. The only answer to the discrepancy was that the farm labor contractors who hauled the men to and from the fields were pocketing the difference. The refusal of farm labor contractors to give the farm laborers a statement as to what their earnings were at the end of the day, inasmuch as they were paid in cash, was prima facie evidence that there was some illegal or unethical activity going on. The demand on the part of the worker for a written statement as to how much he earned places the worker in a precarious position inasmuch as the farm labor contractor in picking the men up next morning to go to the fields can easily refuse to take the worker who has demanded such a thing of him the night before.

The fourth case was that of Mr. H, who applied in April and was discontinued on May 15. There were five children in the family, he was a laborer, had missed his plug-in twice, and was involved in a training program in which he was being trained to be a shoemaker. The county records indicated that he was progressing only "fair" and that in the estimation of the county his progress was not such as would give them a tentative date as to when he would complete his training program and become competitively employable. It was the county's decision, that he should be referred to farm labor and at the conclusion of farm labor they would place him back in the training program on a more intensified basis, and if he could then complete his work as a shoemaker they would continue to assist him until such time as he could become a wage earner as a shoemaker. Again there was considerable discussion back and forth concerning farm labor, travel time, travel distance, low wages, lack of a bona fide job at a specific wage. The discussion included reviewing events from the early months of the year, when Alameda County first began sending men out to pick strawberries at $1.05 an hour. The Assistant Welfare Director had discussed with the labor contractor the possibility of placing some of the men who were not fast enough on a piecework basis of 60 cents a box for strawberries rather than at the $1.05 an hour wage. The Director indicates his Assistant did this because the labor contractor was going to fire the men because of their inexperience and slowness. The Assistant felt that since the men were already there, they should have a chance to pick at the piecework rate and then if they speeded up enough they could be paid at the $1.05 an hour rate. The Director indicated that he would not have the county reverse its original decision in the third case or in this case; therefore, both cases were not granted.

The fifth case was that of Mrs. R, a Negro grandmother who had applied for ATD. The Director indicated that they secured a possibility of a live-in job for her as a domestic. However, after reviewing the case, he agreed that because of her arthritis she would be unable to work and therefore authorized the granting of General Assistance while an ATD application was being processed. Inasmuch as she was taking care of several grandchildren, there was a question as to why she could not be included in the AFDC grant as a needy caretaker. She received about $94 a month for the grandchildren at the present time, but if she were included as a needy caretaker, the grant would go to approximately $160 or $170 a month, an arrangement which could have been made by the welfare department under existing rules.

The sixth and final case was that of Mr. S. This case had two problems, a residence question, and eligibility for ATD. The man was living with a woman who claimed that he was the father of several of her children. Previously she had claimed a different man as the father, and the case had been to a court decision in a Southern state. The case has been on appeal, had been heard by SDSW approximately ten days earlier, and had been forwarded to Central Office with an urgent and priority action attached to it.

As a followup of the meeting at which the six cases were discussed, an SDSW representative reviewed in depth the case of Mr. H, the fourth case mentioned. This was the case of automatic discontinuance of AFDC-U in May 1964 when farm labor became available. The Alameda County Welfare Department had refused to accept three subsequent reapplications, and Mr. H had been given a medical examination and pronounced able to do farm labor. The family had received some AFDC-U assistance in April and May 1964 to supplement UIB of $39 a week. The UIB ended some time in June. Mr. H had been notified by letter in May that assistance was being discontinued because of the availability of farm labor. He never had been previously employed at farm labor, lived on a farm, or had any contact with farm work. He did not receive any employment counseling from the Alameda County Welfare Department. When he telephoned the Alameda County Welfare Department office after receiving the notice of discontinuance, he was told to go to the Farm Labor Office, and was asked if he did not receive in the letter a card referring him there. No such card had been enclosed. He re-received one later by letter. When he telephoned, he obtained the address of the Farm Labor Office, applied there for work, and was sent to a job picking strawberries. After two hours, he was told he didn't know how to do this, was too slow, and was fired. He received cash wages of $2.10, out of which he had to pay $1.30 for round trip transportation and 30 cents for a glass of water. Unfortunately, he does not know the name of his employer, but thought the Farm Labor Office might have this information. On his own, he later went again into this farm area, found work for one day picking peas, but was able to earn only $3. He does not know whether he was working for the same employer as before.

On or about June 11, when Mr. H reapplied for assistance to the Alameda County Welfare Department, a supervisor talked to him. He explained he was fired from the strawberry picking and had earned only $3 the day he picked peas. She told him people earned $8 to $10 a day doing that. He told her he did not know how to do work of this kind. (Besides his lack of experience, Mr. H's natural tempo seems rather slow and he probably cannot work as fast as a small, quick person.) He pointed out that the most he could possibly earn after deductions, would be less than the $39 a week UIB he was then drawing, and he would not be eligible to that if he were employed. (Deductions would have been 50 cents for transportation from the outlying area where he lives to downtown, $1.25 bus fares to places of employment, and 30 cents per glass for water in some places.) The supervisor told him that it was a welfare rule that they could not give him AFDC-U now that there was farm employment. The only kind of help he could get would be General Assistance, and he was not eligible for that because he had not lived here three years. (Mr. H came to California in 1962 from Louisiana. He is Negro. He first lived in San Francisco and had been in Alameda County for about two years.) His only employment had been a little occasional work for a motor company in Oakland. His father had loaned him money to pay rent in new quarters when the family was evicted from their former home for nonpayment of rent, and the Lutheran Episcopal Church had assisted the family some. That organization had called periodically in the home, and knowing of the family's situation, brought them some food last week. The Welfare Rights Committee also had given some assistance.

Mr. H, a member of Union Hall Construction and General Laborers Union, was prevented by lack of money for transportation in June and July from reporting to the Union Hall as required. Consequently, his plug was dropped to the bottom of the board and he was no longer considered for jobs that did come up. He showed a signed card indicating that he had reported on August 3, 7, 14, 21, 28, and September 4 and 11, 1964. This also showed he has moved from an L-12 to a C-7 position on the board. When he gets back on the A roll, he probably will be able to get a job. He returned to the Alameda County Welfare Department three times in June and July to reapply for assistance but each time was told to go to the Farm Labor Office. He has not returned since his third reapplication in July when he was told that his reapplication would continue to be denied. It was after this that he requested a fair hearing. This request was prepared by the Welfare Rights Committee and was formally filed on August 19.

Mr. H had generally been able to support himself and family which included five children and two stepchildren. He grew up in Shreveport, Louisiana, where he was usually employed as a truck driver, and he worked in this capacity during 1956-57. In 1958, he was employed by a lumber company cutting knots. In 1959, he was a truck driver for a drug store in Shreveport, and for some time thereafter drove a truck for a college. Since coming to California in 1962, he had not been able to get into a truck drivers' union. Consequently, he had usually done maintenance or construction work. In February and March 1963, he worked for a firm in San Francisco until work got slack and the firm went out of business. He next worked for a builders maintenance company in San Francisco for a couple of months. He then joined the Construction and General Laborers Union and was employed intermittently in various jobs secured through this union until December 1963. He had little employment during 1964. He is a member of the Army Reserve in which he is classified as a mechanic's helper. He is somewhat hard to understand because of a pronounced Southern accent, and he sometimes did not understand what was said. His education is limited; he wasn't sure of the spelling of the names of some firms and people to whom he referred. It takes time and patience to interview him and get facts. His limitations appeared more cultural than due to lack of normal intelligence. He was very sincere, earnest, and desirous of working. He was never demanding or belligerent. He stated sadly, "I don't know how to do the farm work, and they don't want me around the farms because I spoil things." If he had proper employment counseling or training and necessary financial assistance, he had good potential for supporting his family. He commented that so far they had been able, with the help they received, to manage so the children could eat, without his leaving home. This was not said as a threat but sadly, as a sacrifice he'd have to make it necessary. However, he is still hopeful of securing private employment through the union before things come to that pass. He was informed of his right to a fair hearing, even if he does have work by then, and probably will carry through on the hearing. He seemed satisfied to know his request for a hearing had been received.

The Alameda County Board of Supervisors adopted a resolution on the Welfare Work policy on September 8, 1964, commending welfare actions as follows: be it

Resolved that, without equivocation, it is this County's position that every able-bodied welfare recipient shall work as a condition of entitlement; and be it further

Resolved that this Board of Supervisors does consider farm labor as a legitimate type of employment; and be it further

Resolved that this Board does not ascribe to the anomaly of a person being too proud to work—but not too proud to draw welfare; and be it further

Resolved that this Board does hereby express the utmost confidence in our Welfare Director, that he is administering the County Welfare program in an efficient, business-like manner and in conformity with all the County, State and Federal regulations.

The exploitation of agricultural workers has not notably changed since the 1930's. In the guise of offering "an honest day's work" for not such an honest day's pay, the growers' stratagems, in league with the traditional practices of local welfare agencies, have kept the farm worker as oppressed as he ever was, in relation to the total economy.

In 1966 as in 1936, agreements between the growers, the relief agencies, and the employment departments have resulted in denial of assistance to needy people who show any unwillingness or inability to accept work in the fields. During the WPA era of the 1930's, recipients were removed from relief rolls, and during 1965, they were denied training placement in educational programs for not accepting farm jobs during harvest seasons. The lowest possible wages were offered—25 cents per hour in 1935, and $1.05 per hour 30 years later. Relief recipients were required during both eras to spend hours in travel to their jobs. In 1935, Chambers of Commerce universally praised cheap labor systems, and in 1965, the Alameda County Board of Supervisors passed a resolution in praise of welfare actions which implemented the perpetuation of such systems. In 1935, Solano County relief recipients were ordered into the fields at pitifully low wages and were removed from relief rolls if they refused such work; and in 1963, the Solano County Board of Supervisors signed a resolution petitioning the State Department of Social Welfare to revise proposed AFDC-U regulations providing more income for certain unemployed families on relief than they could possibly have earned on agricultural jobs. In 1966 and 1936, clergymen remonstrated on behalf of farm workers in California after investigating the conditions under which they were forced to work.

In earlier chapters, the generational aspects of poverty and dependency were observed. It is appropriate at this point to observe similar generational qualities in middle class attitudes and systems of oppressing the poor. It may well be noted that generational oppression is as persistent and intractable as generational dependency and probably more harmful to our development toward a mature society. The oppression of the poor and the bigotry in our nation are strange anachronisms in our pseudo scientific era.

Only when traditional oppressive practices toward the poor are restricted, and alternative and more enlightened practices are established in terms of providing greater opportunities to the poor, will the generational aspects of poverty and dependency undergo any appreciable change.

CHAPTER 9

AN EXPERIMENT IN
GUARANTEED ANNUAL INCOME

WHEN INCIDENTS RELATED to the farm labor issue motivated the California State Department of Social Welfare to sponsor improved conditions for the farm worker, the Department took unprecedented action—it adopted regulations in which seasonal farm labor was identified as part-time work for the purpose of giving farm workers eligibility for AFDC-U. The Federal Bureau of Family Services agreed with this interpretation. The effect of the regulation in giving eligibility for AFDC-U, was supplementation of earned farm work income and continuance on aid for those families not earning enough in full-time farm wages to provide their families with a minimal AFDC budget. SDSW Bulletin No. 644 was issued as an emergency regulation May 1965, and was readopted, October 1, 1965. One objective of the Bulletin was to encourage and to make it practical for as many individuals as possible to engage in seasonal farm work even though their full-time earnings would not produce enough to fully support their families on a continuous basis. The Bulletin declared the action consistent with findings and recommendations of the State Social Welfare Board, which spent considerable time and gathered a great deal of information concerning the relationship of earnings of employed families and the amount of aid for which they would be eligible as recipients of AFDC.

Most families, unless they are very large, can earn at least as much as they could receive on aid. The primary group for which this is not true are those engaged in seasonal farm labor, and average size or larger families so engaged earn less than they would receive on aid. In addition, their earnings are adversely affected by multiple factors: Many work for one employer only for a short period of time (some only for one day); there is no security in future earnings; and few of the usual side benefits are available to this group. The State Social Welfare Board pointed out that when the situation of the farm labor family is viewed as a day-to-day situation, it is a self-defeating viewpoint. Not only does it destroy continuity in carrying out the plan of service for the parent and child, but it also gives the family the feeling that welfare has no solid commitment to help them better their condition. Another factor that has adversely affected the interest of AFDC-U families in farm labor has been the delay in restoring aid when they have emergencies or are without work.

THE LONG VIEW

Since the long view requires that every effort be made to maintain continuity of services and provide aid promptly when there is bona fide need, the primary objectives of changes in the regulations were: (1) To encourage parents to accept farm labor employment even though they may not have had previous experience at such work, or are unable to earn enough to maintain their families; (2) to continue services of the county welfare department to these families during periods when earnings do meet need; and (3) to reinstate or change assistance payments promptly when earnings are inadequate or fluctuating.

The proposed Bulletin No. 644 would come to be viewed as an experiment in a modified form of guaranteed annual income.

Bulletin No. 644 was not developed with the guaranteed annual income conception in mind but rather as a response to the need of earlier described, exploited farm workers, and as an antidote to intractable generational systems which sustain the exploitation.

The proposed Bulletin No. 644 regulations were as follows:

Unemployment of a Parent

"Deprivation due to unemployment of a parent is considered to exist when either parent is:

1. Not working at all, and is available for and seeking employment, or receiving training essential to his future self-support, or

2. Employed only part-time.

"If the father is employed full time, deprivation due to the employment of the mother is considered only when the mother has been in the labor market and/or has a valid and workable plan for employment or training for employment, including a satisfactory plan for care of the children, and the ability to work and care for the family.

"Deprivation due to unemployment of a parent ends at the time of the month in which the parent has secured full-time employment and all of the following conditions are met:

a. The employment is expected to continue,

b. The unemployed parent has worked at least one full week, and

c. At least one full week's pay has been received before the end of the month.

Definition of Part-Time Employment

"For the purpose of determining deprivation due to unemployment of a parent under this program, 'part-time employment' is defined as:

1. Employment which normally affords less than 173 hours of paid regular work per month, or less than the number of hours con-

sidered full-time by the industry for the job (as established by the California State Employment Service) if under 173 hours.

Aid is discontinued for a family with a parent employed part-time under this definition when the family is no longer in need, i.e., when a determination is made that net income meets the total family need, or,

2. Employment at farm labor affording irregular, temporary, or intermittent work which provides no assurance of a dependable amount of income shall be presumed to be part-time employment. The presumption that farm work is part-time employment is overcome if:

a. The person has worked for not less than 173 hours in each of the immediately preceding three months, and

b. The employment is expected to continue at or above this level of hours indefinitely beyond the next month.

3. Aid is discontinued for a family with the parent employed at farm labor under this definition:

a. When the presumption of part-time employment is overcome, or

b. At the end of the last month in the calendar quarter in which the family cannot be reached and has not replied to letters or other notices, or

c. There is other tangible evidence such as mail returned because addressee is unknown or left no forwarding address."

CASEWORKER PROCEDURES

Implementation of the newly revised regulations was provided in directives outlining the following procedures for caseworkers.

Informing Applicants and Recipients: When applicants and recipients are being referred to the Department of Employment for work they shall be instructed that they are to work as many hours as the job requires and shall be given information about continuance of aid if their earnings from farm labor are not adequate. They are also to be informed of the procedures they must follow if benefits are to continue. Whenever a parent accepts farm labor, the family shall be given a copy of the brochure, *Information to Farm Workers* as soon as it is available from the State Department of Social Welfare. Persons accepting farm labor employment need to understand clearly their responsibility for securing statements of their earnings and the deductions made by the employer each time they are paid, and of retaining these statements for verification purposes. Any farm worker who has difficulty in obtaining a statement of his earnings should report this immediately to the county welfare department so that the Department of Industrial Relations can be advised of the need for corrective action.

Establishing Amount of Earnings: In establishing the amount of the earnings of a recipient in any period, the county may require submission of a statement of earnings and deductions, and wage statements provided by the employer or other verification if there is reason to believe the recipient is withholding information or reporting incorrectly. The county should inform the recipient of the specified time for reporting income each month and make reporting as simple as possible for the recipient. The reporting time specified should be one that will result in as little delay in payment as possible, but will necessarily be related to the payment method used in the county. Pay records submitted to the county welfare department for inspection are to be returned to the recipient promptly.

Employers and contractors of agricultural workers are required to keep accurate records available at all times for inspection by representatives of the Department of Industrial Relations.* The records must contain information for each employed individual, including name, address, social security number, time of reporting, hours worked, gross pay, and itemized deductions. Employers and/or contractors are required, for each pay period, to give workers written statements of earnings (either as a detachable part of the check or separately on pay day) showing gross earnings, the pay period covered, and itemized deductions and net pay.

If a farm worker reports that he has received no statement of earnings or there is disagreement between the worker and employer regarding amount of earnings and deductions, the case and pertinent facts shall be reported by the county to the office of the Department of Industrial Relations, which has responsibility for the area in which the county is located. If a recipient reports that an employer or contractor has not given him the required statement of earnings or there is a dispute as to the amount of earnings and deductions, the *farm worker's statement of earnings* will be accepted until the Division of Labor Law Enforcement or Division of Industrial Welfare makes its report, unless there is reason to believe the recipient is withholding information or reporting incorrectly.

County Responsibility for Payment and Services and Intercounty Relationships. In recent years, more and more farm workers are establishing home bases from which they operate. They may secure all their work in the "home" county or may work in a number of counties. When a recipient family remains in an established home while one or more members leave for short-time employment or when a home is maintained to which the recipient family will return when not working, the county in which the home base is located has responsibility for determining eligibility, paying aid, and developing

---
*Labor Code Section 1175; Industrial Welfare Commission Order No. 14-61; and Labor Code Sections 92 and 1696.5.

and implementing a plan of services until the family establishes a home base in another county.

When an applicant family remains in an established home while one or more members have left for short-time employment the county in which the family is living is responsible for taking the application, determining eligibility, paying aid and providing services. When the applicant family has accompanied the employed member to another county, whether or not there is a home base elsewhere, the county in which the family is located is responsible for taking the application, determining eligibility, paying and providing services until the family returns to their home base or, if they have no home base, until the family remains in one county for a period of at least 60 days, even though the employed member may stay in the county or go to work in one or more counties. Transfer procedures are initiated at the time the family returns to the home base or remains in another county for 60 days.

Providing aid and services to families of seasonal farm workers requires not only great flexibility, but the closest possible intercounty cooperation in maintaining eligibility, determining the correct amount of grant, and the rendering of services. Since it is particularly important that as much continuity of planning and provision of services as is possible in the circumstances of each individual family be maintained, there should be a two-way, intercounty flow of information about the family.

Services. The following requirements for priority need services in Department Bulletin No. 629, Release No. 6, are applicable to all families with seasonal farm employment.

1. Priority Need for Self-Support Services: All families with a parent employed in seasonal farm work have a priority need for services relating to self-support. Special emphasis should be given to training of the parent and older children to upgrade their skills and abilities and provide opportunities to become self-supporting on a year-around basis. A person engaged in a training project which will enhance his chances of increasing his earnings with greater security should not be referred or encouraged to accept work which will interfere with such training. Since the care of children of farm workers is frequently lacking or haphazard, county welfare departments should provide assistance that will assure adequate and suitable child care during the hours a parent (or parents) are traveling and working.

2. Priority Need for Services for Children with Special Problems: All families with a parent employed in seasonal farm work and children of school age have a priority need for services relating to education. It is particularly important that children of farm workers should be encouraged to remain in school, and provision should be

made to enhance their chances of adjustment to school and to enable them to participate within their capacity. It is most desirable that the farm worker's family remain at home during the school year, even though the father may voluntarily accept employment away from home. Help should be provided to older children to make it possible for them to remain in school and to prevent dropouts. When older children work, they should be encouraged to conserve their earnings for school needs.

3. Priority Need for Services for Children in Need of Protection: All families who do not have a home base but move around to follow the crops have a priority need for services for the protection of the children. Special help should be given to these families to assist them in achieving some semblance of stability for the child.

THE PUBLIC HEARING

Policy development within the State Department of Social Welfare derives from consensus based on varying views which have been mediated through administrative, legislative, and judicial processes. Public hearings held under the auspices of the Department reflect, partially, this process. The Director of the State Department of Social Welfare asked his staff to read into the hearing record correspondence related to Bulletin No. 644. Some communications noted in the hearing record are excerpted as follows:

We have a wire from the Northern California District Council ILWU which urges approval of Department Bulletin No. 644. We have a wire supporting and encouraging Bulletin No. 644 to continue in force from the Central California Chapter National Association of Social Workers. A wire from the Migrant Ministry Project, 1927 N. Beverly, Porterville, California strongly supports Bulletin No. 644. A wire from the Tulare County Grand Jury goes on record as being definitely opposed to Bulletin No. 644. A wire from the Tax Payers Association of Fresno County, endorses the resolution passed by the Fresno County Board of Supervisors opposing Welfare Bulletin No. 644. A resolution of the Board Supervisors of the County of Placer opposes Bulletin No. 644. A resolution by the Board of Supervisors of Madera County opposes Bulletin No. 644. A letter from the County of Santa Cruz, County Grand Jury, goes on record opposing Bulletin No. 644. A resolution by the Board of Supervisors of Merced County opposes the proposed part-time employment of farm labor under Bulletin No. 644. A resolution and interim report opposing State Social Welfare Department Resolution concerning farm labor in Bulletin No. 644, is sent by the Secretary of the Kings County Grand Jury. A statement from the Santa Clara County Welfare Department supports the Bulletin. A wire from the Fresno County Pomona Grange No. 44 opposes adoption of Department Bulletin

No. 644. A communication from the Associated Farmers of Fresno County opposes Bulletin No. 644. A resolution of the Board of Supervisors of the County of Fresno opposes Bulletin No. 644. A resolution from the Fresno County Farm Bureau Board of Directors opposes Bulletin No. 644. A statement from the Social Action Committee of the First Unitarian Society of Sacramento agrees in principle with Bulletin No. 644. A communication from the office of the Board of Supervisors of the County of San Benito opposes Department Bulletin No. 644.

The following statement was presented at the hearing to the Director of the State Department of Social Welfare by his staff: Bulletin starts with the preamble, a general statement containing facts which we would like to read into the record. At the time that the Bulletin was drafted and approved by you and sent out, it recognized that California was in the midst of a seasonal farm labor crisis, and that this was having a large impact on the state's economy. Therefore, one of the purposes of the Bulletin was to encourage and make it practical for as many individuals as possible to engage in farm work, even though the earnings did not produce enough to fully support the family continuously. The Social Welfare Board, the preamble also recognizes, has findings and recommendations as a result of time and information invested that went to the relationship of the earning of employed families in the amount of aid for which they would be eligible as recipients of AFDC. The finding was that generally families with the exception of very large families, earn at least as much as they could receive on aid. Notably, however, there was an exception, and this primary group, which represented the exception were those engaged in seasonal farm labor. And here it was found that the average and larger families engaged in farm labor earned less than they could receive on aid as an average. In addition, the earnings were considerably affected by some factors such as the lack of continuity of work, the tenuous nature of the work and the absence of fringe benefits to this group of people which were generally enjoyed by the rest of the employed population. We, therefore, sought a means of making it possible for these average to large families to engage in farm labor and to encourage this to the utmost degree and to also give them some assurance that their basic needs would be met. To this end then, this Bulletin defines seasonal farm labor as part-time employment...We labeled the objective of the inclusion of these individuals in the part-time definition as: (1) The encouragement of parents to accept farm labor employment even though they may not have had previous experience at such work or they are unable to earn enough to maintain their families thereby; (2) the continuation of services by the county welfare department for these families during periods when earnings do not meet their need; and (3) the prompt reinstatement of, or change in, assistance payments when earnings are inadequate or fluctuating. There has been little doubt expressed by anybody that this group of people is probably one of the most deprived groups which California has, and that not only do we recognize this fluctuation and uncertainty of earnings, but we also recognize that this group, because of its very nature, is probably least able to take advantage of the ordinary services which individuals in communities have available to them. Notably, this is true in health services. And if we look at some of the studies which have been made by the State Department of Public Health in California, it becomes crystal clear that because of their mobility, and lack of earnings there are serious health problems in this group, and they have been unable to avail themselves of the health services of which California boasts. This is also true in education. Time and again, we hear of children whose educational pattern has been disturbed, their learning has been hindered, and their incentive to attend school has certainly been dulled because of any lack of continuity in their educational services. When we talk about child care, we become aware of the lack of provision that is made for supervision of children when both parents are engaged in field work. We have been advised by some of the ranchers regarding the danger of youngsters falling into irrigation ditches or being endangered by machinery or other hazards. So we stress the need for child care in connection with the Bulletin's provision that we expect county welfare departments to give such service at the same time that the families are engaged in seasonal farm work under the part-time definition.

These are the main issues which have been raised around the Bulletin, and significantly, the statements of purpose to help in a service way have never been disputed. Getting the service to families has been raised as an administrative problem, but almost everybody agrees about the need for providing such service and the possibility of giving a better life to this group. Finally, the Bulletin represents a genuine attempt to help a significant and a vital part of the citizenry of this state.

The Director of the State Department of Social Welfare commented that certain references were made to an attempt in Bulletin No. 644 to do something that was rejected by the Legislature. Specific reference was made from time to time about AB1987. The Director asked whether there was any definition in AB1987 of part-time employment. His staff responded that the bill did not define part-time employment nor did it deal with the issue as it relates to farm labor. AB1503, a bill relating to unemployment insurance, defined "partial unemployment" within the concept of the field of unemployment insurance, as any kind of employment which provides less than adequate wages. Both the employment agency and the welfare department use a different concept wherein a person who works a specific number of hours is considered to be employed full time and therefore not entitled to unemployment insurance. We find that under unemployment insurance, there is also a situation in which an individual can work and earn less than his weekly benefit amount, and if he is considered to be working full time, he it not entitled to receive any unemployment insurance for a period longer than two consecutive weeks. AB1503, which would have changed the situation, passed both Houses of the Legislature but did not clear the Governor's desk. The legislative intent was clearly to provide for some support in the case of families or individuals who are earning less than the amount they would be entitled to under unemployment insurance. The SDSW Director stated that to the best of staff knowledge, then, there was nothing before the legislature dealing with the matter of part-time employment as it relates to public welfare.

The Director of SDSW then asked staff to read into the record three case histories which are summarized as follows:

The C family resides in an urban county in the Bay Area, which is a source for a farm labor supply for the coastal counties where harvesting of the crops creates seasonal labor demands. The C family received Aid to Families with Dependent Children on the basis of the unemployment of the father for several months prior to February 1965 when Mr. C found full-time employment. The family contended that Mr. C, the father, did not earn enough to support the family, as they were about $100 short of what they received on AFDC. The maximum participating base for six children with two parents is $337. Mr. C has almost no schooling, he is 28, and Mrs. C is 27. They are the parents of six children ranging from 2 to 9 years old. Mr. C has supported his family from farm work, other seasonal work, including cannery work, and steady work for one year as a poultry ranch-hand and for about one year in a paper salvage plant. General Relief and later AFDC have been sources of support for the family during periods of unemployment. After AFDC was discontinued in February 1965, an appeal was initiated. The appeal hearing disclosed that in April 1965, Mr. C continued to work on a mushroom farm at an hourly wage of $1.35. During some weeks he worked 10 hours a day, with take-home pay of $67. Based on four and one-third weeks in a month, his earnings would have been $290.34. However, there were other weeks when he lost a day or two because of rain, in which case his take-home pay averaged $40 to $50 per week. The family paid $85 rent. They said that after they paid their rent they did not have enough money left to buy food for the family of eight. In the appeal decision, the hearing officer stated that "it is obvious that this family is obliged to subsist at a poverty level even though the bread winner is fully employed. However, there is no remedy to this problem within the framework of the AFDC-U program as presently constituted." ("Presently constituted" referred to the period prior to adoption of Bulletin No. 644.)

The second case is that of a family who was denied AFDC before the adoption of Department Bulletin No. 644 because the father was regularly employed at least 40 hours per week as a farm laborer. The A family consisted of Mr. A, aged 57, Mrs. A, aged 34, and their nine children ranging in age from 3 to 15 years. The father's last job was in a so-called labor camp, but he lost his employment because of the size of his family. Since then they have purchased a house with monthly payments of $74. During a period of unemployment, the family received AFDC, which was discontinued when the father obtained full-time employment as a farm worker. His take-home pay for the week ending March 9, 1965, was $57.23 based on $1.50 per hour. This equates monthly earnings of $248. The pastor of the local church, at the appeal for the family, testified that "their minimal expenses for rent, utilities, furniture, and car payments are $232 per month, not counting food, clothes, and other expenses." The pastor conceded that the children's father is employed at least 40 hours a week, but noted that the family's income or resources are insufficient to meet its needs. In this situation, the brief of the appeal hearing states that "the county recognizes the family's financial problems and specifies that it does not provide financial assistance from county funds. The county, however, explored a variety of sources through which the family might be able to obtain some assistance, including clothes for the children." The decision to deny the appeal for AFDC was based on the finding that the father was employed full-time, notwithstanding evidence that his income from employment is less than the amount for the allowable needs on the AFDC standard for a family comprising the parents, nine children, and an expected child.

The third case is that of Mr. D, who was referred to pick strawberries at $1.05 per hour and earned this regular hourly rate the first day. On the second day, after working 4 hours, his work was not considered satisfactory, and he was laid off. On subsequent days, the farm labor office referred Mr. D to bean picking 70 miles from his Bay Area home so he had to leave for work around 4 a.m. and return home after 8 p.m. The job was paid at the rate of 70 cents a field basket. After paying $1.25 for his round trip transportation, Mr. D took home on the first day about $4 and the second day about $6. Meanwhile, the county welfare agency determined that regular full-time employment was available for Mr. D, and denied his application for aid but continued aid for his stepchildren. The referee, in evaluating the hearing evidence, stated: "We believe that Mr. D is genuinely desirous of finding a way to support his family but needs vocational guidance and other supportive services from the county welfare department." Grounds for granting the appeal for aid were that after the man quit the bean picking job he sought other employment in the city where he lived and that the travel time involved in the bean picking job had been a compelling reason for quitting.

The Director asked to have a letter from the Farm Workers Organization, Porterville, dated March 17, 1965, placed in the hearing record. The letter concerned appeals made by three men who had applied for assistance and were turned down because the welfare department said they had full-time jobs. One had not worked 40 hours in any of the weeks of February and March; another had been employed part-time for two or three days in sugar beets, and had earned only $8 in February; and the third had earned a total of $25 in February. Each of these three men, who had about $100 to support eight dependents during the month of February, were referred to jobs by the Department of Employment, and in no case, were they given full-time work. Nevertheless, the welfare department told them that they were employed full-time, and this was the reason given for withholding their checks. Although it is clear that the welfare department did not investigate whether the men had full-time or part-time jobs, it denied aid on the assumption that the jobs were full-time. This happened in a number of cases. Most men are not willing to make a complaint because the Department of Employment will put down that they refused to work. The welfare department, these men say, will deny your case if you get a bad report from the Employment Department. "Will you please investigate these cases, and also question the Department of Employment and the county welfare department about their practices in determining eligibility?"

Against this background, the Director opened the hearing to testimony that anyone wished to offer with respect to the regulation and particularly with respect to its adequacy and pertinence as a definition of the type of unemployment coming within the provisions of the Welfare and Institutions Code.

The first testimony, from a representative of the County Supervisors Association of California, and in opposition to Department Bulletin No. 644, stated: "It is our understanding that the rationale behind the adoption of this regulation on an emergency basis, which precluded it from proper consideration, was to increase the supply of farm laborers in the state of California. Available data that we've been able to lay our hands on, indicates that purpose hasn't been fulfilled and there is no evidence that it will be fulfilled in the near future. While the intention is perhaps highly laudable, the means are questionable and it doesn't appear that legislative intent has been followed through by adoption of this Bulletin especially if it is given permanency. If this emergency regulation is given permanence, it will be going, in our opinion, directly contrary to expressed legislative intent, when the Legislature objected to AB1987, which would have considerably expanded the definition of part-time labor in the state of California. We think that this is adequate reason for rescinding the emergency regulation which was adopted at a time when the Legislature was still in session, when it was considering AB1987, when there was still some likelihood that the legislation would have been enacted. The ruling has certain other important defects which I will only briefly highlight in the interest of time. We believe that if the Department supplements full-time earnings in farm labor it will be adding encouragement to the continuing low level of wages paid to farm labor employees. We think that the Department is underwriting and encouraging the continuance of low wages paid these people. We think this is nothing more than a farm subsidy. It unjustly classifies the farm laborer as being unworthy of his hire, and relegates the farm laborer to a position of second-class citizenship. It states in effect that the farm laborer is unable to justify by the fruits of his labor a sufficient wage to support himself and his family. We don't believe that this is true, that it's justified. Furthermore, by no stretch of the imagination can the definition of part-time labor be stretched to include entire occupations in which many individuals are employed on a full-time basis. Employment doesn't become part-time because it is one type of occupation or another, it is either part-time or it isn't part-time. No twisting by semantics, philosophy, or good intentions can get around the fact that a person working 40 or more hours a week in any occupation is fully employed. This fiddling with the English language is resulting in significant departures from the status quo in an apparent disregard for the wishes of the Legislature. Furthermore, we believe that if this emergency regulation is given permanence, it will antagonize the general public. Public welfare has always had to defend itself against a variety of unfair charges, the general suspicion that people can take advantage of society's willingness and ability to assist those who are in need, and we think one important position in the defense of the public welfare system has been our ability to state categorically that we do not assist those who are willing and able to go to work when work is available. We believe that if the time comes when full-time earnings should be supplemented by government assistance, the decision should be reached by elected officials, not by administrators assuming the role of the policy-making body. In conclusion, we believe that there has been a clear statement of legislative intent expressed in this regard by the rejection of AB1987, and we hope the Department will so interpret it."

A member of the Board of Supervisors from San Joaquin County testified:

"Although the San Joaquin Valley is the heart of agricultural economy in this state, in fact in the Nation, we of the San Joaquin Valley have found no evidence that this regulation has or will result in more people engaging in farm work or those already so employed being encouraged to work additional hours. The following question was asked of the Valley County Welfare Directors, and I quote, 'In your county, has the implementation of Bulletin No. 644 as of May 24, resulted in additional persons working in agriculture or those already so engaged working more hours?' Responses were as follows, Fresno County, no; Kern County, no; Kings County, no; Madera County, no; Mariposa County, no; Merced County, no; San Joaquin County, no; Stanislaus County, not apparent; Tulare County, not to our knowledge. Ironically, there are indications that the Bulletin has resulted in some reduction of persons engaged in such work. Even with the absence, this harvest season, of bracero labor, valley counties report they have more unemployed parent AFDC cases receiving aid.

"In regard to the welfare standards, there is inevitably diminution of incentive on the part of the motivated individual to aggressively seek agricultural work to the maximum possible extent. As a practical matter under the regulations, if a man works 3 hours per week he cannot be required to put in additional hours, yet historically, farm laborers have worked as much as 10 hours a day, 6 or 7 days a week during a peak harvest season. Although we have not had enough experience to date to provide documentation, it is believed that welfare monetary supplementation will tend to encourage workers to hold their work week to a 40-hour maximum, thereby resulting in a loss of man hours to employers. We are cognizant of the fact that your staff members have stated it is not the intent of the regulation to establish a 40-hour maximum work week. However, we believe this will nevertheless be the practical effect. A press release from your office on this subject, dated June 9 states, and I quote. 'Department of Social Welfare research indicates that the State and the counties will not be spending more on welfare assistance under the new order. On the contrary, federal funds based on a caseload will increase as the caseload increases. Meanwhile the average grant for farm employable families will decrease because they need only partial assistance rather than maximum allowance. This can hardly result in county welfare budget increases. There is no question that the new order will enable more families to qualify for some welfare assistance but the reduced average grant per family plus the increased federal funds will more than offset the additional caseload and related administrative costs.' Queries made to our valley counties and their responses are as follows: By what gross amounts, federal, state and county, inclusive of aid payments and administrative costs, do you estimate it will or has increased your budget request? Fresno County's reply: Increase, $1,816,442; Kern County, $1,129,001; Kings County, specific figure not available but impact significant; Madera County, $669,000. Public welfare in the San Joaquin Valley, both in terms of expenditures and personnel, has a considerably greater impact than that in the state as a whole, and constitutes an area of dire concern to the property taxpayers of our county. It is respectfully requested that you void your Department Bulletin No. 644 for the following reasons: (1) It evidently goes beyond legislative intent of existing law for the reasons just indicated and therefore it does not reasonably and logically fall within the purview of an administrative ruling. (2) It has not served its primary stated purpose, the alleviation of the seasonal farm labor crisis that was particularly acute this spring at the time of the issuance of the bulletin; nor does it offer the prospect of serving its intended purpose when future acute farm labor crises occur during the adjustment period resulting from termination of use of foreign labor. (3) Contrary to the predictions of your staff, Bulletin No. 644 will cost the counties more money for public welfare. In conclusion, we can't help but mention the obvious policy of considering capturing federal funds as free money, nor fail to be reminded of the illusory state predictions of financial relief to the counties through the enactment of Assembly Bill 59 in 1963. The claim of no cost increase to counties is all too reminiscent of the erroneous forecast made in reference to Assembly Bill 59."

The next to testify was a representative from the Social Action Committee of the First Unitarian Society of Sacramento, who stated:

"Our committee agreed with your principles as outlined in Bulletin No. 644. We believe that benefits will accrue to society in general from regulations of this type. Recipients will be able to make a positive contribution to the community without detracting from their family security. The economy of the community will be enhanced by having money which will be immediately spent in a manner which will stimulate basic food, clothing and housing industries. The charge has been made that the program will be costly in terms of time and efficiency. I reject this argument. Human suffering cannot be measured in terms of efficiency. Any program can be smothered in red tape until it dies of suffocation. I hope this program can be made less cumbersome in its application. The argument has been made that this program will subsidize farmers. Farmers are already subsidized, as are airlines, steamship lines, railroad lines, munitions manufacturers, and about half of the major economic activities in the United States. Are we to state that what is good for the healthy half of our population is bad for the less fortunate half?"

A representative from the California Teamsters Legislative Council testified: "The Bulletin itself deals only with a very minor aspect of a very major problem. The poverty of farm workers is perhaps the greatest social problem confronting the people and the State of California. The Teamsters have no simple solution to offer. Our position on the specific matter before you results from our conviction that the scandal of rural poverty will not be ended until the following conditions are met:

1. Wages for farm workers must rapidly rise to equality with wages and conditions of work offered in manufacturing.

2. Unemployment insurance must be extended to agriculture. Incidentally, the payment of unemployment insurance to farm workers would, we believe, substantially lighten the costs of welfare in many rural counties.

3. Agricultural workers enjoy the advantages and strength of collective bargaining.

"We recognize that neither the Director of the Department of Social Welfare nor any individual here present can secure for farm workers any of the three conditions just stated; but our position at this hearing is based upon this consideration. Does Bulletin No. 644 in any way to the slightest degree either advance or impede the attainment of the three objectives?

"It might be argued that Bulletin No. 644, which would permit otherwise eligible recipients to receive financial aid although working long hours at seasonal farm work is, in fact, a subsidy to the farmers' labor costs and therefore tends to keep down farm wages. In our judgment, this argument has a theoretical plausibility that might deceive an academic economist but seems to us entirely without merit. The forces that are making for an overdue increase in wages for agriculture are so strong that the effect of Bulletin No. 644 on agricultural wages can be ignored, precisely as the theoretical effect on the tides of orbiting a satellite over the Pacific can be ignored.

"Does Bulletin No. 644 have any effect upon the possibility of extending unemployment insurance to agricultural workers? Strangely enough, a somewhat similar problem was brought to the attention of the Legislature at the recent session. Under existing law, an individual who works 40 hours in any week is ineligible for unemployment insurance for that week even though his wages are less than his weekly benefit amount. To rectify that absurdity (which closely parallels the absurdity corrected by Bulletin No. 644), the Teamsters introduced a bill, AB1076. The bill was carried by a conservative Republican. We had no difficulty in persuading the appropriate committee in each house that the bill would tend to encourage people to work. The bill passed both houses without a single dissenting vote, but somehow got lost in the Governor's capacious pocket. I mention this simply to indicate that on a problem quite similar to that met by Bulletin No. 644, the Legislature took a unanimous stand on behalf of common sense. Why discourage a man from working by requiring him to forfeit all of his benefits if he works?

"Does the Bulletin now under discussion in any way tend to lessen the prospects for organizing agricultural workers—a matter of great interest to Teamsters who, in fact, have already organized a substantial number of agricultural workers? Admittedly, one sometimes encounters a shortsighted view that organized labor is weakened whenever an administrative agency acts on its own initiative to improve the conditions of working people. There are in some circles (though not among teamsters) 'infantile leftists' who imagine that no gain for working people is a real gain unless it is won by a knock-down-drag-out fight in the Legislature or on the picket line. The teamsters disagree. Where an agency such as the Department of Social Welfare of its own volition arrives at a policy that actually benefits working people, we are for it regardless of our own effort or lack of effort.

"In our judgment, Bulletin No. 644 makes a small but significant contribution to Social Welfare in these respects: Most people would rather earn a dollar than be given a dollar. Admittedly, there are some loafers among agricultural workers, as there are among bankers and bureaucrats. We believe that many persons would rather work long hours as seasonal farm workers than wait for a welfare check; but it is unreasonable, even inhuman to expect any individual to lose income to support his family by reason of working. As we read the regulation in Bulletin No. 644, the assumption that an individual employed as a seasonal farm worker can be considered as working part-time, even though in any particular week or month he is working 40 hours a week or more, is a reasonable assumption. It encourages people to work, it does not penalize them and their dependents for accepting work.

"In our opinion, the policy enunciated in Bulletin No. 644 makes sense not only as encouraging people to work, but as an incentive for them to work in an occupation of vital importance to the economy of the State, particularly now that the bracero program has been terminated."

The next presentation came from a representative of the Golden Gate and Sacramento Area Chapter of the National Association of Social Workers:

"As you may know, this is a professional organization representing graduate social workers. You do have a full copy of the National Association of Social Workers' stand on this matter. We would like to point out that the definition of farm labor as part-time employment allows the social worker and the agency to assure these families adequate income. The poverty level for a family of four is somewhere around $3,000. Under public assistance standards right now, a family of that size would be eligible for $2,220. This is significantly below the $3,000 point. However, if you earned income through farm labor under the definition of No. 644, that same family could at least get $3,084 a year. Now that would place them at the extreme poverty level, and that's the level which we hardly consider to be ideal, but it is more than what a person who is not working would be eligible to have. As you can see, we are not suggesting or advocating the maintenance level of living, but rather we are trying to lift families a little above abject poverty. Secondly, by permitting families with low income to remain eligible for public assistance, medical benefits that are available through the public assistance medical care program can protect the children of farm laborers. The medical care under the Public Assistance Medical Care program is not available under California regulations to the adults in the families, and this is indecent, but we can at least do something for the medical and the dental needs of the children. This availability of medical and dental care to children of farm workers seems little enough that an affluent society can do to protect the health of innocent children and the peace of mind available to parents. Third, the Bulletin can help to give counseling to children in families of farm laborers so that the children can remain in school, and the money that they earn through farm labor can be protected so they will be able to stay in school under the provisions of Bulletin No. 644. The best way in this country to grow up to be a poor adult and untrained manual laborer is to be born into a poor family headed by an untrained manual laborer. The old harangue that children of persons who receive welfare assistance grow up seeing welfare as a way of life, simply doesn't hold water. Children of the poor may grow up and they may later need assistance, but it's the miserable home life that they have endured that has rendered them incapable of escaping the cycle of poverty. Of the young people in California, 25 percent live in poverty conditions, and the worst situations are in families dependent upon farm labor. In 1962, 6,000 children were found illegally employed in farm work, some of them in California. This 6,000 represents the number that we know about, and more than half of them were below the normal grade in school for their age. Among the migrant children who were tested, the retardation rate was 72 percent. We are not prepared to believe that this high retardation rate is a reflection of intellectually inferior parents. Rather, we believe it to be the end product of the neglect of children by a society that is supposedly one nation under God.

"Parents who are affected by Bulletin No. 644 want education and a better life for their children, but what they expect their children will get in life is quite a different matter, as research has repeatedly shown. We permit the social worker to give what he wishes and is prepared to give. This is perhaps even more difficult to accept than the hostile and critical reproaches from some in positions of authority who feel that public welfare ought not to be given at all, or in as degrading a way as possible, if it has to be doled out to what are considered worthless people. It is futile to hope that you can give any kind of casework help to families such as farm workers when you are frustrated at every turn by regulations that exclude anyone who works 40 hours a week regardless of their need. Finally, it would seem useless to complain that Bulletin No. 644 is a subsidy to farm owners when we all know that protective legislation in California and in the nation is not on the books for farm workers. Neither are they protected by other benefits which workers in this economy have. There is some thought in Washington right now to cover farm workers and raise the minimum wage to $1.75 an hour in 1968. To hold out this hope to the men, women, and children who now depend on farm work for their livelihood is not only cruel, it is indecent. The only alternative, morally, to this definition of farm labor as part-time employment is to agitate and immediately pass a state wage law that would be enforced and would require employers in all industries to pay a decent wage. We are not aware that opponents of Bulletin No. 644 are actively engaged in such action at the present time or that they plan to become so. When the average individual earnings in the United States in 1964 from farm work was $913 a year, it makes little sense to go on complaining about a subsidy to growers. This kind of specious argument is merely a smoke-screen, and the real complaint is not against the growers who are hiring the workers but against the farm labor family receiving aid from public funds.

"In summary, I would like to point out that at the present time only one out of five families in need are aided through public welfare assistance. Turnover of staff approximates 40 percent annually in some counties, and it is not only related to inadequate salaries and poor working conditions, but also to how the programs are set up and administered. The problem faced by society and by the social worker is not that too many people come in to agencies for aid, but rather that not enough people see the public social welfare system as a resource for them. We believe that case finding should be an integral part of agency function and that the standards of aid and service should rise, not decline."

A representative of the Agricultural Workers Organizing Committee, AFL-CIO made the following presentation:

"As a temporary measure only, we are in favor of the Department of Social Welfare Bulletin No. 644. This is a short-range answer but not a long-range solution. As much as we would like to see our families have the security of this plan, and as much as we would like to see the children adequately fed, we are opposed to it as a long-term program. If we are going to subsidize farm workers, why aren't the single men and women and the married couples without children who are farm workers included in this plan? They must pay rent, and they must eat, too. This plan could possibly allow the grower or the contractor to offer substandard wages when they would know very well that the welfare department would pick up the difference. The reason we can't endorse this program on a long-range basis is that we would be a party to the endorsement of low wages for farm workers. We oppose this plan on the long-range basis, because we feel the taxpayer should not subsidize a more than $3-billion industry, which is the biggest in the State of California. How long do the taxpayers have to subsidize this labor force for the growers? In the agricultural communities and counties which we surveyed, 65 to 90 percent of the people on welfare are farm workers. Practically 50 percent of the taxes in the county where I live is paid to welfare recipients who are mostly farm workers. We like to boast in California of $120 a week pay, where people are covered by unemployment insurance, social security, health and welfare plans, and a pension plan. But what our farm workers need is not more welfare; what they need is a minimum wage of $2 per hour, unemployment insurance, full social security coverage, federal low-cost housing, and collective bargaining rights, like all workers in the United States."

The Alameda County Welfare Department Director, representing the County Welfare Director's Association stated:

"I may say that some part of the time today I thought I was at the wrong meeting. I can remember a notice that came out that said that you wanted facts, not philosophy. I have heard a good deal of both. I think that we would like to start out by saying that we can't see that Bulletin No. 644 has had a very significant impact, by and large, because we haven't had enough experience operating under Bulletin No. 644 to know. We checked with the counties as a whole, yesterday, and we found that the consensus was that we haven't felt any real result. We don't really see where the plight of the farm laborer has been helped to any great extent at this point in time. I think this is indicated by the fact that in San Joaquin County there are eight families getting supplementation, I think, and there certainly must be many more families engaged in farm labor. In Alameda County, despite some of the comments which were made earlier, there are as of August 2, 14 families with the husband working in the fields who receive supplementation. So we find it extremely difficult to come to you at this point in time and say that the Bulletin is really doing something big for the plight of the farm laborer. Now, as far as getting people into the fields is concerned, and I certainly understood from the wording of your Bulletin that this was part of the intent, we can't see where this has happened to any great extent. The fact seems to be in most of the counties that, just as the gentlemen prior to my speaking said, we are referring through the California State Employment Services substantially more people to the farm labor market who are not being sent to farm labor jobs, so that I don't know where this big crisis is. We do want to say this, that we strongly support the statements made earlier by the California Supervisors Association and by the San Joaquin County Supervisors Association in principle, and I mean by that in terms of the philosophy that was expressed. We don't know anything about the statistics.

"I heard earlier today a challenge to AB-1987, and I thought I heard it said that AB-1987 did not go to part-time employment on a much broader scale than farm labor. I have a document before me here from which I would like to read one paragraph. It says, 'Since the definition of part-time employment proposed by AB-1987 requires a certain number of weeks of unemployment for parents otherwise employed full-time, it is estimated that about 15,100 new families would receive full aid coverage during this period of unemployment. Based on the current study data, the duration of full aid coverage is estimated to be 2.6 months.' Now I don't know what else this means other than that the Legislature did consider AB-1987. I am sure the source of this document is authentic. It happens to be the State of California Department of Social Welfare Research and Statistics Bulletin, published May 17, 1965, giving a preliminary estimate of the effect of AB-1987. So I believe the point made earlier by the two associations that I spoke of was a well-taken point. Earlier reference was made to the fact that we do, in the AFDC program, supplement the full-time earnings of women working under the program and this is true. And, it was also alluded to, although I didn't hear it said right out, that in some counties inadequate full-time earnings have been supplemented by general assistance money, and this is true. Surprisingly enough, this 'vicious Alameda County' happens to be one of them. Now, I would like to point out that in the case of supplementation of the full-time earnings in AFDC, this was not done by action of the Legislature after due consideration. As far as the supplementation of general assistance in the counties, this is left to the legislative body of the county, the board of supervisors, so that there is certainly adequate basis in my opinion for proposing that this type of broad decision needs to be considered by the duly elected representatives of the State of California, because there is no reason to believe that there are not many other part-time employment situations where the earnings of individuals and families are completely inadequate that need to receive perhaps the same kind of attention."

The next presentation came from the Welfare Rights organization by a welfare recipient:

"I work whenever there is a job available. Motels are very good work.They pay well; but it is seasonal work. In Alameda County, I am familiar with, you might say, every motel, and these people are doing their own work now. I also work for very many veterinarians. They call me whenever they need me, but now they don't need me. They are doing their own work. Well, some time ago I decided I would go to farm labor, and a lot of people get the impression you get this welfare check on the first and sixteenth and it encourages you to stay home; you go to your mailbox and you get this check, and your needs are taken care of. That isn't true. That is enough to make you get out and look for a job, but, in Alameda County, where are you going to look for a job? Farm labor, that is it. All right, you get up in the morning. Now it is obvious, the grower wants to make money quickly and quietly as possible. So, when you go the farm, we will talk about beans. It is not the season, but, for instance you are going to work in beans, and you get to the farm labor office at 3:00 a.m. and you would like to make say $8 that day. I mean you are real happy about it, and you are willing to work. Everybody on that bus is willing to work. They would like to make $8 for the day. All right, you get down to the field and somchow or other, they are irrigating here and you have to wait until it dries. But you can go into this field and pick over. You can clean the field up. All right, you do that until 10:00 a.m. Then you can go where the beans are. You know you are really going to make your money then. All right, you get into this field and in the meantime, this farmer he notices there is a bunch of people, but if he had more people he could get his beans that day. So pretty soon you look down the row and here come the men meeting you. You know, you are all. Everybody is in the field. All right, that is fine, we'll say you are fortunate enough, you pick a hamper of beans. You have to weigh them and there is a big long line while you are waiting. While you are waiting to weigh these beans, you are not picking them and you are only getting paid for beans. So, no fooling, I used to tell the welfare worker, I am going to go pick beans, and the welfare worker, every morning he would call the farm labor office (I had two kids) and see did I get on that bus. One morning I told him, 'You know, I got a notion not to go today.' He told my welfare worker I said that, I just said that I had the notion, I didn't say I wasn't going. The most I ever made to my knowledge, (look, I can pick beans because I learnt), I mean, after you are in the field, you learn if you pick with this hand, you learn where the beans are, but I mean any of the farm work, I learned to do it, and at no time did I ever make more than $3 a day. And, out of that $3 do you know what I had to do? I had to pay $1 for me and 50 cents for my kids to get on this bus and my, everybody was real proud of me, and I don't think it is fair and I am quite sure that you wouldn't because most people think farm labor is, you know, it is a snap, but it isn't."

Following the public hearing, the State Department of Social Welfare adopted Bulletin No. 644.

CHAPTER 10

FARM LABOR ISSUES AFTER BULLETIN 644

THE JUNE 1966 Report on Part-time Farm Labor published by the State Department of Social Welfare showed a total of 1,675 seasonal farm labor cases statewide. Of the 58 counties, 34, including Los Angeles, San Diego, Ventura, Contra Costa, San Francisco, Sacramento, San Joaquin and Yuba, reported no seasonal farm labor cases; 16, including Imperial, Orange, Riverside, San Bernardino, Santa Barbara, Alameda, Sonoma and Yolo, reported 24 or less cases; and the remaining eight counties reported from 42 to 442 cases as follows: Kern 442; Santa Clara 237; Fresno 170; Kings 131; Madera 63; Merced 83; Stanislaus 42; and Tulare 360.

By October 1966, the State Department of Social Welfare, through intradepartmental communication, took note of the fact that Bulletin 644 was not being fully implemented by county welfare departments. This was the beginning of a long confrontation, on an official basis, between the proponents and the opponents of Bulletin 644.

THE ISSUES

In January 1967, almost immediately after the newly appointed Director of the State Department of Social Welfare took up his duties, he began receiving protests from the counties regarding Bulletin 644. He therefore requested the author to give him an analysis of the Bulletin, and was advised by memorandum that although Bulletin 644 was promulgated to cope with the farm labor crisis caused by the ending of the bracero program, the problems of migrant farm labor families had been long-standing concerns of the Department. These concerns were stated as follows:

1. Irregular, unpredictable, and inadequate earnings.
2. Lack of a usual place of residence, resulting in children's irregular attendance at a single school; and precluding the development of habilitation and rehabilitation plans for adults and older children in any attempt to break the poverty cycle.
3. Unavailability of emergency and regular medical services at the time they are required.
4. The time-consuming and costly administrative process of closing, reopening, and reinvestigating cases several times in the same year. Authorization of aid, in many instances, could not be

given in time to meet the family emergency, thus causing hardship
and suffering to the family.

5. How could able-bodied, nonfarm worker recipients who
could adjust to the rigorous physical demands of farm labor be encouraged to accept such employment?

Support for the Department of Social Welfare taking some positive steps with respect to seasonal farm laborers came from a number
of sources. In working on possible methods which could realistically
be undertaken to solve these problems, the Department was able to
draw on its long-time success in encouraging AFDC mothers to take
and retain employment by providing supplements to their earnings,
up to full need, and providing needed medical care within the limitations of the Public Assistance Medical Care Program. Since
AFDC mothers' earnings, including those from full-time employment, had been supplemented under this long-existing policy,
Bulletin 644 merely extended the policy and applied it, with some
additional limitations, to the seasonal farm laborer.

The assumption that farm labor is part-time employment is the
major issue upon which opposition to this regulation is based. Part-
time employment permits continuous eligibility for public assistance, services, and medical care; and although supplementation of
earnings is not unique to this regulation, as noted, it is the aspect of
Bulletin 644 that is most frequently criticized.

Another issue identified by the critics of the regulation is that
farm workers should not be singled out for special treatment. We
are in agreement. Staff recommendations favor broadening the part-
time definition to include others who are disadvantaged in their employment due to the irregular, seasonal, and temporary nature of
the industry in which they labor. (This would tend to take the
focus off agriculture and farm workers, and make it easier for the
agricultural counties.) The present definition of full-time employment would not be changed.

The third issue, accusatory in nature, is that supplementary
public assistance reduces the incentive to employment. This is sometimes characterized by the statement that "Department Bulletin 644
provides a guaranteed annual income for farm workers." Present regulations require that a person accept employment if it is available.
Therefore, it is mandatory that one accept employment to the maximum extent that it is available, except where there is good cause
for refusal. Supplementation of earned income occurs to the extent
that it is required in order to maintain a welfare standard of living.
A further concern of the critics is the possibility that women and
children may choose not to work alongside the father. Women and
children should have the right to choose whether or not to work.
There is no evidence that persons normally engaged in farm labor

are receiving welfare assistance as a substitute for their usual work patterns.

In reviewing Bulletin 644 and its effects, several conclusions became apparent. First, the counties have resisted implementing the regulation. In June 1966, when only 1,675 cases were reported under Bulletin 644, there were 34 counties, including some large agricultural counties, which reported no cases at all. Therefore, the effectiveness of the Bulletin is still to be tested. Second, the staff rationale and considered judgments that went to the development of this regulation have not changed, nor is there evidence that the problems to which the Bulletin is addressed have changed significantly or sufficiently to warrant recommending its withdrawal. It was a sound plan when developed, and remains valid today.

On July 19, 1967, an ad hoc committee of the County Welfare Directors Association sent a list of 13 complaints about Bulletin 644 to the SDSW Director, and the Board of Directors of the Association recommended that the Bulletin be rescinded in its entirety. The author and his staff prepared an analysis of the issues for the SDSW Director in respect to the Welfare Directors request by first discussing the philosophical question involved, namely, the Department's primary responsibility to serve needy people regardless of their circumstances. The whole thrust of the Department's activities and of this Bulletin, in particular, is toward that objective. The problems arising from the Bulletin, as expressed by the CWDA's ad hoc committee report, are largely matters of administrative detail and the need for action and resolution. However, if the basic question is whether or not we serve needy people, our position must remain valid, and the Bulletin also remains valid. The problems of assisting farmers to increase the numbers of available workers, the number of working hours available to them, and the like, are not the central issue of Bulletin 644, nor the responsibility of the Department of Social Welfare. It was hoped that by making seasonal farm labor more palliative, recipients could be encouraged to enter this type of employment.

The 13 points raised by the report require some discussion and comment. The first part of each of the following 13 points is the CWDA statement and the second part is the SDSW staff analysis for the Director:

1. After over two years' experience with Bulletin 644, it is apparent that its goal, that of alleviating a seasonal farm labor crisis, has not been attained. In practice, the Bulletin has tended to reduce the number seeking and engaging in such work.

The purpose of Bulletin No. 644 was to encourage seasonal farm labor while alleviating the problems of workers so employed. Because this Bulletin has never been fully implemented by the counties, in fact or in principle, we cannot accurately judge what the full effect would be.

2. Much agricultural employment is necessarily hard, dusty, disagreeable work in temperatures ranging over 100 degrees. With welfare payments making up the difference between net income and need, up to the welfare standard, there is a loss of incentive on the part of poorly motivated individuals to aggressively seek agricultural work to the maximum possible extent.

The thrust of Bulletin 644 is to provide an incentive to welfare families to consider seasonal farm labor as feasible employment. Implementation of that basic philosophy includes a plan of income supplementation to meet economic need, or a plan to reinstate aid immediately when income ceases. With the Maximum Participating Base, most families receive less money when they do not have income. This is particularly true of the larger families.

3. As a practical matter, under the regulation, if a man works 40 hours per week he cannot be required to put in additional hours. Yet during peak harvest seasons, farm laborers work as much as 10 hours a day, 6 or 7 days a week. Welfare supplementation tends to encourage workers to hold their work week to a 40-hour maximum, thereby resulting in a loss of man-hours to employers. Although it is not the intent of the regulation to establish a 40-hour maximum work week, this nevertheless is the practical effect.

The Bulletin requires that the person covered therein works whatever hours are required of his employment and does not in any way limit the amount of hours one can work. In fact, as suggested earlier, the opposite is true. The fact that a person works more than 173 hours in one month does not affect his eligibility for having unmet needs considered.

4. Unless an employer specifies to the Department of Employment that he will accept inexperienced farm laborers, they will not refer inexperienced farm laborers to the Farm Labor Office. Therefore, the Bulletin has not encouraged people from other fields of endeavor to go to work in farm labor.

The Department of Employment's selection of workers and of employer specifications as to employees are beyond the control of this Bulletin or this Department. There is nothing in the Bulletin to preclude referral of recipients directly to the Farm Labor Office* or prevent a county from encouraging able bodied recipients to seek such employment.

---

*However, referral to Farm Labor Office cannot be in lieu of referral to the regular CSES office, which is required by procedures established in the Employment Guide, issued as a supplement to DB 629.

5. The Bulletin is discriminatory in providing preferential treatment to the farm laborer over other classes of workers.

That the Bulletin might be discriminatory by giving preferential treatment to farm laborers is true only in that it was limited to that group of individuals because of factors not usually applicable to other groups.

6. Allowing three months' supplementation of a farm laborer's income when he is fully employed creates an area of injustice to persons in other types of employment whose employment pattern is just as seasonal. Example: construction workers, self-employed persons, and the like.

The extension of aid to irregularly employed, temporary, or intermittent farm laborers should have been a trial of the principles involved which could have been extended to others; whether or not earnings are supplemented during the period of employment depends on the amount of the earnings. The Bulletin provides for a "zero" grant during the months income meets needs.

7. Because of the nature of agricultural work and because of the definition of it as part-time work, a large majority of the farm workers continue to be eligible for a small or zero grant. Unless a farm laborer wants to fully support his family and requests discontinuance, most of these families will be on aid for the whole year.

One of the main purposes of the Bulletin was to eliminate the administrative costs of reopening and reinstating aid when work is not available on a full-time basis.

8. Because of the way many of the farm workers are paid and because many of them are uneducated, it is difficult to accept their statements on our income report forms, and it is difficult to verify the amount of their earnings. If we request verification from the Department of Industrial Relations, the time element becomes a factor.

The rescission of Bulletin 644 would not affect this problem. The employer is required by law to provide the worker with a statement of earnings, and if such statement is not provided, the employer should be contacted. The Department of Industrial Relations should be contacted only as the enforcement agency.

9. There are almost constant monthly contacts with these families and, therefore, the necessity of required quarterly reinvestigations could be eliminated as they do not serve a useful purpose.

The requirement for quarterly reinvestigation is currently under study, not only in connection with farm labor cases, but in connection with all AFDC cases. The requirement should not pose more of a problem in connection with farm labor cases than with other variable income cases.

10. It is difficult and often next to impossible to keep track of the number of hours a farm laborer works and the number of hours he could have worked.

This is a problem basic to Bulletin 644, but is an administrative detail requiring judgment based on knowledge of the general employment situation.

11. Because of the irregularity of hours and wages, it is constantly necessary to hold warrants, and this makes extra work for the social worker and clerical staff.

The problem of the necessity to hold warrants and the subsequent extra work for the social worker and the clerical staff is far less laborious and costly than the previous system of reapplication, reinvestigation, and issuing of warrants. The purpose of the program is to help persons in need and should not be more difficult to administer than other cases with irregular or variable income.

12. With the election of 50 percent federal funding by the State Director of Social Welfare, the small supplementary grants have become a large fiscal burden on rural agricultural counties, thus disadvantaging these counties.

There is some additional cost to the counties under the 50 percent federal reimbursement for aid. At the time the Bulletin was effected, federal matching on a persons count basis was to the county's and State's advantage for small grant cases such as these. However, the new 50 percent matching provides the counties as much or more federal money on an overall basis.

13. The Bulletin is inconsistent with the basic concept of the AFDC program which requires that both need and deprivation exist simultaneously in order for the family to remain eligible. Under the Bulletin, a farm laborer's family remains in an eligible status even though income exceeds need for an indefinite period.

Both deprivation and need still exist simultaneously in these cases. The family is deprived because of the irregular, temporary, intermittent nature of the employment as provided by the definition in Manual Section C-161.41, item 2. If the presumption of part-time employment is overcome, aid is to be discontinued.

THE PUBLIC HEARING

The SDSW Director decided to hold a public hearing on Bulletin 644 November 3, 1967, in Bakersfield, Kern County, the center of the California farm industry, to determine whether he would affirm the bulletin as it stood, modify it, or rescind it. Kern County and Tulare County, adjacent to the North, reported 58 percent of the 3,248 unemployed parent cases working in agriculture as of June 1967; and a total of 80 percent of the cases were in Fresno, Kern, Kings, Madera, Stanislaus, and Tulare counties. Thus, the hearing was held in the region most affected by Bulletin 644 with testimony as follows:

The SDSW Director began the hearing by acknowledging that there were very strong feelings on both sides of the issue and it was his determination that in the interests of obtaining factual information, maximum exposure would be given to the varying view points. He urged those who would speak on the issues to provide him with as much detailed information as possible without duplicating testimony. A staff member opened the discussion as follows:

". . . Department Bulletin 644, entitled 'Part-time Employment Farm Labor', provides for continuation of aid for the seasonal farm worker by redefining part-time employment in the eligibility requirements for deprivation of a child by reason of the unemployment of a parent. The definition provides that irregular, temporary, or intermittent work at farm labor which provides no assurance of a dependable amount of income shall be presumed to be part-time employment. This presumption of part-time employment is overcome if the parent has worked a minimum of 173 hours per month in the three preceding months and is expected to continue at or about this number of hours for the current, the next month, and indefinitely beyond the next month. The Bulletin provides for an assistance payment to the family to meet the difference between the family income and total family need, as computed according to the state welfare standard. If income equals or surpasses total need, then a zero grant is established. Eligibility for full medical care and services of the Welfare Department continues for the family during the months when the zero grant is established.

"Bulletin 644 further identifies the responsibility of the caseworker to: (1) Inform applicants and recipients referred to the Department of Employment that they are to work as many hours as are available. (2) Advise persons accepting farm labor employment of their responsibility to report their earnings promptly to the Welfare Department and to secure statements of their earnings and deductions made by their employers, retaining these for verification purposes.

"There are, of course, other procedures and explanations relating to the policy outlined in the Bulletin such as payment procedures, claiming procedures, and identification of priority needs applicable to services for families with seasonal farm employment;

but detailing these would be lengthy and not essential to this discussion.

"The objectives of Bulletin 644 are as follows:

"1. To make it possible for farm labor, traditionally a low and irregular wage earning group for whom few other social mechanisms exist, such as unemployment insurance, to have the AFDC standard of assistance by providing a partial grant when earnings are not sufficient to meet total needs. (This has been and is established policy for employed mothers in family group cases.)

"2. To reduce welfare costs by providing an incentive to unemployed parents to accept employment in farm labor even though they are inexperienced at this work or cannot earn enough at it to maintain their families.

"3. To help alleviate the farm labor shortage created by the termination of the bracero program.

"4. To enable continuation of services to farm labor families, including full medical care, during periods when earnings preclude but a zero grant. (By definition, priority service needs caused by children's problems.)

"5. To simplify county procedures for reinstating aid for farm labor families during periods of slack employment or emergency in the family, such as illness or injury, eliminating to a considerable extent the reapplication process.

"6. To stabilize farm labor families to enable children to continue schooling without frequent absences, thereby laying a better foundation for their future independence.

"As to the chronology of the adoption of the Bulletin, time does not permit detailed discussion of the events leading to its adoption, but for the record, the Bulletin was adopted on an emergency basis on May 24, 1965, because of the farm labor shortage. After public hearings held May 7 and August 6, 1965, and many presentations on both sides, significant changes were made in the Bulletin and adopted in October 1965. These included instructing applicants to work as many hours as the job required; and requirements for enumerating those conditions which would overcome the presumption of part-time employment as well as provide for discontinuance of aid when the presumption was overcome.

"Of the 22 counties reporting aid to 3,248 families of farm workers under the provisions of Department Bulletin 644 in June 1967, a total of 80 percent were in six counties—Fresno, Kern, King, Madera, Stanislaus and Tulare. Of the six counties, only two—Kern and Tulare, reported 58 percent of the statewide caseload. Statewide, the farm worker caseload ranged from a low of 1,182 in December 1966 to a high of 3,248 by June 1967; and the number of cases decreased in July and August, 1967, as more work became available, to 2,618.

"Comparative data on the differences between AFDC-U farm worker and nonfarm worker families show the following:

"1. Families eligible for AFDC-U as a result of the farm labor policy have an average monthly financial need as established by the AFDC standards of approximately $361 per month, which exceeds the average need of all other AFDC-U families by $52. Such families also have more income available from sources other than public assistance. Average outside income is nearly $144 per month compared to $54 per month for all other AFDC families.

"2. The AFDC-U grant, in combination with outside income available to the family, meets the minimum need standards established by the Department of Social Welfare for over 80 percent of the families aided under Department Bulletin 644, in contrast with slightly over 33 percent of the other employed parent families.

"3. Average unmet need is $9 per month for farm labor families and $28 per month for other AFDC families.

"4. The father of a farm labor family appears to be less well prepared to improve his position in the labor market than the father of other AFDC-U families. He is typically 38 years old, has an average of 5.3 years of school, and is minimally educated. The typical nonfarm AFDC-U father has 5 years more education and is 5 years younger.

"5. More than 80 percent of the farm labor recipients are of minority ethnic background in contrast with 55 percent of the nonfarm labor AFDC families.

"6. The size of farm group families averages 7.1 persons compared to 5.7 persons in nonfarm AFDC families, and the average number of children is 5.1 compared to 3.7.

"7. Families aided under Department Bulletin 644 have an average of 12 years residence in the state."

TESTIMONY AGAINST BULLETIN 644 AND ITS POTENTIAL AS A FORM OF GUARANTEED ANNUAL INCOME

The first to testify against Bulletin 644 was a County Supervisor from Kern County, who was also the immediate past President of the County Supervisors Association of California. As spokesman of the combined membership of the County Supervisors Association of California, the San Joaquin Valley Supervisors Association, and the County Welfare Directors Association of California, he presented the following testimony in their behalf:

"In response to State Department Social Welfare Bulletin 644, entitled 'Part-time Employment—Farm Labor,' the formal position statement and recommendations which I am about to make were unanimously adopted by the membership of these three organizations during regular scheduled meetings. The County Welfare Directors Association met July 20, 1967; the County Supervisors Association of California met on October 18, 1967; and the San Joaquin Supervisors Association met on October 19, 1967. We request that this written and verbal presentation, and the various exhibits hereto attached, consisting of caseloads, statistics, and case examples prepared by those agriculture counties most directly effected by the application of the provisions in Department Bulletin 644, be recognized by you as our full formal testimony for your consideration. It is our recommendation to you that Bulletin 644 be rescinded in its entirety. We make this recommendation to you recognizing that your action rescinding this Bulletin would not disadvantage in any way the needy unemployed farm laborer who would continue to receive financial assistance and agency services under other existing regulations and policies of the AFDC-U program which now are enforced and applicable to all other occupational groups. We believe our position requesting the rescinding of this Bulletin to be a valid one for the following major reasons:

"First, the regulation in its application has failed to achieve its stated objective, that is, to encourage and make it practical for as many individuals as possible to engage in farm work; second, the regulation is class regulation and therefore is discriminatory in its application by treating one occupational group, the farm laborer, distinctly different from all other employed persons in similar circumstances except for their occupation. The attached exhibits, caseload and statistical material developed statewide by your own Bureau of Research and Statistics, will support the testimony.

"Although the San Joaquin valley is the heart of the agricultural economy of the state, after more than 2 years of practical experience with the provisions of Bulletin 644, San Joaquin valley counties have found no evidence that this regulation has or will ever result in more people becoming engaged in farm work or in those already so employed working additional hours. On the contrary, there are indications that this Bulletin has resulted in a reduction of persons engaged in such work, although for the past two harvest seasons the importation of farm workers from Mexico has been drastically reduced, which should have resulted in increased job opportunities for domestic farm workers. During these same 2 years, the AFDC-U caseloads in the agriculture counties have continued to reflect unusual growth, particularly noticeable during the peak harvest season when caseloads should be at an absolute minimum. Such has not been the case, however, as your own statistics will show AFDC-U caseload size in the agricultural counties during these peak harvest months have been much higher than for those same months prior to the implementation of this Bulletin. Perhaps the present harvest season best illustrates the failure of this Bulletin to achieve its objective. At a time when the AFDC-U caseloads have reached their highest harvest season peak since the implementation of the AFDC-U program in February 1964, in a desperate effort to salvage a multimillion-dollar harvest, it has been necessary to take such emergency measures as relaxing the restrictions on Mexican farm workers, using prison inmates, and delaying the opening of some schools in order to use high school students in harvesting the crops.

"We recognize that farm employment is necessarily hard, dusty, disagreeable work which frequently must be carried out in temperatures of over 100 degrees. The effect of this Bulletin, in establishing a guaranteed average annual income with consideration of the personal efforts of the individual to provide for his own support is hardly conducive under these adverse circumstances to motivate individuals to aggressively seek agricultural work to the maximum possible extent.

"The regulation is discriminatory in its application. The application of this Bulletin provides preferential treatment to the farm laborer over all other occupational groups, even though the unemployment of certain other groups such as domestics, gardeners, dairy workers, milkers, construction workers, lumbermen, building trades, and self-employed small farmers may also be seasonal, intermittent, of short duration, and equally unpredictable. Perhaps a prime example of the discriminatory nature of this Bulletin can best be illustrated as follows: Fruit packing-house employees and truck drivers transporting the fruit are now considered to be employed full time if they work 40 hours a week or longer. They would be discontinued from the AFDC program even though their earnings might not meet their budgeted needs under the AFDC-U standard of assistance. On the other hand, the farm worker who picked the fruit in the orchard would not be discontinued from the AFDC-U program under Bulletin 644 even though his earnings fully met his family's needs.

"Perhaps a further comparison of the treatment of the farm laborer and other occupational groups will amplify this point. First, aid may be discontinued to a farm labor case if the person is currently employed, has worked not less than 173 hours each of the immediately preceding months, and is expected to continue at this level indefinitely beyond the next month. For all other occupational groups, aid may be discontinued if the person is currently employed, has worked at least one full week, has received one week's pay, employment is expected to continue, or if income earnings exceed budgeted needs regardless of the amount of time worked. For the farm laborer, during the time that his earnings exceed the budgeted needs, his grant is reduced to zero, thus maintaining medical eligibility for Group 1 services regardless of the amount of income received during this period. No such provision is made for similar medical coverage for other occupational groups. When contact is lost with a farm labor family, aid may not be discontinued until the end of the calendar quarter, and only after the Welfare Department has attempted to locate the family. For all other occupational groups, aid may be discontinued at the end of the month in which contact is lost. The Bulletin is inconsistent with the basic concept of the AFDC-U program that both need and deprivation must exist simultaneously in order for the family to remain eligible. Under this Bulletin, the farm labor family remains in an eligible status even though income exceeds needs for an indefinite period. There are a number of other ways in which this Bulletin is discriminatory in its application, but we feel these examples are sufficient to illustrate the point.

"We do not intend that the testimony just given should be interpreted as a proposal or in support of the extension of provisions of Bulletin 644 to other occupational groups. On the contrary, we believe the present regulations already in existence are sufficient to meet existing needs when applied uniformly to all unemployed regardless of occupation.

"I would now like to make the following additional points which we feel are pertinent to any consideration of the future of this Bulletin.

"1. The provisions of this Bulletin are costly and difficult to administrate. Contrary to the contention of the former State Department of Social Welfare Director at the time of its original adoption, it has not saved the counties money, but rather has resulted in a substantial additional expense, particularly to predominantly agricultural counties, and has proven to be a financial liability rather than an asset.

"2. Adoption and retention of this Bulletin by an administrative ruling of the former State Department of Social Welfare Director has established a major public policy of a de facto guaranteed income without benefit of legislative hearings or debate. It was therefore an innovation against legislative prerogative and does not correctly reflect legislative intent.

"3. The provisions of this Bulletin are not pertinent to almost every segment of the population because of the adverse effect it has had on the available farm labor pool and its discriminatory nature. This truth can best be attested to by every county supervisor and every welfare director who has received numerous complaints and criticism from the public related to this Bulletin.

"4. In conclusion, we submit that the Bulletin 644 was hastily and ill-conceived. We believe that our testimony here today has shown this Bulletin to be an unjust and unfair and unworkable regulation which not only has failed in its objective but also leads to separate and different treatment of a segment of the work force, which represents class legislation. Under these circumstances, we most respectfully recommend your serious and favorable consideration to our recommendation that Bulletin 644 be rescinded in its entirety."

The next person to testify was a representative of the County Welfare Directors Association, who asked to make the following statement to supplement and support that of the Kern County Supervisor.

"The County Welfare Directors Association of California requests that Bulletin 644 be rescinded. In making this request, it is noted that some of the regulations from the Bulletin have been incorporated in the AFDC-U manual, and this manual material is in process of recodification. Bulletin 644 has not yet been cancelled in this process, therefore, whenever we refer to Bulletin 644 we would like to have this construed to include the regulation in the program manual as well as the Bulletin itself. Although we are mindful that the farm laborer may be in a disadvantaged position in comparison with other employment groups, we do not feel that the solution to farm labor problems should be found in the public welfare system.

"We seek repeal of the regulations and we give the following reasons:

"1. After more than 2 years of experience under the Bulletin, it is apparent that the regulations are not fulfilling the stated purpose for which they were established.

"2. The regulations are discriminatory in that they provide different and more liberal benefits than are available to other persons.

"3. It is our belief that regulations, or at least apparent effects of the regulations are contrary to the mandates of law and other expressions of legislative intent.

"4. The Bulletin has had a marked effect on the increase in the AFDC-U caseload and little effect in reducing costs.

"5. Miscellaneous other reasons that did not seem to fit in this pattern. In asking for repeal we are not saying that farm laborers should not be helped when they are unemployed, but that assistance to this group should be on the same basis as is now provided for all other persons.

"I would like to examine each of the five reasons that we have given for requesting repeal. The first of these was that the regulations are not fulfilling the purposes for which they were established and we have taken the purposes as they are written in the Bulletin. The stated purpose of the Bulletin was to encourage unemployed welfare recipients and other unemployed persons into farm work. It is our contention that there is no evidence to support the conclusion that the regulations have developed any new labor supply, and in fact, the caseload increase is evidence that the regulations have developed new welfare cases. In the county package of material that was handed to you by the Kern County Supervisor there are a number of county attachments which give case examples and statistical data to show that, in fact, the opposite of the purpose is true.

"A second stated purpose of the Bulletin was to avoid delays in restoring aid and providing assistance promptly when persons were without work. The county welfare directors' contention is that the immediate need provisions of the regulations are adequate to assure prompt assistance to eligible persons. As a matter of fact, an initial warrant on an initial need basis can be issued with at least equal speed, and in some counties may be issued more promptly than a supplemental grant adjustment—that is, the raising of a zero grant to a dollar amount.

"A third stated purpose of the Bulletin was to provide continuance of services. In this regard, the welfare directors contend that the service regulations can include former and potential types of cases. Those needing social services may be carried without also arbitrarily carrying grant services in every case. What is being provided is continuous paper work for the county welfare departments, and an income subsidy for the farm worker.

"Finally, in respect to cost estimates, although this was not a stated purpose of the Bulletin, there was assurance given verbally and in writing, and here reference is made to the SDSW news release of June 9, 1965, that the farm labor policies would operate at no cost to the state or county. We contend that this may have been true while the state was claiming federal money on a persons count basis. However, this money arrangement was rendered invalid when the state chose the 50 percent matching formula in 1966. We therefore conclude that none of the reasons given for adopting the regulations appear to have any present validity.

"Another reason for asking repeal was that the farm labor regulations are discriminatory in that they provide different and more liberal benefits than are available to other persons. We have therefore set up a chart, and on one side of the ledger show farm labor regulations; on the other side, the regulations as they apply to all other AFDC unemployed parent cases. The farm laborer may remain on aid even though he is working full time where all other cases become ineligible if the individual is working full time. For the farm laborer, he may receive a grant supplement to his full-time earnings if his net income is below the Aid to Needy Children standards. For all other cases, no grant may be received even though the earnings may be no higher than a farm laborer's earnings. Again, on the farm labor side of the ledger, if earnings exceed needs, the welfare grant is reduced to zero and it is continued as an active case. For all other cases, there are no zero grants permitted in the balance of the caseload. For farm labor cases, there are Group 1 medical benefits continued to these individuals who are employed full time. In all other cases, the linkage to the program stops and medical benefits are halted. For the farm laborer, ineligibility does not result until he has been employed continuously for 3 months at 173 hours per month, is currently employed, and his employment is expected beyond the following month. For all other cases, ineligibility results if the person is currently employed, has worked one full week, and has received at least one week's pay. In the farm labor cases, when contact is lost with the family, aid may not be discontinued until the end of the calendar quarter. For all other cases, aid may be discontinued at the end of the month after reasonable efforts have been made to locate the family. As an aside, in respect to the discriminatory nature of these regulations, I believe the SDSW staff member pointed out that we currently have this grant supplement situation in respect to the mother alone, who may be working. I think it is important to point out that in this instance you have both need and deprivation which exist, and this is a long-standing public policy. The contention of the county welfare directors is that in the instance of the farm laborer with the individual employed full time, there is not deprivation within the meaning of an unemployed person.

"Still another reason that the county welfare directors have given for asking for a repeal of the Bulletin is our belief that it is not in accord with legislative intent. Welfare and Institutions Code 11205 provides that it is 'the intent of the legislature that the employment and self-maintenance of parents of needy children be encouraged to the maximum extent and that the Aid to Families with Dependent Children program shall be administered in such a way that needy children and their parents will be encouraged and inspired to assist in their own maintenance.' This provision of the law also obliges the State Department of Social Welfare to take all steps necessary to implement this section. The county welfare directors who administer the program make the following contentions, and we feel that this is supported by the attachments to the material that has been handed to you:

"1. There is no evidence to support the conclusion that more recipients are working or that recipients are working more.

"2. The caseload has increased. The increase of the caseload is more indicative that the regulations are encouraging farm laborers to become welfare recipients than for welfare recipients to become farm laborers.

"3. The rule providing for continuance of eligibility unless the individual has worked at least 173 hours in each of three months is subject to abuse and manipulation to maintain eligibility. Some workers have tended to restrict or reduce the amount of hours they will work to the minimum necessary to stay eligible. It is significant that the State Farm Labor Offices have reported similar observations, and in support of this point, reference is made to a letter to the Director of the Stanislaus County Welfare Department July 10, 1967 from the SDSW Director.

"4. The regulations have provided a negative incentive so that persons lacking motivation tend to work only enough to meet eligibility requirements or to provide an income for their unmet needs on the AFDCU standard.

"5. The present regulations incorrectly place the burden on the welfare caseworkers to get the poorly motivated to aggressively seek work.

"6. The availability of medical care has also provided a strong incentive to make people try to maintain their eligibility for Group 1 medical benefits.

"7. Due to the construction of the farm labor regulations in the stated purpose of encouraging unemployed persons into farm labor, persons who are attempting to get on aid and avoid work become eligible by declaring themselves as farm workers or available to do farm work during periods when, in fact, farm work is not available.

"8. The penalty regulations are not effective for control of the abuses of job refusals because it is possible to become immediately eligible again with a token effort or a promise of cooperation.

"In respect to the question we raised of the Bulletin not being in accord with legislative intent, it is our belief that the political, social, economic, and philosophical issues underlying a government supplementing low income wages should be a legislative matter. Farm labor regulations were adopted in 1965 by the former Director of the State Department of Social Welfare pursuant to his authority under Welfare and Institutions Code 11201, which authorizes the department to adopt rules and regulations to define parttime employment. However, AB 1987, which was in the 1965 Legislature, and would have extended the AFDCU program to supplement the income of low income families, did not pass. We believe the fact that this was turned down by the Legislature was an expression of legislative intent.

"An additional reason that we give for asking for repeal is that we feel the Bulletin has caused a marked increase in the AFDC-U caseload and has had little effect in reducing grants. In the San Joaquin valley counties, about 75 to 80 percent of the AFDC-U caseload are farm workers. The effects of Bulletin 644 are somewhat illustrated by the attached three tables. Table 1 shows that the AFDC-U program began in January 1964 and Bulletin 644 was adopted May 25, 1965. March is a peak unemployment month in most of the valley counties, and employment opportunities start developing in April and increase to a high employment demand during the peak harvest season of August through October. Due to the late adoption of Bulletin 644 in May of 1965, it had comparatively little impact on the caseload that year. Most farm labor cases had already been discontinued, therefore the caseload decrease without the operation of Bulletin 644 can be observed by comparing 1964 and 1965 experience with 1966 and 1967. The figures in the table readily show that in the first two years, over one-half of the caseload was discontinued by the month of June, and by September three-fourths of the caseload was off aid. The 1966 and 1967 figures show a much higher proportion of the caseload remaining on aid. In September 1966 we still had 52 percent of the caseload, and in the last month for which we have figures for 1967—August—we still had 63 percent of our caseload on aid.

"Table 2 shows the average grant paid under the AFDCU program in the eight San Joaquin valley counties. Although the data provides an incomplete comparison, it was apparent that there was less reduction in the average grant paid in these counties after the operation of Bulletin 644 than before it became effective. The 1967 data shows even less grant reduction than in 1966. We believe that these figures tend to show that the farm labor regulations are not resulting in any substantial employment that tends to reduce the average grant paid to these families.

"In Table 3 there are some data that we feel give further indication of the comparative seasonal cost changes prior to and after operation of Bulletin 644. The proportionately higher level of payment during the full work season in 1966 and in 1967 is accounted for by the supplementation of the farm laborers earnings. Under other reasons we have listed three points. For the purpose of the oral presentation I will mention only one of them, the fact that the data on the state statistical report Form CA237 Part D is not an accurate measure of the true impact of Bulletin 644. In this item we are asked to report the number of cases eligible under Bulletin 644. However, the count of cases reported by the counties includes only the zero grant cases, the cases working full-time but receiving a small grant, and cases in which the checks are held during a period of loss of contact. The figures do not include all farm labor cases receiving aid. The figures do not include the much larger number of farm labor cases working only part-time who would be working full-time except for the availability of aid.

"I would like to add that my Board of Supervisors (Stanislaus County) on October 10, 1967, adopted a resolution calling for repeal of the Bulletin 644 and I have been directed to present this at this hearing and ask that it be made part of the hearing record."

The next person to testify was the Director of the Sutter County Welfare Department, who made the following statement:

"We realize that Bulletin 644 was adopted as an emergency measure to hopefully encourage persons in nonfarm employment to move into farm work. As has been stated, we have at this time no evidence to show that this has been achieved. We also realize that farm workers receive minimal wages, that for the most part they have large families, and that very often farm worker families have been deprived of adequate medical care, especially dental care and immunization. However, the farm workers are not alone in this respect. Most low income families are similarly deprived and limited in the amount of medical attention that their families have received, and also in the amount of medical care they receive on an on-going basis. Sutter County supports the position taken by the Supervisors Association and the County Welfare Directors Association, and requests that Bulletin 644 be rescinded and that all persons eligible for AFDC-U be treated equally. When an unemployed truck driver, carpenter, or other craftsman who is receiving AFDC-U finds employment, and receives the first full weeks pay, aid is discontinued at the end of that month or when income meets budget needs, whichever comes first. The family is no longer eligible for medical attention or any of the other benefits that are available to the farm worker. True, we can carry them as service cases and are required to do so if the service needs exist. When an AFDC-U mother obtains employment and her income meets budget needs, her case is discontinued though she has the deprivation factors of eligibility. Her children are no longer eligible for medical care. Her doctor and drug needs are not met, and often this mother finds herself in a position of being forced back on welfare because of needs beyond her capability to meet.

"Another very serious problem that we have experienced in Sutter County and which has also been found in many of the San Joaquin counties is that many of the farm workers who have been receiving assistance are refusing to work longer than 170 or 172 hours per month. Several growers have called our agency in the present harvest season and have bitterly complained that some farm laborers work the needed hours per day, whether it be 8, 10, or whatever, from the first of the month for 2, or 3, or more weeks, whichever it takes to reach approximately 170 or 172 hours, and then leave their jobs often in the middle of the day, informing the ranch foreman that they will return on the first of the following month.

"Earlier in this four days of meetings, a fine speaker described the fallacies of attempting to provide equal educational opportunities for all children, middle-class as well as the poor. We feel that welfare is guilty of this same deplorable practice when we determine that because one is a farm worker, he may be able to stay on welfare for 5, 10, or 15 years under the present provisions of Bulletin 644. Yet a truck driver or carpenter is only eligible until he gets a job and his first week's pay check. Why select farm workers for AFDC-U eligibility from now until all of their children are reared, and why talk about retraining and rehabilitation to get people off welfare and into a self-sustaining role in our society, when we have implemented with Bulletin 644 the means by which we make them dependent and keep them on welfare?

"The Board of Supervisors of Sutter County asks that I bring you this message: Bulletin 644 must be repealed and all AFDC-U applicants and recipients must be treated with equality if welfare is to fulfill its responsibility to the needy and to the people and to those who pay the bill. We have no argument with the factor of unemployment as a deprivation basis for eligibility but it must be the same for all unemployed and it must be related to needs. Deprivation for eligibility purposes no longer exists when employment is obtained in other fields of employment. For equality, it must be the same for farm workers."

Next to testify was the Director of the Tulare County Welfare Department, whose statement follows:

"As the state representatives have stated, 80 percent of the families of farm workers aided under the provisions of Bulletin 644 in June 1967 were in Fresno, Kern, Kings, Madera, Stanislaus and Tulare counties, and Kern and Tulare counties reported 58 percent of the caseload . . . . We did something really quite simple: Since Bulletin 644 was to provide farm labor in our area, we found that the only people who used farm labor were farmers, so we asked them if they were getting farm labor. Here are some of the answers:

"Case 1, date February 25, 1967, the employee in question did not work all the hours available to him. He simply did not come to work, and why should he when you give him money for doing nothing? Case 2, date March 9, 1967, did not work all the hours available to him. The employee is a very good worker when on the job. However, he seems to have more than the usual number of excuses when not working. Some of these excuses are provided by the State Department of Social Welfare. Case 3, date January 1966, did not work all the hours available to him. We really needed this fellow. He left us on the spot with 20,000 chickens and no one to work. Seems like this is what is wrong with welfare. Here we needed him badly and he ups and quits just to go on welfare. Case 4, date January 4, 1967, did not work all the hours available to him. Turned down a 40-hour a week job. He quit me when I really needed a hand and I found that is the way he does everybody he works for. He could have been making $2 an hour and as many hours a day as he wanted. My husband said that there was a lot of people who were drawing welfare who could be working. Case 5, date March 10, 1967, did not work all the hours available to him. This farmer, sir, is from New England, his remarks simply stated he quit. Case 6, June 1, 1967, he worked only 32 hours, others worked 50 hours or more. Case 7, date May 12, 1967, employment of 40 hours a week was available for this employee; he didn't take it. This man has in the past shown a willingness to work although somewhat limited in ability. He seems to have the idea this spring that he should limit his work to an amount that would enable him to get some supplemental welfare. Case 8, May 1966, the employee had 40 hours a week work available but did not take it. Since he would rather be on welfare, he has not worked all the time that was available to him. He could easily make $150 a week. Case 9, date May 10, 1967, employee did not work all the hours available to him. Man is very capable and works very good when on the job. He has 54 hours a week available to him. In the past 14 weeks he has had a total of 756 hours available and has worked only 645 hours. Case 10, July 21, 1967, did not work all the hours available to him. The employee had a 40-hour week job offered which he turned down. I do not belive this man is entitled to assistance. He was given a raise after one week's work and quit. He stated his wife was working at a packing shed so he didn't think he needed to work so he could play baseball. If this man or his family receive assistance I feel it only fair to say I will take it up to Sacramento. Case 11, December 15, 1966, employee did not wish to work over about four hours picking peaches and was told he must work six hours or be replaced because his leaving the field early had a bad effect on the rest of the crew. He elected to be replaced. Case 12, and last case, date December 28, 1966, employee was always a good worker and always willing to do any type of work, but the past year he hasn't been too willing to work . . .

"These answers from employees about the farm workers are not in my judgment an indictment of the farm workers, but rather they are an indictment of Bulletin 644, which provides them not with an incentive to work but incentive not to work. Bulletin 644 should be rescinded forthwith."

The Director of the Yolo County Welfare Department was instructed by the Yolo County Board of Supervisors to request that Bulletin 644 be rescinded in its entirety. In making this recommendation, the Board based its conclusion upon the 13 reasons for rescinding Bulletin 644 as developed by the County Welfare Directors Association.

Next was a presentation by the San Joaquin County Board of Supervisors as follows:

"State Welfare Department Bulletin 644 was adopted as an emergency measure without benefit of a public hearing on May 24, 1965, by the former State Director of Social Welfare. The adoption of this Bulletin was an alleged desperation attempt to help alleviate the farm labor problem by giving economic underpinning to farm workers, thereby hoping to attract more laborers into the fields. Farm labor is necessarily hard, dusty, disagreeable work carried on, for the most part, under difficult working conditions. It is not the kind of work most generally sought by the average laborer. We do not argue that much needs to be done to improve the lot of the farm worker in terms of working conditions, education, housing, and other benefits. However, we propose that Bulletin 644 or any other State Welfare Department administrative device is not the means to be used for such far reaching changes.

"State Department of Social Welfare Bulletin 644 must be abolished in its entirety for the following reasons:

"1. In the more than two years of its existence, it has not solved or alleviated the farm labor problem.

"2. It has, in fact, intensified the problem of making it possible for farm laborers to work fewer hours than before its adoption.

"3. The adoption and retention of Bulletin 644 has established a major public policy of a de facto guaranteed annual income without benefit of legislative hearing or debate.

"4. It is costly and difficult to administer. Contrary to the contention of the former State Welfare Director, it has not saved the County money—rather it has resulted in a substantial additional expense.

"Let us look a little further into each one of these reasons: First, Department Bulletin 644 has not solved or alleviated the farm labor problem. . . . In testimony presented by a member of San Joaquin County Board of Supervisors in 1965, concerning final adoption of Bulletin 644, he stated that the results of a poll of all valley county welfare directors indicated there is no evidence that this Bulletin has or will result in more people engaging in farm work or those already so employed being encouraged to work additional hours. In San Joaquin County, experience has borne out this contention. Secondly, Bulletin 644 has made the problem of the shortage of farm laborers more acute. Even with the decrease in bracero labor, each year we have an increasing number of cases aided as unemployed parents. With welfare payments making up the difference between net income and need up to the welfare standard, there is inevitably diminution of incentive on the part of individuals to aggressively seek agricultural work to the maximum possible extent. . . . Thirdly, Bulletin 644 has established for a select group of workers a system of guaranteed annual income without the benefit of legislative hearing or debate.

"The fact that a different economic system for Americans may or may not be needed is not the issue here. The issue is that such a far-reaching decision as this should stand the test of legislative debate rather than the automatic adoption through an administrative ruling of the State Welfare Director. So far, our legislators have not seen fit to approve this or any similar plan of a guaranteed annual income. . . . In conclusion, we submit that Bulletin 644 was hastily and ill conceived. With over two years experience in San Joaquin County, there is irrefutable evidence that it has not accomplished its stated purpose. Not only has it failed in its objectives, but it is, in fact, harmful to the laborer, the farming industry and taxpayers in general. Under these circumstances, we recommend to the State Director of Social Welfare that he rescind this Bulletin in its entirety."

A letter from the County of Alameda Board of Supervisors was read into the record. Excerpts from it are as follows:

"Your letter of October 10, 1967, gave notice of the Public Hearings on departmental Bulletin 644 and invited comments relative thereto. We will not be able to testify at the hearings scheduled for November 3 in Bakersfield. We would like to take this opportunity to submit the attached statement on farm labor referrals by the Welfare Department. The information is in part the result of hearings by the Alameda County Board of Supervisors in 1965 at which testimony was presented by the Director of the area office of the State Department of Social Welfare, and by representatives of the State Department of Employment and the Farm Labor Office. It also represents the most recent experience of our county welfare department as reported by our welfare director. We hope this will be of some assistance to you in your treatment of this most difficult and significant issue. . . .

"At the time the AFDC Unemployed Parent Program was inaugurated February 1964, the total of 522 cases was transferred to that program from the general relief rolls. It was around this group of recipients that Alameda County had over the years developed a successful referral procedure to the Farm Labor Office with a minimum of difficulty, and in estimation of the optimum advantage to the parties concerned. The free movement of this work force from the relief rolls to available farm labor has been logical, normal, and beneficial to both the individual and the farm economy. Unemployed persons from the city were thereby exposed to opportunities for employment and for development in agricultural skills. Farm labor provided work retention habits which public agencies are now attempting to provide at considerable public expense and was a source of satisfaction and pride for the individual. Unemployed persons from rural areas who drifted to cities looking for work on the off-season were not enticed to remain unemployed in order to receive public assistance.

"The state regulations governing the public assistance programs, and Bulletin 644 in particular, completely change the picture by interposing restrictions. Primary restriction has been the requirement that the referrals flow through state employment service. This system is inefficient and cumbersome. It is not responsive to the unique needs of a welfare agency, and its orientation is such that the normal flow of this labor force to farm labor appears all but choked up. During one period surveyed in 1965, out of 625 welfare referrals to CSES for consideration as farm laborers, only 35 reported for farm labor. At present, the flow of information from CSES to the County reveals a considerably less favorable picture. Out of 1,100 AFDC-U cases currently referred to CSES, we are informed that less than 30 cases were referred to the Farm Labor Office; less than 15 were actively employed full-time or part-time farm labor; and three cases were closed due to failure to cooperate.

"Apart from the low priority which the CSES apparently gives either to finding jobs for welfare recipients or to referring them to the Farm Labor Office, that agency does not keep the county welfare department informed, and it is inconsistent in its interpretation of policy, for example, in referral of skilled or semi-skilled males to farm labor. Also the County was somewhat appalled that the State Department of Social Welfare itself would expect a welfare department to know, as requested in a telegram earlier this month, how many recipients who were available for farm labor had been referred for such and were employed at such, in view of the fact that only CSES can make such determinations and referrals. This inquiry seems to be evidence that the system was hardly working as contemplated and that the respective responsibilities were improperly understood. It would be my recommendation that Bulletin 644 be rescinded and that the ability of county welfare departments to move the available work force to farm labor without undue delay, interference, confusion, and red tape be restored. I would also recommend that the state agencies facilitate employment of public assistance recipients by establishing new procedures and priorities, by offering support, guidance, leadership, and training to the counties, and by developing programs for recipients which will recognize the normal movement of this work force between the welfare rolls and farm labor."

The Secretary-Manager of the Kern County Property Owner's Association testified as follows:

"I have been a member of the Kern County Welfare Work and Training Advisory Committee, appointed by the Board of Supervisors since its inception in January 1964. Many taxpayers in Kern County are deeply concerned about the rapid growth of the assistance program. We feel that everything possible should be done to study all phases and to seek solutions which will relieve the property owner of the heavy burden of taxation he is forced to assume by federal and state legislation. . . . The growth of the AFDC-U program here in Kern County is of particular significance to the purposes of this hearing, dedicated as it is to the reexamination of the provisions of Bulletin 644, which set up special rules and special exemptions for the agricultural worker. Kern County is in large measure an agricultural county where farm labor families make up 90 percent of our AFDC-U costs. It is for this reason that we are vitally concerned with provisions of Bulletin 644. Compare this with San Diego County, where only 15 of the 4,200 cases on AFDC-U qualify because of Bulletin 644. We see in Bulletin 644 regulations that allow able-bodied men who are working 60 to 70 hours a week and sometimes earning with their families over $1,000 a month to remain on welfare, and retain eligibility for medical care. . . .

"If it is decided after this hearing that the provisions of Bulletin 644 are desirable, then this should be the subject of legislative action. Bulletin 644 should be repealed until such action is taken. The welfare program should not be used as a substitute for minimum wage guarantees and unemployment compensation. Bulletin 644 provides discrimination in welfare in California, the guaranteed annual wage based on size of family to a particular group of workers. The same logic could apply to any other low-income worker whose wages did not meet the needs of his family. Why should one special group be singled out for supplementation? There are obvious signs that welfare programs are presently being developed to be the bridge to accomplish the guaranteed annual wage for all. However, this is no argument for continuance of such a guarantee for one segment of our welfare population as opposed to another. Bulletin 644 provides inequity among the counties because Kern and other counties which are largely agricultural are penalized. Nonagricultural counties are given preferential treatment. Bulletin 644 reduces the incentive to work in that there is no reward for the individual head of the family to work extra hours. He can work the minimum and have the deficit made up by the welfare department. . . . Repeal of Bulletin 644 would bring some property tax relief in the year ahead. We vitally need that relief for the health of our economy. The citizenry is expressing growing concern over California's national reputation as the most liberal state in providing benefits in categorical aids. Our state must take stock as to the long-range effects of such a reputation, especially in view of the threatened removal of all residence requirements, and immediately take preventive action. . . .

". . . I wonder whether the attorneys for CRLA are aware of the fact that the County Supervisors Association of California supported AB 59. In fact it is reported that some senators state that CSAC is responsible for the passage of AB 59, the bill that provided for the unemployment word in the welfare laws that makes possible AFDC-U. . . The supervisors now see that Bulletin 644, which was not a part of AB 59, has not been feasible administrative-wise, and they feel that it has been inequitable. So now they are saying that this part of these programs is not workable, and I do not believe that they should be attacked for taking this forthright stand. As far as CRLA goes, it was not my impression that the ani-poverty program was designed for the purposes for which CRLA is being used today. But this is a matter of a hearing in Washington. In regard to the speaker who said the worker should not be obliged to work overtime, I would like to point out that during tomato harvest and cantaloupe time, I know of farmers in Kern County who work from 14 to 16 hours a day. Why is it unreasonable for a worker during harvest to take advantage of work opportunities when they are available? . . . I resent the statement of the speaker who said the welfare director should assume his responsibilities rather than shuffle paper. I'd like to say that I have been close to the welfare department of Kern County for many years and I know from observation that our welfare department has been doing considerably more than shuffling paper."

TESTIMONY FAVORING BULLETIN 644

The following letter from the Director of the Contra Costa County Social Service Department was read into the record:

"Your letter notifying the Contra Costa County Board of Supervisors about the public hearing to be held in Bakersfield, on November 3, 1967, to consider the possible rescinding of Bulletin 644 was referred to the County Health Director and myself for reply. It is our feeling that the Bulletin as structured does not have much effect on this county's welfare department although we realize it greatly affects the valley counties where there is a heavy use of farm labor. We feel however that it does provide an inequity because we have many persons in other seasonal part-time work who are not covered by the Bulletin. Recognizing this, the probable impossibility of expanding such coverage to groups and the probable administrative problems it creates for the valley counties, it is our opinion that the Bulletin should remain in effect. It seems obvious that farm work in California will not become full-time work, and the provisions in the Bulletin should both stabilize and strengthen these families for the benefit of the children. Our health department has had the experience of having to provide considerable health services to migrant farm families because of large fluctuation in income as a result of health problems. We would consider this as a preventive program and a better approach rather than wait until these families become dependent or become eligible for other governmental programs in a way more acceptable to our society, but also more costly in taxes."

The Executive Secretary of the Santa Clara County Farm Bureau testified as follows:

"Today's meeting has been quite an enlightening meeting. I have learned a number of things I didn't know before. One of the most fascinating things I have learned is all the reasons as to why 644 was adopted. Interestingly enough, not one person apparently has the story, at least it hasn't been presented so far, and this is the whole nitty-gritty about 644 and the human problems involved. I'm amazed that welfare directors and people of your class, your training, would say the things you have said here this morning. Now I haven't kept up completely on the welfare field in the last year. Maybe you can and do completely supplant the things that 644 does, and if so, God-speed you. I come here with the recommendation that you adopt the agenda material as it is presented in the agenda. I would like to make certain that you understand that the Santa Clara County Farm Bureau Board of Directors authorized me to speak to this group today and recommend that your proposals as they appear in the agenda be adopted.

"The people I work for are taxpayers, we like to see welfare recipients work, we like to see them get off of welfare; and if the program hasn't worked and hasn't helped, and it hasn't exposed people to the labor market then look to yourselves, first, because where it has been followed through to at least a limited degree it has worked. If it won't work the way it is written up now, take the same concepts and rewrite them so they will work . . . Let's remember back. There really wasn't any particular emergency. The former Director of SDSW was doing his best to manipulate and he did a fine job. He did have the courage to try an idea, and if you in the counties have not had the courage to try it, then I think you ought to be asked to really try it. . . . Our hope with this concept was that it would expose people and keep them with some of their skills if they had them. If they hadn't had skills, maybe it would give the welfare director the opportunity to get a crowbar behind them and say: 'let's get out and get a little work experience, you aren't going to lose any money by it and you might get some work experience.'

"The other thing it did was to simplify the re-entry into the welfare system. The time Bulletin 644 was adopted, if you remember, one of the standard complaints about welfare in the state of California was that if you went off welfare you couldn't get back on for two or three months after you had quit working. So we who sometimes worked in the middle of the winter, would offer somebody maybe a five-day job or a whole month of pruning, and the poor devil would say, 'Look Mac, I would like to, the woman is driving me crazy, the kids are driving me mad, and I would like to get out but you know, I'll lose my welfare.' You know well that this was the situation. Now, if that situation is changed, if instant welfare is available now, maybe this is no longer a valid point. I understand now that we have a better type of welfare, I heard that this morning; I'm glad to hear that. . . .

"We are talking about the down-trodden, the unfortunate, the poor, the indigent, the depressed, the deprived, and the dictionary is full of such adjectives. Basically, if we are going to talk about them as human beings, not things we are going to manipulate, but talk about them as human beings and try to help them really, then everything you do has to be directed on a hand-up not just a hand-out basis. . . . I want to concentrate on the 644 concept, which was to help, not to hinder . . . I speak here today, not to protect farm labor, not to replace braceros, I speak here today because we have a humanitarian issue at stake. I don't speak here because of my own personal connection with this thing in the past other than I happen to know why it was adopted, where it has worked; and if it hasn't worked it's your fault because you should have amended it, changed it, or modified it. You have a new director, these presentations can be made to him and I am sure it can be worked out. But unless you can change the system whereby people who are involved in the particular part of this problem, can continue to get medical attention, you have taken the guts right out of 644 and destroyed it and hurt the people for whom we are concerned."

The next organization speaker was the agricultural relations representative for the American Friends Service Committee, who gave the following unqualified support to the continuation of the provisions of Bulletin 644 and for its incorporation in the manual:

"Working in Tulare County, it has been our experience that the provisions of this Bulletin work to provide a very essential basic service for great numbers of people. The number of people served in the valley counties appears to us to be good evidence of the essential nature of this program and of the fact that it is being used. We feel that a program to provide basic minimum income support and to provide basic minimum necessities of food, clothing, housing, and medical care are absolutely essential and perhaps increasingly so in view of the developing farm labor situation. We would like to present several recommendations for improvement in conduct of the program. One of these is with regard to the matter of translation. It would seem rather unusual that in a county like Tulare, where 70 percent of welfare recipients are Spanish-speaking, that an applicant would have to be advised to bring in a translator with him. This is the case, however, and most of the cases with which I have had personal contact where a person has been improperly denied have involved a failure of communication. I also find that very frequently people will bring in friends or neighbors who may not be equipped to understand the intricacies of welfare regulations, or perhaps a child who has been held out of school for the purpose.

"Secondly, it seems to me that there needs to be a basic change of attitude on the part of the welfare department. There needs to be a presumption of the existence of need rather than a presumption of noneligibility. Again, in the cases in which I have had personal contact, there seems to be a searching on the part of welfare workers for loopholes whereby aid may be denied. Thirdly, I would suggest that the State Board of Social Welfare investigate very carefully what the additional cost to taxpayers is for programs such as this by virtue of the fact that recipients are denied coverage under unemployment insurance. Perhaps this could be done on a very simple basis, by ascertaining whether the persons who have been receiving aid under AFDC-U for farm laborers would have been eligible for unemployment insurance under normal circumstances at the time that they received the welfare assistance.

"I would like also to comment on some of the testimony of the Kern County Supervisor, given on behalf of the County Welfare Directors Association and the Association of County Supervisors. The Supervisor appears to base his criticism on the grounds that the program has failed to induce an increased labor supply and that it has failed to reduce costs to the welfare department. I would submit that neither of these are appropriate for a welfare department. He attempts to attribute to Bulletin 644 the entire increase in the caseload on welfare during peak labor months. It seems to me that he overlooks any effort to evaluate the vast changes that are taking place in our agricultural economy and in our labor force. He overlooks the influx of labor families from the Southwest; he overlooks the fact that there is a constant and very large annual decrease in the amount of man-months of farm labor generally. For example, the total decrease paid farm labor in the United States from 1965 to 1966 was $38 million. The County Welfare Directors Association representative commented that the solution to these problems should not be provided through public welfare. We would agree, but the device which offers us a solution to these problems which is currently in force through Bulletin 644 should not be rescinded until such time as more effective or more appropriate programs are available, such as unemployment insurance. Finally, to the Tulare County Welfare Director's comments, and I say this advisedly, since I also live in Tulare County, I think the evidence he has offered of individual case information should be regarded strictly as hearsay until such time as evidence from the other side of the cases has been heard."

The research director of the California Labor Federation, AFL-CIO, made the next presentation.

"The California Labor Federation is a statewide organization representing some one and one-half million AFL-CIO members in this state. Over the years, the Federation has taken a most active interest in the entire question of farm labor and in ways to improve the lot of the agricultural work force. Reflecting this interest, we are here today in order to make our views known regarding Bulletin 644. In our view, the Bulletin cannot be examined in a vacuum. It must be viewed in light of past and present developments in the field of agricultural labor. Its impact, favorable or adverse, must be examined in a context broader than that of other regulations affecting welfare recipients. . . . theoretically, under Bulletin 644, welfare recipients and their families benefit because the regulations improve the standards of living of farm workers' children. Obviously this goal has merit and it perhaps should be extended to all other low income families. Unfortunately, there are other less pleasant or desirable consequences of this Bulletin. It has been repeatedly documented that farm workers in California and elsewhere are extremely low paid, generally work sporadically, and enjoy few if any of the working conditions usually taken for granted by workers in most other industries in this state and Nation. This sorry fact is recognized in Bulletin 644. To continue this point another step, it also has been long recognized in California that growers enjoy a privileged place in this state's economy. They benefit, unlike most other industries, from the research and development sponsored by the University of California. The advantages of this are obvious, the growers spend little if any of their own financial funds on research; instead, that research is financed by the general tax payer. Some growers receive federal subsidies for not producing, and many are benefactors under federal reclamation law of large-scale, interest-free, 40-year loans. Also, unlike any other industry, they continue to profit from federal programs supplying them with supplemental labor from abroad. In sharp contrast, their work force is not covered by the basic Federal labor laws, which guarantee most workers the right to organize and bargain collectively with their employers. I am referring to the National Labor Relations Act, enacted 32 years ago. Nor are they covered by unemployment insurance. The implication is obvious in terms of welfare loads and costs. Even their Social Security and minimum wage coverage under federal law is far below the general standard. In short, growers are the direct beneficiaries of numerous governmental programs. On the other hand, their employees have been purposely excluded from the legal protections and benefits extended to most other workers since the 1930's. Apparently now, some of the growers want to abolish Bulletin 644 in order to insure that they have a totally captive labor force at their beck and command. As an aside, I can't help but feel that this is just another example of the general approach taken by so many people today on any program that is aimed at benefiting other people.

"The crux of the matter regarding Bulletin 644 is the impact of its regulations and requirements, and the parallel regulations, requirements, and procedures of the California State Department of Employment. The present situation seems to be that a welfare recipient can and is referred to a farm job under the following conditions, or should I say more appropriately lack of conditions.

"(1.) No guarantee regarding the minimum hours of work by day or week, and no maximum hours of work daily or weekly are set. In fact, Bulletin 644 states that when applicants and recipients are being referred to the Department of Employment for work they shall be instructed they are to work as many hours as the job requires, whether 12, 14, or 16 hours.

"(2.) Transportation problems revolving around getting to the job and the distance the welfare recipient may be forced to travel to a job which, in many cases, can be unreasonable.

"(3.) Males, to the extent they may be covered under the Federal Fair Labor Standards Act, would receive a minimum wage guarantee of only $1 an hour. Females, on the other hand, are covered under the State Industrial Welfare Commission order affecting agriculture, and would receive a minimum of $1.30 an hour.

"The minimum wage paid welfare recipients sent to do farm work is a major concern to us. We feel the situation as it now exists is unfair and inequitable. As we see it, the situation is one where growers can use welfare recipients at as low as $1 per hour while required to provide, under Public Law 414, a minimum of $1.60 an hour. In other words, domestic workers are treated less favorably than foreign workers. In fact, welfare recipients, as it stands, can and are depressing overall farm worker wage rates. While we recognize that workers on welfare are not the proper vehicle for raising overall farm wages, the reverse of this is that they should not be used to depress farm rates . . . Nowhere in California is the prevailing farm wage rate near $1 per hour. Yet, as we understand it, the male welfare recipient may receive only $1 per hour. This appears illegal and to us is morally indefensive. The California Labor Federation urges the Department of Social Welfare to revise Bulletin 644 to include, at least, provisions for minimum and maximum hours of work daily and weekly; provisions outlining travel time, transportation distance, and means required; provisions setting the minimum to be paid to any welfare recipient referred to farm work at $1.60 an hour now, and a $1.65 an hour beginning February 1, 1968. To do otherwise, in our view, is to depress or hold down farm labor wage rates and thus work a severe hardship on all farm workers as well as on welfare recipients.

"To sum up, the concept underlying Bulletin 644 is humanitarian. To achieve this in a meaningful and realistic way, however, the changes we recommend should be made. So many references were made this morning to all the horrible things that this Bulletin does and doesn't do. In terms of the growers, it doesn't give them enough workers, people are lazy, the county welfare administrators are in a horrible situation because they have to work harder. Quite honestly, I can't bleed any at all for the county welfare administrators. It seems to me that their job is to enforce the law, and I wish their concern was with the welfare recipients and their children rather than with the shuffling of paper.

The next presentation was made by the Diocesan Director of Catholic Charities for the Diocese of Fresno, who was also the Chairman of the California Association of Catholic Charities Directors. In behalf of these organizations, and in opposition to repealing the State Department of Social Welfare Bulletin 644, he made the following statement:

"My main concern is with the plight of the farm worker, a group of American citizens almost totally lacking government protection and assistance. Our migrant and residential farm workers consist of the poorest of the poor in our land. Farm workers are specifically excluded from the National Labor Relations Act; from unemployment insurance provisions; and for many, from minimum wage coverage. The purposes for which Bulletin 644 was introduced are valid ones:

"(1.) To encourage parents to accept farm labor employment, even though they had no previous experience at this type of work or were unable to earn enough to support their families.

"(2.) To continue medical care and other services of the welfare department to families during periods when earnings meet financial needs.

"(3.) To simplify procedures for reinstating aid promptly when earnings are inadequate.

"I feel that the Bulletin rulings should be retained, despite some administrative difficulties. We are at a point in history when farm workers are beginning to organize themselves for purposes of collective bargaining. They are beginning to have dignity and self-respect as workers. We must not take from them the very minimum protection and assistance which they now enjoy in virtue of Bulletin 644.

"Bulletin 644 is no large government endowment. At best it allows a farm worker family to live at the level of poverty established by our government. While some may object that the Bulletin discriminates in behalf of farm workers, this is really not true. No other class of American workers remains as abandoned and impoverished as the seasonal farm worker. Some object to the program's continuance because of the cost. Granted everyone is anxious to reduce government spending, but is this program really that expensive when compared to the billions of dollars of government subsidy for the rest of the agriculture industry? Why is it that we become so alarmed over assuring a farm worker of earning a poverty income, but never raise our voices to question subsidies to other participants of the agriculture industry? I am not opposed to the subsidization of agriculture, as long as both farmer and farm worker receive equal treatment.

"Many of our farm workers are Americans of Mexican descent. Their living and working habits do not always fit the Department's requirements for maintaining residency for precise periods of time, nor for recordkeeping according to all the regulations. Their rugged way of life is no Utopia, and I am certain they would welcome a way out of it. The real issue is whether or not we will bow to arguments of alleged economy when the living situation of the farm worker is already so pathetic. All of us have a commitment to this impoverished group of citizens—a commitment which is in reality a moral and social responsibility.

"One of the agonies of our times is the way we respond to the needs of the poor. What we should really be discussing today is methods to uplift the State's farm workers, and to make it possible for them to share in the abundance of our State's resources. Instead —and quite ironically—our response is often repressive. For some inexplicable reason, at times society tends to turn against the poor as if to make an already depressing cycle of dependency more intolerable.

"I appeal to you, on behalf of our State's farm worker families, to retain Bulletin 644's provisions. If changes are to be made, let them be in favor of the farm worker. Listen to the farm workers.

Hear their problems and their pleas for help. Let us respond to their needs openly, honestly, and with a response that will reflect our State's genuine concern for their well-being. Let California serve as example to the Nation of our deep commitment to these, the most neglected of our poor."

Next, the representative of the Legal Aid Society of Alameda County: "We are for the most part an urban organization, but we also see clients who have been subjected to some of the experiences that were so glibly described this morning. . . . I am concerned about a great many people in our state, including farm workers, but perhaps also about some of those who could with straight faces stand here as allegedly responsible people and proclaim the most inhumane, obscene standards I have heard put forward in public for some time. There was a woman who stood here and testified that she, of her own knowledge as an experienced Welfare Director, knew that children in this state were being subjected to improper medical care and she wanted farm kids subjected to the same thing. There was a man who stood up here this morning and said that his experiences as Supervisor in a county in this state had led him to be concerned with the needs of the poverty stricken people. But that same gentleman later permitted another supervisor's representative to stand here and enunciate policies that could not possibly have been more oriented toward other sets of needs if they had consciously done it. I will go through some of these arguments. We were told that Bulletin 644 should be abolished because it was a disadvantage to the other needy people, that the farm people got things they should have but the farm people were getting by accident. We were told that by every speaker this morning, people who run county departments in this state.

"Welfare is for needy people. People who are in need of money to live, people who are in need of money to permit their children to have decent medical care should have any benefits extended to them, not cut back. We were told that the regulation had failed, that it was not practical or effective to make more workers for the farm. Were we told that the wages are low on the farms, and were we told about those welfare recipients who beg for a wage that will get them off of welfare, as opposed to a wage that keeps them barely at the welfare standards and without medical care for their families? We were told that the Bulletin had not resulted in a reduction of caseload and therefore should be eliminated. Somehow, despite the counties' conscious administrative efforts, this Bulletin identified a need. Having recognized it, are we now to slam the door in the face of those needy families? We were advised that caseloads were lowest before welfare Bulletin 644 was adopted. Shall we return to that enlightened era? We were told that these policies are inconsistent with the goals of the AFDC-U program. We were told that they were inconsistent with legislative policy. I submit that the allegedly responsible people who made this testimony this morning had better read some of the sections on needs.

"This program, and every welfare program in this state supposedly is supposed to help people, not just growers who need cheap farm labor. If you starve people too long they might start burning the fields like some people have started burning our cities. Need is not something that evaporates because you choose to make like an ostrich about it. If people need the assistance then let us in a responsible fashion, within the standards of the law, apply our system to satisfy their problem. We were told that the present regulations are sufficient to meet existing needs. In Alameda County, one woman in a wheelchair who had taken a temporary job because she would like very much to be self-supporting spent 60 days getting requalified for Aid to the Disabled when the job was lost. Now any county administrator who can stand up here and claim that existing procedures are efficient, and that when a case is closed emergency aid is in fact given, has committed quite a sin of omission.

"A recent public hearing in Alameda County, an intake worker testified that she was forced to send men to farm labor whose grants for Aid to the Disabled came through that same week. Now I wonder how the administrators can so glibly read their regulations and decide they are solving problems and we don't need the procedural device of keeping a case open. We were told that this program is a financially, de facto, guaranteed income. Well, thank God for that. Someone told you that it is at least a guaranteed poverty income. That's a great benefit in our culture! It does keep you from starving very little more. With $145 or $192, can some of you research gentlemen who present yourselves as authorities, figure out how far that money goes? In my own county, rents are less than half the prevailing cost, and I cannot believe that farm workers are better off than urban slum dwellers when I look at the rural hovels I drove by getting here. We were told that the solution to the farm labor problem is not in the welfare system and I agree. I submit to you that the SDSW should deal with the problem, namely, help needy people; and the growers should find the economic means to pay a competitive wage and hire people at a better rate, and if they can't do it, then they should worry about their problems without subverting the welfare system. Whether the gentlemen who spoke this morning want to be honest about welfare or not, the people this afternoon have talked to you of humanity and of need. The people this morning talked to you of abuse and manipulation to obtain eligibility. Did anybody mention the abuse and manipulation to obtain discharges from welfare? Were you told about the lady who had to give up her clerical job because her child needed an eye operation, and the clerical job just barely covered needs, and nobody bothered to consider any possible extensions under existing regulations to let her go through the week that the eye operation was necessary?

"You were told that people who can make it on welfare won't work. Well, I don't blame them, if a public official can stand here and glibly say that it's wrong because they didn't work an alleged available 53 hours a week when he didn't bother to tell us what the overtime rate of pay was or how backbreaking the 53 hours might have been, or the health condition of the person who supposedly was assumed capable of performing the duties. I was outraged this morning. I think that public officials are supposed to tell the truth about their jobs and not distort operations. Their job is to identify and meet needs, and if there is an inequity because other people in need are not being served, then in my opinion you should serve them also. And before the SDSW blindly runs down the path of wiping out something that for a change is accomplishing good for human beings I would caution you that there may be some technical points involved. We have been allowed to get very broad on the policy here because the Director was interested in finding out what the spirit of the community was, but before us on this formal agenda are specific regulation changes and I would like to make some technical observations about them. The repeal is not before us and it is my opinion that before any kind of repeal could go into effect it would have to be posted for another public hearing, and I assure you I will arrive armed with statistics and whatever else will be needed to deal with this situation.

"It is completely correct that recurring unemployment is not just in farm labor. It is completely pathological to deal with unemployment in farm labor in an abusive fashion rather than trying to reach it elsewhere when you get the time and the money. Something that someone else tried to say this afternoon is so otherwise incredibly absent from this hearing today that I want to call it to your attention: Welfare recipients are people, they hurt, they hurt when they are spit upon, they hurt when they are kicked in the teeth and if they hurt enough and if they don't resort to rioting and bombing and burning fields as well as slums, then they get apathetic and they become a kind of living dead. It happened in concentration camps and it can happen to us whether you like to face it or not. You get the welfare recipient who is so limp he can barely tell his story, let alone think he has got a right. We don't need any more repressive techniques in this system, people who are cut off come into my office because they are scared to death to go back to the welfare department to be shamed. A father who is unemployed has it even harder than my woman in a wheelchair, his job petered out, and he has got to prove what he did with every cent of that money. That is a degrading experience and he'll starve himself, keep his kids out of school, as will the mother, before they subject themselves to that crucifixion again. Taxpayers cannot afford to be penny-wise and pound-foolish, and if the county welfare departments are not willing to tell the taxpayers the truth, then the SDSW had better enforce it despite them if that's what it boils down to. You may save a penny now, and later spend two million dollars rebuilding Watts. If you don't give them the administrative relief of not having to wait 60 days to requalify, don't give them medical care for their families, eventually I assure you, you will pay. You will pay for the next generation that never learned how to cope because the parents got lethargic through no fault of theirs, or you will pay in this generation which is grimly beginning to talk back, even on the farm.

"I am for modification of 644. I am for strengthening it and seeing to it that the counties which so manifestly this morning do not intend to apply it unless they are hit over the head, are in fact hit over the head. I am for extending it to the urban communities that need this kind of relief as soon as the money is there to make that possible."

The next representative, from the Marysville office of the California Rural Legal Assistance, made the following statement:

"For those of you who may not know, California Rural Legal Assistance is a nonprofit corporation funded by the OEO. We have nine legal aid offices in rural areas in California. Many of our clients are farm workers and we have had a lot of experience representing many of them in welfare matters as well as other matters. We have approximately 30 attorneys in the field dealing with farm workers problems on a day-to-day basis. The people who attacked Bulletin 644 this morning stressed two points: 644 discriminates against farm workers, and it doesn't provide growers with cheap labor as it supposedly was intended to do. None of these people discussed whether Bulletin 644 helped to further the purpose of the AFDC-U program, which is to help needy children and make them productive members of our society. This seemed to be totally irrelevant to them. I would like to discuss this issue, and to my mind this should be the only issue. Does this Bulletin help needy children and will its elimination hurt needy children?

"The position of CRLA is that we urge retention of Bulletin 644, and even more important than that, we feel it should be enforced because right now many of us have the feeling it is really a scrap of paper and it wouldn't make much difference if it was repealed because it's not enforced.

"It seems to us that the State Department of Social Welfare has two major interests in this matter of Bulletin 644, both of which compel its retention and taking further steps to see that it is enforced, to see the county departments comply with it. These interests are first, getting eligible needy children on aid and keeping them on aid so long as they are eligible, so they can use welfare for the purpose for which it is intended, helping them grow up to become productive members of society. Secondly, you should be concerned with giving farm worker families incentives to stay in farm work and maximize their work output. Well, let's look at this first point, getting eligible needy children on aid and keeping them there while they are eligible. How will this be effected if 644 is repealed? I think I can testify on this matter from actual experience. We represent people in Yuba and Sutter Counties. In the course of representing people who live in Sutter County, we have found that Bulletin 644 is not complied with by the Sutter County Welfare Department, so it is just as if it wasn't there, or repealed, so we have a test case to see what it would be like if it was repealed. What happens up there is if a farm worker earns more than his needs, according to the needs schedule, in one month he gets notice of action telling him he is cut off of welfare, totally in violation of 644. We have had fair hearing decisions pointing out to Sutter County this is the rule, but they are still doing it.

"This situation apparently is happening elsewhere. I notice from the statistics given us this morning, that in June of 1967 there were 3,248 open cases on AFDCU for farm workers in this state. This was decreased to 2,600 in July and August as more work became available. Now if 644 was being obeyed there wouldn't be this reduction, more work becoming available doesn't necessarily knock people off aid under 644. You still keep the case open, the guy gets a zero grant but you still have an open case. So we have 600 cases where apparently the law was violated according to his statistics. I wasn't aware of it before today, but apparently Sutter County is not unique. Now let's look at the effect of this. We are taking a situation where we don't have any 644 and what happens? The first thing we have observed in our program in dealing with farm workers is that the whole public attitude toward welfare has been imbued in them. Welfare has been given a public image that it's for the greedy, it's a hand out, and it's not dignified, and these people feel more strongly about it then some of the most vicious opponents of welfare. They don't want to go near it. A lot of this is because of the public attitude and because when they have gone in for welfare, when they have friends that have gone in for welfare, they have found they have to beg for it or grovel for it, even to get a food order.

"There isn't dignity in the intake process which might give people a good feeling when they go in, so they just stay away from it, they don't like it. Now what does this mean? When it starts raining in November and these people can't work they are eligible for welfare with or without 644. Instead of going into the welfare department to apply for aid, which is the only place they can go, since they are not eligible for unemployment compensation, they put it off. First they live on their savings, and when that runs out they get another loan on their car or pickup truck, loan that up to the hilt, then they borrow from friends, get a little sporadic work. Meanwhile, the bills pile up, and kids need medical attention and clothing. We have had many cases where parents don't send their kids to school because they can't pay for their school lunches and their clothes are in such bad shape they don't want their kids to be seen at school like that. So the people are eligible in November and December, but often they never go in, they last the whole winter and spring without welfare. This spring was so bad with the late rains, a lot of them just had to go to the Welfare Department in March and April. They could have been eligible three months before, but they go in March or April, some even in May, and finally apply for aid, and even then, most of them were denied. . . .

"Actually, without 644 they have to make three applications a year and they don't want to make one. Now we have 644 and it has to be enforced or it is worthless. If we have it and it is enforced, these people can make one application for aid and they are on aid if the conditions of 644 are met . . . Another problem with making this application is that even those who do make the application and are clearly eligible, often can't get aid. A hostile rural welfare department can make the intake process pretty rugged. They can think of some pretty fancy ways to keep someone off aid, and I am sure you are aware of that. So they don't want to go and when they do go they often don't get on aid and the kids suffer because of it. And that's the main effect of 644, and no one has talked about it today. Most of the speakers opposed to it apparently have had no connection with farm workers, have never seen these problems, have never seen this issue. The main thing 644 can do is avoid that continual application process.

"The second point is the interest of the State Department of Social Welfare in keeping farm workers in farm work and working. It has been suggested that 644 stops the incentive to keep working. Well I think this is totally untrue. First of all it has been my experience and the experience of the other CRLA attorneys that the great majority of farm workers want to work and don't want to live on any type of welfare aid where they can possibly avoid it, where they can possibly avoid the injury to their kids. They want to work as much as they can. The Tulare County welfare director has these

12 pieces of paper which indicate certain people don't want to work. I could have brought thousands of these pieces of paper concerning people who want to work so bad that they have never applied for welfare aid, and struggled through the winter. You can think up these horror cases and find a few people like that in any system. Go out and talk to some of your business friends and see what they did on their income tax returns. It is ridiculous to take in 12 pieces of paper, all hearsay, none of which really has anything to do with 644. If it's true they don't want to work, there are enforcement mechanisms already on the books, totally independent of Bulletin 644 to keep them off. The county welfare departments should be enforcing these. It has been my experience they do enforce them; this is one place they live up to the law doing everything they can to get these people off.

"Concerning 644 itself, it is my belief it actually provides one of the greatest incentives to farm workers to work hard and earn money way beyond their needs according to the needs schedule. One thing people haven't talked about is the fact that under 644 the farm worker can earn way beyond his needs in a given month and still keep his Medical card. I can't state any stronger than the prior speaker did that my opinion in this argument that Bulletin 644 discriminates in favor of farm workers and therefore we should knock out 644 is so absurd on its face that I don't think that it requires much further comment. Other people are suffering, so why should these people not suffer? Let them suffer along with the rest. I don't see how they said it with straight faces. Well, in conclusion, I and the other CRLA attorneys urge you to retain Bulletin 644, extend it to these other classes of people that are now excluded from these benefits, don't cut out the farm workers, but include the other people, and enforce 644 and make the counties comply with it."

The next speaker was the Social Workers Union representative from Los Angeles who testified as follows:

"So many things have been said, and many of the things that have been said are the kinds of things that our union wants to associate itself with, namely the testimony of the Legal Aid Society of Alameda County and of the California Rural Legal Assistance as well as that of the California Social Workers Organization, and particularly the testimony of the California Labor Federation representative and the concrete suggestions on how we can help to shore up the effects of 644. But I want to say a couple of other things: I want to say that there are some basic inequities in our welfare system, and that social workers recognize this. I want to say that there are terrible inequities between the states and between one part of one county and another part of it; and there are terrible inequities between different categories of aid. I want to say that Bulletin 644 goes part of the way towards meeting some of the inequities that farm workers have suffered under in this state for a very long time. Some of the witnesses representing the growers, the Supervisors Association, and unfortunately, I have to say the County Welfare Directors Association, are missing the point of what the AFDC-U program is supposed to be about. It is supposed to be about providing certain necessary services to people who need those services and to meeting needs as they exist. . . .

"I want to say that 644 has to be shored up. It has to be made tougher. The reason that I say this is that social workers resent very bitterly being made part of what often becomes a referral service or an employment agency for a miserable industry that does not do anything to strengthen family life or make the lives of children and their families any better than they are. And let me remind you again that the purpose of the Aid to Families with Dependent Children program is to strengthen family life, to make lives better, and to bring people into the mainstream of society. In many of the valley counties there is continual pressure, particularly at harvest time, to refer people to agriculture regardless of the needs of the family. Apparently the needs of the industry come before the needs of the family and the needs of the children.

"In Stanislaus County, when a new case at intake shows up, there is an immediate, automatic referral to the Farm Labor Office, with a certain amount of pressure to make sure that this happens fast. I'm going to give an example of how this works in Santa Clara County, which is in many ways one of our better counties here in California. This is a county that has a fairly large agriculture caseload. At the insistence of the Board of Supervisors and the politicians, on September 19, the Chairman of the Board of Supervisors sent two fellows from the Farm Labor Bureau of the Department of Employment into the welfare office in San Jose to set up a desk in the waiting room. Initially, they were thrown out by welfare management. Additional pressure came on September 29, the Farm Labor Bureau people showed up again with the desk, and all applicants for aid had to go to that desk directly, rather than first seeing a social worker. By all applicants for aid I mean disabled, AFDC-U, General Assistance, people over 65. Everybody had to go through, because there was a good deal of pressure from the prune growers. One member of the Board of Supervisors is a prune grower. At this point, a union committee headed by the president of our chapter in Santa Clara County had a number of meetings with the intake division chief and it became quite clear that the staff of the department was not going to tolerate this kind of activity, particularly in a department that had a relatively good record as being a social service agency.

"The desk is still there, the referrals now come from social workers rather than as people come through the front door, but the pressure is also still there. Social workers are supposed to refer all 'appropriate clients', meaning physically able to do farm work. There are a number of mothers with six or seven kids who are physically able to do farm work, undoubtedly, but some of these mothers may lack babysitters, they may lack all sorts of other things. In this case, mothers presumably are supposed to take the kids into the fields with them. Actually Santa Clara County social workers won't refer many mothers to farm labor, and in fact, I don't think they refer any. But it has been reported to me that members of the Board of Supervisors have said that they believe that the fields are a good place for AFDC-U mothers and their children. It's this type of policy, coming from the supervisors of one county who are obviously not terribly different from the supervisors of most counties, that makes the operations of Bulletin 644 as an integral part of our AFDC-U program of services to children and services to families in need often a touch-and-go affair. . . .

"What we want to do is to be able to work together with management to make sure that the AFDC-U programs and our other service programs, inadequately financed as they are, will meet as many needs as possible. We want to be able to do this with our departments and with backing from our boards of supervisors. Frankly, I've lost a good deal of faith in the possibility of this ever happening on a local level, and as a matter of fact, I'm not really so sure that federal-state social security programs or welfare programs really belong in the hands of five-man boards of supervisors, but really should be administered by the Federal Government itself and by the state agencies. In conclusion, Mr. Director, we want 644 to be retained, we want it to be made an integral part of the regulations, we want other guarantees built into it that people do not have to take any kind of job just because they are referred to it and the employment is available, because if the conditions are miserable, if the wages are unlivable, then this becomes obnoxious employment and does not help to restore decent family life, if it has been destroyed, or maintain a strong family where it does exist."

The next person to speak was a farmer, who contributed the following:

"I am of the emphatic opinion that the California State Department of Social Welfare program under AFDC-U and Bulletin 644 is a necessary and a sound program. If the citizens, taxpayers, farm producers, the present Reagan administration, and the State Department of Social Welfare, if we individually or collectively have any moral conscience at all, we have to support this program or come up immediately with a sounder and more just program. It is immoral that farm workers' annual income is kept at the poverty level for many because of seasonal unemployment and because wages are kept low as a result of farm workers not having the protection of the law to guarantee collective bargaining for higher wages. It is also immoral that farm workers are given second-rate status by not being eligible for unemployment insurance as most workers are. The program being considered here is the only program that our state has come up with to move in the direction of justice and morality for unemployed seasonal farm laborers. It would be emphatically immoral and an economic disgrace if the program were cancelled out or watered down. It is minimal.

"The present program gives a foundation from which to accomplish two basic rights in the interest of farm laborers—that the program is carried out in full compliance with Bulletin 644, and the unemployed farm worker receives comparable treatment to an unemployed industrial worker, who only has to be unemployed for one week in each year to qualify for unemployment insurance payments to bring his income in every succeeding month in the following 12-month period up to the rate established for him by the Department of Employment. The program serves to subsidize not the worker, but the farm producer, who pays no unemployment insurance tax because it would provide a seasonal farm worker with a minimal income which the basic $1.40 per hour farm wage is inadequate to provide. It must be stated parenthetically that $1.40 has been the basic wage during periods of surplus workers and periods of high unemployment in the 12-month period prior to this date. Example number 1 in the Appendix of Bulletin 644 is a true-to-life example to drive home this point. It requires $406 per month to provide minimum requirements for a family of eight. The welfare department only grants $337. At $1.40 per hour, it would require 32 working days to earn $406, and 27 days to earn $337. Farm producers and citizens in general should be grateful for this subsidy to growers so that those who labor to produce our crops can provide their children with minimum living requirements under this program. It must be emphasized that this program is designed primarily to protect children of seasonally unemployed farm workers. Growers and state agencies are concerned with keeping workers available in the labor market. It has been definitely proven that since the elimination of the bracero program that when wages are raised to respectable levels, laborers will go into the fields and produce the crops. The program isn't the hindrance. Wages are the hindrance.

"As citizens, more particularly as rural citizens, we have to honestly recognize that unemployment is a tremendous factor in annual incomes of many workers and we have to honestly recognize the need for a flexible, practical program to compensate for this fact of life. I come from Sutter County where tree crops and tomatoes are the major users of farm laborers. In a 12-month period in Sutter County, there are three normal periods of unemployment amongst farm laborers; namely October 1 to November 15, between harvest and pruning; February 15 to May 1, between pruning and thinning; June 15 to July 15, between thinning and harvest. Every season there is added unemployment caused by periods of inclement weather. In Sutter County, the previous 12 months experienced two abnormally extended inclement weather periods with accompanying excess unemployment, namely, November 15 to December 15, 1966, and March and April of 1967. In our county, workers experienced much unnecessary suffering because our Sutter County Welfare Department was not geared to this program. Workers were deprived of the prompt aid they were entitled to. One of the greatest assets of this program before you is that the annual nature of the program eliminates the delays and suffering that come with establishing eligibility at intermittent occurrences of unemployment. A permanent status of eligibility for medical aid under the program insures consistent medical care for seasonal workers subject to low annual income periods or periods of no income at all. This is a just program. If you kill it, those that cause this to happen should hang their heads in shame. There is a crying need for a uniform application and enforcement of the program in every rural county in the state. The real farm workers are not spongers off welfare funds. They have pride and are reluctant to seek welfare assistance. Many families suffer as a result of this pride. Others suffer because of the humiliating treatment they received in some county welfare departments. There is a very real need for a whole new approach towards eligible unemployed farm workers."

The next presentation, by the California Social Workers Organization, a voluntary association of social workers employed in governmental and private agencies throughout California, was as follows:

"Many of our members are directly employed in providing public assistance aid and services. Others serve those who are not eligible for public assistance. We are in a unique position, therefore, to evaluate public assistance programs and their effects. And, from the beginning, it is important to remember that social workers are taxpayers, too. We recommend that the provisions of Bulletin 644 be continued and that they be included in the Public Social Services Manual. We are talking about a program to aid needy children, perhaps the neediest children in California, the children in families who follow the crops.

"Bulletin 644 has probably helped to stabilize the domestic farm labor force. In the process, the children of farm labor families have been enabled to live more nearly like other children. Our recommendation is based on practical considerations. These are well illustrated by quoting from a letter received from a social worker whose caseload includes farm laborers assisted under the provisions of Bulletin 644. This letter stated that there are 'fringe' benefits to Bulletin 644. More and more children are at their proper age level in school. In the past, a 16-year-old, whose classmates were 13 or 14 years old, was ripe for becoming a drop-out. Now, there is greater appreciation of education on the part of parents and children. More English is spoken in the home. With the fear of bare existence eliminated, more and more children who work in the summer have been motivated to put some of their earnings in a special savings account for their future educational needs.

"We recognize that public welfare payments may not be the ideal way to stabilize farm labor families and the economy in which they live. Until we can devise better ways, however, we urge the retention of this one."

Next, a representative of the Madera Community Service Organization, composed mostly of Mexican-Americans, stated as follows:

"We learned from the newspapers that a group of county politicians are trying to abolish Bulletin 644. This would cause great hardship in our home county of Madera. There is almost no employment available for people except farm work. Men and women work when they can but farm work is seasonal and poorly paid. If families who depend on farm work for a living were denied aid it would result in wholesale starvation and hardship in counties such as Madera. These are the same politicians who oppose unemployment insurance for farm workers. They criticize the people who are trying to make conditions better for the farm workers, then they turn around and complain that there aren't enough farm workers to work in their fields. They don't care about the poor. They are trying to take food out of the mouths of the poor children whose only sin is to be born into a family of farm workers.

"In Madera County, we are familiar with another abuse of AFDC-U and Bulletin 644. Workers of the Madera County Welfare Department went from door to door of welfare recipients and demanded the children and the mothers work in the raisin harvest. Conditions in nearly every vineyard violated the child labor laws of California. They made mothers of small children desert their children and work under conditions that violated the laws of California about employment of women in agriculture. Welfare to families has been cut off because mothers and children did not work under conditions which were abolished in civilized parts of America 50 years ago, and they were so proud of the fact that they removed all these families off of welfare and these children were in need that they publicized it in all the papers. Nineteen families with little children, some 5 and 6 years old, were taken off of welfare.

"If you change Bulletin 644 at all, you shouldn't allow the counties to cut off people because the kids don't go to work in the fields. You shouldn't allow the counties to cut off people because the mother of a preschool aged child doesn't work because she wants to give her child the love and security that only a mother can give at home with her child, taking care of it properly. The welfare department should be told not to send recipients to employers who violate the labor and sanitation laws, or to labor contractors who violate the labor contractor rules. You shouldn't allow the counties to cut off welfare because a mother refuses to work for an employer who violates Industrial Welfare Commission rules about employment of women in agriculture. There are a lot of labor abuses in the valley and you shouldn't let the welfare department become a part of them. The State Department of Social Welfare didn't create the problems, but it should recognize them. If the politicians want to do something about farm worker problems then let them pass a decent minimum wage law, and get unemployment compensation for farm workers. Also, they compared the farm worker with persons in other industries. If you are a truck driver you are covered by unemployment insurance, you belong to an organization. All the social workers belong to an organization. All the farmers belong to an organization. And yet, the farm worker is not organized, he is downtrodden. They want to make a slave out of him. And if anyone stands up to defend him, he is—I can't explain any more. In closing, I would like to say that the Madera County Community Services Organization does not want Bulletin 644 rescinded until wages are sufficient so that a farm worker can earn enough to support his family, and he is covered by unemployment insurance so that at the time that he is not employed he will not have to go and ask the welfare department to support him and his family."

CONCLUSIONS

The preceding testimony covers a wide variety of argument for and against the continuation of Bulletin 644. As might be expected, the special interest groups representing the farmer and the tax payer opposed the measure. Special interest groups identified with the public assistance program and the people it serves largely supported Bulletin 644. There were some exceptions to this. A rancher and a farmer organization supported the Bulletin, and the most important deviation from expectations of support for the Bulletin was in the position taken against the Bulletin by the County Welfare

WORK RELIEF TO REHABILITATION

Directors Association and individual welfare directors. Only one welfare director (Contra Costa County) spoke in favor of the Bulletin. This strange phenomenon, while unexpected, has been characteristic of positions taken by the Association for many years. A highly gratifying development is noted in the client advocacy by the Economic Opportunity Act-sponsored California Rural Legal Assistance, Legal Aid Society, and by religious organizations.

Following the hearing on Bulletin 644, the Director of SDSW took the question under advisement for later decision. Soon after the hearing, Public Law 90-248, designed to modify the Community Work and Training program, was finalized by Congress. There appeared a distinct possibility that provisions of the Federal law would change the definition of unemployment in such a manner that Bulletin 644 would be nullified. The Director of SDSW decided to withhold a decision on the Bulletin pending clarification of the Federal law.

President Johnson signed Public Law 90-248 on January 2, 1968. When the provisions of the law were clarified by March, they clearly indicated no change in the definition of unemployment. The State Department of Social Welfare Director then decided to reopen the issue and personally visit four counties, two of which tended to favor Bulletin 644, two which opposed it. After these visits he prepared a list of 13 items which reflected questions and issues raised during the course of his county discussions. The author developed a response April 24, 1968, to each of the questions raised and reaffirmed earlier recommendations that Bulletin 644 be retained.

On May 1, 1968, the Director of SDSW made a decision to modify rather than rescind Department Bulletin 644. The modification was designed to retain the essential features of the Bulletin, thereby insuring the virtues of the Bulletin for children, such as continuity of family income, health care, and education. The modifications were essentially of three kinds:

1. The establishment of a provision which would require a case review at the end of 3 months on aid to determine if full employment in farm labor would be expected to continue for 2 months; and if the two-month employment was anticipated, the family would be discontinued from public assistance. The former regulation provided that the family must be considered to have full employment indefinitely, so the essential change was a modification of the indefinite rule to a two-month rule.

2. The establishment of a new provision in the regulation providing for discontinuance of a family from public assistance when the parent failed to work the number of hours considered usual for currently available farm labor. The regulation provided that the county welfare director, in cooperation with the Department of

Employment, would designate what would be a normal work day for the type of crop during peak period.

3. A two-month averaging principle was established in the regulation for those families where the wage earner was working more than 173 hours. This rule accommodated some of the questions raised by counties regarding the complexity of the program, and would have no serious impact on the families themselves.

The three provisions completed the Director's modification of the regulation. The Director was under extreme pressure to rescind the Bulletin, as evidenced by the representations at the November 1967 Public Hearing. Subsequent to that hearing, continuing representations from county boards of supervisors and welfare directors had occurred requesting rescission of Bulletin 644. On April 30, the Director met with the State Senator from Tulare County, who strongly petitioned him to rescind Bulletin 644 and arranged a meeting of the Senatorial Committee with the Director to be held on May 5, 1968, to receive the views of this Committee on the subject. The Director advised the Senator that he would be glad to attend such a meeting and interpret the decision which he would have made. The Senator was most disappointed that the Director was unwilling to delay the decision, since it was hoped that the Senate Committee could persuade the Director to rescind the Bulletin.

In some respects, the actions which the Director took on Department Bulletin 644 could be viewed as substantive, but in considering the totality of the effect of the changes and the political pressure on the Director, it was apparent that this was a powerful position against compromising the basic thrust of the Bulletin in the sense of preserving the benefits for families and children. Bulletin 644 had become a symbol for the poor and their advocates. They were surprised and pleased at the continuing support of the Bulletin by the Director, who was a farmer, and a former member of a Board of Supervisors. The regulation was adopted by the Director on May 1, 1968, without further public hearing. The Director agreed to hold a public hearing in November 1968 to review the impact of the regulation in its modified form.

On May 14, 1968, the California State Senate passed the Senator from Tulare County's Resolution, SR 179, which recommended that the State Social Welfare Director rescind Bulletin 644. The Senator defended his resolution as follows:

1. The Bulletin grants special privileges to one group of workers which are not granted to others.

2. It constitutes the granting of a guaranteed annual wage to fully employed farm workers through administrative action rather than through more appropriate legislative action.

3. The Bulletin has not resulted in the provision of more domestic farm workers as allegedly intended.

4. The boards of supervisors of the major agricultural counties oppose the Bulletin, and report it is throwing an extra burden of time and money on local welfare departments.

5. The Bulletin is ruining the initiative of farm workers in that they do not need to work full time, but draw full-time pay because the welfare payments make up the difference.

The tremendous local and state power thrown into the defeat of progressive regulations designed to upgrade the lives of poor people has been a powerful instrument against change. Our brief historical review of the farm labor phenomenon in California clearly illustrates the patterned opposition involving local and state approaches to defeat of any action which would alter working conditions. The union uprisings of the 1930's and 1940's were successfully stifled, in improvements sought, by patterned power tactics of a similar kind used today. While the power of the California farm industry is fully revealed, it is sad to observe, concurrently, the powerlessness of the farm workers themselves. The testimony on Bulletin 644 reveals an increasing expression of concern from people-oriented groups, but their testimony before the California Senate was not sufficient to persuade defeat of SR 179.

The Governor, the Administrator of the Health and Welfare Agency, and the Director of the State Department of Social Welfare received copies of SR 179. Although the resolution did not have the power of law, it was a highly persuasive instrument.

THE DEMISE OF BULLETIN 644

On November 8, 1968, the Director of the California State Department of Social Welfare conducted a public hearing in Carmel, California, at which testimony on Bulletin 644 was received. The SDSW staff report to the Director indicated that the program operated smoothly the preceding year, and this was corroborated by a representative from the Farm Labor Office of the State Department of Employment.

Presentations were made at the hearing by the County Supervisors Association of California, the County Welfare Directors Association, and the Kern County Property Owners Association duplicating statements made at an earlier public hearing held November 3, 1967, at Bakersfield. Each organization strongly opposed the continuation of Bulletin 644. The only spokesman for the Bulletin at the Carmel hearing was a representative of CRLA. The hearing was low-keyed on the subject, and SDSW staff concluded that pressure, although continuing, had lessened against the Bulletin during the past year. In some respects, the low-keyed protest seemed almost ominous, possibly a facade to cover assurances already received, and unfortunately, proponents for the program were not out in force as at previous hearings. At the conclusion of the presentations the SDSW Director took the matter under advisement for later decision.

The following week the Director met in a regular session with the executive staff of SDSW and announced that he had decided to rescind Bulletin 644. The stated reason for this decision was related to concern about a new earned income exemption in federal Public Law 90-248 signed by the President January 2, 1968. The law provided that the first $30 plus one-third of the remainder of a public assistance recipient's income would be exempt from consideration in computing a public assistance grant. The Director explained that he had received complaints from the agricultural counties regarding some high grant cases which exceeded $1,000 per month for a family where several members of the family worked at farm harvest. While these cases were rare, the Director feared public reaction.

The unexpected decision generated considerable reaction and discussion from the SDSW executive staff. As a staff member, the author's rebuttal to arguments for the decision was as follows: The same large grant issue had arisen the previous year, when Economic Opportunity Act earned income exemptions created a few similar large grant situations, and since protests from the states had generated corrective legislation from the Congress, new protests from the Director and other state directors to the federal administration and the Congress on this issue would surely generate new corrective action; since the issue was larger than the farm labor problem and covered other nonfarm labor-connected AFDC earnings, it would require corrective action irrespective of action taken on Bulletin 644; and finally, the great values of Bulletin 644—stabilizing family life for farm workers, providing continuity of education for children, augmenting family income, and providing continuity of medical benefits—should not be jeopardized by recission of the Bulletin.

Although these arguments plus persuasive considerations by other executive staff formed a unanimous rebuttal by program staff against recission, the Director's decision to rescind the Bulletin was not altered. Although unstated, it was apparent that once more the power wielded by the Establishment overwhelmed the impotent poor.

An eagerness to regain cohesion for the Establishment was revealed by the vehicle used to announce the decision three days later, on November 14, 1968, at the California County Supervisors Association annual meeting. The news media reported the Directors decision of recission as follows: "The state's seasonal farm labor policy, which says families of farm workers are 'underemployed' and therefore eligible for welfare aid regardless of how many hours the parents work, will end January 1, 1969. The announcement was made by the Director of the State Department of Social Welfare during a panel discussion before the County Supervisors Association of California, which vigorously had opposed the policy. The regulation was fought bitterly by county welfare departments and boards of supervisors in the Sacramento and San Joaquin Valleys. The SDSW Director told supervisors he decided to repeal the bulletin because, 'There have been cases of enormous gross income in some farm worker families during the seasonal work period, especially in the families which have teenage children working in the fields.' Supervisors from agricultural counties, asked about the effect of the repeal, said they could not estimate the reduction in welfare costs. The SDSW Director estimated it could mean 'a couple of million dollars in savings, statewide in the total program.' The administrative officer of Kings County said the impact would be 'considerable.' The chief administrative officer of Stanislaus County said 'It will certainly cut welfare costs in agricultural counties. And it will cut administrative costs because welfare caseloads will be reduced for at least part of the year.' Reducing welfare costs usually has a high priority at supervisors asociation's meetings and this one is no exception." The news media gave no report upon the reduction in human benefits occasioned by the repeal of Bulletin 644, nor was there any public expression of regret at the loss of human values occasioned by the repeal of the Bulletin.

Thus, while in 1968 the nation sought new welfare approaches favoring experiments involving the upgrading of benefits for low income families, the State of California negated an emerging leadership model for under-employed persons found in Bulletin 644. In retrospect, we look back to John Steinbeck's *Grapes of Wrath*, and Carey McWilliams' *Ill Fares the Land* and *Factories in the Field*, written in the 1930's and early 1940's, deploring the sordid conditions in which farm workers lived and worked. We view the continuation of such conditions with little change during the 1950's and 1960's. The world hardly notes the dilemma, and continues, now as then, to stand still while these conditions persist. The advent of the AFDC-U program in February 1964 reactivated an understanding by SDSW that conditions, in fact, had not changed in farm labor practices. The Alameda County issue and subsequent study by SDSW brought back into focus the exploitive practices of the counties, involving the conspiracy of established systems to sustain the practices. The revelation of such exploitation and deprivation of the families inspired Bulletin 644 enactment by the SDSW in 1965. We have reviewed in detail the sustained protest against the Bulletin and then its demise—effective January 1, 1969. What is required in this nation to institute permanent reform?

The agricultural power structure maintains low wages and poor working conditions, and strongly opposes welfare subsidy of poor families. Concurrent with these conditions, the corporate farm industry powerfully influences the continuation of its governmental subsidy. The Federal Government pays the J. G. Boswell Company, Kings County, California, $4 million not to grow cotton; The Rancho San Antonio Company, Fresno County, California, $2.8 million not to grow cotton; and the South Lake Farms, Kings County, California, $1.3 million not to grow cotton. The U.S. Sugar Corporation, Hendry County, Florida, receives a $1.2 million subsidy not to produce sugar; and the Hawaiian Commercial and Sugar Company of Honolulu receives $1.3 million for not producing sugar. In 1967, the Federal subsidy program paid one-third of a billion dollars to 6,579 growers, individual or corporate. Portions of this subsidy inevitably supported the growers efforts to downgrade agricultural labor and fight Bulletin 644—a meagre farm labor subsidy in comparison to the grower subsidy.

Few problems in our society have persisted so stubbornly as those of farm workers and migrants. The brutalizing effects of continuous unemployment and poverty; the shocking facts of malnutrition, poor health, and disease; the debilitating waste of young lives in child labor, in meagre education, and in wretched housing —these things are well enough known to lie heavily on the conscience of large sections of the American public. But one of the curious characteristics of this problem is that too often these facts of deprivation are rediscovered every few years, widely publicized, loudly lamented, and then pushed aside. Significant of these hearings is that California is not permitted to forget.

Bulletin 644, by no means a cure-all, represented the inception if a more humanized official approach to the problems of *all* impoverished minorities as well as to the specific problems of farm workers and their families. Opposition to the Bulletin represented not only the special interests of farm labor employers, but also the traditional viewpoint of the "haves" in private industry and local governmental agencies toward the "have-nots."

What can be said about injustice of the kind described in the testimony? The repetitive nature of the testimony brings forth clearly the nature of the issues and the injustice. It is generally conceded that if a man, his children, and his children's children are all, in turn, subjected to the same humiliations and oppressive tactics which have marked farm labor and public assistance to the poor for more than 30 years, a regressive family trend may eventually be noted in terms of "generational dependency." It is not as readily recognized that if an agricultural hierarchy of the 1960's perpetuates the oppressive practices of the early industrial barons (whose own grandchildren have long since become philanthropists), it displays a regressive generational trend of another kind, perhaps even more insidious because of the power held and wielded to avoid change.

CHAPTER 11

THE CALIFORNIA COUNTY WELFARE DIRECTORS ASSOCIATION
—The Establishment

"WELFARE" HAS BEEN DEFINED variously as a blessing; as a condition of health, prosperity, and happiness; or as a state in which comfort and success contribute to the sense of well-being of the individual. A "state of welfare," in which the welfare of citizens is promoted largely by governmental effort rather than by private organizations, is a term used today largely in a contemptuous sense by opponents of such a state for the impoverished individuals who are most in need of such promotion.

The County Welfare Directors Association (CWDA) is an important segment of the welfare power structure in California. One would anticipate this group to defend the rights and needs of the clientele it serves to insure representation of the poor in administrative and legislative discussions and actions. The CWDA has not represented the poor in California, but conversely has taken positions favoring the opposition—the County Supervisors Association, taxpayer groups, and farmers associations. It is sad that the poor were not only without defense by the CWDA during hearings on Bulletin No. 644, the CWDA itself implored the Director of SDSW to take action to rescind the Bulletin. This paradoxical situation has such deep roots and has disturbed the normal check and balance system to such an extent that it will be given further consideration here.

THE CONFIDENTIAL BULLETIN

Public welfare services in the State of California are rendered through state supervised and county administered programs. The State Department of Social Welfare promulgates rules and regulations which the counties must then administer. Each of the 58 county boards of supervisors maintains responsibility for appointment of its own county welfare director, an administrative arrangement which has traditionally developed a conflict of interests between objectives sought by the State Department of Social Welfare and those dictated by the county board of supervisors. A county welfare director tends to be more responsive to his board of supervisors which has the power to hire and fire him.

The County Welfare Directors Association works closely with the State Department of Social Welfare during the rule-making process. Joint committees of varying kinds are established, and the welfare directors, through their Association, always make presentations to the State Department of Social Welfare Director at formal hearings on rules and regulations. Similarly, the County Welfare Directors Association has a tie-in with the California County Supervisors Association.

The April 1965 issue of the Confidential Bulletin published by the County Welfare Directors Association, contained an editorial regarding the effectiveness of the joint Relief Advisory Committee consisting of county welfare directors and representatives of county boards of supervisors, pointed out that the membership of the Joint Committee included approximately ten county welfare directors, a majority on the Committee, and stressed the importance of maintaining communications and improving relations between the welfare directors and the supervisors.

In November 1965, the Confidential Bulletin further editorialized on the relationship between the county welfare directors, the State Department of Social Welfare, and the county supervisors, suggesting that the arrangement in California was not a sound one from the standpoint of established and accepted principles of administration, but the fact that it had worked fairly well gave credit to the people involved rather than to the system itself. It noted one of the fundamental principles of sound administration —that authority must be accompanied by responsibility, whereas in the California welfare system, authority rests at state and federal levels, and responsibility rests at the county level. Although the adage that "a man cannot serve two masters" has been universally accepted through the ages as a truism, California's county welfare directors have been for many years attempting to serve, at the same time, conservative boards of supervisors and liberal State Directors of Social Welfare. County supervisors employ and discharge county welfare directors, set their salaries, vacations, and sick leave policies, while the State Director of Social Welfare tells these directors what they must and must not do. Such a situation, under the best of circumstances, is uncomfortable for the county welfare director, who finds himself frequently doing something under state direction which is contrary to the desires and philosophy of those who have the power to remove him from office. The importance of local government and its proximity to the people was emphasized in the editorial which also suggested that the majority of the county welfare directors in California are content to be a part of local government in spite of their split responsibility.

In an earlier Confidential Bulletin, dated February 1963, an edi-

torial identified the problems associated with the split in administration of public welfare in California, suggesting that county welfare directors should take whatever position they believed sound
but should not expect the state staff to agree when the basic issue
is one between liberality and conservatism in welfare matters. It
recommended that since it was most difficult to reach agreement
on fundamental issues, perhaps the best decision would be to let
each group speak its piece and then allow the State Department of
Social Welfare to make appropriate rules in accordance with its
view of the situation. If issues were, in the final analysis, incapable
of resolution, the conflict then should be taken to the Governor
and the Legislature, through the California County Supervisors
Association.

In May 1966, the Confidential Bulletin again spoke to this issue
in an editorial, noting once more the conservative administration
expected by the county boards of supervisors. It complained about
the development of state and federal regulations without satisfactory advance planning: failure of state and federal agencies to give
adequate attention to procedures, methods, and housekeeping functions necessary to facilitate development of programs; initiation of
programs and services in advance of public acceptance and without
adequate interpretation to the public; and development of programs
at a more rapid rate than that at which local agencies were able to
administer them.

As noted earlier, the County Welfare Directors Association
assumed a negative position toward Bulletin 644 and this characterized well-known patterns. Although the development of laws
and regulations providing assistance, training and education for
employment to poor persons in the State of California represented
a landmark in the state's social welfare history, it was sad that few
noted the importance of this event. Characteristically, the County
Welfare Directors Association in their February 1964 Confidential
Bulletin, issued the same month during which this important regulation was passed, commented that California had established an
unenviable reputation for a persistent pattern of crash programs
in public welfare. It stated that while other states appeared to be
able to progress in an an orderly and systematic manner in the
area of welfare legislation, California attempted great leaps forward
and as a result was faced with considerable confusion, chaos, and
some backsliding. It deplored the important federal legislation
which provided for services which the State of California also made
operative, and particularly lamented the adoption of AB 59. Its
comment that the federal and state legislation represented more
change in welfare programs in California than the sum total of state
legislation since 1935 appeared to be an admission that California

had produced very little in the preceding 30 years. This editorial observed that the philosophy of the services program was sound and proper, pointing the direction in which public welfare must travel, and that controversial AB 59 was good, bad, or indifferent, depending on individual philosophy, but that together, they represented too much, too soon. It concluded that their simultaneous enactment hampered rather than aided the orderly process of public welfare in California, and recommended a moratorium on legislation, pleading that future legislators should forego the temptation to author additional changes in welfare law until California could digest the existing programs. It was unfortunate that the spokesman for the poor in the State of California—the County Welfare Directors Association—took exception to the fine social welfare legislation developed during the preceding months.

After the 1965 Watts-Los Angeles riot, considerable discussion emerged regarding the adequacy of local county administration of welfare programs and the possible development of a state system of service centers which would, in some respects, become advocates for the poor. This created a great deal of concern on the part of some county welfare directors who, through their boards of supervisors, went on record as being in opposition to such an arrangement for service centers because it seemed inconsistent that one part of the welfare system could become an advocate for the poor in opposition to another part of the system.

The March 1966 issue of the County Welfare Directors Association Confidential Bulletin stated that there had been considerable finger-pointing at county welfare departments by present and former members of the State Department of Social Welfare on grounds that county welfare in general and social workers in particular should bear a major portion of the blame for the unfortunate attitudes and activities of some of the rioters. Assertions had been made that county welfare departments were very unpopular with the poor and that in the Watts district it ranked second only to the Police Department as a disliked function of government. The editorial concluded, nevertheless, that the majority of social workers in public welfare were basically good people, genuinely interested in the welfare of others.

It is a fact, one which most welfare directors will acknowledge, that the County Welfare Directors Association is, in effect, a captive organization of the County Supervisors Association. The County Welfare Directors Association maintains a very conservative line and emphasizes maintenance of the status quo in most of the positions it takes on regulatory material. County welfare directors to a large extent, individually and collectively, do not represent the clientele which they serve; nor do they champion the rights of the poor, or acknowledge their need for aid and services in the effective manner expected of a professionally dedicated association. This leaves the public welfare recipient without an effective spokesman before the county boards of supervisors and the Legislature, except in the form of the State Department of Social Welfare.

An editorial in the April 1966 issue of the Confidential Bulletin characterized the conservative approach of the County Welfare Directors Association, speaking against the people helped by welfare programs and criticizing the expenditure of money for program improvements. One of the issues was AB 59, which the Association had envisioned as a means for tremendous savings in county money. This editorial saw little evidence of any savings three years after AB 59 became law, but ample evidence of tremendous increases for public assistance expenditures in California, including the counties' share. It noted that one of the arguments for adoption of the AFDC Unemployed Parent Program in AB 59 had been that a father would no longer have to leave his family to obtain assistance, that this would have the effect of reducing desertion, and that with the decrease in desertions there would be a resulting decrease in the number of applicants and recipients of aid. The editorial states that no one in official welfare circles had yet explained why the number and percentage of applications for dependent children, which are based on desertion, have continued to increase. With regard to State Department of Social Welfare Bulletin 644, designed to alleviate the crisis in farm labor in California, the editorial stated that casual observation would reveal no noticeable impact on the farm labor situation, and in a small percentage of cases, farm laborers had actually been encouraged to leave their jobs or report for work on a sporadic basis. The Director of the State Department of Social Welfare took exception to this editorial in a letter which clarified some of the issues and suggested that a most disturbing element was a viewpoint based on evaluating all program development primarily from the impact it had on the size of the welfare rolls and the total cost involved, and that while this certainly was a legitimate concern, savings should come not as a primary objective but as a by-product of the major rehabilitative efforts provided those in need.

The Confidential Bulletin dated June 1965 contained an editorial on the State Department of Social Welfare Bulletin No. 644 relating to farm labor, stating that the Bulletin was poorly drawn, ill-conceived, and untimely, and did not take into account human nature, because some individuals will not work except under coercion or dire necessity, and there is no provision for this group of individuals in terms of penalizing them when they terminate their employment. It considered Bulletin No. 644 ill-conceived because it presumed to resolve a crisis in the farm labor supply but created a permanent dependence by the workers upon low wages and welfare supplementation, and stamped these persons as second-class citizens whose labor is not worthy of hire; complained that since Bulletin No. 644 was adopted as an emergency measure, it was untimely in that it ignored county budgeting problems for administration and assistance purposes; and claimed that after many years of effort, the public has been persuaded that public welfare does not support those who are willing and able to work when employment is available, and that now we must advance the idea of supplementation of wages of those who are willing to work but who are not paid a wage commensurate with public assistance grants. The editorial opinion was that this would aggravate negative attitudes of the taxpayer towards public assistance; that some would view Bulletin No. 644 as a liberal move but it actually was a backward step and a death blow to hopes for permanent improvement in the farm labor situation, because at a time when farm wages were at last on the increase, and there appeared to be hopes for unemployment insurance for farm workers, this tended to drive a nail in the coffin of any hopes for continued improvement. The editorial concluded that Bulletin No. 644 penalized the farmer who paid adequate wages and subsidized the farmer who did not; that it condemned the farm laborer to an existence built on low wages, welfare subsidy, and no hope for enactment of legislation to provide the social insurance protections enjoyed by other American workers.

The following month, July 1965, the Confidential Bulletin printed another article dealing with Bulletin 644, and expressing concern about the State Department's administrative review of Alameda County in respect to its referrals of AFDC applicants and recipients to farm labor. This article took note of the fact that the SDSW survey was bitterly critical of practices which attempted to recruit and refer a maximum number of recipients and applicants to farm labor. An earlier article in the February 1965 issue of the Confidential Bulletin had quoted one SDSW Deputy Director's (the author's) description of farm labor as "one of the saddest chapters in the history of man's inhumanity to man" and his statement that recipients and applicants should be trained out of farm labor. The article suggested that this approach continued to be the party line of the Department until April 30, 1965, when the State Department of Social Welfare Director wrote letters to all county welfare directors urging that caseloads be examined to determine the ability of clients to perform as agricultural workers, and suggesting referral of those who had not previously been considered available for farm work, including the physically handicapped, those available for only part-time work, and those who did not have transportation or housing. The July 1965 article calls this a far cry from the conclusions drawn in the Alameda County survey, and further notes that on May 24, 1965, the SDSW Director issued an emergency measure, the infamous Bulletin No. 644, which defined farm labor as part-time employment and required families to be kept on welfare rolls on a year-round basis. This article concludes that theoretically, all farm laborers were back on welfare on May 24, after having been taken off aid on April 30. In this same issue, it was reported that the County Welfare Directors Association had corresponded with the California County Supervisors Association, questioning the advisability of the State Social Welfare Director's issuance of emergency regulations on matters which have traditionally adhered to the public hearing procedure for enactments by administrative agencies. It was reported that the Executive of the California County Supervisors Association shared the concern of the welfare directors regarding the action of the SDSW Director, were advised that he would discuss the matter with the Administrator of the Health and Welfare Agency, which agency had responsibility for the welfare program and that the results of this discussion would be relayed to the County Welfare Directors Association. It was also noted that at a meeting of welfare directors from the San Joaquin Valley area, primary consideration was given to Bulletin 644 and its implications for welfare administration, some alternatives to Bulletin 644 had been developed, and objections to the Bulletin had been voiced.

In September 1965, the Confidential Bulletin reported on a meeting of the County Welfare Directors Association Board of Directors on August 5. The Alameda County Welfare Director, who had collected materials from several counties relating to Bulletin 644, reported that the San Joaquin Valley Supervisors Association had protested the unorthodox manner in which Bulletin 644 was adopted, commented on its disregard of legislative intent, and proposed that the County Welfare Directors Association endorse the position taken by the San Joaquin Valley's Supervisors Association. A representative of this Association stated that it planned to base its objection to the adoption of Bulletin 644 on the grounds that legislative intent was violated, and announced that the Mother Lode Association, the San Joaquin Valley Association of Supervisors, and individual county board spokesmen would present statements in opposition to Bulletin 644. The Santa Clara County Welfare Director stated that if the real purpose of the regulation was to supplement farm labor, it should be initiated by the Legislature. The Madera County Welfare Director expressed concern that county money used in cases covered by Bulletin 644 was greater than the federal subvention to these cases, thereby adding to county costs. After considerable discussion, the Ventura County Welfare Director moved that the County Welfare Directors Association endorse the statements made by the San Joaquin Valley Supervisors Association and the California County Supervisors Association, and the motion was approved.

The State Department of Social Welfare held a public hearing on August 6, 1965, and the principal item on the agenda was the readoption of Bulletin 644, related to farm labor. There was a sizable audience at this meeting, and testimony was taken from opponents and proponents of the measure.

Those who approved the readoption of Bulletin 644 included: The First Unitarian Society of Sacramento; the Santa Clara County Farm Bureau; the National Association of Social Workers; the California Teamsters Legislative Council; a Business Employees Local Union from Alameda County; the California Social Workers Organization; the Agricultural Workers Committee of the AFL-CIO; the Welfare Rights Organization; a private citizen from Alameda County; the East Bay Progressive Labor Party; the Madera County Community Service Organization; and the Citizens for Farm Labor.

Those who testified against the readoption of Bulletin 644 included: The California County Supervisors Association; the San Joaquin Valley Supervisors Association; the Butte County Board of Supervisors; the Welfare committee of the Northern California Supervisors Association; the Chief Administrative Officer of Stanislaus County; the Madera County Board of Supervisors; the Tulare County Welfare Advisory Committee; the Chief Administrative Officer of Kings County and the Kings County Grand Jury; the County Welfare Directors Association of California; and the Fresno County Board of Supervisors. It should be noted that the Los Angeles County Bureau of Public Assistance submitted a statement declaring its position on the subject was neutral.

In November 1966, the County Welfare Directors Association Confidential Bulletin contained an editorial on evaluating Bulletin 644, which originally was adopted on May 24, 1965, and revised October 1, 1965. It noted that in the Central San Joaquin Valley, families receiving AFDC under the Unemployed Parent portion of the program averaged $7\frac{1}{2}$ persons per family, and that it was obvious that such large families living on seasonal employment and low wage scales would have difficulty in maintaining standards of living comparable to that of the average American family. It granted that Bulletin 644 had without question raised the standards of living for farm labor families because it established a guaranteed annual income, but questioned its beneficial effect in regard to the supply of farm labor, which was alleged to have been one of the purposes of Bulletin 644. It was noted that the farm labor population by and large was an honest group, willing to work, but that a small percentage did not possess these characteristics and Bulletin 644 worked to their advantage. The editorial concluded by suggesting a study of the effect of Bulletin 644 before expansion or change, and that a thorough and objective examination be made of its purposes and its achievements. This editorial was strange as it said nothing new, all of the points having been made in previous issues of the County Welfare Directors Association publication, although the tenor was a bit more moderate than in some of the earlier critical positions taken by the Association. Inasmuch as this editorial was written in November of the 1966 election year, it might have been partially designed to bring the issue to the attention of the new administration. Finally, on the issue of Bulletin 644, as far as the County Welfare Directors Association was concerned, it should be noted that very little solicitude was expressed for people it served. There were no case examples of the advantages achieved for families, nor any assessment of administrative simplification in welfare agencies which were inevitable results of Bulletin 644.

THE PARTNERSHIP

After the 1966 election, the new and conservative Governor of California took no chances in his appointment of the Director of the State Department of Social Welfare. He appointed a rancher who was also a member of a local county board of supervisors. The new SDSW Director stressed the importance of state and county relationships. The County Welfare Directors Association Confidential Bulletin took note of this fact by printing, in late 1967, the following editorial, signed by the President of the County Welfare Directors Association and the Director of the State Social Welfare Department: "The Partnership Working—A truly working State-County partnership in welfare administration in California has long been sought and has in fact emerged on our scene in recent months.

"PL 90-248 has called for extensive policy review and consideration, as well as much detailed work to plan for implementation of a comprehensive Congressional shift in plan and direction.

"The State partner invited the County partner to participate from the beginning. The County partner responded. The result is State and County staffs working on policy committees and task forces to produce the best possible accommodation to changes in the various aspects of our welfare programs in California.

"County government and county welfare directors have responded magnificently to the request for operating specialists to man the task forces with State staff. State staff has done yeoman work in materials preparation, anticipating Federal guide material, and testing of mutual ideas against the Federal scene.

"We do not have to wonder any more whether a State-County partnership is possible. We have the ingredients—the leadership of a State Director who believes in it, and the good faith of State staff and the counties in response to it.

"It is ironic that it comes at a time when the welfare system is under its worst attack, and when the perennial bill for State Administration has a tailwind behind it.

"If the partnership can work, perhaps the system can.

"And the partnership is a fact these days."

In 1968, after the SDSW Director had sustained Bulletin 644 and had taken a few other actions against the wishes of the Association, rumblings began to be heard that an editorial of protest should again be printed. The "Partnership" seemed to be deteriorating once more. And in an editorial in the October 1968 Confidential Bulletin the attack on Bulletin 644 was renewed. The Editor of the Confidential Bulletin characterized the "lowly farm laborer" as rising through welfare regulation to "an exalted and envied position," while the "dishwasher" receives no such benefits. Inferring discriminatory practice, the Editor regretted that he couldn't assign the "top welfare administrator" the task of convincing the dishwasher that he should occupy a lower status than the farm worker. Thus the campaign continued and the editorial became the softening up prelude to the SDSW Director's hearing held on Bulletin 644 in November 1968.

On October 9, 1968 at a joint public meeting of county and state welfare directors, the Tulare County Welfare Director vigorously criticized the Director of the SDSW because of a communication issued by him on the Old Age Security Program which contained a critical tone against counties. During the course of this discussion the SDSW Director took note of the worsening state-county relationships and spoke for its possible improvement.

If the event reveals the strategy, the Governor's next move might be interpreted as an antidote against the possibility that his appointed SDSW Director was going soft on Welfare. Apparently against the wishes of the SDSW Director and his boss, the Director of the Health and Welfare Agency, the Governor appointed the District Attorney from a rural county as Assistant to the Health and Welfare Director, to be responsible for Welfare Matters, effective May 1968. The new appointee was described in news media as a hard-hitting and highly controversial action man, vigorously critical of public welfare. The National Association for the Advancement of Colored People later characterized, through the news media, the former District Attorney as a man "whose punitive, retrogressive attitudes and actions are a public record . . ." that he "pushed extremely punitive and constitutionally questionable proposals to harrass welfare recipients."

The described events are similar to those occurring in the administration of Governor Brown who differed with his Director of the SDSW over welfare policy. A news release dated August 18, 1966 stated that the dispute between Governor Brown and the Director of SDSW was a "long-standing conflict between the SDSW and the Supervisors Association." The Governor sided with the Supervisors Association in the later phase of the controversy —a complaint against the SDSW Director for approving state contracts with organizations representing welfare recipients. The Governor contended such contracts, which he ordered cancelled, amounted to a state subsidy for lobbying purposes. The SDSW Director resigned September 1, 1966. The influence of the powerful County Welfare Directors and Supervisors Associations directly contributed to the SDSW Director's resignation—a long sought objective on the part of these Associations.

To further illustrate welfare directors' and boards of supervisors' advocacy of entrenched power systems, let us consider their successful resistance against a proposed state system of advocacy of the poor.

THE MULTISERVICE CENTER

Multiservice Centers were proposed by Governor Brown shortly after the 1965 Watts riot to attack the causes of poverty, and to overcome the sense of defeat which had become tragically evident in the deprived areas of California. The Multiservice Center was conceived as a new effort utilizing the traditional constellation of services which were currently available but dispersed in a variety of agencies.

To the extent that public services were available to meet needs there were several reasons proposed explaining why services were not fully effective:

Facilities were situated in areas which were not easily accessible for disadvantaged persons; transportation was a serious problem for some of them.

Services were buried in an array of fragmented, complex local, county, state and federal institutions; many persons were unable to identify and reach needed services.

Poverty and hopelessness provoked fear and distrust of government institutions, and reluctance to request services.

The underlying assumption of the Multiservice Center concept was that coordinated planning by a professional staff of a variety of agencies could make available to disadvantaged citizens a meaningful program of services. It is not enough to make the services available, however, since they must first be accepted by the people themselves as offering some hope. Multiservice Center personnel went to the people for help in defining the problems and sought new methods of making services both available and acceptable.

The Multiservice Center attempts:

To make families and individuals self-sufficient and productively employed members of society;

to eliminate fragmentation of the individual through interdisciplinary and interagency planning to meet his needs;

to bring needed service to the citizen in the general area of residence;

to reduce the citizen's cost for transportation to obtain services;

to provide a "one-stop" service in the sense that most needs can be arranged from a centralized location;

to provide a continuity and a coordination of services by different agencies to meet the needs of the individual;

to place responsibility for coordination and continuity on the agencies rather than on the individual;

to provide services when they are needed rather than when they can be obtained;

to reduce duplication and confusion for the individual and the agencies;

to improve citizen awareness of the services available through improved public information and communication by direct contact;

to improve the confidence of disadvantaged citizens in turning to government for services which are needed and for which they are eligible;

to reduce the isolation of the disadvantaged from their government and their community by involving them in the process of identifying the needs and the services to be provided in a Multiservice Center.

to reduce feelings of hopelessness, dismay, and frustration by a direct attack on the conditions of poverty and by creating a climate which encourages upward mobility or "somewhere to go";

to mobilize all community resources to eliminate conditions of poverty and need.

State agencies represented in the centers include:

Social Welfare	Public Health
Employment	Office of Economic Opportunity
Fair Employment Practices	Motor Vehicles
Apprenticeship Standards	Consumer Counsel
Vocational Rehabilitation	Youth Authority
Veterans Affairs	Mental Hygiene
Corrections	

Services in the centers were grouped according to functional relationships which appeared logical to those seeking help with their problems, such as housing, employment, education, and health. The Center was designed to eliminate the referral of persons seeking help to some other agency and the demoralizing effect of recounting the problem to a never-ending stream of intake workers.

In summary, the following principles were applied in establishing Multiservice Centers.

Identification of services needed in the area with the help of the community residents.

Establishment of a cluster of services which logically belong together regardless of the agency or governmental level. Housing agencies closely together of services which require continuity.

Avoidance of a "service" center which is nothing more than another referral stop.

Clients must be made to feel that their problems are receiving prompt attention.

Implementation Areas

Multiservice Centers were originally planned for South Central Los Angeles, East Los Angeles, Oakland, San Francisco, South San Diego, Venice-La Playa, Bakersfield, San Bernardino-Riverside, Long Beach, Fresno, Vallejo, and Stockton. These areas were selected on the basis of racial concentration, income and educational levels, unemployment, and housing conditions.

Every effort was made to encourage participation by nonstate agencies, such as public schools, county hospitals, law-enforcement agencies, county welfare departments, private social-service agencies, Economic Opportunity Act community-action projects, the offices of district attorneys and public defenders, health departments, and housing authorities.

Organization

To achieve improved services by each agency and a better co-ordination of services it was necessary to strengthen departmental resources and to improve the availability and coordination of state and local services. The coordination of the vast network of community services has been an objective long sought. Differences in sources of authority, interest groups, and attitudes of departments of government presented the major obstacles to the successful operation of state service centers.

Recognition of these differences prompted the state to introduce two new concepts to state services, namely the creation of a Center Manager position with line authority over all personnel in the Center; and the establishment of an intake unit servicing all departments.

Thus, the built-in obstacles traditionally present in an organizational model featuring autonomous, functionally related units would be eliminated. Under the new model all departments would sacrifice a certain amount of autonomy in the interest of the greater objective of concerted unified service focused on the client. This proposal created problems of other kinds associated with federal-state-county legal, administrative and fiscal requirements of individual agencies which complicated ability to fully accommodate the unified administrative concept.

All functions and activities of the centers would be directed by a manager reporting to the Office of the Governor's Cabinet Secretary. Agency staff engaged in the work of the Center would be under the direction and control of the Center Manager. Managers and staff were to be civil servants. Procedural or policy questions which affect established agency practices were resolved by the Cabinet Secretary in consultation with the Agency Director.

Reaction from local welfare administrators to the Multiservice Center idea and particularly to participation by the State Department of Social Welfare were initially cool for several reasons:

First, there was, strangely, some opposition to the improvement of the local welfare operation. State and county relations conceivably could be strained by the addition of another monitoring device. The County Supervisors Association in which welfare directors are influential passed a resolution opposing further authority to the State Department of Social Welfare.

Second, county welfare directors expressed the view that such a program of direct services duplicates the functions of local welfare departments; and that supervision of local operations and provision of complaints procedure are assigned to the state welfare agency in the context of present law and should not be duplicated in a Service Center.

Third, opponents remembered an earlier special-project proposal by the State Department of Social Welfare to *organize* recipient groups; this proposal was abandoned.

County welfare arguments had theoretical validity yet didn't resolve the concern of some individuals and organizations about the lack of appropriate responsiveness of some county welfare departments to the needs of the poor.

THE MISSION OF THE STATE DEPARTMENT OF SOCIAL WELFARE

The original mission of the State Department of Social Welfare was identical with that of the Multiservice Center. In addition, the department set for itself the following specific objectives:

Provide short-term counseling based on principles of self-help, rehabilitation, and cooperation with other agencies in solving individual problems.

Counsel welfare recipients and potential recipients in obtaining public-welfare assistance, and other public community services such as legal aid.

Assist in developing protective services to families and children through the local welfare departments.

Extend the department's complaints and appeals procedure by employing personnel in the Multiservice Centers.

Train low-income persons to bridge the communications gap between residents and public services, and to provide jobs.

Increase awareness in the department of existing programs in meeting the needs of low-income persons.

Work with public and private agencies in mobilizing community resources in meeting the needs of persons in the target areas.

Assist local welfare departments to add programs which will better serve persons from target communities.

Client Counseling

One of the functions of the State Department of Social Welfare was to provide social workers to work with a Multiservice Center team. For practical reasons, one agency would maintain a service file on the client. Representatives of other departments would be brought in to develop the "prescription program." This was the basis for the "functional-team" concept. A client may be sent to a person in the Social Welfare Department because his problem appears to be primarily a social one. The social worker may determine that the client needs public assistance and may refer him to the nearest welfare office. In addition, an employment counselor may arrange for a training program at the nearest skill center. Conceivably other services, such as rehabilitation, may be indicated, which would result in the consultation of a rehabilitation counselor.

Seeking solutions to complaint problems was originally to constitute the most common activity of the Social Welfare Department in centers. Complaints involving clients from the Service Center areas would be handled by Center personnel; an attempt would be made to find a solution in cooperation with the nearest county welfare department.

For example, in the Watts Multiservice Center a system for processing complaints was agreed upon between the Los Angeles Bureau of Public Assistance and the State Department of Social Welfare. Clients with complaints regarding denials, reductions, or delays in receiving aid would be interviewed by SDSW staff at the Center.

If the complaint appeared to be justified, a social worker or aide from SDSW's staff would call the local welfare program supervisor and discuss the problem. Thus the activities of the Service Centers would merely supplement the services of the county departments.

Another activity in which social welfare staff would be expected to play a major role was to be information and referral to assure that clients became connected with the helping agencies. Unlike the passive referral role of some agencies, this job called for suggesting an appropriate referral and for assuring that the client had the means for getting to that resource. In some cases an aide would assigned to transport the client.

Aides and Training Program in Multiservice Centers

The objectives for an aide program were as follows:

Bridging the gap between the middle-class-oriented professional and the client from poverty areas.

Employing local persons in the solution of problems in their own community.

Facilitating services to other disadvantaged persons coming to the Center.

Providing a training experience and income during the training period for the purpose of gaining permanent employment.

Two hundred aides and three training officers originally appeared in the Service Center budget. The Center was committed to the use of nonprofessional persons as social-services aides because of the opportunity for employing local persons in the solution of problems in their own community; in order to provide experience and income during the training period; and to help to close the cultural gap between the professional social worker and the needy persons in the poverty area.

Tasks for which aides were to be trained and used included the following: (a) To provide temporary care of children in the child's own home during emergency periods; (b) to provide transportation related to other services; (c) to facilitate communication between the worker and members of the family, including language interpretation; (d) to work with selected families to carry out the case plan for teaching and providing support to parents through discussion and participation of the aide and family in designated activities (purchasing, preparing food, finding more adequate housing, keeping the home clean, providing clothing for the children, arranging for medical, dental, educational, vocational, and related services).

The Multiservice Center conception has validity in terms of serving the poor where they live, through coordinated rehabilitative centers. During the first six months of 1967, 82,000 persons were served by the centers. An average of 700 persons monthly were placed in employment. However, the demonstration of success is not entirely one of coordination. In fact, coordination of services for more effective performance has become a cliché, tried often and failing usually to relieve the totality of the problem in the poverty area itself and in the hundreds of other poverty areas in the state. The Multiservice Center has demonstrated, more importantly, the great need for provision of services in poverty areas—and the eagerness of impoverished people to utilize rehabilitative services. The provision of multiservices in urban and rural poverty areas throughout the state is needed. The value of Multiservice Centers has been demonstrated. The strategy now must include the development of a long-range plan for progressive establishment of the services throughout the State of California.

MULTISERVICE CENTERS—SUMMARY

Governor Edmund G. Brown initiated the Multiservice Center concept in response to the 1965 Watts riot in Los Angeles. He designated his Cabinet Secretary to develop the plan. Concurrently, the State Department of Social Welfare (SDSW) was proposing to the Federal Welfare Administration experimental centers fulfilling an advocacy role—advocate for the poor seeking help from sometimes unresponsive, middle-class helping agents. The SDSW Advisory Board had engaged extensively in "conversations with the poor" before and after the Watts riots. The State Social Welfare Departmental Director was persuaded by the Board study and the

Watts events that advocacy was a method needed to provoke change. The original Federal project request was in excess of $400,-000, and when the Governor's Multiservice Center idea emerged, it was jointly agreed that the project would be included in the Multiservice Center budget. All references to advocacy, however, were deleted from the project proposal.

The earlier-described proposal for Multiservice Centers was discussed with county welfare directors, who opposed the idea of advocacy by the State against its county instruments (welfare departments). Boards of Supervisors protested and prepared resolutions against the welfare part of the plan. The SDSW role in the Multiservice Center plan was gradually downgraded until it became little more than a consulting role to other agency personnel in the centers. Direct work with welfare recipients and potential recipients served by the Center was ruled out for SDSW personnel.

The focus was changed to that of encouraging the local welfare department voluntarily to provide services in the Center or nearby rather than SDSW staff. Under these different terms, the federal project, which had been approved by the Welfare Administration in Washington, D.C., was not activated.

Multiservice Centers, as they were conceptualized in the early California State Department of Social Welfare project submitted to the federal agency were designed to serve as advocates for the poor. The protests of Boards of Supervisors and county welfare departments resulted in gradually trimming the function of Multiservice Centers until they were shorn of any vestige of advocacy. They became multiservice rehabilitation centers, with state social welfare services virtually eliminated, although other state agency services were provided by the centers as earlier described. The primary action agencies in the Multiservice Centers became the Departments of Employment and Rehabilitation.

When Governor Ronald Reagan took office January 1967, he reduced the number of planned Service Centers from thirteen to six (South Central Los Angeles, East Los Angeles [Watts], San Diego, Venice, San Francisco, and Richmond). The Governor believed the Multiservice Center concept could be demonstrated as readily in six centers as in thirteen.

Multiservice Centers in California, as an experiment, are emerging, not as advocates of the poor, but rather as more effective instruments to provide services having two important qualities: (1) Association in one location of the various rehabilitative services now in diverse locations, and (2) location of centers in areas where the poor live.

In regard to the advocacy question it is, in fact, probably too much to expect of government that it shall develop systems which are adversary to itself. Moreover, if government in fact perpetrates the injustice, it is asking too much that it prosecute itself for the violation. Some attempts have been made to insure justice in the form of appeal and administrative fair hearing arrangements. The establishment of an Ombudsman has been sought in California. These methods reflect the more orderly, systematized efforts of overcoming arbitrary administrative actions but generally are unresponsive to broad injustices. If government itself cannot afford effective advocacy of clients groups, this may show the way for private enterprise and philanthropy to carve a role for themselves as advocates of the poor. Private social service agencies and philanthropic foundations should examine this field as part of their future work.

Two kinds of advocacy must be considered: (1) That which works with the individual client in his indigenous environment; and (2) that which represents the poor at the legislature and with the administration. The latter may influence more substantive change although work with the legislature and administration may be enhanced by the orderly, nonviolent protest in the street as background against their deliberations.

This brief administrative case example illustrates the coalition of entrenched power structures—the Boards of Supervisors and County Welfare Directors—effectively stripping Service Centers of state welfare advocacy of the poor.

The County Welfare Directors Association has maintained tight control of its organization, has established itself firmly as a captive organization of the conservative California County Supervisors Association, and has generally opposed progressive legislation for the State of California. The welfare directors themselves understand this, they plead, and attribute the problem to duality of supervision which they receive from the State Department of Social Welfare and the county supervisors. Since the supervisors have the power to hire and fire them and because they are responsible to them for their budgets and general administration of the programs at the local level, the welfare directors suggest that this requires that they be more subservient to the supervisors than anyone else. At first glance, the rationale that the welfare directors have established for their attitudes and actions appears to be logical. There are other factors, however, which must be studied and understood. If the welfare directors as a whole were fully trained professional social workers, one would question whether their actions would be the same. Professional identification would equip them with fuller understanding of the dynamics of human behavior and the needs of people for improved conditions, and their actions might move in a more liberal and humane direction in spite of the conservative interests of the county boards of supervisors. County welfare directors, in effect, could be supportive of progressive movements, assist the State Department of Social Welfare in program development, and join together as a state-county unit to confront the conservative actions of the county supervisors and this would be a more rational arrangement inasmuch as federal and state agencies are the primary source of money for public welfare and of rule-making and the setting of standards.

County welfare directors in California have largely been untrained and, in effect, have been groomed for their positions by the California County Supervisors Association and the County Welfare Directors Association. After a new county welfare director has been appointed, his rise in the ranks in the County Welfare Directors Association will be in direct relationship to his ability to conform to the expectations and traditions of his peers. The County Welfare Directors Association has a code of ethics which all members of the Association are expected to follow carefully. Since the established system is one which reflects the attitudes of untrained administrators and easily accommodates the conservative attitudes of the county boards of supervisors, the influence of the peer group becomes very important in determining the role which the county welfare director will play in the state scene as a whole and in his own local community. Although some county welfare directors do have professional training in social work, they are a small minority, and in most cases, they too find the influence of the peer group, combined with that of their boards of supervisors, so overwhelming that they generally accommodate the attitudes and beliefs of the Association and follow established practices and procedures, both statewide and locally.

The author was a county welfare director with full professional training. He observed the conditions and expectations of the County Welfare Directors Association, and was astonished at one of his first meetings with the Legislative Committee of the County Welfare Directors Association, when the Committee Chairman recommended that the Association take a position against legislation to establish the Aid to Disabled program in the State of California. As the Association was about ready to vote against this progressive legislation, the author stood up, and protested, and began to speak in favor of its adoption. The Committee Chairman firmly suggested that he remain seated. During six years tenure as a county welfare director, the author remained a minority voice of the Association.

The incompatibility of the state-county welfare system in California is apparent and must be modified and changed. It is unreasonable to expect that county welfare directors under the present arrangement can ever accommodate fully the expectations of improved services and assistance to people. These conditions cannot easily be resolved. They require fundamental change and rearrangement of the administrative patterns in the state or, short of that, placing the power of appointment of county welfare directors with the State Department of Social Welfare. Recognizing the necessity for change it must also be understood that there is no magic in administrative change from county to state administration. There are 28 states which have state administration of welfare programs, and some of these programs are as poor as or even more restrictive than those in California. Nevertheless, fundamental change must occur to insure the development of an enlightened program.

The mediocrity which characterizes county welfare administration in California has its counterpart in many other states, notably in the state of New York, where welfare programs are state supervised and county administered, as in California. At a 1968 organization meeting of county welfare directors held in New York, a state welfare authority from California gave a speech in which he proposed several welfare program improvements. The spokesman for the county welfare director organization of New York responded to these proposals with the flat statement that "welfare was operating very well as it was, in New York," and he "could see no necessity for considering change."

Meetings of associations of county welfare directors, whether in California, New York, or elsewhere, proceed in an atmosphere strangely unrelated to the causes of the people served. The directors have become so absorbed in reviewing regulations, discussing fiscal impact, and deploring extra administrative burdens created by new rules, that an unknowing observer might conclude that the end product of all this administrative zeal was some sort of gadget or inanimate gizmo instead of the real issue—human lives.

State welfare directors in the 50 states follow the pattern of the 58 county welfare directors in California in their lack of attention to the needs of the people they are supposed to be serving. Newspaper reports in April 1968 of hunger in the United States contained accounts of a "Report of the Citizens Board of Inquiry into Hunger and Malnutrition in the United States," which declared that in 256 counties, 10 million people suffer unremitting hunger. The report stated that 47 of these counties are in Georgia, but the Georgia welfare director stated: "As bad as the situation is in Georgia, its not as bad as the committee painted it." The report stated that 27 of the 256 counties are in North Carolina, and the welfare director in North Carolina stated: "We are aware that there are many poor persons without food and other essentials of life, including proper shelter and clothing," adding that his department was doing its best to help the destitute. In Virginia, which has 14 hunger-struck counties, the Welfare Director said some hunger and malnutrition problems stem from "eating and buying habits." The opportunity to exploit the "Hunger Report" by state welfare directors favoring poor people was without precedent, but the state welfare directors were cautiously defensive and unresponsive.

Similar responses occurred in reference to another landmark action. A Federal Court in Connecticut ruled that residence requirements for welfare eligibility in that state were unconstitutional. The State Welfare Agency appealed the case to the Supreme Court. Similarly, in California, on April 22, 1968, when residence requirements for welfare eligibility in the Aged, Disabled, and AFDC programs were discontinued on order of a Federal District Court, the Chief of California's Health and Welfare Agency stated the following day that the court order would add $24 million annually to welfare costs in California. He declared: "We are humanely concerned with the plight of the needy, but California taxpayers are strained now in meeting their own obligations without undertaking to pay the obligations of other states." This Health and Welfare Administrator, a former District Attorney, did not express a lawyer's interest in the constitutional question raised by the Federal courts as to the rights of individuals to travel freely from state to state.

Welfare directors in Connecticut and California allowed their offices to be used by the power structure in those states against the interests of the poor people they served without a public protest against the injustice. Is it possible that our affluent society cannot really afford to feed, house, and employ poor people and insure them justice? One should rejoice at the landmark decisions which shattered over five centuries of unjust residence requirements in England and the United States, and anticipate a favorable Supreme Court decision on the question. Yet, state social welfare directors are caught in the same bind as county welfare directors in that they are subservient to their respective power structures.

The progressive actions of a former California SDSW Director placed him in disrepute, and Governor Edmund Brown frankly acknowledged this as a political liability to his campaign for re-election as Governor, a post which he later lost to Ronald Reagan, although a few months prior to the election, Governor Brown had incited the Director's resignation. This event illustrates clearly the consequences for dedicated welfare directors who take actions favoring poor people in opposition to actions desired by the power structure. And, without the emergence of more sophisticated power structure leadership, humanely concerned for the welfare of poor people, we remain buried in Elizabethan poor law philosophy and practice.

At a meeting in Washington, D.C. of state public welfare directors in July 1968, the 32 directors attending were strongly critical of new federal welfare regulation proposals. The group as a whole developed U.S. Department of Health, Education and Welfare (HEW) resolutions which were discussed with officials, recommending outright abolishment of the federal requirements for welfare advisory committees which were to include one-third membership from welfare clientele. The state welfare directors were strongly opposed to a requirement that legal counsel be provided by the welfare departments to recipients requesting a fair hearing; they opposed the federal recommendation that public aid be provided to welfare recipients whose grants had been terminated and who were appealing the decision of the welfare department through the fair hearing process, asserting that such a rule would greatly increase the numbers of persons on public welfare; and they opposed the Work Incentive Program on grounds that Departments of Employment in the various states would be incapable of providing an adequate service to welfare recipients.

The secretary of HEW had promulgated some of the proposed regulations on the basis of commitments he had made to a delegation of poor people who had marched on Washington, D.C. in May of 1968. The violent protests of the state welfare directors against these substantive changes in regulations characterize traditional approaches of the established welfare system, and were strikingly similar to the protests of county welfare directors against state-federal regulations. In fact the hopelessness for change had become so apparent to the HEW secretary that he discussed at this meeting with the state directors the concept of need for change in welfare organization. He proposed the federalizing of public assistance programs to provide a national standard of assistance and service, recommended that the program be administered by the federal agency in all of the states and counties, and proposed accommodating the possibility of contracting with states for administration of the program in appropriate circumstances. Thus, while some state observers who view the hopelessness of change in county welfare practice advocate state administration, federal welfare system observers with a similar sense of hopelessness for change in state administration seek federal administration of welfare.

While the feeling of hopelessness of change in traditional welfare beliefs is largely shared by social work personnel, the difficulties inherent in controlling the California system, which includes state supervision and county administration of welfare, is noted in the Governor's *Survey on Efficiency and Cost Control* by a conservative welfare survey team in November 1967. The report clearly indicated lack of state control, and stated specifically that "Many counties have been successful in blocking most control attempts by SDSW."

The well-being of people in this nation should be a national concern and not subject to the vagaries of state and local regulations and financing. Such an approach can be found in already developed national programs such as those administered through the Department of Labor.

It has been demonstrated that both state and local welfare directors are generally not helpfully oriented to the people their programs serve. Rather, the orientation is toward the power structure, and concern is more with fiscal problems than with human values. Historically, public welfare officials have been able to remain successfully responsive only to their power structure. But the times reflect changes which require responses from other forces in the community. With improvements in communication channels, everyone hears and knows about current issues and generally wants a part in policymaking about those which affect him. The Economic Opportunity Act focused on this through provision of programs which include participation by poor people in policymaking bodies. The concept of participation, however, can be overdone. The objective to be sought for poor people should be that of enabling them to overcome their poverty and gain participation in the broader issues of community life—not as members of a minority or an oppressed group but as full-fledged citizens. This does not alter the value of participation of the poor in policymaking which concerns them, but rather establishes a perspective of long-range objectives for the poor.

It is absolutely essential that executive staff administering welfare programs become professionally oriented to the needs of people, maintaining of course, appropriate perspective in reference to fiscal feasibility. The welfare executive, however, must not capitulate easily when strong program representation is needed. To do so disturbs the check and balance system. Normally there are sufficient fiscal and management experts available to carry the torch with respect to their expertise. If there is anything at the heart of work in the welfare field, it is the optimism one must carry for human capacity to change and for human values per se. If the welfare executive does not have this persuasion he literally should go into another line of business which favors his particular approaches. Welfare directors have failed to resolve contemporary problems of administrating people-serving agencies. New social developments provide challenges beyond the capacity of the obsolescent administrative practices which characterize welfare admin-istration in most places today. Present conditions require an attitu-dinal stance, a level of expertise, a sense of urgency, and a quality of judgment rarely found in welfare leadership at the legislative and administrative levels of practice. Some county and state wel-fare directors are making improvements when it is safe for them to do so; a few others are effecting change with risk. But mainly, welfare directors, both state and local, are afflicted with the black-sheep syndrome, which prescribes practice in conformance with the herd, irrational as it may be.

When state social welfare systems run counter to local expecta-tions, other forces eventually emerge to counteract them. An earlier chapter described the successes of CRLA in use of the fair hearing process as a method of upholding the rights of welfare recipients. A state legislator took note of this development.

In the 1968 Legislature, a California State Senator, from Tulare County, a conservative agricultural county in the San Joaquin Valley, initiated legislation which would transfer the fair hearing process from SDSW to the Office of Administrative Procedure, Department of General Services. The fair hearing process was es-tablished at the inception of the Social Security Act in 1935 to provide a relatively independent and objective review of actions taken by a welfare department and with which a public assistance recipient disagrees.

Fair hearing practice in California has provided social workers as hearing officers. The welfare progam in California is county administered, while the fair hearing process is administered by SDSW, thus providing the objectivity needed. The Office of Ad-ministrative Procedure of the Department of General Services is staffed by attorneys who have little orientation to the social wel-fare program. Some states, however, have placed the hearing process with similar administrative procedure bureaus. The SDSW recom-mended against the transfer of this function, and the proposed legislation was defeated. Later, in July of 1968, the Governor's Office ordered an experiment in use of the Office of Administrative Procedure to conduct fair hearings in the large San Joaquin agricul-tural area where Tulare County is located, and in San Diego and Orange Counties, also very conservative counties. The question arises in reference to this action as to whether or not there is any association between the work of CRLA in some of the rural coun-ties of California which emphasized responsibility of these counties in implementing a fair hearing process, and the action taken by the Governor to transfer on an experimental basis the fair hearing process of the Office of Administrative Procedure.

The federal welfare agency initiated in July 1968 a regulation

which would require the representation of welfare recipients at
hearings by attorneys employed by state welfare departments. Considering the movement of placement of the fair hearing process
with attorneys in the states, the federal action appears quite appropriate to insure proper representation of the recipient's rights. Nevertheless, the State Welfare Directors strongly protested this federal
action.

When California agricultural counties become alarmed about
suspected encroachment upon their traditional beliefs and practices,
they seek redress in the State Legislature. In 1963, when the State
Social Welfare Board, under its policy-making power, ordered
counties to upgrade county welfare staff standards through provision of a $400 minimum wage and requirement of an educational
level of B.A., county reaction was violent and retribution swift.
Hardly a year passed before the counties had influenced the Legislature to destroy the power of the State Social Welfare Board.
State legislation simply changed the Board from a policy-making
to an advisory Board. Historical, patterned practices involving intergovernmental power play predicts future practice, as noted in the
present struggle against established fair hearing process. The poor
are impotent against such combinations of power against them.

What further connection can be made between earlier chapters
on man's emotional, illogical distortions of unemployment and dependent people and the present chapter illustrating welfare directors' irrational subservience to outmoded belief systems. Perhaps
the strongest linkage between the disinherited and the Establishment is their common tendency to cling to their own status symbols no matter how inadequate to the crises in which they find
themselves. Fear of losing the togetherness shared in a specific
belief system prevents recognition of the fact that the system no
longer functions. Motivational factors change, power symbols
change. Economic and other controlling factors change. Morally
responsible men within the Establishment must be willing to change
their attitudes even at the risk of incurring the disapproval of their
peers, if they are to contribute to civilized survival. The main
trouble appears to be not that man is excessively aggressive but
has developed the capacity for excessive loyalty and devotion, and
has a stronger need than any other species to belong, to attach
himself to a person, a group, or idea. One possible reason may be
the protracted helplessness and dependence of the human infant;
another may be the increased dependence on solidarity and cooperation of our primate ancestors when they took from the forest
to the plains and turned into carnivorous hunters of prey bigger
and faster than themselves. Only in homo sapiens did the cohesive

forces within the group develop into fanatical loyalty to tribe, totem, and its later symbolic equivalents.

Most civilizations throughout history have been quite successful in taming individual aggressiveness and teaching the young how to sublimate their self-assertive impulses. But we have failed to achieve a similar sublimation and canalization of the self-transcending emotions. The number of victims of individual crimes committed in any period of history is insignificant compared to the masses cheerfully sacrificed ad majorem gloriam, in blind devotion to the "only" true religion, dynasty, or political system. We implicitly recognize in "blind devotion" the uncritical nature of the self-transcending urge to form attachments to a person, group, race or system of beliefs, and we may learn to recognize the essential difference between such primitive identification and the mature forms of social integration. Social integration preserves the autonomy and responsibility of the individual in the social whole, whereas identification implies partial or total sacrifice of both, a surrender of the critical faculties, of moral responsibility, in some respects representing a regression to infancy or to the "womb" of the Church, in others, resembling hypnotic rapport, and in extreme cases, producing the phenomenon of mass hysteria in overt or latent form. As to its origins, some clues are perhaps provided by factors previously mentioned—the long infantile dependence and strong social interdependence characteristic of our species.

There is also the peculiar ability of the human brain to sustain belief-systems, rooted in emotion, which are incompatible and in frequent conflict with its reasoning faculties. The result is the split-minded, schizophrenic mentality, which seems to be inherent in man's condition and is reflected in his absurd and tortured history. The consequences of this built-in schizophyrenia range from so-called normal behavior, where emotional bias distorts reasoning only within tolerable limits, through neurotic and psychotic disorder in the individual, to the collectively held beliefs in irrational causes to which we are emotionally committed in blind devotion and militant enthusiasm.

PERSPECTIVE

It is not the intent of this chapter to establish a rationale for phasing out public welfare as an effective instrument of social intervention. The revelation is designed to objectify some of the substantive problems of public welfare with the hope that this will aid in overcoming the obstacles to effective services.

The position of the County Welfare Directors Association often differs from the official stance of the welfare director when he returns to his individual county. The CWDA is dominated by a few agricultural counties. Urban welfare directors are less vocal in meetings and often, if they differ, they cast no vote, or declare a neutral position. Some welfare directors have excelled in program development and all have some elements in their programs which are good. Below the welfare director level in the administrative hierarchy are hundreds of dedicated, sincere and competent social workers, supervisors and administrative staff. Some social workers' unions have championed the cause of improved services to the people they serve. Yet if the welfare director is unresponsive to human need, the most dedicated staff cannot influence the system to change. In some respect, the staff is as impotent as the clientele itself against entrenched, unresponsive power systems. It is difficult to portray substantive problems in the welfare system since the revelation distorts the welfare image, obscures the good work that is done and clouds the great future the welfare system has for provision of an effective services program. The author believes public welfare's destiny will be that of a sophisticated public social service agency at the local level. The obstacles to the achievement of this goal are many and varied. Yet with all its problems public welfare has a heritage of some service of a kind that will form a foundation for its future role as a compassionate, responsive, professional system of intervention for all persons.

It must be reemphasized that just as the actions of the County Welfare Directors Association do not represent the best interests of the clientele it serves, similarly their actions often do not represent dedicated staff of welfare agencies. This paradox reemphasizes the earlier expressed strange unrelatedness of the actions of the CWDA to the real world of its staff and clientele.

The Establishment, as reflected in the Associations of Welfare Directors and County Supervisors, have held to outmoded beliefs and practices in spite of the evidence of their dwindling power and effectiveness. They continue to seek, through earlier described power plays, the preservation of their outmoded systems. They fail to recognize that the intellectual and scientific era is displacing the Establishment and the ferocity of the Association's death throes reassure them that they retain power long since waned. The most naive reformer will agree that the welfare directors and members of the county boards of supervisors reflect the will of the people in their community. Education and science have been essentially overwhelmed by ignorance, tradition and mythology in affairs of public welfare. This is no excuse for lack of exercise of enlightened leadership except that unenlightened electorates tend to elect and appoint their own models. However, education and science is emerging as a powerful force in the society and will inevitably displace ignorance and apathy.

CHAPTER 12

THE WAR ON POVERTY

As ESTABLISHED PUBLIC WELFARE SYSTEMS at local levels have strongly resisted reform, the federal government has sought, on a large scale, to induce improved responsiveness to the needs of the poor, even at the expense, where necessary, of bypassing the Establishment. The War on Poverty was declared official in 1964. The overall strategy planned against poverty emerged through the Economic Opportunity Act. The resources needed to carry out a frontal attack required the authorization of funds to be administered by the Office of Economic Opportunity, and the mobilization of community resources at local levels to give tactical support.

THE ECONOMIC OPPORTUNITY ACT—1964

The President's Message on Poverty and the proposed implementing legislation—The Economic Opportunity Act—were transmitted to Congress on March 16, 1964. The measure called for the creation of a new Office of Economic Opportunity, and for six major programs designated as: (1) Youth Programs (Job Corps, Work-Training Programs, and Work-Study Programs); (2) Urban and Rural Community Action Programs; (3) Special Programs to Combat Poverty in Rural Areas (Grants and Loans, Family Farm Development Corporations, and Cooperative Associations); (4) Employment and Investment Incentives (Incentives for Employment of Long-Term Unemployed, and Small Business Loans); (5) Family Unity Through Jobs; and (6) Volunteers for America.

As summarized by the President, the new Act would provide five basic opportunities:

"1. It will give almost half a million underprivileged young Americans the opportunity to develop skills, continue education, and find useful work.

"2. It will give every American community the opportunity to develop a comprehensive plan to fight its own poverty—and help them to carry out their plans.

"3. It will give dedicated Americans the opportunity to enlist as volunteers in the war against poverty.

"4. It will give many workers and farmers the opportunity to break through particular barriers which bar their escape from poverty.

"5. It will give the entire nation the opportunity for a concerted attack on poverty through the establishment, under my direction, of the Office of Economic Opportunity, a national headquarters for the war against poverty."

The bill was introduced in the House of Representatives by Phil M. Landrum (D-Ga.) as H.R. 10440 and referred to the Committee on Education and Labor, Rep. Adam Clayton Powell (D-N.Y.), Chairman. In the Senate it was introduced by Pat McNamara (D-Mich.) as S. 2642.

Office of Economic Opportunity (Title VI). There would be created, in the Executive Office of the President, an Office of Economic Opportunity, headed by a Director who would have the function of coordinating existing federal agency programs related to poverty and to initiate and formulate guidelines for the new programs as authorized by the Act. "The Director," the President said, "will be my personal Chief of Staff for the war against poverty. I intend to appoint Sargent Shriver to this post."

Youth Programs (Title I). Nearly one-half of the total projected expenditure was allocated to the three youth programs in Title I: Job Corps, $190 million; Work-Training Program, $150 million; and Work-Study Program, $72.5 million. The Job Corps, which would be administered by the Office of Economic Opportunity, would provide education, vocational training, and work experience in residential centers for male youths aged 16 through 21. Enrollees would be provided with quarters, subsistence, clothing, recreational and health services, and a living allowance of $30 to $50 per month. Enrollment would ordinarily be for a maximum of two years. Upon termination of enrollment, each individual would receive a "readjustment allowance" at an amount not to exceed $50 per month. It would also be possible for part of this allowance, up to $25 a month, to be paid directly to a dependent, with matching funds to be added by the Corps.

It was planned that the Job Corps in operation would consist of two different kinds of facilities—conservation camps and training centers. Individuals would be assigned to conservation camps if they were so lacking in basic academic skills that they could not undertake vocational training, or had problems of attitudes and resistance to learning. A new environment which would encourage achievement was an important consideration. They would be given training in reading, writing, arithmetic and speaking, and would work under experienced members of federal conservation agencies, such as forest and park rangers, or members of the Bureaus of Indian Affairs, Land Management, or Reclamation. During the first year, there would be 15 or 20 thousand enrollees assigned to conservation camps of 100 to 200 persons. Upon leaving the Corps,

these enrollees would be guided by counselors to placement opportunities or further vocational training through the U.S. Employment Service.

Training centers for the Job Corps would offer more intensive
and advanced education and training to persons ready for this experience, some of whom might come as "graduates" from conservation camps. The centers would be housed at unoccupied or
under-utilized military camps, and would range in size from 500
to 5,000 enrollees. For the first year, the expected strength of the
training center program would be between 15,000 and 20,000—the
same as for conservation camps.

The Work-Training Program was designed to provide useful
work experience for unemployed youths, both male and female,
aged 16 through 21, in locally sponsored work projects in their
home communities. Projects could be developed and conducted by
any agency of state or local government, including Indian tribes,
or by an approved nonprofit private organization. Typically, these
would be hospitals, welfare agencies, schools, and parks. Projects
could offer full-time or part-time employment to young people.
Assignments might be in such jobs as nurses' aides, hospital orderlies,
clerical workers, cooks' assistants, waitresses, building maintenance
and landscape assistants. The program would be coordinated with
vocational training and educational services adapted to the special
needs of the enrollees. For the first two years, federal funds could
pay up to 90 percent of the costs of projects, and thereafter, up
to 75 percent. Administrative responsibility would be delegated
to the U.S. Department of Labor. When operating at full strength,
it was estimated that this program would provide employment for
200,000 young men and women of whom 30,000 would be working full time; 60,000, half time; and 110,000, either quarter time
throughout the year or full time during the summer months.

The Work-Study Program would provide part-time employment—not more than 15 hours a week—for college students from
low-income families. The federal government would pay 90 percent of the cost the first two years, and 75 percent thereafter, with
the educational institutions paying the rest. It was estimated that
during the first school year, the program, under the administration
of HEW, would employ 130,000 undergraduate students earning
$500 each, and 15,000 graduate students earning $1,000 each.

Urban and Rural Community Action Programs (Title II). One
of the major features of waging the War on Poverty was the proposed authorization of funds to be administered by the Office of
Economic Opportunity "to provide stimulation and incentive for
urban and rural communities to mobilize their resources, public
and private, to combat poverty through community action pro-

grams." The OEO would serve as a focal point for coordinating
the various federal programs in support of community programs.
A community might be any urban or rural or combined geographical area, including but not limited to a state, metropolitan
area, county, city, or town.

Plans and grant applications would be developed by local community action organizations, either public or nonprofit private,
and broadly representative of their communities. Funds and technical assistance would also be made available to the community
organizations to assist in the development of the community action
programs and to provide information concerning the various federal resources available. Procedures would also be established for
the participation of state agencies in community action programs,
including provision for the referral of applications to the state
governors for their comments. Relevant services of existing agencies as well as other new or expanded services would be brought
into focus on the needs of low-income individuals and families
under the community plan. These might include, as determined
by the community, expanded and improved service, assistance,
and other activities and facilities in the fields of education, employment, job training and counseling, health, vocational rehabilitation,
housing, home management, welfare, and other related fields.

Federal funds would be paid directly to the individual community action organizations, or, when appropriate, OEO would
allocate funds to other federal agencies who would then pay the
costs of their assigned functions under local plans through established channels. Elementary or secondary school education programs participating in a community plan, however, would be administered by the public educational agencies principally responsible for these functions in the areas involved. Typically, this would
be local school boards. No child could be denied the benefits of
such a program because of irregular enrollment in the public
schools. Tentatively, administrative interpretation suggests that
each community plan proposal would be evaluated on the basis of
the following criteria:

1. Does it demonstrate a basic knowledge of the facts of poverty in the area?

2. Does it propose to attack the real causes of poverty?

3. Does it promise effective solution of the problems which it
identifies?

4. Are there community organizations which will work together to carry out the plan responsibly, speedily, and efficiently?

5. Is the community itself dedicated to the achievement of the
goals, and willing to contribute its own human and financial resources towards the objectives?

The federal share of the Community Action Programs would be up to 90 percent for the first two years and up to 75 percent thereafter. The nonfederal share could be either in cash or in kind, including the services of volunteers. The bill also provides that: "To the extent feasible, and consistent with the provisions of law governing any federal program and within the purposes of this Act, the head of each federal agency administering any federal program is directed to give preference to any application for assistance or benefits which is made pursuant to or in connection with a community action program approved pursuant to Title II of this Act." The sum of $340 million was allocated to the support of Community Action Programs for the first year.

Poverty in Rural Areas (Title III). An appropriation of $35 million was allocated for the first-year operation of a program to meet some of the special problems of rural poverty. This three-point program would:

1. Authorize loans of up to $2,500 to low-income rural families to purchase or improve farm land, to participate in cooperatives, or to finance nonagricultural enterprises for supplemental income. It was expected that such grants would be made to 45,000 farm families at an average of $500 each, and supplemental loans from the Farmers Home Administration could also be made.

Promote and support the organization of nonprofit corporations for the purchase of quantities of land which would be resold in units not larger than family size farms to low-income farmers. It was estimated that this program initially would benefit about 2,500 families who would acquire about 80 acres each.

3. Authorize loans to local cooperatives furnishing essential production, processing, purchasing, or marketing services, supplies, or facilities predominantly to low-income rural families.

Employment and Investment Incentives (Title IV). A program to promote jobs for the long-term unemployed and to assist small businesses authorized the federal government to make or guarantee loans for the establishment, preservation, or expansion of business ventures which would result in the employment of long-term unemployed and members of low-income families. Loans would be limited to $25,000 for each new job created. Most businesses, local in nature, would be in depressed areas beyond the reach of the Area Redevelopment Administration (ARA) program. Loans would be administered by ARA and would be limited to areas having an approved Community Action Program.

Family Unity Through Jobs (Title V). The provision most specifically and directly involving public welfare agencies called for a major expansion of the authorization established by the 1962 welfare amendments (Social Security Act, Section 1115) for conducting experimental, pilot, or demonstration projects under the Public Assistance categories. The 1962 amendments authorized the U.S. Department of Health, Education, and Welfare (HEW) to waive state plan requirements for approved projects likely to assist in promotion of the objectives of the Public Assistance (P.A.) titles. Such projects could be financed through open-end federal appropriation with matching funds in accordance with the regular P.A. formulas. Expenditure of an additional $2 million per year was also authorized to pay necessary project costs not covered by matching funds.

Title V was designed, through increased federal support, to enable and stimulate the states to expand opportunities for work, training, and basic education for heads of low-income families. This new title would apply to the AFDC category only, and would cover projects offering a combination of job training, counseling, and actual work experience. Unemployed male or female heads of families receiving AFDC assistance could be assigned to such projects. In states which had not adopted the unemployed parent program, projects could be set up to which unemployed male non-AFDC parents could be assigned if they otherwise qualified for assistance. Wages would be paid on the basis of budgeted need, plus allowances for additional expenses incidental to employment and training. The program was also envisioned to provide basic literacy education and vocational training (but not work) for AFDC fathers and mothers if adequate day-care facilities could be made available to their children. The sum of $150 million was allocated to HEW for the Family Unity through Jobs program.

Volunteers for America (Title VI). A national corps, Volunteers for America, was established under the Office of Economic Opportunity. Enrollment was open to individuals 18 or more years of age who could meet prescribed selection criteria. They would be trained for one month and assigned to duty in a variety of placements, such as health, education, or welfare services on Indian reservations, for migrant workers and their families, in facilities for the mentally ill and mentally retarded, or with the Job Corps or Community Action Programs. No one could be assigned to any activity under state or local sponsorship without the consent of the governor. Volunteers would normally enroll for a period of one year. They would be provided with quarters, subsistence, medical care, and a living allowance as needed. Upon leaving the service they would also be paid an accumulated stipend of $50 per month. It was projected that by the end of the first year, enrollment would reach a strength of 5,000 volunteers, with one half assigned to state and local programs and the other half to federal programs and federally assisted institutions.

An Economic Opportunity Council would be established to consult with and advise the Director of OEO, who would be the Chairman. Other Council members would include the Attorney General; the Secretaries of Interior, Agriculture, Commerce, Labor, and HEW; the Housing and Home Finance Administrator; the Administrator of the Small Business Administration; the Chairman of the Council of Economic Advisers; the Director of Selective Service; and others as the President might designate. In addition, a National Advisory Council would be established to review operations and activities of the OEO and to make recommendations. Membership would consist of the Director of OEO as Council Chairman and not more than 14 additional members who would be representatives of the public and of appropriate fields of endeavor, all appointed by the President.

The Economic Opportunity Act of 1964 (P.L. 88-452) was signed by the President on August 20, 1964. Although exhaustive debate in both the Senate and the House led to the adoption of a number of amendments, the general framework of the measure remained substantially as introduced. The bill was first passed by the Senate on July 23 by a vote of 62 to 33, and by the House on August 8 by 226 to 184. The House version was then adopted by the Senate without amendment on August 11, thus obviating the need for a joint conference. The authorization was for three years ending July 30, 1967. The appropriation, however, was for only the first year, so that in each succeeding year, Congress must renew the money authorization.

The six titles of the Economic Opportunity Act provide several work and training programs for youth and for persons on public aid; self-employment loan programs for marginal farmers and small businessmen; a "domestic Peace Corps" called "Volunteers in Service to America" (VISTA); and an open-end program of federal grants to localities to stimulate and draw together a variety of local social services. The Act was designed to give OEO maximum flexibility in working with state, local, and private organizations. OEO's Director was authorized to contract with the states to obtain technical aid for localities which would develop Community Action Programs, and to utilize services and facilities of the states and their subdivisions. For three of the programs (Work-Training, Work-Study, and Community Action), there were modest provisions for equalizing distribution of funds among the states.

The bill also included provision for state participation: VISTA volunteers could be dispatched to a state only with the governor's consent, and in the Community Action Programs of Title II, the OEO Director was instructed to "facilitate effective participation of the states" and to refer project applications to state governors for comment. Flexibility in dealing with the states was deliberate on the part of Administration staff members when drafting the bill, because they wanted to avoid the limitations traditionally imposed at state levels upon federally funded grant-in-aid; and they wanted to cut through the layers of bureaucratic state administrators and private professional associations in order to reach the poor. Community Action Programs were apparently designed to bypass the entrenched institutional systems and their middle-class orientation, which persisted in stifling all innovative approaches.

An important feature of the Economic Opportunity Act of 1964 was its new approach to federal-local relations. Title II authorized community-wide planning and implementation of poverty related programs. The vehicle for this purpose, the Community Action Agency (CAA), is a public or private nonprofit agency which can coordinate a locality's existing resources for combating poverty.

The program was designed to restructure social services through use of new fiscal methods, alternatives to the traditional special-purpose grant-in-aid, and an approach to the concept of the block grant. Although the Budget Bureau originally became interested in Title II as a potential method of coordinating federal programs and bypassing traditional agency jurisdictional lines, there is evidence that the furor engendered in practice cooled the earlier enthusiasm.

The Act specified that a Community Action Program was to be "developed, conducted and administered with the maximum feasible participation of residents of the areas and members of the groups served," and this concept of broad community participation appeared in memoranda from the time the war on poverty was first proposed. Another innovative aspect of the CAP approach was its wide-angle view of geographic and political boundaries. The Act speaks of "communities," not of cities, towns, counties, or metropolitan areas, and although CAPs frequently parallel existing political subdivisions, such boundaries may be crossed for functional purposes of planning or implementing poverty-related programs.

Under the Act, at least 10 percent of CAP funding must come from the locality, although this may be in the form of nonmonetary, in-kind contributions, such as staff time or office space; and CAPs must be capable of mobilizing existing local service systems, such as schools and welfare agencies. A method of control was also established to assure adequate inter-community consultation by means of a check point procedure. Project proposals are required to be checked with the chief elected official of the community, the local director of the state employment service, the director of the county welfare department, the school superintendent, and other appropriate officials. By requiring involvement of those with a stake in the welfare programs, CAPs have developed new approaches to sharing in the democratic process, even extending, in some instances, to the inciting of war on City Hall itself.

The distrust of some community action groups has been directed both toward local politicians and welfare professionals, on grounds that such middle-class oriented groups are reactionary and unconcerned. Their solution has been to destroy entrenched local power structures by mobilizing neighborhood-based protests. Such groups appeared to be encouraged in this sort of action by some OEO staff, and the agency's emphasis on the likelihood of need for such action by the poor may have led many prospective agency applicants to comply with the "participation" requirement. CAP grants had also included programs directly aimed at general political education and activation of the poor. More conservative forces later modified these practices to move CAPs back toward the middle-class complacency they had sought to disturb.

Local power structures are being challenged to absorb the demands of the poor; and the War on Poverty, in providing education, training, and services, has become an instrument for mobilizing the poor as a political force. Ultimately, these developments may have a significant effect upon the advancement of man's right to work.

THE MANPOWER DEVELOPMENT TRAINING ACT

The Manpower Development Training Act (MDTA), passed in 1962 against a background of high unemployment, a growing labor force, a widening impact of technological change, and the first nationwide program for training and retraining the unemployed which also authorized a program of manpower and automation research, was expanded by amendments in 1962 and 1965. The Act provided that research programs on manpower requirements, development, and utilization be carried on to answer such questions as: In what occupations are there existing or foreseeable shortages of workers? What are the benefits and problems resulting from automation and other technological changes? How can we tell in advance what effect certain changes will have on workers' jobs? What practices of employers and unions make it hard for workers to move from job to job, and what practices facilitate this movement? What methods can best provide useful work experiences and training for inexperienced youth?

Research data shows that by October 1, 1965, projects for over 449,000 persons in the United States had been approved under MDTA. Of these, 387,000 were institutional (in school) trainees, and 62,000 were on-the-job trainee projects. Approximately 75 percent of enrollees in institutional training complete their courses, and 75 percent of those who complete training find jobs soon after graduation. Completion and placement rates are higher for on-the-job trainees. MDTA experience proved that some people can be helped through education and training even though too few were hard-core welfare recipients.

In fiscal 1966, plans were made to train and retrain 250,000 persons under MDTA programs. Only about 15 percent of the MDTA trainees in California were public assistance recipients. In some places in the United States, MDTA has been utilized inappropriately due to political pressures, and in one instance, large urban newspapers used it for training their employees in the new color process, at government expense. (The poor public assistance recipient does not have such power to influence governmental systems, so those who need training the most receive the least.) MDTA has solicited nurses who left the field for marriage or other reasons, and provided retraining courses for a substantial number of them, although most could easily have purchased such training. Since welfare recipients have potential for nursing careers, one questions why MDTA did not recruit and train them. In some respects, this may be likened to the extensive adult education courses provided largely to educated people, seldom to the uneducated. There has been little commitment to the hard-core poor, who have been written off as unlikely candidates.

NATIONAL ALLIANCE OF BUSINESSMEN— JOB OPPORTUNITIES

The President, aware that substantive change was not evolving as hoped, through bypassing established systems, sought alternatives for change through engagement of the power structure itself. What better symbol of power could be found than private industry?

In early 1968, President Johnson formed the National Alliance of Businessmen (NAB) and appointed Henry Ford II as its chief. NAB established a plan called Job Opportunities in the Business Sector (JOBS) and set up 50 field offices in the United States. The goals of the program were to secure 100,000 jobs for the hard-core unemployed by July 1969; to provide 200,000 summer jobs to youth in urban centers in 1968; and to find 500,000 jobs for hard-core jobless persons by July 1971. By May 1968, JOBS had secured 83,000 pledges for the hard-core unemployed. The test will come when industry struggles with the deviant and often nonconforming life styles of the hard-core unemployed, but if tolerant patience prevails, rekindled hope for the hopeless will emerge.

The federal government provided $106 million for the 1968-69 fiscal year to reimburse companies for extraordinary expenses incurred in hiring and training persons with low productivity, paying as much as $3,500 for each hard-core unemployed person who is trained and hired.

The failure of some training programs for these unemployed has been based on the lack of jobs after training, and NAB seeks to correct this serious deficiency. At Ford Motor Company, among the 3,500 people hired over a 6 month period from the Detroit ghetto, the turnover was less than among other persons hired during the same period. Although this was unusual, it illustrates the potential of some hard-core unemployed.

Other early reports on NAB are less hopeful. Some of those recruited from the hard-core unemployed turn up at industial plants for training and then disappear. Their tardiness, lack of adjustment to the plant, and absenteeism tend to disillusion the well-intentioned industialists who hire them. NAB's failure to recognize the need for social services may ultimately lead to failure of the program. Private industry should provide training and employment but cannot be expected to tolerate undue disturbances of staff, training, and production routines. The provision of opportunity alone may not be enough to overcome deep-seated attitudinal, social, or psychological problems. Concurrent with NAB placements, there should be made available social and other services, as needed, to support the trainee through early adjustment experiences.

It is encouraging to note that a recent issue of a business magazine[1] captured the essence of contemporary domestic problems in the United States today in three separate articles which, respectively, humanized the poor unemployed; illustrated that rehabilitation programs must be meaningful, not role-playing; and sounded an alarm of possible revolution in America.

In the first of these articles, Leo Beebe, Executive Vice-Chairman of the National Alliance of Businessmen, emphasized that business, in order to eradicate some of the national sickness, must become more tolerant of the deficiencies of hard-core unemployed persons. He advocated tolerance about the absenteeism and tardiness which is a way of life for some, and suggested painstaking personal counseling to motivate reliability—a far cry from traditional punitive, crack-down approaches.

In the second article, David Wellman, a social worker, described the failure of a California Department of Employment project in Oakland which stressed teaching hard-core youth how to take job examinations and how to apply for jobs. Techniques included taking mock tests, conducting mock interviews, and visiting places where jobs might become available. No job training was provided, and the youthful participants ridiculed the project.

The third article gave the viewpoint of Harvard sociologist, Thomas F. Pettigrew, who stated that conditions similar to those which gave rise to the French and Russian revolutions are present in the United States today. He observed parallels in the living conditions which improve at a much faster rate for the dominant group than for the subordinate one; in the status inconsistencies between educational achievement and job level increase, as the Negro's educational level exceeds his occupational status; in the expectations of change among the depressed lower class which outpace real changes; and finally, in the broadening of lower class perspective which leads to a comparison of their conditions with that of the dominant group. Pettigrew saw peaceful alternatives to revolution only "if the oligarchy gives ground," as in England after the French revolution.

These articles not only synthesize some of our major problems, they also seem to give some hope for eventual solutions when conservative spokesmen see danger and seek to deal with it in a meaningful and humanitarian manner, rather than by such simplistic approaches such as improved armament for the police. Men of good will may be moved to modify traditional approaches of the Establishment. At least, cautious optimism about the final outcome of the War on Poverty may be no longer purely in the realm of fantasy.

TITLE V: FAMILY UNITY THROUGH JOBS

The purpose of the Work Experience Program authorized by Title V of the Economic Opportunity Act was "to expand the opportunities for constructive work experience and other needed training available to persons who are unable to support or care for themselves or their families." Up to 100 percent federal financing was available to stimulate the states to adopt work and training programs to help unemployed parents and other needy persons to secure and retrain employment or to attain or retain capability for self-support or personal independence. The objectives of Title V were to be accomplished through use of the provisions of Section 1115 of the Social Security Act for experimental, pilot, or demonstration projects in public assistance. Such projects could be related to any of the titles of the Act; work and training could be provided under a variety of arrangements; and recipients could also be furnished with money payments, medical care, and social services, as appropriate. It was anticipated, by the Welfare Administration in the Department of HEW, however, that the greatest emphasis would be placed on expansion and improvement of community work and training programs authorized by Section 409 of the Social Security Act, and on concomitant expansion of the Aid to

Families with Dependent Children Unemployed Parent (AFDC-U) segment. The purpose of Section 1115 was to encourage states and localities to explore and experiment with original methods of promoting the objectives of the public assistance titles of the Social Security Act—to strengthen family life and to offer constructive help to individuals and families in their efforts to achieve self-support or self-care. Section 1115 permitted a waiver of statutory conditions in the public assistance titles of the Social Security Act; allowed receipt of federal mtaching at the usual rate of expenditures that would otherwise not be matched; and permitted the use of federal funds to pay the nonfederal share of public assistance expenditures.

Under Title V, states could utilize the flexibility permitted by Section 1115 to extend the work and training approach to recipients in any of the public assistance categories and to other needy persons, provided there was some relationship of the person aided to one of the federal-state public assistance programs, and the objectives of these programs were likely to be promoted thereby. States could experiment with more liberal eligibility requirements and definitions of unemployment in order to reach the hard-core unemployed. With respect to all participants involved in work and training programs, local welfare agencies could provide services related to the priority need for self-support and personal independence such as health care, family counseling, and employment counseling.

The work and training projects that could be developed under Title V were as varied as the needs of the participants. Preference was to be given to those projects which were components of community action programs under Title II of the Economic Opportunity Act, and use was made of the basic adult education provision therein. Also, use was made of other programs which played key roles in solving the overall problem of unemployment, including public employment services, programs under the Manpower Development and Training Act of 1962, and the Vocational Education Act of 1963.

Since Title V provided that the Work Experience Program would be carried out through use of Section 1115 of the Social Security Act, it was necessary to follow the administrative pattern applicable to public assistance programs. State public welfare agencies applied to the Bureau of Family Services, of HEW for federal funds to finance a work and training program under Title V. If approved, the Bureau of Family Services made a grant of funds to the state, and the project was administered by the state or by a local welfare office under the supervision of the state welfare agency. Work and training programs thus funded provided a resource for communities in attacking the causes of poverty. Funds were available to support, on an experimental, demonstration, or pilot project basis, programs "designed to help unemployed fathers and other needy persons to secure and retain employment or to attain or retain capability for self-support or personal independence" as part of the public assistance programs.

Procedures for granting work and training projects made coordination with community action programs relatively less complex than with other federal-state programs. Approval of any project recommended by a state remained with the federal government, and among the criteria for approval, coordination with a total community poverty activity received priority. When such activity was being developed in a community, the local public welfare director had an essential part in the developmental process. The Bureau of Family Services of HEW originally identified the kinds of work and training projects that could be developed under the provisions of Title V, ranging from basic work experience and literacy training in preparation for simple entry jobs in the labor market or more extensive vocational training, to the development of the utmost skills and abilities within the capacity of individuals.

Programs which could be initiated and developed under the resources of Title V were classified under one or more of the following three broad types of suggested work and training projects:

1. *Work projects designed to develop and to prevent deterioration of good work habits, attitudes, and morale.* In most of these assignments, special skills were not required and no planned skill training was to be offered. Work would usually be performed under close supervision. The plan required that selected participants in such projects were to be encouraged to improve their basic education through adult education courses, and that they were to be upgraded, as qualified, to more constructive work and training projects.

2. *Work and training projects designed to improve or conserve existing skills.* Workers were to be given opportunity to use their skills and through this useful job experience and optional related vocational instruction or adult education were to be enabled to increase their employment opportunities.

3. *Work and training programs designed to develop new or improved skills through the planned coordination of work experience, training, and related instruction.* Participants were to be carefully selected on the basis of ability to absorb training and instruction. Work projects closely geared to producing well-trained workers for a competitive labor market were necessary to carry out the purposes of the Economic Opportunity Act.

CALIFORNIA TITLE V PROGRAM DEVELOPMENT

The Federal Bureau of Family Services established an Office of Special Services to assume responsibility for the administration of the work experience program under Title V of the Economic Opportunity Act. The Office of Special Services received all new Title V project requests from the states for complete evaluation. When the staff was ready to make recommendations for approval of a project it was presented to the Commissioner.

On December 10, 1964 the author took eight California Title V projects to Washington, D.C., in order to expedite their processing. Three of these projects involved establishment of a training program in day care centers in San Francisco, Ventura, and Santa Clara Counties. The federal staff was unprepared for requests of this kind, expecting projects more directly associated with work experience and training. It took a couple of days time and considerable discussion before they finally accepted day care training centers as appropriate for financing from Title V funds. The following is a summary of the discussions held.

Day care centers were acceptable on the basis of certain conditions:

1. They were to be established in accordance with standards developed by the State Department of Social Welfare.

2. To the extent that day care centers would serve mothers in work experience or training in ways other than those generally provided in the centers, the nature of the training assignments were to be completely identified and fully reported. Since Title V dealt only with work experience and training, the federal agency had to be assured that the day care which would allow such training would be directed toward an acceptable educational or vocational plan.

3. When Title V money was requested to purchase day care for children of participants in projects from private or other public resources, the costs would first have to be met from grant and income within the maximum grant structure. Only after this resource was used, could Title V money be used to purchase day care. This followed the general principle that all available state and local resources must be utilized before Title V money could be sought.

Work Experience and Training-Connected Expenses: The federal agency would grant Title V money for the provision of work experience and training-connected expenses to participants in Title V projects. Such expenses would include transportation, lunches, work clothing, and the like. These expenses would first have to be met from grant and income to the extent that they could be met within the maximum grant. Title V money would be used when the grant resource was exhausted.

Medical Care: Medical care could be provided through use of Title V money under the following conditions:

1. Medical care would be provided only to the participant in work experience and training and not to other members of the family.

2. Medical care would be provided only to enable the participant to engage in work experience and training. The intent was to exclude medical care which might be desirable but was unrelated to the vocational plan.

3. Medical care would have to be provided from the combination of grant and income within the maximum grant before Title V money could be used.

4. Each project would have to provide a statement that medical care would be made available to the participant irrespective of the source of payment for this care.

Supporting Service Standards: It would be necessary for county welfare departments requesting Title V money to declare that the participants served in the project would receive casework and other services consistent with SDSW service standards; that is, the caseload size could not be more than 60 cases per worker, supervisory formula five to one, etc. The federal agency was also concerned about the development of some system of vocational assessment for all participants to insure appropriate placement in training and education. Non-public assistance cases which are served by Title V projects could be fully staffed with technical work experience and training personnel plus casework and other supporting personnel as a direct federal charge. In such Type II projects, however, the federal agency would require caseload and other standards to be at least equal to SDSW standards for public assistance recipients.

Record Keeping and Reporting: The General Counsel was extremely concerned with the need for Title V project records to fully reveal whether participants were being appropriately served in terms of the intent of the Economic Opportunity Act. That is, Title V participants would have to be engaged in work experience, vocational training, or educational or vocational training, or educational programs which would upgrade their skills and move them toward employment. Accordingly, it would be necessary to identify the full nature of the educational or vocational placement, and each project would be required to declare its agreement to keep appropriate records and make reports.

Work Experience and Training Projects: Two of the California projects requested Title V money to provide staff to supervise the work experience and training project per se, one in Shasta, the other in Los Angeles. The Shasta request was denied because it appeared that the staff was to serve projects already set up and functioning. The Los Angeles staff requests were approved with modification. The following principles were developed:

1. When county personnel was to be used to supervise work experience and training projects, as when the county park staff would provide supervision, no question would be raised about providing supporting staff employed by the agency to work with project supervisors. For example, a project coordinator might be employed who would generally supervise all of the projects and would examine the nature of the training assignments to determine that the training component was being met.

2. When project supervisory staff and materials were to be requested from Title V money, these special conditions should prevail:

   a. The project would have to be new and of a different kind and for some special reason than ongoing projects already served by agency staff.

   b. The project should have particular pertinence to improving the individual living conditions of the poor. For example, project supervisors for a unit of public assistance recipients who would repair homes of other public assistance recipients would be a most acceptable project from the standpoint of employment of personnel and provision of materials.

   c. If the project would benefit a poverty community, such as Watts in Los Angeles or Hunter's Point in San Francisco, project supervisors could be provided through use of Title V money. For example, in the development of a children's play field from a vacant lot in a poverty community, it would be expected that the local community would provide the materials. However, exceptions would be allowed to this condition in special circumstances where the community itself was impoverished and unable to provide materials.

The author introduced to the federal agency and strongly supported the proposals in b and c above.

Research: Title V money would not be made available for projects essentially identified as research. An example of this would be found in the Los Angeles request for Title V money to research the vocational testing systems and methods to especially accommodate public assistance recipients. The federal agency rejected this because it was essentially for research and would not accomplish Title V objectives, except indirectly.

Wage Incentive: The Santa Clara County project raised the question of provision of wage incentives. The federal agency was sufficiently interested in this to consider a later review of the request. To the extent that the federal could accommodate it at the time, it appeared that a Title V project could be established to provide for a work experience and training participant who was also a public assistance recipient. In addition, either as a training stipend or as a worker trainee stipend, an arrangement would be made whereby an individual would receive a payment of wages for work performed in accordance with prevailing wages for such trainees. The monthly amount provided would be one or both of the following:

1. An amount to accommodate all work-connected expenses, payment for day care, and payment for medical care.

2. An additional amount over and above anything which could be identified in the needs budget, similar to the exempt income provisions for the aged and blind, and designed to provide incentives in AFDC. Since the federal staff was skeptical of this unless provision was made for a maximum, it was tentatively suggested that $25 per month be considered as a maximum for the incentive item which would go beyond budgeted need, as a starting point. This arrangement was later denied by the federal agency.

Fully Employed Supplementation: Several items in the Contra Costa project were related to requests for Title V money to provide work experience and training and supplemental income to employed low wage earners with large families. The federal agency had no question about the provision of money for the work experience and training costs and for expenses connected with such training. However, they did question their ability to supplement the income of fully employed persons, since it was believed to be precluded in their own law. The author suggested that they deal with this, then, in terms of modifying their definition of unemployment to include those who are unemployed at least four weeks during the course of a given year; or those whose income is less than SDSW maximum grants, considering size of family and income. The federal agency denied this proposal (note its similarity to Bulletin 644).

Full Need: Since the federal agency wherever possible encourages states to meet full need it requested that welfare departments establish the requirement that full need be met in all Title V projects. The author pointed out that California had not arrived at any conclusions on this as yet, and therefore we should deal with the subject in terms which could accommodate the movement of the eight projects being submitted. It was finally agreed that the federal agency would accept our projects as at least partially meeting their full need requirement on the basis that we were sixth in all of the states in adequacy of grant; and we would make it a condition of all of our projects that work-connected expenses be met, and medical care and day care services be provided in some manner. The Commissioner agreed to accept our conditions as fulfilling expectations that Title V projects would serve persons receiving full budgetary allowances although later a federal requirement was established that full budgetary need of each Title V participant family must be met.

Participant Exploitation: The federal agency was concerned about exploitation of work experience and training participants. SDSW regulatory material must accommodate this in some manner. While the federal discussion occurred in relation to private industry, the author suggested that SDSW should be similarly concerned with county, city, state, or federal projects as well.

Purchase of Service: The federal agency was wary of any request for purchase of service, and raised substantive questions about such requests from the Los Angeles and Shasta areas. In Los Angeles the purchase was to be from private industry and private trade schools, while in Shasta the purchase was to be made from the Department of Employment. The federal agency planned to follow its assistance rules in this regard, which generally meant purchase through state agencies, and asked that we request a waiver for purchase from private resources. In addition, they were very skeptical about purchase of services from such state resources as the Department of Employment. We were able to resolve this for Shasta County by identifying in the project that the purchase would be from the state college. This was acceptable. The rationale for this, of course, was that the Department of Employment should have been providing such services in its normal program.

The federal agency approved, with modification, the eight projects taken to Washington, D.C., by the author and subsequently a number of additional Title V projects were also approved.

SOME CALIFORNIA TITLE V PROJECTS AND OBJECTIVES

Los Angeles County: Enrich and expand existing work experience and training program in the south central area of Los Angeles County. Funds provide transportation, child care, medical care, and other training-related costs; repair and improve housing owned and occupied by public assistance recipients, and rehabilitate poverty areas through utilization of work experience workers, including costs of construction supervisors, transportation, purchase of material, and rental of equipment; and establish training through private industry and private vocational schools as an expansion of the work experience training program.

Los Angeles County (Day Care Centers): Provide funds for

establishment and operation of four day care centers under contract
with the Willowbrook School District, Enterprise School District,
Westminster Neighborhood Association, and Henderson Community Settlement of the Second Baptist Church. Funds requested
for renovation of buildings, provision of equipment, construction
of playground areas, and operational expenses, including staff salaries, educational supplies, and food. The four centers provide day
care services for 336 children and in addition provide work experience training for public welfare recipients such as child care and
teacher assistants, cooks, housekeepers, typist clerks, and custodians.
Project includes considerable outlay for building space procurement
and renovation due to shortage of adequate and satisfactory building space for child care in the south central area in Los Angeles.

Madera County: Multioccupational training programs designed
to return AFDC mothers and fathers to the labor market: Provide
farm tractor operator course and preventive maintenance; train unskilled laborers as milkers for dairy industry; hold remedial education classes in cooperation with the Madera School District to assist
recipients in raising literacy level; provide training courses designed
to prepare AFDC mothers for employment as homemakers and
child care attendants; provide language classes for non-English
speaking AFDC parents; and provide general clerical training in
typing, shorthand, and filing machine operation.

Ventura County: Establish two day care centers to serve a dual
purpose: Provide training for AFDC mothers for employment as
homemakers, housekeepers, food service employees, and in other
service occupations; and provide day care for children of AFDC
parents who are participating in this and other programs.

San Francisco County: Establish a training-day-care facility
to provide a Home Service Training Center in which AFDC mothers will be trained in basic fundamentals of house cleaning, meal
preparation, sanitation, and other skills required of homemakers,
housekeepers, and other service employees; a child care facility
for children of the mothers in training; and training for mothers
who will seek employment as day care center workers.

Santa Clara County: Expand existing work experience and training program for public welfare recipients to include: Intensive
vocational, social, and basic education and homemaker services on
a demonstration basis for a selective group of 100 hard-core, long-
term recipients; year-round help to 600 families with seasonal unemployment or erratic work histories; intensive and continuing services aimed at providing stability in employment; formal training
in various personal services areas (homemaker aide, home health
aide, personal attendant, transportation aide), followed by on-the-

job training providing services to old age, disabled, and other public assistance recipients; establish a special day care facility to provide adequate child care for AFDC mothers undertaking training; and training for selected recipients as child care aides.

Contra Costa County: Expand existing work experience and training program to include incorporation with Contra Costa County and cities of Richmond and Pittsburg in establishing training programs in county hospitals, social service, probation, and health departments, county schools, public works, recreation and parks; and incorporation with a home visiting service of Contra Costa County to establish a training program for housekeepers, homemakers, and home managers whose services will then be utilized by several county agencies and by the community; and expand services to the physically and mentally disabled through the purchase of services from the State Department of Rehabilitation. Another Contra Costa County project was the establishment of a research and demonstration program to determine the most effective remedial education methods in conjunction with intensive casework services.

Kings County: Training tractor operators and other farm machinery operators as well as general community work and training programs for skill development.

San Luis Obispo County: Expand existing work experience and training program in five vocational areas: Cooperation with Department of Parks and Beaches to improve facilities in a public park (Nipoma Park), with supervision, technical assistance, plants, and supplies to be provided by the county department of parks and beaches, and sprinkler system and material to be provided by the Nipoma Men's Club. Training in the school district to work as teacher aides in schools. Cooperation with clerical staff of county welfare department in training program to provide concentrated clerical training in organized class to be followed by on-the-job clerical work experience. Training program in homemaker-attendant aide and general area of home services to the aged, disabled, and others in need of assistance in living independently. Cooperation with Atascadero State Hospital in establishing training programs in food services, laundry, clerical, fire fighting, security, groundskeeping and crafts and trades available in the state hospital, this program to be incorporated into the existing employee training program at the hospital. In addition, literacy and remedial education classes sponsored by the hospital will be utilized for public welfare recipients.

Lake County: Four basic training programs: Self-help housing repair for 75 families from the Indian villages at Big Valley, Scotts

Valley, Robinson Ranch, and Sulphur Bank, including provision of materials, training in building trades, and literacy training. Because of the unique problems of legal entanglements involving their land and property holdings, legal consultation will also be provided under this project. Provide instruction media and production technician training; food processing training, and surveyor training.

Sacramento County: Expand existing job development and placement program through provision of additional staff, vocational consultation and assessment; extend work experience and training services to additional AFDC recipients in cooperation with staff from the Department of Rehabilitation presently stationed in the county welfare department; and extend such services to the physically and mentally disabled (ATD) and Aid to the Blind recipients.

After the 1965 Watts riot in Los Angeles, the author and the Los Angeles Welfare Director visited the smoldering ruins of the Watts central business district and planned a Title V project for unemployed, able-bodied single persons who normally did not qualify for public assistance. Simplified methods of granting aid were established. The applicant simply declared his resources and income, if any, and eligibility was established forthwith. A flat grant of $150 was provided, and later was increased to $175. Training and education was largely purchased from private resources. Casework counselling was provided by the welfare agency. This Title V project emerged as one of the most meaningful in the State of California. A case example is illustrated in the appendix of this book. The following is a description of the project.

LOS ANGELES COUNTY'S PROJECT FOR ADULT TRAINING

A significant step forward in training program attitudes may be observed in the following report from Los Angeles County:

Beginning April 1, 1966, the Los Angeles Department of Public Social Services initiated the Project for Adult Training (PAT), a unique manpower training program serving the hardest of the hard-core unemployed. This has been an unusual opportunity to demonstrate what can be done with low caseloads, decent subsistence allowances, and a relatively expansive range of training opportunities. The project was undertaken with regular public assistance staff lacking formal training in social work or vocational rehabilitation. The primary quantitative justification of the PAT program must be in its superior ability to reach truly hard-core recipients and help greater numbers of them to get through to decent jobs.

The attitude of the Department of Public Social Services is that a program's responsibility begins when an eligible applicant walks through the door. Some manpower training programs assume statistical responsibility for a client only when he is assigned to training, although this may be two to three months after he has "walked through the door." By this time he has survived all of the testing, counseling and waiting without any really meaningful action going for him—specifically subsistence and training. This process weeds out the marginally motivated or unstable client. Conversely, in making an almost immediate commitment along with money and training, PAT takes in the clients that other programs exclude. PAT's philosophy has been to accept for training any hardcore person who is eligible in terms of the basic criteria. Practically none are excluded at the point of intake because of poor training potential or other judgmental areas.

Of the 1,272 originally eligible clients accepted for PAT since its inception, 240 graduated, and of that group, 184 are currently employed, or more than 95 percent are in jobs for which they were trained. With the current favorable labor market, the expectation is that 95 percent of those successfully graduating can ultimately be placed, although these figures do not reflect this because at any one time, 20 to 30 recent graduates may still need help in the area of job search and job preparation. An additional 480 clients are still engaged in training. The remaining 552 eligible clients have ranged in their responses from those who would not return after the first interview to those who completed substantial portions of their training programs, and 11 percent had to terminate because of arrest and incarceration. Another view of these terminations is illustrated in the following table:

DISPOSITION OF ALL TERMINATED CASES

Received no training	10.3%
Received 1-20 percent training	21.8
Received 20-40 percent training	12.6
Received 40-60 percent training	6.9
Received 60-80 percent training	6.9
Received 80-100 percent training	28.8
Terminated with job upgrading	12.7

Thus, if "successes" can be defined along a continuum from those who complete 80% or more of their training to those who actually graduate and receive upgraded jobs, the PAT success factor to date is 463 clients, detailed as follows:

152	Completed 80 percent or more training
240	Graduated (expected placement rate 90-95 percent)
71	Terminated with less training but obtained upgraded employment
480	Still in training
329	"Unsuccessful drop-outs"

It is still too early to measure precisely the extent to which PAT strengthened its efforts in the second year. With a precipitous start in April, 1966, inexperienced staff, and a one- to two-month social worker strike, the first year must be viewed as relatively unstable. From January 1, 1967 through August 31, 1967, PAT approved the cases of 540 clients, of whom 136 are now employed; 304 are still in training; and 100 terminated before graduation. Of the 100 terminations, approximately 40 completed at least 80 percent of a training program or, notwithstanding the amount of training received, obtained employment which represented a distinct upgrading in terms of their previous vocational achievements.

A crucial goal for any poverty project is to consistently reach and serve the original group contemplated. The objective of PAT was to reach the hard-core adult hopelessly trapped in the cycle of poverty, discrimination, and ghetto existence. Approximately 56.3 percent of all adults approved by PAT have served jail or prison terms in excess of six months, and of this group, 33.6 percent have histories of narcotic offenses. In terms of ethnic status, age, and average education, the following is a comparison for male trainees:

	Negro	Mexican-American	Caucasian
Percent of total	68.6	22.8	8.6
Average age (years)	28.5	28.8	27.8
Average education (years)	10.6	10.2	10.7

Type of Training: PAT continues to make predominant use of private trade schools. Approximately 90 percent of our clients receive this type of training. It is our experience that private trade schools tend to be better at the sort of training we need than any other training resource. PAT has not had access to on-the-job-training slots to any significant extent. What experience we have had strongly suggests that clients with ghetto backgrounds are not ready for direct transition to private employer on-the-job training.

In the past we have been unable to make significant use of the public school system. The vast majority of courses offered are on a semester basis and for these there would only be a few times during the year that the client applying for training would be available for enrollment in such courses. Moreover, clients are almost entirely trade-oriented. They want the type of training whose tempo and subject matter lead to quick and early job placement. In many instances the length of time required by the use of public schools would build up prohibitive subsistence costs which would more than wipe out any savings of the cost of training.

Public school officials, during the past year made rapid strides towards the concept of the vocational center. Several are now in existence in downtown Los Angeles and offer courses in advanced welding, electronics, TV and radio repair, to mention a few. PAT intends to make maximum use of such resources since they are now competing favorably with the private trade schools in terms of cost, duration, and quality of job preparation.

Methodology: PAT continues its emphasis on early client involvement in specific training and job preparation activities. It is believed that the client must feel very soon that "things are happening." Accordingly, in almost all cases, once a client is found eligible, he is assigned to a specific training program and school. He is also granted early financial assistance whenever needed.

The program continues to avoid the use of testing and measurement. Many clients are suspicious of testing, having been precluded innumerable times in the past from job and educational opportunities because of testing. The project sought professional opinion concerning the validity of testing and its use for the socioeconomic groups served and was advised that there are few norms and that little basis exists for the prognostication of success. Since the project was not interested in high possibilities of success, but rather in working closely with the very groups for whom success is rated as a low possibility, there was good reason for avoiding the use of tests. The only current theory which is used to justify testings is that the results are given to the client to help strengthen his decision concerning the choice of a career. It is hard to see, if the professional cannot really decide what the tests mean, how the client can use them to strengthen his decision.

During the second year of the project the major change of method was an increased emphasis on pretraining and job preparation. In many instances the client from the ghetto has a set of attitudes and values which were necessary and useful for his previous means of adaptation. These do not function as well in the semi-middle class atmosphere of the trade schools, or for the later conditions of employment. Accordingly, intensive group and individual counseling have been initiated before the client reports to the school, and after graduation, before he seeks employment.

In terms of the counselor-client relationship, the Department sought to create a direct "leveling type" of relationship—one in which the worker must respect and understand the hard realities of the asphalt jungle. There was an attempt to minimize the caseworkers concept of professionalism as involving a superior-subordinate relationship. It was necessary to work with problems of "standoffishness" and reserve. It was difficult for some middle-class workers to accept or even understand how manipulative and aggressive one must be to survive in the ghetto. The Department established sensitivity training with the help of professional psychi-

atric caseworkers and psychiatrists to deepen caseworker understanding of these problems.

Counselors have been intensely active in working with the
schools and have direct and close contacts with school personnel,
especially the instructors and other direct line staff.

Caseworkers have stressed the "pivotal case"—the one identified
as having important problems in the way of training and job preparation which could go one way or the other and in which casework intervention could make a difference. This is partially to
avoid caseworkers being over-involved with clients who present
multiple problems far beyond their capacities to serve.

Community Workers: On the second year's renewal, four community workers were granted to PAT. The problems that followed illustrate some of the difficulties in implementing new projects. Preliminary work with the Civil Service Department had been
completed in October 1966, supposedly to a successful termination. Notwithstanding, it took several months more before Civil
Service had approved, in final form, the community worker class
and produced a usable list for recruitment.

Eligibility Audit: A singular feature of the PAT program was
the noninvestigation of eligibility except for a 10 percent sampling
of cases, and on these 10 percent a regular public assistance investigation of these cases was conducted. On all cases, as an additional
check, a clearance was made with the Department of Employment.
The sampling procedure was designed to reveal any undeclared receipt of unemployment or disability insurance. It would also show
earning records for the past year. The latter would reveal employment at skills which would revise our judgment as to the hard-
coreness of the client. It might also show current employment
which had been undeclared. In *no* case was any client found ineligible due to fraudulent misstatements. This should not be surprising.
The vast bulk of the clients have either been desperately poor or
they have supported themselves in the past by marginal or illegal
activity.

Community Relations: The PAT program enjoyed outstanding
relationships with the various community agencies; but most notable was the establishment of good working relationships with the
full spectrum of the the militant action groups, bar none.

THE CONTRA COSTA COUNTY PROJECT

Contra Costa County developed a program of another kind as
illustrated by the following report: This Progress Report covers a
14-month period (May 1, 1966 through June 30, 1967) involving

both Title V EOA and the regular Community Work and Training Programs of the Contra Costa Social Service Department.

Persons received Vocational Services 2,576

Trainees enrolled in training programs 1,163

Persons obtained employment 1,251*

Not every able-bodied adult on welfare can instantly be put into job training. The work training projects cannot handle that many trainees at one time; social workers and vocational counselors need time to gather and evaluate the information necessary to fit the individual to the training; obstacles standing in the way of training cannot be removed overnight. For example: There are 26,517 children represented in the AFDC caseload. There are 4,042 welfare families in Contra Costa County with children under 5 years of age. Care must be arranged for the children before their parents can enter job training.

On June 1, 1967, Vocational Services had screened out 2,251 of those parents most obviously ready to benefit from training. Of this group, 549 were assigned to some sort of training. The remaining 1,702 are unassigned—waiting for training. It is with these two groups that this report is concerned.

In the 1,784 cases where the information was available, statistics show that while 1,280 welfare recipients picked for services have licenses to drive, 504 do not. Some 1,112 own a car, but 1,139 must depend on public transportation. Of the car owners, only 536 report carrying insurance on those cars. In a county as large as Contra Costa, where public transportation is almost unavailable in some areas, the lack of a car and a driver's license is a definite problem in assigning an unemployed person to training programs. Many advertised jobs calling for minimum skills are out of the reach of those without transportation.

Of 2,251 welfare recipients scheduled for or assigned to training in Contra Costa County, 182 felony and 1,051 misdemeanor convictions were recorded. Since these were cumulative figures, one person may have accounted for more than one of the convictions.

More than half of the welfare recipients screened had not finished high school and a few had no schooling at all. (It is estimated that there are 1,800 non-reading AFDC parents currently receiving assistance, some of whom have attended school, some who have not.)

---

*In addition, 974 adults obtained employment and left the welfare rolls through their own efforts.

Education by stated grade completed:

Grade Completed	Percent Assigned*	Percent Waiting†	Grade Completed	Percent Assigned*	Percent Waiting†
None	2	2.0	12	35	32.0
1-4	2	3.0	13-15	7	5.0
5-7	6	5.0	16	0	0.5
8	8	8.0	17+	0	0.5
9-11	39	44.0			

> *With an education you can have*
> *a much better life.*
> **(Handwritten excerpt from training class 1966-67)**

> *In five year I would like to be a filler cleork and be able*
> *to Send my chrieldren to College.*
> **(Handwritten excerpt from training class 1966-67)**

Not all unemployed welfare recipients are ready for immediate vocational skill training. Willingness and ambition are not enough to qualify the young woman who wrote the above for placement in an office to learn the file clerk's skills she dreams of using. She needs basic education first.

Within the limits of the available funds, welfare recipients, assigned to job skill training, education or a combination of the two, are given extra money in addition to the regular grant. Under Title V, for example, an extra $45 to $125 a month is given to cover additional food, clothing, and incidentals. Actual child care costs and transportation expenses to and from training, special clothing such as uniforms or work shoes, and union fees and dues if necessary, are allowed. These dollars are granted only to those in full-time training leading to employment. The training allowance is given only for actual training time spent and absences result in cut funds.

Mary A. was 30, a divorcee with four children. She had a 9th grade education plus some night courses. She needed training that would allow her to support her family. The LVN Course at Junior College was her answer. For three semesters she ran her home and studied also. She is now employed as an LVN.

Of the 1,163 people assigned to the various training programs in the 14-month period covered here, 908 were assigned to Title V

---

*Assigned to training are 105 men and 385 women.

†Awaiting assignment are 802 men and 959 women.

Projects (including education) and 255 were funded and assigned to the County financed training.

Adult Basic Education: Greenleigh Project Summary—
In the Spring of 1966 the Social Service Department, five school districts, and Greenleigh Associates cooperated in a Federally sponsored research project on adult education. A total of 517 students were enrolled in Basic Education classes. No student tested at more than a 4th grade reading level although 21 percent of those enrolled had a 9th grade or higher education. Forty-seven percent had less than a 5th grade education.

The Teacher Brough Dictory from The Libuary.
(Handwritten excerpt from training class 1966-67)

One of the questions most frequently asked of those involved in the Greenleigh Project was, "Who are these people? Where did they come from that they can't read or write?" We do have compulsory education in California, questioners kept pointing out. Did the students come from other countries? Statistics from Greenleigh data show the following breakdown:

Birthplace	Percent	Race	Percent
California	10	Caucasian	31
Puerto Rico	1	Negro	45
Mexico	11	Spanish	18
N.E. United States	2	Other	6
Southern U.S.	59		

Length of time in this area	Percent
Lived in Calif. 10 years	73

I wonted to come to school. I don't Know things.
(Handwritten excerpt from training class 1966-67)

The Greenleigh Project answered many questions about Adult Basic Education, the most important of which was that adults can and *will* return to school and that they *can* learn the 3 R's—and often far more rapidly than children are expected to cover the same objective. Almost 70 percent of the Greenleigh students had been out of school ten years or more. The average reading level was 2.7 grade at entry. Sixteen weeks later the average grade level was 4.6; 25 percent of the students scored above 6th grade level and 11 percent above the 8th grade level at the end of the instruction period.

I am learning and enjoying it.
(Handwritten excerpt from training class 1966-67)

Grade achievement scores tell only a small part of the story. Adult students learn much more than reading and writing in basic education classes. Their new academic skills help them in their shopping, their family relationships, in their ability to take initiative and responsibility, and to get along with new people. Their confidence in their ability to succeed grows.

When my child graduates from highschool
I would like her to go to College.
(Handwritten excerpt from training class 1966-67)

Seventy-seven percent of the adult students in the Greenleigh Project had children. The general population census figures in California show 3.0 persons in the families of the general population. The families of the adult students averaged 4.1 people per household. The students had an average of 3.69 children—an average that included a young, single man and an older couple with ten children all living at home. Particularly important is their new attitude toward school and learning. These adults are determined that their children will stay in school and learn. The adult students know first hand just how difficult is the life of a dropout.

I am always telling my children to stay in school.
I always use myself as an example.
(Handwritten excerpt from training class 1966-67)

I thinks reading is fun now.
(Handwritten excerpt from training class 1966-67)

When the Greenleigh Project was completed in May 1966, the students wanted to continue learning. They realized it would take much more than a fourth grade ability to get a job. Business and industry almost always require a high school diploma, its equivalent, or a passing score on a company administered test. The adult students aimed at passing the General Education Development Test (GED) which is a universally accepted substitute for a high school diploma. Enough money remained to continue classes until the middle of June 1966.

I want to learn how to read and write.
I think I should learn more.
(Handwritten excerpt from training class 1966-67)

In February 1967, the Richmond Unified School District entered into a contract with the Social Service Department. The Contra Costa County Board of Supervisors allocated funds to reimburse the school district for their actual cost of operating five basic education classes and two classes for those who tested above the 8th grade level.

The 227 prospective students were picked by Social Service Counselors and tested by Richmond adult school. Of this group 80 percent had attended school at least through the 8th grade. Of the prospective students seven percent had no more than a 3rd grade education.

There was a wide variation in student achievement on the tests. Some entered class needing only brush up learning in missed high school courses. A few entered unable to even write their names. All needed education before job skill training. The 42 prospective students (19 percent)* tested at above the 8th grade level. These students made up the two advanced classes. There were 98 students in basic classes (elementary level) split roughly into three grade group levels. The 87 prospective students went onto a waiting list. A few were put into classes to replace those who dropped for various reasons. The rest, plus some who were tested later, are still waiting for their chance at education.

Results: Prior to termination of classes in June 1967, these students were counseled and their achievements tabulated (out of 42 students, 19 passed the General Education Development exam) after 16 weeks of half day classes. Classes—though not as many—are continuing with students who seem most likely to be future job holders being placed in classes first. The waiting list grows longer and it is hoped that more classes can be started when funds become available. Mt. Diablo Unified School District provides full-time day classes in Concord and West Pittsburg. Enrollment is not restricted to welfare recipients. Emphasis is placed as in other schools on small classes where individualized instructions may be given.

I want to do for my family and my self
and also help others if they need help
(Handwritten excerpt from training class 1966-67)

---

*Note: Although 80 percent of those tested had gone to the 8th grade or higher, only 19 percent scored above that level.

DISPOSITION SUMMARY OF 52 STUDENTS:

37 *completed Training:* 33 working; 4 seeking employment.

9 *Incomplete:* 5 not qualified; 4 health or emotional problem.

7 *Miscellaneous:* 3 married; 2 other school; 1 deceased; 1 child had heart surgery.

WORK TRAINING PROJECTS

It is impossible to completely detail all of the kinds of work training programs that were in progress during the 14-month period. They were many and varied. The biggest group of trainees were in the clerical, health and other service occupations. Some went into semi-professional training, others into skilled and semi-skilled occupational training. It all depended upon the abilities and interest of the trainee and the recommendations of the vocational counselors and social workers. Perhaps a description of a few of the specific programs and some individual case histories will give an idea of the work training projects.

Joan C., 21, was a single woman with one child. She could type and had once worked for six weeks but now her self confidence was completely shattered and she was terrified to look for work. V.S. placed her in an office where she was trained as a receptionist, transcriber on dictaphones, and in office practice. Her self confidence grew; her appearance improved. After six months of training, Miss C. found full-time clerical employment.

Many public agencies in the area have taken welfare recipients needing on-the-job training. (This is not as easy as it sounds. Trainees need much more supervision and attention than regular workers.) Some of this work training is on the semi-skilled and skilled level and is very successful in that often the trainee learns for the first time that he really enjoys a type of work he had never considered before. For instance, men who have spent their lives in the heart of an urban ghetto find gardening a new and fascinating experience and so bring interest and enthusiasm to the work.

Oakland U.S. Naval Hospital decided to participate in a Work Training Project after the Vietnam conflict cut the number of nurses aides and dental assistants to a serious low. Eight AFDC mothers were enrolled in Nurses Aide Training. They commuted from Richmond to the Naval Hospital, a distance of 35 miles each day for 12 months. They were rotated through all phases of a nurses aide training program including pediatrics, orthopedics and laboratory work.

Both the trainees and the hospital profited from this training program, The girls graduated ready to take their places in any facility, civilian or military, and the hospital had their services while they learned. These girls will have no problems now when they fill out application blanks asking for "special training" and "recommendations." They are on their way to successful futures immediately, with 7 out of 8 currently employed.

A Dental Assistant program was established. After applicants were screened through written exams and dexterity tests, formal training began in October 1966. The women who were chosen for training learned to receive patients, have records and x-rays ready for each appointment. They studied dental x-ray techniques, adjustment of x-ray equipment, processing of x-ray film, basic dental anatomy, the proper precautions against over-exposure to x-ray, assistance in restorative dentistry and oral surgery, and prosthetic dentistry. The trainees learned to maintain dental records and provide chairside assistance. Although this training program is not completed, it has attracted nationwide attention in other Naval installations. The initial response was positive and the trainees have excellent opportunities for employment.

As part of the Greenleigh Project discussed earlier, nine former AFDC mothers who had been given several months of work experience training in different departments or agencies, were then hired as Community Aides. They were given specific training in their new job responsibilities and civil service ratings as employees.

They have helped to make the program a success by recruiting students, following up on absenteeism, arranging for child care and transportation, changing doctor's appointments which interfered with school attendance—acting as trouble shooting liaisons between home and school, welfare and education.

These aides are still working for the Department. They are supporting their families. If these nine women work only six years, the money saved in welfare payments to them will completely pay for the educational costs of the entire three-state, seven-county Greenleigh Project.

Jane C. was 26, the mother of four and separated from her husband. Although she had once worked in an office, her clerical skills were rusty and her self-confidence at a low ebb. The V.S. Counselor assigned her to a Work Experience and Training Program in an office. After only two months of on-the-job training she was employed by the University in one of its offices.

Between May 1, 1966 and June 30, 1967 almost two thousand (1,983) people left the Contra Costa County welfare rolls because they found employment. Over half of them (1,254) needed the help of Vocational Services before they could find work. When a parent applies for public welfare, Vocational Services is only one of the many services provided by the Social Service Department. Each applicant is reviewed immediately to determine their need for vocational counseling, training or job placement.

Others need a different kind of help—emergency financial help in a time of family crisis; the advice of an outsider such as a Social Worker who could see their problems clearly and help them work through them—or perhaps direction for the future. Timing is important—someone to talk to about work, how to get a line on a job or just a few leads which haven't been explored before. This may mean the difference between facing the stigma of being on welfare or live as a parent who knows the feeling of being self-supporting once again.

Jerome B. at 38 had an 8th grade education, three children and 20 years of steady employment. Then he was seriously injured in an auto accident. His usual work was impossible. He had always wanted to be a draftsman. V.S. placed him in basic education classes and after only one month of intense studying, he passed his GED test. Although he was offered training to become a draftsman, Mr. B. wanted a job because being on welfare was too hard on his family. He is now working and taking night courses in drafting.

JOB PLACEMENTS—1961 to 1967

Year	No. Placements	Year	No. Placements
61-62	131	64-65	188
62-63	191	65-66	662
63-64	216	66-67	1,073*

SUMMARY (Contra Costa County)

Some people have a tremendous amount of native ability that has never been recognized. They are way above average in intelligence and determination. Marcia J., for example, went from a second grade reading level to secretarial school in less than a year. Mike B. went from bare literacy through to a GED Certificate, a civil service exam and into a very good job in 13 months. He is now studying law at night. These are the exceptional ones who, without help, would have never taken their rightful place in the world.

Jim B. attended "special classes" through 12 years of public school and could barely read and write at the end of that time. He lost his only job—as a laborer on a construction crew—because he was too slow and did not work well with others. Jim resented teasing; he also resented supervision. He felt people made fun of him because he wasn't very smart. Eventually V.S. sent him to a sheltered workshop to develop good work habits and to prove to him

---

*Note: Does not coincide with the 14-month period covered by this Annual Report (May 1966-June 1967).

there *was* some kind of work he could do. Today he is happily working for $2.50 an hour as a landscaper in a housing development.

Some welfare recipients need only a few months of specialized training in a specific skill. Others need basic training first in just being at the same place at the same time every day and the forming of a regular work pattern before specialized training would be helpful. Still others, starting in at the lowest basic education classes, will need several years of help before being ready for the labor market. This makes it very difficult to arrive at any sensible percentage of success for the total efforts of Vocational Services during a specific period—if success is considered only employment.

By June 1967, 52 percent (244 out of 471) of those who have completed an educational or vocational training program have found work. This figure naturally will rise as more and more trainees find jobs after completion of training. The California State Employment Service and Social Service Department will continue to assist them in their efforts. Out of the total enrollment in all programs, Adult Basic Education, Work Training Projects and Vocational Training Programs, there are many who are not yet counted in the "success" column. There are people such as Jose who is learning English and upholstering at the same time, going to school eight hours a day at two different locations.

There are people like Margaret who could not write her name six months ago and now can read the newspapers, help her children with their homework while doing her own, and whose son was a school dropout at 14 and is now in high school classes every day.

It was difficult to define or to judge success in Vocational Services in Contra Costa County except on the basis of individual cases.

I would like to be working and have a Steady Income.

(Handwritten excerpt from training class 1966-67)

EVALUATION OF TITLE V PROGRAM, 1964-1967

The accomplishments of the Title V work and experience training program from its inception in December 1964 to July 1967 could be noted nationwide in reports of economic benefits, through reduced welfare costs, to all members of the communities involved, as well as in the human values of restoring dignity to project participants by providing them with the opportunity to train for meaningful work.

No structured, scientific study has been made, to date, of the Title V program, but a tentative evaluation may be projected on the basis of favorable or critical findings made during the two and one-half year period after inception.

The Report of the Senate Committee on Labor and Public Welfare on the Economic Opportunity Act Amendments of 1967 includes the statement: "It is highly significant that many of the persons successfully trained under Title V are people who have been clients of public welfare for some time but were not helped until the advent of Title V. Title V placed new resources—especially trained personnel—added financial incentives at the disposal of the welfare department . . . the Committee has found that the work experience and training program is reaching the hard-core unemployed for whom it was intended. Some of the work performed is a notable public contribution. In the best operations, significant proportions of the participants raise their employability, obtain jobs, and get off welfare. In many places it has helped to strengthen and broaden the work of public welfare agencies." Of the total number of trainees assigned to the program, about 23,800 had left because of illness or disability, transportation or child care problems, or increased resources that made them ineligible. Of the rest, 67 percent had reached the program objective of improved employability. Either they had completed their training and were looking for jobs, or they were immediately employed or had gone to advanced vocational training as a result of having qualified through their Title V training.

The Title V program has concentrated on improving the education of the hard-core poor. By June 1967, almost 60 percent of the 169,000 trainees in the program had either received adult basic education (63,700); had taken high school equivalency courses (8,500); or were enrolled in full-time vocational education (25,000). In addition to employment and educational achievement, other important benefits for trainees were changes in outlook related to a future break in the poverty cycle; remedial medical attention; and a heretofore unknown kind of security which improved their ability to carry out roles as breadwinners and parents.

By mid-1967, the training pattern conformed closely to distribution patterns for poor families, with 60 percent of all training in urban areas; 40 percent in rural areas; and approximately 39 percent of the total trainee population were non-white. During the 3 year period since inception of the Economic Opportunity Act, $56 million in Title V funds had gone into projects in the 182 poorest counties of the Nation—a larger investment in these areas than in any other "economic opportunity" program.

Since improved earning power is ordinarily the most important and most closely appraised factor of success in a work experience and training program, it is noteworthy that preliminary analysis of a three month followup study has shown that more than 75 percent of the trainees who found employment immediately after leaving the project were still employed three months later; that their earnings ranged from $74 in part-time employment to $667 per month; and that they averaged $273 monthly, or 80 percent more than the average monthly AFDC-U payment of $152.

A number of influential newspapers commented favorably on the results of the work experience and training program, particularly the reduction in public funds needed for assistance payments when families become self-supporting. In Connecticut, the *Hartford Courant* reported on February 22, 1967, that "Very largely as a result of the training the number of cases of welfare-supported families receiving aid to dependent children of unemployed parents has been reduced from a normal figure that ran as high as 2,500 to the almost incredibly low figure of 300 State-wide. Some 1,000 families, representing about 4,000 people, have been removed from the welfare rolls as a direct result." An estimated $3 million was saved in Connecticut's relief costs.

The Lawton, Oklahoma, *Constitution* reported on August 5, 1967, that "Nearly 1,000 persons who would have been dependent on State welfare funds now are gainfully employed as a result of a work and training program fostered by the Oklahoma Department of Public Welfare." This was accomplished over two years in 29 counties. For example, in the period from April through June 1967, 74 cases which were removed completely from the welfare rolls had received about $160,000 a year in welfare payments. Their earnings now amount to approximately $234,000 a year.

During the first 18 months of the Title V program in several counties in Michigan, about 1,055 participants terminated training to take jobs. Of these, 840 left the assistance rolls entirely, resulting in savings of $133,560 a month, and 214 had their grants greatly reduced. The group's income increased $137,760 a month over their former welfare payments. Estimates for future employment, including over 3,100 still in training, indicated total savings of $172,515 a month in assistance payments.

When the Economic Opportunity Amendments of 1967 were being debated in the House of Representatives, Congressman Alexander Pirnie said, "I cannot stress enough the importance of leadership to the success of this overall (anti-poverty) effort. Let me cite what I feel is a dramatic illustration. For two and one-half years the Oneida County, N.Y., Department of Social Services has operated a work experience program. Three Federal grants, totaling $818,214, have been awarded to help finance this facet of our local war against poverty. The funds have been used to train unemployed heads of families who lacked sufficient education or basic work skills to become employable. The results achieved are most impressive.

"To date 379 individuals have 'graduated' from the work experience program and are now on the job, laboratory technicians, shoe repairmen, heavy equipment operators, groundskeepers, etc.

"These 379 individuals have 1,825 dependents, including themselves. Prior to participating in the work experience program they were receiving $90,202 per month, or $1,082,424 per year, in welfare payments. They were being supported by the taxpayers.

"Now, these same 379 individuals are working. They are earning $112,942 per month, or $1,355,304 per year. They are taxpayers. They have found a new meaning in life, new direction. They have dignity and pride and we are proud of them.

"There are presently 240 enrollees in the program and they are headed along the same path. Soon, they too will be earning their way.

"All this was made possible by anti-poverty grants, by a program that places its greatest emphasis on 'opportunity.' We are receiving and will continue to receive very sizeable dividends from what, by comparison, must be termed a modest investment."

The Kentucky Commissioner of Economic Security, reported to the House Education and Labor Committee in Washington that Title V achievements included the planting of 2,700,000 trees to halt mountain erosion; construction of 230 miles of road; repair of 6,400 miles, 600 foot bridges and 500 car bridges and repair of 1,000 others; construction of 30 public buildings, such as schools and community centers, and additions to 57 buildings. He added that these achievements plus the benefits of job experience and training, adult education, and the salvation that has become possible for thousands of children of jobless parents make sense because they offer the kind of weapon that is most likely to advance the war against poverty in cities and rural areas throughout the country.

Private employers in many communities sponsored work-training programs and found the results promising. The training ranged from food service occupations to welding and dental technician skills. In Connecticut, the National Oil Burner Institute accepted participants for training as skilled workmen in the oil heating industry. In Baltimore, Maryland, the Chesapeake and Potomac Telephone Company of Maryland, the Baltimore branch of the Western Electric Company, and a dozen other local industries, which cooperated in the Title V program, found that trainees were making good progress and that more would be employed "as soon as applicants qualify."

The Title V program as well as earlier community work and training programs have demonstrated that problems of the hardcore unemployed extend beyond a lack of opportunity or lack of education and training. The apparent success of Title V programs arose from the association of social services (casework, child care, homemaking) with the educational and vocational plan.

The 1962 Social Security Amendments placed emphasis on the association of social services with other services in the interest of rehabilitation. The Amendment objectives were to assist the individual to develop his capacities for personal and economic independence and fulfill his appropriate family role; enable him to use his own personal resources or the resources of family and community to meet his needs; help maintain his sense of individual dignity and worth; and help him assume his appropriate role as a citizen using community services to meet his needs and contributing to community life within his capacity.

Under the 1962 Amendments, caseload standards of not more than 60 cases per worker were required. Selected caseloads requiring intensive work and extensive time required a standard of not more than 25 to 35 cases. Supervisory standards of not more than five workers per case supervisor were required. Provision was made for visits as frequently as required, but not less than once every three months to assure that current knowledge was maintained about each member of the family and to provide for continuity of services. These standards were to be in effect by July 1, 1963.

Under Title V procedures, the applicant for public assistance comes to a county welfare department when his own resources are exhausted or insufficient to maintain himself and his family. County welfare departments represent the human concern of the community, the State, and the Federal government, not only in the provision of financial assistance, but also in marshaling the services and resources available to help the applicant realize his potential in eliminating or reducing the extent of his dependency. In this respect, the financial and social services of the county welfare agency are not simply supporting services for educational or manpower programs in the community, but are the central service to which other resources should relate. The hard core, the impoverished group, is best known to county welfare departments.

The effectiveness of combining social services and employability planning and preparation has been well demonstrated. As reported by the participants themselves, the investment made by county welfare departments in Title V projects has provided better tools for caseworkers to carry out their objectives; and county welfare administrators have had better opportunities for positive interpretations of public welfare programs and for dispelling the concept of the "work-shy" stereotype which has been conveniently misused in certain quarters of every community.

The provision of coordinated social services and vocational and educational services within a single welfare agency is a key feature in the message this book seeks to communicate, and the Title V program has provided informal evidence of the validity of this concept. Viewing the situation with a different perspective, Dr. Sar A. Levitan of George Washington University, reported to the House of Representatives' Committee on Education and Labor on July 12, 1967, in connection with an evaluation of Title V: "State and local welfare agencies . . . were ill prepared . . . had little or no experience with training or placement and awareness of labor market operations . . . (and welfare officials) seemed to take the position that their activities constituted a separate universe from other manpower and anti-poverty programs and that they had little to learn from other agencies."[2] As an advisor to congressional committees, Levitan strongly contributed to legislation transferring work experience and training functions from welfare agencies to labor agencies. Yet Levitan and other such experts were not aware that many served by Title V projects were not merely unskilled and unemployed—they were often caught in difficult personal and domestic circumstances. Some were illiterate, some were unmotivated. Most were well-known to local public welfare agencies, but others were not even included in unemployment statistics because they no longer actively sought work and had given up.

It has been said that Title V projects were, in a sense, "training the untrainable and finding employment for the unemployable." Public welfare agencies, in recognition of the need for providing work and training programs to meet the special requirements of this group, have long sought help from other agencies, usually to little avail. In some instances, after despairing of ever obtaining such services elsewhere, they started their own and some of these were well under way and showing good results long before the War on Poverty emerged. Therefore, when provision for work experience and training was included in the original Economic Opportunity Act in 1964, public welfare agencies looked toward it hopefully as a resource for fulfilling long-felt needs.

During August 1965 the author met with federal representatives for the purpose of discussing complaints about program details, reporting requirements and delays in processing Title V projects at the federal level. These discussions brought forth the following unfavorable comments about fiscal policies at the federal level:

1. The $112,000,000 appropriation for the 1964-65 fiscal year was depleted; and the 1965-66 appropriation which had not yet been provided by Congress would range from $150,000,000 to $300,-000,000. It was anticipated that $90,000,000 of this appropriation would be utilized for renewals of 1964-65 projects. Of projects pending August 1, 1965, California had 13 awaiting action in the

federal office and six in process in the offices of the State Department of Social Welfare.

2. The scarcity of federal funds was related to the following:

a. Use of substantial amounts for initiating unemployed parent programs in states where such programs had not previously existed, therefore requiring in addition to vocational training and educational costs, the federal government funding of 100 percent of the public assistance costs and the draining off of education and vocational training money for use as public aid.

b. Establishment of a federal regulation which required the provision of full budgetary need to all Title V participants. In California, where maximum grants preclude the provision of full need in about one-third of the cases, a substantial amount of money would be required to provide the need, again, draining off training money to supply aid money.

3. The development of a cost allocation system required the use of Title V money for certain administrative costs not directly related to the provision of training to Title V participants.

Such usage of Title V money tended to drain off large portions of it originally intended for achieving the essential objective of the program, namely that of educating and vocationally training public assistance recipients. This became most apparent when the federal agency could not authorize funds for pending state projects planned to offer the important aspects of training and education. These substantive fiscal policy decisions had the effect of watering down the original legislative intent that public assistance recipients be trained and educated: The substitution of federal welfare administration objectives of promoting in additional states the development of unemployed parent programs and the upgrading of standards of assistance.

In addition to these hindrances, administrative actions which also adversely influenced the implementation of this important legislation were taken as follows:

1. Project approval responsibility was held closely to the central office of the Federal Welfare Administration. Regional offices did not have the power of project approval although they participated considerably in project development.

2. The program was designed to be administered on a one-to-one project basis as opposed to the development of a statewide plan.

3. Program procedures were developed on a detailed line item basis rather than through development of standards and criteria against which project audits could be developed, for example, it was required that the precise make and cost of each piece of equipment such as a desk or typewriter be established, rather than issuance of specifications for authorized purchases.

4. Unreasonable reporting requirements were established, such as the requirement of a considerably detailed weekly report on each project.

5. A requirement was established that a federal representative visit any approved, over-$1,000,000 project in the early stages of the project. While this was unreasonable in terms of available federal staff able to conduct such visits, it carried other implications of direct federal welfare project supervision which raised substantive questions in states regarding the state function.

Let us now consider some of the above listed points in greater depth. The National Social Welfare Assembly issued a statement April 10, 1964, regarding the Economic Opportunity Act, Title V. The Assembly concurred in the objectives of the Title, but called attention to the fact that while the Economic Opportunity Act proposed important measures to alleviate poverty, public welfare grants, the basic public measure for such alleviation, were actually declining. The Assembly stated that in the seven months between April and November 1963, the national average of payments to needy individuals and families went down in all categories despite enlarged federal financing provisions and rising costs of living. The author concurs in the concern expressed by the Assembly about inadequate levels of public aid to individuals and families. It is strange, however, that this deficiency in public welfare should be stressed in the context of a discussion around the values of the Title V work experience and training program in the Economic Opportunity Act. A preferable position, in the author's opinion, would have been to endorse the provision of opportunity to public assistance recipients to improve their educational and vocational skills leading toward employment. The Assembly then, in another context, could have expressed concern about the necessity for upgrading levels of public welfare grants. Yet this position exemplified and became predictive of events to follow.

The Commissioner of Welfare strongly supported the view that public assistance should be upgraded in Title V projects. This was to be accomplished in two ways:

1. It was agreed that focus would be placed upon the development of AFDC-U-type programs in states which did not have such programs. In this circumstance, the Economic Opportunity Act would completely fund from federal sources the cost of the public assistance grant as well as the cost associated with the provision of training and education.

2. It was further decided that in those states which had maximum grants or ratable reductions on grants, the participant in a Title V project must receive his full budget. In other words, the maximum or the ratable reduction would be disregarded and the federal

agency would provide the difference between such maximum or ratable reduced amount and what the appropriate budget need would be.

These policy decisions resulted in an expenditure of more money for public aid to recipients than was provided for the education and vocational training of the participants in the Title V programs. While the author strongly agrees with the desirability of upgrading the level of grants, he disagrees with inappropriate actions taken in this situation. The area of disagreement is in respect to utilization of money appropriated for the upgrading of vocational skills and educational levels for purposes other than that objective. In other words, it appeared inappropriate to utilize federal monies designed to upgrade individuals educationally and vocationally for purposes designed to improve the public assistance programs in the several states. As a result, a large number of potential projects in these various states could not be funded because of the depletion of the initial appropriation in the fiscal year 1964-65. In addition to the assistance provided Title V participants, the federal agency also provided for work-connected expenses such as transportation, day care for children, lunches, and special clothing. This, in the author's view, was an appropriate expense and properly associated with the training or educational experience. It is strange, indeed, that the author must criticize upgrading assistance grant levels which he strongly believes must be upgraded, yet the overriding priority issue was determining in this instance.

Another major complaint regarding the administration of the Title V program was related to the tightly-held responsibility for project approval in the Central Office of the welfare administration in Washington, D.C. Responsibilities were not delegated to the regional offices of the federal agency nor to the state agencies. The author worked directly with the federal welfare administration on a number of Title V projects in the State of California during the early stages of the program and strongly recommended, with others, that the welfare administration establish general standards and criteria associated with project operations, and delegate authority to the states for administration of the program in accordance with normal operations of the welfare programs where such delegations are routinely made to states for administration. The federal agency, however, disagreed with this approach, and persisted in administering the program from the Central Office. The administration was on a budget line item basis and involved minute details of project development, an example of which would be the outlining of the cost and manufacturer's name on each piece of equipment such as a desk, typewriter, etc. Moreover, if the project director wished to transfer a few dollars from one line item to another line item within the overall budget, this could not be accomplished without Central Office approval. The central agency, furthermore, established detailed reporting requirements, requiring telephoned reports weekly on the status of projects. The nit-picking nature of the program caused considerable dissatisfaction on the part of staff at all levels and considerable turnover in staff resulted. Protests from county welfare departments regarding these procedures mounted daily.

A third problem associated with initial phases of development of the Title V program related to the quality of the training and educational projects. To a large extent, most of the initial projects became little more than an extension of work relief and work experience programming which had previously existed in many states. Gradually, however, the federal agency improved its standards and established stricter requirements. As a result, the quality of the programs improved.

President Johnson, in a message to the American Public Welfare Association in 1963, remarked that the 1962 amendments to the Social Security Act provided vital new tools with which to reduce dependency, help many of our needy towards self-reliance, and prevent poverty where it threatens. It is now clearly recognized that objectives of this kind are dependent upon action taken by the states to provide the necessary social and rehabilitative services that are spelled out in the new legislation. Before the advent of Title V, 18 states had developed AFDC-U programs and of these states, only ten included work experience and training programs. After Title V of the Economic Opportunity Act emerged, four more states adopted the program, making a total of 22 states, 12 of which had work experience and training programs. In California and most of the other 11 states, the work experience and training programs largely evolved as a continuation of work relief, which had relatively little effect on employability. There were exceptions to this in California counties such as San Mateo and Santa Clara, where effective training programs were developed. The early unemployed-parent programs with their work experience and training components may have aided in the overall development of such programming by giving impetus to the idea of Title V in the Economic Opportunity Act. Such pilot programs, in effect, focused national attention on the possibility that the employability of some public assistance recipients could be improved.

Irrespective of deficiencies in the early welfare administration of the Title V program, the author acknowledges that the effectiveness of the program was gradually improved to the point where it provided a meaningful service to large numbers of public assistance recipients who would not normally be caught up in training or educational programs through other institutional systems such as employment and education. Departments of employment, vocational rehabilitation, and education have traditionally served individuals who were ready to receive such services, but these agencies were not equipped to provide services to the hard-core unemployed, and their practices largely ruled out such individuals, returning them to the public welfare agency where they would receive aid in idleness. Therefore, the placement of the Title V program under welfare administration seemed an appropriate delegation of responsibility to insure that public assistance recipients would receive the services needed to upgrade themselves educationally and vocationally. However, other agencies, particularly departments of employment, have questioned the validity of the placement of this program in the welfare administration, and Federal legislators have also raised questions about this arrangement.

In 1966, amendments to the Economic Opportunity Act were proposed to place responsibility for work experience and training programs with the Department of Labor. H.R. 15111 was introduced in the House of Representatives and assigned to the House Committee on Education and Labor. A major feature of the proposed amendments was the division of program responsibility between the Department of Labor and the Department of Health, Education, and Welfare, and a move in the direction of transferring the administration of the work experience and training program to the Department of Labor. The Secretary of the Department of Labor testified that in his opinion such a transfer would be desirable. The Secretary of HEW, testified also before the House Committee on Education and Labor, stating that the people served by the Title V programs had traditionally been neglected by the employment agencies and other normal channels through which people enter the job market, and concluded that reaching this group was essentially welfare business. The Commissioner of the Welfare Administration, Department of Health, Education, and Welfare, stated that welfare agencies dealt with persons at the bottom of the barrel —those without education or work skills, and generally burdened with serious family and health problems, and emphasized that they needed a wide range of services in order to gain any opportunity for moving into the job market. She pointed out one of the distinctive features of the program besides the range of services which it offered—that it was basically a family-centered program, and most appropriately operated within a welfare setting. It was concluded that the movement of the past five or ten years toward uplifting public assistance recipients would be negated if the program were removed from the welfare administration.

On July 13, 1966, the American Public Welfare Association

(APWA) took a strong position against the transfer of Title V from the welfare administration to the Department of Labor, in testimony before the Senate Committee on Labor and Public Welfare. APWA emphasized that many of the people served by Title V were not merely unskilled and unemployed, but rather were more often caught in difficult personal and domestic circumstances; some were illiterate and some unmotivated. APWA also noted that while public welfare had long recognized a need for providing work and training programs to this special group, and had sought help from other agencies, it was usually to little avail. APWA particularly noted that welfare agencies in the past had little success in engaging the interest of the Department of Labor or its agencies in doing something for the people served by welfare programs. To remove the Title V program from welfare would in effect continue welfare responsibility for the hard-core poor, but without the resource of Title V, which was initially designed to help the group. APWA emphasized the social service and training elements as being closely related and that a division of these components would dissolve the essential ingredients which made the program successful. APWA emphasized that it represented the opinions of most of the state welfare directors in the nation and strongly urged that the committee not take the proposed action of transfer of the Title V program from welfare administration to the Department of Labor.

On October 17, 1966, the House of Representatives and the Senate, concurred in an orderly transfer of the Title V program from the Welfare Administration to the Department of Labor. It was proposed that the welfare administration was authorized to continue the Title V programs through June 30, 1967; after that date, it could complete existing programs begun prior to June 30, 1967; but in no case could it continue to administer the program beyond June 30, 1968. In addition, provision was made for division of responsibility between the Department of Labor and the Department of Health, Education, and Welfare. The Welfare Administration would assume responsibility for pretraining services, basic maintenance, health, basic education, day care, family counseling, and similar supporting services, and would purchase from the Department of Labor those services under the Manpower Development and Training Act which included testing, counseling, training either on or off the job, and classroom instruction where needed, effective July 1, 1967.

REFERENCES

1. Business Management, Vol. 34, No. 3, June 1968.
2. Economic Opportunity Act Amendments of 1967: Hearings . . . . Part 3, p. 1670 ff., Washington, U.S. Government Printing Office, 1967.

CHAPTER 13

CONGRESSIONAL TESTIMONY

THE TEMPER OF THE FEDERAL CONGRESS in 1967 caused apprehension in public welfare circles regarding the future of Community Work and Training and Title V programs. Evolving programs in public welfare, while deficient both in quality and quantity, offered hope for the future. The prospect of losing hard-fought gains through transfer of these programs to the Department of Labor was disheartening.

Since 1954, the author has advocated and developed educational, vocational, and casework services for public welfare recipients at county and state levels and had actively participated in federal programs. When responsibility for part of the Title V program was transferred by Congress to the Department of Labor, the author was invited to participate with HEW representatives in policy discussions with the Department of Labor. These 1967 meetings were filled with conflict over the issue of grossly divided responsibility and the impossible conditions that such division would bring about. A compromise was finally reached. Later in 1967 it became apparent that the Title V transfer was only a skirmish, with the bigger guns being directed toward a complete transfer of work experience and training programs from Welfare administration to Labor. The author testified before two congressional committees in July 1967 against such an eventuality as follows:

Great concern has been expressed throughout the nation regarding social conditions which require correction. Attention has been paid to poor housing conditions, slums, ghettos, and the deteriorated commercial and residential cores of many large cities. The life of the poor has been generally deplored, and it has been recognized that poverty, hunger, inadequate housing, poor medical care, and marginal living conditions are inconsistent with the affluence of the remainder of society. Students of public welfare have identified generational qualities of poverty, pointing out that dependency on public welfare, and the immorality, amorality, and similar characteristics attributed to the poor are apparently being transmitted from one generation to another since it is extremely difficult, although not impossible, for an individual caught in a poverty-stricken family to escape. However, generational poverty does not need to exist, given an improvement in the individual's own qualities.

While we place blame on the individual for his defects, we have insufficient concern for the contribution to these defects made by society as a whole. Such problems persist, not because they are unseen, but rather because there is no commitment to overcome them. If society were committed to overcoming the physical and cultural blight in our large cities and rural areas, the economic blight of unemployment and poverty, the human blight of dependency, mental and physical illness, immorality, and delinquency, it could move by scientific method to overcome these conditions. A society which is capable of solving the problems of space travel is capable of assuming an objective, scientific approach to solution of the problems of poverty. There are no simple answers, however. Solutions to problems of unemployment and poverty cannot be found in oversimplified guaranteed minimum income or negative income tax proposals, which could establish a system of money payments in association with idleness similar to relief itself.

Most people must be engaged in meaningful activity in order to be at peace with themselves, and it is this simple truth which refutes any relegation of man to a life of idleness. . . . (A portion of the testimony is deleted here since it is repetitious of discussion in earlier chapters of this book.)

As a result of unemployment, the family is also profoundly affected. Children suffer through the loss of prestige with their peers, and through disturbed parental relationships which often lessens the warmth and affection of parental care. The continued presence of the man in the home during the working hours, leads to marital friction. One of the few values of work relief during the depression, noted by a number of observers, was the restoration of a normal family living rhythm. The wage earner regained respect for himself and from his family and peers even though the work had lesser status because of its association with relief. If a father experiences chronic unemployment, but the mother works, the son's identification process with his father becomes disturbed. The generational aspects of dependency to the extent that it exists may be ascribed partially to chronic unemployment which has established the parental dependency model for the children.

Our task is clear—we must set forces in motion which will modify our culture to the extent that each person, irrespective of age, physical or mental condition, will be able to serve society in some meaningful manner. Social, psychological, medical, occupational, and other services must be established in public welfare agencies to focus on the achievement of this objective and to remove obstacles to such achievement. It is apparent that social casework, psychiatry, and medicine cannot significantly assist people who are without hope of achieving their own concepts of a meaningful role in society. Help must be provided in conjunction with concrete activities which will give hope to the individual in emerging from the bounds of his environment. Assistance may be offered in the school which corrects functional illiteracy, in the work experience program which provides work habits and restores hope of purposeful functioning, and finally, in the work which represents the goal of a meaningful life. The helping roles of social workers, physicians, psychiatrists, and vocational counselors should be interwoven with such activities.

In public welfare we are beginning to understand that many of the people we serve cannot go from dependency to a more meaningful life without concerted intervention. It is often the training, work experience and group association which have remedial value, just as casework, medicine, and psychotherapy are the formalized therapeutic tools; and these latter therapies should be needed less and less as hope for improved functioning increases.

The major objective of public welfare should be to remove these obstacles within the person and his environment which deter him from full self-realization. The person is caught in a dependency role as he becomes less and less productive, receives fewer satisfactions in life, is subjected to more humiliating experiences, and has so little hope of achieving productivity again that he adapts to the meagre satisfactions of a lesser and more dependent role in society. On the other hand, the joy and happiness which is experienced in productive activity establishes a sustaining quality and anticipation of continued favorable adjustments to the environment.

It is the responsibility of public welfare agencies to insure that every person, irrespective of age, disability, sex, race, or religion, is provided with services which remove obstacles to his engaging in meaningful activity consistent with his capacity and with appropriate protection for other members of his family unit. If we start with the conviction that every man is for the most part motivated toward such goals, and keep in mind that to some extent he is not so motivated, we can examine and treat the obstacles which prevent full self-achievement. Many such obstacles may be readily identified by the characteristics of public assistance recipients.

In California, among typical recipients of AFDC-U the average age of the mother is 31; that of the unemployed father, 35.

The average AFDC mother has completed 9.7 grades in school; the father, 8.4, and 70 percent of the total have had less than a high school education, with actual competence almost always at a lower level. Known health problems existed in 39 percent of the family group cases and in 32 percent of the unemployed cases. Mexican-Americans comprised 22 percent of the family group cases; 35

percent of the unemployed cases. Negroes comprised 30.2 percent of the family group; 20.3 percent of the unemployed.

Over 21 percent of the adults had no marketable skills, and 21 percent of the mothers and 10 percent of the fathers were physically or mentally handicapped. In family group cases, 11 percent of the mothers, and in unemployed parent caseloads, 20 percent of the fathers were employed but at a level not high enough to take them off aid.

In the family cases, the usual occupations of the mothers were: domestics, 15.4 percent; other service, 27 percent; unskilled labor, 10.6 percent; farm labor, 7.8 percent, and 25 percent had never been employed. In the unemployed caseload, 26 percent of the fathers were unskilled laborers, 24 percent farm workers, 27.5 percent skilled or semiskilled workers, and only 0.6 percent had never been employed; and 44.3 percent of the mothers had never been employed.

California has sought improved methods of intervention. One of the ten states with a Work Experience and Training program prior to the advent of Title V of the Economic Opportunity Act of 1964, some of its county community work training projects date back to 1951. These included a rehabilitation and evaluation workshop, remedial and skill training in classrooms, and work habit and skill on-the-job training in government agencies. Several counties have had special staff for over ten years to provide vocational counseling, develop and coordinate projects, and provide liaison with the staff of state agencies concerned with rehabilitation, employment, and education or with their local counterparts.

Since 1951, statutory enactments and California Department of Social Welfare regulations have increasingly stressed the requirement of self-support activities, and since 1963, this requirement has been mandatory throughout the state. As a condition of aid, every able-bodied AFDC adult must become engaged in education, vocational training, or work experience; and each California county is required to establish a work experience and training program in its welfare department. All employable recipients of AFDC-U are referred to local offices of the Employment Service and are required to keep their applications active. In addition, disabled and trainable AFDC-U recipients are referred to the Department of Rehabilitation.

The experience of California indicates that an expansion of this program in its welfare system is now in order without duplicating the training and placement opportunities offered by other agencies. Any expansion of skill training and placement activities by other agencies will necessitate heroic efforts by the welfare system to bring its clients to the level of personal functioning which would allow them to compete with other disadvantaged persons for these new training opportunities. The greatest need is for expanded pretraining facilities, and for increased staff development efforts to overcome those prejudices of social workers, clients, and the public which have contributed to the erroneous but generally held belief that welfare recipients are almost all unemployable or untrainable, the fathers do not want to work, and the mothers should not work because to do so would harm their children.

The Work Experience and Training program and Title V program have shown that when adequate supportive services are provided, motivation increases and the children in the family gain from the parents' increased self-confidence. The participation of the parent in a carefully organized basic education program and evaluation-motivation-conditioning work experience project (or, if necessary, a sheltered workshop for these purposes), gives the child a model to emulate. The role of the social worker in this process, is to evaluate, with the help of specialists, the personal and family needs of a potential trainee, particularly in the realm of physical and emotional strengths and weaknesses. The present services program, with increased staffing, must continue so that it can be thoroughly assessed, and arrangements must be made, supported by adequate legislation and appropriations, so that proper child care, transportation, work clothing, tools, books, and other resources are made available. Individuals and families who are not ready for referral to pretraining activities need group services, casework, and occasionally psychiatric services.

The welfare system requires a specialized staff which closely relates to the social work staff and is also in constant liaison with the education, rehabilitation, and employment services available in the community to coordinate the activities of those services with the needs of the clients. At the pretraining level, the vocational staff must be in consultation with the social work staff to enable the latter to make meaningful referrals to them for further service. The vocational staff must coordinate the referrals to the other departments to avoid an avalanche of paperwork and duplication of effort. The referrals to the schools and agencies must be made only after a carefully prepared vocational-educational plan is developed with the client. All components of pretraining service must be analyzed and resources found so that timely and effective referral can be made. The liaison work of the vocational staff will assist other departments in scheduling and programming their efforts at a level to best serve the particular needs of welfare clients.

California has had several programs that provide comprehensive pretraining and preconditioning services. The sheltered workshop in San Mateo County combines the strengths of individual and group counseling with evaluation of on-the-job techniques to give the recipients insight into their strengths and interests while developing work tolerance and improving their motivation. Ventura County's Title V day care training centers, which the county has now taken over under its ongoing Work Experience and Training Program, provide not only day care but training in home management and child care, plus grooming, basic education, and work habits, to AFDC mothers who would otherwise not be acceptable for skilled training. The success of this program has been so great that other cities in Ventura County are requesting similar centers. Santa Clara County provides a team of a social worker, vocational counselor, and homemaker to help clients and their families deal with the multitude of problems which have prevented them from becoming organized for upward mobility. This project also provides the same services for those who have temporarily succeeded in obtaining a training spot or a job but are predictably doomed to failure in the near future. Riverside County has developed a self-help project which enables trainees to learn auto repair, using recipients' autos on which to train, thereby providing transportation for some so that they can more readily take skill training. County funds were found for the cost of repairs, an average of $30 per car. In Lake County, a Title V project trained Indian welfare recipients in home repair, carpentry, and cement work on their own homes and those of other welfare recipients.

An agreement has been developed between the State Department of Social Welfare and the California Department of Education to train welfare recipients as teachers' aides in the Preschool Compensatory Education program and in child care centers. Nurses' aides, attendants, case aides, and home health aide courses have been operating in a number of California counties training welfare recipients to serve aged and disabled recipients or to provide day care services to AFDC recipients. In San Mateo County, more than 100 AFDC mothers graduated from the nurses' aide training program and there has been a 100 percent employment record for the graduates. Other counties combined group counseling with individual guidance for basic adult education and small work habit projects. The foremen or supervisors were given consultation by a vocational counselor-coordinator who observed and directed the trainees toward self-confidence and reliability. Basic adult education is often given on the project site and relates to the work being done, such as gardening. Although skills are learned, the skill training is coincidental with attitudinal development. Group activities organized for spouses of trainees help them to participate in and develop respect for the efforts of the trainees. Attitudinal changes, combined with observations and recommendations of the foremen, often enable the pretrainee to convince the employment service and an employer of his potential, whereupon he can go directly to paid employment without the step of skill training. Mass referral of hard-core recipients, without individual assessment, group effort, vocational counseling, or support through the social worker, will result in expensive lost motion and further demoralization. Failure to legislate and appropriate funds for pretraining services will cause the majority of welfare recipients to remain unacceptable for training and employment opportunities.

During the 1965-66 fiscal year, combined efforts of new manpower, education, and poverty programs resulted in nationwide participation by more than 100,000 persons in training under the Manpower Development and Training Act (MDTA). Of the 23,096 trained in California, only 3,105 were welfare recipients. National plans for 1966-67 were to train and retrain 250,000 persons under MDTA. In California, during the first ten months, 21,562 were trained, of which 2,321 were welfare recipients. Very few of the hard-core poor qualified for MDTA training because of the difficulty in developing adequate training techniques for this group. Of 500,000 persons eligible for help under the work experience program of the Economic Opportunity Act, nationwide, only 65,000 actually participated in 1966. In California alone, during 1967, 200,000 adults were on AFDC with additional thousands on the Aid to Totally Disabled (ATD) and Aid to the Blind (AB) programs; 50,000 aid recipients were either working or in welfare work experience and training programs; and placement of a total of 90,000 in such pograms was sought by the end of the 1967-68 budget year. Even if MDTA had concentrated all of its national resources in California, it would still have fallen short of meeting the needs of the State's welfare recipients and other poor people. Therefore, we question whether manpower agencies can expand their activities rapidly enough to fill this training need as required now and in the future.

In accordance with 1963 statutes and regulations adopted under them in California, the establishment of a Work Experience and Training Program by the welfare department in each of the 58 counties became mandatory. As a result, hundreds of work experience projects are currently operating in governmental agencies under the auspices of these welfare departments. Such resources should not be destroyed until alternate resources are immediately and fully available.

There has never been any question about the role of manpower agencies in providing vocational training and employment placement. Welfare departments have been referring recipients to manpower agencies for 32 years, with varying results. As manpower agency resources are improved, referrals from welfare will continue, with the hope of placement of increasing numbers of people. These resources should not be weakened by extension to the hard-core unemployed or to those women with children who are not ready for skill training. The conditioning, motivating, and pretraining services for such recipients must be provided in the welfare agencies, and the pretraining services, in order to be comprehensive, must include traditional services plus occupational therapy. Work Experience and Training programs in public welfare departments will play an important role in the California State Department of Social Welfare policy of launching a major thrust in this field.

Two high-tension areas in California—Watts in Los Angeles and Hunter's Point in San Francisco—are Negro ghettos. After the Watts riot in 1965 and recognition of its roots in problems associated with unemployment, a public welfare Title V project was established for single adults (many of them absent fathers of AFDC children). Although approximately 50 percent of the unemployed men and women accepted for vocational training and education in the Watts area had criminal records, 60 percent of the total number of trainees completed the program and of these, 95 percent obtained jobs. According to a social worker on the Watts project, the majority of the 40 percent who failed to complete the vocational training "couldn't be reached" because they were returned to jail. To prevent or reduce such recidivism, public welfare social services for the criminal must be enriched. It has been observed in Watts and elsewhere that the most hardened criminal is in fact very naive about how to make his way legitimately, and has little understanding as to how to proceed to obtain a job and live as other people do.

Although the underlying tensions associated with overcrowded living conditions, poverty, and unemployment are universal throughout ghettos in the United States, such tensions tend to grow even worse in areas like Watts and Hunter's Point, where close proximity to great affluence further accentuates the ghetto dweller's poverty and increases his sense of isolation to the breaking point.

Some progress is being made in Watts. In this area with a population of approximately 600,000, the unemployment rate, which was 17 percent before the riots, has been reduced to approximately 12 percent. The unemployment rate of the 50,000 populating the Hunter's Point area is also about 17 percent, 73 percent have less than high school education, and 31 percent have not completed grade school.

The poor on public welfare have multiple handicaps to overcome, often before vocational training can begin. A woman who succeeded in the electronics training program in Watts failed to find employment. She was obese, passive, and poorly motivated. The welfare department arranged for her placement in a sheltered workshop which offered further work experience in electronics for three months. In this setting, she slowly regained confidence, proceeded to control her weight problem, and gradually emerged as a more self-sufficient person. She is now fully employed and doing well. The pretraining in this situation, although delayed, was an absolute necessity and involved not only the sheltered workshop experience but the thoughtful counseling of the social worker and physician.

A private trade school specializing in welding has been working with unemployed men from the Watts area referred by Title V projects. About one-third of these men who had failed because of personal problems now receive pretraining guidance and counseling plus continuing supportive services. The welding school manager stated that he could teach welding to persons with less than a fourth grade education and that he has placed illiterates and deaf mutes in employment. The placement success for those certified by the school is 100 percent, with a large backlog of standing requests for more graduates.

The impact of intervention by governmental agencies in Watts has been augmented by the dedicated work of a volunteer business executive. Encouraged by California's Governor, this outstanding citizen mobilized private industry to make jobs available to the poor and to minority groups in Watts and other tension areas. He emphasized that the individual must offer a skill to the employer and that poor social attitudes which create problems on the job will not be tolerated by employers.

On my most recent visit to Watts, I was encouraged by the movement toward upgrading skills and reducing unemployment, a striking contrast to the desolation and smoldering embers of August 1965. Watts may be symbolic in its lesson of riot and the subsequent responsiveness of the community, the state, and the nation in attempting to overcome the root causes found in unemployment and its accompanying exigencies. While the culture of poverty may be better understood now, the poor also have awakened to the desperate nature of their plight. One Watts man who had been unemployed but is now in training stated recently that he had not realized before the riot that he lived in a problem area or that as an individual he was on a dead-end street. Apparently the "invisible poor" have problems which are invisible not only to the middle-classes but also to themselves. The awakening of the poor in this decade creates an even greater urgency for amelioration of their problems.

My most recent visit to Hunter's Point in San Francisco stands out in sharp contrast to the Watts visit. Since the riots at Hunter's Point were more recent and much less intense than the Watts rioting, perhaps this accounts for the difference. Hunter's Point is a desolate area located between the opulence of the peninsula to the south and the gilded hills of San Francisco. Hunter's Point has its hill also looking out over a huge auto wrecking plant; odorous Butchertown area, and Candlestick Park, home of the "Giants" baseball club; and the water of the Golden Gate. While Hunter's Point hill could have a "Top of the Mark" it has instead at its top a boarded up "shopping center" out of business except for one small liquor store. The housing at its top is dominated by a former Federal Housing Project now run by the City and County of San Francisco; some of its buildings are abandoned, standing empty with broken windows and those buildings in use are rundown frame structures characterizing the slum appearance. Signs in the windows of the projects proclaim a "rent strike." The principal industry of Hunter's Point is the U.S. Naval Shipyard. As a result of the San Francisco Welfare Department's requests that the Navy open the shipyard to welfare recipients for work experience and training, nine AFDC mothers were recently placed at the base as dental assistant trainees. But the need is for men's work experience and this has not been made available at the base. The staff of the Hunter's Point offices of Employment, Welfare and Economic Opportunity stated that the overriding cause of tension and riot is unemployment and that the need is for training centers and educational opportunity. The unemployed in Hunter's Point, inarticulate and unskilled in the art of regular work habit and job seeking, have all been registered at the employment office but cannot be helped without pretraining. Either no jobs materialize for them or when jobs are offered they often cannot take or keep them. As of July 1967, there were practically no educational or training programs in operation in Hunter's Point. Reliance was mainly on referral to other resources in the city and these were admittedly meagre. This is a major contrast noted between Watts and Hunter's Point—the latter having hardly started to move on substantive rehabilitation programs.

We have developed a brief, conceptual framework establishing that most men are strongly motivated to be engaged in meaningful work and that some are prevented from expressing this urge to work by personal, medical, psychological, and social impediments; by deficiencies in education and vocational training; and by the unavailability of resources for work and training-connected expenses, day care, or sufficient income to cover daily needs.

Many avenues for action are opened by the foregoing conceptualization. Work must be made available to every man through normal sources of employment or governmental provision of work for the unemployed; deficiencies in education and training must be corrected in a goal-directed employment framework by manpower agencies and educational facilities; money may be provided as educational or training stipends—not in the form of public relief; and social, psychological, attitudinal, and medical problems must be diagnosed and overcome by public social welfare agencies. It should be public welfare's purpose to fulfill the social service responsibility. Federal and state governments seek fundamental reform in traditional welfare services, moving the system from relief-giving to a service function, and, in fact, federal legislation has moved in this direction through the 1956 and 1962 Social Security Act amendments. Nationwide, over 3,000 public welfare offices with thousands of social workers already provide many sophisticated services: adoptions; day care; foster care to children and adults; protective services to children and adults; guardianship; intensive case and group work; and a myriad of other services. Additionally, in California, the State Department of Social Welfare assumed responsibility on July 1, 1966, for all mental hygiene institutional leave patients, receiving a transfer of over 500 professionally trained social workers.

Public welfare, then, is a rich resource with a potential for service much greater than its present practice. Welfare will be a social service agency—not a manpower or an educational agency. But public welfare must have an employability development service available to coordinate with its social services. We need to promote morale and the habit training virtues of work experience now being developed by federal agencies or we need to build these through the use of sheltered workshops.

While it is now argued that all public welfare work experience sites should be placed under manpower agency supervision, there are more compelling arguments in favor of another approach. Public welfare has no quarrel with those manpower agencies which provide skill training and placement of welfare recipients in employment. On the contrary, for 32 years we have sought this objective through regularized referral procedures. It is gratifying to find that others now share our concern for provision of employment opportunity to the disadvantaged. Although the meagre resources now made available are insufficient, we must be cautious about raising jurisdictional controversy between manpower, education, and public welfare factions before money is provided for skill training and education needs. Since the effect of this might be the premature drying up of an important resource, it is suggested that training programs be continued in public welfare until such time as manpower agencies can absorb this function. Acceptance of the role of public welfare in the occupational therapy context is of primary importance. As manpower agencies assume more comprehensive roles in skill training, public welfare can gradually redirect its resources to the pretraining activities which involve the conditioning, motivation, and evaluation of recipients through the use of work experience projects and sheltered workshops, as well as to the provision of social services and the other helping services and resources.

The preceding testimony by the author stimulated a number of questions from the Congressional Committee. The following excerpts are from the *Examination of the War on Poverty: Hearings Before the Subcommittee on Employment, Manpower, and Poverty of the Committee on Labor and Public Welfare, United States Senate, Ninetieth Congress.* This report was published by the U.S. Government Printing Office, Washington, D.C., 1967, and comprises the First Session hearings on Senate Bill 1545. The Bill was to "provide an improved Charter for Economic Opportunity Act programs to authorize funds for their continued operation, to expand summer camp opportunities for disadvantaged children, and for other purposes . . ." The excerpts follow:

SENATOR CLARK: Mr. Simmons, would you take over now? I read your statement with great interest and I note that you summarized it very well indeed on pages 17 to 20. I think your, if I may so call it, psychological approach is extremely interesting. Since I have read it perhaps you would like to spend 3 or 4 minutes in highlighting the points that you think should be of the greatest interest to this subcommittee.

STATEMENT OF HAROLD E. SIMMONS, DEPUTY DIRECTOR, PROGRAM DEVELOPMENT, CALIFORNIA STATE DEPARTMENT OF SOCIAL WELFARE

MR. SIMMONS: Thank you, Senator Clark, for reading that rather lengthy statement.

SENATOR CLARK: It was very interesting.

MR. SIMMONS: I have tried to conceptualize in the first part of the material the meaning of work to man because I think it is the fundamental issue. If we fully understand this, then it is easier to make decisions about the next steps that must be taken.

SENATOR CLARK: Does this mean, and correct me if I am wrong, that you are not much of an advocate of a guaranteed annual income for work?

MR. SIMMONS: Well, I covered that briefly in my paper, and to the extent that it is associated with idleness, with individuals who have potential for employment, I would not favor a guaranteed annual income. To the extent that you deal with it in terms of family allowances as they have in the other countries for families, say, larger than four, I would see the possibility of utilizing this arrangement but to do so you would need to establish some minimum wages that are appropriate for the family of four and consistent with decency and health standards.

SENATOR CLARK: My own reaction would be that whether or not the guaranteed annual income regardless of work is a good idea or not, I am expressing no opinion on that, the problem is the pragmatic matter of practical politics in the Congress.

Would you agree with that or not?

MR. SIMMONS: Senator Clark, I would approach it this way, if I might suggest a course of action: I would seek solutions that put men to work or train them or educate them first and then I would deal with this question with what was left over, if you will.

SENATOR CLARK: Now how do you feel about that migratory labor problem in your State, and how do you feel about Hunter's Point and Watts? As you know, we spent 3 days out there. I came back from California with not very fixed views as to what should be done under the poverty program in the general category of welfare.

MR. SIMMONS: In reference to the first part of your question, Senator Clark, the migratory problem, it seems to me that this is the issue of minimum wages and appropriate working and living conditions associated with it.

SENATOR CLARK: And including shelter.

MR. SIMMONS: Yes, very much.

SENATOR CLARK: I saw those people out there in the area of Stockton. I was very much impressed with the housing which had been provided for both the single man and for the families where they had housing but I also saw these families camped out on the side of a ditch living under conditions of shocking poverty, and I came to the tendered conclusion that all that was really needed was some more housing and a little more food.

How do you feel about it?

MR. SIMMONS: This would help a great deal. The problems of the migratory labor have persisted for decades, literally, and it is sad that we have not moved more rapidly in accommodating ourselves to these problems. The solutions are certainly not easy.

SENATOR CLARK: How about the employers? Are they doing as much as they should be required to do, the cherry farmers and also the larger planters on the west side of the valley?

MR. SIMMONS: There is a great deal in the literature, Senator Clark, which suggests that part of the problem is a grower problem in the sense of perpetuating inadequate wages and not dealing with the poor living and working conditions surrounding the vineyards and the orchards. I think, however, we can not dismiss this by placing responsibility entirely on the grower, I think it is a problem that society must deal with in some manner.

SENATOR CLARK: Do you see any difference relatively in terms of acreage of smaller fruitgrowers on the east side of the valley and the phrase that has been used perhaps unfairly, feudal landlords on the west side of the valley? Is this a sociological problem or has somebody been pulling my leg?

MR. SIMMONS: Senator Clark, as I recall Cary MacWilliams in his book, *Factories in the Field,* which was written in perhaps the early 1940's, spoke precisely to the point that you are making and he makes a good case for the position that you take.

I am not an expert on this personally. I think there may be some relevance but again I don't feel that you can deal with the issue unilaterally just in that context. I think there is a myriad of factors involved.

SENATOR CLARK: I am sure it is very complicated but I wonder if you think most of it could be solved with more money.

MR. SIMMONS: I feel that a great deal of it could be solved if the individual received adequate wages. In fact, that principle, it would seem to me, would apply to all segments of the economy.

SENATOR CLARK: Simply your view is that the minimum wage has been a very adverse factor in the economy of the migratory worker in California?

MR. SIMMONS: Yes, sir, it is.

SENATOR CLARK: You have no sympathy with them?

MR. SIMMONS: I believe it is imperative that we establish an adequate minimum wage.

SENATOR CLARK: You do not think this is going to destroy that economy?

MR. SIMMONS: I don't think so. I think the economics of this would be that if it costs more to produce agricultural products the consumer in the final analysis must pay higher prices.

SENATOR CLARK: Were you sympathetic with eliminating the braceros?

MR. SIMMONS: Yes.

SENATOR CLARK: Do you think Americans will do that labor?

MR. SIMMONS: Yes, I believe they will if given appropriate wages and working conditions.

SENATOR CLARK: You do not think that would result in products being priced out of the market?

MR. SIMMONS: I don't think so, personally; no, sir.

SENATOR CLARK: Now just say a word or two about Hunter's Point and Watts. What will welfare do with that?

MR. SIMMONS: Let me tie this in with the earlier comment I made, Senator Clark, the meaning of work to man. In 1933, if you remember, in my testimony I speak of a doctor from Philadelphia, who identified the stages through which men go who are unemployed, feelings of loss of hope and frustration. At one stage he identified rebellion on their part as being a specific, and it seemed to me that his comments in 1933 are pertinent to the conditions before us today in Hunter's Point and in Watts; that is, an underlying problem is unemployment and idleness. We must overcome these conditions, and to the extent that we are successful I feel this will to a large degree resolve the problems of tension in these communities.

SENATOR CLARK: You know a thing that startled me about both Hunter's Point and Watts, being an easterner from a large city which has had its share of urban slums, was you go out there to Hunter's Point and it looks pretty good; the buildings are run down but the location is magnificent, there seems to be pretty good roads getting in there and back, the view over the harbor can't be beaten, the people giving no indication of unhappiness and yet a week later there was a riot. You get down to Watts and you see single houses with flower gardens, people wandering around the streets looking relatively well dressed; you see no real evidence of hunger and yet the next week there may be a riot.

How do you account for that from the welfare point of view?

MR. SIMMONS: The tensions of man, Senator Clark, are difficult to perceive on the face of things. I had the privilege of going through the Watts area almost immediately after the riots there when the buildings were still smoldering and observing, as perhaps you and others have in surrounding areas where the people live, the homes are single-dwelling homes.

SENATOR CLARK: It does not look very different from Alexandria or Arlington. This is what fooled me. Perhaps you could enlighten me on that.

MR. SIMMONS: As I say, it is a deceiving phenomenon but the physical appearance is no gauge of how people feel. You can't see the crowded conditions under which people live in these single-dwelling homes. There may be two families or three families living in one small home.

SENATOR CLARK: I am sure that is true, and I agree you can't see it driving around in a black Cadillac from the outside but I would be almost certain it was not even in the same category from C Street right down here in Washington and within a stone's throw of where we are talking about, or Brown Street in Philadelphia or

448

Harlem, because there is so much real estate there, you can spread out. Maybe I am wrong.

Tell me if I am wrong.

MR. SIMMONS: I would suggest that the situation is a universal one, whether it is Watts or Harlem. The conditions have similarities and the tensions and the problems have similarities and the appearance of these communities has little relevancy to the underlying tensions.

SENATOR CLARK: Very deceptive. You think the important thing is the job?

MR. SIMMONS: Yes, sir; I think this is the overriding thing.

SENATOR CLARK: Of course, behind jobs there must be some education, some technical skill, some vocational training. We went through a center set up by a wonderful fellow, you probably know who he is, an automobile worker. I imagine though education is important I think transportation is important, too. They don't seem to be able to get in and out of Watts.

MR. SIMMONS: The McCone commission study of the Watts riot identified transportation as a key element. The people were not mobile, they could not move from where they lived to jobs or opportunities that would lie elsewhere in the city.

SENATOR CLARK: Do you agree with that?

MR. SIMMONS: Yes; I agree this is extremely important.

SENATOR CLARK: You have an extremely heavy welfare role in **Hunter's Point and Watts?**

MR. SIMMONS: Restate that.

SENATOR CLARK: The California Welfare Department, I am not sure that the department of social welfare, but that State.

MR. SIMMONS: The State department of social welfare is a supervising agency, the program is administered by the counties.

SENATOR CLARK: I see. So all you have is an oversight over the expenditure; but are they State funds or local funds?

MR. SIMMONS: It is Federal, State, and local funds. We are the supervising agency and we write the rules and regulations governing the welfare operations.

SENATOR CLARK: But you think that your department of social welfare can solve this poverty program or make a substantial impact on the solution of the poverty program in California, or do there have to be other forces? Are you really sort of a holding operation?

MR. SIMMONS: We feel that the welfare agency has a dynamic role to play as one of the important components of a rehabilitative approach. We certainly would not expect to do it alone, we think the manpower agencies and the rehabilitation agencies of other kinds are important components as well. Three years ago, four years ago, 1963, we established in welfare the unemployed part of the

AFDC program and we had such strong feelings around the importance of people being kept busy that we wrote into the law and into the regulations that every able-bodied AFDC recipient must be engaged in an educational program, a vocational training program, a work-experience program, or in employment. That is a condition of aid in California. And to implement this the law required that a work-experience and training program be established in each of the 58 counties by the welfare department. These programs are in effect and there are literally hundreds of projects operating today to serve public welfare recipients. We have close to 200,000 adults receiving AFDC in California and almost 25 percent of them are engaged in such programs.

The Governor of the State of California and our new director are hoping to make a major thrust in moving larger numbers of AFDC recipient adults into these programs, and this is the crux, I think, of my testimony. I see the role of welfare in terms of the pretraining role; conditioning people, motivating, evaluating, working carefully with them to prepare them for the skilled training. This goes back to your point, Senator Clark, regarding the case in Mississippi. Some people are not ready to be referred to skilled training and we think welfare has a role in this because of the association of the helping services, the social work, medicine, the day care, and also this other ingredient which is what I termed in my paper a kind of occupational therapy. It encompasses the concept that work literally is therapy.

You can apply all of these other services to little avail if the man or the woman is not able to get hold of something to do to feel a restoration of hope out of that action.

SENATOR CLARK: I thought you made that point very well in your paper, and I was very much impressed with it.

SENATOR CLARK: Now you three gentlemen are all in the welfare area and you know the priority problem which exists in the poverty program where the funding, I don't think we are being unduly pessimistic, is certain to be inadequate and therefore, we have to determine where the dollar will do the most good.

Of course, you gentlemen are to some extent in the welfare business, and it would be very unusual indeed if you didn't feel that the welfare dollar went at least as far as the services dollar or perhaps the Job Corps dollar.

I would like to have you, Mr. Grais, just take a minute or two and if the other gentlemen would like to chip in to tell us why you think that Title V in the other areas which depend on your duties by overseers or administrators of welfare departments, that you can spend a dollar of poverty money just about as well or better than any of these others?

Mr. Grais: Well, this is my view, Senator. As I said before, we have a chance now to break the cycle of dependency—these two- and three-generation families on public assistance. I am thinking not only of the man of the family but also of the children who see the father going to work, and they have someone to look up to that they can be proud of. They learn that welfare does not have to be a way of life. We have people in St. Paul who had three genera- tions on assistance, and some have not worked for 15 years. This program is proving to us that these men can be placed in employ- ment. In fact, we had this work and training program in the county budget, and we were requesting $137,000 to expand it just before Title V was enacted. However, when the Title V funds became available, we immediately took advantage of the program and ex- panded our work and training efforts. I think that if a dollar is to be spent in welfare today, it should be spent in rehabilitation, not only for the individuals on welfare but for the generations that follow them.

Senator Clark: Thank you very much. Do either of you gen- tlemen want to add anything to that?

Mr. Simmons: I would like to support what Mr. Grais has said and add another comment or two. I feel that the Federal Govern- ment which is providing the leadership must develop a sense of com- mitment, which is emerging in the Economic Opportunity Act, but which is incomplete at this point; a sense of commitment which in- sures that every man has an opportunity to be at work and which does not exclude any man. The generational problem that Mr. Grais speaks to is important in that a man with a family would be ex- cluded from employment because he is 50 years old or "hard core." The children in that family would be adversely affected if their father maintains the idleness model.

So rather than considering the reduction of programs like Title V we should be moving in the opposite direction and be developing a design that establishes programs of training and education for all persons who need it and employment for all persons who seek it. . . .

Public welfare has been referring welfare recipients to man- power agencies for 32 years since the inception of the Social Secu- rity Act in 1935. This is a regularized procedure that we follow with varying results.

Now to the extent that the manpower agencies can more read- ily fulfill placement and training responsibilities, this certainly would be all to the good. I have personally no quarrel with this but I do think that the Department of Labor should deal with those individuals who are ready for skilled training and not engage them- selves in supervision or other kinds of activities in relation to the occupational therapy components which I have identified in my paper. I believe that welfare must have available to it within its administration the work experience component and a sheltered workshop component to provide the therapy that these elements offer as a part of the service programs.

MR. HALLMAN: Would you include basic literacy or adult education as a part of therapy or as a part of manpower?

MR. SIMMONS: I would include adult education courses of certain kinds. Let me explain what I mean. We are trying to set up a plan whereby every public assistance recipient in AFDC will receive at the point of intake a long-range vocational plan. Now some of the women, obviously, won't be ready for employment maybe for 5 years, because they may have small children, but they still should become engaged in an educational program that will ready them for employment at some later date.

A woman may enter in an adult education program that only consists of 2 hours a week course, for example. Now surely this should be a responsibility of public welfare.

MR. HALLMAN: Does it matter who runs this? What if there is a good program run, what if the adult education department is doing a good job in adult literacy? Would it not be appropriate for them to run this course, including for welfare recipients as well as others?

MR. SIMMONS: At the present time we make contracts with Education or other resources to provide this and I would hope that we could retain the privilege of working in that manner to insure that programs are designed to meet the needs of the people that we serve.

MR. HALLMAN: My point is should you not go where the capability is in each community rather than saying that welfare shall run all of these services every place in the country or that employment security shall run all these services? To get the services for welfare does not necessarily mean that the welfare department needs to run.

MR. SIMMONS: There is apparent logic to the position you take. It is difficult to refute but there are subtle points. It is my experience, having been in public welfare for over 20 years, that the administrative agency that has the responsibility for the people has a primary concern and can more effectively mobilize resources to meet the needs of these people than any other system and I think they need to retain some prerogatives in this respect. Otherwise, we will continue to take the "cream" off the top, if you will, of those people who may be ready and the majority of the people on welfare will continue to remain unserved.

Dr. Sheppard: Can you see any sign that the Labor Department is gearing up to take an occupational therapy approach at the Department of Labor approach?

Mr. Simmons: The interpretation that I have received of the Department of Labor position on the operation of work experience and training programs in the occupational therapy context is that the Department of Labor should assume responsibility for this function. I disagree with that position.

Mr. Hallman: They assume responsibility but the Department of Labor does not run any program at all. They contract it out through some local group. Would one of their local affiliates do it or how would it be administered?

Mr. Simmons: This is precisely to my point. They could contract with some other agency to provide the work site. We have literally hundreds of projects serving thousands of people in operation right now and we don't contract for this. We receive the training services, the work experience service free of charge from the governmental agencies.

Our only cost goes to the staffing which maintains supervision and general administrative responsibilities. It would seem to me unwise at this point when the manpower resources are so meagre to dislocate an arrangement that welfare has of this kind.

Mr. Hallman: Was there anything to prohibit them from contracting back where there is capability?

Mr. Simmons: I presume one could do this but it seems like rather an unusual way of administering a program.

Mr. Hallman: Mr. Grais, what is your understanding of the arrangements which will exist after July 1?

Mr. Grais: We had a 3-day head-bumping session with the Department of Labor last month. Mr. Simmons was there. It was my understanding that the welfare department would be responsible for pretraining and the referral for occupational training. The director of the project would be from welfare and would be in charge of the entire program.

Mr. Simmons: The arrangements that were considered in our discussion didn't alleviate my concern because it established that at any worksite, whether it was a conditioning or motivating worksite or a skilled training worksite, the Department of Labor would assume full responsibility for operation of that irrespective of how they do it, through contracts or otherwise.

Now our position is that the welfare agency should continue to administer that part which deals with the pretraining. As you know, there is a pretraining phrase in the Title V law itself, and this would be in my view a reasonable interpretation of that phrase.

MR. HALLMAN: So what you are saying is not that the law necessarily needs to be repealed but that there needs to be an interpretation on the pretraining to give considerable breadth to the welfare department's role.

MR. SIMMONS: Yes.

MR. GRAIS: The welfare departments have worked with these people and have given them service to assist them in their daily living. Sometimes they go to extreme lengths to assist them, such as getting Jack Jones out of bed at 7 o'clock in the morning and taking him to the job.

I would like to see the welfare department have the responsibility for the program and the determination of the individual's need. Let the Labor Department be responsible for training but with the direction of the entire project coming from welfare. In addition, these projects which are successful should be left intact and not be the responsibility of the Labor Department. I cite such successful projects as we have in St. Paul, for instance, in Cleveland and those that are real successes.

MR. HALLMAN: Mr. Hobson, do you have any further comments?

MR. HOBSON: Yes, I just want to say that our concern is at that step when you say in effect you turn them over to Labor to find the job training and train them. Is that all the past history of labor and the indications which we have gotten in our conversations with the Labor Department as they have come around to the various States to plan for this July 1 turnover, under this new law is it their indication that these people won't get the consideration? In other words, that the job training will in many instances be at too high a level and that the Labor Department does not have the facilities to help these people and to help motivate them further and to re-motivate them and to give them the helping hand and the pushes and the shoves and all the rest that the welfare department does do daily, and is equipped to do with their services.

In other words, what we are fearful of is that the thing will collapse because these are not the kinds of labor pool people that the Labor Department is used to operating with.

Did I make myself clear?

MR. GRAIS: Yes.

MR. HOBSON: That is the fear we have.

MR. GRAIS: I am quite against the Labor Department taking over. It appears to me that a two-headed monster has been created, and it is my prediction that we will be here again a year from today, looking at the problems which have resulted because I don't think it is going to work.

You can't have two bosses. What we are now trying to work out is an accommodation with the Labor Department whereby the welfare departments have the principal responsibility and the Labor Department has responsibility for the vocational training and placement. The welfare department would transfer money to the Labor Department for the people on its rolls which it refers for training. In other words, we are hiring the Labor Depatment to give the service which we cannot provide ourselves in those instances where we cannot provide it. It so happens that in our town we have a magnificent relationship with our employment service. Even so, when we send people down to the employment security office, they seldom get a job unless the way has been paved for them. One of the requirements when a man is accepted for welfare is that the individual must report weekly to the employment office. This procedure seldom results in job placement. The people on welfare are not the kind the employer calls for. The employer wants a man who has a skilled background of one kind or another. Most often, our people do not meet the requirements, or they would not be on relief.

We work with MDTA, and we work with the other manpower agencies in the city, and this is true around the country. In many places, however, the relationship between agencies and the department is not as good as it is in St. Paul.

MR. HALLMAN: Two weeks from now we will have representatives from both Labor and HEW before the subcommittee, and at that time we will be asking them about what is going on, and your background will be very helpful.

MR. GRAIS: I would like to be here more often, but I have drugstores to run, and I have been here three times in the last two weeks.

MR. SIMMONS: In the fiscal year 1966-67 there was a national expectation of 250,000 MDTA trainees. In California as of April 21,562 persons were trained through MDTA and 2,321 of these were welfare recipients.

Now, this is good, we are beginning to move. However, we are hoping by the end of the next fiscal year to have up to 100,000 AFDC recipients in California engaged in educational or work experience or other kinds of training programs either provided through other resources or through our own resources. At the present time we have literally thousands of people engaged in these kinds of programs.

To the extent that other resources can be brought to bear and pick up this training for those who were not in the preconditioning, the pretraining category, I would say this is great, but we should not develop legislation which interferes with the vast resources of States like California in this field already, recognizing that there are nine other States at the present time, I believe, who also have work experience programs.

We should not abandon these. There is legislation that may have this effect in 5710 that deals with the overall work experience and training programs.

In other words, 5710 picks up the essence of the provision in Title V, namely, the transfer of all welfare work experience and training programs to Department of Labor, and I believe that we should deal with this more cautiously.

Certainly we should move and develop our manpower programs but we should not establish legislation which will interfere with ongoing systems which, as I interpret 5710 would be done; that is, it would interfere with the Federal matching money that public welfare receives to support such programs at the present time.

MR. HALLMAN: Gentleman, your testimony has been very helpful to us, and as I said, it will help us prepare to ask the departments some very deep, searching questions on this.

CHAPTER 14

THE WORK INCENTIVE PROGRAM

IN 1967, THE 90TH CONGRESS passed a new Work Incentive Program law (signed by the President January 2, 1968) offering hope to millions of public assistance recipients through the provision of opportunity for education and vocational training, but begrudgingly couched the benefits in terms savoring of petulance and outright hostility against those for whom the legislation had been enacted.

Although one of the guiding principles which had motivated the legislation was the development of the latent potential of each individual, the language of the statute singled out unmarried mothers for services "preventing or reducing the incidence of births out of wedlock," and predicted the failure of such services thus: "then when the State agency has reason to believe that the home in which a relative and child receiving aid reside is unsuitable for such child because of the neglect, abuse, or exploitation of such child, it shall bring such condition to the attention of the appropriate court or law enforcement agencies." Moreover, to insure enforcement of this aspect of the law, the legislation provided for "entering into cooperative arrangements with appropriate courts and law enforcement officials . . . including the entering into financial arrangements with such courts and officials to insure optimum results under such program." Thus the American gift for ineptitude in the behavioral sciences is once more revealed—in the expectation of overcoming human problems through the strengthening of law enforcement.

While the Congress provided generously through Public Law 90-248 for vocational training and education for welfare recipients, it limited aid for specified absent parent cases so that "the average monthly number of dependent children under the age of 18 who have been deprived of parental support or care by reason of the continued absence from the home of a parent . . . for any calendar quarter after June 30, 1968, shall not exceed the number which bears the same ratio to the total population of such State under the age of 18 on the first day of the year in which such quarter falls as the average monthly number of such dependent children under the age of 18 with respect to whom payments under this section were made to such State for the calendar quarter beginning January 1, 1968, bore to the total population of such State under the age of 18 on that date." By thus forcing the limitation of aid and giving priority of entrance into vocational training to unemployed parents, failure of the program in relation to the maligned absent parent cases was at least partially insured. It would have been more logical, in view of the stated objectives of the legislation, if the Congress had given first priority of referral to vocational training for the target group—unmarried mothers.

The myth of "local responsibility" for sharing in the provision of public aid was perpetuated by the Congress through the requirement of a 20 percent contribution to the Work Incentive Program by the State or local jurisdiction, with the welfare agency assuming final liability for this amount. While manpower programs of other kinds were funded more generously by federal subventions, the poorest, most needy, hard-core segment of society was subjected to the vagaries of local financing.

Despite the inconsistent mood of the Congress and the contradictory provisions of the law, the author considered the Work Incentive Program (WIN) as historical social legislation with positive potential for providing opportunity to poor people, though he had testified against this eventuality before Congressional committees and continues to harbor doubts about the effectiveness of a manpower agency in serving the needs of hard-core public welfare groups.

BACKGROUND

In 1967, when the first session of the 90th Congress amended the Social Security Act, it provided for the cessation of community work and training activities and for the establishment of a Work Incentive Program. This cancelled the experimental Community Work and Training program which had been operated in 11 states by the Department of Health, Education and Welfare and replaced it with a permanent program to be administered by the Department of Labor. Since the Work Incentive Program is directed exclusively towards AFDC welfare recipients, it is an extremely important program for serving the target welfare population instead of screening them out as too "hard-core" or not "economically feasible" as in previous manpower programs.

Legislative developments and relations between the Department of Labor and the Department of Health, Education and Welfare across the past five years are important to our understanding of the nature of this new program, since they serve as models for it in terms of interdepartmental administration and program content.

Earlier efforts to provide manpower services for welfare clients came about as a result of 1962 amendments to the Social Security Act. Title IV, Section 409 established an Experimental and Demonstration type progam for the states on an optional 50-50 matching basis. Under Section 409, a state could develop Community Work and Training programs for public assistance clients, but the concept was slow to catch on, and though 22 states passed enabling AFDC-Unemployed Parent legislation, only 11 operated such programs of Community Work and Training which served about 12,000 trainees. In general, worthwhile and sound goals were set forth for these programs in the Social Security Act of 1962, but because the funding formula placed heavy burdens upon state and local tax resources, administration at the local level was inept, the impact of the programs was limited.

In 1964, the next significant development came with the enactment of the Economic Opportunity Act. Title V of that Act provided for work and training programs which could be 100 percent federally financed and made available to public assistance clients and other selected needy persons. The Act designated HEW as the delegate agency in these programs, which were wholly operated by State and local welfare units. In a relatively short time after enactment, all but Alabama had Title V programs in operation. The total number of trainees reached a peak of approximately 114,000 during 1965, and because of decreased funding, declined to approximately 40,000 by early 1968. The Economic Opportunity Act also established the Neighborhood Youth Corps. This program and other adult programs added later were conducted by the U.S. Department of Labor and provided work experience training for over 265,000 welfare recipients by early 1968. Concurrently, other legislation created programs with similar goals. In 1962, Congress passed the Manpower Development and Training Act, which was modified and enlarged by the Congress in 1962, 1965, and 1966 to incorporate the evolving experience of the program into the basic legislation. In 1966, the Congress specifically enlarged opportunities for welfare recipients in skill training programs and provided for transfer of the work experience training aspects of the Title V (EOA) program to a substantial degree by incorporating them into the Manpower Development and Training Act.

In 1967, prior to the enactment of the Work Incentive Program, the author participated in early policy discussions conducted in Washington, D.C. by representatives of the Department of Labor and HEW. The discussions were designed to implement legislation requiring a change-over of administrative responsibility for the Title V programs from HEW to the Department of Labor. The policy changes were hard-fought, each side of the controversy maintaining its initial intractable position. Each department retained part of authority and control, resulting in an almost untenable fragmentation of responsibility.

The basic concern of the Department of Welfare was that existing Title V programs, many of which were quite effective, should not be disturbed during the life of the project, and that its tremendous efforts expended in employment of new staff, establishment of hundreds of work experience projects under governmental auspices, and contracting with scores of educational and vocational training agencies should not be impinged upon by national realignments of authority. Moreover, there was skepticism regarding the effectiveness of the Department of Labor as a helping agent to the hard-core poor. For 30 years, while those in the ranks of welfare had uselessly referred able-bodied welfare recipients to employment, and the files of Labor Offices everywhere became cluttered with "registrations" of welfare clients, the employment effort screened off the cream of these referrals to favor very critical employers. The Department of Labor was viewed as employer-oriented and as a resource for placement of only the best qualified employee applicants, whereas the Department of Welfare had few well-qualified employee candidates on its rolls. Also, it had become apparent to many that new manpower programs springing up in the early 1960's were only a token resource and that welfare clients were essentially not employable, considering their deficiencies in attitude, education, and vocational skills. When new training and education programs had first emerged under the auspices of the Economic Opportunity Act and the Department of Labor manpower programs, those in welfare had anticipated more help. Title V, designed exclusively for welfare recipients, emerged as the primary resource for them. But historical and traditional practices of middle-class oriented employment and educational systems created a hopeless feeling that Department of Labor operations would never develop a crusade for welfare recipients.

In view of its acknowledgment that those in welfare had persuasive arguments for retaining work experience and training programs, what could the Department of Labor offer as a rationale for wishing to take over Title V and later, the entire program? After the advent of federal legislation which established welfare's responsibility for community work and training programs and the later Economic Opportunity Act Title V program, Department of Labor personnel began to feel apprehensive about potential fragmentation of their traditional functions. National, state and county employment department personnel began to disparage welfare efforts, became competitive with them, and began initiating presentations to legislatures favoring transfer of all employment and training func-

tions to the Department of Labor—a highly successful effort, incidentally, considering later Title V and Work Incentive Program
legislation. These early efforts went largely along the legislative
route, and no employment crusade emerged at any level of government which espoused the realignment of existing manpower
programs to favor welfare recipients. However, later cooperative
alignments did emerge as national goals were set by the Department
of Labor to insure at least a modest 18 percent of MDTA training
spaces be reserved for welfare recipients.

The reluctance of employment department systems during the
early 1960's could be matched by similar reluctance among those
in welfare. Welfare had its own set of traditions and attitudes,
seeking to create an image of itself as a social service agency, yet
practicing as a relief-giving system with sixteenth century law and
folklore as its standard. Welfare, of course, was only the instrument
of traditional beliefs and myths strongly held by the citizenry,
leaderless legislatures, and welfare administrations. The uninspired
leadership offered small hope for emergence of a strong social service agency supportive of goals of employment for its clientele.
Failing in the provision of social services, there was even less expectation of success in the development of community work and training programs. The record in 1968 clearly shows failure in welfare
to provide "self support" social services to welfare recipients as
provided for in the 1962 Social Security amendments. Rather,
gamesmanship in state and local legislatures and welfare administrations had consisted of acquiring the 75 percent federal administrative
subvention prize (an increase of 25 percent) with minimum change
in traditional practices. Welfare administration at the federal level
had designed an ineffective service policy which, in 1962, the author
predicted would result in little more than a new subvention formula
for state and local governments with little service benefit to the
welfare recipient. The combination of poor federal policy development and uninspired state and local administration resulted in continuation of an ineffective social service program at local levels.
Nevertheless, there were some exceptions, and the national requirement of caseload size reduction to a maximum of 60 cases eventually developed a foundation for the strong service emphasis demanded by the new Work Incentive Program.

As welfare systems were slow to implement social services
toward self support, they were even more unresponsive to the need
for development of community work and training programs. Five
years after the 1962 Social Security Act amendments provided for
an experimental community work and training program for public
assistance recipients, only 11 states were conducting such programs.
Largely, welfare administrators acknowledged that they had no

interest in administering work and training programs, believed that this was not their proper function, and expressed the belief while administering archaic and debilitating work relief programs. Welfare departments modified these attitudes somewhat when the Economic Opportunity Act, Title V program offered 100 percent federal subvention for the work experience and training programs. In the early days of the Title V program, some counties threw federal money into work relief, against federal policy, and it took months afterwards to move toward the more constructive types of programs found in the 49 states administering Title V programs by early 1968.

The earlier welfare and labor program experiences led to eventual realization of the need for expanded work and training programs for AFDC recipients and enriched labor-welfare understanding and the possibilities inherent in the kind of coordinated agency effort which can capture and effectively utilize the distinctive expertise in each department. Under the new WIN program the Department of Labor would provide for placement, vocational education and training, and public works; and the Department of Health, Education and Welfare would provide the social and rehabilitation services inherent in the new title of the federal welfare administration, such as casework, child care, group-work services, and other appropriate supporting services. The historical labor-welfare relations and the evolving understanding underlying them provided some capacity to link together large and complex programs into an effective system. Neither role was to be diminished, but each department had new opportunity and challenge to expand proper expertise in directions appropriate to its distinctive function.

The significance of the 1967 amendments to the Social Security Act which provided for the Work Incentive Program lies in a major shift in public policy relative to the welfare client, with major emphasis on his rehabilitation rather than on his long-term maintenance, and in the combining of social and rehabilitation agency resources with a single manpower funding source into one of the most comprehensive manpower rehabilitation programs yet envisioned.

The operation of the Work Incentive Program together with other training programs was delegated to the Bureau of Work-Training Programs, U.S. Department of Labor, by the Secretary of Labor. It was the intent of the Bureau to operate the program in the various states and cities of the nation through state and local employment offices wherever this was feasible and productive, and to work through other public and private agencies when necessary or desirable, with the agency operating the program at the local level responsible to the Bureau for the manner in which the activities were conducted and funded. For the manpower agency, this meant great readjustments in attitudes, administrative arrangements, fiscal realignments, and perhaps most important, interdepartmental relationships. These relationships required respect for the expertise of each department and the proper application in good faith, of a joint effort which would be more than challenged by their hard-core unemployed clientele. The deficiencies which had precluded job achievement for these clients were of many kinds: social, psychological, cultural; educational and vocational; poor work orientation and habit; loss of hope of attainment; and resource gaps in terms of child care, transportation, and work connected expenses. Each department needed to devote full attention to the task of improving its respective system toward effective interdepartmental relations which would enhance the efforts of both in reaching and helping these welfare recipients.

GENERAL PURPOSES

The purposes of the Work Incentive Program are to increase the employability of those over 16 years of age and out of school who receive welfare, place them in meaningful and permanent job roles, and thus effectively remove them from the category of welfare recipients. It is the further purpose of this program to meet the client at his level of experience and motivation and move him through an experience of work, training, and education into a position in the nation's labor force which offers the greatest utilization of his potential. The major purpose of the program is not just training, but employment with a future—*the training of individuals and placement in jobs where they have a chance to grow, careerwise, wherever possible*. To achieve this objective, it was considered necessary to utilize the full scope of the manpower service and programs established within the Department of Labor, and to coordinate nationwide utilization of manpower efforts in making a significant impact on the problem of reduction of increasing welfare rolls. The basic principle guiding such utilization of manpower resources was to be the development of the latent potential of each individual within a context of flexible programming.

Both the individual and the community gain when an AFDC family is enabled to become self-supporting. The experience of a number of programs indicates that many heads of households can attain self-support and that they desire to do so. There are, however, many serious handicaps confronting AFDC parents, particularly mothers. In enabling them to become self-supporting and increase self-respect, they may also be helped to overcome some of these handicaps.

PROGRAM CHARACTERISTICS

Identification of some of the ways in which the WIN program differs from other manpower programs may help in gaining an understanding of the total management and program processes which were developed.

1. *Client Group*—The only persons eligible for service in this program are those individuals identified as "Aid to Families with Dependent Children" (AFDC) clients by the welfare agency. This definition includes all adult members of the family and youth over the age of 16 who are not in school full time and who are receiving AFDC.

2. *Mandatory Features*—The law provides that state and local welfare agencies must refer all "appropriate" individuals on AFDC for employment or training. Individuals thus referred are considered as part of the Work Incentive Program. To prevent misunderstanding and clarify the manner in which the program would operate, the Act sets forth a number of categories of individuals who could not be considered as "appropriate" for the Work Incentive Program. Each member of the family who has attained 16 years of age and is not in school would be considered appropriate for referral except one who is ill, incapacitated, or of advanced age; is so remote from a project as to preclude effective participation in work or training; is a child attending school full-time; or is a person whose continuous presence in the home is substantially required because of illness or incapacity of another member of the household.

All recipients of assistance under this title not referred to the Secretary of Labor, including the foregoing exceptions who wanted to take advantage of the new opportunities to become self-supporting could request referral, and persons making such request would be referred to the Secretary of Labor.

If an individual referred to the Work Incentive Program refuses to accept work or undertake training, an opportunity for a fair hearing must be provided before an impartial body, for purposes of determining whether good cause existed for such refusal. If good cause is determined to exist, then the state welfare agency is so notified, the individual is no longer considered a participant in the program, will retain public assistance status, and maintenance grants cannot be cut off. If it is determined that good cause does *not* exist, then the state or local welfare agency is notified and the individual is provided 60 days of counseling and reassessment. Following this period of counseling, the state agency may deny public assistance benefits to the individual (but not necessarily the family) if the individual still refuses to participate.

3. *Size of Program*—The program must be established in each political subdivision of a state in which the Secretary of Labor determines that there are significant numbers of AFDC recipients who have attained the age of 16. In addition, however, the Secretary of Labor must use his best efforts to establish programs in whole or in part in all other political subdivisions or provide transportation to a neighboring area where there is a progam. Although the Work Incentive Program would be in a buildup period for about two fiscal years, it was obvious that Department of Labor field agencies should be prepared to receive all referrals made by welfare and to provide the manpower services available either to accomplish the rehabilitation of the client or to involve him in a special work program. No later than July 1, 1969, state public assistance plans must include provisions for a Work Incentive Program if it is to be approved. Ultimately, WIN must be prepared to provide meaningful manpower services to the public assistance clients of more than 3,000 counties in the states.

4. *Effective Date and Program Duration*—Any state could enter the Work Incentive Program on April 1, 1968, if a modification of the state welfare plan was approved by that time. Following April 1, 1968, states could enter at their option until July 1, 1968. Beginning on July 1, 1968, the Work Incentive Program became effective in each state unless "a statute of each state prevented it from complying with the requirements of such amendment" as of that date. In any event, all states were required to enter the program by July 1, 1969. This series of effective dates provided for a limited but rapid phasing-in process. Enabling state legislation was not necessarily required. Only the existence of preventive legislation could exclude a state after July 1, 1968, and then only until July 1, 1969. All other manpower programs with the Department of Labor had legal limits relative to duration; but the WIN program did not. Department of Labor testimony before Congress projected an average maximum training period of about one year. There was a maximum limit placed upon an average training period for work experience and institutional training, but this did not apply to individuals. This meant that an individual could be moved much further up the employability ladder than had been possible in other programs.

5. *Incentive*—The WIN program has several built-in incentives to encourage the public assistance client not only to participate in the program, but also to take employment. Although the effect of these incentives cannot be measured, they should not be underestimated. Cash incentives include earnings, exemptions, and direct payments. If the individual is employed or involved in on-the-job training he receives an earnings exemption covering the first $30

wages plus one-third of the remainder. The amount thus exempted would not be deducted from the welfare grant to which he would otherwise be entitled. Incentive payments of up to $30 a month are provided to all persons involved in work experience and classroom or institutional training, an amount paid in addition to the maintenance grant. The earnings exemptions are applicable to welfare recipients in all manpower programs, including those not specifically funded by the Work Incentive Program, i.e., Economic Opportunity Act programs.

The law also made mandatory the provision of child care services for small children of mothers while involved in any aspect of the Work Incentive Program as well as during the initial stages of employment. Another significant incentive involves retention of welfare status by the individual after becoming employed and until such time as his ability to participate in productive employment is assured. This provision by itself would go far to encourage the public assistance client to participate in paid employment.

FEDERAL MANAGEMENT

Federal administrative responsibility in the WIN program may be clarified by reviewing the following organizational provisions:

The current relationship between the welfare administration and the manpower administration differs significantly from the relationship previously established in Title V, in which the manpower component was supplied by the Department of Labor for a program developed and managed by the welfare agency. Title IV had assigned full responsibility for the development and administration of the manpower program to the Department of Labor, and the welfare agency role rested primarily in the determination of employability, and the orderly referral of employable recipients, while concentating its activities on the provision of social services to the public assistance family group and the enrollee. The administrative responsibility for the WIN program is now placed with the Bureau of Work-Training Programs, although legislative history indicates that the program should be carried out through the system of State Employment Service offices "wherever feasible and productive." The intention of the Department of Labor to move in this direction was stated in a memorandum of the Secretary of Labor which set in motion a realignment of responsibilities within the manpower administration in his department. To carry out both the legislative intent and departmental policy, it was obvious that the State Employment Service offices would have to share with the Bureau of Work-Training Programs a great deal of responsibility for mounting the WIN program in the field. Guidelines for the working relationship were developed by a task force which was appointed to accomplish the reorganization. In the national office, when staff members from both the Bureau of Work-Training Programs and the United States Employment Service worked together to develop program models and procedures, the author was privileged to become the only representative of welfare to serve on this National Labor Task Force during January and February of 1968.

FIELD ADMINISTRATION

The changes which evolved in regard to the relationship between the manpower administration and the field agencies had a far-reaching impact upon total program management concepts within the Department of Labor. In the past, work experience functions had been carried out by local government and nonprofit organizations; on-the-job training activities involved several types of organizations both public and private; and institutional training activities had been, in large part, the responsibility of the State Employment Service offices in cooperation with public and private educational establishments. WIN brought together for the first time in the Manpower Administration all training functions and support services, whether conducted in the classroom or at the work site. In order to make maximum utilization of State Employment Service agencies in this program, their previous role at the local level required change, and under the direction of the Bureau of Work-Training Programs, they became involved in operations which included not only those functions they had traditionally performed, but also an expanding redirection of their role in other manpower services. This did not necessarily change the existing relationships with the Office of Economic Opportunity relative to work experience programs under that legislation.

PROGRAM COMPONENTS AND CONCEPTS

WIN program components were designed to deal with the broad range of problems which must be faced in training welfare recipients for jobs. The specific terms used to designate the components are considered descriptive, but since they do not show the operating processes involved, care must be taken to avoid any implication of rigidity in their applications. The components which contribute to the removal of the individual from dependency upon welfare and give him maximum freedom of choice in becoming a meaningful, full-time member of the labor force, are as follows:

1. Initial Assessment.
2. Orientation.
3. Employability Evaluation and Planning.
4. Work Internship.

 5. Work Experience.
 6. Institutional Training.
 7. On-the-Job Training.
 8. Followup On-the-Job Training.
 9. Basic Education.
10. General Educational Development.
11. Job Engineering.
12. Job Development and Job Placement.

INITIAL ASSESSMENT

Initial Assessment covers a period of a week or more, during which time an individual receives one or more counseling interviews and appropriate tests. A conference will be held between the employment counselor, the welfare caseworker, and the individual client, at which time a decision will be reached with respect to the next step to be taken. Alternatives are: (1) Nonacceptance of the individual into the program due to refusal to participate; (2) referral to job placement services, to other training situations; or (3) to an apprenticeship situation; and continuation into the next phase of the program.

Orientation—Each program provides for a period of intensive orientation and preliminary job education for those persons not immediately job-ready. The period of orientation varies from two weeks to four weeks maximum. Observations of work experience and training programs for the disadvantaged, experimental and demonstration programs such as JOBS NOW, and programs under Title V of the Economic Opportunity Act show that this orientation period is necessary but that *it must be kept as brief and intensive as possible*. The individual is counseled regarding the nature of the program, its purposes, and the variety of opportunities available to him as a result of his participation, and is given intensive education in the essential elements involved in securing and holding a job. Orientation covers such areas as neatness, relationship with fellow employees, promptness, avoidance of absenteeism, employers' expectations, the handling of difficult personal situations on the job, the purpose of testing, counseling, and job referral, and the handling of grievances.

In general, the orientation is designed to provide meaningful insights into average office or industry requirements, and to prepare the enrollee for the new or unusual circumstances which may confront him. Techniques involve seminars, group discussions, roleplaying, and preliminary guidance in tests and interviews. Vocational counseling begins during this period, together with the development of an employability plan.

All persons entering into the program participate in the orientation except those deemed completely job-ready. Following the orientation phase, the individual is assigned to one of the program work and training components or is referred directly to a job. This may vary from project to project, but in any event, a basic core of participants in the orientation will be ready for job roles.

Employability Evaluation and Planning—Each enrollee participates in a continuous process of evaluation and planning which is designed to move him into a job through the most appropriate work and training route. Evaluation of the individual's capability begins during the first week of orientation and extends throughout his participation in the program. The evaluation of capabilities is balanced by knowledge of labor force needs and of the mechanisms available for education and training.

The employability plan is the key concept which relates to manpower development. Since this plan is never final, but undergoes constant change as the trainee moves through the program, it assists in maintaining continuity without rigidity. Employability planning is an extremely flexible, goal-oriented mechanism through which the individual will be moved into equitable job roles at whatever point is most appropriate in his job training.

At several points in the program, the employability evaluation and planning process provides answers to critical decisions. At the end of the orientation period, it provides the basis for deciding the direction of the enrollee's future program activities. During work internship, it evaluates the individual in his relationship to various internship roles. During one of the several work and training activities, it provides the basis for determining the individual's readiness to enter into permanent job roles. Upon the completion of work experience or instructional training, it provides the basis for determining whether the enrollee should enter into a followup on-the-job training activity, be moved from one type of training experience to another, e.g., work experience to institutional training or OJT to work experience, or receive basic education or GED, and under what conditions.

Work Internship—Work internship is a specialized program component lasting approximately 10 weeks. Its purpose is to provide further insight into the initial problems of training specific individuals for job roles, and to uncover not readily perceivable potentials within the individual. During the period of work internship, the enrollee will participate in from two to four distinctly different work situations.

Work internship is designed to deal with two issues which confront a program designed to deal with welfare recipients—unforseen personal or work related problems which may inhibit the enrollee's progress, and the unforseen capability of the enrollee to advance to higher skills. Review of the many manpower programs involving welfare recipients and other disadvantaged persons reveals that a number of problems arise during work and training experience which are relatively unforeseen until the individual is placed into a working situation. In addition, the chronically unemployed may have extremely limited points of view regarding the types of jobs available and the skills required. On the other hand, programs dealing with the disadvantaged place them too often in jobs which have relatively low skill requirements, and because they successfully handle such jobs roles, they are left there without consideration of the fact that they might successfully handle more meaningful job roles with higher skill components. Some who do well in custodial jobs may also do well in jobs requiring greater skill and providing more hope for upgrading.

Work Experience—Work experience is the assignment of an individual to a job situation in which he performs duties under the supervision of the regular employer as well as under supervision and counseling by project staff. He receives training through the performance of work tasks while developing a broad range of work related skills and understanding. He is not anticipating employment in the particular agency or organization in which he is working. In addition to acquiring skills, the individual is motivated and given more adequate perception of himself in relationship to the world of work through performance on the job site.

Because of the limited or negative experience of the chronically unemployed and welfare recipient plus many hindering personal and social problems that must be overcome, entry into the competitive job market requires a larger variety of services and experience than normally would be given to individuals seeking employment. This includes relationships with supervisors and fellow workers, relationships of pay to work produced, the manner in which one must approach a prospective employer, such necessities as promptness, cleanliness, regularity, and a knowledge of job alternatives. *Training the unemployable for the world of work provides an experience which provides a body of knowledge far beyond the skill qualifications for performing a particular task.*

The participant in work experience or training does not engage in a series of random, unrelated activities, but is carefully guided into a world of work where the inter-related nature of actions taken and duties performed must be necessarily understood. Agencies seeking to provide work experience or work training to the chronically unemployed must insure that the nature of the work required of the enrollee on the job site and the quality of the supervision provided are such that he can begin to structure skill patterns. The enrollee must be clearly distinguished from the normal participant in the labor market by virtue of the fact that he has not previously been given sufficient work opportunity and guidance to provide this type of knowledge. Many enrollees will be involved in the New Careers type of experience and a sizeable proportion will receive concurrent education, usually of the basic remedial nature as they participate in the work experience training. Work experience extends for an average period of 26 weeks, although this varies considerably according to the type of job role in which the individual is involved.

Institutional Training—Institutional training in WIN is similar to that developed under the Manpower Development Training Act for over 60,000 welfare recipients. It is a combination of classroom vocational, education and workshop training generally coupled with basic education, and can in most instances be coupled with on-the-job training experiences. The average period of training is 28 weeks.

The type of training provided in this program component varies from low level or semi-skilled occupations to highly skilled ones, including those of the key punch operator, heavy equipment operator, or clerk stenographer. The training may be provided either by public or private agencies according to the needs of the individual and available facilities.

The program is designed for the individual and is aimed at his entry into the labor market at a competitive level. Enrollees will generally remain in training until they have completed the experience, but the employability evaluation process will aid them in securing a job at any point in their training where this is deemed appropriate. It is estimated that 33 percent of the trainees will enter into a job before completing the full course. The system is flexible and is directed towards the specific problems of the welfare recipient.

On-the-Job Training—In on-the-job training, the enrollee is placed for training in a work situation where it has been indicated that he will be hired upon successful completion of training. He receives wages paid by the employer in accordance with the wage scale prevailing in the job role to which he is assigned. The employer receives compensation for excessive waste of materials and for costs of increased supervision or training. The program may include instructional periods or may be coupled with education.

During the period of on-the-job training, the individual is carefully coached by vocational counselors and caseworkers. The utilization of this program component has been shown to be particularly successful in dealing with employment problems of the disadvantaged, including those on welfare. It requires, however, a close staff relationship to the enrollee, and the development of special understanding on the part of the employer seeking to provide a job for the individual. Enrollees who successfully complete on-the-job training have, in reality, already found their job role and place of employment.

Followup On-the-Job Training—Followup on-the-job training is a specialized program component designed to bridge the gap between the training and the experience of being a wage oriented member of the labor force. In many instances, welfare recipients, because of past negative experiences, experience anxiety at the thought of leaving the welfare role for a job in private industry. The fear of failure together with the problems of re-entering the welfare system if failure does occur, lead many persons to consciously or subconsciously reject job opportunities.

The enrollee is placed into the job situation after going through referral and hiring procedures. The job he is working on is the job he is expected to retain. He receives a salary, nearly normal supervisory attention, special coaching concerning problems, and the employer is similarly assisted. No training expense allowance is made, and the amount paid to the employer for supervisory training and waste of materials is only half of the compensation paid for such items in on-the-job training.

The advantages of this approach lie in the fact that it allows the individual to enter the world of work in a wage oriented fashion and receive coaching on special problems encountered during this transitional period. It further allows the individual to remain technically a part of the welfare program for a brief period without being dependent upon assistance payments. Wages received during this period will offset assistance payments. This type of training lasts for eight weeks.

Basic Education—A substantial number of welfare recipients have less than the minimum education necessary to continue participation in the world of work. It is estimated that 50 percent of the enrollees will need some basic education. The length of time required will vary according to the individual, but will average 14 weeks. Experience in dealing with welfare recipients and other disadvantaged persons reveals that such education is more meaningful and more useful to the individual when coupled with vocational experience like work experience, institutional training, or on-the-job training. In addition, the Department of Labor has for some time recognized the need for a specialized curriculum which couples vocational goals with the experience of the adult and his educational needs.

General Educational Development—General educational development programs are aimed at those who have approached the completion of high school by entering junior or senior high school, and whose future vocational progess is dependent upon having the equivalent of a high school education. It is estimated that five percent of the enrollees will participate in this high school equivalency program.

Job Engineering—In its most practical sense, job engineering involves sophisticated determinations of how the utilization of manpower can be most effectively redesigned within an institution to achieve the highest level of quality in delivery of services with available personnel. To accomplish this, however, there must first be a comprehensive and functional analysis both of occupations and service systems. Such analysis may lead to effective redivision and reallocation of tasks of workers, ranging from the lowest to the highest in authority, responsibility, and skill. The effort to carry this through would be termed job engineering or redesign of agency positions in either subprofessional, support, or auxiliary categories. These new positions utilize the skill and the potential skills of individuals trained in this program. In addition, persons filling these newly designed jobs can aid in overcoming sizeable manpower gaps in health services, education, welfare services, law enforcement, and many other occupations. Individuals in these positions would not be performing make-work tasks. They would have responsible job roles with every reasonable anticipation of advancement in accordance with normal personnel practices. Such jobs are not subsidized; they are created in answer to the sometimes desperate manpower needs within various portions of our economy, public and private.

The redesign and restructuring inherent in job engineering cannot be easily separated from issues of upward mobility, quality and accessibility of services, types of training and education available to trainees and regular staff, certification, accreditation, civil service, and merit systems requirements, and the permanency of work situations in agencies following initial training periods. To maximize the potential of new positions, careful consideration must be given to structuring them to allow for upward mobility in a system of ladders or lattice work which permits movement of persons, regardless of level of skill or responsibility, to different, more responsible positions. Training and education must be carefully related to the kinds of jobs engineered and the types of ladders used for mobility. By necessity, this directly affects methods of certification of skills and education, and civil service requirements, which set basic standards for public service jobs. Standards involved in certification, accrediting, merit systems, and civil service obviously will have to be studied and revised where necessary to permit the establishment of new categories of positions, regardless of where on the spectrum of achievement and responsibility the job engineering occurs.

Job Development and Job Placement—Job development and job placement are familiar words in the lexicon of manpower services. In the context of this program, it refers to the development of a wage-paying job role in either the public or private sector through the specific cultivation of employers. Job development begins early in the program and is aimed at securing a meaningful job role related to the experience of the trainee. It implies assurance that the employer will give priority to the hiring of participants in the program.

Job placement actually moves individuals into permanent jobs. It utilizes openings already available and those acquired during job development activities. The concept of job placement referred to here includes special vocational counseling related to the specific placement and also job adjustment services that are required as the individual begins his new work role. Job development and job placement activities will be required by all individuals in the program, including those directed to jobs immediately following orientation, those involved in on-the-job training, and those moving from any work experience or training component into employment. Job placement services will be provided to all individuals entering into employment regardless of whether they have completed program activities. Job development and placement activities will be continuously related to the process of employability evaluation and planning, and these two components represent the dual approach to both the client and the employer.

Local Operation of Project—The operation of the WIN Program revolves around the central principle of retaining flexibility in working with the individual while utilizing all available manpower resources in a coordinated and integrated fashion. The application of this principle to projects at the local level has a number of obvious results. Three, however, are worthy of special mention. First, the project will rely upon job engineering and job development together with specialized job placement, not simply on regular labor market channels. Second, the approach to the enrollee with problems is based on a follow-through concept rather than on accepting him as a dropout. Third, the project will continue the followup procedure after placement instead of terminating contacts with the person placed.

STRUCTURED WORK INCENTIVES—PROGRAM COMPONENTS

The WIN Program described by Congress identifies three components—regular employment, education and training, and special work projects. Although each component is backed by all the required manpower and welfare services, the program is not limited to these elements.

All persons referred by the local welfare agency to the Work Incentive Program are initially interviewed to determine whether they are currently job-ready. It has been estimated by the Bureau of Employment Service that as many as 20 percent of all persons referred will be ready and capable of accepting and performing meaningful employment in the regular economy without undergoing training. Thousands of persons leave the welfare rolls each month because of employment. The program must insure that they are given the maximum opportunity to obtain meaningful long-term employment and that their capabilities and potentials are not overlooked in favor of temporary menial job placement. Those not entering directly into employment undergo intensive orientation and evaluation prior to being referred to various types of training opportunities.

The key to success of the Work Incentive Program is an ongoing developmental relationship between the client, the counselor, and the social worker. Participants may be placed in or recycled to assessment services, training, or employment as individual needs dictate. Prior to entry into training, each individual will be given an "employability plan" which will state general goals and outline the developmental activities necessary. This plan will be changed and/or elaborated upon as problems develop and as the capacities and skills of the individual come to life through the training and work process. At the local level, those directed to the manpower agency by the welfare agency will be referred to three types of opportunities in the following components:

Regular Employment and On-the-Job Training—In the first component, the manpower agency would inventory the work history of each person, using aptitude and skill testing to get a clear picture of his employment potential. Those with work skills needed in the locality would be referred to potential employees and as many as possible could be moved immediately into regular employment. Others might be moved into on-the-job training slots under federal training programs.

Upon termination of an initial orientation period those individuals deemed to be immediately available for placement in employment (including OJT) would be provided with labor market information by an interviewer and job market analyst. Employer contacts and job development efforts would be immediately initiated in the client's behalf and if suitable employment failed to develop, job restructuring efforts would be undertaken. Should these efforts be unsuccessful because of the client's outmoded or obsolescent job skills, deficiencies overlooked or underemphasized during initial counseling, he may be rephased to participate in certain exploratory activities to remedy the deficiencies or he may be given brief re-

fresher training to sharpen skills dulled through lack of use. It is
anticipated that a sizeable number of welfare clients will qualify
in this category without additional services.

Institutional and Work Experience Training—In the second
component, those who need some form of training, classroom, or
work experience would be assigned to training suitable for them
and for jobs available in the area. During the training period, they
would receive their public assistance grant plus up to $30 a month
as a training incentive. The type of training available would include basic education, teaching of skills in a classroom setting,
employment skills, and work experience. Only public employers or
private nonprofit employers organized for a public purpose could
be used in work experience projects.

Those considered not job-ready would be given the opportunity
to engage in an intensive employability development program related to individual needs, and the vocational plans identified initially in the first orientation component would determine the nature
and extent of services given. Uppermost in the mind of the counselor would be the client's need to acquire job skills through work
experience or institutional training, supported by basic education
and high school equivalency (GED) where necessary. Those not
ready for skill training would be exposed to work experience situations to develop motivation and good work habits and to enable
further exploration of their abilities and interests. Basic education
could be introduced at this stage as part of the vocational activity.
Not only can opportunity for recasting vocational goals and plans
on the basis of these experiences be afforded at this stage, but flexibility in redirecting vocational plans and arranging various combinations of training and supportive services would also be encouraged at every point in the client's developmental process.

Special Work Projects—Under this third program component,
the Department of Labor would enter into agreements with public
agencies or private nonprofit organizations for special work projects
to employ those found to be unsuitable for training or for whom
jobs in the regular economy cannot be found at the time. Participants in these projects would receive wages from their employers
for the time worked instead of their regular assistance grants, and
the grant for each participant (or 80 percent of the wages, whichever is less) would be paid by the state welfare agency to the manpower agency. The manpower agency places this money in special
accounts to reimburse employers for a portion of the wages paid to
participants, and one or more such accounts would be maintained
in each state. The Secretary of Labor would contract for this type
of work on the best terms he could negotiate, and the amounts paid
by him to employers would depend on those negotiations but could

not be larger than the funds provided by the state welfare agency. The Secretary of Labor negotiates each special work project in order to obtain a contribution to the wage payment from each employer which fairly represents the net value of the services which the employer receives from participants. It is expected that in many cases the Secretary can arrange for sufficient contribution from employers to preclude the need for all of the funds provided by the welfare agency.

An important factor of the third component special work projects is that in most instances the client would no longer receive a welfare check. The money paid by employers would be a "true" wage, subject to all income, social security, and other taxes just as in regular private employment. Each participant receives the minimum wage required by law if any is applicable to the work he performs. Wages earned are excluded in determining need in computing the amount of the client's assistance grant. Participants are thus guaranteed that their total income while engaged in the project will equal at least the amount of the assistance grant to which they are entitled plus 20 percent of the wages paid to them by their employer under the project. In no case does the state welfare agency pay a total which is more than the maintenance grant would have been.

The agreements between the Secretary of Labor and public or private nonprofit employers for operation of these projects will determine the following provisions:

1. The portion of the wage to be paid by the employer and the portion to be paid by the Secretary.

2. The wage rate to be paid to each participant and the number of scheduled hours of work per week.

3. Access by the Secretary to the premises where the work will be conducted.

4. Termination of any agreement by the Secretary after reasonable notice.

When all the available resources of the first and second components of the program have been fully applied to the client, and it is determined that regular employment or skill training is not currently suitable, he is referred to the third or special work project component, and the counselor and aide who have been working with the client will bring him in contact with an employment specialist. After reviewing the case, the employment specialist determines which type of work is appropriate. If a vacancy exists, the client is targeted into that program; if not, the employment specialist takes steps to create a job for the client, works closely with an employer relations representative and the counselor or aide, carries out negotiations with the employer concerning work conditions and related matters, and enters into a contractual relationship with the employer. The counselor or aide maintains continuous contact with the client, and the employment specialist maintains continuous contact with the employer. When later significant changes occur in the work situation, a reassessment of the client's status is made by the counselor. Reassesssments will be made at least every six months, with or without significant changes in the job client relationship, and when deemed appropriate by the counselor, the client will be provided extra supportive services or will be recycled into other phases of the Work Incentive Program.

The Secretary of Health, Education, and Welfare takes appropriate steps, under the provisions of the bill, to assure that payments from state welfare agencies to the Secretary of Labor are made in a timely manner to insure that the regular payments to special work project employers can be made by the Secretary of Labor in accordance with agreements for operation of the projects.

Each state is authorized to establish one or more review panels with authority to approve the establishment of all special work projects in which participants are to be employed by private nonprofit organizations. During the first full fiscal year of operations, 1969, and for public agencies only, the Secretary of Labor was authorized to pay into such accounts the difference between the amounts paid by state welfare agencies and the wages paid each participant. In effect, the Federal Government paid the state agencies' share.

COST, EVALUATION, AND OTHER GENERAL PROVISIONS

Under the law, federal contributions to the cost of Work Incentive Programs could not exceed 80 percent of the total cost. The 20 percent nonfederal contribution would be in cash or kind, and was required to be arranged for (but not necessarily paid by) the state welfare agency. The amount of employers' contributions to wages under the special work projects and the cost of evaluation are not included in computing the cost of a program.

In the event that a 20 percent nonfederal contribution is not made in any state, the Secretary of Health, Education, and Welfare can withhold amounts due that state under other specified titles of the Social Security Act until the amount so withheld together with the amount of any nonfederal contribution made within the state equals 20 percent of the cost of the Work Incentive Program. Any amounts so withheld are transferred to the Secretary of Labor for use in paying the cost of work experience programs within the state and must be considered as a nonfederal contribution. This is an explicit expression of the determination of Congress that this program shall be fully and expeditiously implemented.

Evaluation and Research—Provision is made for evaluation and research in connection with the Work Incentive Program. The Secretary of Labor conducts such evaluations jointly with the Secretary of Health, Education, and Welfare. Many anti-poverty program problems today can be traced to failure to maintain a proper system of evaluation. High priority is placed on assuring appropriate evaluation. Despite the full responsibility in the Labor Department for the operation of the Work Incentive Program, the Secretary of Health, Education, and Welfare must play a vital role in evaluation since his agencies will have the responsibility for referral and the provision of social and welfare services. The Secretary of Labor can authorize research on evaluation techniques so that those now in use may be perfected and new techniques may be developed.

Continuation of Services—Services related to the Work Incentive Program and provided by the Secretary of Labor may continue for such period as the Secretary determines necessary in order to qualify a client for full employment even though he is no longer eligible for an assistance grant. Such followup services indirectly reduce AFDC rolls by substantially cutting the number of families returning to welfare from unsatisfactory working experiences.

Average One-Year Enrollment—The Secretary of Labor designs the programs so that the institutional and work experience training component is limited to an average training period not exceeding one year. It is recognized that restoration to employability of those on welfare is not an easy task, and that problems accumulated for decades cannot be solved overnight; but since unduly prolonged training benefits no one, the provision for training is designed to permit an intensive training program that will move participants to self support in the shortest possible time.

Relocation—The manpower agency may assist participants to relocate their residence when necessary in order to enable them to become permanently employable and self-supporting. Such assistance may not exceed the reasonable cost of transportation for the family and its household goods and a reasonable relocation allowance. Relocation assistance may be given only to persons who will be employed at their place of relocation at wage rates which will meet at least their full need, as determined by the state to which they will be relocated. No participant may be forced to relocate. The Congress envisioned only limited use of this provision. The average cost of each family thus relocated is estimated at only $360, while the first year savings would average five times that amount.

This concludes the general description of the WIN Program. We will now review public social welfare considerations. The author, as Chairman of a Department of Labor Task Force Sub-

Committee, prepared the following materials related to nature of population groups, provision of social services, child care section, and activity centered therapy proposals.

The WIN program was designed exclusively to serve AFDC recipients, who could be broadly characterized according to family composition and achievement level as follows:

Family Composition—The AFDC caseload, in terms of family composition, is divided into four parts:

Absent Parent: This category approximates 67 percent of the caseload. The family consists largely of a woman as the head of the household with approximately three children.

Incapacitated Parent: This group, largely of families with the male head of the household incapacitated, consists of approximately 18 percent of the caseload.

Unemployed Parents: This represents a small number, approximately 60,000 cases or 6 percent of the caseload in 21 states.

Widows with Children: Only about 7 percent of the AFDC caseload consists of widows with children.

Other: Comprises 2 percent of the caseload.

Achievement Level—Statistical evidence available in public agencies showed that in 1968, typical AFDC parents were low achievers. The adult had little education and functioned approximately at three grades lower than the grade level achieved; had little if any vocational skill, and at best, intermittent work experience. To the extent that work had been obtained, it was in menial, low-paying jobs.

The combination of family characteristics had produced adults with low aspiration and meagre hope of greater achievement, the so-called "hard-core" candidates for rehabilitation. Moreover, the children in these families tended to mimic parental attitudes which resulted occasionally in "generational poverty." It was, therefore, imperative that consideration of the target population include the out-of-school unemployed youth living in the AFDC family.

The importance of fully understanding the nature of the caseload cannot be overemphasized. The Work Incentive Program would be working largely with women whose social, psychological, and attitudinal characteristics are profoundly deficient and disturbed, and with whom loss of hope of employment goal achievement is all-pervasive. Such problems and deficiencies cannot be overcome quickly. They require endless patience, nonjudgmental attitudes by employment, welfare, and education staff, and more important, flexibility in local program development. Guidelines should not, for example, fix an educational program at four weeks when possibly eight or more weeks would be required by some of the trainees.

Evaluation of Individual—Before referral to the Work Incentive Program, the welfare agency would evaluate the readiness of the individual, as a potential employable. This judgment would take into consideration the social, psychological, and physical conditions plus the need for child care. A favorable evaluation would accommodate an early referral to WIN, and an unfavorable evaluation, related to problems in one or several of the qualifying elements, would require application of appropriate services to enable the client to overcome obstacles which deter achievement of employment. The welfare agency would provide a full range of service appropriate to the problems presented.

Provision of Continuing Welfare Services—In addition, welfare would provide services to all individuals referred to WIN in order to support the adjustment of these individuals to the training and employment goal, but the services would remain in the context of the agency's prescribed function. In summary, the function of welfare is to prepare an individual for referral for employment and training and to provide appropriate services while that individual is in training.

Goal-directed Welfare Services—Since effective utilization of employment resources is essential, the welfare agency would refer all potential trainees. Those with physical, emotional, and child care problems would receive effective services from the welfare agency to insure removal of obstacles and to prepare as many for training and employment as possible.

The welfare agency would develop, as authorized by federal law, a range of family and child welfare services directed to the objectives of improving individual capacity for self-support and self-care; maintaining and strengthening family life (home and money management, counseling, family life education, family planning services, consumer education and protection, housing and legal services); and fostering child development, parent education, and child care services. The welfare agency would be responsible for program content, administrative arrangements and realignments to provide social work, family life education, health, and other services to the target population, and in collaboration with other community resources, must deliver a range of services to meet immediate and long-term problems of the families.

Some members of Congress recognized that much patient work would be needed to improve levels of living and personal and family functioning to assure continuity of care of children, reduction in out of wedlock births, and readiness for training or employment.

Referral Priorities—The welfare agency, in making referrals to the Department of Labor, would give priority to the following goups:

1. AFDC-U fathers, within the first 30 days of application for aid.

2. Out-of-school youth, male and female, age 16 and over, not employed, and not planning to return to school. (Federal legislation authorized the continuation of AFDC to youth 18 to 21 years of age, enrolled in a school or in technical or vocational training.)

3. AFDC mothers with suitable child care plans.

4. Other individuals over 16 in the home who determine to be ready for referral (incapacitated fathers or other caretaker relatives).

5. Mothers ready for training or employment, but lacking suitable child care plans or other enabling services.

6. Referrals from activity centered therapy and other readiness programs.

In each state or area, these priorities would receive joint consideration, and by mutual agreement would be scheduled as to sequence, timing, and estimated numbers to represent a realistic approach to varying case problems.

Child Care Services—Federal law emphasizes that any "such relative, child, or individual who is referred to the Secretary of Labor . . . is furnished with child-care services . . ." Child care services are public social services which substitute for or are supplemental to care given by parents for children living in their own homes or away from their homes for less than 24 hours a day. These services are part of a child care plan developed by the agency with parents for purposes of maintaining and strengthening family life.

In 1968, there were places for 473,000 children in licensed day care facilities. By 1969, only 200,000 additional children, including children of AFDC mothers who have taken jobs or entered into a training program, can be accommodated. The projected increase in facilities is not nearly large enough to take care of anticipated need. The demands for day care services which will occur as the result of Public Law 90-248 alone, would mean at least a doubling of facilities. In addition, new methods of care will be developed, and night care of children, as well as before and after school supervision, will also become pressing as mothers take jobs with odd hours of employment.

There was expectation on the part of Congress that the states would act quickly to provide child care and other supportive services for parents or relatives who are in training or employment since child care resources were in short supply. It was urgent, therefore, that the welfare agency clarify the numbers of children in need of a child care plan, the ages of these children, the kinds of resources needed, the priorities in terms of geographical locations and groups to be served, the responsibility of each state for setting and maintaining standards, and the methods of financing these resources. It was equally urgent, in spite of pressures to move quickly, that the states develop programs to include the three essential elements of social, educational, and health services, and avoid purely custodial care.

Child care service plans must be established with reference to the following basic considerations:

1. Child care services must be furnished where needed to make it possible for the mother to take advantage of work and training opportunities and participate in the Work Incentive Program.

2. Agencies must be prepared to provide and support a variety of methods of child care. There is no definition of child care services in the Act, but by mandating the establishment of a progam for *each* adult, the intent of Congress seems to be that the provision of supportive services, such as child care services, will take into consideration the particular needs of each child and adult: (a) Families differ in their child care needs; and no single method of child care will be suitable for all families, since there is no common denominator for such needs. (b) Day care services and homemaker services, which are cited as child care services in the Committee reports, can be construed as prescribed methods of child care although they are not the only acceptable methods. Many parents will prefer to establish a child care plan in their own homes or with relatives or neighbors. The costs of such plans will be federally reimbursed.

3. It is the responsibility of the states to assure that adequate safeguards and protection are provided for children whose parents are not available to provide care for part of the day, that the care provided is appropriate for the child, and that specific standards of care are met.

4. Since sufficient resources for the child care which must be provided do not presently exist, agencies must develop their own child care resources and must promote expansion of existing resources. Employment and welfare agencies must cooperatively establish child care training centers and on-the-job experience programs including child care with day care focus; a homemaker program; housekeeping services; general maintenance work; cooking; attendant care (for OAS and APTD welfare recipients); and home health, case and community aides. Child care training centers should be located in poverty areas where welfare recipients live, and should care for recipients' children, including those of center trainees and other welfare mothers. The trainee homemakers will receive training and on-the-job experience in the homes of other welfare recipi-

ents such as the aged and disabled. The training program should be administered by the employment service.

Referrals of children to child care training centers would be made by the public welfare agency; referrals of trainees, by the Employment Service. The center would determine vocational aptitude of the trainee and make appropriate placements in the center. The welfare agency would establish child care standards for the center, provide ongoing evaluation of the program, and render casework and other supportive services, as needed, to the trainees and children.

In summary, the Sub-Committee emphasized, the child care responsibility of the welfare agency would be carried out through a variety of methodologies to insure resources of appropriate quality and kind for all Work Incentive Program trainees and employables. In some circumstances, such as in a child care training center, the welfare agency would work cooperatively with the employment agency in combining services and resources to provide new child care and training programs in local communities.

Interdepartmental Collaboration and Arrangements—The author emphasized in his work on the Department of Labor Task Force Committee that inter-agency welfare and labor agreements must stress the importance of close collaboration between the welfare worker and the employment counselor in all case activity. Required collaborative arrangements were therefore proposed as follows:

1. Joint consultation between the social worker and the employment counselor to develop a case plan within a specified period after referral by the welfare agency.

2. Conferences which evaluate periodically (at least every three months) the progress of the case, needed actions, or changes in plans.

3. Joint participation in an Interdepartmental Case Review Committee.

4. Interdepartmental liaison.

5. Interdepartmental training progams.

Policy: Interdepartmental relations between the employment and welfare systems must be characterized first, by a clear understanding of respective functions and second, by the development of reasonably flexible interdepartmental arrangements which facilitate the work of the employment counselor and social worker. Such arrangements must fall within a prescribed perimeter.

Liaison: The need for communication at each level of administration between the manpower agency, the social and rehabilitation service agency, and the education agency is imperative and should not be restricted or obscured by structured formal agreements. Each agency should designate a liaison representative familiar with the respective roles and functions of his department at every level of operations. The representative will disseminate information within his organization on basic policies, objectives, and operational responsibilities. Meetings of liaison representatives will be called as necessary for the exchange of information, reviewing program evaluations, and progress reports and the representative in each department and at each administrative level will be responsible for arrangements necessary to conduct on-site evaluations or visits. Every effort should be made to coordinate visits to worksites and training facilities to avoid unnecessary interruptions of work and training schedules.

Interdepartmental Case Review Committee: In recognition of the need for close interdepartmental coordination and cooperation at the local level to effectively serve AFDC recipients, and the need for interdepartmental arrangements to deal with special situations, problem cases, and respective areas of responsibility in providing services to the AFDC family group, an Interdepartmental Case Review Committee was proposed by the author at the local level with an employment counselor, a social worker, a representative from education, and a community service worker as permanent members. In addition, representatives from work training and experience projects, OJT projects, an employer, medical or psychiatric consultants, or other individuals familiar with the work or training situation would be asked to participate in review discussions. The members of the Committee jointly review the following cases:

1. All cases of questionable readiness for referral to the Employment Service, including incapacitated parent cases.

2. All cases where there is a question of refusal or referral without good cause will be reviewed prior to requiring a fair hearing to determine if the problem is subject to solution without a hearing.

3. All cases where trainees are experiencing problems of adjustment resulting from unseen personal, family, or work related problems which cannot be resolved by social worker-employment counselor consultation.

4. All cases where trainees seek a fair hearing will be referred for evaluation prior to the hearing.

The Department of Labor accepted the recommendation for the Interdepartmental Case Review Committee and included it in policy directives.

Continuing Services Following Employment: The Departments of Labor and Welfare must establish interdepartmental agreements to insure continuity of services and assistance for persons needing supplemental help after placement in employment or special work projects. These continuing resources will be of two kinds: social services, employment counseling, and other appropriate services as needed; and medical care, child care, and supplemental work-connected expenses as needed to continue the individual in employment.

Interdepartmental Training for Joint Intervention: The National Labor Task Force Sub-Committee emphasized the importance of joint work between the departments of employment, welfare, and education in serving the individual client toward his employability goal. It is necessary that all field level personnel understand the respective roles of each department in order to achieve this goal. One of the instruments for achieving the objective is the development at all levels of government of an interdepartmental training program. This program will generally pursue the following policy criteria, standards, and practices:

1. At the federal level, the Bureau of Work-Training Programs of the U.S. Department of Labor will establish an interdepartmental committee to be responsible for the development of a joint training system, program content for the operating staff at the field level, and methodology through the intergovernmental system for achieving the training goal. The Bureau will assume chairmanship of the interdepartmental training committee, which includes representation from Social Rehabilitation Services, the Bureau of Employment Security and the Office of Education.

2. At the state level, a counterpart interdepartmental training committee will be established and will include representation from welfare, employment and education, and the chairman will be the employment service representative. This committee will establish state policy, taking into account federal standards and criteria in respect to the state training program. The employment service will administratively implement the policy established by this committee.

3. At the county level, an interdepartmental training committee will be established consisting of representatives from the departments of welfare, employment, and education. The chairman of this committee will be the employment service representative. The employment service at the county level will be responsible for administering the departmental policies prescribed by the interdepartmental committee, taking into account federal and state standards and criteria.

As guidelines for the training committee activities at each of the three levels of government, the following principles were proposed:

1. Training of the employment counselor, the social worker, and the educator, in broad context, will be a joint training effort. Content of the program and policies associated with its length will

be established by the county interdepartmental training committee within the framework of prescribed policy from federal and state interdepartmental committees. Each of these committees at the varying levels of government will keep their prescription of policy within a general framework so that descending levels will have flexibility of policy development appropriate to their functions. In narrow context, each of the departments of employment, welfare, and education will train respective staff in terms of upgrading functional expertise.

2. The training program must become an integral function of the welfare, employment, and educational systems and cannot be delegated to educational or other kinds of training resources. An exception might be found in training programs which deal with general practice in the respective fields. Each agency must retain full responsibility for training in the specific practices associated with the administration of the Work Incentive Program.

3. The two Departments (DOL and HEW) should set aside sufficient funds to accommodate the staffing and associated costs of the training program at all levels of government. To the extent that training personnel will be required for individual agencies, such as welfare and education, it will be expected that their training staff will be augmented to provide the supplemental staff required for the welfare and educational input in the joint training program.

4. A major thrust of the interdepartmental training program will be that of identifying clearly the respective roles of the employment counselor, the social worker, and the educator. In addition, strong emphasis will be placed upon the interdisciplinary collaborative touch points, such as the Interdepartmental Case Review Committee, the initial referral process, and the continuing reevaluation of case progress.

5. Provisions must be made for a year-round continuing program designed to offer progressive year-round training to original staff; to assure that every new staff member entering the program receives the complete training; and the local training unit will be required to prepare and present a feedback report, through channels, to the interdepartmental committees. This report will capture the elements of practice which reflect policy problems and make proposals for policy improvements that strengthen the training process.

The Sub-Committee report on training as outlined above was not included in later WIN policy releases.

The author, in his work on the Department of Labor Sub-Committee, strongly emphasized the necessity of sheltered workshops to be administered as part of a services program by public welfare. Department of Labor staff was opposed to any work activity being conducted by public welfare and the Chairman of the Policy Development Committee rejected the author's original proposal on the subject. The author revised and clarified the proposal and gave it a new title: Activity Centered Therapy. The Chairman finally agreed that Activity Centered Therapy programs should be administered by public welfare. Chapter 15 of this book will consider in detail, the nature of Activity Centered Therapy.

The Work Incentive Program has great potential for rehabilitation of public welfare recipients. Established employment, welfare and education systems must overcome traditional bureaucratic, unilateral approaches and mold an interdisciplinary, cooperative instrument of intervention for public welfare clients. We will now review the development of the WIN and social and rehabilitation programs in California to test the potential of interdisciplinary effort in rehabilitating welfare recipients.

CHAPTER 15

CALIFORNIA'S WORK INCENTIVE AND SOCIAL REHABILITATION PROGRAMS

CALIFORNIA'S INTEREST in the Work Incentive Program was represented in Washington, D.C., at meetings with the U.S. Department of Labor and the Social Rehabilitation Services Agency during February and March of 1968. The author, from the California State Department of Social Welfare, and a member of the California State Department of Finance who was also present, made it clear that California was strongly desirous of receiving an allocation of as many WIN slots as possible. Since the initial allocation for the last quarter of the 1967-68 fiscal year was pegged at only 5,100 slots for California, the author protested that this was insufficient. The allocation was increased to 8,000 by the Department of Labor after the February meeting, at which the federal agencies had requested written statements from state representatives, and the California delegates collaborated in a written recommendation of support of the 8,000 slot allocation.

FUNDING THE "WIN" PROGRAM

The WIN formula as prescribed by law allocates an 80 percent federal contribution and a 20 percent state or local contribution for the support of the program. The author recommended to the Director of SDSW that since the WIN program is administered by the Department of Employment in California, the 20 percent state or local funding should be secured for that agency budget and that it should be a complete state contribution as opposed to a formula which would require local participation. These recommendations were made in spite of the federal legal requirement that if the 20 percent could not be secured from the state or locality, it would be deducted from welfare payments to the state from the federal agency. The Directors of SDSW and of Employment agreed with these two principles, and recommended legislation to accommodate the objectives, namely, a bill which would appropriate money to the Department of Employment for the full 20 percent of state-local cost of the WIN program.

489

During the meetings of March and April 1968, discussions were held between the Department of Employment, Department of Social Welfare, and the Department of Finance. The Department of Finance took a strong position against acceptance of an 8,000-slot allocation to California and sought to limit subsequent fiscal year allocations, a decision which ran counter to recommendations by the Departments of Employment and of Social Welfare and which negated earlier departmental representations, both orally and in writing to the federal agencies. The Department of Finance not only made strong representation in meetings in California on this subject but sent a representative to Washington, D.C., to negotiate a modified plan and to seek understanding of how many slots the Federal Government might mandate. In spite of SDSW protests, the Department of Finance position prevailed and a formula eventually emerged which prescribed that California would not participate at all in the WIN program during the April-June quarter of 1968 and would finance only 12,000 slots in the fiscal year 1968-69, several thousands of slots fewer than the Federal Government would have been willing to make available to California.

It is paradoxical that while these negotiations were transpiring to limit the availability of training and educational resources for poor people that a California Lieutenant Governor's Committee on work training and placement was putting together recommendations for employment of such poor people. This unusual phenomenon is difficult to explain. It is possible that methodology was the key feature, based on the Governor's position, which tended to favor upgrading of educational and vocational skills for the poor through use of private resources, as opposed to development and expansion of governmental programs designed to help the poor. Our understanding of the needs of poor people for training and education suggests it will take the combined talent of government and private resources to accomplish these goals, and that such resources should complement one another. The achievement of full training, education, and work for the unemployed poor through private resources has often been attempted without success. One is reminded of the committee hearings and discussions during the Hoover administration in the early 1930's, when committee recommendations which similarly sought ameloration of problems of employment through private auspices were not successful.

The California Legislature accepted the recommendation of the Department of Finance and the Governor. No funding was provided for the last quarter of fiscal 1967-68; and the 1968-69 fiscal year was funded at the 12,000-slot level even though the U.S. Department of Labor had assured California a minimum of 15,000 WIN slots. The cost to California for the 12,000-slot WIN program was 3.3 million dollars. It was estimated that Welfare's phased-out Work Experience and Training program provided over 16,000 slots, so the impact of WIN during the first year of operation in California meant a net reduction of training slots.

While political and administrative adjustments and alignments were evolving in California, the author was advised by a Department of Labor representative of a strange development in Washington, D.C. The Department of Labor had allocated eight million dollars of their 1968-1969 WIN budget to Component 3, Special Work Projects. This amount was reserved for special request from the 50 states. It was learned in March 1969 that the Department of Labor had allocated five million dollars to West Virginia, leaving only three million remaining for the remainder of the states. While information was difficult to obtain on this transaction, it was alleged that a political deal was arranged with the Governor of West Virginia whereby the state would use the money to provide labor for the state and would pay the welfare recipients involved one dollar an hour wages from the allocation. This strange political arrangement would be inequitable to other states and recipients, and the alleged one dollar rate of pay for recipients is reminiscent of work relief practices. That the Department of Labor is vulnerable to political pressure was revealed earlier in reference to some MDTA actions and it was hoped that the WIN program would escape this fate. If the WIN program is to achieve the great destiny implicit in its early beginning, alleged political arrangements of this kind must be thoroughly investigated and appropriate controls established to insure that such nefarious arrangements do not occur.

A number of issues which required resolution in California before implementation of the WIN Program could be completed are presented in the following outlines:

Requirement that AFDC Families be Referred to WIN. Federal Public Law 90-248 provided for a new Work Incentive Program in place of the present Community Work and Training provisions, to be administered by the Department of Labor, through the nationwide network of state employment offices, for appropriate welfare recipients referred by welfare departments. The amendments defined precisely the characteristics of those against whom states could not apply sanctions for refusal to participate in the Work Incentive Program, and included:

Children under age 16 or going to school;

Persons whose illness, incapacity, advanced age, or remoteness from a project precludes effective participation in work or training;

Persons whose substantially continuous presence in the home

is required because of the illness or incapacity of another member of the household.

Such persons, however, must be referred if they request referral to a Work Incentive Progam unless the state determines that participation would be inimical to the welfare of the person or his family. Within these limitations, states were required by July 1, 1968, to refer promptly all appropriate children and relatives receiving AFDC and other appropriate individuals living with the family whose needs were taken into account in determining need for aid by the family.

It was apparent to SDSW that the WIN Program could not possibly accommodate all eligible AFDC adults for several years, estimated at approximately 80,000, and it was recalled that part of the objection by some groups, of Public Law 90-248, was the apparent federal mandate that all adults be referred to WIN. In order to soften the mandate and at the same time insure that all appropriate adults be referred to the WIN Program, SDSW developed regulatory material which set up priorities for referral and which at the same time prohibited involuntary referrals of women to the WIN Program. It was believed that if a mother was unwilling to receive education and training, this state of mind on her part revealed a social or psychological obstacle which the welfare departments should seek to overcome through use of social services. The SDSW regulations required referral on a priority basis to the WIN program as follows:

1. Unemployed fathers would be referred immediately.

2. AFDC mothers who were currently participating in the Community Work and Training Program or Title V, and volunteered, would be referred.

3. Youths 16 years of age and over who had left school or training would be referred.

4. AFDC mothers with no preschool children, and not currently involved in Community Work and Training or Title V, would be referred to WIN if they volunteered to be referred.

5. AFDC mothers with preschool children who volunteered would be considered for referral if such referral would not endanger their children.

These criteria will fully accommodate all possible WIN training slots within the next few years and clearly avoid forcing AFDC mothers into training and education. The regulations do, however, require referral of unemployed fathers to the WIN Program.

The SDSW Director's hearing on June 13, 1968, received representation from a variety of groups, including the California County Welfare Directors Association, a welfare rights organization from Alameda County, the Alameda County CRLA, a social worker's union from Los Angeles, the Alameda County Legal Aid Society, and the National Association for Social Workers.

The California County Welfare Directors Association was generally supportive of the regulatory material, raised a number of minor questions, and the major issue—whether emphasis should be given to voluntary placements in education and training as opposed to participation through force. The Association strongly favored retention of sanctions which would require engagement, and showed little understanding of the dynamics of human behavior which suggest that most people are motivated to engage in such programs, and when they are not, it represents obstacles which the Welfare Department should assist the individual in overcoming.

The welfare rights organization representative, a very fluent and effective speaker, a welfare recipient from Alameda County, emphasized the importance of social workers maintaining helpful attitudes and approaches in working with recipients. She suggested that many workers did not try to understand and help overcome the problems of recipients but really created more problems for them; and she affirmed the author's contention that welfare recipients do want to become educated, trained, and employed. She indicated, however, that many recipients have been upset by current training programs which provide skills but no employment, and cited cases where individuals had been trained in a skill center in Oakland and then were incapable of obtaining work. In some cases, such persons were again trained for another type of work, and still failing, their consequent discouragement and disallusionment was very upsetting. She noted that this tended to give the rehabilitation programs a bad image with welfare recipients and hoped that the new program would avoid these problems. She said that "welfare recipients are tired of going through routines and finding nothing which helps reconstruct their lives."

The general approach in the testimony by legal representatives of CRLA and Legal Aid was one which sought modification of the rules to protect the rights of recipients. A major concern, which also was shared by the social worker's union, was the proposal in the regulations which developed a county plan concept. This proposal was designed to place more responsibility on the counties for declaring their welfare service objectives in a county plan, as opposed to the traditional detailed rule-writing by the SDSW. The protest went to the question of the intent of the counties to develop sophisticated programs, and the charge that counties must be ordered by the state to improve their programs. The social worker's union went so far as to suggest that the county plan proposal favored the Supervisors Association proposal developed a year or so earlier and entitled Cal-Flex. The Cal-Flex proposal recommended

WORK RELIEF TO REHABILITATION

more flexibility in regulations, and the delegation of responsibility to the counties. The author recognized the dangers inherent in the county plan concept but considering the lack of progress of services development in counties under old regulations believed that on balance the county plan approach needed experimentation. One virtue it had was the provision of hope that more sophisticated counties could move for the strengthening of services without being hampered by limiting state regulations which have the effect of maintaining uniform mediocrity amongst all the counties.

This public hearing in California on the WIN Program was mild and orderly compared to reactions of welfare advocates in other parts of the nation. The voluntary approach taken in respect to referrals of women to the WIN Program softened the reaction. The following excerpt from a welfare rights organization publication illustrates the adverse reactions of many persons to the WIN program:

"The 1967 Anti-Welfare amendments to the Social Security Act include a so-called Work Incentive Program (WIP) to force AFDC recipients to accept work or training or get cut off of welfare. (To make the WIP program sound better, the welfare bureaucracy has decided to call it the WIN program) . . . We are against forcing mothers to work. We are for meaningful jobs with adequate pay and proper child care for all women who wish to work and for adequate income for all women who choose to work fulltime as mothers caring for their own children."

Definition of Unemployed Father. Public Law 90-248 provided that effective January 1, 1969, if a state wishes to provide AFDC for children of unemployed fathers, the state plan must, except as specified in item 1. (b) below:

1. Include a definition of an unemployed father:

    (a) which shall include any father who is employed less than 30 hours a week, or less than ¾ of the number of hours considered by the industry to be full time for the job, whichever is less; and

    (b) which may include any father who is employed less than 35 hours a week, or less than the number of hours considered by the industry to be full time for the job, whichever is less.

2. Provide for payment of aid with respect to any dependent child when the following conditions are met:

    (a) His father has been unemployed for at least 30 days prior to the receipt of such aid.

    (b) Such father has not without good cause, within such 30-day period prior to the receipt of such aid, refused a bona fide offer of employment or training for employment.

(c) Such father (1) has six or more quarters of work within any 13-calendar-quarter period ending within one year prior to the application for such aid, or (2) within such one-year period, received unemployment compensation under an unemployment compensation law of a state or of the United States, or was qualified for such compensation under the state's unemployment compensation law.

A "quarter of work" with respect to any individual means a period (of three consecutive calendar months ending on March 31, June 30, September 30, or December 31) in which he received earned income of not less than $50 (or which is a "quarter of coverage" as defined in section 213 [a] [2] of the Act), or in which he participated in a community work and training program under section 409 of the Act or any other work and training program subject to the limitations in such section 409, or the work incentive program established under part C of Title IV of the Act.

The strange effect of these provisions of the federal law in California is that of excluding from the WIN Program, a number of recipients of AFDC-U, because California has been supplementing the income of persons receiving UIB and did not prescribe other exclusions listed in these provisions. As California counties evaluated the impact of this, it became apparent that up to 50 percent of the AFDC-U fathers would be excluded from the WIN program in such highly industrialized counties as San Francisco, and it was anticipated that for the state as a whole, an average of 22 percent of those receiving AFDC-U on July 1, 1968, would be excluded by the federal plan. This exclusion would be not only from federal financial participation in the AFDC-U grant payment, but would also exclude referrals of such persons to WIN. The most amazing feature of the federal act is its exclusion of needy unemployed families from public aid and from training and education. In 1968, California decided to continue its AFDC-U program intact event though the federal subvention for about 22 percent of the caseload would not be received. This created the dilemma in which approximately 78 percent of the fathers could be referred to WIN as federally eligible, and the remainder must rely on resources of the state and county to receive education and training toward employment.

Training-Connected Expenses. In view of past reluctance of county boards of supervisors to appropriate training-connected expenses for the Community Work and Training welfare participants, the author strongly recommended to the Director of SDSW that for WIN, these expenses be completely funded from federal-state sources. To rely on local resources would jeopardize the implementation of the WIN program through the county delaying provision of money or through its insufficient or total lack of appropriations. There was an expectation on the part of Congress that states would act quickly to provide child care and training-connected expenses for persons referred to the WIN Program. The Director agreed with this objective and recommended such an arrangement to the Legislature, which was only partially responsive.

AB 1595 enacted by the Legislature provided $500,000 to match federal funds for child care and training-connected expenses of WIN participants. The Legislature required, however, that two-thirds of the nonfederal share cost of these services would be carried by the state; the other third by the county. In other words, during the 1968-69 fiscal year, the federal share would be 85 percent, the state share 10 percent, and the county share 5 percent. For California, this still was a fundamental change of federal-state-county fiscal responsibility. Traditionally, all administrative costs in California's county-administered, state-supervised welfare program have been shared by the federal and county governments without state participation. The distinction is made here between program costs involving public aid itself, which is shared fiscally by federal-state-county, as opposed to the costs of administration of the welfare program at the local level, which is shared only by the federal and county governments.

It is a paradox that SDSW, a state agency, would supervise and write regulations which are binding upon the county agencies and which would influence administrative costs without the state itself having any financial involvement. In respect to the training-connected expenses for the WIN Program, the Legislature's insistence that the county continue to share in the cost created the very problem which the state agency had tried to avoid, namely, the involvement of counties. To illustrate the nature of the problem, consider county X, which predicted training-connected costs for the WIN program of $500,000. The county share would be $25,000, a very small contribution for such a large expenditure. The county method of budgeting requires, however, that the total $500,000 be submitted to the board of supervisors for inclusion in the welfare budget. This requirement places the burden upon the county welfare director for augmentation of his already large budget by another one-half million dollars, and in some communities this is a difficult process irrespective of the large reimbursement from federal and state governments. Moreover, it is a process which takes time, and in the early months of the WIN Program, participants were not receiving reimbursement for training-connected expenses on time.

The SDSW instructed county welfare departments regarding the definition of training-connected expenses, namely, the costs of transportation (an average of $20 per participant per month), and miscellaneous personal needs (to be covered by a flat grant of $25 per participant per month). The Department of Employment interpreted the welfare responsibility as also including the costs of books and supplies, small tools, safety gear, and special uniforms. These different interpretations did not come to light until a case situation arose in one of the counties, setting off a long series of interdepartmental policy discussions. The Department of Employment submitted a request to their federal counterpart for interpretation and received a favorable reply, allowing them to cover such expenditures as small tools, books, supplies, and the like. Even so, the Department of Employment did not believe that AB 1595 provided the necessary authorization for them to proceed. The Interdepartmental WIN Policy Committee spent several sessions discussing the item and because it remained unresolved, the issue was later referred to the Directors of the two departments, who were also unable to reach agreement. It was then discussed with representatives of the Department of Finance who believed the issue required a legal interpretation. The legal staffs of the Welfare and the Employment Departments then reviewed the matter and concluded that the SDSW interpretation was appropriate. Accordingly, almost two months after the activation of the WIN program, it was finally resolved that Employment would cover the cost of training-connected expenses such as small tools, safety gear, and books. During that two-month period, county welfare departments, without definitive instructions, were improvising. One county sponsored luncheons in order to raise money for the items; in another county, the WIN staff of the welfare department voluntarily assessed themselves to meet the items of need; and in a few other counties, expenditures were made without regard to whether federal reimbursment could be claimed.

Single Payment Plan. Another feature of the California program is a cooperative welfare-employment recipient payment plan. The author is persuaded that the social outcast effect of the AFDC program upon adults and children must be offset in every manner possible, and that a plan for a single payment from the Department of Employment partially overcomes this. The arrangement combines the assistance grant, the training-connected expenses, and the WIN stipend of $30 a month for each trainee. The child care payment is not included, but is separated as a vendor payment to the child care vendor.

Through Assembly Bill 210 enacted in August 1968, California specifically provides that: "Pursuant to Section 5012, the depart-

498 WORK RELIEF TO REHABILITATION

ment shall pay a training stipend from the manpower development fund to each participant in an institutional and work experience and training program each month equal to the sum of an amount not less than the grant for which he would otherwise qualify under the aid to families with dependent children program, plus an incentive payment of not more than thirty dollars ($30) per month, payable in such amounts and at such times as permitted by federal law . . ." In response to the new law, a system was devised by which the initial referral of a WIN trainee triggers the initial combined payment upon acceptance of the individual as an enrollee by the Department of Employment. The referral form incorporates the grant amount which is utilized by the Department of Employment with the incentive payment for the first month's payment. Subsequently, after acceptance as a trainee by the Department of Employment, the regular social welfare payroll is segregated between case recipients (not enrolled in the training program) and those enrolled in the WIN program for whom no checks are issued by social welfare. This latter portion of the regular monthly payroll is sent to the Department of Employment as their authorization to continue the welfare portion of the combined stipend payment. Any "adjustments" necessary in the welfare grant are automatically incorporated in the authorization to the Department of Employment. It is apparent that the federal single-state-agency requirements are fully met, inasmuch as Social Welfare assumes full responsibility for eligibility and grant determination, and the role of the Department of Employment becomes essentially that of a paymaster, much like auditors in some counties who issue checks to persons upon authorization from the county welfare department. The above reflects the law and the proposed regulations but the single payment procedure was not to become operational before July 1, 1969 because of Department of Employment machine problems.

Reporting. Both the welfare and employment systems have need for a substantial amount of data concerning funding of the program and social and vocational attributes of participants in it, and much of this data is required to be reported both to the U.S. Department of Labor and to the U.S. Department of Health, Education, and Welfare. In order to eliminate the duplication of data collection systems, the decision was made in California to assign the Department of Employment responsibility for data collection both for their own needs and for those identified by the Department of Social Welfare. In this way, the Department of Employment collects some information for which it has no other use except to report to the welfare system. The entire responsibility for identification of informational needs for the welfare system remain with Social Welfare. To some degree, this tightens the welfare responsibility since it becomes extremely difficult, if not impossible retroactively, to call upon the system for additional information which was not anticipated in the original plan—and not inserted into the system. This is a problem, however, that is inherent in the development of a single reporting system, although it may be more difficult to modify because of the multidepartment arrangement.

The objective sought through a compatible reporting and data collection system is not only that of joining two agencies by means of the system, but also of establishing an intergovernmental system of data collection and reporting for county, state, and federal governments.

Interdepartmental Policy Committee. The SDSW and the Department of Employment in California agreed to the establishment of a top-level policy committee involving Deputy Directors and their staff. This committee would develop policy, serve as a communication medium, and provide an opportunity for confrontation on hard, unresolved issues. If the policy committee could not reach agreement, the unresolved issues would be referred to the Directors of the two departments for resolution. In the early, hectic days of the WIN program, this committee served a very useful purpose.

Education and Training Program (ETP). On June 13, 1968, the Director of SDSW conducted a public hearing to review proposed rules and regulations for the WIN program and other supportive programs. During the early months of 1968, it had become apparent that the insufficiency of WIN slots because of relatively small federal appropriations, and because of the California action which limited WIN training slots, there would be insufficient education and training resources for welfare recipients. The slots available for the fiscal year 1968-69 would not cover 16,000 persons, the approximate number served in 1967 (combination of community work and training programs and EOA, Title V programs). To accommodate this deficiency, a long series of negotiations were conducted with the federal Social Rehabilitation Services (SRS) agency to gain federal recognition of a state services program which would accommodate education and vocational training pending full WIN development.

California's position, as stated in the following correspondence to HEW and in state instructions to the counties, covered the rationale for the proposal. The letter follows:

"Our Department and the county welfare departments are becoming increasingly concerned that the WIN program in California will probably be unable to provide within the next fifteen months for sufficient training slots to accommodate even the number of trainees we now have enrolled in our Community Work and Training and Title V programs. It is expected that this lack of training slots will exist in both the 26 WIN-funded counties and the 32 non-funded counties.

"We are convinced, therefore, that we must take immediate action to avoid eliminating services and benefits to people who are now receiving them. To do otherwise would not only disregard the needs of the individuals involved but would also create serious public relations problems. Any lessening or termination of recipient participation in social rehabilitation and training programs promotes idleness, would retard our steady movement toward the self-support objectives of our public assistance programs, and would result in seious breakdown of morale and diminution of the individual's sense of self-respect and self-worth.

"It appears to us that there is clear provision in the Social Security Act and in federal policy for us to administer these essential program activities within the framework of the public assistance services programs with federal financial participation of 75 percent (or 85 percent). Our plan is outlined in the attached Circular Letter which we propose to issue to our counties within the next few days.

"It is the intent of our plan that recipients who cannot be immediately accommodated in the WIN program will be continued in programs that will provide a learning or training experience, and offer the participant an opportunity for achievement and accomplishment while preserving or developing skills that enhance movement in the direction of self-support. In some instances this will involve arrangements under which the recipient is afforded the opportunity to learn-by-doing in a public agency or facility. The critical point to which we wish to draw special attention is our need to have federal assurance that under these arrangements, we can continue to receive federal reimbursement for the assistance payments made after June 30, 1968, to recipients who engage *voluntarily* in such activity. Without this assurance, we have little chance of heading off a rapid deterioration between now and July 1, 1968, in programs and opportunities that now exist in this state.

"It is understood that unless the provisions of Section 409 of the Social Security Act are extended as we have urged, that it will be necessary for us to modify our own regulations to discontinue involuntary recipient participation and the application of wage credits in relation to the welfare payment. This we are prepared to do.

"In view of the need to have definite direction in this matter and so that we may not be put into the position of having to take steps to terminate existing programs because of the lack of a federally-approved plan, we must have an early reply to the proposal embodied in this letter and in the attached Circular Letter."

The proposed Circular Letter follows:

"The Social Security Act Amendments of 1967 make Section 409 of the Act inoperative after June 30, 1968. As a consequence:

"a. We will lose our authority to claim federal reimbursement on any assistance payments made to recipients after June 30, 1968, in the form of payments for work performed on work-training projects established and administered under Department Bulletin 636 or as Title V projects.

"b. Administrative expenditures which are attributable to the administration of work-training projects as presently constituted for recipients engaged in these projects, will not be subject to federal participation after June 30, 1968.

"The repeal of Section 409 will not affect the organized group instruction element of Department Bulletin 636. This activity is an integral part of the program of social services the state elected to provide under PL. 87-543 and could have been carried on even though we had not also elected to have a community work and training program under Section 409.

"In light of these circumstances, there is serious danger of an intolerable drop in the level of this type of self-support activity on behalf of public assistance recipients during the interim period when the Work Incentive Program is being established and brought up to the operating level of the existing program. The purpose of this circular letter is to convey the actions taken in order to prevent this occurrence and to establish our intentions with respect to operations to be carried by the counties, including the 26 currently scheduled for initial inclusion under the WIN program.

"1. The Governor has requested the California Congressional delegation to seek the extension of Section 409 of the Social Security Act.

"2. We have reviewed the problem with the Department of Health, Education and Welfare Regional Commissioner of Social and Rehabilitation Services and have been informed that the approach as outlined in this letter is consistent with federal law.

"3. We will adopt appropriate changes in State regulations to designate our continuing effort as 'social rehabilitation service' and to put the plan outlined in this letter into effect, while concurrently repealing policies that will be inconsistent with the WIN program and in conflict with federal law when Section 409 becomes inoperative.

"Plan of Operation

"California public welfare agencies will proceed toward full implementation of PL 90-248 as rapidly as possible, guided by the conviction that not only is it essential that there be direct movement of people toward employment, but that it is equally essential that there be a strong, continuing social service program designed to build and maintain individual morale, self-esteem, feelings of self-worth and constructive aspirations, and to otherwise assist needy persons toward the goal of self-support. In accordance with this philosophy, and in view of the need to assure an orderly redistribution of responsibilities among Employment, Rehabilitation, Education, and Social Welfare, the State and County Welfare Departments will have both an *interim* and a *continuing* objective.

"Our *interim objective* is to provide for termination of work projects on July 1, 1968, and to convert such opportunities into social rehabilitation services and/or training activities in order to maintain persons in training and activity-centered programs to the extent that this is necessary and essential, pending the assumption of responsibility for such of these activities as appropriately belong to the Department of Employment, Department of Rehabilitation, or the Department of Education. The maintenance of this effort will be considered a complementary service as provided by State Regulations PSS 56-101 and federal policies. The administrative expenditures attributable to these services, e.g., training and activity-connected costs, as well as costs of child care and county welfare department personnel, will continue to qualify for federal financial participation of 75 percent (or 85 percent).

"In order to comply with federal law, at such time that Section 409 becomes inoperative, State regulations will be changed concurrently:

"1. To make participation in County Welfare Department-sponsored training and rehabilitation service activities voluntary on the part of the recipient; and

"2. To discontinue all 'wage credit' policies.

"Our *continuing objective* is to reorient the emphasis of public social services and to build up a stong and effective self-support program to be known as 'social rehabilitation service,' in compliance with Section 402(a) (15), Social Security Act. Proposed policies and procedures for this are being developed by the State-County Policy Committee's Task Groups on Work Incentive and Public Social Services.

"In subsequent weeks we will act on this notification by adopting and promulgating the policies and procedures necessary to put this plan into full effect."

The federal agency gave approval to temporary provision of education and vocational training programs under their Services regulations. Accordingly, the regulations before the Director of the SDSW incorporated three major features—provisions concerning the WIN program; provisions enabling the counties to provide educational training programs (ETP) through welfare program funding; and provisions for social rehabilitation services (SRS). The first two were designed to serve the individual who was ready for an educational and training program; and the SRS program was designed to serve those who were not WIN-ready (those whose physical, psychological, and social problems precluded effective engagement in an educational or training program). It was agreed that the ETP program would be temporary, pending the capability of the WIN program to serve all persons ready for engagement in training, and the ETP program would be available to counties which had not been designated as WIN counties, and to WIN designated counties which could not serve all WIN-ready welfare recipients.

The federal piecemeal approach to the rehabilitation of public welfare recipients was further complicated by lack of comprehensive coverage of able-bodied recipients in WIN. Welfare departments would still need to provide vocational training and education to able-bodied General Assistance and non-federally eligible AFDC-U cases. Thus a dual system of education and training would continue to be maintained by Employment and Welfare departments with Welfare continuing to serve WIN-ready and eligible recipients who could not be served by WIN because of insufficient slots, General Assistance recipients and non-federally eligible AFDC-U recipients. While Welfare was grateful for the strong support of the WIN program, the obvious question was raised that if Welfare had to continue provision of vocational training services to substantive numbers of welfare recipients why didn't the Congress provide the WIN money to Welfare to augment their existing training programs?

Concurrence

In order to insure that the ETP program would develop as a temporary supportive program to WIN rather than a competing program, and in order to comply with federal requirements, the SDSW and Department of Employment agreed to policy which required that the Department of Employment would give "concurrence" to the local welfare agency for the operation of the ETP program. The initial criteria for concurrence were that sufficient welfare referrals should be made to fill all WIN slots and in addition, the quality of the ETP program was to be reviewed by the Department of Employment to insure sophisticated training programs rather than work relief projects.

In the initial stages, SDSW had preferred an arrangement whereby the two programs would run concurrently, with insistence placed upon WIN referrals. SDSW was aware, however, that 16,000 AFDC recipients were in educational training programs and many more were ready for placement. Considering these large numbers, it was anticipated that the 12,000 slots allocated to California could be readily filled through transfer of all AFDC fathers, the priority group, to the Department of Employment programs, and through transfer of as many AFDC mothers as would be needed to accommodate the total number of WIN slots available. Following this arrangement there would have been no loss of time on the part of welfare recipients in training or education.

The Department of Employment, however, was reluctant to follow this procedure, fearing that training resources might not be transferred from the welfare departments to the WIN program and that the better qualified welfare recipients might be held for ETP rather than referred to the WIN program. Accordingly, the Department of Employment mandated that no new referrals be made to ETP in any county until it was apparent that WIN slots could be filled. The suspicion of noncooperation from welfare departments was expressed by an Assistant Director, Manpower, California Department of Employment, on October 2, 1968, in the following statement made to an interstate group of Employment agency officials: "What appears to be another serious problem is the failure of the county welfare agencies to refer WIN enrollees to our offices. Between September 3 and September 19 we received exactly 248 referrals from 26 county welfare departments. There we were with 47 offices and over 500 staff and practically no enrollees! After energetic prodding by our state welfare department the flow of referral documents increased and by September 25 we had 699 referrals. I have a sneaking hunch that this matter of depending on the welfare system is going to be a big problem for us. I get the impression that Welfare doesn't *want* to refer their cases to WIN and when we get our enrollees into training and into employment we are going to have *big* trouble with the 'earning exemption' and 'payment of necessary expenses' policies. I hope I'm wrong because these kinds of problems will '*un*motivate' our enrollees in a big hurry."

That some of these apprehensions were unfounded is illustrated by the fact that in California, at the end of six months of WIN operation, 36.000 WIN referrals had been made by the welfare departments to the Department of Employment. The Employment offices were incapable of processing so many referrals, and at the local level asked welfare agencies to slow down on the referral process. As it became increasingly apparent that several thousands of welfare recipients would not be served by the WIN program during fiscal year 1968-1969, the author requested meetings of the

Welfare-Employment Interdepartmental Policy Committee to establish criteria for concurrence, so that welfare agencies could commence operating their ETP progam. During meetings held on the subject, the Department of Employment proposed that they would not give concurrence in any county until the WIN slots were filled in that county and the Employment agency had approved every welfare training and education slot being considered for recipient placements. The author and his staff strongly protested these proposals because the filling of WIN slots by Employment could take as long as a year in some places where the time was needed for careful processing; and it was unreasonable to expect Employment approval of all training and education programs, since many would involve single recipient placements. The author made the alternative proposals that concurrence be given when welfare referrals exceeded allocated WIN slots, whether filled or not, by 100 percent; and that welfare be given project approval by agreeing to follow general project standards set by Employment rather than by a one-by-one project approval. The Employment representatives on the Policy Committee refused to accept these alternative welfare proposals, with one representative going so far as to suggest that he viewed ETP as a competing system, that he would resist giving concurrence to any county, and that he believed WIN would provide training for all AFDC recipients. He professed no concern for those persons unserved for months or years during the phase-in period of WIN. Since the concurrence issue could not be resolved at the Policy Committee level, the author referred the issue to the Director of SDSW with the recommendation that the issue be dealt with only at the state level, the objective being to reach interdepartmental agreement between the two state departments rather than to subject each county to the concurrence process as present agreements prescribed.

Analysis of the concurrence issue reveals that each of the departments was confronted with difficult problems. The SDE believed it had a mandate to become the manpower agency for WIN-ready AFDC recipients even though they could not serve all of the recipients needing training. The SDSW was concerned about the large numbers of AFDC recipients remaining idle during the phase-in period and those who might not be served for a few years because of inadequate WIN resources. The issue was complicated by the fact that the Federal Congress did not adequately fund the WIN program to cover all AFDC recipients and then concurrently discontinued welfare training programs during the phase-in of the WIN program. The SDSW sought to remedy the congressional lack of foresight by developing ETP as a supplemental phase-in program.

A statistical analysis reveals that the specific number of welfare enrollments of work experience and training (Title V) and community work and training recipients in March 1966 was 21,283. Later, when the Federal Congress began to reduce Title V allocations and phase the Title V program into the Department of Labor, the impact was noted in California by a lessening of participants in the programs. The community work and training and the Title V programs were abolished on July 1, 1968, which cut the number of participants in training programs to 8,100 in California on that date. Subsequently, the low point was reached in September 1968, at which time only 5,000 persons were in training and this number began to slowly increase, with the implementation of the WIN program to 12,000 by December 1968. The number of AFDC families receiving aid in California in March 1966 was 158,000, rising to 215,000 in September 1968. Therefore, AFDC recipients in training in March 1966 was 13 percent of the total on aid at that time and this was reduced in September 1968 to less than two and one-half percent. Appropriate congressional and administrative planning could have avoided this serious reduction in welfare trainees, through the development of an effective phase-in program which would allow retention of welfare training programs during the build-up of the WIN program. The reductions in the welfare training program should have occurred only as the WIN program was able to accommodate the totality of AFDC recipients needing training. Not only did the Congress fail to anticipate the described problems and fail to develop appropriate phase-in approaches, it expressed its impatience with increasing AFDC rolls by placing a "freeze" on the number of AFDC recipients who could receive federal participation in the AFDC grant. The Congress somehow expected that the magic of rehabilitation in the WIN program could overcome the incidence of dependency in spite of inadequate funding and the inevitable delays in accelerating the implementation of a new program. As a result of protests from states, Congress later decided to delay implementation of the "freeze" one year.

The congressional lack of planning and foresight is a chronic problem, noted earlier in regard to congressional requirements that beginning July 1, 1967, the Secretary of Health, Education, and Welfare was required to gain concurrence from the Secretary of Labor before making a decision to renew an existing Title V project. The Title V program was to be phased-out by July 1, 1969, although most projects ceased by December 31, 1968, upon the advent of the WIN program. The interdepartmental, DOL-DHEW, discussions at the federal level were heated and hard fought as to proper departmental jurisdictions during the phase-out of the Title V program. The Congress lacked insight into an elementary principle of administration, namely, that you should not give administrative power to one agency to be invoked over another agency. The delegation of power must be clear-cut to each agency. The DOL, then, having received the power over DHEW in the Title V controversy sought similar power in the California WIN-ETP controversy, and this created arguments which were just as hard fought at the state level. In fact, the key word in both the state and federal interdepartmental disputes was "concurrence." In each of these disputes, the question was not in the form of an argument over the shift in responsibility for administering welfare manpower programs, but rather was focused on the muddled, joint DOL-DHEW administration of welfare programs during the welfare phase-out period, caused by lack of clear-cut delegation of authority and responsibility by the Congress. In effect, all of the power systems were so motivated to transfer so-called manpower responsibility from DHEW to DOL that the focus centered on that crucial struggle, while the needs of AFDC recipients became temporarily obscured.

And in March 1969, as the Department of Employment was becoming overwhelmed with the 36,000 California WIN referrals from welfare, they decided to suspend enrollment of welfare recipients for the WIN program until July, 1969, except for enrollment of unemployed fathers who were mandated by Congress to be recipients for the WIN program until July 1969, except for enrollment of unemployed fathers who were mandated by congress to be referred. As the Department of Employment searched for answers to their own problems of slowness of enrollment and assignment of recipients, they found that to process a single WIN participant it required 97 different transactions by WIN staff alone, not considering welfare forms!

These are a few of the issues emerging during the early implementation of the WIN program in California. Scores of issues were settled in an orderly and cooperative manner by the Interdepartmental Policy Committee during the early months of the program. Yet the concurrence issue which was difficult to resolve was crucial, and the poorly resolved issue regarding state financing of the WIN program was also a critical issue. Poor people became the victims of the clumsy and bureaucratic administrative and legislative systems during the phasein of the WIN program, even though the WIN program provided more long-range hope for opportunity through upgrading of education and vocational training than could possibly have been attained through the welfare system. Yet a strange circular system had emerged whereby the California Governor's office and the Legislature limited the number of potential WIN slots for welfare recipients, and later, the Department of Employment, competitively sought to thwart welfare effort to augment insufficient WIN slots. One's feelings become strangely mixed in viewing the potential and the hazards in the changing system. Finally, in January 1969 the concurrence issue was settled. It was agreed by the two departments that an interagency concurrence agreement would be signed at the state level without further involvement of the counties. This agreement provided for continuation of the ETP program under SDSW administration, to supplement the WIN Program. It was fully agreed that the ETP Program would cease when the WIN program could serve all WIN eligible AFDC welfare recipients.

And while hard administrative negotiations were being held in Sacramento, the WIN orientation group meetings held in the counties were beginning for some public welfare recipients. Four reports prepared by Department of Employment orientation group leaders follow:

From the start, the group tended to their own needs. A man's car broke down, so he called another man in the group to arrange a ride. One man stated he needed tires, another man in the group said he could help on tires as he had some old ones in his garage. One of the men in the group read an ad in the paper for a job he thought one of the other men could qualify for and he gave him all the information to apply for the job, which the man did. The group advised one of the men, a waiter, to change occupations because he stated it was difficult for him to smile and he didn't think that was part of the job as a waiter. A young man in the group wore sandals to the sessions. One day he reported barefooted stating he left his sandals in his car. The group took objections to his being barefooted and voted he go get his shoes, which he did."

"During the first week of Orientation all but two of the eight members were interested in what the Program had to offer. The two individuals indicated that they were preoccupied with family problems. For example, one individual was worried about his wife who was about to have a baby. He had very few clothes for his wife, baby or himself. Also his welfare grant had decreased to such a degree that it had made it impossible for him to pay his rent. The other individual had similar problems, but he was more concerned with getting a job NOW!"

"Mr. A. was a member of my first orientation group. Mr. A. was 35, a Mexican National, and his English was limited. For the last four years his only work had been seasonal, as a farm laborer. He completed the sixth grade in Mexico and is presently attending ABE classes to get his American citizenship. He is highly motivated and sincere and his attendance in class was perfect. His employability plan called for work training at Patton (in the Cabinet Shop) along with continuance in basic education. In the last hour of orientation when he was told to report to Patton for his chest X-ray and finger printing, he got up from the table and stood by the window and hung his head. When asked what was troubling him, he stated, 'If I know I be finger printed, I walk out first day.' The perspiration popped out on his forehead and he stated. 'I 'fraid.' The group tried to help him. We all knew there was no problem of arrest. He had the sympathy of all of us and everybody tried to talk to him to find out why he was so frightened. We found out that when he came to this country seven years ago, he was forcibly finger-printed. The experience terrified him. The group explained to him why this was necessary and that it was really for his protection. He kept saying, 'I know, I know, but I scare. I could have job a year ago at Kaiser, good job but they tell me I have finger prints. I leave, I scare.' Two of the girls in the group tried to show him how it was done and he stood there and watched. He seemed to be interested but he wouldn't try it himself. All the time he was talking, he had goose pimples on his arms. I asked him if it would help if I went out with him to Patton. He said, 'No, this something I got to do myself. I go home, I take a cold shower and I think about it over the week-end. If I decide not to go to Patton, I come in and see you.' I told him it was all right and that we would still try to help him, but I hoped for his sake he would go to Patton. The following Monday morning when I got to work, he was waiting for me. He said, 'I have trouble with my car, but I go. I still scared but I go and try; you mighty fine lady and I try for you.' I arranged with the coach to take him out there. I phoned the training officer at Patton and explained the situation and he thanked me for telling him and said they would be as gentle as possible. When the coach returned, he said, 'He got finger printed all right; he closed his eyes and turned his face away, but he got his finger prints taken.' I feel the orientation group, because of their compassion for this man, helped him overcome his problem. The value of the 'group type orientation' was evident in this case."

"One of the young women in the group was a 19-year-old whom we will call Marilyn. She had run away from home at 13 and had a baby at 15. She had never married, had a 10th grade education, no work experience and no self-confidence. She has been on Welfare for 2 years, 1 month. Her appearance and grooming were very poor. She cracked her knuckles, used four letter words, and was very bitter and abusive toward her parents. The fourth day, after using a four letter word in reference to her father—the room became still. The silence was deafening. After what seemed like hours I asked, 'Why is everyone so quiet?' Then the entire group began to tell her why. They didn't like her language, her knuckle cracking or her abusive references to her parents. She immediately agreed that she had bad habits. For the rest of the session the group kept urging her to return to school, complimented her on her grooming. Her appearance, self-confidence and language improved daily. On the last day of orientation after everyone had said their goodbys, she burst back into the room where I was alone. She threw her arms around me and said, 'This has been the most wonderful experience of my life. I didn't know there were such wonderful people in the world, as the ones I've met in this class.' She sobbed as though her heart were broken. She told me I was the best friend she ever had. I feel, again, that because of the group, this girl has benefited from the personal relationships and reinforcement provided by others in the same circumstances. Also the knowledge that she had the WIN team behind her gave her the self-confidence she needed."

Comments from four participants in the WIN Program were recorded as follows:

"I feel that the Orientation Sessions of The Win Program were rather interesting and helpful to me because they illustrated the problems that most people like myself face, when trying to secure employment. Also, it provided a great deal of insight into the backgrounds, personal problems, and abilities of the people that are on welfare, and it destroyed a lot of the myths we are led to believe about the stero-type welfare cases that are unskilled, poor educated, indolent, lazy and all they want is a hand-out. But, this is not the case, as I have found out. They are human beings, with real needs, but due to circumstances beyond their control, they are unable to fullfill them. Hence, I feel that I am not the only one with problems. Also, I feel that with some assistance most of us will eventually be able to stand on our two feet."

"I think that a good number of us were pretty much down in the dumps when it started but that most will have a high morale and a different attitude after finding that we are not alone in our situation."

"These last two weeks have given me a spark. I lacked confidence in what I am attempting to do. Everyone on the WIN team bubbles with enthusiasm about me, complimented me on my good points, criticized the bad points. It has given me the good feeling that each of these people can help me and are just as anxious for success as I am."

"She is genuinely concerned and interested in my present and future. Her enthusiasm for this program has been contagious. Her interest has added to my self-confidence. Her eagerness for my success has given me added incentive to fulfill my plans and eliminated many doubts as to my success. I also feel she has learned with all of us and more times than not she has been as accepted as one of us, rather than the leader over us. She acted like she really cared what happened to each and every one of us."

The author's expectation of success of the WIN program was reaffirmed by the early administrative and case successes in spite of the various legislative and administrative impediments. Yet, the coverage of the WIN program was incomplete for public welfare recipients. The following case examples illustrate the problems of Aid to Disabled (ATD) persons who should also receive vocational rehabilitation.

Mrs. P, 55 years old, who lives with a married daughter and four grandchildren, is separated from her husband. She is receiving a General Relief grant, and her daughter receives an AFDC grant. Mrs. P had a twelfth grade education, has worked in a laundry, and managed a large apartment building. She has a cervical spine ailment and activity is medically restricted. ATD was granted.

Mr. H, 59 years old and married, had a fourth grade education, and worked as a seasonal farm laborer most of his life. He has emphysema and degenerative disease of the spine. In spite of these ailments, the examining physician stated that if the patient had a better mental outlook he probably would be able to do most kinds of work, short of prolonged heavy labor. ATD was granted.

Mr. Z, 21 years old and single, resides with his parents. He had an eighth grade education and has worked only occasionally at bucking hay. Three years ago he received multiple stab wounds and a concussion when attacked by other persons. Since injury and surgery, he has had epileptic seizures and diminished mental comprehension with an IQ of 64. ATD was granted.

Mr. W, 49 years old, lives with his wife and minor child. He had a sixth grade education, worked as a laborer, auto mechanic, and body and fender man. He received an AFDC grant for the preceding four years because of unemployment. Mr. W has epilepsy and an IQ of 65. ATD was granted.

Mr. D, a 19-year-old single man who is living with relatives, receives an ATD grant. A referral for ATD was made by the Monterey County General Hospital, where the claimant had been under care several months after being struck by an automobile, suffering a compound fracture of the leg and kneecap. Mr. D completed the sixth grade in school.

Mr. D was steadily employed at the time of the accident at his occupation of milking cows. This occupation demands excellent leg flexibility; he had to bend and unbend his knees from twelve hundred to thirteen hundred times a day. The doctor advised him that, although his leg will improve, it is doubtful that he will be able to return to work in his own particular skill. Although improvement is expected, the left leg is weak, and Mr. D is unable to bend his knee except very slightly. He has limited use of his left foot. When he is in bed, for example, he has to move his left leg with his hands.

Mr. D was hospitalized in December 1967, but the referral to apply for ATD was not made by the hospital until June 1968. Mr. D had been under continual medical care by an orthopedic surgeon and incurred bills totalling $7,000.

The physician advised the welfare department that Mr. D could do no hard labor from four to six months. The doctor wrote: "It is my feeling that the fracture of the femur though clinically united, is certainly not mature and 100 percent solid. Within another four to six months, this fracture will undoubtedly go on to solid union and cause no more difficulty to the patient other than the angular deformity and shortening which is now present. The patient's problem, mainly, is his knee joint. He has had a good result following his patellectomy and now has a good range of motion though certainly not a complete range of motion. His limited range of motion is probably due not only to the patellectomy which would possibly limit his full flexion somewhat but also due to adhesions of the quadriceps mechanism to the fracture site. Though the patient is young and has a better chance to gain a good range of motion, I feel that he will probably always have some limitation of full flexation of his knee joint. In addition, the patient has instability of his knee joint due to laxity of his collateral ligaments and cruciate ligaments, probably due to ligamentous injury at the time of his injury. This instability will be permanent and it is doubtful that any surgical repair will improve the stability of his knee. I would think, therefore, that the patient will always have considerable trouble with this knee and he would certainly have difficulty doing any job which required stooping or squatting or climbing. Since the patient's present job is dependent upon being able to do these things, I would think that the patient should be considered for retraining in some type of work which would not require stooping, squatting or climbing. Also the patient should probably not do any work requiring walking on uneven ground as his knee will be subject to twisting or straining."

It is apparent that Mr. D could work in another occupation but this would require training and education. Mr. D's eligibility was determined, not on his potential for retraining, but on his incapacity to return to his former occupation. In effect, the emphasis of Mr. D, the agency, and the physician was to focus on the disability to qualify Mr. D for public aid as a totally and permanently disabled person at age 19.

And there is another group of people on the fringes of public welfare who are denied assistance as illustrated by the following case examples.

Mrs. D, 47 years old, was married in 1945, had two sons, and was divorced in 1957. By 1968, her children had left home, her savings were exhausted, and she was plagued with a variety of health problems. She was a former tuberculosis patient and had residuals of an elbow fracture and arthritis. Mrs. D's meagre work history consisted of short-term clerking in a drug store, practical nursing, babysitting, and housework. At the time of application for the Aid to Disabled program, Mrs. D was depressed and in a highly nervous state. Her application was denied because her physical condition was not sufficiently disabling.

Mr. H, age 49, has a 44-year-old wife and two married daughters. He had a fifth grade education and no special training. He worked 19 years in a lumber mill. He terminated this employment following a leg injury resulting from a fall through an unprotected hole at the mill. Mr. H has severe emotional problems, right eye removed, chronic bronchitis. The family was without any source of support except $137.90 monthly benefits from Old Age, Survivors and Disability insurance. His application for ATD was denied.

Mr. J, 54 years old, lives alone in a small apartment. He separated from his wife 10 years ago. His children, aged 17 and 18 live with a grandmother in another state. Mr. J had a fourth grade education. He was employed as a tire recapper for 10 years. He received a back injury when a tire fell on him. He also was employed as a janitor and furniture mover. He hadn't worked for over a year because of back trouble. He received $35.56 Industrial Compensation plus a meagre General Relief public assistance grant. His application for ATD was denied.

These persons who were denied aid could return home only to become more disabled so that they eventually qualify for aid.

These case examples and hundreds of thousands more, in the nation, illustrate that our welfare programs and services are misdirected. (California has 120,000 persons receiving ATD.) The primary focus of programs should be on the provision of services which reinforce the strengths of the individual, with adequate training stipends—not public aid—to provide sustenance during the rehabilitation process.

The future of public welfare is to be found in the provision of social and rehabilitation services. While a good foundation for this new destiny exists in all welfare agencies, the road to fully developed, sophisticated rehabilitation programs will be long and troubled. Social and rehabilitation services will eventually provide child welfare, including adoptions, protective services, foster home care, day care, and services to emotionally disturbed and retarded children; services for adults, including marriage counseling, social services to the emotionally disturbed, mentally retarded, alcoholics, drug users, unmarried mothers, and dischargees from mental and penal institutions; and guardianship programs. Another essential service—the rehabilitation of persons toward meaningful activity—will involve the painstaking process of rebuilding broken bodies and minds and restoring hope and motivation through application of a variety of social services and through activity centered therapy. Activity centered therapy will become the hub of public welfare rehabilitation programs because only through such occupational therapy will once hopeless men and women be able to regain confidence in their capacity for engagement in a meaningful life and understand that it is no longer necessary to prove incapacity to gain life necessities through welfare eligibility.

Although it has been established that work fills many functions in life, some may not become aware of its importance until the possibility of losing a job of significance becomes a reality. Gainful employment furnishes income, fills in the hours of the day or night, and aids in maintaining physical vigor and vitality. A pattern of comradeship and contact with others helps to establish status in family and community. Beyond this, however, a sense of satisfaction in new experiences and a chance to be creative and to continue working give life enduring significance. Work has meaning for each individual; work loss or unsatisfactory replacement in retirement because of disability creates major problems of adjustment. Work or its equivalent must be recognized as a common human need with respect to economic independence, social status, the satisfaction of living, and the continuance of life itself. Contempt for work is the mark of a decaying society. Work is the best way of increasing longevity. When disability requires transfer from an active to an inactive program, it produces discontent, unhappiness, and illness. When purposeful work is replaced by aimless living, neurosis and depression appear.

Organisms, organs, and tissues tend to die when they no longer serve a useful purpose. An aimless existence is intolerable to nature. The debilitating effects of advancing years cannot be laid entirely to structural changes brought on by age. Loss of incentive, loss of driving power—that something which keeps an individual in motion and in tune with his fellow man—changes the person from a contributing to a parasitic member of the social group. When he begins to be aware of the signs of approaching decay, rehabilitation can reverse the trend.

Rehabilitation programs such as Activity Centered Therapy, as conceptualized in federal meetings, was considered for adoption in California. After discussions here initiated with the Welfare Director in San Mateo County regarding his interests in adapting his department's sheltered workshop into an activity centered work program, he developed a proposal which was submitted by SDSW to the federal agency for approval of federal services subvention. The federal agency fully agreed with the proposal and the San Mateo County program was viewed as a model of activity centered therapy for other counties in California, as well as a blueprint for a substantive future rehabilitation role of public welfare in the nation. Adaptations of the original concept to the California scene emerged as follows.

ACTIVITY CENTERED THERAPY

Introduction: The limited potential of some hard-core welfare recipients requires specialized effort on the part of the welfare agency. Functional incapacity and disability are not always apparent, particularly in recipients with an outward appearance of adequacy. The referral of functionally disabled recipients to WIN would create problems for WIN as well as for the individuals themselves, and although they are limited in number within the program, it is important that their needs are met effectively. The welfare program must include among its resources a service facility for determining and restoring functional capacity to the extent possible. Damaging life experiences require specialized activity centered therapy to rekindle a sense of personal identity, self-worth, and progressive adequacy in the individual, and such strengths must be sufficiently developed to give him a reasonable chance of success.

Program Goals: The goals of an activity centered therapy program are: To serve the needs of the community by providing such therapy for recipients of Aid to Disabled, Aid to Needy Blind, Old Age Assistance and AFDC; to provide a wide range of social development activities to assist clients in becoming trainable and/or employable and to provide a resource for determining and restoring functional capacity to the extent possible for hard-core welfare cases.

Administrative Goals: Administrative goals of activity centered therapy are to demonstrate projects under direction of the public welfare department, and through public welfare contracts with private agencies, and to coordinate the program between welfare, education, WIN, and vocational rehabilitation agencies through appropriate administrative devices such as case review committees, advisory committees, and interdepartmental methodologies of varying kinds. Goals would include demonstrating the use of volunteers, indigenous case aids, and interdisciplinary intervention in the form of medical and social case work, social group work, occupational therapists, and other appropriate specialists, as well as private industry and government as contractors to provide vocational-oriented activity for participants in a meaningful form. Additional objectives would be the development of methods of evaluating effectiveness of varying administrative arrangements and the case results of activity centered therapy as a means of preparing hard-core public welfare recipients for education and vocational training programs under auspices of WIN and vocational rehabilitation agencies.

Disabling conditions that require treatment: Functional handicaps may involve such conditions as chronic alcoholism, drug addiction, mental retardation, a temporary physical handicap, parole from a mental institution, mental illness and other aspects of personality and character disorders. Major impairments among AFDC incapacitated fathers (18 percent of caseload) are due primarily to disease of the circulatory system, mental and personality disorders, arthritis, and other diseases of bones and organs of movement, and diseases of the respiratory system. In some instances, family disorganization, desertion, or child welfare and delinquency problems will have a direct bearing upon capacity for employment. The level of literacy may always be a compounding factor which limits severely the ability to develop personally and cope with the circumstances of self-support and family responsibility in present day society.

These illustrations cover a wide range of physical and emotional conditions which may require intensive therapy over a period of time. Activity centered programs will be used to restore feelings and aspirations for engagement in the work world in a meaningful manner. Progressive task situations will be adapted to individual circumstances and combined with treatment of contributing marital and other family factor problems—all essential in the therapy if lasting change is to be accomplished.

Methods of Intervention: Disabling conditions will be as varied as the life conditions and experiences which contribute to the need for adjustment. Recipients with functional handicaps may be identified through personal histories of erratic and irresponsible behavior, court or prison records, or cycles of hospitalization and physical incapacity brought on, possibly by self-defeating goals and patterns of living. Defensive adaptation of the individual to his condition of dependency and apathy may be difficult to overcome because of its chronicity, which generates loss of hope. Since individuals with these deep-seated problems are not easily reached, they may respond best in an institutional setting where routines are established and treatment is constant through use of interdisciplinary approaches involving medical, social, and occupational therapy.

Personal change can be accelerated also by establishing the sort of group identity and consciousness which has been demonstrated as a powerful force in self-development. Engagement of a group in activity centered therapy may provide mutual support experiences and communication may be established between members of the group. Often a group can discuss why they are unemployed and provide "feedback" of possibilities of change that is readily accepted. Group feelings can lead to mutual support and sharing of individual experiences and feelings. The similarity of feelings in task activity may lead each participant to less severe self-judgment, greater self-acceptance of himself as a person with capabilities, and hope of restoration of lost capacity for independent functioning.

Activity centered therapy projects will aim to provide services to meet the following needs of recipients: Self understanding; Self sufficiency; Prevention of deterioration; Meaningful activity; Group associations—the cultivation of healthy interpersonal relationships; Learning activities—self-improvement, community improvement; Social skills, communication skills; Occupational activity association; Development of positive attitudes toward self and society; Maintenance of morale and motivation; Gaining involvement of individual.

In summary, state public assistance plans must provide for treatment facilities to serve the most severely damaged, hard-core group of individuals and families. There must be assurance that individuals will be referred for work experience and training only when there is a reasonable chance for effective employability planning. Referral of individuals with serious disorders would prejudice and severely handicap success of the program. Therefore, an activity oriented treatment facility for such persons will be an essential component of the program. Medical, social, and psychological services alone will not be adequate unless they are applied in the situation where the individual can literally use his hands to feel and talk his way out of his disability. Effective social services must accompany and progress with the activity centered therapy, directed toward ultimate referral to vocational training and job placement.

Activity oriented treatment centers will fulfill the following expectations:

1. Provision of a place where severely handicapped clients can participate in a regular schedule of activities.

2. Evaluation of the assigned recipient's interests, aptitudes, abilities, temperament, and motivation for retraining.

3. Provision of opportunity to engage in purposeful activity, thereby gaining for the individual a sense of achievement, renewal of hope of improved functioning, and increased self-respect and feelings of self-worth.

4. Provision of individual and group counseling and other therapies when indicated.

5. Clients exposed to the activity center process should have a better chance for personal adjustment and possible referral to WIN or other types of vocational rehabilitation programs.

6. The activity center can be used as a showcase to demonstrate to employers and community workers that severely handicapped AFDC recipients and the blind and disabled can engage in useful activities.

7. Prognosis for successful training and ultimate employability for some recipients may appear unrealistic. For such persons, the center may provide continued activity and thus prevent further deterioration; for acceptable persons, consideration of referral to WIN (component three) may be possible.

8. Emotional and social ills of clients referred to the center will be inventoried and periodically evaluated during the overall process.

Legal base and funding: For provisions of activity centered therapy, federal financial participation will be available to the state welfare agency at an 85 percent ratio for the first year ending July 1, 1969, for full cost of operations for AFDC cases. In subsequent years, federal participation will revert to 75 percent. Public Law 90-248, January 2, 1968, under Title II-Public Welfare Amendments Part I, paragraph (h) is as follows: "Notwithstanding subparagraph (A) of section 403(a) (3) of the Social Security Act [as amended by subsection (c) of this section], the rate specified in such subparagraph in the case of any State shall be 85 per centum (rather than 75 per centum) with respect to expenditures, for services furnished pursuant to clauses (14) and (15) of section 402 (a) of such Act, made on or after the date of enactment of this Act, and prior to July 1, 1969."

Through extensive case review and analysis the author concluded that up to 20 percent of the California Aid to Totally Disabled caseload had potential for rehabilitation toward employment. In addition in March 1969, the author participated in a case record review of all of the AFDC incapacitated parent cases in a small rural county, 81 cases in number. The results of this case review were surprising. A total of 49 adults were identified as having self-support potential after the provision of needed rehabilitation services. In other words, 61 percent of the incapacitated parent AFDC caseload could move from welfare to work as a result of provision of appropriate services. In the United States, about 18 percent of the AFDC caseload are incapacitated parent cases. Therefore, rehabilitation of this group of recipients has the potential for the reduction of the total AFDC caseload by a full 10 percent. Activity Centered Therapy will become one rehabilitation resource for incapacitated public welfare recipients.

SAN MATEO COUNTY SOCIAL REHABILITATION ACTIVITY CENTER

A case review by the author of selected trainees at the San Mateo County Social Rehabilitation Activity Center supported the need for a concentrated service activity program to selected public assistance recipients. It is recalled that the theoretical formulations in respect to this service proposed concentration on emotionally disturbed persons and persons in conflict with the law. The following are case examples of such persons served in the San Mateo Center.

Emotionally Disturbed or Mentally Deficient

Miss A, a recipient of Aid to the Totally Disabled, was referred to the Activity Center in June 1967. Miss A had been in a mental institution for about one year prior to her referral with a diagnosis of schizophrenia. In addition she had epilepsy and had been a juvenile delinquent. Her epilepsy would become exacerbated under severe stress, but was under drug contol otherwise. Although the social worker thought the outlook for Miss A was hopeless, she was referred to the work shop for further clarification of potential for rehabilitation. She spent five months on a simple task of bagging ear phones for an airlines contract. Then she was graduated to power sewing machines involving the construction of wine bottle jackets for another contract. After two months, she was placed into a combination receptionist-typist position and at that point became very responsive and motivated. She was able to take criticism and work well within prescribed limitations. She expressed vocational interests at this time to become a nurses' aide and was placed in such an assignment. While her absentee rate was high in her earlier assignments, she missed only one day in three months on the nurses' aide assignment.

She had two epileptic seizures; one occurred a week before graduation from the nurses' aide course; the second occurred one hour before graduation. She attributed this to her excitement about the event and indicated she had never graduated from anything before. Miss A was placed in employment within a month of her graduation.

Miss A had severe social problems in the work situation. During her initial assignment in the workshop, she would use a variety of techniques to shock other trainees and staff. Her conversation generally centered around sex, with discussions involving how her boyfriends would proposition her. As her adjustment in the workshop improved, her need to shock others lessened, and at the point of her graduation from the nurses' aide program, had completely disappeared.

Miss A's living arrangement with her family was very unsatisfactory, and the social work staff was working with her toward an eventual move toward independent living. Her adjustment in the family, even so, had improved. The Activity Center staff had been very supportive of Miss A, and in their view, this was a key factor in her improved adjustment.

This case is a very good example of the necessity for engagement in an activity centered therapy program to improve socialization of the individual. It is apparent from the description of Miss A's behavior that placement in a normal educational or training program without the supportive and permissive atmosphere of the Activity Center would have failed.

Miss B, age 25, single, a recipient of Aid to the Totally Disabled, had spent seven years of her life in a mental institution as mentally retarded, caused by a psychosis. She was returned to her family and was employed there essentially as a babysitter for her siblings, but was very unsatisfactory because of her violent outbursts of temper. Miss B was placed in the activity centered therapy workshop in April of 1968. She was started on the airlines contract job, where she felt rejected by her coworkers. She was explosive and profane while on her job in the early stages of placement. As she gradually adjusted, these characteristics became minimal. The social worker saw Miss B as strongly motivated and as having potential for full-time employment. The general assessment of staff was that this woman was not mentally retarded and could become a productive person. Work of the staff was directed toward stabilization of the individual in training and working toward improvement of her living arrangements.

Miss C, a 23-year old recipient of Aid to the Totally Disabled, had been diagnosed as a chronic schizophrenic. She had no history of mental institutionalization, had completed the 12th grade in special classes, and was living with an emotionally disturbed mother in a gloomy house with 14 cats. Miss C had been referred to the Department of Vocational Rehabilitation by a welfare department social worker in 1967. The DVR psychiatrist rejected Miss C for training pending psychiatric treatment. He advised her that she was emotionally blocked and that became a label which she continued to use in discussing her problems. Miss C was very nervous with outward manifestations of constant wringing of the hands. In early 1968, a social worker referred her to a mental health clinic. They rejected her because her condition was not in crisis. She was then referred to the activity centered therapy work shop in May 1968. Her appearance was bizarre, with long hair falling over her shoulders and face, and she spoke in a high, shrill voice.

Miss C's initial placement was on the bagging of ear phones on the airline contract. Her performance was very good and she was promoted quickly to a contract involving the assembly of straw flowers. The progress that Miss C had shown in five months was phenomenal and could not have been predicted. The workshop staff clearly believe that Miss C will be ready for full employment within a few additional months.

Miss D is a 19-year-old girl on the ATD program. She was diagnosed as mentally retarded and was placed in a hospital for mentally retarded from August 1967 to January 1968. This placement resulted from expression of sex problems with siblings and subsequent complete rejection by the family. Miss D had an illegitimate child who was subsequently relinquished for adoption.

Upon her return from the institution, Miss D was placed in an adult boarding home. She was then referred to the activity centered training program in May 1968. She expressed considerable difficulty in her relationships to other trainees, would sit on men's laps in the Center, and persistently used foul language. Through a socialization process involving individual and group therapy and work activity in the Center, she completely overcame her obnoxious behavior within a period of four months. By the time of the case review, she was engaged in the straw flower project, had developed good relationships with other trainees, and the staff fully believed that she would become employable and independent. The evidence of mental retardation was lessening as her adjustment improved.

Persons in Conflict with the Law

Mr. E, a 26-year-old single man, was a member of a family which had spent a long period of time on public welfare. His juvenile arrest record dated from age 13. He came to the department of public welfare on General Assistance because of a broken arm in 1964. Mr. E's employment record has been very poor, mainly menial labor, such as car washing and day laborer. He was usually laid off or fired from these jobs because of an extremely bad temper. He had been referred to the Department of Vocational Rehabilitation, where he failed to cooperate, and to the Department of Employment MDTA, from which he was dismissed after three days because of disruptive behavior. In March 1968, he was entered into the Activity Center workshop and received a variety of assignments there. While he was still in the workshop in August 1968, the continuing disruptive behavior and other kinds of relationship problems were so great that his continued placement in the work shop was questionable. In other words, the socialization problem for this individual is so great that the present program of the activity centered therapy probably cannot accommodate it. This may suggest the need for refinement of the program or development of alternate programs for this type individual.

Mr. F is a 20-year-old Negro living in the ghetto in San Mateo County and receiving ATD. Mr. F had completed the 11th grade in special classes. At the time of the case review in August, he was in jail on an assault with a deadly weapon charge. He had stabbed his brother because the brother was choking the father. The brother was seriously wounded, but did not die. Mr. F has serious emotional problems combined with epilepsy, which is under drug control except when he drinks. He lives at home with his six siblings and mother and father. The mother works and the father has a small business. The father is an alcoholic. In addition to Mr. F's delinquency and epilepsy, he also is of borderline intelligence and emotionally unstable. He has had sporadic menial labor, such as dishwashing. He viewed himself as a very bad person. When under emotional stress, he would drink, usually have an epileptic seizure and would commit theft. He has been in and out of jail a number of times.

Mr. F entered the Activity Center workshop in August 1967 where he remained until May 1968, at which time he was jailed again. The social worker and vocational counselors in the work shop worked closely with the probation officer, and during the few months Mr. F was in the program, he showed remarkable improvement. He liked carpentry, so was assigned to a soft drink crate repair job. While he clowned a great deal to gain attention on the job, his adjustment there improved. He began to feel exploited during the period he was not receiving ATD and was spending considerable time in the workshop without pay. Accordingly, he was transferred to a neighborhood youth corps and received pay, but maintained also a continuing role in the workshop group therapy program. He responded well to this new arrangement.

During the period of placement in the work shop and neighborhood youth corps, Mr. F continued to get into trouble, although decreasingly so. On one occasion he was arrested for petty theft in San Francisco and was given a short jail term to be served during weekends. On one weekend he returned late to jail and then had to be referred back to the District Attorney's Office. The social worker accompanied him before the judge and sent the judge a letter outlining his improvement while in the workshop. On the basis of this, the judge relented on a three-year term which he was considering, and placed Mr. F in an honor camp for six months. The social worker continues to keep in touch with Mr. F during his incarceration and Mr. F is looking forward to a continuation of his vocational training program when he is released from the honor camp.

The NAACP reported that while Mr. F was engaged in the workshop he no longer became involved in street fights. He so valued the approval of the social worker and the vocational counselor that the staff has absolute confidence that Mr. F can be rehabilitated toward independent living and employment, although they recognize it will require a number of months to complete the process. It is important to note that the resocialization process for individuals like Mr. F requires patience, continuity of relations with the staff, whether in the workshop or in jail, and it requires time, as much as two to three years. In Mr. F's situation, the continuity of staff relations and the appearance of the case worker with him before the judge were of inestimable value.

Mr. G, a 27-year-old Negro receiving General Assistance, had a common-law wife and two children. He was a high-school graduate with two years of college and had held a variety of jobs, including mining, aide for juvenile hall and the Humane Society and dishwashing. He lived with his mother and had a younger brother in a mental institution. He was referred to the Activity Center in October 1967 and was placed in an electronics assembly project. He was later arrested for assault and battery on his common-law wife and for driving without a driver's license. He had extreme difficulty in adjusting to confinement and was ultimately placed in solitary confinement where he showed serious deterioration. The social worker maintained contact with him in jail, arranged for a medical examination, and Mr. G was ultimately diagnosed as a paranoid schizophrenic.

Mr. G maintained strong interest in returning to the activity centered therapy program for further work. The social worker attempted to make arrangements for him to become involved in some aspect of the work while in jail, but the authorities there were not cooperative. At the time of the review of this case Mr. G was still in jail. The evidence is strong, however, that when he is released he will have a starting point again in society as a result of the continuity maintained with the activity centered training staff.

Mr. H is an 18-year-old man with a 17-year-old wife and one child receiving AFDC. He is on parole, resulting from a burglary and assault charge. He has an eighth grade education. He was placed in the Activity Center training program in May 1968 and was started in a basic education class. Within a few days he found a job in which he failed very quickly, and he returned to the Center with his 19-year-old brother, who had also been involved in delinquent behavior of various kinds. His brother asked to be entered in the basic education program and the Center agreed to accept him. The brother has since been accepted in a neighborhood youth corps program and is progressing well.

Within a short period of time, the Center staff discovered that Mr. H was very artistic. The staff arranged a referral to DVR and that agency enolled him in an industrial design course. Mr. H continues to relate to the Center and participate in the adult education program. The Center staff describes Mr. H as being highly motivated, and the staff has great expectations that he will become self-supporting and that his delinquent behavior problems will not recur. The socialization and retraining process for Mr. H will undoubtedly take much less time than was required for treating the chronic conditions described earlier.

Medical and Social Problems

Mr. J is a 33-year-old Negro, single, receiving ATD. He has had an eighth grade education. His right side is hemiplegic with his right arm held in a bizarre position. He also has a crippling condition of one leg although he is fully ambulatory. He has been able to work in the past sporadically as a janitor and errand boy. He is very interested in horses and has some experience in training them. He has not worked full time since 1963 and has been on public assistance since that time. The medical diagnosis revealed that he was a congenital luetic and had a stroke when he was about 3 years of age. The mother was a Christian Scientist and refused all medical treatment. The activity centered therapy staff arranged medical treatment which has improved the use of the arm. Mr. J has engaged in workshop activity since April 1967 and has also become a student in the basic education course. His attitude toward his condition has gradually improved and he is highly motivated toward work. He particularly appreciated the attention given his medical condition and the improvement that has resulted.

Mr. K is a 55-year-old married man with four children receiving AFDC. He had a fifth grade education and at one time was a journeyman marine electrician. He has not worked full time in the past ten years, and is a confirmed hypochondriac. Even though complete medical and dental care is available through the AFDC program, he persists in carrying with him a broken set of dentures, explaining that he can't work because of his physical appearance. Mr. K was referred to the activity centered therapy workshop in February 1968 and persistently failed appointments until he was finally seen in May. The work shop staff has been unable to engage Mr. K in any of the workshop activities or help him in his search for employment. When discussing the possibility of employment in San Francisco as a marine electrician, he declined because of his fear of hippies, and because his wife would be unfaithful while he is gone. The problems of Mr. K are reflective of a small group of similar individuals with severe emotional deterioration, loss of hope, and adaptation to dependency. Mr. K is probably incapable of filling a journeyman marine electrician position, considering his educational background and lack of experience in the past ten years. In analyzing the case, it was agreed that the Center staff would discontinue efforts in reengagement of Mr. K in his original specialty and would begin his engagement in workshop activities such as electronic assembly with the objectives of restoring work habits, providing hope of return to work, and improving morale. It is further hoped that support from the Center staff will assist in the reduction of irrational fears and attitudes. Mr. K is clearly the type of person who needs preparation for more intensive educational and vocational training work available in the WIN program.

Mr. J, 40 years old, has a wife and three children. Prior to the development of a heart ailment he had worked steadily for 14 years. After two years on AFDC, he stated that his wife and children viewed him as a bum. He entered the county welfare department activity centered therapy program, was placed on a work project at 15 cents per hour, gradually increased to $1 per hour based upon his increased productivity. Mr. J reports that the attitude of the family toward him is one of respect, a complete reversal of earlier attitudes. The physician called the social worker to state that he didn't know what was being done for this man but to do more of it, since the improvement in his physical condition was phenomenal. Mr. J progressed to employment in the welfare agency as a staff aide. He could not obtain private employment because of insurance restrictions for employment of handicapped persons.

In reflecting on the review of cases in San Mateo County, several methods of treatment and other suggestions for program improvement emerge as follows:

1. Clarification of social worker and vocational counselor roles is needed. It was observed that the vocational counselor often performed a social worker's role while the social worker served only as an eligibility technician. It is suggested that social workers be assigned to the Center, since such a service program is primarily a social work responsibility. It would be an added benefit if social workers could be vocationally oriented. The function of determining eligibility would be performed by personnel within the welfare department who would not assume social work responsibility for activity centered therapy for hard-core welfare recipients. The San Mateo Center is fortunate in having two workers who combine the attributes of social work and vocational orientation.

2. Emphasis should be given to the importance of continuity of service, wherever the individual may be—jail, hospital, or elsewhere. The Center worker should assume responsibility for work

with the families of clients as well as with the individuals initially referred to the Center.

3. The Center must obtain a wider variety of occupational activities to accommodate the interests of many individuals, must become more rehabilitation oriented, and less production oriented. In other words, the work engineer may need to be replaced by an occupational therapist. Continued emphasis on utilization of other resources, such as Neighborhood Youth Corps, and DVR, is important in maintaining continuity of service from the Center and continuing class work if appropriate. To increase variety of placement for Center trainees, consideration might be given to placement in county government work experience programs, retaining responsibility for case management at the Center.

The theoretical framework for the development of an activity centered program originally contemplated more emphasis on treatment than on the vocational aspects, since it was assumed that activities of most kinds, whether or not they had relevance to the individual's interests and capacities, would be beneficial. A review of the foregoing case examples suggests that this assumption is invalid. Accordingly, it is suggested that at least a tentative vocational assessment be made to provide some understanding of individual work interest and potential. The activity assignment can then become adaptive to those interests and aptitudes. Vocational planning activity, whether long-range as in the Center or short-range as in the WIN program must be appropriate to the individual's concept of what he wishes to be. Consider, for example, the young woman who became most responsive to the work activity of her program only when she became engaged in nurses' aide training. Her earlier assignment involving the airlines contract work had no relevance to her interest and long-range goal. This suggests the possibility of breaking down work activity in such a way that the Center could offer something short of the full nurses' aide training program and still provide a goal-directed incentive to such an individual, thus accelerating the therapeutic process.

It may be concluded, after case review and discussions with the vocational counselor and the social work staff of the Center, that the original theoretical formulations of activity centered therapy have been affirmed. When the required patience, time, and ingenuity are provided, the results are strikingly successful.

HUMBOLDT COUNTY

During the summer of 1968, the author met with the welfare director from Humboldt County and SDSW staff in San Francisco to discuss the client self-help project submitted to SDSW for funding. Initiated by a group of recipients, the idea of this project was to develop a woodworking workshop for the fashioning of useful objects from redwood lumber mill scrap. Other work projects were to be considered at a later date. The group agreed to basic criteria based on the activity centered therapy model, with some variations to adapt to the particular situation in Humboldt County, as follows:

1. The selection of candidates for engagement in the project would be from the non-WIN ready group of AFDC recipients, including the physically incapacitated and those who are psychologically and socially nonfeasible for referral to WIN or to public welfare education training program.

2. Discharge from the activity centered therapy program would be based on the individual's rehabilitation to the point where he could be referred to WIN or ETP for vocational training and education. If the individual requires long-range engagement in the Center because of mental deficiency or chronic social, psychological, or physical handicaps, he could be retained in the workshop as a departmental employee or in a continuing trainee status.

3. The program would include the following components:

(a) A compensatory educational program adaptive to individual needs and not necessarily appropriate to a vocational objective. Part of the objective might be that of socialization.

(b) A type of work activity that should be vocationally oriented to the long-range vocational interests of individuals. The focus here, however, is not on vocational training per se, but rather on remotivation of the individual and on improvement of his morale through activity that has true relevance to his interets.

(c) Staffing in the Humboldt project may vary from the San Mateo model. The group work, social work, medical, and other appropriate disciplines will be utilized. The County is considering, however, the possibility of some assignments to the workshop directly from the eligibility bank of cases not normally served by a social worker. The experiment would be that of determining how many cases could be served without specific reference to the social worker, keeping open, however, the possibility of referral to a social worker when indicated. This is a very impotant feature, since we need to know whether it is possible, through environmental manipulation apart from therapeutic disciplines, to achieve rehabilitation objectives derived from the satisfaction gained in the activity centered program and group sessions.

4. It was agreed that in this project a training or work stipend based upon minimum hourly wage standards would be provided the individual. The author's initial difficulty with this proposal was based on the belief that monetary incentives were not necessary to engage welfare recipients in educational training, and the tend-

ency, in view of this belief, to overlook the fact that there are surely many advantages to monetary incentives, particularly to such an economically deprived group of people. The San Mateo project did not provide economic incentive and gained considerable success in its operation. Even so, a case was reviewed in San Mateo County of a man who felt he was exploited when he continued to work in the workshop without reimbursement at a time that he was discontinued from ATD. The therapy for this man became his engagement in a NYC project which provided reimbursement. The provision of incentive payments now appears to be a very desirable element for the purposes of this project.

The differences between the Humboldt and the San Mateo workshop models are as follows:

1. The self-help aspects of the Humboldt program will be emphasized. Split-offs from the activity centered therapy program may occur which engage recipients full time for remuneration in the self-help context.

2. Incentive payments in the Humboldt activity centered therapy program will become an important differential from the San Mateo model.

3. In respect to staffing, the Humboldt project will experiment with the provision of activity centered therapy, excluding the "one-to-one" casework process.

LOS ANGELES COUNTY

Introduction: As a first step toward providing activity Centered Therapy, Los Angeles County intends to start small on a *pilot* basis, and expand as more information becomes available about SRS, and as they gain more expertise. Initially, they will follow a two-pronged procedure: Some clients will be referred directly to other community resources providing ACT; and other clients will be provided services within the agency by the social worker, district counselor, or by referral to the Toy Loan facility which is being converted to a pilot Center; and in some instances, a combination of the two procedures may be feasible. Los Angeles County's plan, the main thrust of which is toward the Activity Centered Therapy Program, follows:

Objectives: Major goals are to provide specialized rehabilitation and activities programs directed to the improvement of social functioning and adjustment of aid recipients; provide prevocational activities to enable AFDC clients, inappropriate for WIN referral, to prepare for later involvement in vocational training for self-support; provide activities involving vocational skills and work experience for limited numbers of AB, ATD, and OAS clients whose employment is a feasible goal; evaluate and refer categorical aid recipients to appropriate community agencies or, after evaluation, recommend such referrals to the social workers; and develop and maintain effective liaison with other agencies which provide services for aid recipients.

Description of the Center: The Los Angeles County Department of Public Social Services proposes to utilize their present Toy Loan facility as a pilot Center. During the period CWT was in effect (early 1964–June 30, 1968), AFDC clients were assigned to Toy Loan. The facility provided under a workshop type climate, a gentle form of preconditioning training. Toys donated from the community through service clubs and private agency toy drives were repaired and assembled by clients under the guidance of Los Angeles City School instructors. These toys when refinished, were then made available to underprivileged children in some 37 toy lending centers scattered throughout the County. In addition, remedial and vocational classes were offered to clients assigned.

Toy Loan can now be easily adapted to provide the basic ingredients for a SR Center. Many of its activities can continue as is, except vocational training for AFDC clients. They will provide, in addition, more professional staff, and new activities such as evaluation, group counseling, and special classes geared to SRS. The facility is being enlarged to handle some 300 clients at any one time. Clients may be assigned for periods up to 90 days, or an average of 45. On this basis, the Center can serve some 2,400 clients a year.

Activity Centered Therapy Operations:

1. Selection of Recipients—Social workers will select AB, ATD, and OAS recipients for SRS to improve their social adjustment. A few will be selected who could benefit from vocational training to the point of self-support. AFDC clients, not appropriate for WIN services, will be selected to improve their social adjustment and family functioning to the point where referral to WIN may be feasible.

2. Referrals to the Center—Clients selected for SRS by social workers will be referred through the District SRS counselors. In general those referred to the Center will be those who could benefit from the evaluation which the Center provides.

3. Services at the Center—Each client will receive evaluation from professional staff at the Center. When the goal of WIN involvement is feasible, the evaluation shall indicate the steps necessary to achieve ultimate self-support. For those with disabilities, the evaluation shall indicate the steps needed to achieve a better functioning life. SRS counselors at the Center will determine the appropriateness of any referrals to other community resources and will act as liaison for social workers and District SRS counselors, and no referrals will be made without social worker involvement.

Work therapy for recipients in all aid categories will be provided when appropriate. A "sheltered" or "gentle" work climate will be utilized and will not include a wage concept or work production pressure. Examples of such work therapy are doll repair and toy refinishing. On-going evaluation of the client's progress by experienced counselors will be an integral program component. Work behavior patterns; ability to acquire occupational skills; development of work habits, attitudes and tolerance; and social behavior suitable for successful job performance will be individually appraised. The training should afford each participant every opportunity to reach his maximum capabilities.

Clients will be encouraged to attend existing adult education classes within the community appropriate for SRS. In addition, prevocational classroom instruction will be made available for participants at the SRS Center. Some will be classes regularly funded through the Los Angeles City Schools such as Sewing, Woodshop, English as a Second Language, and Basic Education. Other classes, not available through the Los Angeles City Schools, will be purchased—prevocational subjects specifically designed for welfare recipients, such as Parent Education, Education for the Mentally Retarded, Consumer Education, Home Management, and Understanding Family Programs. Initially, some ten such classes are planned with others to be added as needed.

Small group meetings will be conducted by the Center's group workers to orient clients and assist them in gaining insights to social adjustment, family functioning, and their ability to engage in a plan for eventual self-support. Information gained about and by clients at these sessions may result in helpful referrals to other community resources.

Each of two group workers will each conduct two 2-hour sessions daily for 15 clients. All 300 clients assigned will receive group counseling initially and at least every week thereafter.

Group cultural activities designed to instill confidence and generate heightened morale and self-esteem will be conducted. Such activities will be a learning process in that they may bring out latent skills a client may possess. Included in these programs will be study trips, play-acting as a means of overcoming speech defects, and research projects in minority group history.

Five additional counties—Shasta, Santa Clara, Tehama, Kings and Glenn requested help in development of activity centered therapy programs. The Welfare Department in Shasta had in operation a very fine sheltered workshop. The additional funding available through the model plan would enable the county to strengthen the program in accordance with the model standards. Kings, Tehama, and Glenn counties had sheltered workshops operating under private auspices but serving essentially welfare recipients. Each of these counties agreed to transfer the function to public welfare for funding and operation in conformance with model standards. SDSW staff provided consultation leading to arrangements for the necessary changes.

Thus, the State of California found eight counties interested in developing activity centered therapy, an extremely gratifying development. The author was unaware of this latent interest, expecting to initiate only the San Mateo program by 1969. Each of the counties was enthusiastic about the program and its potential. Moreover, each county cited strong support for the program by its Board of Supervisors and the community, and anticipated no trouble in gaining appropriation for the local fiscal share of costs.

The Social Rehabilitation role of public welfare in California is clearly established. For the WIN program, the welfare role will be that of provision of supportive social services and child care programs. For non-WIN persons, the social and rehabilitation function will be emphasized in all of the 58 county welfare departments, for ATD, Blind and AFDC incapacitated parent cases.

CHAPTER 16

A DESIGN FOR
INCOME MAINTENANCE, EMPLOYMENT
AND SOCIAL REHABILITATION SERVICES

CONCERN ABOUT POVERTY has been intensified by the startling contrasts between the poor and the affluent and by the extent and persistence of the poverty which affects 40 million persons in the United States, and goes beyond one individual lifetime into generational poverty for entire families. Numerous authors have weighed, measured, and counted the poor and their meagre and deprived environment and others have contrasted the advantages of the affluent with the miseries of the poor. These and many other books and articles have reaffirmed the necessity for change if this democracy is to survive and maintain respect in the world community, but the development of a rationale for change is not enough. Provincial self-interest continues to hold more of the affluent aloof to change than otherwise, although within certain groups, they tolerate minor, billion-dollar skirmishes against poverty.

The rediscovery of poverty in the United States, through literature and the militancy of the disaffected, has upset comforting myths about equality, revealing the extent to which poverty exists, its corrosive character, its lingering effects, and how the growing disparity between incomes can reduce the poor to a permanent state of inequality with their more affluent countrymen without quite starving them out of existence or giving them the opportunity to improve their status.

Poverty can be measured from two viewpoints: In the standard approach, income level is specified as the poverty line; in the relative approach, a specified percentage of the population is considered poor, since changing conditions relative to other groups in society reflect trends toward or away from equality. While most past studies have used the standard approach, most of the recent studies use the relative approach, placing the poor at between 20 and 25 percent of the total population, and some assert that this poverty line is too low by current American standards. Several have pointed out that it is disgraceful that any segment of the population within a rich society can be designated as "poor," and some, like Leon Keyserling and Herman Miller have suggested that the economy has not drastically improved conditions of the low-income population since World War II.

The author feels great concern regarding the conditions in our society which require correction: the poor housing conditions, slums, and ghettos, the deteriorated commercial and residential core of our large cities. Poverty, expressing itself in the hunger, inadequate housing and medical care, and generally deplorable living conditions of the poor, is recognized as highly inconsistent with the affluence of the rest of society. The common denominator of these conditions is historical repetition. Recent studies of public welfare have expressed concern about the generational qualities of poverty, pointing out that the dependency on public aid, the immorality, and other degrading characteristics of the poor are transmitted from one generation to another. The unfortunate aspect of this accusation is that it is partly true. Poverty, in fact, is persistent throughout the generations, because it is extremely difficult for an individual caught in a poverty family to escape, although not impossible. It is only the exceptions to the rule which seem to prove to some that generational poverty does not need to persist, that the individual victimized by poverty can, somehow, improve his own qualities.

Need for improvement is directed more often toward the unfit individual than toward societal problems. We blame the individual for his deficiencies and concern ourselves too little with the deficiencies of society as a whole. Society's problems persist, however, not because they are unseen, but rather because there is no commitment to overcome them. If society were committed to overcoming the blights in its cities and rural areas, it could move in a scientific manner to accomplish this, much the same as it moves to place man in space and on the moon. Society would assume an objective, scientific approach to the problem and proceed to solve it.

In each generation, some men reflect upon the possibilities of an improved society. In 1887, when Edward Bellamy[1] projected himself to the year 2000, he stressed the need for each person to be treated and viewed in the same light as one race, a member of one human family. He could think of no feature of civilization as it existed in 1887 more repugnant than the way in which society treated its dependent classes. He observed the contemptuous attitudes toward some menial occupations, noting that persons of culture and refinement would never condescend to engage in such activities. In other words, he was aware of the difficult conditions placed upon certain occupations, that service in them was reserved for the poor, and that these underprivileged persons received added contempt from general society for being menials and poor.

Bellamy envisioned that by 2000, man would not consider life worth living if he had to be surrounded by a population of ignorant, boorish, coarse, wholly uncultivated men and women, finding himself in the same plight as did the educated minority of 1887. He questioned how a man could be satisfied merely because he perfumed himself to mingle with a maladorous crowd, or how, living in a palatial residence, he could enjoy such living if the windows on all four sides of the house opened into stable yards. He believed that such a man could be little better off than those actually living in squalor and brutishness around him, and likened him to one who is up to his neck in a nauseous bog, solacing himself with a smelling bottle. Bellamy stressed the importance to every man of having for neighbors intelligent, companionable persons, and stated that the nation could do nothing more important than to educate his neighbors.

Bellamy deplored the practice in England of educating some to the highest degree and leaving the masses wholly uncultivated, establishing thereby a gap between the two groups without any means of communication. He noted that in England in 1887, riches debauched one class with idleness of mind and body, while poverty sapped the vitality of the masses by overwork, bad food, and pestilent homes, and the labor required of children and the burdens laid on women enfeebled the very springs of life. Conditions envisioned for the year 2000 were quite the opposite, with the establishment of most favorable conditions for the young, and the accommodation of labor to the capacity of the individual. He was particularly optimistic about the life of women in the future noting that their career ambitions were as normal as those of men. He commented that marriage need not separate women from the normal interests of society, that only in pregnancy would they withdraw temporarily from work, and afterwards, would likely resume their places in the work world.

When Bellamy envisioned himself reporting his ideas to a wealthy group of citizens in London in 1887, he also foresaw the results of that report as follows: "I have seen humanity hanging on a cross! Do none of you know what sights the stars look down on in this city, that you can think and talk of anything else? Do you not know that close to your door a great multitude of men and women, flesh of your flesh, live lives that are one agony from birth to death? Listen! Their dwellings are so near that if you hush your laughter you will hear their grievous voices, the piteous crying of the little ones that suckle poverty, the hoarse curses of men sodden in misery, turned half way back to brutes, the chaffering of an army of women selling themselves for bread. With what have you stopped your ears that you do not hear these doleful sounds? For me, I can hear nothing else. Silence followed my words. A passion of pity had shaken me as I spoke, but when I looked around upon the company, I saw that far from being stirred as I was, their faces expressed a cold and hard astonishment, mingled with extreme mortification and anger. The ladies were exchanging scandalized looks, while one of the gentlemen had put up his eyeglass and was studying me with an air of scientific curiosity. When I saw that things which were to me so intolerable moved them not at all, that words that melted my heart instead had only offended them with the speaker, I was at first stunned and then overcome with a desperate sickness and faintness at the heart. What hope was there for the wretched, for the world, if thoughtful men and tender women were not moved by things like these!"

Although Bellamy regretted that the anguish which he felt and which was so clear and all-important to him was meaningless to others, and that he was powerless to change conditions, he finally accepted the inevitable—that until conditions for change were ripe, innovations could not be expected with any rapidity. He knew, however, that should such time arrive when society would show concern for and determine to overcome the mortification of the poor, then the scene would shift with an almost magical swiftness. That precise time had not arrived by 1969 but the trends indicate that it may be placed in motion in the 1970's.

It is to be deplored that the "practical man" in contemporary society still holds the traditional beliefs of Bellamy' contemporaries, and that the hard-core nature of modern middle-class culture is as intractable in its opposition to change as is poverty itself.

In 1817, Robert Owen[2] wrote a book associated with his hope for a Utopia, and expressing concern about the conditions of mankind at that time, because, as he noted, in Great Britain and Ireland in 1817, the poor exceeded 12 million persons or nearly three-quarters of the population of the British Islands.

Owen established the principle that one's own happiness can only be attained by conduct that promotes the happiness of the community. He believed that any society which allows destructiveness of the happiness of those excluded, will inevitably engender opposition from the justly injured feelings of the excluded in proportion to the extent of the exclusion, and that the result of this will be to diminish the happiness of the privileged. He thought that the governing powers of all countries should establish rational plans for the education and general formation of the characters of their subjects, and that children should be trained from earliest infancy in good habits, rationally educated, and their labors usefully directed. He was persuaded that such individual understanding and education would impress them, giving each an active and ardent desire to promote the happiness of every other individual. He noted that such conditions would not necessarily ensure health, strength, vigor, and happiness of the individual, since his perception of human behavior and potential was profound. But he had also noted that children were, without exception, passive and wonderfully contrived human compounds, and that by means of accurate, early, and subsequent attention, founded on correct knowledge of the subject, they might be developed according to plan. He understood that there was considerable variation between children, yet they had a universal characteristic, a plastic quality which could be ultimately molded toward rationality.

The fundamental truth observed by Owen in 1817 was that children are products of their environment. If the environment is conducive to development of conditions designed to establish a model of societal expectations, then the child will fulfill the expectations, but if conditions of poverty and deprivation exist, the child's model will be impaired and his later actions deviate. Owen understood the importance of the family and of educational models to the child. He noted that the child who has been rationally instructed from infancy will readily discover and trace the source of the opinions and habits of his associates and why they possess them; and will also have acquired reasons sufficient to exhibit the irrationality of being angry with an individual for possessing qualities which he had no means of preventing. Owen understood that a child becomes the product of his environment, that his behavior is occasioned by his early experience and understandings, and that his behavior is therefore rational, even though it may deviate from the norm in society. Owen went too far when he suggested that there should be a national system concerning itself exclusively with the formation of character and general amelioration of the lower classes, in his terms. He was confident that any community could train its citizens to live without idleness, without poverty, without crime, and without punishment, for he asserted that these conditions represented errors in the various systems prevalent throughout the world and were necessary consequences of ignorance. Owen believed that the formation of character should be accommodated by improvement of education and provision of it to every individual, and that no child should be excluded from an educational experience. While one might not go so far as to establish a national system for the purpose, these are objectives which we seek today, and they can be attained through rational arrangements without need for central control.

Owen also believed that it was important to furnish honest and useful employment to all, and that it was the responsibility of government to ensure that training and employment were available to every man. He recommended that to the extent employment was not available to all persons through the normal operations of industry, it should be provided on useful, national projects so that the public could derive advantage comparable to the expense of the projects.

Having observed the necessity for society to assume responsibility, with the family, for all children from the very earliest age, Owen suggested that children's personalities are formed very early, that the child's disposition is correctly or incorrectly formed before his second year, and that many durable impressions are made by the end of his first year. He believed that uninstructed and ill-instructed children would suffer injury in the formation of their characters during these early years and that the community should provide playgrounds and other arrangements for small children almost from the time that they could walk. This same belief is finding expression today in programs such as Headstart, operated through the Economic Opportunity Act.

Owen deplored the erroneous belief that each man forms his own character, is therefore accountable for all his sentiments and habits, and merits reward for some and punishment for others, and stated that a man's character was always formed for him by his predecessors, who gave him the ideas and habits which generally governed and directed his conduct. Since he had observed that general public opinion in the early 1800's had been directed by a combination of prejudice, bigotry, and fanaticism, derived largely from ignorance, he insisted that education for those who were poorly taught should become of first importance to the welfare of society and that it was particularly important to assist the child in understanding the connection between the interest and happiness of each individual and the interest and happiness of every other individual.

The fundamental errors which Owen protested in 1817 were certainly more pervasive than those which exist today, since it was common for six- and seven-year-old children to work in spinning mills and other labor from six in the morning to seven at night, six days per week, and ignorance and poverty were more widespread, yet elements of those conditions and of the attitudes of men persist today to a lesser degree. When Owen deplored the legal and institutional arrangements which perpetuated such conditions, he interpreted them as stating, in effect: "Remain in ignorance and let your labor be directed by that ignorance: for while you can procure what is sufficient to support life by such labor, although that life should be an existence in abject poverty, disease, and misery, we will not trouble ourselves with you, or any of your proceedings: when, however, you can no longer procure work, or obtain the means to support nature, then apply for relief to the parish; and you shall be maintained in idleness."

Owen believed that anyone acquainted with the dynamics of human nature would understand that men, women, and children could not be long maintained in ignorance and idleness without becoming habituated to crime; that idle poor existed in England in such large numbers because they had been permitted to grow up in gross ignorance, and when they were willing to be trained to useful labor and productive employment, the opportunities for this had not been provided to them. Owen believed not only that all men were ready to acquire knowledge and habits which would enable them to produce far more than they needed for their support and enjoyment, but took issue with Malthus by suggesting that even though the world population was adapting to the quantity of food raised for its support, Malthus had never told anyone how much more food could be created from the same soil by intelligent and industrious people than by those who are ignorant and ill-governed. What Owen maintained in 1817 still holds today—every man must have the opportunity for engagement in meaningful employment, and to the extent that the private and public economy does not accommodate this, some provision must be made to ensure that every man is so engaged.

The attitudes of society toward the unemployed, the dependent, and criminals are emotional and unscientific, yet deeply ingrained. Men with scientific backgrounds in economics, medicine, the physical sciences, law, and biology lose contact with the scientific method when dealing with emotionally charged issues of deviant human behavior. Yet the study of man calls for the most scientific expertise for solutions to the problems caused by such behavior, and requires perspectives which are not limited by a specific cultural orientation.

Stuart Chase[3] noted the entrenchment of traditional myths about people and welfare by examining a typical "Middletown." There were 38,000 people in Middletown (Muncie, Indiana), when the Lynds first arrived with their small survey staff in 1924. The great boom of the 1920's was fairly launched, buoyed up by the soaring automotive industries. Middletown had been chosen among many candidates because it was typically American, manufacturing was diversified, with the glass jar business prominent, and farmers came in from the rich surrounding corn lands to Saturday market at the county seat. The Lynds returned to Middletown to check their findings in 1935, after ten years had gone by—four more years of boom, then six of depression. They wrote another report on it, called *Middletown in Transition*. The extent to which the nation had faltered in its economy was incredible. By 1933, Middletown's storekeepers had lost 57 percent of their business compared with

1929, and another six percent were struggling to survive. Building construction fell to five percent of the 1929 figure, while factory payrolls were cut in half. Motor car sales dropped 78 percent; gasoline sales, only four percent, because the cars were old but people kept on driving them. Loan sharks did a thriving business. When General Motors tore the machinery out of their big plant and left town, it looked as though the end had come. A full quarter of Middletown was on relief. Yet for two years following the stock market crash, the leaders of the town refused to admit that their symbols of progress—self-help, bigger motor cars, and bigger bank accounts and land values—could ever be tarnished.

In a chapter entitled "The Middletown Spirit," the Lynds preserve for the curious historian the credo of Midwest America in 1928. No fewer than 172 beliefs are categorically set down. Here is a sample lot:

1. Economic conditions are the result of natural order and cannot be changed by man-made laws.
2. We always have had depressions and always will.
3. Men won't work unless they have to.
4. Any man willing to work can get a job.
5. The individual must fend for himself, and in the end gets what he deserves.
6. You can't change human nature.

Chase observed that Middletown had learned nothing from a world war, a crazy stock market boom, and a depression which had made beggars of a quarter of its people. Like many other communities, Middletown wore a suit of symbolic clothes cut from an outdated pattern, and now aware of its shabbiness, continued to wear the ancient garment because there was no replacement. Simple faith was gone. Profoundly disturbed, but clinging to its tattered belief system, Middletown could find no way out of its dilemma.

There is a general concept in our society that public welfare recipients might better be retained on aid than rehabilitated toward employment. Some of the traditional bases for this concept are as follows:

1. Since most welfare recipients are poorly educated and lacking in skills, they would be trained for work of an unskilled nature which is low-demand to the extent that they are placed on a job that would displace someone else who ultimately would come on welfare. Therefore, there is no advantage to the preparation of such individuals for work.

2. Welfare recipients have handicaps involving social, psychological, medical, and motivational problems. The investment of

time and money in overcoming these obstacles would be too great for such provision of services to be economical.

Economic advisers generally hold that full employment cannot be maintained without inflation. Because the economist knows well the monetary hazards of inflation but little about the human hazards of unemployment for men and their families, to his mind the dangers of inflation or other economic hazards transcend human risk. Such men will rationalize human degradation on public relief as a necessary and therefore desirable condition to economic stability. Knowing that men can control and sustain the economic conditions in which they live, the humanitarian would create full employment and avoid inflation by seeking other methods of control than by reducing jobs. The economist sometimes seeks strange methods to regulate the economy. He has killed pigs, plowed grain into the soil, paid farmers to hold their land idle while families succumb to starvation in the United States and abroad. When will a President of the United States appoint a Council on Human Affairs to seek greater balance between the affluent and the poor, and to supersede, but make use of the limited services of the Council of Economic Advisers, whose sole objective at present is to balance the budget at the expense of those who can least afford to pay?

Statistics compiled by the U.S. Departments of Commerce and of Labor over the past 20 years have provided one basis for the rationale that high unemployment rates are the most effective antidote for inflation. The following chart illustrates this theory:

WHEN UNEMPLOYMENT IS HIGH, INFLATION IS SLOW

During 10 years of high unemployment in the last two decades: Unemployment averaged 5.8 percent, price inflation 1.3 percent.

	unemployment rate percent	inflation rate percent
1949	5.9	-0.6
1950	5.3	1.4
1954	5.5	1.5
1958	6.8	2.6
1959	5.5	1.6
1960	5.5	1.7
1961	6.7	1.3
1962	5.5	1.1
1963	5.7	1.3
1964	5.2	1.5

Note: Inflation rate is the increase in average price of all goods and services produced in U.S.

WHEN UNEMPLOYMENT IS LOW, INFLATION IS FAST

During 11 years of low unemployment in the last two decades: Unemployment averaged 3.8 percent, price inflation 3.3 percent.

	unemployment rate percent	inflation rate percent
1948	3.8	6.7
1951	3.3	6.7
1952	3.0	2.2
1953	2.9	0.9
1955	4.4	1.5
1956	4.1	3.4
1957	4.3	3.7
1965	4.5	1.9
1966	3.8	2.6
1967	3.8	3.1
1968 (est.)	3.6	3.7

Source: U.S. Depts. of Commerce, Labor.

Economists have decided that when unemployment rises to about 5.5 percent, prices rise at 1.5 percent annually; when it is decreased to 3.5 percent, prices increase by 4 percent, and they have warned that when government attempts to lower the jobless rate below 4.5 percent by stimulating total demand, this is likely to bring sharp increases in costs and prices. It is apparent that economic sophistry of this kind will become a theoretical barrier to the emerging programs for promoting education, training, and full employment. Yet a statistical association between two aspects of the economy does not necessarily establish a cause and effect relationship in spite of after-the-fact analysis which seeks to support the association. A myriad of other coincidental associations could be established.

The economist must play an important role in our society, and planning which seeks order in the economy to avoid high inflation or severe depression is necessary, to be sure, but the urgency of the issue relates to the proper placement of the economist in the order of things. The economist is a specialist who should "be on tap and not on top." Social engineers and planners should advise the politicians regarding the absolute minimum below which human values shall not fall, and should deliberate upon the optimum conditions needed to stabilize the economy within the framework of the criteria of civilized human values.

Human values dictate that all able-bodied adults must be engaged in work, therefore absolute full employment must prevail. The economist must examine this phenomenon and make appropriate recommendations not only for economic but also humane adjustments. Surely our society can remain free, capitalism can thrive, and human dignity can be maintained all in the same framework of endeavor. Let us go even further and state that prosperity and freedom for private enterprise should become the natural by-products of full employment. Present-day public relief policies, social unrest, and riots are symptoms which reflect the inadequacies of our social institutions. The advent of education, training, and full employment for all the people will ameliorate social unrest.

The human suffering occasioned by the great depression of the 1930's triggered forces of social reform, and taught us that we could no longer allow our economy to follow traditional patterns of boom and bust. The Full Employment Act of 1946, misnamed because it has never provided full employment, provided a vehicle for large-scale economic planning through development of executive and congressional economic advisory and planning mechanisms. While social reform also followed the depression in the form of OASI, unemployment insurance, minimum wage legislation, and mortgage and deposit insurance, the major thrust was still economic. And as we view the need today of even more substantive reform, we find ourselves still relying on so-called experts in economic theory to fashion the remedy.

An economic rationale must take human values into consideration. Public assistance recipients must be rehabilitated toward employment irrespective of the obstacles. It is important that every individual be enabled to make a major contribution to society. If denied this opportunity, he will become engaged in defensive activities such as criminal behavior, running counter to his own and to the basic interests of society, or he may be easily recruited for riots in the streets. Engagement of each individual in a major activity is extremely important to his family, his children, and his spouse, who lose respect for him if he is not engaged in work as the other members of society are. Moreover, prolonged dependency and nonwork establish a model which the children may ultimately come to view as acceptable even though humiliating, thereby establishing a climate for generational dependency.

In addition to the human values, it is possible that some economic values might accrue also through rehabilitation of welfare recipients. The potential for welfare recipients to become trained for skilled jobs is relatively low, although experience has shown that some recipients have capacity for higher education and in fact have gone to college with help. Others have been rehabilitated for skills such as welding, which in some localities is a scarce labor commodity. Economic as well as other benefits accrue to the rehabilitated individual. Improvement of self-respect and status prevents individual and family deterioration involving medical, psychological, and behavior elements. In some circumstances it has been noted that the feeling of self-worth on the part of mothers engaged in education and training programs has had direct relationship to the establishment of a marital plan which contributed to independence and improved family living. Innovations in new career developments have opened up jobs that never existed before, involving indigenous case aides, homemaker and attendant services and teacher aides. To the extent that individuals are placed in employment without displacing other workers, their contribution to the economy becomes significant.

Man's right to work must become a paramount approach. We must exercise our ingenuity to educate, train, and rehabilitate all persons for work, and when work is not available for those trained, the Federal Government must become the employer of last resort and provide work.

Considerable attention is being given to the possibility of augmenting income of the poor. Proposals are wide-ranging, but all maintain a common element—supplementing income to a point

fixed above poverty level. The concern for the poor and their plight
is not new. History indicates that other attempts have been made
to supplement income of the poor in a rational way. One of the
most significant attempts occurred as early as 1795 in England, when
the justices of the county and other persons met at Speen, the center of a district in England known as Speenhamland, near Newbury,
to consider a proposal to fix agricultural wages by law. They agreed
that they should recommend to the farmers that wages be raised,
but concluded that this would be insufficient to provide living
wages to families. They therefore decided to supplement wages
(see Chapter 9 discussion on Bulletin 644). A plan was developed
whereby, as the price of bread rose or fell in cost, the amount of
supplementation to the wage earner and family would similarly rise
and fall (modern cost-of-living increases). In addition, plans provided for a differential in the supplemental rate to families, dependent upon the number of family members (current practice in public
welfare). Thus, in effect, the plan provided a double-graduated
scale, varying according to the price of bread and the size of the
families.

The arithmetical precision with which the proposals seemed to
regulate relief gave the plan a scientific glamour, and many thought
it a fine development. In fact, Malthus agreed that he could not
see what else could have been done under the circumstances. It
was the hope that the plan would aid the "useful poor," those able
and willing to work. It was generally believed that the plan would
cost much less than to allow a family to regress into a state of indi-
gence where they would need to be fully maintained by the public.
This plan was soon adopted throughout all of England and was
known variously as the Berkshire Bread Act and the Speenhamland
Law. The English Parliament adopted the law in 1795. The plan
spread from agricultural labor to the weaving industry in the urban
areas, and to various other industries as well. The laboring poor
came to believe that they had a legal right not only to relief from
immediate destitution but also to a regular, minimum payment for
maintenance of themselves and their children, whatever their capacity or industry might be. Between 1795 and 1830, the family
allowance standard had dropped by one-third, a result to some
extent, of criticism by many of the plan (an eventuality which
must be contemplated in reference to current guaranteed annual
income proposals).

Lonsdale[4] reported some of the problems associated with the
Speenhamland Law:

1. Farmers were forced to employ pauper labor, which was a
burden on them. One farmer reported that he had tried to keep
two excellent laborers, but that he was obliged to discharge them

because authorities forced him to take on two paupers instead, since they had to be cared for anyhow. Farmers found that the paupers were unskilled and incapable of performing an adequate job.

2. It was believed unfortunate that the able-bodied adult should look on the parish as his paymaster; a part of the year he might be supported by wages, part of the year he would receive wages plus parish pay, and another part of the year he would receive only parish pay.

3. It was believed that because of the availability of the parish allowance, irrespective of the value of the labor itself, that this tended to deteriorate the quality of the labor. However, in one circumstance in a village, the commissioner found that while there was plenty of work to be done in a railway yard a few miles from the village, the able-bodied men refused to work there and went to the parish instead, which gave them relief.

4. It was found that taxes increased considerably because of the larger sums of money paid for relief.

5. It was believed that the availability of public relief in lieu of work deteriorated the morale of the poor. Moreover, it was found that individuals would plan for marriage and immediately after the ceremony apply to the parish for placement on the relief list.

6. Lonsdale quoted commissioners who described the system as follows: "Drink and dissipation, indolence and insolence, deception and dependence, have become the familiar characteristics of the English laborer. We do not believe that a country in which the distinction between the pauper and the independent laborer has been completely effaced, and every man ensured a comfortable subsistence, can retain its prosperity, or even its civilization." (See Chapter 9 discussion of Bulletin 644, and note the similarity of arguments today.)

Nicholls,[5] who was a Poor Law Commissioner and a secretary to the Poor Law Board, was very critical of the Speenhamland Act, noting that the wages of labor and the relief from the parish rates became so commingled that one could not be separated from the other. He suggested that the evil of the program fell heavily on all classes, rich and poor alike; the rich paid more for worse labor, and the poor were compelled to receive the equivalent for their labor in a form that was repulsive to their feelings of independence and self-respect.

The Webbs[6] noted the political problems engendered by the Speenhamland Act. While it was agreed in the early 1800's that the

Act had failed, it was extremely difficult to gain political action to repeal the law. Everybody agreed about the evil results of the practice, but no one dared to vote against it. Finally, following the publication of a Royal Commission Report, a new poor law act was passed in 1834 which abolished the provisions of the earlier Speenhamland Act. This act went to the opposite extreme by declaring that all relief to the able-bodied, except in well-regulated workhouses, was declared illegal. The provision was gradually enforced and it was anticipated that all types of outdoor relief would cease within a few years.

Although the Speenhamland Act was developed over 170 years ago, it still serves as an example of problems which might be anticipated in contemporary society, given a similar arrangement. In essence, it would appear that the problems of the poor should not be associated, in terms of solutions, with the general working society. That is, the problems of unemployment and inadequate wages should be isolated and dealt with in their own right. Since the movement toward a minimum wage would greatly assist in the upgrading of living conditions of the poor, it represents one important remedy. (The author agrees that stop-gap measures such as Bulletin 644 should not substitute long-range goals of adequate minimum wages and standards).

Another important approach will be found in the movement to upgrade the education and vocational skills of each individual, so that he may be better prepared to bargain in the labor market. It is also imperative that there be assurance of work for all men either in private industry or through provision of needed work in the public sector to the extent that it cannot be found in normal industry and governmental work.

The Full Employment Act of 1946 committed the Federal Government to a policy of eradicating unemployment. The act stipulated that the continuing policy and responsibility of the Federal Government would be that of promoting maximum employment, production, and purchasing power. This Act was a real commitment that the Federal Government combat unemployment. Out of the Act came increased governmental action in economic planning, The Council of Economic Advisors, the annual report on the economic condition of the nation, and the careful fiscal planning which has resulted in the avoidance of severe depressions during these past two decades. The prolongation of prosperity has indeed improved economic conditions in the Nation and has contributed greatly to the reduction of unemployment. Concurrent with these developments, however, cybernetics has made great inroads in the economy, resulting in the partial automation of many industries, consequent reduction in employment, and the maintenance of a persistent unemployment factor.

The benefits of the Full Employment Act of 1946 are in the improvement of economic planning and consequent reduction of wide swings in the economy which produced high inflation and depressions in the past. The conception of full employment must go further; it must deal with the placement of all residual unemployed in some type of employment, whether private industry or governmental. It is what is missing in the Full Employment Act of 1946, and it is what the war on poverty today is all about. It appears that the Nation has finally come to realize this breach in the employment situation and is now proceeding to find a remedy.

Part of the problem of chronic unemployment stems from society, part from the individual. The official war on poverty seeks only to overcome the individual problem. Society understands that many skilled positions go unfilled while many unskilled workers remain unemployed, and that it is important to equate available manpower with available jobs. What is not as well understood is that when balance between these factors is achieved to the greatest extent possible, one must still examine the economy to determine where gaps remain, and then ensure that work becomes available for the residual unemployed—those who are the most uneducated, the most lacking in skills, the most physically and emotionally ill, and those who are most depressed because of the debilitating effects of unemployment. Any war on poverty must overcome these handicaps, in order to win the struggle for the rest of society.

Many pessimists in society today believe that automation will result in vast unemployment, and that society therefore must learn how to live without full employment. This belief is partially responsible for considerable discussion today about guaranteed incomes to all persons, whether they work or not. Such theory development derives from an economic point of view which disregards the fundamental need of man to be engaged in gainful activity. Automation and other cybernetic outcomes must be viewed as a release of man from hard labor, as freedom from distasteful jobs, and as a challenge which society must consider in producing other types of employment and occupational interest. Automation and computerization should in no way be a threat, because they can really liberate man from menial and demeaning tasks. New kinds of employment which serve mankind must be developed to ensure that all men may continue to be involved in meaningful work.

Despite President Johnson's declaration in his 1965 Manpower Report that in The Great Society, each individual must have a fair chance to develop his abilities, engage in productive and rewarding activity, and enjoy the self-respect and economic security which flow from full use of his talents, society has never fully understood the personal tragedy of unemployment and its social and individual consequences.

In considering the total unemployment picture, proper perspective with regard to the public employment office cannot be overemphasized. While it is true that this agency's services require considerable improvement, there is no question that its function is important, primarily for the unemployed; secondarily, as a recruitment source for private industry and government. Unemployment arouses varying degrees of fear, uneasiness, and apprehension in every individual but particularly so in the public assistance recipient, whose situation is compounded by economic stress.

In Sheppard's and Belitsky's exposition on the social and psychological factors of job-seeking behavior and anxiety of the unemployed,[7] they noted that anxiety was higher when unemployed workers waited longer before starting their job hunt; when they checked fewer companies the first month of their unemployment; and among older workers (39 years of age and over), when they applied only at companies which they had heard in advance were seeking new employees or when there seemed to be less probability of their job finding success. Finally, among all who did find jobs, the higher their anxiety, the greater the probability that work was found through the public employment service, rather than by direct application to a company. When asked to choose the best way to find a new job, those who chose the public employment service were higher in anxiety, on the average, than all the others. This underscores the importance of a public employment agency serving as an intermediary or buffer between the jobseeker and the ultimate employer, particularly for very anxious and fearful persons seeking employment. It is apparent that chronic unemployment is based partly upon the psychological makeup of the individual, and upon his lack of education and vocational training.

In 1963, after Kalish[8] conducted a statistical study of the unemployed, he concluded that lack of education and training make the unemployed the most vulnerable members of the labor force. He suggested that job security could be institutionalized to some extent but that in the long run, education and training would provide more permanent protection against chronic unemployment than any other factor.

Economists evaluate "tolerable levels of unemployment" and "tolerable levels of inflation"; they define "deficient-demand unemployment" as an economic condition which can be changed by raising aggregate demand without conflicting with other economic policy goals; and they explain "structural unemployment" as the difference between the lowest rate of unemployment attainable by aggregate demand measures and a still lower rate attainable only by allowing the economy to reach an unacceptable level of inflation. To translate, what the economist believes is that whenever inflation reaches an unacceptable level, appropriate policy steps must be taken to remove as many people from the labor market as will help restore the economy to a noninflationary status.

In 1966, economists contended that the trend toward a lower unemployment rate could be attributed purely to aggregate demand policies. While the rate of structural unemployment had been rising, it did not show any substantial increase after 1957, although many analysts, both structural and aggregate demand theorists, believed it would. It therefore appears that the rate of structural unemployment has risen simultaneously with that of some deficient-demand unemployment. Questions as to the nature of the hard-core unemployed is a public policy issue involving debate over whether structural unemployment has worsened during the latter part of the postwar period.

Have increases in structural unemployment caused the total rate of unemployment to rise? According to Gruber,[9] the answer is "No." His findings show that in no class of workers most affected by unemployment has the unemployment situation worsened relatively; and the rise in total unemployment since 1945 is taken into account.

Have poorly educated people experienced greater difficulty than before in attaining employment in the latter part of the postwar period? Gruber believes that they have experienced relatively greater structural unemployment problems, even after the rise in the total rate of unemployment is considered. A comparison between 1950 and 1960 unemployment and participation rates, by classes of educational attainment, provides evidence for Gruber's belief.

Has the rise in structural unemployment made it more difficult to return, through the use of increased aggregate demand, to the four percent unemployment level that was experienced from 1955-1957? Gruber concludes that the return to the labor force of those poorly qualified who have become unemployed since 1950 will create problems of greater magnitude than in earlier periods of high unemployment, and thus, the total rate of unemployment made up of the marginal workers entering the labor force will increase. There is a lack of available statistical evidence to confirm this. However, it can be stated that, although overall structural unemployment has not worsened since 1954, structural problems for those with little education have increased during the postwar periods.

Gunnar Myrdal declares our thesis in other words: "It will not prove possible to change over the American economy to rapid and

steady growth and full employment without taking vigorous measures within the American nation to induce greater equality of opportunity and of standards of living."[10] He believes that meeting
material goods needs of the poor is not enough; that we must also
improve the construction and organization of communities; improve "human care" of incomplete families, the sick, the aged,
children and youth; and provide a higher level of cultural attainment throughout the country. Myrdal views unemployment as
damaging for adults and their families, who become "a substratum
of hopeless and miserable people," isolated from the rest of the
Nation, and believes the remedy can come only from large-scale
reform based on social justice. In contrasting the American economy
with his native Sweden, Myrdal notes that in his country, more
money is spent on the prevention of unemployment than on depression by retraining workers and transporting and rehousing families,
while America's record in this regard is spotty. He states that the
United States must introduce vocational training as a regular part
of the educational system in a manner which avoids dead ends and
allows horizontal and vertical movement in employment itself, and
that youth training plus retraining of older workers is a necessary
and urgent function of government.

When Myrdal emphasized the potential of unemployed men
becoming "unemployables," he showed that the answer to unemployment, "a damaging way of life," is not more insurance or public aid, but rather employment itself. Stressing the need for a
planned, radical improvement in the quality of labor, which would
involve huge expenditures for training, retraining and education of
the unemployed, Myrdal insists that such programs must be tied
in with long-range economic planning.

In the United States, economic planning has traditionally been
left to private industry. To the extent that labor exploitation, mis-
use, or unuse has been a consequence of such planning, it has been
viewed as a byproduct of democratic government and more beneficial than evil, since reserves of unemployed labor keep costs low,
profits high, and stimulate the economy to further expansion. Meanwhile, marginal relief for the exigencies of the unemployed poor has
kept them near starvation and motivated for work when it became
seasonally or economically available.

Unemployment and poverty must not be viewed as an economic
issue but rather as a human one. The premise has been established
that all men must be engaged in meaningful work; that work is an
essential human need; and that the consequences of nonwork are
individual and social disorganization. An important byproduct of
employment for all men would be reduction of poverty and improvement of economic prosperity. To the extent that social, psy-

chological, or physical obstacles interfere with man's impulse to work, appropriate services can be provided by public social services agencies to overcome these obstacles, and work therapy can be provided as an important service adjunct.

Economists have been advising government in the United States for three full decades regarding the intervention required to stabilize the play of market forces. Planning has become a recognized necessity to insure coordination and regulation of the national economy. Short-term and long-term forecasting has resulted in modification of policies involving commerce and finance. Control of the cost of borrowing money is a primary regulator. Increased interest rates counteract inflationary trends and reduction in these rates stimulates the economy during periods of deflation.

A variety of other actions influence the economy. The government plans to increase public spending during periods of deflation and decrease it during periods of inflation. The Federal Government uses the income tax as a method of economic control. Spendable income is increased to combat deflation through tax decreases, and money flow is lessened by increased tax rates. Social security programs, enacted in 1935, provide a strong stabilizing element through continued purchasing power for retirees, the unemployed, and public assistance recipients.

The Full Employment Act of 1946 was planned to develop pressure toward full production of goods, provide full employment, and establish mechanisms for regularized, governmental economic planning. And now we find it works so well that when unemployment goes below four percent, it overheats the economy. Inflation rather than deflation has been the continuous worry. Economic planning has produced stability in the economy and has dramatically reduced the unemployment hazards of earlier decades. Economic theory was responsive to needs of the time by placing responsibility for depressions and unemployment on an imbalance between aggregate demand and supply, opening up a rational way for the state to raise investment and production, and to create employment simply by raising expenditures while reducing taxation. We must applaud the economist for great success in stabilizing the economy and reducing unemployment. The protest of this book goes, however, to the deficiencies remaining in our society which do not yield to economic planning. The residual unemployed are the hard-core poor who have personal, social, educational, and vocational deficiencies which no amount of economic planning can overcome. If it is fully established that unemployment rates under four percent cause inflation, it is inevitable that the economists will sacrifice the four percent unemployed to maintain stability!

It is imperative at this late stage that the social scientist become more fully engaged in planning for the conservation of human resources. Economic planning has focused upon intervention relative to material things and fiscal processes, with success. Where the work of the economist leaves off, the task of the social scientist begins; and the economist must then reexamine and regulate the economic situation after the social intervention. The residuals of mass poverty, the chronic and gross inequality of opportunity, and the myriad of social problems of the poor must be relieved through social intervention.

The author reviewed several hundred Aid to Disabled cases in welfare departments in 1969. The desolation, degradation, and hopelessness in the lives of such men and women, viewed one by one, leaves an indelible imprint upon the observer. Realization that each individual has the potential for change, given opportunity, leaves the observer with a zeal to overcome the dilemma. The simplicity and naivete of the people so entrapped becomes evident through reading of many case histories; and one recognizes that with such limitations, the possibility of self-propulsion out of the poverty trap is impossible. Yet, their responsiveness to meaningful intervention is noted. The twenty-year-old man receiving ATD, had epilepsy, was mentally retarded, and had a variety of disabling physical defects. He became so motivated upon entry into the San Mateo Social Rehabilitation Activity Center that he was rehabilitated and found employment within ten weeks, and was excited about his forthcoming marriage. Such examples are frequent, although most welfare recipients require much more time, patience, and multidisciplinary intervention. Yet the author remains impressed at the latent talent wasting away because doors have not been opened. Even the most hardened criminal is, more often than not, found to be unbelievably unknowing and naive, according to social workers serving parolees, but he also has a motivating force which can be released when the right spark, symbolized by education and training, is struck. Effective and total social intervention must be provided for each person, one by one, so that he can realize his full potential.

Society must do everything possible to train, educate, and place in employment all able-bodied men and women. When this objective is achieved, problems of underemployment may still occur, requiring some form of program to provide minimum living standards, particularly for large families. In addition, supplementation of other types of income, for retired persons as an example, will be required until benefits become adequate. A variety of proposals are emerging.

GUARANTEED INCOME APPROACHES

With the current commitment to wage war on poverty, various proposals have been advanced to supply additional income for the poor. The ultimate goal is to raise the income of the poor and to eliminate poverty. The Social Security Administration has estimated that the addition of $11.5 billion would permit the 34.6 million persons designated as poor in 1963 to escape poverty.

NEGATIVE INCOME TAX

The most widely discussed proposal is utilization of the federal income tax machinery as a vehicle for providing income to the poor. The law, providing now only for the collection of taxes, might be extended to include grants based on family or individual needs.

A negative income tax would allow individuals or families whose income is below the taxable level to claim the unused portion of their current exemptions. Such a plan would tend to spread the benefits thinly among most of the poor. The negative income tax, operating through the existing personal-income tax mechanism may be based on one of two approaches. In the first approach, an official minimum income level would be established, and payments to the family or individual would be used to make up the difference between actual income and the official minimum. The second approach, emphasizing that the poor cannot take advantage of personal exemptions, would allow to the individual all or a portion of unused exemptions. Both approaches allow incentives to recipients to obtain additional earnings from work.

Among the many specialists in this field, Tobin, Schwartz and Theobald advocate the first approach; Friedman the second; and Lampman both the first and second. Tobin recommends payments to a recipient by the income-tax administration of $400 per family member if the family has no income from any other source; a couple with three children would therefore receive $2,000. The subsidy would be reduced by $33\frac{1}{3}$ cents for every dollar the family earns; or conversely, the family is encouraged to work because it improves its position by two-thirds of every earned dollar. At an income of $1,200 per person, the subsidy would become zero, and above that level the family would pay taxes in the conventional manner.

Schwartz has a similar proposal, but incorporates another feature. Any family or individual whose anticipated income falls below a predetermined minimum would receive a subsidy called a "family security benefit" for the amount of the difference. The official minimum would be related to price and productivity indexes. As a work incentive, Schwartz would permit the partial retention of earnings, but would reduce the family security benefit by a percentage that would increase as earned income rose.

Theobald advocates the adoption of an economic floor called "basic economic security" of $1,000 for each adult and $600 for each child, and appropriate deficiency payments to individuals or families whose incomes are below the floor. As a work incentive, Theobald would permit the retention of a flat ten percent of other income.

Friedman suggests either a proportional negative tax rate, such as 50 percent of unused exemptions, or a progressive set of rates similar to that proposed by Lampman. A positive work incentive is maintained in all the second-approach proposals because when the negative tax payments diminish as earned income rises, each extra earned dollar always brings a higher disposable income. Under Friedman's proposal, assuming an official living standard for a family of four of $3,000, and family exemptions plus deductions of $3,000, the family would pay no taxes, but on any income above that amount would pay taxes. If the family had no income, it would receive $1,500—50 percent of the difference between the standard and earned income (nothing in this case). With an earned income of $2,000, the family would receive $500, or 50 percent of the difference between the $2,000 of earned income and the $3,000 standard. This is a compromise plan in that it guarantees income to cover 50 percent of the poverty income gap, although Friedman would accept the progressive set of rates such as Lampman proposes.

Lampman would apply a flat negative tax rate of 50 percent of the difference between a family's total income and a predetermined poverty line income. Partial retention of the earnings from work would be permitted as a work incentive. The payment of 100 percent of the difference between actual income and poverty line income is rejected by Lampman on grounds of cost and adverse work incentives. In addition to his version of the first-approach proposals, Lampman offers the following two versions of the second-approach: (a) families and individuals with incomes below the level at which income tax is payable would be permitted to claim a flat 14 percent of their unused exemptions and deductions; and (b) a scale of progressive negative tax rates from 14 percent to 40 percent is suggested, the rate increasing with the amount of unused exemptions.

These guaranteed annual income approaches seek a universal method of providing income to masses of poor people in a simplified manner and in specified amounts of money so that family income will not fall below a stipulated minimum. Although some proponents view income guarantee as a complete substitute for public welfare, in the author's view this is an unlikely consequence.

Guaranteed income would tend to impede the development of adequate wages because of reduced pressures upon employers to raise wages, and would probably stabilize and sustain poverty for large numbers of people because of the inevitable meagreness of the allowance. We are currently experiencing this in the inadequate social insurance and unemployment insurance benefits which require welfare supplementation. Even more regrettable would be stabilization of the deficiencies of the affected group receiving the gratuity.

The facade of resolving poverty through provision of guaranteed income is merely another way of releasing society from concern over the poor person's deficiencies in education and training and in social and health characteristics. It would become an easy excuse for doing nothing about many substantive problems other than those involving money, which besiege the poor. Simple answers to complex problems of poverty will not resolve the issue. Society has been trying for centuries to wish problems of poverty away to no avail.

FAMILY ALLOWANCE

The proposed family allowance plan which is also receiving much discussion today, consists in a payment to all families with children in specified age groups without regard to family income. Payment might, for example, be $25 per month for each child under six, and $10 for each child from six to eighteen. This plan would particularly benefit large families and families with preschool children. A variation of the plan would not pay allowances for the first two children, but would pay $25 per month for each later child. At the other extreme, another plan would pay $50 per month for each child (at an estimated cost of $41 billion annually). The administration of a family allowance plan would be relatively simple. Each person with custody of a child—parent or guardian—would file a statement indicating the child's age and relationship, and would receive an allowance for the child in monthly checks.

Because of the interest in the United States, in a family allowance program we have analyzed existing welfare schemes in five countries—Canada, Denmark, France, Great Britain, and Sweden. Particular attention has been placed on the methods of financing various welfare programs and their income redistribution effects. Well-defined programs to eliminate poverty do not exist for the reason that there has been little or no preoccupation with the subject. Defined levels of poverty in these countries do not exist. In each country, there is a reliance on standard social welfare measures, including the family allowance, to accomplish the placement of a minimum income floor for everyone. However, with the exception of the family allowance, the other measures are also used in the United States, and any variation that exists is simply a matter of degree. None of the countries used what is called "negative" income taxation, nor is there any interest in using this approach. The person who thinks that the European countries are doing things better than we are in the whole area of social assistance may be disappointed.

The family allowance has been suggested as a device which can eliminate poverty in the United States. In the five countries examined, the family allowance comes close to what can be considered a guaranteed income. In France, it is a very important social welfare measure, and as a transfer payment represents around five percent of national income. The allowance is based on a step progression—22 percent of a base minimum income of 328 francs in the Paris area for the second child, 33 percent for the base for the third child, and 33 percent for subsequent children through the sixth child. The allowance can constitute a sizeable proportion of personal income for lower income families. For example, for an average French worker with an income of $190 a month and with children, the family allowance would amount to approximately $38 or 20 percent of the average income. In 1961 the estimated percent of monthly family allowances to average gross monthly earnings of French production workers was 28.7 percent.

The family allowance is of lesser importance in Great Britain. It was introduced in 1945 as a part of the social welfare measures adopted by the Labor government. In the 22 years since the family allowance has been in existence, the rates have been changed only three times. In terms of real income, the allowance is less important now than when it was introduced. In 1961 the family allowance constituted 5.7 percent of the average production worker's monthly wage.

In Sweden the family allowance is payable to all families regardless of the number of children, unlike France and Great Britain where the first child is excluded. The allowance is a flat 900 kroner a year ($175) for each child and is financed out of general tax revenues. With average family income amounting to more than $5,000 a year, the allowance would represent a small percentage of total income to the typical Swedish family. However, for lower income families with several children, it can constitute a sizeable percentage of total income. The allowance has not kept pace with the cost of living, and as a percentage of personal income has declined since its inception in 1948.

In Denmark, the family allowance does attempt to discriminate between families on the basis of income. Families below a prescribed income level receive a general allowance which is over and above the regular family allowance. This general allowance decreases as family income rises to a standard which is considered a minimum income level. The family allowance is used as partial compensation for a series of indirect taxes, the latest of which is the value-added tax.

In Canada the family allowance was introduced during the period immediately following the Second World War. Current payments are $6 a month for children under ten, and $8 a month for children ten to 16. Payments are low for a high-income country such as Canada, but are of importance to low-income families with a number of children. The family allowance also varies in importance between regions in Canada.

In the five countries, family allowances also include benefits in addition to allowances for children. Examples are marriage, prenatal, maternity, and housing allowances. There are also allowances for dependent persons other than children and for such categories of the population as disabled persons and orphans.

In general, the following statements sum up the characteristics of the family allowance as it is used in the five countries.

1. With the exception of France, it is financed out of general tax revenues. In France, it is financed from a tax on the employer.

2. The reasons for adopting the family allowance are diverse. In France, the primary reason for its adoption was to increase the birth rate. In Canada and the United Kingdom, the reason was Keynesian in nature—the need to stimulate aggregate demand after the end of the Second World War. The Beveridge plan and its Canadian equivalent, the Marsh report, recommended the adoption of the family allowance as part of the general social security system.

3. In Great Britain, the family allowance must be declared as income for tax purposes; in the other four countries, it does not constitute taxable income. Exemptions for children are not permitted under the Danish and Swedish tax systems—they were replaced by the family allowance. Regular exemptions for children exist under the British tax system. In Canada, the exemption is $300 per child receiving the allowance and $550 for other dependents. In France, the family quotient system enables a wage earner to split his income for tax purposes among all dependents.

4. The family allowance, for the most part, has not kept pace with the cost of living. With the exception of France, it does not constitute a significant source of income to the average wage earner. To the low-income groups, however, it can be a significant source of income.

5. All families receive the allowance. No attempt has been made to differentiate on the basis of need.

The family allowance has been suggested by some Americans

as a device that can be used to reduce the extent of poverty that exists in the United States. It would appear that this would be a rather inefficient approach to the solution of poverty.

The family allowance is payable to all families under current arrangements in the five countries examined in the study. This means that if the system were adopted in the United States, a considerable amount of wastage in terms of payment to non-poor families would occur. If, for example, a $10 a month allowance is paid for all children under 18 in the United States, the cost would be approximately $8.5 billion. Approximately one-fifth of all children live in poor families. This would mean that around $2 billion would go to poor families and the remainder to families that are not in need. The family allowance, as a transfer payment, would not be subject to the personal income tax, so it would result in a gain for upper income families who already enjoy a form of family allowance in exemptions and deductions for their children. The current $600 exemptions could be taken away, and the allowance used in their place. This is the normal arrangement in countries using the allowance. However, the merit and political acceptability of the arrangement is doubtful.

The family allowance could be limited to poor families with children. For example, in 1964, 15.9 million children would have been classified as poor. If a family allowance of $10 a month per child had been applied, the cost would have been $1.9 billion a year; if an allowance of $30 a month per child had been used, the cost would have been $5.7 billion a year.

If, for example, the Swedish family allowance of approximately $180 a year per child, were transplanted in the United States, the cost would be approximately $12.2 billion a year. However, the Swedes do not permit exemptions for children, so part of the $12.2 billion cost would be recovered by the elimination of exemptions for children in the United States.

The French family allowance would cost an estimated $30 billion if it were used in the United States. Unlike the Swedish allowance, it is a rather cumbersome device which excludes the first child in a family from an allowance. The rates also vary depending on the number and ages of the children.

Canada, Denmark, and Sweden have a "double decker" arrangement of old-age pensions. One pension is general in that a basic amount is paid to everyone who reaches a certain age. The other pension is related to earnings. Both pensions combine to provide an income which can amount to a substantial proportion of income which was earned during the years of employment. Canada has adopted a guaranteed income supplement program which, when combined with the regular old-age pension, currently provides a guaranteed income of $107.10 a month to a single pensioner. Old-age pensions in both countries are tied to a cost-of-living index.

There is little or no interest in negative income taxation of the type proposed by Friedman, Tobin, and others in the United States as an antipoverty device. The reasons vary from country to country. In France, there is no official recognition that poverty exists. In the other countries, there is recognition of the fact that many families do indeed live on incomes which are well below half of the average or median family income. There has been no formal attempt to delineate between who is poor and who is not poor.

Transfer payments through the government sector play an important role in income redistribution in these countries. When transfer payments are compared to household income, the percentage is higher in the five countries than in the United States. In France, transfer payments represent 19 percent of household incomes compared to 6.5 percent in the United States.

However, taxes expressed in terms of their relationship to gross national product are considerably higher in most of the five countries. In Sweden, all direct and indirect taxes and social welfare contributions represent 43.6 percent of the gross national product, compared to 27.3 percent in the United States. In Great Britain the percentage is 35.4. There is also a reverse side of the coin. Over the period, 1960-64, real consumption of households increased 31 percent in Sweden, 36 percent in Great Britain, and 59 percent in the United States. In Sweden, for every dollar increase in household income during this period, 34 percent was absorbed by increased taxes compared to 15 percent in the United States.

While a number of other nations have family allowance systems, the author does not recommend such a plan for the United States. A family allowance plan would relieve some of the fiscal problems of large families, but its weaknesses are apparent. The cost would be enormous since it covers all families rich and poor, and the benefits would remain meagre, thereby perpetuating the poverty of the target group—the poor; it is a form of wage subsidy which tends to hold down wage rates by reduction of pressure on employers; it would reduce the need for individuals and society to upgrade education and training of the poor, thereby retarding the possibility of increasing their earnings in a manner offering hope and dignity; and finally, it is governmental paternalism for all families, antithetical to personal freedom and independence and in effect, a form of large-scale public relief. Thus, the author strongly urges that the United States avoid establishing one more paternalistic instrument to perpetuate poverty—the family allowance system. The family allowance is an instrument which seeks to placate the poor, thereby avoiding a little longer, the development of programs which will strike at the causes of poverty.

UNIVERSAL DEMOGRANT

Another proposal for income subsidy is the "universal demogrant" plan, which would pay a "social dividend" to each man, woman, and child and replace all welfare payments. The scheme would be financed by a proportional income tax and would cost up to $50 billion annually. This plan would have most of the disadvantages of the negative income tax proposals as well as all of the objectionable features listed for the family allowance plan.

Opposition to the universal demogrant plan, the negative income tax proposals, and the family allowance relates to their potential for prolonging, rather than relieving poverty, and the ways in which all of these plans not only conflict with the incentive to work and learn new skills, but move toward governmental paternalism for all.

Alan Wade[11] advocates the guaranteed minimum income for all persons and the abolishment of public assistance programs as they are presently known, because it is his belief that they are grossly inadequate in terms of the levels of public aid payments made throughout the nation; and that the administrative climate is generally based on the insidious, paranoid, and restrictive preoccupations which stem from the poor law heritage. His contention that grants are too low and are provided in conjunction with restrictive eligibility requirements will be generally supported by those who are knowledgeable in the field of social work, but his recommendations for abolishment of public assistance programs on the assumption that a guaranteed minimum income would resolve the financial needs of poor people is open to question.

It has been noted that under the Speenhamland Act of 1795 in England, grants decreased over a period of three decades by one-third. We have no assurance today that any guaranteed minimum income arrangement would be sufficient, in terms of long-range practice, to provide adequately for families. Our Social Security Act of 1935 established a social insurance program which was designed to eliminate the need for public assistance. Yet social security allowances are so meagre that they fall far short of the poverty line for the aged, the disabled, and the families for whom the program was designed. In California, 70 percent of the aged recipients of public assistance also receive federal social security benefits, and the nationwide average is 50 percent.

Although state and local public aid must be provided to supplement inadequate social security benefits, the inadequacy of such benefits for the aged, the disabled, and the unemployed is not necessarily an argument against the development of a guaranteed minimum income. It does suggest, however, that if an insurance program designed to help the poor continues to fail in its purpose because of inadequate grants, the provision of sufficient funds would be even more difficult under a program which is disassociated both from insurance and from payment for work performed. Moreover, precipitous elimination of public assistance programs and substituting minimum income for them would impede the current movement of such programs toward functioning essentially as public social services. A more gradual modification must take place as the functions of the public assistance system, including the provision of full employment are replaced by more appropriate income maintenance arrangements. At this time it is not yet possible to determine whether the function of public assistance programs is actually in transition and being adapted from money-giving to public services. This changeover will require a number of years, and there is need to devise methods for accelerating the process.

Apart from the administrative and political problems associated with modification of the public assistance system and the establishment of a minimum income program, other important factors such as human feelings and needs are involved in such a change. The 39-year experience of the Speenhamland Act program established that the morale of the people served was seriously affected, that the satisfactions normally gained by engagement in meaningful activity were somehow lessened when it was understood that income was available whether work was accomplished or not. Under such circumstances, the efforts to overcome unemployment or underpayment for employment go to the search for supplementation through a relief system, rather than to a search by society for improvement of the individual's competency through vocational training or a search for methods of improving the wage structure.

Wages should not be supplemented with relief, but should be increased to the point where they become adequate to support a man and his family. Laborers should not remain on low wages, but should be educated and trained so that their performance and income can be upgraded. Society must seek these objectives. To do otherwise, through the development of subsidy methodologies, irrespective of work, would stifle any potential improvement in a social system which malfunctions to the extent that a minimum income arrangement would appear as a form of alleviation.

It is true that there is urgency to overcome poverty, but the urgency must be expressed in the form of providing opportunity to individuals, not in relief to compensate for individual and societal inadequacies. Although man may develop satisfying life goals apart from meaningful work in the distant future, it is now difficult to conceptualize a society without individual life patterns of engagement in service activity. Until that millennium arrives, the meaningful work values which sustain our cultural patterns and belief systems should not be undermined. Our growth and development as a nation will depend upon our response to the needs of man in society, and history has shown that when such needs are ignored or cultural values lost and not replaced, the people become apathetic and the culture sinks into oblivion.

The author's position, favoring a form of guaranteed income for farm laborers, as in the Chapter on Department Bulletin 644 but opposing it for others, may appear to be, but is not paradoxical. On the one hand, Bulletin 644 goes to the maintenance of temporary arrangements to insure adequate income for the farm laborer family and to insure living necessities and health care for his children. The author is also in favor of such temporary arrangements for other workers until a long-range program emerges which will insure adequate employment for all, and to the extent that this is not possible, the author favors the provisional form of supplemental income. On the other hand, guaranteed annual income plans fail to take into account the primary importance of providing education and training for productive employment and then insuring that jobs are available. In other words, the negative income tax proposal, while allegedly beneficial in reference to bringing everyone near the poverty level, creates other kinds of hazards associated with social values and goals.

Two issues are involved—the first being education, vocational training, and employment for all persons interested and capable; the second, inadequate income in social insurance and public assistance. The following alternative proposals are based on the author's belief in man's wish and need for engagement in meaningful activity with dignity and self-dependence.

INTEGRATION OF SOCIAL INSURANCE AND PUBLIC WELFARE PROGRAMS

In the United States today the public welfare program supplements the inadequate benefits of the OASI program. In California, for example, 70 percent of public welfare's Old Age Security recipients also receive OASI benefits. California has established a simplified eligibility process involving a declaration of resources by the recipient as opposed to earlier complex methods. Since the eligibility mechanisms in welfare can be likened to the current OASI process itself, there is no continuing justification for two governmental agencies serving the same population group in respect to the money payment process. The source of funds for the two programs could remain the same at present, but at some future date the integration of funding arrangements should be considered. One imperative would be to raise OASI benefits to adequate cost-of-living levels. This process in itself would essentially eliminate the need of public welfare for aged persons, and in addition, large numbers of disabled persons could be removed from welfare rolls and integrated into the OASI program for money payment purposes.

As the OASI program becomes the money payment agency, the public welfare program would become the social and rehabilitation agency. The public welfare agency social service program would serve OASI recipients plus other population groups as needed. Activity center therapy programs would become particularly adaptive to the needs of the aged and disabled. As major reorganization is considered, it would be desirable to place the vocational rehabilitation agency in the welfare agency at the local level. These two agencies certainly have similar social and rehabilitative roles to perform in the future.

SUBSTANTIVE ABSOLUTE MINIMUM WAGE LAW

The human equation is the most important component in commerce, agriculture, and industry, yet machinery and equipment receive more protection and care than labor in some occupations. Human labor must be paid for in sufficient amounts to support the wage earner and his family in decency and health. A minimum wage must be established. It is important that every family have a wage earner receiving an adequate income. Supplemental income programs should not be considered until adequate wages prevail. Our affluent economy must yield on this crucial issue to avoid continued pauperization of large numbers of wage earners. Thus, an absolute requirement of any reform movement involving guaranteed annual income must begin with a "guaranteed" minimum wage provision—a substantive extension of the provisions of the Fair Labor Standards Act of 1938.

What is an adequate minimum wage and to what size family should it apply? It is suggested that the wage should not be so meagre that it keeps the wage earner alone in decency and health; nor could it realistically be so ample as to provide for a wage earner, his wife, and their ten children. But, the minimum wage should be sufficient to support the average American family—the wage earner, his wife, and two children in reasonably comfortable circumstances. Let us assume that in the year 1970, $4,800 per year would be sufficient for a family of four. Congress would mandate that amount as the minimum wage for every wage earner in the United States, thereby insuring that the majority of family units could live on such wages without supplementation from public welfare. Congress would add a cost-of-living clause to the minimum wage legislation to insure automatic escalation of the $4,800 amount in accordance with annual increases in living costs.

Who pays for the increased cost of production? Current market fluctuations show that as costs of machinery and labor increase, costs of goods increase, efficiency is improved, marketing methods are modified, research is enriched, and a myriad of other factors are adjusted. Thus, the public pays for part of the increased cost, and improved efficiency absorbs another part of it. The minimum wage ingredient, however, must be uniform throughout the Nation. A compassionate employer cannot survive if he pays one dollar an hour more in wages than his competitors elsewhere in his state or outside it. If the farmer in California raises wages, his competitor in Florida may capture the market with lower prices. The issue is national in scope. In keeping with the General Welfare clause on the regulation of commerce in the U.S. Constitution, the Congress is authorized to establish a national minimum wage, and such wage must be substantive, rather than a token offering.

WORK AND TRAINING FOR THE UNDEREMPLOYED

One of the most economically deprived groups in the United States is the large family, low-wage earner combination. This group of families must receive special attention in a manner which respects their right to independent, wage-earning status. Typical of the many letters received in welfare departments from members of such families are the following:

"I write to you, director of the state of Calif, for you to give me a reason that I live in my economic situation. My wife & I have 12 in our family & she & I make it 14. At times I earn good money & at times I earn little, but I live at times very poorly in my economic situation. . . I have to pay something to the doctor when I am sick. My children & I asked for help following the medical bill, but did not get it. . . I live on the ranch where I work. . . I have 9 children in school which we live quite far from. I work to pay doctors, for food, school clothes, automobile. . . but only God knows and I want you to give me an explanation, because I can't explain it to myself, why I see other people with less of a family & they have medical welfare & they travel in very good cars. . . I don't know what to say, but study my case because I need your help."

"I am the mother of five wonderful children; two in perfect health; one, bad asthmatic; one, a slight cerebral palsy; and my little girl wears straps around her deformed legs and she cannot talk, she is very slow, so far the specialists from the county clinic haven't found the cause of her difficulties. We all love her so much! We try to make her talk and make her do things for herself; she is so beautiful and sweet! please do something for the education of handicapped children; there are some children so much worst then mine! My husband was a truck driver and doing good until he had an accident and then a stroke; he is forty-two years old. He is not supposed to drive trucks any more so he took a job as a janitor in a school rather than stay on welfare; he doesn't want charity, but he is making less now than if he'd stayed on welfare; after paying our bills, there's barely enough left to eat, he takes home $341.89 a month; this is to take care of a family of seven! We cannot get financial help from the welfare because the job is steady. (If it was part time, we could get help!) We can't even get medical, I cannot take my little girl back to the specialist for her legs, because he doesn't wish to bother under the cripple children program, I cannot afford to go back to my own doctor to be checked regularly (I had cancer). We were so much better off on welfare! Please pass a law to help the men that want to help themselves rather then loaf around waiting for the welfare check. I know that an awful lot of men just won't work, they rather take advantage of the welfare but can you blame a man with a big family for wanting to stay on welfare? Why should they work for less and deprive their children of more food and medical care? Is my husband selfish for wanting to work and depriving the children? He is a veteran of two wars; he wants to do what's right and be a good American. Please do something. I am certain that there would be fewer men on welfare if they could get some help if the wages weren't high enough to provide for their family, and the help would be much lower then if they didn't work, saving the state an awful lot of money."

In planning work and training for the underemployed large-family worker, two basic elements must be considered: development of a method of upgrading skill and earning power of the large-family wage earner; and development of a method of augmentation of income during the period of skill training.

In regard to upgrading of skill and earning power, the following three basic principles will be established:

1. Outright family allowance or subsidy will not be provided, but the augmentation of income will have relevance to a training stipend and work setting.

2. Every large-family wage earner will be provided the benefits of the program, irrespective of his personality, education, and vocational skills. There will be no dropouts or pushouts. The program will be adaptive in quality, variety, and training time span to accommodate every situation.

3. The program will be funded and administered by the Federal Government as part of its responsibility for the "General Welfare."

The low wage earner will be provided an on-the-job work and training assignment in private industry, in regular governmental work, or in especially designed federal work and training projects. The income provided will be a combination of wages for work performed plus a training stipend. The regular work week will include the time expended on education, skill training, and work experience. The wage earner will not be required to seek public assistance for any portion of his earnings or stipend.

It is important to accommodate every large-family, low wage earner in the program. From study of the individual's interests, capacities, and motivation, a long-range work and training program can be worked out for him. The limitations of one individual may require persistence in the program for ten years, while another may graduate to a high paying job within six months. The program must maintain the firm commitment to continue the individual's participation in the program as long as the condition of large family and low income persists. He will remain until he graduates to a high paying job or until he can support his family because it has decreased in size.

The Federal Government will completely fund the total cost of the program. Since conservation of human resources is a "General Welfare" function provided for in the U.S. Constitution, it should receive priority before other generally accepted functions of the Federal Government which deal with natural resources, and subsidies to farms and industry, and the like. In this program, there must be no requirement of state and local participation in funding, and no requirement of transfer of funds from welfare, social security, or unemployment compensation to support the program.

Responsibility for administration of the program will be placed with the Department of Labor, Work Incentive Program (WIN) Component 3, Special Work Projects. This WIN Component 3, which will be modified to accommodate the provisions of the program, is recommended because it is a part of an education, training, and employment system. It is anticipated, therefore, that continued emphasis would be given to the upgrading of skills, and that employment counseling and placement would also be available for the higher paying jobs sought. The WIN Program concerns itself with hard-core persons and would be expected to exercise ingenuity in the development of a viable training and employment program. In addition, since the WIN Program works cooperatively with departments of public welfare, it is anticipated that such departments would be available to provide social services.

In regard to development of a method of augmentation of income during the training period, the following two basic conditions are required:

1. The participant's income will derive from two sources—the fair value of work performed or the minimum wage, whichever is the greater; plus a variable training stipend determined by the number of family members based upon the income tax formula which provides child exemptions of $600 per year or $50 per child per month.

2. The wage-stipend income level will vary only as work production or family size varies, and it will be maintained indefinitely until the participant is placed in regular employment at a wage equal to or in excess of the wage-training income.

The following case example illustrates the application of the two conditions listed above:

Mr. A. has a wife and 9 children, earns $380 per month as a janitor, and enters the WIN Component 3 program for work and training. His work performance is low, so his wage is figured at the minimum wage established for a family of four, $400 per month. The training stipend is determined by the number of children (less 2 already covered by minimum wage formula). The $50 per child allowance multiplied by 7 children amounts to $350 per month. The sum of the wage and training stipend would amount to $750 per month for the family. Mr. A. may increase his skills so that the $400 wage component could be increased to $500 within four months. In such a circumstance, the training stipend would be reduced to $250 per month.

The concept of training stipends lends dignity to the participant and to the training process, as opposed to the social outcast concept characteristic of public assistance. Moreover, the process is standardized and acceptable in our society. An analogy is found in training grants, largely governmental, which are currently provided for professional training in medicine, social work, law, and other occupations, and which usually provide special allowances for dependents. It is estimated that the average length of time required to complete training for the underemployed will not exceed that required for the professional.

The personal destiny of one person is as important as that of another. Who can measure the respective contributions each will make to society? Every man must have the opportunity to fulfill his maximum potential, whether professional or otherwise, and when this objective is achieved, an important by-product will be the enrichment of society itself.

The Canadian Prime Minister, in a debate on family allowances, quoted statistics showing that 84 percent of all Canadian children under 16 years of age were dependent upon only 19 percent of the gainfully employed. He stated that since the burden of raising the next generation was carried by less than one-fifth of the working population, it was only fair that a portion of the burden of support should be shared by all. A primary objective of the Canadian family allowance program has been cited as the provision of equality of opportunity for all children and the same could be said for a work and training program for the underemployed in the United States.

Social surveys conducted in England, and cited in the Beveridge Report,[12] revealed that one of the major causes of poverty was the fact that breadwinners had families that were too large in relation to their wages. In fact, of all the poverty in England, roughly one-quarter to one-sixth was the result of failure to relate earned income to family size.

Two important and hoped-for results of the proposals for work and training for the underemployed emerge: the upgrading and enrichment of the life style of the wage earner; and the provision of needed income to his family. Success in achieving these objectives would result in a beneficial influence upon the children as they see the parent in school, in training, and ultimately in an important job. We have not been able to measure the adverse influence of the degraded parent ideal upon children, but we postulate that it is profound. Thus, it is extremely important that we over-extend ourselves to upgrade the life style of the present generation to insure reduction of generational poverty and degradation in subsequent generations. Finally, an important by-product of the enrichment of life style for this selected group of large family wage earners will be enrichment of the society itself. A production-work oriented society will enhance its value systems, increase social tranquility, and decrease social unrest.

WOMEN AT WORK

We have sought to establish that women in the United States are not only at work but when given a choice, will select work rather than public aid. The American culture should accept this phenomenon and develop its programs and institutions accordingly. Men and women want work, not relief. Therefore, AFDC and AFDC-U should be abolished. Such a proposal appears, on the surface, to be harsh to women and children, yet the real cruelty lies in the failure of the AFDC program during the past 35 years. The alternative to AFDC will be found in the variety of programs which prepare women for work, serve women at work, and provide unemployment insurance to women temporarily out of work.

Education and vocational training will be provided all women who require job preparation. This should preferably be provided during youth, but when such youth programs fail, adult programs will fill the gap. The adult programs will be adaptive to the variety of difficult problems. Questions of length of training, the woman's economic feasibility for work, attitudinal obstacles, and problems of other kinds will be dealt with and resolved. For example, one woman may be functionally illiterate and require as much as five years in education and training before employment is possible. Another woman, a high school graduate, may have strong aptitude for teaching, and therefore, require five years of college training. In each circumstance, the training program must adapt appropriately to the optimum potential of the individual and not become short-circuited because of expediency, such as placing the high school graduate in a clerical job, thereby avoiding the expense of a long training period.

During the education and training period, the woman will receive a reasonable (nonhumiliating) training stipend, which will provide basic family maintenance, training-connected expenses, and child care costs, and will vary by size of family and training program requirements.

VOCATIONAL EDUCATION FOR CHILDREN

In 1961, President Kennedy appointed a panel of experts to take a national look at vocational education for children. The panel found that essentially the educational institutions in our nation were not providing vocational education to children and adults who need it. Approximately 80 percent of the children in elementary schools at that time would not receive a college degree and yet the schools were providing vocational education nationally to less than 10 percent of the youth in the 15- to 19-year-old bracket. As a result of the revelation of these glaring inadequacies, the vocational act of 1963 was passed by the Congress and this has had important results nationally. Increasing emphasis is now being placed on vocational education which combines general education with work experience in business and industry, providing one-half days for each of these experiences. Some schools are beginning to introduce youth at a much earlier age to the world of work through innovations in the 4th, 5th and 6th grades.

While the President's panel revealed that less than 10 percent of the youth were served in vocational education classes in 1961, we are now serving in excess of 25 percent of the youth in such classes, but this is still insufficient when we realize that most of the high school graduates must go job hunting immediately after graduation without having had any kind of job training. Considering the neglect of vocational education, it becomes easier to understand why large numbers of adults are incapable of finding work because of poor preparation and ending up on public welfare.

It is imperative that the educational system in all of the schools in this nation prepare each child vocationally, or for entrance into college. The school must become adaptive to the needs and interests of the children so that no child drops out of school without appropriate preparation for his life work. The vocational educational act of 1963 which has started in this direction must be augmented to insure the achievement of these objectives.

We should shift the emphasis in this nation of our social security and public assistance programs from elderly people to children. This does not mean that we neglect the elderly, but rather that while we serve adults and elderly people, we shift our prime interests to children. To the extent that we are successful in the development of effective programs for children an inevitable by-product will be an improvement of the conditions for adults and the aged because of the consequent more satisfying life role for the individual resulting from vocational preparation during formative years.

GUARANTEED FULL EMPLOYMENT

The Full Employment Act of 1946 has strongly contributed to reduction in wide economic swings. A relatively stable economy has evolved with unemployment becoming stabilized at approximately the 4 percent level. The economic mechanisms utilized to achieve this economic stability have been sophisticated and effective, but have now reached their maximum potential, since they rely upon the 4 percent unemployment rate as a control element against inflation. Human value judgments must now displace all other considerations, and the 4 percent unemployment rate should be reduced to zero. To the extent that such reduction cannot be met through normal employment channels, the Federal Government must become the employer of last resort, through the establishment of a *Special Employment Program.* The Federal Government must, belatedly, establish a labor subsidy program, although subsidy is a poor choice of terms when one considers that the work will be useful work designed to improve natural resources and overcome resource depletion and contamination. In addition, it will conserve human resources through appropriate service and cultural activities. We repeat, men want work, not relief or prolonged unemployment compensation.

GOVERNMENT: THE EMPLOYER OF LAST RESORT

To insure that every person is guaranteed an opportunity for full employment, the Federal Government must become the employer of last resort. In the United States there is a great need for increased public service employment in such fields as health, education, recreation, housing, neighborhood improvement, maintenance of streets and parks, rural development, beautification, and conservation. In addition, there is a rapidly growing need for services to people in child care centers, rehabilitation programs, hospitals, nursing homes, public and nonprofit social agencies, correctional institutions, and mental hospitals. Also, care of persons in their own homes requires attendants, homemakers, caretakers of children, home health aides, visiting nurses, friendly visitors, and transportation aides. Thus, the need for public service employment greatly exceeds the total number of persons who are unemployed or underemployed.

The Federal Government, through the Secretary of Labor, should make 100 percent grants to federal, state, and local governmental agencies or to nonprofit organizations to provide employment to every man, woman, and child who has been unemployed for a period of 30 calendar days, and for whom the Department has determined that further education or vocational training is not indicated or available. The Federal Government will insure that wages are paid at the prevailing rate, and in no case lower than the minimum wage.

The Work Incentive Program described in Chapter 14 should become the manpower resource for administration of the special employment program. Present cumbersome financing in the WIN program should be abolished, and as a substitute, the Federal Government should subsidize the program 100 percent. Even so, the cost would be lessened for the Federal Government by returns to the participant in wages from the work site, discontinuance of large numbers of AFDC and ATD men and women recipients, and substantive reduction of unemployment benefit payments.

In the initial stages of the program, Congress must authorize three million special employment jobs. Ultimately, the program must become open-ended to accommodate all persons needing employment of this kind.

The value of using Component three of the WIN program would be the provision of ready access to training and education opportunities plus the employment placement which is the other resource of the manpower agency. Every effort should be made to place participants from the special employment program back into regular employment. For some persons, job placement may not be possible. One of the virtues of the program would be its provision of long-term employment for those who could not otherwise be employed. The major challenge to the program would be to overcome the obstacles to regular employment of all participants.

COMMUNITY REDEVELOPMENT

Unemployment hits some communities harder than others. Automation, declining industry or agriculture, and natural disasters are a few of the causes of high unemployment rates. Once started, the decline of the economic life of a community feeds upon itself, becoming chronic and accelerated in tempo. Although people have deep roots in their community and are reluctant to seek employment elsewhere, one remedy to high unemployment in depressed regions is found in federal manpower programs in the form of relocating families to areas of high employment. High employment areas in the United States are found in the most heavily populated urban centers and in the cities which are heavily congested, over-populated, and smog-ridden. Transportation problems are overwhelming, with clogged freeways and practically no rapid public transportation available. The transplantation of families from relatively pleasant, familiar environments to a complex and hostile urban atmosphere creates fantastic burdens for the displaced family.

One of the criteria used by industry in opening additional plants is the availability of a surplus of appropriate labor in the new locations. Accordingly, high employment areas tend to draw more industry, become more congested, smog-ridden, and generally more unsatisfactory as places in which to live. The chronicity of this spiral may have more serious social consequences, in the long run, than those which result from problems in areas of unemployment. Manpower relocation programs require reevaluation since they generate such serious social consequences. Other alternatives must be examined. Community redevelopment programs should be established as one alternative, and special work programs, as previously outlined, should be utilized in communities of high unemployment on a continuing basis. In addition, federal manpower and commerce experts should be available for consultation to the community regarding potential new industry, agriculture, or governmental contract work.

Rehabilitation of communities should become the major policy thrust for depressed areas. For decades, the social problems created by the migration of people to urban areas have been viewed as components of a natural and irreversible trend. Yet, careful study indicates the potential for reversing the trend through a variety of voluntary arrangements, short of governmental control. Community redevelopment councils composed of industry leaders *can* evaluate and recommend specified voluntary industrial development in depressed areas; an intergovernmental council on redevelopment *can* be established in each depressed area to recommend special work projects; a federal interdepartmental council *can* be established to recommend federal contract allocations to depressed areas; and a federal-state task force *can* provide consultation to local redevelopment councils. These are a few of the constructive redevelopment possibilities and mechanisms. Once the downward trend is reversed in a community, the increased prosperity often feeds upon itself, thereby enabling the community to become self-sustaining.

The urgency of constructive approaches is emphasized by the fact that throughout the Nation, there has been a marked tendency for people to migrate from farms, rural areas, and small towns to larger centers of population. The bulk of population growth continues to be registered in metropolitan areas. Among the 30 largest metropolitan areas, those which experienced the most rapid growth during the 1950's have generally continued to be the fastest growing in the current decade. Seven metropolitan areas in California, three in Texas, and two in Florida are listed among the 30 highest ranking metropolitan areas in numerical population growth during the 1960's. In California, where the population of the cities has increased about one and one-half times as rapidly as that of the non-metropolitan areas between 1960 and mid-1968, more than 90 percent of all Californians now live in officially designated Standard Metropolitan Statistical Areas, and the congestion and smog in the largest of these, Los Angeles, have rendered the community unfit for human habitation.

The many proposals for a guaranteed annual income are essentially unrelated to common human needs. The frames of reference have largely evolved from the minds of men who are economists, and their proposals have little relevance to men, women, and children—their aspirations, their basic need for dignity, for congenial family life, and the fundamental need for a meaningful life in the broader social group. The proposals for guaranteed annual income, with their meagreness, promote continuation of poverty and make it uniform; with their implication of non-work, they deprive man of meaning and purpose in life; and with their formulas and governmental paternalism, foster bureaucracy and dependency.

In the economic process, labor must no longer be treated as a pawn to be manipulated for checkmating inflation and to hold down the price of labor. In economic terms, labor is a mass of faceless men; 4 percent unemployment is a statistic with relevance only to inflation or as a desirable barrier against labor bargaining for increased wages. Look at the unemployed, one by one. They are people degraded, those who lose hope when idle hours lengthen into days and weeks and their families get caught up in the anguish and turmoil of their disrupted lives. This poignant truth has not yet penetrated man's acquisitive, exploitive, and unbridled greed. Bellamy and others have noted the phenomenon in the past, with regret, yet the injustice persists. It is clearly evident that society must concern itself with the well-being of each individual man, woman, and child, not en masse; and after that, economic formulas can be applied for the good of all.

The guaranteed annual income formulas prepared by the economists are designed for robots and machines, not for men. Where are the social engineers, the social psychologists, the social workers who understand the dynamics of individual and group behavior? These are the men who must construct the conceptual framework for development of a proposal which will allow men to engage in a meaningful life and receive an income for their contribution which will maintain their families in decency and health.

In the final analysis, the fundamental issue is work. Every man must be guaranteed the right to work; the right to opportunity in the form of education and training so that he may fulfill his maximum destiny in his chosen field of endeavor; and the right to be provided with the helping services of medicine, social work, and other therapies to overcome obstacles precluding engagement in a meaningful life. These elements must become the basic rights of all men and they cannot be displaced by economic mechanisms which create surpluses of labor; which allow a 4 percent unemployment rate; which sanction early retirement or nonwork; which pay for prolonged unemployment or disability, and which allow persistent underemployment and consequent poverty.

THREE-YEAR PHASE-IN

It is recommended that the first three years of the 1970's be devoted to phasing-in the new programs in a manner which will allow for their evaluation and enable intelligent implementation of the later phases. The following programs should be considered for phase-in during the three-year period:

1. *Integration of Public Welfare Program (OAS) with Social Insurance Program (OASI).* The following arrangements will be considered:

a. Increase all grants to a minimum of $100 per month per person, and for those whose grants exceed this amount, increase the current grant by 5 percent.

b. Increase the $100 minimum and all other grants by 5 percent annually until an established standard of decency and health is reached. At the point the standard is reached, establish a cost of living increase which will automatically adjust grants in conformance with revised cost of living standards.

c. Strengthen public welfare services programs to insure needed social services, attendant care, and other types of services required by the aged, including OASI beneficiaries and former welfare recipients.

2. *Vocational Training and Education.* The vocational training and education program patterned after the Work Incentive Program must be made available to all unemployed, underemployed, and able-bodied persons who have not been in the labor force. This program will serve public assistance recipients, recipients of unemployment insurance benefits who have been unemployed over 30 calendar days, and any other citizen in the community who requires upgrading of educational and vocational skills to compete successfully in the labor market. The program will be administered by the Department of Labor and could be accommodated through expansion and strengthening of the WIN program as follows:

a. Establish a 100 percent federal funding arrangement to insure that the WIN program does not vary widely state by state because of differential state fiscal capacity, and to fully express the federal responsibility for conservation of human resources.

b. Provide open-end adequate federal funding to insure that *all* WIN eligible men and women receiving AFDC become engaged in a training and education program, and not be subjected to a welfare supplemental ETP or other improvised type of program.

c. Expand Component 3, special works projects, of the WIN program to accommodate one million persons the first year, and an additional million in each of the following two years until the proposed three-million goal is achieved at the end of the third year, at which time the program would become open-ended. The effect of this would be to establish the Federal Government as the employer of last resort, and insure full employment to every able-bodied person. This provision expands the present WIN program from its exclusive focus on AFDC, and extends it to all unemployed persons who are seeking and capable of employment.

d. Extend vocational education for children. It is recommended that the Federal Government increase its subvention of education through use of vocational education as the vehicle. In other words, the Federal Government will concentrate its funds for education in those areas which are specific to vocational education. During the three-year phase-in period beginning in 1970, the Federal Government will increase its vocational education subvention to the local school districts by 25 percent in each of the three years. Beginning in 1974, the Federal Government will support vocational education at a 100 percent subvention rate on an open ended budget basis to insure that every child requiring vocational preparation will receive such training.

3. *AFDC Interim Provisions.* To accommodate the objective of abolishing the AFDC program, the following recommendations should be considered during the three-year phase-in period:

a. The AFDC program should remain essentially as it is (except for items e. and f.) as far as federal legislation and regulations are concerned. The emphasis during this period would be placed upon significantly reducing the number of persons served.

b. At least 20 percent of the AFDC adults and their children will be transferred from the AFDC program to the WIN program each year. The WIN program will be modified so that each of these welfare recipients will receive a training grant which will include dependents' allowances, and each will be discontinued from public assistance for purposes of money payments. At the end of the three-year phase-in, more than 60 percent of the AFDC recipients will have been transferred to training programs. The federal agency will establish an evaluation council to make recommendations regarding the provision of aid or further training and education to the residual AFDC group.

c. Protective services to children in AFDC families should be strengthened to insure that such children receive proper care and attention, and are not subjected to neglect and abuse.

d. Social services and child care services should be strengthened within the welfare departments to facilitate the adjustment of each individual to WIN placement or to employment. The welfare agency will retain full responsibility for the provision of social services and child care to persons in the general community served by the WIN program, whether they are receiving public assistance or not.

e. The residual federally subvented AFDC program will be subject to uniform federal standards for aid payments which, in turn, shall be reasonable standards of decency and health.

f. All requirements related to liens, recoveries, responsible relatives (except parents' responsibility for minor children), man-in-the-house rule, suitable home requirements, and any other such restrictive provision shall be abolished by federal law to insure uniform application of public welfare laws throughout the Nation.

g. In June 1968 in California, the AFDC-FG and AFDC-U programs served 207,055 families with a total of 621,055 children; a total person count of 815,621; and at a total cost of one-half billion dollars annually. It is statistically projected, on the basis of past experience, that the number of persons who would receive AFDC-FG and AFDC-U in 1970 would increase to 268,500 families with 778,800 children; a total person count of 1,031,600. The AFDC recipient rate for 1,000 children under age 18 was 90.9 in 1968 and was projected to increase to 110.7 as of June 1970. This evidence clearly establishes the urgency for correction of the social and economic conditions which lead to such large increases in dependency and emphasizes the need to develop rehabilitation, employment, and money payment programs to serve this group and reverse the alarming trend in AFDC program growth.

4. *Activity Centered Therapy*. The public welfare departments will initiate Activity Centered Therapy (ACT) programs (as described in Chapter 15) to serve AFDC incapacitated parents, ATD recipients, and blind recipients of public welfare. Each welfare agency will develop an ACT program and arrange for the purchase of additional services to the extent that they are available in the community. The ACT program will become the center for providing social services, including group work, as a means of rehabilitating persons served by the welfare agency. In addition, the program will become a focal point for provision of services to individuals who do not require activity centered therapy. For example, an individual might require only social services plus an adult education program at the outset of his rehabilitation process without participating in the center program. The ACT program will be 100 percent federally financed and the participants in the program will receive training stipends and wages where indicated, as employees of the welfare agency, rather than as recipients of aid payments.

5. *Aid to Totally Disabled*. The ATD program will be modified as follows during the three-year phase-in period:

a. Of the ATD program recipients, 20 percent will be transferred to ACT each year.

b. Of the ATD recipients, 12 percent will be transferred each year to the OASI program for aid payments at 100 percent federal cost.

c. The residual ATD program will be carried by public welfare departments in conformance with present law and regulation, except that federal law will establish uniform, adequate levels of money payment.

d. The public welfare agency will strengthen its social services to serve all present or former ATD recipients.

e. All requirements related to liens, recoveries, responsible relatives, and any other such restrictive provision shall be abolished by federal law to insure uniform application of public welfare laws throughout the Nation.

f. In June 1968 in California, the ATD program served 129,000 persons at an annual cost of one quarter billion dollars, and this program was projected to serve 162,000 persons by June 1970. The recipient rate per 1,000 persons was 11.7 in 1968 and would move to 13.8 by 1970. The evidence clearly establishes an urgency for correction of the social and economic conditions which lead to such increases in disability and dependency, and indicates the need to develop rehabilitation and money payment programs to serve this group and thereby reverse the alarming trend in ATD program growth.

6. *Aid to Blind.* The AB program will be modified in the following manner:

a. Of the AB caseload, 20 percent will be transferred to the ACT program each year.

b. Of the AB recipients, 12 percent will be transferred to OASI each year for money payments at full federal cost.

c. The residual AB program will continue to be carried by the public welfare department and will be subject to uniform federal standards for aid payments in conformance with reasonable standards of decency and health.

d. The public welfare agency will strengthen its social services to serve all present or former AB recipients.

e. All requirements related to liens, recoveries, responsible relatives, and any other such restrictive provision shall be abolished by federal law to insure uniform application of public welfare laws throughout the Nation.

7. *General Assistance or General Relief Programs.* These programs will be modified in the following manner:

a. The Federal Government will expand its emergency aid program to provide federal subvention to all needy persons irrespective of existing categories associated with age, disability, etc.

b. The federal agency will provide subventions to the states for General Assistance Programs in conformance with the AFDC matching formula.

c. Of the former General Assistance recipients, 20 percent will be transferred each year either to the WIN program or the ACT program at full federal cost.

d. The residual federally subvented General Assistance program will be subject to uniform federal standards for aid payments which conform to reasonable standards of decency and health.

e. All requirements related to liens, recoveries, responsible relatives (except parents' responsibility for minor children), man-in-the-house rule, suitable home requirements, and any other such restrictive provision shall be abolished by federal law to insure uniform application of public welfare laws throughout the Nation.

RESPONSIBILITY OF PUBLIC WELFARE AGENCIES

Public welfare agencies have offices in all of the 3,000 counties in the United States and in addition, in the hundreds of sub-offices in the larger metropolitan areas. Public welfare is close to all people in the United States, and has established an image for service as well as for the provision of public aid. Some services have been provided to the total population as well as to recipients of welfare. Child welfare programs involving adoptions, licensing of foster homes and institutions, protective services for children, and day care services have been of benefit to the total population irrespective of the economic status of the persons served. The 1962 Social Security Amendments emphasized the importance of services to public welfare recipients and others, and implemented the provisions of the law by increasing federal subvention to 75 percent of the cost of such services. Thus, the public welfare agency is a well-established and effective instrument for the provision of such services. There is need for considerable improvement in the quality of services provided by public welfare departments, but there is also great potential for such improvement.

In serving the needs of the total population, public welfare departments must become more effective as social service agencies. These services may be provided directly or through purchase from other agencies when appropriate. The public agency should, however, concentrate on those population groups for whom there are no other services in the community. Recipients of OASI should have a full complement of public welfare services available, since this group is most vulnerable to social problems. The OASI agency should provide money payments to this group and should be prepared to develop appropriate referral mechanisms to insure that the problems of these clients will be referred to a public welfare agency.

The public welfare agency will establish an effective social services and child care program for persons engaged in education and training in the WIN program and in other vocational rehabilitation programs, and will coordinate these services with the education and training provided by other agencies.

The public welfare agency will continue to serve children in need of protection and in need of special services, such as adoption and foster care. In addition, the agency will provide the family with individual counseling services, if needed; will develop, administer, or purchase child care resources for mothers engaged in education or training programs, or in employment; will develop arrangements whereby services are provided to all persons needing them, on a free basis if necessary, and on a graduated fee basis when families have sufficient income to carry part or all of the cost. The agency will also set standards for child care resources, and will continue to perform its historical function of licensing and otherwise improving family homes and institutional programs for children.

The public welfare agency will assume responsibility in the local community for special groups, such as returnees from mental institutions or those who have potential for placement in a mental institution; and for returnees from penal institutions and those who are at risk for law violation. It must be recognized that the agency is in direct contact with most people who are potential for institutionalization, for psychogenic disease, for family breakdown, or for neglect of their children. In the interests of prevention, it is important that these persons be served early by an effective social service agency, and public welfare should fulfill this responsibility.

Finally, public welfare must continue to carry the responsibility for those residual population groups on public assistance who are not served in other programs. This would include emergency assistance needed because of some family disaster; residual programs for women with children who, for some reason, cannot be accommodated in vocational training with stipend programs; and any other unforseen individual or family problem requiring short-term support. This public assistance function will cover a relatively small group of people and will be characterized particularly by its short duration.

The range of services which should be provided by the public welfare agency should include the following:

1. Information, advice, and referral services

2. Advocacy and legal services

3. Personal counseling, rehabilitative, and therapeutic services, and family casework

4. Personal and home health aides, especially to assist the aged, the handicapped, the ill, and families in need of help in the home

5. Homemaker services for families, the aged, and the ill

6. Beginners' day schools, providing child development programs involving activity with parents

7. Educational enrichment for adults, including opportunities for adults and youth to improve basic education skills, to pursue cultural interests, or to supplement and extend their formal education

8. Family planning services

9. Volunteer placement and opportunity services

10. Protective and foster care services for children and the aged

11. Community care services for those recently hospitalized or

institutionalized or for those capable of avoiding such institutional care by being given access to comprehensive help in the community
    12. Activity centered therapy programs.

Cash payments under this residual public assistance program should be fully assumed as a federal responsibility. The funding required for administration of the social services should become a federal-state responsibility, excluding local responsibility for funding. The federal-state formula should be 90 percent federal and 10 percent state.

*   *   *

It is becoming increasingly clear that public welfare agencies fail to meet the needs of the people they are supposed to serve. In addition, it is evident that public welfare staff members are finding very little satisfaction in their work. They complain that the benefits to clients are inadequate; that clients are made to feel like second-class citizens; and that the programs seek to disqualify rather than help people. Strikes of social workers have cited these issues even before expressing concern about their own working conditions and salaries. The vocal protest made in such strikes represents less than 1 percent of the working staff; but the silent protest which incorporates a much larger percentage, is found in the staff turnover. Public welfare departments in California reported a 50 percent loss of staff in 1967, and in 1968, the condition worsened to the point where 58.8 percent of the staff left public welfare jobs. Only 8 percent of those leaving public welfare obtained employment in another public welfare agency. This is a silent protest against the public welfare system as it currently operates.

Some administrators blame the professional expectations and federal rules which result in oversupervision of the workers. It is suggested, however, that administrators must look to more substantive issues. They must consider that a member of a public welfare staff is a creative individual, not a detective; and that his supposed function is to deal with professional services which rehabilitate, not to become bogged down in nit-picking regulatory details which add to the client's problems rather than relieving them. It is important that the image of the public welfare worker be reestablished in terms of service, and this will also create problems, because many incumbent public assistance workers will become lost when the nit-picking details are removed, and they will not fully understand what must be done in the way of services. The separation of services from public assistance has created problems which can be overcome only through administrative understanding and retraining. The public welfare system demands change of a substantive kind, and it will be better to accommodate change through fundamental modification of the program rather than through piecemeal ap-

proaches which can only complicate further the problems in public
welfare administration.

Public welfare has been described as a form of government-
sponsored poverty. Over 9 million of the almost 40 million Americans on the edge of poverty are receiving public welfare payments
which do not conform to general governmental standards for minimum human decency and health. Even this low level of income
varies widely between states because there is no national standard
for welfare payments, and recipients in some states receive only 25
percent of what is given in another state. The Federal Government's
war on poverty is strange in the sense that government must wage
war on itself, since it is a major contributor to poverty—in welfare,
social insurance, and unemployment insurance. What nature of
government is this, that it will provide monetary benefits to the
poor to relieve their distress and by its own standards provides much
less than is needed—often adding indignity as well?

The 1968 Report of the National Advisory Commission on Civil
Disorders states that our public welfare system materially contributes to the tensions and social disorganization that have led to civil
disorders; that welfare is designed to save money instead of people,
and that it tragically ends up doing neither. The Commission decries
the welter of administrative practices which remind recipients that
they are considered untrustworthy, promiscuous, and lazy; which,
through residence requirements, prevent assistance to newly arrived
persons in a state; which violate privacy through regular searches of
recipient's homes; and compound problems through inadequate social services.

Depressions in the United States have clearly revealed that when
men cannot find work they become sick, and the community in
which they live also becomes sick and decays. There has been no
national commitment in the entire history of our Nation to overcome unemployment for once and all. Too little was provided in
the depression years, and present war on poverty programs are only
token attempts to overcome the problem. The overriding issue is
simply to put all men to work who are ready and able to work, and
for those not able to work, to help them become ready.

Social reform of the kind proposed here will place responsibility
for the general welfare of people squarely upon the Federal Government—where it properly belongs. The United States can no
longer tolerate the unevenness of welfare programs in the various
states in terms of the meagre aid and services provided. Moreover,
archaic local practices such as residence laws, liens, and responsible
relative laws can be abolished under more sophisticated federal
leadership. If these programs are left as they are, reforms will require at least another 100 years at local government levels. It is be-

coming increasingly apparent that poor people cannot and will not wait.

The Federal Government must assume fiscal responsibility for the programs proposed by the author in this chapter. This includes the social and medical services which will be required to serve the variety of programs outlined. The precious national human resource can no longer be relegated to the fiscal vagaries of local and vengeful power structures.

Social reform as outlined, in the final analysis, will offset the necessity for political reform. The author strongly supports the American heritage and dream which enables each individual person to seek his own destiny, to fulfill his own potential. The proposed program of social reform is designed to augment this objective through provision of opportunity of education, training, and employment so that each person can fulfill his greatest potential. And if that potential for some is less than the competitive market can use, then the government must provide the opportunity for expression of the limited powers of some men through the special works programs. Through this process, weaker men may work with dignity and gain the respect of their families and communities rather than being condemned as social outcasts because of their weakness. The American society must insure that every man and woman is caught up in a constructive manner in the work of the Nation. When this occurs in a meaningful way, society itself will be greatly strengthened, not weakened, as some rugged individualists believe.

History has clearly revealed that social structures tend to collapse when confronted with fundamental change in conditions. Anthropologists have proved that a culture which is cut off from its past will inevitably wither and die. The American people, their systems, and the political establishment have not changed some of their beliefs and practices since the Nation was formed two hundred years ago. And this is now causing civil unrest of a kind which is threatening the vitality of the country. This American internal conflict today requires synergism of a special kind, merging the past into the present through deliberately constructed phase-in methodologies to resolve this dichotomy. We speak in this book of fundamental legislative and administrative change that is needed. The proposals have relevance to basic change in value systems as well as methodologies. Yet, how can these changes be brought about when politicians who have power to modify our systems must mimic the attitudes and beliefs of those persons least well-educated, least thoughtful and most steeped in the traditional, outmoded beliefs which inevitably will destroy them. It is surely possible in this scientific era to construct change systems which will preserve valued, traditional, democratic beliefs and institutions and at the same time discard useless ones; thereby frustrating both the anthropologists' prediction of inevitable societal destruction if we do change, and the anarchists' rationale for impelling us to oblivion if we do not change.

REFERENCES

1. Bellamy, Edward: Looking Backward. New York, Houghton Mifflin Co., 1887.

2. Owen, Robert: A New View of Society: or, Essays on the Formation of the Human Character Preparatory to the Development of a Plan for Gradual Ameliorating the Condition of Mankind. London, R. and A. Taylor, Printers, 1817.

3. Chase, Stuart: The Proper Study of Mankind, Revised Edition. New York, Harper & Bros., 1956.

4. Lonsdale, Sophia: The English Poor Laws. Westminster, England, King & Son, 1902.

5. Nicholls, Sir George: The History of the English Poor Law. London, John Murray Company, 1854.

6. Webb, Sidney and Beatrice: English Local Government; English Poor Law History, Part 1; The Old Poor Law, London, Longmans, Green & Company, 1927.

7. Sheppard, H. L. and Belitsky, A. H.: The Job Hunt, Baltimore, Johns Hopkins Press, 1966.

8. Kalish, Carol B.: A portrait of the unemployed. Monthly Labor Review, 89:7, 1966.

9. Gruber, W. H.: The Use of Labor Force Participation and Unemployment Rates as a Test for Structural Difficulty, Poverty and Human Resources Abstracts. Paper presented at a Meeting of the Industrial Relations Research Association, December 1965. Ann Arbor, Michigan, November-December, p. 71, 1966.

10. Myrdal, Gunnar: Challenge to Affluence. New York, Pantheon Books, p. 7, 1963.

11. Wade, Alan D.: The guaranteed minimum income; Social work's challenge and opportunity. Social Work, 12:94, 1967.

12. Beveridge, Lord William: Social Insurance and Allied Services. New York, Macmillan Co., 1942.

Rehabilitation:
SOCIAL WORKER–WELFARE RECIPIENT
Dialogues

● *The author, as Chairman of an American Public Welfare Association Regional Conference Program Committee, developed a panel of former welfare recipients and their social workers to engage in a dialogue on the welfare rehabilitation process. The author, members of the Program Committee and the audience were profoundly affected by the personalities and the rehabilitation process as revealed in the dialogues which were recorded as they were presented and are reproduced on the following pages.*

AMERICAN PUBLIC WELFARE ASSOCIATION
WEST COAST REGIONAL CONFERENCE
Hotel Biltmore, Los Angeles - October 8-11, 1967

REHABILITATION:
SOCIAL WORKER-WELFARE RECIPIENT DIALOGUES

Chairman: *Paulene Myers*, Actress, Motion Pictures and Television, and Trustee Motion Picture and Television Relief Fund, Hollywood

Vice-Chairman: *Verrill Rogers*, Executive Director WAIF-ISS, Los Angeles

Participants:

Maricopa County, Arizona
Nancy Chase, Social Worker
Mrs. Diaz, former recipient

Ventura County, California
Judy Alexandre, Social Worker
Mrs. Miller, former recipient

Ventura County, California
Richard Richards, Rehabilitation Services Counselor
Mrs. Smith, former recipient

Los Angeles County, California
Evelyn Schwaber, Social Worker
Mr. Washington, former recipient

Recorder: *Margaret A. Klein*, Training Program Supervisor, Ventura County Department of Social Welfare

* * *

Verrill Rogers: Good morning. My name is Verrill Rogers and I am the Executive Director of WAIF, International Social Service. WAIF is a broad-based child welfare program and before the morning is over you will understand why I have become so involved with Title V.

The Chairman of this session is Miss Paulene Myers, Broadway, Television, and Motion Picture actress. Miss Myers is also a Board Member of the Motion Picture Relief Fund and serves on their case-review committee.

Should I say . . . we are both social work oriented? Certainly we have both been affected by our experiences the past few months.

It has been said, "It is the righteous taxpayer's almost automatic assumption that the state-county welfare programs are too soft . . . that they support too many drones who make no effort to support themselves. And the War on Poverty is getting nowhere."

Miss Myers and I couldn't agree *less!*

The qualities which have made our country strong and have contributed to the development of leadership are matters of mind, heart, and action, and the greatest of these is action. Whether it

587

is voting and doing so intelligently on the basis of information, both pro and con; participating in the political party of our choice; contributing as an individual, or as a member of a group, to some aspect of service to our fellowman and exerting our personal sphere of influence in the molding of a favorable climate of public opinion, without which nothing can succeed. Action is the keynote of effective leadership.

There has been effective leadership in Title V, and Miss Myers will prove how effective this leadership has been.

Never has there been greater need for our democratic ideals to be meaningful and clear-cut. Never have organized groups with programs for helping people held so significant a place in our social structure; for the health, or even survival of a democratic society, is dependent on the services performed by its citizens. So it is incumbent on all citizens to have the wit and the will to develop and use the social leadership and coordinated approach necessary to ensure a strengthening of these democratic ideals I mentioned, for it is only as they are "practiced as they are preached," that they can be anything more than a smoke screen behind which too many people and organizations operate as if these principles did not really exist.

What you and I do, or fail to do, as practicing citizens, may have incalculable results, for there is a tragic sort of determination about events and trends and attitudes now in progress. We could be reminded of the sign that was posted at the beginning of a road that stretched out across the prairie in the middle west: "Choose your rut carefully. You will be in it for the next 500 miles!"

We must make every citizen in this country a productive, constructive consumer, or we will have a chronic, disgruntled dependent. We will either provide the resources for rehabilitation and prevention, or we will pay, now and forever, more and more money for welfare.

Miss Paulene Myers will take you through a living experience which will prove there *is now*—and there *can be more*—help and hope for many.

Miss Paulene Myers. . . .

Paulene Myers: Thank you Verrill. Imagine being in a rut for 500 miles! Well, I do believe that we are being jolted out of that rut now.

Early in May, Miss Rogers, whom I did not know at the time, called me, at the suggestion of Mr. William Kirk, whom I *did* know, to recruit me for Mr. Harold Simmons, whom I also did not know! Now, Miss Rogers didn't know *me* either, but Mr. Kirk said that I was just what she was looking for (whatever that was), and taking his word for it, she foisted me onto poor Mr. Simmons, who was stuck with me!

I want to say in passing that Mr. Kirk is the Executive Director of the Motion Picture and Television Relief Fund, and I am a member of the Board of Trustees. The Fund is set up to help care for the aged and needy in our film industry. For the past three years, I have worked on the committee which reviews these cases with our social workers. It has been for me a most rewarding assignment.

Anyway, there I was on Harold Simmons' Review Panel, which was responsible for this session, wondering why I was always the "schmo" who couldn't say "no." Then something wonderful happened to me. On July 27 I met the other panelists for the first time. The dynamic Verrill Rogers, who charmed me into the whole thing. Dorothy Druschel, wonderful, warm Dorothy Druschel of San Francisco, Associate Regional Representative for Special Services, Bureau of Family Services, Department of Health, Education, and Welfare. Then, the boss, Hal Simmons, pleasant, easy, knowledgeable, who immediately gave us homework to do for the next morning's meeting. It was his presentation made before the House Committee on Education and Labor in Washington on last July 14. If any of you have not read it, I would certainly suggest that you do so.

So, armed with all the background of the Title V Program set forth in Hal's presentation, we met early the next morning with Mr. Ellis Murphy, Director of the Los Angeles County Department of Public Social Services, his staff assistants, and the three worker-recipient teams they had selected for our review. Tom Goff, Los Angeles County Editor of the *Times*, was also on our panel that morning. In Mr. Murphy's opinion, "Mr. Goff is a thoroughly professional newsman, with an excellent background knowledge of welfare activities." I agree with that opinion. Well, Tom Goff seemed overwhelmed that morning, as we all were, by the evidence of rehabilitation and rebirth revealed by the former recipients who came before us. It was not easy to select a first team to bring before you today, but we managed.

Our next review was in Ventura on August 4. We had trouble *finding* that place, and when we finally drove up, a wide-eyed, anxious staff literally tumbled out of the building to greet us with relief that was visible for a block. Howard Rourke, the Ventura County Director of Social Welfare, had arranged for us to have lunch, and then he proudly produced his teams. Howard sneaked in *four* teams instead of three, and they were all so wonderful, we couldn't select just one, so we came away with *two* teams from Ventura. 'Ray! for Ventura County! Also on our panel that day was

Mr. Julius Gius, Editor of the *Star-Free Press*. I will tell you of Mr. Gius' reaction to our session later.

On August 29, the panel traveled to Phoenix, Arizona. Now, that took a bit of doing, what with Dorothy Druschel juggling dates in Alaska; and everyone praying that I wouldn't work that day—except me, secretly, I always want to work!! Verrill with a big bash for WAIF the night before—somehow, we all made it! It was hotter than those well-known hinges, but we lunched and met air-conditioned Jack Knight, Director of the Work Experience Program —Title V, State Department of Public Welfare, produced his teams, and we selected a jewel for you.

Now, it is my privilege to present to you the wonderful people who will participate in this session. The first dialogue will be given by Nancy Chase, Social Worker, and Mrs. Diaz, former recipient, from Maricopa County, Arizona.

Mrs. Chase: This morning I would like you to meet Mrs. Diaz, who is 26 years old, the mother of four children. She is the sole support of her children, as well as her father, who, because of ill health, is unable to work. Originally from Texas, she came to Arizona in 1961. Mrs. D., will you tell us something of your life in Texas before you came to Arizona?

Mrs. Diaz: I was borned in Heresford, Texas. It is small town in sout' of Texas. I was oldest of seven children. My Mama die when I seven years old. The youngest, only two month.

Mrs. Chase: Did a relative or housekeeper care for all you children then?

Mrs. Diaz: Oh, no! We a very poor family. Seven kids and not much moneys. My father, he work, but he don' make much. He make barely enough for us to eat, so there no money for to pay somebody to take care of us kids. I took care of us all since my Mama die. Nobody else to take care.

Mrs. Chase: While you were growing up, did your father work steady?

Mrs. Diaz: Pretty steady, yes, but so many kids and they don' pay him much. Then he got sick a lot and couldn't work.

Mrs. Chase: Since you were taking care of all your brothers and sisters, you pobably didn't have much opportunity for schooling, did you?

Mrs. Diaz: I try my bes'. But, I had to quit after sixth grade. I miss too much days from school and there not enough money for nothing at home. Not even food.

Mrs. Chase: Did you go to work then?

Mrs. Diaz: Work in fields is what I did. That only thing for me to work, in lettuce fields, onion fields, potatoes, cotton. You name it, I've picked it.

Mrs. Chase: How much did you make doing this work?

Mrs. Diaz: Oh, I don' know. It different with different crops. Sometimes 75 cents a day, sometimes maybe even $1.25 a day. Sometime they give us onions to take home and no money. But who can feed on just onions? The money was what we need.

Mrs. Chase: Who took care of your brothers and sisters while you worked in the fields?

Mrs. Diaz: Me! Who else gonna do it? They go to the fields with me. When they old enough, they go to work too. After work, we all go home. It was not much of a home. It had dirt floors and walls were just pieces of wood. When it rain or get cold, the walls don' keep nothing out.

Mrs. Chase: You married at an early age, didn't you?

Mrs. Diaz: I ran away and marry only a little while. I wanted to have a little fun and get away from all the work and all the kids. So what do I do? I have four kids of my own now.

Mrs. Chase: How long were you married?

Mrs. Diaz: One month only the firs' time I marry. Then I leave my husband and come home to my Daddy and the kids. My husban' he don' wanna work. He don' wanna do nothin'. He make me work to support me and him both, so I go back home and have my baby.

Mrs. Chase: Mrs. D. married again in 1961, and by her second husband she had three more children. This man was a transient farm laborer—that is to say, he followed the various crops from state to state. The family arrived in Arizona to pick the lettuce crop, but when that work was through, the family ran into real trouble.

Mrs. Diaz: Oh, Nancy, did we have the troubles! I couldn't speak English like I do now—only a few words I knew when I was a maid in Texas for a lady. I just know words like "mop" and "clean" and a few words like that. Everybody in my town in Texas, they all speak Spanish—no English. They most all poor and don' have much moneys for education. No chance to learn English.

Mrs. Chase: Yes, but there is quite a large Mexican-American group in Phoenix in the area where you live. Did you find it hard to communicate with them?

Mrs. Diaz: It a funny thing. Mexicans in Phoenix, you ask them a question in Spanish and they answer you in English.

Mrs. Chase: Then Spanish is not the main language spoken in the home then?

Mrs. Diaz: Not in Phoenix, except maybe in the homes of the older people. Most Mexican-Americans want to speak English like everybody else, like the rest of the Americans, so they don' use the Spanish much at all. That's why when I come to Phoenix, I hadda learn the English pretty fas'.

Mrs. Chase: You certainly speak English well now.

Mrs. Diaz: My kids—they're the ones. No Spanish for them at all. They raised in Phoenix, so they jus' speak the English. When my brother got marry in Texas a year ago, I go back for the wedding. Nobody believe those kids are mine because they speak English so good. Even my own relatives say, "how come you kids speak English so good?" "How come you know English now?" They so surprise.

Mrs. Chase: What sort of work did you do when you were first living in Arizona and there were no crops to pick?

Mrs. Diaz: Anything I can get—dishwashing, motel maid, housecleaning, scrub floors, anything. My kids gotta eat and have shoes. If I don' work, then my husban', he won't work. If I work, then he work too. But there not much money and so my husban' he say he gonna go to California and Colorado to pick new crops and he say I should stay in Phoenix and he send me money to live. He go all right, but he don' send any money. Jus' maybe $20.00 every three or four months. There was no food, and I couldn't get steady work. I didn't have any training and maid work not permanent.

Mrs. Chase: How did you support the children?

Mrs. Diaz: Finally, I start to apply for Welfare, but I don' want to do this. I want for to support my own kids. I want my kids to know I work for them, not jus' colleck the Welfare for doin' nothing. I don' want to jus' sit back with my arms folded. But before I apply for Welfare, lady from Title V come to see me. I didn't know what was Title V, but she explain it is for training and education for people like me, so I can get a job after I have the training. She explain the Home Management Class to me and ask if I want to be in the class.

Mrs. Chase: Why *did* you decide to enter the class?

Mrs. Diaz: Nancy, all my life I want education, but I never have the chance. I wanna do the best for my kids. No father anymore for them, so now I must do it. This is my chance to help myself and my family.

Mrs. Chase: (directly to audience in explanatory form) The Home Management course was designed to help people like Mrs. Diaz make the best use of what they had and could afford on very limited incomes. For example, many people qualified to receive Surplus Commodities either did not get them, though eligible, or if they did get them, didn't really know how to use them. The cans of powdered milk, powdered eggs, canned meat, corn meal stayed on their shelves unopened. The Home Management Advisors helped the women learn how to use all these commodities effectively, economically, and in many different ways. It has been estimated that with the use of Surplus Commodities, these families save over one-third on their monthly food budget. Tours were taken to acquaint these women with various agencies that could be of service to them and their families such as Family Debt Council, Planned Parenthood, Legal Aid, etc. Comparative shopping tours were taken so that the women would learn how and where to shop for their best values. Effective cleaning methods were demonstrated in the homes to help the women upgrade the quality of their housekeeping. Good grooming was emphasized, and a first aid course was given to them. This is how Mrs. Diaz spent her first two and a half months in Title V. This was considered to be Phase I of the rehabilitation program planned for her. Mrs. Diaz, tell us some of the things you learned in the Home Management class that were particularly helpful to you.

Mrs. Diaz: Most of all I like the teaching of the Surplus Commodities. I never knew how to use them before. My brother-in-law, he a cook in a fancy restaurant in Phoenix. He would never eat the Surplus Commodity meat—always said it was terrible, like dog food. When I learn to make Tamale Pie, I send him over a piece, but I don't tell him it made from the Surplus meat. He come over and he say it is delicious and so good he wants some more even. I tol' him it Surplus meat and he was so surprised he couldn't hardly believe me.

Mrs. Chase: Tell us about the help the first aid section of the class was to you personally.

Mrs. Diaz: That wedding I tell you about in Texas that I go back for? That was right after my home management course was over. While I'm there, my Aunt's house burned down and all the fire department is is volunteer people. Some of my cousins and relatives are in it. The house is burning, but they get my Aunt out of it. They put her on the ground but she not breathing. All the womans standing around crying and the mens think she dead too. I ran to her and give her the mouth to mouth resuscitation like they teach me. I keep doing it and my relatives think I am kissing her goodbye because she is dead. They don' know what I'm doing. Finally she start breathing again and was all right. All my relatives and friends ask me how I learn this and I tell them the Welfare in Arizona taught me how and I tol' them the other things Title V taught me. They could hardly believe me 'cause the Welfare in Texas don' do nothing like that for the people.

Mrs. Chase: How do you mean that?

Mrs. Diaz: When I live there the Welfare lady come once a month just to check. That's all they do. Not like Arizona.

Mrs. Chase: (explanatory-narrative form to audience) When Mrs. Diaz came back to Phoenix, she entered the second phase of her training—the Day Care Program. This consisted of half-day basic education, which included basic arithmetic, English, spelling. The other half of the day was child care and development instruction. This covered the various emotional and physical development levels of the growing child, problems of the working mother, problems in the "fatherless" home, nutrition and health. During this two and one-half month second phase, Mrs. Diaz raised her reading level from fifth to almost eighth grade level.

Mrs. Diaz: The education—that's one of the parts I like the bes'. Education is so important. My kids, they're proud of me for going to school. They proud I'm gonna be a somebody and not a nobody. We Spanish-speaking people kind of funny. The womans they sit home with their arms folded. They don' get jobs. They sit home with the kids alla time. They *think* they know how to raise their kids, but they don'.

Mrs. Chase: What do you mean by that?

Mrs. Diaz: Befor' I have the Day Care class, I think I know everything about raising up the kids. The kids were always around my skirt. When I go to fields to pick crop, the kids go with me. Alla time they never away from me. But day care teachers teach us it not always so good to have kids with you alla time. It good for them to play with other children and be with other people sometimes too.

Mrs. Chase: Did it bother you to be away from the children while you were in training during the day?

Mrs. Diaz: At first it seem so strange and the kids they not used to have nobody else to take care of them. Then they start learning new things, games to play, things to make and bring home, new songs, and so they were happy. The day care teachers teach me about child development, how you should be patient with your kids and not jus' hit them when you mad at them, but to listen to them and try to find out why they do it. They teach you how kids act at different ages so you know what to expec'.

Mrs. Chase: Did this Day Care class help change your attitude any?

Mrs. Diaz: Oh, yes! For the first time I start thinking maybe it not too late for me to learn new things. I thought before maybe I was too old already to learn new things. But then I think maybe it isn't too late to really help myself and my kids. I don' want to sit at home in that dark room with my hands folded. I want my kids to be proud of me.

Mrs. Chase: (narrative form to audience) After the second phase of Mrs. Diaz' training from Title V, it was time to initiate the third and last part of her rehabilitation. While she was going through phases one and two, a great deal of intensive counseling was being done with Mrs. Diaz. During these sessions, actual vocational training was discussed at some length in order to arrive realistically at a type of training that she wanted and could handle. She evidenced a strong interest in Nurses Aide work and so she was placed in a Nurses Aide class that lasted five months. Tell us something of your training, Mrs. Diaz.

Mrs. Diaz: I always wanted to do nursing and when I get this chance, I thrilled! At first I was little scared, but after the first few days everything was fine. Nancy found a lady to take care of my kids so I didn't have to worry about them while I'm training.

Mrs. Chase: Was all your training at the hospital?

Mrs. Diaz: No, before the Nurses Aide classes start, we have a two-week prevocational class. The instructor from Title V tell us about Nurses Aide work, what we do exactly, what an employer expec' from us, how we should act with the patients, how much money that kinda work pays, what kinda problems a working mother have, how we should always call if we be late or sick. We had physical examinations, chest x-rays, and then we went to Saint Luke's Hospital for training.

Mrs. Chase: What were some of the areas you studied during your training?

Mrs. Diaz: Well, we learn how to take blood pressures, and temperatures. They show us how to make the beds the special hospital way, how to serve the patient's food, how to move them and then in the afternoon we learn from books and charts about the parts of the body, diseases, medicines, and things like that. That was the first three and one-half months, then we are placed in the hospital itself on the floor with the patients for the last month and a half.

Mrs. Chase: Of the entire Nurses Aide class of 20, Saint Luke's Hospital reported that Mrs. Diaz was one of the best of the trainees and certainly one of the most popular with the patients themselves. She seemed to have that special knack for saying the right thing, being cheerful and interested in each of the patients she attended. Mrs. Diaz was hired at Maricopa County Hospital just days after graduation from the Title V Nurses Aide class.

Mrs. Diaz: I was so happy when I get my job! My kids, they are so proud of me. For once I'm gonna be able to have steady money coming in to take care of my kids. I'm working! I'm somebody, not a nobody. For once I can buy things for my family like furnitures that look nice, not all torn and broken apart. I even got me a washer. Before, I had to do all the washing by hand, but now I even got the washer. And I work for it—not just sit home and colleck the Welfare. You know, we taxpayers don' approve of paying taxes for somebody to do nothing. If they can work, they should work, not sit home.

Mrs. Chase: What effect did obtaining full-time work have on your children, Mrs. Diaz?

Mrs. Diaz: They know I work hard, but they know they don' have to be scared anymore 'cause it's steady. They don' have to worry to see if their Daddy send money anymore like they used to. They're proud of me.

Mrs. Chase: What are your plans for the future?

Mrs. Diaz: Right now I'm making $262.00 a month, but I'll get a raise soon. I going to try and get my GED now by going to school nights. Then maybe I learn typing and get to be a Nurses Aide Clerk. But most of all, I'm sure of is that I'm gonna make sure my kids get the good education! All this I have now and Title V is responsible for all of it. Even my glasses. When Nancy find out I don' see so good, she had an eye examination for me and Title V pay for glasses even. When I was in Nurses Aide training, they pay for my uniforms, books, and watch, too. If I gotta problem and want help, I call Nancy and she come over and talk to me and give advices. She tell me she never too busy to talk to me. I wanna thank all the Title V people for helping me so much. You took me out of the dark room!

*   *   *

Paulene Myers: I told you she was a jewel! Now for our next dialogue. This one is from Ventura County, California. Miss Judy Alexandre, Social Worker, and Mrs. Miller, former recipient.

Miss Alexandre: I am so pleased we were asked to come to Los Angeles and tell of our close association under the Title V Program. Quite a bit has happened to you during this past year. Would you tell our audience about it.

Mrs. Miller: As I look back, I marvel at all that has happened to me. The whole thing started a year ago last May. I remember that distinctly because it was my birthday and I was sick. I was a waitress. I had been working for weeks with a kidney infection. I believe this was the beginning of my problems. Then my husband walked out on the children and me. I didn't realize what had happened until the following day. It suddenly dawned on me that here I was broke and sick, five kids to take care of and feed. I got hysterical and fell to pieces. Luckily, a waitress friend of mine came by and took me to the doctor. I was under heavy sedation for several days then.

Miss Alexandre: What else did your friend do for you?

Mrs. Miller: She did many things besides coming to the house and taking care of things whenever she could. She went down to the city manager and told him the situation and asked him if there was any way that the city could help me. I didn't really expect to receive help, but he sent $40.00 up for the family to help buy food. This was a Godsend, because we really needed it. I think this just goes to show you the advantage of living in one town for so many years.

Miss Alexandre: As I remember, your son was graduating from high school about then.

Mrs. Miller: Yes, I think this is one of the things that brought me out of it. I realized that graduation was drawing near and I had to attend the graduation ceremonies and all that went with it. He had done so well in school. He was president of the student body and I knew I had to be there, so I had to straighten out. I just couldn't let him down.

Miss Alexandre: Then what did you do?

Mrs. Miller: I guess I just realized I had to do something, so I applied for public assistance. I saw an intake worker and he arranged for Surplus Commodities for us and had me sign some papers to give us more help. The commodities certainly came in handy. In about three weeks, I received a grocery order and I went to the Bayless Market and stocked up. In the meantime, I applied for my disability insurance.

Miss Alexandre: What were you to receive disability for?

Mrs. Miller: It was for the kidney infection, because I wasn't able to work. With the disability insurance and the commodities we managed to scrape by until my 90-day waiting period was over and my assistance checks started coming in.

Miss Alexandre: How did you happen to go to the Mental Health Clinic? You were also receiving benefits based on your emotional problem. What other help were you receiving for that problem?

Mrs. Miller: I started attending the clinic at General Hospital, because I knew I couldn't afford to pay a private doctor. To top it all off, my son came down with mononucleosis and had to have shots every day. I was real mixed up at the time. I was feeling hatred for my husband and had developed a shame or guilt complex over the separation. It was a shock. Although we had been separated before, the first two times it was my idea, and I think it was a blow to my pride that he walked out on me finally. I was in a terrible state of mind. One day at the clinic, I asked the doctor for some salve for my eyes, which were red and scaly and inflamed from crying so much. She had given me some tranquilizers previously, and I guess she realized the situation. She told me, "Well, the only thing I know is for you to quit crying and your eyes won't be red." Well, that did it, and I started crying. So she called a nurse and had me taken to the Mental Health Clinic. I saw the Chief Psychiatrist there, and he arranged for my first appointment with a psychologist.

Miss Alexandre: You mentioned that the psychologist was quite a help to you and going to the clinic helped to get you going again. Can you relate some of your feelings about going to the Mental Health Clinic and exactly what the psychologist did for you?

Mrs. Miller: He helped me in many ways. One, I think most important, was the fact that he was someone to talk to, and just knowing it was confidential was a help in getting it off of my chest. Another thing, I had grown to the state where I didn't want to face anyone. I didn't want to go out of the house, go to the store. I'd send the children. I just wanted to stay in the house and sleep and escape my problems that way. I didn't want to see anyone or talk to anyone. After several interviews, he began to get through to me and made me realize that I needed to quit hibernating and get out and see and talk to people and possibly go back to work.

Miss Alexandre: Was it at this time that you were referred to the Rehabilitation Unit of our department?

Mrs. Miller: Yes! The last thing in the world I wanted to do then was to face anyone and go to work, but he suggested that I see the Rehabilitation Counselor. He looked at my background of employment and suggested that I consult the Department of Employment.

Miss Alexandre: Quite a few people were trying to help you solve your problems in that short period. From Disability and Intake, Mental Health Clinic, the Medical Clinic, Rehabilitation Counselor, and now, the Department of Employment. Was this all beneficial to you?

Mrs. Miller: Yes, because everyone I was seeing was helping me. Each did what they could and sent me on to someone else. It was bringing me out of myself, giving me a lot of help. Most important, everyone I saw understood. I had three interviews with Employment discussing jobs and what I would like to do. They arranged some testing for me. One was manual dexterity. Another was an intelligence test, and there was a Kruder Vocational test. There were jobs available, but other than waitress or packinghouse work, they all required a high school diploma, and I didn't have one. They said that I had scored so high on the tests that I could take advantage of this GED, equivalent to a high school diploma, and there was one coming up in December. They suggested that I try taking the test and see if I could get my diploma and then come back and see about a job.

Miss Alexandre: How much education did you have?

Mrs. Miller: I completed the ninth grade. I took some math books and went home and tried to study on my own. This was very frustrating, I found it very hard to remember things. I recall my son coming home from college in the afternoon. He would find me sitting at the dining room table in tears, and he'd say, "Mom, what's the matter?" I'd say, "These darn things, I'll never learn any of this math."

Miss Alexandre: He was a help to you?

Mrs. Miller: Yes, all the children were. They would sit down for hours and help me find why I couldn't get a certain problem done. The 14-year-old was in eighth grade at the time and helped me with Science and World History. The 10-year-old helped me with my multiplication tables, which I had to master all over again. I remember the day I helped my 10-year-old with her multiplication tables. That was quite an accomplishment.

Miss Alexandre: I think it was at this time that we thought maybe the training center could help you get your GED faster. An appointment was set up and I remember you sitting in the lobby and you weren't anxious to see anyone at all. You had brought a friend with you and when I came in you were ready to leave and go back and sell Stanley Products.

Mrs. Miller: Well, I hadn't done too well at home studying, and I chickened out on that December GED test. I definitely wasn't ready, I had sold Stanley Products before, so I thought this was a way out.

Miss Alexandre: What finally motivated you to stick it out?

Mrs. Miller: Well, I guess my thinking about a good job, other than waitress work or selling. My children had graduated and I guess I wanted a high school diploma. They had all done quite well. I wanted the feeling that Mom could do it, too. I guess I wanted to be like them.

Miss Alexandre: Then did you see the Rehabilitation Counselor?

Mrs. Miller: Yes, and we decided I'd go to the center.

Miss Alexandre: How did you feel when you first went there?

Mrs. Miller: I didn't feel like facing anyone. I still was afraid of people and these were strange faces, and a strange place. My son was a good standby through the whole thing. I guess he realized that if he didn't take me and come back for me in the afternoon, I might leave. He dropped me off and I walked in terrified, and I thought to myself, "Ye gods, what am I doing here?"—you know! And if I had a car, I guess I would have left. But, within a week I began to be relaxed and feel a little at home.

Miss Alexandre: Did the other trainees at the center help you get this feeling?

Mrs. Miller: Yes. I think just knowing that they were trying to do the same thing that I was doing and were having the same difficulties was a help to me. It was very hard at first. I think it was having to get up and dressed, getting breakfast, fixing my face, and getting on my way.

Miss Alexandre: What was so difficult about this?

Mrs. Miller: Well, I had been home for quite a while and it was quite a change to have to get up and get ready to go somewhere early in the morning. After I had done it for awhile, I started thinking—this is what I'll have to do if I get a job.

Miss Alexandre: During this time, although I know that you probably told yourself "It's not worth it," you really did keep yourself going and you did learn. How were you feeling about the approaching test?

Mrs. Miller: It is hard to describe my feelings of dread of the GED test. But I wanted desperately to pass it. I knew that I would be letting a lot of people down—my children having so much confidence in me; the Instructor who devoted so much individual time to each of us; the trainees and employees at the center; everyone seemed concerned and interested in all of the women that were preparing for this GED test. The Instructor saw to it that we had trial testing and words of encouragement, telling us we could really do it, and everyone at the center, even the kitchen help, went out of their way to make things nice and easier for us.

Miss Alexandre: You really felt support from the center?

Mrs. Miller: Yes. Some of those ladies had it real rough, a lot rougher than I did, because they had little children that they had to get up in the morning, toddlers they would bring to the center. I was grateful that my youngest was not the age that I had to do that, too.

Miss Alexandre: The test did actually come—I mean you did take it. Will you tell us how you reacted to this test?

Mrs. Miller: The test was given at the college. It had five areas of testing, one each night for five nights. Math was my rough subject, but I was lucky enough to get English Literature the first night! I felt that I did fairly well on it. We met at the coffee shop after the testing each night and when I heard some of the remarks about that math test, I went home and crammed on Algebra and Geometry. We had been told no studying during the week, but I felt that I had to.

Miss Alexandre: In the coffee shop gatherings, when you would come together, your talks weren't always too positive, I gather.

Mrs. Miller: No, but we managed to get through the test and none struck out. We all knew we were going to fail it, but once you start something like that, you have to follow through. We had several days that we had to wait until we found out the results of the test. We sat around and made our pessimistic plans for the future. Some of us, some of the women, decided they would just go out and get any kind of a job.

Miss Alexandre: What were your plans?

Mrs. Miller: Well, at the time I was feeling badly because I knew I had failed the darned thing, and I wanted to pass it. Although I heard the other women saying, "Well, I'm going to go out and get a job and the heck with this," I waited for someone else to say, "Well, gee, I'm coming back, because this is what I want to do." I wouldn't have minded studying further, if I had to, to prepare for the next test. It was a good place to be, and I felt at home there.

Miss Alexandre: After the week of waiting and you did get your results, did you continue to get support or were you left on your own then?

Mrs. Miller: No. We finally got word of the results, and, surprisingly, we all did quite well. We had an opportunity, each of us, to talk to the Rehabilitation Counselor. Most of the women knew what they wanted to do. That wasn't the case with me. I had been thinking only of the goal of getting that diploma. I wanted a job, but what kind, I didn't know.

Miss Alexandre: Were any suggestions made to you at this time?

Mrs. Miller: I told the Counselor I didn't know what I wanted to do. I wanted a well paying job, because my children like to live well! During the testing at the Department of Employment, I rated high in "Persuasiveness." I was told that I should work with people. I mentioned this to the Counselor, and he, in turn, told me about the possibility of employment at the School for Girls.

Miss Alexandre: Did you file an application for employment there?

Mrs. Miller: Yes and no. The next morning I think I felt better than I had in ages. I was so full of vigor and vitality I could have gone to work that day. So, I went to the School for Girls and walked in boldly and got the shock of my life, because no one would talk to me about an application. A woman came out and said, "Well, haven't you heard? All the state jobs are frozen." I said, "Well, all I want to do is put in an application." She said, "We aren't taking any. The jobs are all frozen." Well, needless to say, I went out of there with a slow, depressed walk. But, I still wasn't licked. The

Counselor had mentioned the 3-M Company in Camarillo, which also paid well. I went over there and applied. They informed me that they were doing no hiring at the present time, but they would keep my application on file.

Miss Alexandre: I think about this time you began to slip back emotionally. Was that when a friend told you there were vacancies again at the School for Girls?

Mrs. Miller: Yes, a lady I had been riding with to the training center called me. She had passed her GED and was in further training at the center. She said our Instructor had told her to call me and let me know that they were definitely taking applications at the School for Girls.

Miss Alexandre: But before you went, wasn't there a month or so that you were doing something else?

Mrs. Miller: Yes, I went back to selling Stanley Products. I knew that I had to do something, because I went home and I got back in the same old rut. I didn't take care of myself, slept every chance I could get. I found out that just getting a high school diploma is no magic charm. But my heart wasn't in selling. So I went back to the School for Girls; they let me in this time. I filled out the application and had an initial interview, and was set up for the written test.

Miss Alexandre: How was the written test?

Mrs. Miller: It was another difficult test, and I was afraid I had failed it. But, to my surprise, they asked me, "Well, what day would you like to come in for your oral interview?" Things just kept getting harder all the time. That oral interview was another experience. Two staff members asked a lot of personal questions about my former employment, about how I would handle different situations. I knew—no matter what—I had failed that test.

Miss Alexandre: But you didn't fail it, did you?

Mrs. Miller: No. Within about a week and a half, I received word through the mail that I had passed, both written and oral examinations, and to report to work. So, I became a Group Supervisor at the School for Girls.

Miss Alexandre: It seems amazing when you think back that just a year ago you were at home, quite emotionally upset, didn't want to see anybody, didn't want to talk to people, but gradually through the year you got to a point where you are working with people, where you are very much influencing their lives. How do you feel about it all now?

Mrs. Miller: It is difficult to explain. I know that most of my co-workers have a college education. I have come a long way and all I can do is try my best. It means security for my family, financial security. I've got a 14-year-old that I know is going to want to go to college. It gives me a good feeling to think that I have had this chance to be doing something that other women with a college education are doing. I know that none of this would have been possible, had it not been for the help of so many people along the way. From the time that I went up to the door of the Welfare Department to the day I went out at the center, I think, is the best thing that ever happened to me.

* * *

Paulene Myers: Our next dialogue is also from Ventura County. This time we have Richard Richards, Rehabilitation Services Counselor, about whom you heard previously, and the former recipient, Mrs. Smith.

Mr. Richards: Mrs. Smith, you have successfully completed a Welfare Department training program and you are now gainfully employed. Will you tell our co-workers here at the conference your story?

Mrs. Smith: Yes, I'd love to. I'd like to tell you how much I appreciate what the Welfare Department has done for me. I hope what I have to tell will help somebody else in a similar situation.

Mr. Richards: How long have you been off welfare?

Mrs. Smith: A little over a year.

Mr. Richards: It sounds as if you have done a good job. It's made you self-supporting for all this time. Tell us how all this began!

Mrs. Smith: I was 13 when I was first married, and I had my first child when I was 16. Because we were so young at the time, the marriage just didn't succeed. Unfortunately, about a year after my daughter was born, we were divorced. Knowing what I know now, I wouldn't advise anyone to be married at that age.

Mr. Richards: How did you happen to marry at such an early age?

Mrs. Smith: I had too much responsibility at home. I didn't have a mother and we moved an awful lot. From the time I was about nine years old, I had to do all the housework and cooking for myself, my younger sister and my father.

Mr. Richards: Were you ever married again?

Mrs. Smith: Yes, I was married when I was 18.

Mr. Richards: How was this marriage. Was it any better?

Mrs. Smith: It was better than the first time. I was older, which made a lot of difference, not that I was old enough though, because I was still quite young. The second time I married a man 13 years older than myself.

Mr. Richards: How long did you remain married to your second husband?

Mrs. Smith: About three years, until I was about 22.

Mr. Richards: What has happened to you since your second marriage?

Mrs. Smith: Well, it was shortly after that that I met my youngest child's father. This is when everything started going bad. We were unable to be legally married until my divorce was final. Therefore, we lived together in a common-law marriage. We tried to get married, but it seemed like we never had enough money for it, which is a very handy excuse. I had a child from him, but this didn't seem to make the marriage any better. It was during this time of living with him that it seemed like I was in a living hell.

Mr. Richards: What do you mean by that?

Mrs. Smith: Well, starvation would be a good example. It was very upsetting and very degrading when the next door neighbor had to bring food. Not had to, but brought food over, knowing my predicament at that time. They knew I needed food for my three-month-old baby and my other children. My husband, as usual, was off somewhere busy spending what little money he earned, gambling, drinking, or otherwise.

Mr. Richards: What effect did this have on you, when your neighbors brought the food over?

Mrs. Smith: Well, it's kind of hard to explain. I was . . . well, to put it quite bluntly, I just stood there and cried.

Mr. Richards: What happened after that, when did you become involved with the Welfare Department?

Mrs. Smith: It was sometime during the time that I was living with him, probably one of the times when he was off on a drunk. We had next to nothing in the house to eat. I don't know the exact date; anyway, it was during this period of time when I made an application for welfare.

Mr. Richards: What do you remember of your early experiences with the Welfare Department?

Mrs. Smith: My first social worker helped me a lot. She listened to me and seemed to try to understand me and my predicament. She didn't criticize me or make me feel ashamed or anything. She was very understanding. Of course, the best thing was her helping me get on welfare so I could have a regular meal for my children. This was very important to me. She also was the best listener I ever had. She helped me open my eyes to the way I was living.

Mr. Richards: How else did she help you?

Mrs. Smith: She helped me with housing. It was during this time that Port Hueneme City was going through a redevelopment program, you remember. Anyway, our house was to be torn down and we needed to move. The social worker tried to help me move into the Colonia Housing Project, but they said they wouldn't accept my three children.

Mr. Richards: Oh, why was that?

Mrs. Smith: Because of their different last names. So, my worker and I continued looking for housing until I found my present place.

Mr. Richards: What else do you remember from the Welfare Department?

Mrs. Smith: I had several social workers who only came by for a visit or two, so I don't remember them. There was my last social worker, who played a very important part in my life.

Mr. Richards: How did he help you?

Mrs. Smith: First, he helped me tremendously with my oldest daughter. I was having an awful lot of trouble with her at that time. She was in a very large, deep state of depression. She was like this for over a year. She was completely withdrawn. She wouldn't laugh or she wouldn't play like other children. She was quite disobedient and very stubborn.

Mr. Richards: How did this social worker help you in this situation?

Mrs. Smith: He helped me to understand my daughter and why she was like this. There had to be some reason why she was like this, and he brought it to my attention. He showed me that it was a combination of the way we were living and the way I, myself, reacted to her. I think he was better than any psychiatrist.

Mr. Richards: Are you and your daughter getting along better now?

Mrs. Smith: Oh yes, we laugh and play together; we weren't even able to be together before.

Mr. Richards: Are there any other ways in which he or the Welfare Department has helped you?

Mrs. Smith: There have been several ways I was helped. He helped me also by introducing me to the training program that the Welfare Department had.

Mr. Richards: Had you worked at all prior to this?

Mrs. Smith: The only work I had was in the frozen food plant, where I worked off and on for about five years. This was seasonal and wasn't adequate for supporting my family.

Mr. Richards: What type of training did you get through the Welfare Department?

Mrs. Smith: I took clerical training at the training center in Oxnard.

Mr. Richards: How did you get started at the training center?

Mrs. Smith: Through this last social worker of mine who referred me to a counselor at the Welfare Department, for some sort of job or education evaluation.

Mr. Richards: Did the counselor help you? Did he tell you what sort of training would be appropriate in your case?

Mrs. Smith: Yes, I had a couple of interviews with him and we decided that the clerical field at that time was best suited for me.

Mr. Richards: What were some of the problems you had to overcome at the beginning in order to start training?

Mrs. Smith: Babysitting was the main one. I was told that the training center could help me with the care of my children. I couldn't take advantage of this service though because we lived too far from the center for my children to walk to it after school. Therefore, the Welfare Department helped me by paying a sitter to watch the children while I was in training.

Mr. Richards: How about transportation? How did you get to the center?

Mrs. Smith: I had my own car, but there was the problem of the auto expenses. This, also, the Welfare Department helped me with. In fact, they gave me a lot more money than usual so that I could take part in the training.

Mr. Richards: Had you had any clerical training or preparation in high school?

Mrs. Smith: No, I wasn't even a high school graduate. I had only about a seventh grade education at that time. I realized I had a very long way to go.

Mr. Richards: What were some of the plans that were made to help you bring up your education?

Mrs. Smith: I started night school, their regular program, while going to the training center. I was glad to be at the center because it gave me the opportunity to study even more than just going to school like most people usually do.

Mr. Richards: In other words, you not only were able to do some of your homework at the center, but to get help on it, if need be. How did you feel about the program at the training center?

Mrs. Smith: I liked being there a great deal. We worked beyond clerical training. We discussed grooming and had outside people come in and discuss various subjects. I felt at home there. There wasn't the nervous tension one might expect in a training situation. After all the time and help everyone there gave me, I began to worry about letting them down.

Mr. Richards: Can you give me an example of some of the special help you are referring to?

Mrs. Smith: Yes, I was still in my first semester in high school when they enabled me to take a civil service clerical test. I was just in training for the GED test and didn't have all the qualifications for the Account Clerk test. Even so, the training center made arrangements with the County Personnel Office so that I could take the test with my GED still pending. Boy, was I nervous! Unfortunately, I didn't pass, and I thought I had really let everybody down.

Mr. Richards: But, you kept on in training didn't you?

Mrs. Smith: Oh, definitely, they gave me the encouragement to continue by saying how well I did in the test, considering my employment background and my level of education. Therefore, I continued studying even harder for the GED test. Along with my regular work at the center and homework from night school, I was given other classes at the center and books so that I could prepare myself for the GED.

Mr. Richards: Did you take the test?

Mrs. Smith: Yes, the Welfare Department helped me to go to Los Angeles, including extra money for expenses, to take the GED test. I passed the test, which then enabled me to qualify for a clerical job, just as if I had a high school education.

Mr. Richards: Well, what was the next step?

Mrs. Smith: Next, I was an account clerk trainee for Ventura General Hospital. While there, I was able to take the account clerk test again, and at this time I passed it with a very good score. In fact, I was sixth in standing out of about 35 others that took the test.

Mr. Richards: Did you get the job at this point?

Mrs. Smith: No, I was on the eligibility list and continued the on-the-job training. I had just passed the test and was very worried about my first interviews. I spoke to one of the staff members, and told her I was very nervous about the oral interview end of it, the do's and don'ts of an interview.

Mr. Richards: What did this training center staff member do to help you at this time?

Mrs. Smith: She enabled me to speak to a county personnel official. She gave me the do's and don'ts of an interview. When the interview with her was completed, she said I didn't have much to worry about and that I would probably be very successful. She also mentioned that she would be glad to hire me since I had already passed the test and they needed a girl at the Welfare Department. I preferred not to, though, because I felt I would have the feeling of still being on welfare.

Mr. Richards: Where did you finally go to work then?

Mrs. Smith: I got a lead to a job, or what I thought was a job, at Point Mugu, and I went for an interview. At the time they interviewed me they didn't need anyone. The personnel manager, however, said that there was a new sub-contractor coming in that day and that he would be in need of a secretary. I was called in for an interview. At this point, the sub-contractor hired me and I went to work. I have a feeling that the job resume the training center helped me to prepare played a big part in my getting this job.

Mr. Richards: How did you do on your first job as an office clerk?

Mrs. Smith: I found to my amazement that what the personnel manager told me concerning this sub-contractor just starting out was certainly true. We had a small trailer to work in and one working typewriter, a filing cabinet, and that was it. I had to set up the complete clerical procedure and do everything.

Mr. Richards: Are you still with this company?

Mrs. Smith: No! I was transferred from the sub-contractor to the primary contractor, as a senior clerk.

Mr. Richards: Are you still with the primary contractor?

Mrs. Smith: No, in the spring of this year, he lost his Federal contract. For a short period I was again without work and beginning to worry a great deal, but luckily I landed a new job with Ventura County and that's where I'm working now.

Mr. Richards: Since you're earning your own money and you are not on welfare anymore, do you feel your family is doing any better or not?

Mrs. Smith: Well, I think we're a much happier family. I'm very independent and my children are just happier children, they can laugh like other children do now. We can afford the little things we couldn't afford on welfare. I was receiving $190 a month for my three children. Well, now I'm earning $365 a month. When I'm working, I'm like a new person, I just feel alive. I still have problems, but I know now that I can work things out.

Mr. Richards: How old are your children now?

Mrs. Smith: I have a girl eleven, a boy seven, and a girl three-and-a-half years old.

Mr. Richards: Thank you so much, Mrs. Smith, for speaking with me and sharing your experiences. Do you have any suggestions as to how we could improve our program?

Mrs. Smith: Yes, if there could be some sort of bus service to the training center, I'm sure this could help a lot of people. Even though

I had my own car, I saw a lot of other people having difficulty getting to the center regularly.

* * *

Paulene Myers: Our last dialogue today comes to us from Los Angeles County. The Social Worker is Mrs. Evelyn Schwaber and the former recipient is Mr. Washington.

Mrs. Schwaber: Mr. Washington, we know each other, but our audience doesn't. Could you give us a little bit of a background on how you and I came to know each other as well as we did?

Mr. Washington: Well, I went in his office one day and he asked me would I be interested in going to school, and I said yes. "Well, what would you want to go to school for?" "Well, I want to go for barbering." "Well, you come back and see me in a couple of weeks, and I'll see what I can do." So I went back and in the meantime I checked the barbering schools and I gave him a rundown how much the cost was and what have you, so I came back and I told him, and he said, "Well, we'll see what we can do." So then I explained to him that I had a police record in this way and the other, so, "Well, we'll check it," so in the meantime he says, "Well, you go to the school that you want to go to. You go and file an application." So I went and filed the application and she says, "Well, there will be a waiting period." So I waited, and I just did get in in time because they—well, I don't know how to explain it—anyway, I had waited, but I would have had to wait 90 days, but she, the lady at the office, rush my application and check it. So she checked it and the lady called me one evening and told me, "Well, Mr. Washington, the barber board accepted it." So, when the barber board sent me a letter, I told them about my record and I sent them a photostatic copy of it, of my record and everything, and they sent me a letter back and told me, say, well, if I get into any trouble, notify them during the process of going to school, so, and that's the way it all started. So now I had a lot of problems in school when I started.

Mrs. Schwaber: Mr. Washington, in your arrest record there was one particular thing that we talked about. Do you remember the assault with a deadly weapon? What did that come from?

Mr. Washington: Well, at that particular time I had a temper. So, this is the same thing that happens to me when I'm at school—I have a temper, but I learned to control it through, by, well, I would say, more or less, by the social worker, you know, because every time I would have a problem, well, I would call and I would go down and talk to her, and she would talk to me, and each time, well, I don't know, it's just something that she explained to me, well why this and why that, and you got to have rules, you got to have regulations, and I have to comply with them, so I learned this and then, like I said, and furthermore, when I was in school I had a lot of problems, you know, but actually I learned to get along with the people—accept the rules and the regulations. That was the whole problem was that I just didn't comply with the rules and regulations, but I learned to do this because I know that what I was going to school for was something that I wanted because I had went from this job to that job and no way to keep a job, and I would go to where you could get a decent job and the first thing they would ask you, well, what have you been arrested for, and I mean you got to tell the people, and once you tell them they say, well, I'm sorry, we're not doing no hiring. So, I got the chance to do something for myself, so I say, well, I'm going to go on and do it because I don't want to be facing this problem of "I'm sorry, we're not doing no hiring," you know. So I went on and I got on down and accepted the facts and I got myself under control and I went on and I finished the course, and I completed it, you know, and I'm proud and I appreciate what I got and I appreciate what she did for me, you know, and helping me along and talking to me, because, otherwise, I mean, a lot of times I really—I didn't want to give up, but a lot of times, I mean, the things I had to deal with in school with the instructors, I mean, I would think about if I would like to give up. I said, no, I can't give up now, you know, got to go along with it, and I mean the day that I completed the course and finished, and then when I got my results back from the Board, I mean, the best day of my life that I can ever recall, you know, I mean I don't think nothing else can be no better because I'm going to have something now— I'm going to have something now that I don't have to go nowhere and they say, "I'm sorry we're not doing no hiring," because I'm qualified to cut hair and I have a license for this. So, I mean, if there's an opening, I can fill it, but before I go some place and they say, "Well, I'm sorry we're not doing no hiring," or they say "What are you qualified to do?" Well, at the present time I wasn't qualified to do anything, but I am now and I can say that I appreciate what I got, and it did a lot of things for me and it changed me altogether, you know. So, I don't know, before we came up here it's a lot of things I thought about I could say, but I mean now, I don't know how.

Mrs. Schwaber: We had a great deal to talk about and we learned quite a few things as we were talking—things that I hadn't realized were on your mind, too. And I learned something from you, if you recall. We were talking about some of the benefits that you got out of this, and you mentioned something. First of all, even before we were talking about the benefits that you got out of the program, we were talking about how you were really, in a sense, the same person, having the same temper, having the record you had when you came to us, and yet you managed to control all of this. You managed to stop yourself from doing the things that you had done before. Now, what was it—do you remember what you told me?

Mr. Washington: Well, I can say I feel like this—like the old saying says—'a wise man changes, but a fool never changes.' Some people sleep all their lives and some wake up, and I was just fortunate enough to wake up in time to come to myself, because the things that I was doing wasn't benefiting me, you know, it was all against me, you know, so I say, well, it's time for me to wake up and do something for myself. And, like I told you, like it say in the Bible, I mean, because I looked at it every day, I read the book and it says without education there's no elevation. You know—I mean if you're not qualified for something, you can't get it.

Mrs. Schwaber: Do you remember also what you said about if you had gone into something else?

Mr. Washington: Oh, yeah, well, if I had took mechanics or upholstering or something, I would have flopped out, because it wasn't what I wanted, you know, and so I took what I wanted, because if you go to school for something you don't want, you're wasting the people's time and money and your time, too. So, I knew this, so that's why the first day that I told you when you asked me what I wanted to, I told you what I wanted to do—well, I mean, I could have told you, well, I want to go and be a mechanic, knowing that I don't want to, but I would have went on and wasted the time and the money and everything for something that I wouldn't have been a success at, because like what I have now—like I told you—I intend to be one of the best barbers—not the best—but I intend to be one of the best. It's something that I want, but if I had picked something else that I didn't want, well, I'd just have been wasting time, wasting my time. I knew this.

Mrs. Schwaber: Well, one of the things you're telling us, then, is that if the training program for anyone is to be successful, you do have to consider what the person wants.

Mr. Washington: Right. And also, the individual himself—he has to know that he wants this, because a lot of people say, "I'm going to school just for the money." I never had this idea in my mind. I had the idea in my mind that I wanted to go to school for something that I want, that's going to benefit me, that I'd appreciate somewhere later on, because as far as the money goes, the thought had never crossed my mind. But a lot of people do go to school in different programs for the money. A lot of them do this because they don't stay in school long—maybe four or five months

—and in the process of going there, they don't do anything. I've seen this happen. I've seen students drop out. I've seen students put out for low attendance and what have you. Well, they say, "I don't want to cut hair anyway." I say, "Why did you come to school? You shouldn't go for something you don't want. If you want dressmaking, you should go for dressmaking, not barbering." I tell people, "Now, you're hollering about you want a job, you want this, and you want that. Well," I say, "you can't get this if you're not qualified for it." The guys say, "Man, I can cut hair as good as you can." I say, "If you can good as I can, what are you doing about it?" I say, "You're sitting here telling me about it. I can show you on the wall I have a license to cut hair. Do you have one?" He said, "No, but I still cut hair as well as you." "Well, don't tell me about it, because I don't have to tell you, you can see for yourself. This is something that I want to do." I look at these people; they go to school for various things that are not what they want. They say, "Well, I should have went for something else." That's why I tell anybody that when you go to school, you go in a program, you pay, however you go. Go for what you want, something that you want.

Mrs. Schwaber: Could you help us out. Have you any way of helping us to know when a person really wants something?

Mr. Washington: Well, I don't know. I'll put it like this. If a person wants something, you can tell what he's going to school for. You can tell how he's doing, if he's got a project he's working on, or whatever it is, you can tell how he's doing, because it's the same way in biology—when you have a test on biology, or whatever, you can tell if the student has studied or not. Whatever comes up or how he's doing on his haircutting at a certain period of time. Say, in a period of six weeks he should be able to turn out some pretty nice hair if this is what he really wants to do. It tells, because if a person is interested in something, it shows. But if he's not, it will show, either way.

Mrs. Schwaber: You mentioned waste of money. How could we avoid that in the beginning? By not even sending a person to school? Do you think there's any way we can judge that?

Mr. Washington: Well, I couldn't say. I couldn't tell because, like I said, once he starts, after a period of six weeks, or whatever it is, you can be able to tell whether it's money being wasted or not. You can tell by the attendance he keeps, because if it's a few times —you can't get there every day—there was a few times when I couldn't get there every day, but I had reasons for the times I couldn't be there.

Mrs. Schwaber: Would you say, then, that we should really give people a chance at what they think they want?

Mr. Washington: Yes, they should be allowed a chance, because a lot of people say, "Well, they won't give me a chance." I was allowed a chance—I feel the next person should be allowed a chance. Like I said—in time you can tell. Time will tell. If you're interested in what you're doing, if you're in a body shop, or whatever kind of trade you're in, if you're interested in what you're doing and they got other students there, you say, he's getting A's and B's on these tests, I'm going to get B's, too, because this is what I want and I want to get all I can out of it.

Mrs. Schwaber: Let's go back to the beginning when we first met. If you recall, we talked a little bit about some of the past work that you had done. What kinds of work were some of those?

Mr. Washington: Well, I washed dishes, bus boy, waiter, stock boy, and truck driver. I had just about every job you can have as far as common labor. I've did it all.

Mrs. Schwaber: Do you remember when we were talking together, I questioned your going into barbering, with all the background—you even had some truck driving.

Mr. Washington: Well, all the things that I did, I didn't like. Like I told you, if I had picked something that I didn't like, I wouldn't have went. I'd have wasted time. It's got to be something that you want. All these last jobs that I had, I didn't stay on them long. I worked maybe five or six months and I quit because I wasn't satisfied with what I was doing. If it wasn't that I couldn't get along with the man on the job, it was always something that I would find. I think it would be me most of the majority of the times, because I didn't like what I was doing. Out of all of these various jobs that I've had, I never had one until now—what I got now—that I like. I enjoy what I've been doing now.

Mrs. Schwaber: Well, how did you know that you were going to be a barber?

Mr. Washington: I didn't know. Like I told you, it took all this time for me to realize what I was really supposed to do. When I was going to school, my father wanted me to be a musician, and I took music lessons and I was doing fairly good, but what he wanted me to be wasn't what I wanted to be. Any individual, you can put all your money on him and what have you, but if it's not what he wants to be, it's just not going to work. Like I explained to you— it took me all this time to realize what I really was meant to be was a barber. So, because out of all the things that I did, this is the only thing that I've had success in—I mean really completed and really enjoy what I've been doing.

Mrs. Schwaber: So what you're really saying is when a person is successful at something, or feels he is, that this is the one thing that counts the most with him.

Mr. Washington: Right! Because I feel that this is what is really meant for him to do in life. You know—you got lawyers, you got doctors, you got politicians—if you were meant to be a politician, well, no matter what you do, in the long run you're going to be a politician, if this is really what you want to do. I feel that every person is something that he was meant to be in life. Some find out, some don't. Some people sleep all the way through and never know. When you got kids in school, like when I was going to school, they say, "Well, when you grow up, what do you want to be?" Well, I never did really think about what I wanted to be, and I'd think of different things, and I'd say no, I didn't want to be that. I didn't know what I wanted to be. It took all this time for me to really know what I really wanted to do. What I'm doing now, this is what I want to do. If I live 30 years, well, if I was meant to cut hair, well, I'm going to cut hair. It's the only thing that I'm going to ever do—it's the only thing that I want to do.

Mrs. Schwaber: Barbering seems to have a very special meaning to you. Outside of the fact that you like the work, there's something extra special about it that you mentioned to me that's different from a lot of other jobs.

Mr. Washington: Well, one thing, there's a number things that I like about it. Another thing is, it's clean, and you get to meet different people, important people, some—some are not. You meet a variety of all types of people. You never know who you are meeting. The barbering profession—barbers—he's all around. If he's a baseball player—whatever the customer likes—that is what you got to like, too, regardless of whether you like it or not. If I say I don't like baseball, well he says I got this other customer that does. They talk baseball and so I talk baseball, too, but I always talk what I have seen a little bit of because I never get too far out with it because I know he knows what he is talking about because this is the game he likes. And you got a lot of them that like boxing—I mean, I like boxing—you might talk about that. Whatever kind of customer you got, you got to talk what he likes because if you don't agree with what he agrees to, he is going to be mad. You got to go along with him. That's one thing. When you get off at night, you're not tired. It's a clean job, people respect you.

Mrs. Schwaber: And respect is very important.

Mr. Washington: Very important, very important. I mean, just like I look back on things in my past that I have done, you know, I didn't have any respect. People looked at me and said I was no good. But I don't live like that anymore. Like I said, people see me, they never know I've been in jail unless I tell them, and if they would ask me, I would tell them. People ask me, "Well, you're not ashamed?" I say, "No, I'm not ashamed that I have been in jail. When I went it was that I was asleep and I didn't have myself together. It was just a mistake. I'm not supposed to be still doing time." And they laugh. I just woke up in time to stay out, because going in and out wasn't benefiting me. Each time you get a little older and you still don't have nothing. If you do 30 days, that's 30 days out of your life you can never replace, and in 30 days you lose sight on the world. Like, what I got now, I know that in order to—if I'm going to be a barber, people come in and say, "Where's the barber?" I say, "Well, he's in jail." Every half the time you're in jail and half the time you're cutting hair—well, sooner or later, I won't have no customers. I don't have any reason to violate the law. I got to comply with the law in order to keep my license, which I expect to keep my license.

Mrs. Schwaber: You've learned something very important. You had to change yourself a little bit, but you found it worthwhile. What are you doing now when you go around talking to the youngsters?

Mr. Washington: Yes, I tell them you say you want to write and you want a job writing—in order to get the job you want, you got to be qualified. You can't go take the man's job and you're not qualified. If you go to school and educate yourself—whatever you want to go for—I'm not telling you to be no barber like me—be more than me—get you a high position or a higher profession—get you something out of it. As long as you stay around these pool halls and stand on the corner and drink your wine and holler about your rights, the white man ain't going to give you anything, because you're not qualified for this. Some say, yeah, you're right, you're right. Well, maybe so. I say, man, you tell me you don't know—I say well now you just face it. How are you going to go down here and get a job and you don't know anything about it. But you want to take the man's job. When the man pays you his $4.00 an hour, you expect to go in and get $4.00 an hour, and you're not qualified—you haven't finished high school and still you want that job. Take, like me, I didn't finish high school, and I can't get that job because you go somewhere to apply for a job, that's the first thing you hassle with—did you finish high school. That lets you out right there. You're out right there, automatically out. But if you got your trade or something that you're qualified in and you prove that you got the qualifications, the man can't refuse you the job—he got to give it to you. But if you're not qualified, he's not going to give you nothing—turn the doors on you. So, as far as you hollering about you want your rights, you want this and that, and you want what the white man has, how do you think you can get what he has? You educate yourself, you go to school. Some of them, once they get their profession or trade, they still go to school. They don't stop. But one of you guys, you can have something going, but you stopped. You give up right there.

Mrs. Schwaber: You didn't get it when you were in high school and you didn't get it when you came out. I would suspect that there were many reasons that you didn't do it, but possibly one was that there wasn't the training available for you or because you couldn't afford it.

Mr. Washington: Right. Like I told you, I didn't stay in school and I had to take these $50 and $60-a-week jobs—and you got a family, well, it's just actually enough to keep you from starving to death—and I never would have had enough money to pay for the course and buy the tools, too, and wouldn't have the time to go to school and the time to study, because on those jobs working long hours and you get off at five, the best thing you can do is take your bath, and that's it, and be ready for the next day. So I would never have had the time. When the opportunity came to me, I got it and I appreciate it. I didn't waste any time when I went to school because I got a chance to go for something that I want—I'm being paid to go for this, and I'm going on for it, not because I'm being paid for it, but because I'm getting a break that I had never had before. Like I told you the day I came to the office—I always get the bad breaks when I go for a job. They ask me if I been arrested. I mean, you can't tell the people you haven't, because they check it, and they can say you've lied right there. You have to tell them like it is. Say, "Yeah, Mr. Man, I'll tell you what—you come back in a couple of days and we'll see." Well, I know him, he's telling you then he doesn't want to tell you he's sorry he can't hire you— he tells you to come back in a couple of days. Well, I wouldn't go back because I know what he is going to tell me. I took an examination for the city to ride on the garbage truck. The man told me, "I'm sorry—you passed the test all right . . ." (you know, when I went for the interview) . . . "you did all right, you passed it, but one thing . . ." I said, "Well, yeah, one thing—I know—my record is bad." ". . . otherwise, we would hire you." Everytime you have these letdowns, you go to these places, you say, "Well, I'm in a bad bag, so I might as well stay in this bag."

Mrs. Schwaber: Yes, but you're out of the bag now.

Mr. Washington: Yes, I'm out of the bag now. Like I say, I appreciate it. Like I tell everybody whether you've been in jail, or wherever you've been, standing on the corner is wasting your time. These things I have done myself and I know it's nothing there. I didn't finish high school. I got grown too quick. I wanted to be on my own. I didn't have time for school. People would tell me that was older than I, they say you better go on to school because there is going to come a time for you to get a job. I'd say I'm going to get a job. But it happened to me. I found out the hard way. That's why I tell the youngsters now to go to school. At least go to high school if you don't do anything else, because I know how it is.

Mrs. Schwaber: Aren't you saying something else? Aren't you saying that if you have a record this keeps you in a bag and you never get out of the bag.

Mr. Washington: Well, if you don't want to get out of the bag, I'll put it like that. I wanted to get out of the bag because I knew sooner or later I would say, "Well, I'm off in this bag and they won't let me out, so I might as well do something else." I didn't think like that. I said, "I know somewhere I'm going to get me a break somewhere along the line."

Mrs. Schwaber: Well, something let you out of the bag, and what you're saying is that if others in the same spot you were in were helped to get out of the bag, they'd stay out. Do you remember when you were talking about some of the things that you thought added to training—you mentioned something—of course you mentioned how you felt about having that certificate, how you were proud of it—but you mentioned something else that I hadn't even thought about.

Mr. Washington: Like I said, I don't have to look for a job anymore. Anywhere I go in the State of California, I got a job. If I go in a shop and barber, I just hang my license up and go to work. I can take my tools and my license and catch a freight train and get off in a town and work maybe two days and go on to the next town, as long as I'm in this State, and everything I told you—that a lot of people look upon barbering as a trade—I don't—I look upon it as a profession—because due to the fact that a trade, I can leave here and go to Arizona and show the man my qualifications for this trade and go to work. But I can't do that with what I have because I don't have a license in that state to cut hair. I only have a license in the State of California to cut hair. That's why I say it's a profession. If I go into another state, I got to get a license for that state. If I had a trade, I could go in and work anywhere I wanted to, like I can work anywhere in this state on my license, but not in any other state. That's why I look upon it as a profession and that's why I'm proud of it.

*   *   *

Paulene Myers: My thanks to the teams who traveled here to show you how Title V programs can work. Would you like to thank them, too? (applause)

Now, back to Mr. Gius. He summed up a long and glowing account of his afternoon with the Ventura teams by writing: "It has inspired hope in people who had little to hope for, given them dignity through self-reliance. I would say that is the ultimate goal of public charity."

One hundred years ago, a very old black woman—she was 86 years old and making her last public appeal for human rights—said of the freed slaves: "Give them land in the West where they can find themselves and soon they would be a people among you. We've earned enough land for a home. They say, 'let them take care of themselves.' Well, they can't do that because you took all they earned away from them—ain't got nothing. Give them land—have teachers learn them to read, and then they can be somebody! It would be a benefit to you all and God would bless the whole of you for doing it."